THE OTHERS WITHIN US

Advance Praise for *The Others Within Us*

"Robert Falconer is such a stimulating author, and his books so well written. I am always learning a lot and having so much fun as I read him."

—Anibal Henriques, Head of Sociedade Portuguesa
de Psicoterapias Construtivistas, Portugal

"As a traditionally trained psychiatrist and psychopharmacologist, I have noticed how usual treatments often fail to adequately relieve my patients' psychic pain. With the techniques that Bob Falconer has taught me, the people I work with and I have a new set of astoundingly effective tools. They are far from the range of traditional medicine but, as Bob demonstrates in this book, many of these tools have been used in one form or another for most of human history. As with Bob's previous books, this one has been exquisitely researched and scientifically documented. It is a treasure for anyone who is looking for new ways to heal."

—Charles H. Silberstein, MD, Medical Staff, Martha's Vineyard Hospital Medical
Director, Island Counseling Center, Martha's Vineyard Community Services

"This book is a landmark for helping those in Western cultures reorient their perspective in meaningful ways in the paradigm shift from physicalism to the primacy of consciousness. At the same time, Falconer has written this far-reaching tome in an inviting, conversational style, making the expansive ideas accessible and practical in the universal charge of reducing human suffering."

—Rev. Rachel Rivers, MA, D.Min., Pastoral Psychotherapist & Spiritual Director

"I'm so grateful for what Bob is both modeling and teaching on the subject of "the others within." It's... so needed and important... I'm also so grateful for the way Bob demonstrates both the strength of holding a clear boundary but also how powerful kindness and compassion can be, even to those forces that would seem the least likely to warrant any."

—Stephen Chee, MD, MPH, MA, MTOM, LAc, Certified Internal Family
Systems (IFS) Therapist, Quadruple Board Certified: Family Medicine,
Integrative Medicine, Medical Acupuncture, Oriental Medicine

"Bob Falconer's knowledge about what IFS terms "unattached burdens" is comprehensive. With his clear writing style, extensive case examples, and voluminous review of literature on related issues, his new book *The Others Within Us* will become an essential reference for those working in this field."

—Tom Holmes, PhD, author of *Parts Work: An Illustrated Guide to Your Inner Life* and
Parts Work: A Path of the Heart: Healing Journeys Integrating IFS and Spirituality

The Others Within Us

Internal Family Systems,
Porous Mind, and Spirit Possession

Robert Falconer

Great Mystery Press
greatmysterypress.com

ISBN: 979-8-9878588-0-6

Printed in the United States of America

Dedicated to
Seonghee Son

Table of Contents

Foreword by Richard C. Schwartz, PhD xiii

How to Use This Book xxi

PART 1   THE FULL CATASTROPHE 1

CHAPTER 1   Violence, Healing & Parts 3

CHAPTER 2   Internal Family Systems Therapy 11

CHAPTER 3   A Case That Changed My Life 23

CHAPTER 4   Interesting People on a Winding Path 45

CHAPTER 5   Interoception 71

CHAPTER 6   A Basic Outline of Dealing with Unattached Burdens 87

CHAPTER 7   Cheat Sheet 109

CHAPTER 8   More Cases 111

CHAPTER 9   Other Modern Therapies 169

PART 2   THIS CHANGES EVERYTHING 195

CHAPTER 10   Other Cultures & Anthropology:
Non-Western Examples 197

CHAPTER 11   A Totally Eurocentric View:
Spiritual Presence Experiences in the West 223

CHAPTER 12   The Porosity of Mind 261

CHAPTER 13   Personalism 287

CHAPTER 14   Guides & Discernment 297

CHAPTER 15   Advanced Cases 353

CHAPTER 16   Conclusions 403

Afterword 415

Selected & Annotated Bibliography 419

Research Bibliography 423

Index 457

Acknowledgments 477

About the Author 479

Foreword

This book is a synthesis of massive research and substantial clinical experience, but I will begin this foreword by laying out my fears about its being published. First, its subject is a phenomenon that I have been reluctant to teach or write about for fear that Internal Family Systems (IFS), the model of the mind that I've spent my adult life developing, would be discredited, particularly in bastions I hope to continue to influence, such as traditional psychiatry and psychology. With its assertion of the natural multiplicity of the mind — that there are no bad parts — and the existence of an undamaged, healing Self, IFS is enough of a challenge to the prevailing paradigm of the mind without adding the topic of this book — what I have come to call unattached burdens (UBs). For the past forty years, I have been trying to sell IFS to a skeptical therapy community and to the public. Especially in the early years, I encountered enormous resistance and occasional verbal attack. Now that IFS has reached a huge level of popularity and acceptance not only in psychotherapy but in many other areas, why revive that skepticism and jeopardize all these gains by writing about this topic?

Several years ago, my friend and colleague Bob Falconer became fascinated by UBs and specialized in releasing them. Despite my cautions, he became determined to write about how IFS can be used to work with them and has done so in the book that follows. So, this foreword is my attempt to clarify my position on UBs and on how the book can help people unload them.

My second fear is that by writing on this topic, we will contribute to a mistake I believe to be common around the world. Too often extreme protector parts are misunderstood and assumed to be evil entities or demons and, consequently, subjected to exorcising rituals. Initially, many protectors resemble UBs in declaring that all they want to do is hurt or destroy the person they are in or other people. If threatened, these protectors will maintain or escalate their extreme positions, which can result in damage to that person or others. If, on the other hand, protectors are approached with curiosity and even compassion, eventually they will reveal their protective intention and can be transformed into their natural, valuable states (Schwartz and Sweezy 2020). Regardless of how UBs are approached, they will not reveal positive or protective intentions because they only want to do harm or create havoc, but it can take time and patience to distinguish them from protectors.

Follow the Data

As I have explored people's inner worlds over the past forty years, I've tried my best to be an objective reporter of what I have observed. I first encountered this UB phenomenon over twenty five years ago, at a point when the foundational principles of IFS were well established. I was quite shaken by the encounter because up until then I was convinced that there was nothing bad inside people — just parts in extreme roles. I had developed IFS by following my scientist father's advice to go with the data even if it takes you well outside your paradigm, and the data around parts and Self already had me far from home. Because I had gotten that far with this open-minded approach, however, I stayed curious about UBs and asked the parts of me that wanted to deny or dismiss them to step back.

I'm not the only one who considers himself a scientist and has had to put aside prejudices in order to study what are typically considered religious or spiritual phenomena. Psychologist David DeSteno has examined the psychological value of many religious practices and writes:

> Over the past few years, as I've looked back at the results of my studies and those of other researchers, I've come to see a nuanced relationship between science and religion… It's not that I've suddenly found faith or have a new agenda to defend religion… Like any good scientist, I'm simply following the data without prejudice… Doing this doesn't require accepting a given theology — just an open mind and an attitude of respect. Not doing it risks betraying our principles. If we ignore that body of knowledge, if we refuse to take these spiritual technologies seriously as a source of ideas and inspiration to study, we slow the progress of science itself and limit its potential to benefit humanity. (DeSteno 2021)

I've tried to take a similar approach to the study of UBs.

Having now divulged my fears, I want to speak for the parts of me that know that this book can help many people. I have worked with a number of clients who felt hopelessly resigned to living with scary impulses or believed that, at their core, they were evil. I felt stuck with many of those clients because their parts weren't responding the way one would expect and didn't until we found and unloaded the UB. After that, they felt tremendous relief, inner spaciousness, and more access to Self. So, most of me is glad this book is now available to therapists and clients. Bob has done an impressive amount of research on how the UB phenomenon is understood and dealt with around the world, and he lays out clear guidelines and examples for using IFS to unload them.

My History with UBs

In the late 1980s and through the 1990s, I was interested in whether the principles and practices of IFS would hold up even with highly traumatized and pathologized clients. I actively took on the most challenging clients I could find — people carrying heavy-duty diagnoses such as dissociative identity disorder, borderline personality disorder, severe eating disorders, and so on. I also consulted for several years for a residential treatment center for juvenile sex offenders called Onarga Academy. There I worked with parts that had molested children or raped women. I was amazed to find that even those parts, once approached from the clients' Self with respectful curiosity, would share their secret histories of how they were forced into their extreme roles when the client had been abused as a child and how they came to take in the energy of their abusers. I was excitedly concluding that there really were no bad parts.

A number of these clients were suicidal, with histories of serious attempts. I was finding that having them ask, from Self, what the suicidal part was afraid would happen if it didn't kill the client would begin a process by which we could heal the parts holding intense pain whom the suicidal part was trying to protect the client from, thereby freeing the suicidal one to take on a different, often life-affirming role. Then I tried it with Nikki's suicidal part. The part wouldn't talk to her, so I shifted to "direct access," an IFS technique in which I asked to talk to it directly, and the following conversation ensued:

Me: Why do you want to kill Nikki?

Part: Because she's bad and deserves to die.

This answer was a common first response among the clients with whom I was working, so I wasn't concerned at this point. In response to the next question, most suicidal parts soften and reveal their protective role.

Me: What are you afraid will happen if you can't kill her, though?

Part: I'm not afraid of anything. I just want her dead.

Me: Okay, but what would be good if you were able to kill her?

Part: It wouldn't be good or bad. It's just what I want to do.

I went on and on with different versions of that question, and the response was variations on the theme of it just wanting to kill her and having no other intention. I began to panic because this was a direct challenge to the "no bad parts" conclusion I was so excited about, and was teaching, after years of conversations with all kinds of inner citizens. Maybe my basic premises were wrong!

I noticed that this suicidal one seemed less developed and more one-dimensional than most parts. It had a very narrow range of responses or beliefs and often repeated the same words over and over. So, out of left field, I tried a question I'd never asked before:

Me: Are you a part of Nikki or something else?

Part: I'm not a part of her. (From here on out, I'll call it the suicidal voice.)

Me: What are you then?

Voice: I'm just here to get her to die.

We continued to go in such circles until I decided to talk to Nikki again.

Me: What was it like to listen to me talking to that thing?

Nikki: It was scary but also somehow reassuring. It has never felt like the other parts we've been working with. It's always felt foreign to me.

Me: Do you want to see if we can send it out of your system?

By then IFS was quite developed, and I was doing unburdening with clients' parts where, once the part felt fully witnessed by the Self and was retrieved from where it had been frozen in the past, we would ask if it was ready to unload the emotions and beliefs it carried from the trauma. If the part was ready, we would offer a menu of the elements, and the part would pick one to send its burden off to and then send it out of his or her system through light or fire or wind, and so on. It occurred to me that maybe this suicidal one was simply an extreme belief — a burden like those we sent out that had been attached to parts — but somehow wasn't connected to a part. In other words, it was floating around freely in the client's inner world, wreaking havoc and having no positive intention. If that were true, we should be able to send it out in the same way we sent out attached burdens.

Me: Are you ready to send it out?

Nikki: It's getting bigger and more threatening, and I'm afraid of it.

I had found, in working with scary parts of clients, that if I could get their fear to separate so they were in Self and consequently calm, confident, and courageous relative to the part, try as it might to keep scaring the client, it couldn't, and it also no longer had any power. It seems that nothing has power inside people when they access a critical mass of Self. So, I helped Nikki convince her scared parts to go into a safe inner waiting room and let Nikki and me handle the thing. (I had to get my scared ones to separate, too.) Once she was in Self, we continued.

Me (firmly): Tell this thing that because it's not a part of you, it can't stay in you any longer and we're going to send it out of your system. (I later learned that it's possible to reassure these unattached burdens that we're sending them to be transformed into something good because they often seem scared to leave. All this can be done with compassion as well as firmness.)

Nikki: It's still trying to intimidate me, but it can't, so it now seems resigned.

Me: Okay, Nikki, bring in the light and have it shine on it. How does it react to the light?

Nikki: It seems paralyzed or something.

Me: Okay, ask the light to take it to where it belongs and just watch until it's fully out of your system.

Nikki (after a few minutes of silence): It's gone.

Me: How do you feel without it?

Nikki: Much lighter, and my parts seem very relieved.

Over the past thirty years, I have run into more of these seeming bundles of inner nastiness. Not all of them are suicidal. Some seem to want to hurt or get power over others. Some just seem lost. Initially some clients don't want to unload them, fearing that their power or protection would leave with the UBs, so we had to first work with parts that depended on them. I find UBs more in people who have spent time dissociated from their bodies — who have, for example, had multiple surgeries, been physically or sexually abused, or taken a lot of drugs. It seems that the embodiment of Self is protective — they can't penetrate Self energy. This is why it is important for therapists to fully embody Self whenever they do therapy and particularly when working with clients who contain UBs.

Porousness

This brings up the topic of porousness, which Bob also discusses in this book. I was not aware that burdens could transfer between people until I began learning from clients about legacy burdens. For example, I was helping a client get curious about his intensely harsh inner critic. While he interviewed it, it said that it took in its critical voice from his father. This seemed similar to what psychodynamic therapies call "internalization," so I didn't think twice about that answer. But then the part conveyed spontaneously that his father got that voice and angry energy from his grandfather, and my client began seeing scenes of combat and abuse related to the source of this harshness that were clearly not from his lifetime.

As I encountered similar experiences with other clients, I began using the term *legacy burdens* for these beliefs, energies, and emotions that were transferred across generations. The topic of legacy burdens has become a huge one in the IFS world, and I distinguish between:

- those that came down through the generations from an earlier trauma in the client's family (lineage burdens)

- those that are carried by a client's ethnic group but may not be directly related to their particular family (ethnic burdens)
- those that float around in the culture or country the client lives in and are absorbed simply by living there (cultural burdens)

I later learned that there is scientific evidence from the field of epigenetics for the cross-generational transfer of extreme beliefs and emotions. (Rachel Yehuda has published some five hundred articles, many dealing with the intergenerational transmission of Holocaust trauma. See also Dias and Ressler 2014.)

The point here is that it seems that burdens (extreme beliefs and emotions) can enter people, especially when, as I mentioned above, the people are not fully embodied. While this seems weird and took me time and lots of evidence to believe, I don't feel the need to look to metaphysical or spiritual answers to understand the UB phenomenon. I'm a big subscriber to the law of parsimony — that an explanation of a thing should include the fewest possible assumptions that allow for it to be worked with effectively. I'm also an empiricist in that I try to stay close to the observed data and avoid grand speculation. Most of what I have written derived directly from reports of clients as we explored and experimented with their inner worlds.

The Pragmatic Approach

The UB phenomenon fits nicely into the IFS paradigm of parts, Self, and burdens. It's just that these UBs aren't in or on parts and have a certain independence, hence the name "unattached burdens." Some of them aren't as unidimensional as the one I described above, so it can be harder to distinguish them from parts. For some reason, however, when asked if they are a part, they generally don't lie, even though they seem to have no morals otherwise and lying might get me to back off and not send them out.

As Bob so thoroughly documents, most cultures other than our Western rationalist one see UBs as inhabitants of the spiritual world and have quite elaborate and sometimes violent rituals for expelling them. I believe that if two inner laws became more widely known, some of the ritual, and all of the violence, would be discovered to be unnecessary. Those laws are:

- When a person accesses Self to the point of not fearing UBs, they lose all power.
- When you fully embody Self, UBs can't penetrate to begin with, and if one has, you can send it away quickly and often without a lot of help.

Thus, just as in the healing of burdened parts, access to Self makes all the difference.

I'm also not taking the hyper-rationalist position that there are no spiritual elements to the phenomenon. That position strikes me as arrogantly closed-minded and contradicts most of the rest of the world. My inclination all along in developing IFS has been to stay as close to the data as possible and focus on the healing aspects of the discoveries. In another book (Schwartz and Falconer 2017), Bob and I explored the amazing similarities between the IFS conception of Self and how it is described in every spiritual tradition. As a result of that research, do I now believe that Self is something like God in us, as many of those traditions do? That does seem like the most parsimonious explanation for its invulnerability to trauma and natural healing wisdom. So, I do lean in that direction these days but try to keep my mind open to other explanations, and I don't impose that belief in my teaching.

For now, seeing UBs as free-floating extreme beliefs, energies, or emotions that can be unloaded, rather than as spiritual entities that possess people and are to be battled with, seems to work well. Bob frequently cites the radical pragmatism of William James as a big influence on him. I'm not sure Bob's is an accurate interpretation of James, but I've always taken the position Bob cites that the best path is to focus on how inner systems work and how clients describe them, without worrying too much about what they are ontologically. I like to think of myself as an anthropologist of these inner tribes, although unlike most anthropologists, I have intervened to try to heal or change them. Whether or not you believe the inhabitants of those tribes (the parts) are human-like beings, relating to them as if they were creates the most healing. At this point, I consider UBs to be far less human-like (even though you can interact with them) than parts. Instead, I believe they are the manifestation of extreme beliefs and emotions that our minds personify. Sending them out of the system as soon as possible seems to work well.

After forty years of studying these fascinating inner worlds, I know a lot about how they operate and how they can transform and heal, but what they actually are remains a marvelous mystery. It is that mystery that drives me to keep studying them. In retrospect, my ignorance of intrapsychic models was an advantage as I entered this inner territory forty years ago because I was forced to have what Buddhists call "beginner's mind" — to listen carefully to what my clients reported and believe them instead of fitting those reports into presumptions I brought with me. I've tried to keep that same mindset with the UB phenomenon and not automatically fit what I find into the belief systems of other cultures and shamans, even though they've been at it much longer than me. I'm interested in Indigenous perspectives and do compare notes with them, but also try to stay open to discoveries that don't fit other belief systems, Indigenous or otherwise.

Guides

Bob also touches on another phenomenon I've been reluctant to discuss but have extensive experience with — what I and many spiritual traditions call *guides*. Guides started showing up in clients' systems at about the same time as UBs. Different clients, with very different backgrounds and religious beliefs, spontaneously began saying things like "a beam of light has suddenly appeared, and I'm getting the message from it that I'm on the right track" or "I see a hazy figure who is embracing my little girl, and she feels extremely comforted" or (sobbing) "I'm feel so loved. I'm not sure where it's coming from, but it feels great!" Often these experiences followed intense, scary retrievals and unburdenings. I thought to myself things like "Isn't it nice that she has some parts who are cheering for her and actually helping out?"

I would ask the clients to thank these parts and ask about their role in the system, and clients would say some version of "It says it's not a part, but it does want to help." When I had clients ask what it was, they would usually get vague answers, but sometime the guide would be direct and tell them it was there to help them on their path and would give them comfort or valuable advice about the problems they were facing. Subsequently, I have encountered guides in many clients, and their effect has always been salubrious. Some clients form ongoing relationships with them and begin sessions with reports of what their guides have been teaching them.

Are these spiritual encounters or simply manifestations of higher levels of consciousness within these clients? Similar to UBs, I can stay agnostic on that question because my focus is on their impact rather than their origin. As Bob describes, he and I are not the first explorers of the psyche to encounter guides or UBs. The best known of these pioneers was Carl Jung, who had the courage to write about these phenomena and also tried to avoid spiritual explanations. In 1945, he wrote to theologian Victor White, "I never allow myself to make statements about the divine entity, since such would be transgression beyond the limit of science…" While Jung has had an enormous influence on psychotherapists and on many aspects of our culture, his work is rarely taught in rigorous academic circles largely because he dared report on such mysterious findings.

So, we come full circle — back to my fears of IFS being discredited because Bob and I are sharing our experiences with this phenomenon. Anyone who spends time exploring their own or their clients' inner worlds will eventually encounter what we are describing. My hope is that enough people, academics included, are now using IFS and having these experiences that they will be harder to dismiss than in Jung's time. Whether or not that is true, it feels good to no longer keep these data secret.

—Richard C. Schwartz, PhD, founder of Internal Family Systems Therapy

How to Use This Book

This is a big book, and it can seem unwieldy. It is intended to set the standard in this field and is almost encyclopedic in scope. I want to cut it down to size so it is friendlier and easier to use. This book summarizes more than a decade of research and clinical experience. Of course, I hope you read it all cover to cover, but this is not necessary. For all readers, Chapter 3, "A Case That Changed My Life," is important. If you are a helper or therapist, the most important part of the book is Part 1, "The Full Catastrophe." The core of the book for you will be Chapters 6 and 7, which contain explicit and detailed recommendations on how to deal with unattached burdens — the others within us.

For the more general-interest reader, the second half of the book, "This Changes Everything," might be more important. Part 1 shows that certain kinds of phenomena occur in psychotherapy that do not fit in our current worldview at all. Part 2 explores what this implies for our conceptions of mind, cognition, and person. These questions should concern every thinking human. Hopefully, the general-interest reader will gain enough from the first section to have a grasp of the basic phenomena, but these readers do not need the detailed "how to" material.

For all readers, please read only as many case studies as appeal to you. Each case study shows the subject from a slightly different angle, resulting in a detailed three-dimensional image, but they are not necessary to follow the gist of the text. This is also true of the survey of similar occurrences in non-Western cultures and different eras of our history. It is like the blind people and the elephant. The one who touches the tail says the elephant is like a rope. The one who touches the leg says the elephant is like a tree. The one who touches the ear says, "No, it's like a sheet of leather." Having all the different viewpoints creates a rich and detailed picture, but it is not necessary to an understanding of the book. Read the ones that attract you.

It has been said that extraordinary claims require extraordinary evidence. This book does present extraordinary claims. This is another important reason I have included a plethora of different cultures and case studies. Actually, I edited out a great deal of material, as you can appreciate if you glance at the research bibliography. Hopefully, I have included enough to make even the most hardened skeptic think twice.

Feedback, comments, and corrections are very welcome. Please send them to my website: robertfalconer.us.

The Full Catastrophe

CHAPTER I

Violence, Healing & Parts

We are still possessed by autonomous psychic contents as if they were
Olympians. Today they are called phobias, obsessions… neurotic
symptoms. The gods have become diseases.

—C. G. Jung

The purpose of poetry is to remind us
how difficult it is to remain just one person
For our house is open, there are no keys to the doors,
And invisible guests come in and out at will.

—Czeslaw Milosz

Those who look outside dream. Those who look inside awaken. Carl Jung said
something like this about a century ago. Yet most modern science refuses to
look inward and takes the word *subjective* to almost be synonymous with dubious or outright wrong. Many, possibly most, other cultures value the subjective
realms of interoception — the perception of internal sensations — more than we
do and know these territories in greater depth. When we explore our inner world,
we find it is at least as vast as the external cosmos. It's like looking at the night sky.
Imagine looking at a small spot in the night sky as big as a quarter, held at arm's
length. Pick a spot that seems blank. With a small telescope, a few stars appear.
With bigger and bigger telescopes, more and more stars, then whole galaxies, are
there. With the best sensors, the cosmic background radiation appears, a remnant
of the big bang. Distant not only in space but also in time — billions and billions
of years ago. A similar progression occurs as we focus inward. The near realms are
somewhat familiar. Modern psychology, especially parts work in Internal Family
Systems (IFS), is giving us fairly accurate maps. The farther in we go into what
Aldous Huxley called the antipodes of the mind, the odder the flora and fauna
become. Fewer people have explored these realms, and those who do are often
labeled psychotic or mystics.

This book follows my journey as I pursued healing: the lessening of human suffering for myself and my clients. This pursuit relentlessly took me into deeper and deeper waters. Many people, especially those who worship at the altar of materialism and science, might think I am totally wrong. I want to gently remind them that it is always the outlying data — the data that don't fit our current theories — that lead to new discoveries and change paradigms. As Colin Wilson showed in his book *The Outsider*, it is usually those who do not fit in who lead the way onto new ground.

This book will very briefly reprise my long focus on healing trauma and my settling on IFS as the most respectful and potent therapy for this work. Following that will be a summary of the basics of IFS parts work. Then the focus will shift to the other within: the denizens of the antipodes of our minds — the things, beings, and energies we find inside us that are not part of our personal life histories. The vast majority of this book will be about the farther reaches of the mind.

Some ten years ago when I was in my early sixties, I was quite content with my work. I saw myself as a hard-nosed, battle-tested trauma counselor. It had taken decades for me to cobble together a model of trauma therapy that satisfied me. I felt I had a solid basic grasp of psychological realities. But then some events happened that I could not ignore or deny. They led me to a much-expanded view of psychology and the mind. I hope that at least a fraction of the excitement, confusion, and wonder I felt comes through this narrative of my meeting with the others within.

It seems important to give a basic outline of my healing journey so you have a better sense of whether or not I'm trustworthy since the subjects we will be discussing are very odd. I was born into a family in New York City that, from the outside, looked okay; middle class and churchgoing. But on the inside, there was addiction and violence. I shy away from the word *evil*; it's not really acceptable in polite discourse these days, but it may well apply to my family. I was molested and beaten throughout my childhood by my father, my mother, and my older brother. Both parents were addicts. My father drank a six-pack of beer every evening, and that didn't count as drinking. He often drank a lot more as well. My mother was a binge alcoholic but more of a prescription drug addict.

For most of my childhood, my father had his gay lovers and fellow child molesters living in the house with us, and they also molested and beat my brother and me. They were heavily involved in sadomasochism. The abuse was often extreme. As is true of most children who are badly abused, I learned how to dissociate. I could numb my body to most pain. I could leave my body. My body would become almost catatonic. This ability to become impervious to most physical pain is not unique to me; many severely abused children develop it. It is a lifesaving skill. Andrew Vachss, who worked for a time as the warden of a locked juvenile detention facility, said that some of the children there were almost impossible to control or subdue because they could numb out all pain and would continue fighting and resisting even when their arms were broken.

Pia Mellody describes three levels of dissociation in abused children. In her first level, the child dissociates and experiences themselves as sitting beside their body while it's being abused. In the second level, the child experiences themselves up on the ceiling looking down at the scene. In the third level, the child leaves the room and the house entirely and goes off into other realms. I experienced all three of these levels, and in a painfully ironic way, this dissociation opened me to deep inner subjectivity. There is a terrible irony in the fact that this third level of dissociation is so similar to profound spiritual experiences. When my father realized that I could become numb and thereby escape the pain he was inflicting, he started to focus on suffocating me until I lost consciousness. This I could never numb out; it seems there's a biologically hardwired response. It created in me an overwhelming full-body panic state in which I would exert all my energies to try to breathe again.

Waterboarding — the suffocation torture the US government has inflicted on prisoners — is an extreme form of torture, even though there is no blood and it leaves no scars. I do not think these events would really qualify as near-death experiences, but often when suffocated unconscious, I felt a merciful female presence that was sweet and wonderful. This precious contact while in the very depths of my worst hell may have been what allowed me to survive and then, much later, heal. With my child's mind, I came to hate and resent this merciful female presence because she kept sending me back to that room where my father was tormenting me. Later I came to miss this presence terribly and struggled to reestablish communication. For many years, the image I had of my existence as a spiritual being was a soldier in a frontline trench with a radio, trying to call back to headquarters. There was nothing on the radio but static. These early experiences let me know unequivocally that there are realms of the mind that we are normally completely unaware of and that these realms can be very important for not only our health but also our very survival.

When I was a teenager, my brother committed suicide. He was a year and nine months older than me. He was a star child overachiever, while I was the family's problem child, the identified patient. My mom was institutionalized several times for her mental illness. My father was murdered when I was twenty-one in a crime that remains unsolved. (It wasn't me — I was over a thousand miles away at the time.) My guess is that he abused the wrong person's child. By all odds, I should be a junkie, in prison, or dead like my brother. But now in my seventies, I am essentially a happy man, and I feel that I have contributed something to the world because I have spent most of my life helping other men with histories like mine. How in the world did I end up with such a good outcome from such a terrible beginning? I believe meeting that merciful female presence was very important, and there are many, many things — some seemingly quite trivial — that changed the whole course of my life. I have worked hard and consistently at healing for many decades but, more fundamentally, much of my healing seems to have come as a gift.

As a young boy, I had no idea how to play with my peers, and I was always isolated and in trouble. I fought a lot and was thrown out of several schools. I felt unwanted, rejected, and despised both at home and in the world. I was becoming bitter and hard. Amazingly, in ninth grade, I was admitted to a small religious school. One day, another freshman hit me with a spitball; I cornered him in the coatroom and had him by the lapels of his jacket. I was about to start beating him up, but for some reason I put him down and brushed off his coat. Since then I have never hit anyone in anger. This small event was a watershed for me. I could so easily have been thrown out of yet another school and taken the road that soon would have led to prison.

In high school, a young woman, Ruth Chu, and I had what could be dismissed as a puppy love affair. But I had never experienced human kindness before, and she was truly kind to me. I kept expecting betrayal or something horrible, but she was true and kind and gentle. This astounded me. I didn't know humans could be that way, and it opened a thin ray of hope in my dark life, creating a crack in the concrete shell of bitterness and anger I had been building around myself. There were other incidents like this as well.

All during middle school and high school, I was drinking large amounts, and I was well on the way to becoming an alcoholic like my father. Being drunk provided temporary relief. This was the late 1960s, and fortunately, when I went to college, I started taking LSD and other psychedelics. Even though there was no therapeutic supervision, the experiences these chemicals and plants provided made me lose my desire to drink. For years I didn't drink any alcohol at all and even looked down on people who did. Later I did drink again, but it was never with that addictive energy. For many years now, I have not drunk at all — it just sort of faded away. It was not a big struggle for me, as I know it is for so many.

After I got out of college, I started a small, hippie-sized independent business in remodeling and construction. It was psychologically almost impossible for me to work for or with others, so it was me and my dog in my pickup truck. Also, I had always been athletic and started competing in tennis tournaments. Between the physical exhaustion of my work and athletics, along with some pot and later wine, I was able to sort of slouch along through life. Then my lower back gave out, and overnight I could no longer play tennis or do the intense manual labor I had been so proud to do. My world collapsed. Luckily, at this time I found a therapist, Patricia Alexander Weston, who understood trauma, child sexual abuse, and subpersonalities. This was very rare in those days. Pat called the subpersonalities "the insiders." These are almost exactly the equivalent of what IFS calls "parts." I have worked with Pat ever since then — more than thirty years now, even though she is retired and no longer taking clients.

I realized that I was a mess. I was basically suicidal. But I made up a list, with the idea that if I really was going to kill myself, I should try certain things first, and only when I'd done them all, if they didn't make me feel better, then I would kill myself. And as I checked things off the top of the list, I kept adding more to the bottom. One of the things on my list was getting a master's degree in psychology, studying psychotherapy, and finding every healing modality I could.

For some forty years, I've lived near Esalen. I've attended over 140 workshops and have been introduced to many cutting-edge therapy techniques and many of the leaders of the human potential movement. Some of them are wonderful, and others have caused far more suffering than they cured. The first therapy in addition to the steady work with Pat that really helped me was Ericksonian hypnotherapy, the work founded by Milton Erickson, MD. I never met him, but I met his oldest daughter, Carol, and she became my first major teacher. She ran my master's program, and I studied hypnotherapy with her for years. The hypnotic trances took me back to realms that were very much like the extreme dissociative states I'd experienced as a child. It was good to learn how to enter, explore, and leave those states voluntarily. There is a fascinating interplay of voluntary and involuntary in hypnotic trance. You can largely enter voluntarily, but the images that appear often seem autonomous, like the images in a dream and, as I would learn later, like our parts, or subpersonalities.

Then through her I met Jack and Helen Watkins, the developers of ego state therapy, which is a kind of parts work based on hypnosis and is very powerful. They were great teachers for me. With them, I came to more deeply experience that there are independent parts of me that are often unknown to my normal, conscious mind. Esalen is where Gestalt really took root in the United States. That, of course, is another form of parts work. There were many great teachers of Gestalt at Esalen: Christine Price, Mariah Fenton Gladis, and many others. I absorbed that world and swam in it. Here was a whole group of therapists who found ways of working with all these independent parts and helping them interact and grow together.

I also studied with Pia Mellody. Pia is a registered nurse whose focus has been on inpatient addictions treatment and the treatment of codependence. She calls her work post-induction therapy. She took parts work to a new level because she knew that there weren't only the wounded parts that the Gestalt people and many other therapists had begun to recognize, but there were also what she called the "adult adapted wounded children." These are parts that work to protect the younger wounded parts, but they are also children, not fully adult. This was a precursor to Dick Schwartz's concept of protectors. Mellody's understanding of addiction, especially love addiction, has shaped much of my life.

There are many other kinds of parts work as well. Roberto Assagioli, the founder of psychosynthesis, was very important because he showed that, as we come to realize that the human mind is made up of parts, it also opens us to deep spirituality. This is a fundamentally important understanding. Assagioli, like most other modern therapists, felt the need to conceal the stranger and more spiritual depths of what he discovered. He did write and speak openly of the spiritual and the higher self, but he also concealed quite a bit. His students related that he had two libraries: one in a public place with books that were academically acceptable in his day, and a private library filled with books on occultism and mysticism. Hal and Sidra Stone developed Voice Dialogue, which again is very much a parts work model, based on the realization that we're not one unified thing but instead are made up of many parts with whom we need to relate. We need to dialogue with them — not dominate, control, or eradicate them. We need to form relationships with them.

While I was following all these trails, I was also deeply involved in the survivors' movement. During the '70s and '80s, trauma and child sexual abuse were assiduously ignored by most professional therapy schools and the big academics. They pretended it didn't exist. It was actually an activist grassroots movement that forced the schools to recognize how crucial trauma and specifically childhood sexual abuse is in the psychological development of many. I was one of the very first men to publicly speak about having been sexually abused as a child. I got involved with a survivors' healing center, which was literally a storefront service provider for survivors here in Santa Cruz, California. One of the major founders of the survivors' movement was Ellen Bass, a poet and writing teacher. In her writing classes, women wrote about having been abused. At that time, it was safer to bring this to a writing teacher than to a therapist! Tremendous changes have taken place in the decades since then. Now the very institutions that pretended abuse didn't exist are teaching it as though they knew about it all along.

The evolution of our understanding of PTSD is very similar. The major academic institutions denied that it existed for a long time. It was the Vietnam veterans' rap groups who knew this stuff happened. They got together and, with the help of psychiatrist Robert Jay Lifton, organized a movement and put political pressure on the government. It was this pressure that forced the academics to accept PTSD as something real and forced them to include the diagnosis in the *Diagnostic and Statistical Manual of Mental Disorders*, which is the bible of psychopathology in academic America.

So, these big changes have occurred within my lifetime. Having watched this process with child sexual abuse and PTSD has given me a healthy skepticism about the academic authorities on psychological healing. Despite all the degrees, high academic honors, and position, they have been fundamentally and disastrously wrong about the basics of psychological healing. It was also during this period, mainly in the 1980s, that multiple personality disorder was first widely recognized. This is the most extreme version of parts — of the fragmentation of mind. This concept was also strenuously resisted by academia and only accepted when it was forced on them.

MPD

Multiple personality disorder (MPD) is now called dissociative identity disorder (DID). It is almost always the result of severe childhood abuse and trauma. The splitting of the parts is so flagrant that they often do not even know each other. Walls of amnesia separate them, and they can take control of the person serially. For our purposes, there are three important issues that come to light in this early work. One is the stunning and uncomfortable fact that we can be taken over by parts of ourselves — that we are not truly the masters of our own homes. There exists a dynamic structure in our minds that allows parts to hijack us and get us to act in ways that we regret and do not understand later. This unsettling fact is one reason that the whole idea of parts work has been so strenuously resisted.

The second issue is the belief, which came from this work, that all parts are the result of trauma. Considering the population that these early therapists were working with, reaching this conclusion is understandable, almost inevitable. But it is wrong. Clinicians see milder forms of this separation of parts in all of their clients. It slowly became clear that this parts structure is normal, beneficial, and healthy. Trauma exacerbates the healthy separation and makes it extreme and damaging. However, trauma itself does not create the separation.

The third discovery from this era that is important for IFS and our work is one that is often ignored because it does not fit easily into the existing modern worldview. This is the internal self-helper, or ISH. This was first written about by Dr. Ralph Allison. He noticed in many of his MPD patients that there was a wise and kind presence who knew all of the alters and what they had been doing. This

ISH could offer valuable suggestions for therapy. Dr. Allison asked several of his colleagues if they also often found this ISH. They did. They didn't know what it was, but it was so helpful that they made practical use of it in their work. The ISH is a predecessor of the IFS concept of the Self, which Dick says is the most important discovery in his model.

CHAPTER 2

Internal Family Systems Therapy

In about the year 2000, I started learning about Internal Family Systems, a type of therapy that was developed by Richard Schwartz and many others about forty years ago. At the time, I was deeply entrenched in Esalen and Gestalt, and it took me another ten years to abandon the Gestalt world and other modalities I had learned and become almost entirely an IFS therapist. I believe it is the most potent and respectful of all these parts work models for several reasons. One of the most fundamental reasons for the power of IFS is that it is profoundly respectful. It respects not only the client but also each of the client's parts. This is a radical shift from the one-up, expert position of diagnosing and pathologizing that most therapists have been trained in.

In the twenty years I've worked with IFS, and especially in the ten plus years I've devoted my professional life almost exclusively to it and to learning about it, I've helped train thousands of therapists in this method. I've been on staff at more than twenty official trainings, have led many of my own IFS workshops internationally, and coauthored the book *Many Minds, One Self* with Dick Schwartz. (Everybody who knows him calls him Dick.) I have also assisted Dick at many of his trainings, including at Esalen. IFS is very simple in its basic principles but not at all easy to master. IFS is first and foremost a model of psychotherapy but has grown to also be used in education, coaching, mediation, law, business, and as a way of living. It offers us a new way of being with ourselves and a new worldview.

Before he developed IFS, Dick was working as a family therapist and was quite prominent in the field. He coauthored what is perhaps the most frequently used textbook on family therapy and was a tenured professor at a young age. To prove that this kind of family therapy was all that was needed in order to heal psychological distress, he did an outcome study with a group of families who had bulimic children, most of them daughters. He rearranged the family systems in just the way he was "supposed to." The belief in family therapy back then was that if you took these therapeutic steps, the symptoms would disappear and the people would be healed. However, that didn't happen. His outcome study showed that his method was not working as he expected. The bulimic children were still bingeing and purging.

Unlike many academics, Dick took the data seriously rather than fudging or discounting it. He got curious about what was going on and started interviewing the bulimic daughters. When he interviewed them, they started talking about parts of them. "When I get upset, a part of me just wants to eat and eat and eat so I don't feel the pain, and then another part of me hates me for doing this and is disgusted and makes me vomit." As Dick started learning about this parts structure, he had the idea that maybe he could apply the systemic way of working that he'd used with external families to the internal family — the family of parts inside each person.

One big advantage that Dick had is that he had almost no training in intrapsychic work; all of his training had been in family systems theory. Therefore, he didn't have to unlearn any theories or move any aside that would cloud his fresh perceptions of what was going on in his clients. He was able to listen deeply, clearly, and respectfully to these people, and he says they were his major teachers and the real source of this model.

As he started working with them, he had one client who was also a cutter. This is actually a fairly common phenomenon; people typically cut themselves on the forearms or body, and it seems to work to relieve emotional pain. One day Dick decided that once and for all he was going to join forces with the parts who didn't like the cutting and force the part who was cutting to agree not to cut. He set aside an entire afternoon to meet with this client, badgered her relentlessly, and had her badger the part who did the cutting until that part finally agreed to stop cutting. The next week when she came to her next session, she had a big gash down her face. Dick sort of fell back on the couch, shocked and dismayed. His work had backfired, and he said out loud, "I can't win this battle." The part who had been doing the cutting said, "I don't want to win this battle either." Dick got truly curious about this part. "Well then, what do you want, and why are you here?" Dick says that this moment was the real birth of IFS. He got curious about the parts and let go of trying to control them or push them around. Instead he treated them with respect.

Dick found that many of the techniques of family therapy that worked in the outside world also worked in the inner world. When communication between two parts was difficult, there was often a third part, like a third family member in the outside world, who was getting in the way. In the outside world, just asking that third person to step back led to better communication. This strategy worked in the inner world as well. Dick was getting excited about this realm, which was new for him. However, many of his clients, after big sessions with powerful emotional release, would have untoward events. They'd have a car wreck going home, or they'd pick a fight with their spouse, or they'd have a high fever. Dick started realizing there was a very delicate ecology in the inner world. He became concerned that perhaps he was doing more damage than good and needed to give up on this project of working with the inner parts of people.

This led to another major innovation of IFS — the realization that some parts are protecting the system and other parts often carry extremely difficult emotions that are buried. Most therapies just rushed toward these hurt parts that carry these difficult emotions. Dick realized that it was crucial to honor the protective parts and get their permission first. Once this was done, there was very, very little pushback when trying to contact the hurt parts.

Another core concept in IFS seems very simple but, like the idea of multiplicity itself, it revolutionizes therapy. This idea can be stated as "parts are not their burdens." Burdens are the extreme emotions, belief systems, and other energies that young parts took on when they were deeply hurt. These burdens are not who the parts are; after the parts feel fully witnessed, we can help them unload these burdens so they can return to their beneficial natural state.

Dick became convinced that he had come across something of value that could significantly help reduce human suffering. He had the great courage to quit his tenured position and has spent the approximately forty years since that time developing and spreading IFS. For many of those years, he was on the road, speaking and leading workshops, as much as two hundred days a year. Many others have joined him and added to the model. Now IFS is incredibly popular. There is a waiting list of over ten thousand people for the Level 1 training in the United States. IFS is now also being taught all over the world — across Europe as well as in China, Korea, Pakistan, Vietnam, Australia, New Zealand, Russia, Canada, the Middle East, and more.

So what is this model? What is IFS, and what are its basic ideas? First and foremost, humans are multiple. In a sense, we all have multiple personality disorder, or DID, but in most cases it's not, in fact, a disorder. This multiplicity is not the product of trauma — it's natural, healthy, and beneficial. This basic realization, when all its implications are followed, revolutionizes the way we work with people and how we view ourselves. It really is a game changer. This idea is not new. Plato had a multiple model of mind. In one of his dialogues, Socrates is talking to one of his students, and they say that the very fact that someone could disagree with themselves and have a debate inside their head about what to do next shows that the mind is multiple. They just moved on as though this was practically self-evident. In fact, internal dialogues have been found in every culture in which they have been looked for. Many philosophers besides Socrates have had a multiple model of mind. Yet this idea has been very unpopular in the West.

To me, it's like the Copernican view of the universe. We're no longer the center of the universe, no longer one unified thing. It's a humbling realization. In Hermann Hesse's novel *Steppenwolf,* the hero realizes he has two parts and then learns that he actually has many more. Hesse writes of his hero, "Harry consists of a hundred or a thousand selves, not of two. His life oscillates, as everyone's does, not merely between two poles, such as the body and the spirit, the saint and the sinner, but between thousands and thousands. Every ego, so far from being a unity, is in the highest degree a manifold world, a constellated heaven, a chaos of forms, of states and stages, of inheritances and potentialities. As a body everyone is single, as a soul, never."

Hesse's novel contains an entire eloquent section about why modern society has had to squash this idea over and over. But it keeps rising again. Carl Jung's idea of complexes was very much a multiple model of the mind. He wrote, "The so-called unity of consciousness is an illusion… we like to think that we are one but we are not, most decidedly not." He held that we could be taken over by these smaller parts of us — in his language, these complexes.

We want to think we are fully in control of ourselves and masters of our ship, so this idea of being made up of parts that can take us over is quite difficult for many people. Dick realized that you could consider these parts as things or as full subpersonalities with all the characteristics of a person. Early on, he would say we can show clinically that if you treat them as full subpersonalities, you get better results. But now he's much more blunt and basically says they are full-spectrum subpersonalities. One reason this is so important is that if we view them as things, drives, or forces, we may tend to treat them cruelly, without respect or care. We also tend to ignore their ability to change and the potential gifts they bring. When we instead see them as full-spectrum people, usually children, it is easier to see their value and to feel real respect, care, and love for them. All parts are welcome.

Dick had another discovery that he says is his greatest discovery. In addition to the parts, there's also something inside each of us that he calls Self, with a capital S. Very often with his early clients, a part would appear that seemed wise and calm, and he'd ask, "Who's that part?" And they'd say, "Oh, that's not a part — that's who I really am, that's myself." So, he took their word, *Self,* and called it Self. Self is who the person really is. It's always the witness. It's the eyes looking out into the world. It's the awareness, and it's characterized by eight C words. (Dick loves alliteration.) The eight Cs are: curiosity, compassion, courage, confidence, clarity, calm, connectedness, and creativity. Dick says this is who we really are, and anytime we're not feeling these qualities to a large degree, a part has taken us over — has hijacked us. I'm sure it's pretty obvious that most of us spend the vast majority of our lives hijacked by parts.

Another thing that Dick said about Self that was absolutely life-changing to me, and to many of the people I'd been working with, is that it cannot be damaged or even dirtied. It's like the sun on a stormy day. A disastrous storm can blow down the trees and cause mudslides and destroy your house, but when the clouds part, the sun is still there — undirtied, undamaged, untouched. I had been told that with a childhood like mine, the most I could ever expect was a miserable little life and that I should take a lot of meds and not get too hopeful. I was told that since I'd never had the early attachment experiences I needed, I would always be operating at a deficit. Dick said no — this Self is who you really are, and it is undamaged and undirtied. That is a very important, and potentially life-changing, message for big T trauma survivors. In my experience, this is true. No one, no matter how terrible their life experiences or earlier behaviors, is fundamentally damaged goods. No one. We all are this radiant Self, and this fundamental health can never be taken from us.

Here's the basic map of IFS. Each of us has parts, who are all full, 360-degree subpersonalities, and we also have a Self. Parts come in two basic varieties: protectors and exiles. Exiles are the wounded inner children that many other forms of psychotherapy have found. We all, even those of us with the most benign childhoods, have to exile many parts of ourselves as we grow up. It's part of being enculturated. As one humorist has said, you can't become an adult without being adulterated. But for those of us who have experienced any kind of trauma, exiles are often the parts that bore the brunt of the pain that otherwise would have overwhelmed the system, and the rest of the system locked them away in some basement of the mind so we could go on.

These encapsulated parts want to get out, and when they're triggered by something in the outside world, they can come roaring up and take over the whole person. To contain these parts, there's a whole realm of protectors, who come in two varieties: managers and firefighters. Managers do their best to prevent exiles from ever being triggered. They make life safe and keep people away who might do anything that would remind the exiles of their pain. Firefighters are parts who come up *after* exiles have been triggered. Their job is to put out the flames of strong emotion at any cost, and they really don't care very much about collateral damage. Addictions are usually firefighters, for example. Managers are proactive and tend to be socially approved. Firefighters are reactive, and they're often not very welcome.

But in IFS we welcome them all. We welcome and respect all the parts. Regardless of their behavior, we realize they all have good intentions and are all trying to keep the system alive and afloat. Welcoming all the parts, like many things in IFS, sounds simple and easy. We think we can just go right by that, easy, done. It's not. It's very, very difficult. With my history of sexual abuse, it was very hard for me to welcome parts of others that would sexually abuse a child. I hated them, and I couldn't find any Self to be with them. I spent many years working with sex offenders, and it took close to a decade of inner work before I could really welcome those parts. So "all parts are welcome" is a very simple concept, but it's not easy to implement.

Why would we want to welcome these extreme parts? The reason is that we can then help them change in a fundamental way rather than just try to imprison them forever (which never works anyway). The managers, even though more socially approved, can also be very destructive. The overworker, the internal critic, the perfectionist — all of these can become extreme as well. Parts are forced into extreme roles by the trauma they had to experience and then contain.

When released from these extreme roles, all parts are of value and helpful to the system. They all have great gifts to bring. Very often the exiles, whose pain led us to lock them in the deepest internal dungeons, are actually the most sensitive and innocent of our parts. Of course, they are the most hurt by abuse and trauma. Welcoming them brings back an exquisite sensitivity, a great gift. Healing in IFS is like starting with a civil war and helping it change into an orchestra or a choir. Each one of these parts is valuable and has wonderful things to contribute. They all are welcome. We don't want to blend them all together and make a single bowl of mush. In an orchestra, we need all the different instruments — violins and cellos and flutes and trumpets and vocalists and more. It's the same inside.

The basic path of an IFS healing starts with finding a part to focus on. Very often this is quite easy — they're right on the surface. For example, someone's full of rage or fear. We find the protectors involved, check with them, and get their permission to connect with the vulnerable parts they are protecting. We don't expect protectors to change their behavior right away. We just want their permission to go inside and help the exiles they've been protecting. If they don't grant it right away, we listen respectfully to their concerns until they feel comfortable relaxing back. Once they've granted access to an exile, we meet the exile and witness it completely, finding out whatever it wants us to know about how hard it was back when it took on the burdens it carries. Then we help this exile come forward in time to a safe and comfortable place. After that, we help it let go of the extreme emotions, beliefs, and energies — the burdens — it took on back then. Only then, when the exile is unburdened, safe, and free, do we ask the protector to consider changing its behavior.

This is quite a revolutionary approach to healing. Many forms of psychotherapy, including most cognitive behavioral therapy, are essentially about increasing the strength of the managers to control the system. This can be helpful, but it leaves the basic underlying dynamic unchanged. If we do this, much of our life energy is spent on our parts fighting and struggling against each other. When we can free the exiles and release the protectors from their extreme roles, there's much more life energy and joy as well as the eight C qualities of Self.

The real healing in IFS takes place between the client's Self and the client's parts. It's not something we therapists bring in from the outside. We trust that each client has deep, healing wisdom inside themselves, and we respect that. In IFS, we ask some important, almost magical, questions. One is: "How do you feel toward that part?" Then we wait until we hear one of the C qualities. If there is no Self there, we work with whatever parts are interfering with the connection until Self is present. This process develops that inner Self-to-part connection. This Self-to-part relationship is the primary locus of healing. It stops the civil war and turns the client's inner system into a cooperating orchestra or team.

This is a very, very brief summary of the basics of IFS: We are multiple. We are made up of many parts, and this is a good thing. We need all the different instruments in our orchestra. We also have a Self, which is characterized by the eight Cs, and real healing comes from helping people connect to their own Self. All parts are welcome. They all have things of great value to bring to the system, and they all have fundamentally good intentions. They're struggling to survive and help the whole system survive. When people are able to stop the internal civil war and their parts befriend each other, huge amounts of energy are released, and people become much more creative, peaceful, loving, and positive.

IFS is not merely a therapy method that treats pathology. It becomes almost a way of life. When someone cuts you off in traffic, you can realize when an angry part of you has hijacked you and wants to scream obscenities. You can love that angry part and welcome it with humor and friendship. That's very different from the way most of us react. IFS can also become a spiritual path in welcoming this Self energy more and more deeply into our lives. In addition, it can help us be more forgiving and loving with others because we realize that sometimes when they're acting in ways that are offensive to us, a part has hijacked them and it's not all of who they are — it's just a part.

The author Michael Ventura said, "You are not one person, you are many people, you are a community of moods and selves under one name. Parts of you aren't even human, they're part mammal, part reptile, part rose, part moon, part wind. And life is a question of which parts are dominant — which, in effect, possess you. (I think most people walk around possessed by the dullest parts of themselves; this, the worst state of possession, is called normal)" (quoted in Weller 2015, 59). The psychiatrist and philosopher Iain McGilchrist referred to this multiplicity with the delightful phrase "the field of you."

Farther Reaches of IFS

IFS has some rather unsettling implications, and this book will focus on probably the most unsettling of them. But let's mention a few of the other ones first. Parts have parts. Parts have a structure like the structure of a person. They have a Self and parts, and their parts come in two varieties: protectors and exiles. This becomes very important clinically when dealing with dissociative identity disorder (formerly multiple personality disorder) because in these people, where the walls between parts are so strong, you're always talking to one part or another — you can't yet talk to an overarching Self. And then you work with the parts within that part, and sometimes the parts within the part within the part.

This reminds me of a story about a gentleman, from India I think, who was asked, "What does the world rest on?"

He replied, "The world rests on the back of a tiger."

"What does the tiger rest on?"

"The tiger stands on the back of an elephant."

"What does the elephant stand on?"

"The elephant stands on a turtle."

"What does the turtle stand on?"

"From there, it's turtles all the way down."

In some ways, the IFS Model is as unsatisfying as that — it's parts all the way down. Arthur Koestler called this kind of organization a holarchy. The parts are holons; they're nested systems, one inside another, with basically the same structure. This is very much like the mathematics of fractals. So that's one thing about IFS that's quite odd. The same concept also works in the other direction: we are parts of bigger systems, which in turn are parts of still bigger systems... This reminds me of a bit of doggerel from my childhood: "Big bugs have little bugs upon their backs to bite 'em, Little bugs have littler bugs and so on, ad infinitum."

If you start thinking about Self, what is it? It seems to be something within a person. People experience it by going inward, and in that sense it seems sort of like a particle. But then as we look at parts, they also have a Self, which also seems to be a particle within them. But Self also somehow seems bigger than that. Dick now says Self can be experienced as a particle or a wave — either way. The wave reality of Self is almost as though Self is a field. This also gets us into ground that's uncomfortably spiritual for many people. I am reminded of a theologian who was asked, "Is the divine immanent or transcendent?" He just said yes. Self is both in us — a particle, immanent — and somehow beyond us — a wave, a field, transcendent. Dick now explicitly acknowledges the similarity to the Indian concepts of atman and brahman. Brahman is the divine at large in the cosmos, like Self as a field. Atman is the Self within us — Self as a particle. A classic Hindu statement of realization is the Sanskrit *tat tvam asi*, which means "Thou art that." The atman is the brahman. Dick has also suggested that enlightenment in IFS terms might be shifting the sense of identity from our usual manager parts to our Self.

Another thing that's very unsettling to some people about IFS is that as you go inside and meet all of a person's parts, you come upon things that do not come from their individual life history. Some of this is to be expected if you stop and think about it. As evolutionary psychology has demonstrated, much of our mind comes in modules — our computer comes already programmed with all these subroutines — so all that stuff is in there. But also, there's what IFS calls *cultural burdens*. Americans typically have the cultural burdens of racism and consumerism and extreme individuality as well as certain other characteristics that we took in from our culture. We also have what IFS calls *legacy burdens*. A legacy burden is a complex of extreme emotions, beliefs, and energies that has been passed down from our ancestors. Pretty much every other culture on this planet, from hunter-gatherers to urban civilizations, recognizes the importance of ancestors. They are worshipped or placated, honored and feared. Our culture has largely sneered at this as the superstitions of primitives, but the so-called primitives were right. They were onto something important. The science of epigenetics makes it clear that these multigenerational transmissions exist — there's hard scientific evidence for them. We do inherit things that our parents experienced that are not transmitted to us through genes. When I was in high school and college, we were taught that this idea was ridiculous.

The most important experiment about multigenerational transmission was conducted by Brian Dias at Emory and Kerry Ressler at Harvard (Dias and Ressler 2013). Dias had noticed that in his community — the poor Hispanic community in Atlanta, Georgia — addiction and mental illness seemed to run in families. He wondered if there was any way this could be biologically inherited, so he designed a very clever experiment to test it. He took a male rat and exposed it to a chemical that has a relatively pleasant smell, somewhat like cherries or almonds. He paired that smell with electric shocks until the rat had a startle response when it was just exposed to the smell. This created a classically conditioned reflex. Then he took the semen from that rat and artificially inseminated a female rat. The female rat never met the male rat and was never exposed to the smell. When she had her pups and they were mature enough, they were exposed to the same smell, and they had the same startle response!

So this acquired characteristic was heritable, and there was absolutely no behavioral connection between the original male rat and these children. This startle response continued for generations. There are many other experiments like this now. We know it happens. So psychologically, traumas that happened to your ancestors can affect you. This has also been very clearly demonstrated in the children and grandchildren of Holocaust survivors. Rachel Yehuda of the Icahn School of Medicine has published over five hundred papers in this area that include powerful evidence of biological as well as psychological dimensions to these legacy burdens. A well-studied syndrome of feelings and behaviors occurs in these people. So, we know it happens, there's hard science behind it, and we can work with it using the IFS parts model.

Even stranger, some things inside get in a person's system that are not legacy burdens, they're not cultural burdens, and they're not a part of the person's system. IFS has come to call these "unattached burdens" (UBs). We don't really know what they are, and they don't fit any accepted theory. Like the experience of internal guidance or guides, they have no place in modern materialist thinking. Many therapists find this entire area so awkward and unsettling that they ignore it when it comes up. Nevertheless, unattached burdens occur, and IFS has developed pragmatic ways of working with them. What IFS calls unattached burdens and guides will be the main focus of the rest of this book.

The story of Hungarian physician Ignaz Semmelweis is very instructive. In Europe during the early 1800s, childbed fever killed a large proportion of the women and newborns who were in a hospital for the birth. This fever would rage through the wards. Doctor Semmelweis was the head of one of these clinics, and he realized, I think by accident, that if he washed his hands with chlorine until they were slippery between patients, it would stop the spread of childbed fever. He knew that this would not be a popular idea, so he didn't publish it, but his students were very enthusiastic and started bragging about the results on their ward. When Semmelweis started defending his hand-washing practice, he was attacked by the other doctors. They called the practice ridiculous, saying, "Are you saying our hands have put this disease in all these women? Are you accusing us of being the cause of this disease?" The debate became more and more violent. Semmelweis became quite unsettled. He was fired from his job and then may have had a mental breakdown; at any rate, he was locked up in a mental institution and died there a few weeks later as a result of a beating from the guards. It wasn't until decades later when Lister's theory about the bacteriological cause of disease provided a theoretical framework that what Semmelweis had discovered could be accepted and used. Not only did he die unnecessarily — probably hundreds of thousands of women and babies died because the academic establishment of the day couldn't accept something they lacked a theory to contain.

Another, lighter description of the problems of introducing radical new ideas comes from the German philosopher Arthur Schopenhauer. He said that all important advances go through three phases. At first they are ridiculed and mocked, and their proponents shunned. Second, they are argued against vehemently. Third, they are accepted as self-evident.

Dick has been very concerned about my writing this book because he thinks it might be used to discredit IFS. What we're discussing here will have no academic framework that can contain it right now. I will suggest some in the second part of the book. But I keep in mind what happened to Dr. Semmelweis as something that both sobers me and gives me courage. If this book contains ideas that are absolutely unacceptable to you, I hope you blame me and not Dick. I do not speak for Dick or IFS directly — I've gone farther than he does into these strange waters. The basic method of IFS is well established, it's evidence-based, and it's used very successfully in many places all over the world. Dick's fear is that these weird, extreme realms that I am fascinated by will be used to discredit it. If it seems weird and extreme, it's probably me and not Dick or IFS.

CHAPTER 3

A Case That Changed My Life

I will not commit the fashionable stupidity
of regarding everything I cannot explain as a fraud.

—C. G. Jung

There is only one portal to knowing; the portal is I do not know.

—Sadhguru

About ten years ago, I was on the staff of a Level 1 IFS training in a sweet, picturesque college town in Michigan. One of my duties as a program assistant was to lead triads, or practice groups. Each group had three participants plus me; one would take the role of the therapist, another would be the client, and the third would be the observer. The people in the therapist and client roles would do IFS sessions, and I would directly intervene during sessions to help them learn IFS in a very hands-on and personal manner. This has always been the most pleasurable, exciting, and challenging part of doing these trainings for me. It's always new and fresh. During this particular practice group, I was working with a male minister and pastoral counselor who was in the role of the therapist. The client, who was the clinical supervisor at a large agency, was a woman in her fifties.

In working with her, the man in the therapist role found a critical voice. Now, inner critics are very common in IFS — they're a type of part that almost everybody has. They're usually a protector, and specifically a type of manager. But this one was relentlessly mean, fierce, and negative. I had the feeling it wasn't really a part of her, that it was an unattached burden (UB), and I had only a vague idea about how to deal with them from my own training, but not much experience. The man who was in the therapist role was not doing well. I said to him, "I think this is something you haven't had any training in. Would it be okay with you if I took over the session?" He gratefully agreed.

I started working with this woman about this thing in her. It was relent-lessly negative. Usually, with an inner critic, you can find out why it's criticizing, such as it wants to keep the person safe or motivate them or improve their lot in life. There's a good intention in there somewhere. We looked for this energy's good intention over and over. I would ask her, "Can you ask this thing why it keeps criticizing you so harshly?" It would just say things like, "I want to cut her down to size." I'd ask, "What's good about cutting her down to size?" "Well, then she wouldn't be so arrogant." "And what's good about her not being arrogant?" "I just want to destroy her." It just kept stating negative things. This is the first important indication that something is not a part of a person's system. Parts always have a good intention. It may be hard to find, but it's there. Even suicidal parts have a good intention. Usually, it's the last refuge when the pain is unbearable. It's an apex protector — the highest firefighter. The part thinks it can stop the pain this way.

This thing didn't seem to have any good intention. The next thing I'd been trained to do was to have the client ask it directly, "Are you a part of me?" She did this several times, and it kept evading the question. This critical voice sounded more and more hostile. I asked her if she could see anything or if she had any im-ages of what this critical voice looked like. She said, "Yes, it looks like a bloodshot eyeball." As she focused more on the imagery, she said, "Oh, it has legs, too — they're sort of like the legs of a goat. So, she had this internal dreamlike image of a bloodshot eyeball with the legs of a goat, and it just kept criticizing her, and it wouldn't answer the question "Are you a part of my system?" when she asked. I encouraged her to keep calmly and steadily asking. At one point, she reported that it yelled at me, "You're supposed to be a teacher; that's a very stupid question. Don't you have anything smarter to ask?" I laughed a little and said, "Yes, it may be a very stupid question, but it's a very simple question. Are you a part of her?" For a long time, it just kept evading the question. Finally it roared, "No, I'm not a part of her — I'm a much more powerful and beautiful being, and I'm going to crush her like a worm, the same way I'm going to crush you." There was an ensuing silence.

Okay. This thing is not a part of her system. It has no good intention — it just wants to damage her. It's what we call an unattached burden. We were able to get it out of her system. We will discuss in great detail how to do this later. Luckily, in this early case, it was relatively easy. We called for light to fill her inner world and told the bloodshot eyeball thing that it could no longer stay in her. It tried to sneak back in disguised as a little girl exile part, but it was one of the most bizarre-looking little girl exile parts you could ever imagine. The disguise wasn't very good, and we got it out completely. Then I was able to debrief the group calmly, telling them that this was an unattached burden, we run into these sometimes, they're fairly rare. I then closed the group and took everyone back to the main class.

After that, we had a staff meeting, and my body temperature probably dropped three or four degrees. I was very cold and couldn't get warm, even with blankets and people holding me. That was very weird. I also became somewhat irritable. Some of my friends were joking with me about this, saying, "Bob's the ghostbuster," and I was really angry and snappish and had to apologize afterward. As my body temperature came back up and I started normalizing, I wanted to pretend the whole thing hadn't happened. It was a fluke, a once-in-a-lifetime coincidence or strange experience. I was starting to write it off and go back to my hard-earned, trauma-oriented view of psychopathology.

As the workshop ended, I started getting long emails from the woman in the client role who'd had this thing removed from her. The emails scared me because she seemed to almost be having a manic episode. She was saying things like, "Oh, the light in the airport is so beautiful — I haven't seen colors like this before" and "I can feel deep love for all the people in the airport." I was starting to get quite worried. Then she sent an email that dramatically increased my fear level. She said, "Bob, I didn't tell you or any other people in the workshop this, but when I was a young woman, I tried to kill myself many times and was institutionalized many times." Now I was really scared. Visions of malpractice danced in my head. Then she wrote something that changed my life. She wrote, "Bob, you're the first person to ever take me seriously when I talked about the nonhuman inside of me, and you have changed my life. Back then, if I tried to talk about this, they gave me electroshock and a lot of drugs. I have not talked about this to anyone for decades. Thank you." When she said that, I knew I would not be able to just ignore this and pretend it hadn't happened. Well, what *had* happened? What in the world could this possibly be? With hardly any special tools or skills in this area, I had been able to help this woman make a big change. Was it purely the fact that I accepted that she could have something inside her psyche that was not a part of her? Did my basic IFS knowledge of our parts structure help?

I have followed this woman since then, for over nine years now. She has continued to feel that the experience was very liberating and life-changing. The outward signs in her life indicate that she is flowering and growing and enjoying new depth and richness. I truly didn't know what to make of this. It seemed impossible. It didn't fit my trauma model of the human mind at all. But I reluctantly came to think, maybe my trauma model is still valid, but it's only a small part of a bigger picture. Perhaps the trauma model must be contained in something much, much larger. I expressed curiosity about this stuff to a lot of the people in the IFS world. They'd mostly heard of unattached burdens and maybe even seen one or two small ones, but nobody was focusing on it. Nobody wanted to — it was sort of weird and ugly and creepy. As word got out in the IFS world that I was interested in this topic and willing to work with it, I got more and more referrals. As a result, I've now had quite a bit of experience with unattached burdens. And because of this rather odd situation, my clientele is skewed. I can't tell how common this is in the general population because people who have this experience have been sent to me so often.

Quite early on in the process of learning about these things, I focused on trying to figure out what unattached burdens were, but I put that on hold and instead kept my attention on how to help the suffering human being in front of me. This change in focus is very important. My goal as a therapist is to reduce human suffering — not to pursue my research agenda at the expense of my clients. Also, answering what these things were seemed overwhelmingly difficult, impossible, and impractical. I know that no matter how fancy my theories, they may not make a difference in the lives of my clients. Insight is very often not curative. I went back to William James, who talked about radical pragmatism and radical empiricism. You work with what you're given. The more extreme pragmatists said what works is what's real. I disciplined myself to stay focused. How can I reduce human suffering? What works when this is how people describe their experience? What works when things like this appear in a client, or in myself?

I trained myself to not get into fancy theories about what unattached burdens are, what they could possibly be, or anything like that. For most people, the temptation is to jump into either trying to find out what these things are or to rigorously deny their existence or defend it. These issues are in a distant second place for me. The fact is, people experience unattached burdens. They will report them to you if you show any openness. These types of phenomena have been reported throughout Western history and in almost every human culture. They do not fit our modern materialist ideology, but it seems painfully arrogant to refuse to study a phenomenon because we have no theory for it. As William James wrote, "There is no source of deception in the investigation of nature which can compare with the fixed belief that certain kinds of phenomena are impossible." Another advantage I have in terms of doing this work is my age; at this point in my life, I am old. I don't need to defend a career or establish a place for myself or have academics approve of me or any of that. I can pursue what appears real to me and what relieves human suffering. This choice of the basic question to ask about these phenomena has determined the course of my research for the past decade.

Here is a case that is perhaps more typical of unattached burden (UB) work. This is the first fifteen minutes of a one-hour session. During these fifteen minutes, the therapist and client found and removed a UB that had been blocking work with the client's parts. The rest of the session was traditional IFS focusing on family-of-origin work. Notice that this UB is sort of flat and two-dimensional. It is capable of responding to questions, but it shows very little understanding or emotion. This session was done in a workshop by an IFS senior trainer whom I will call George. There were about thirty people in the room.

George: So, let's all go inside. Let's bring a lot of Self energy to Helen as she does this. Okay, there's a lot of energy here for you.

Helen: I can feel it.

George: Good. So, did you have something in mind?

Helen: Yes. I have a part that is this narrator, commentator, that lives behind my left eye, and it drives me insane, and it, it's just going all the time. There are brief respites, but it gets particularly loud in the middle of the night, and it won't let me go back to sleep. I don't think it ever goes to sleep.

George: Yeah, a lot of those parts don't. Okay. So, it's right back here, and as you notice it there, how do you feel toward it?

Helen: I really hate it, and I'm really frustrated with it.

George: Yeah, I understand why. Will the part that hates it give us the space to get to know it and maybe help it? Just check and see.

Helen: Yeah, it's softening.

George: Okay, good. How do you feel toward the narrating part now?

Helen: Curious.

George: So, let it know. Just see what it wants you to know. Don't think of the answer — just wait for the answer to come from that place in your head.

Helen: It wants me to know how hard it's been working.

George: Yeah. How do you feel toward it as you hear that?

Helen: Some compassion.

George: Let it know. Maybe ask why it's working so hard and what it's afraid will happen if it didn't do this narrating thing all the time.

Helen: That I would let my guard down.

George: Okay, and then what would happen?

Helen: I'd be vulnerable.

George: And then what would happen if you were vulnerable?

Helen: It's… it's afraid that I'd disappear.

George: Disappear. Does that make any sense to you, Helen? It does? Is it okay to feel all this?

Helen: Yeah.

George: Yeah. So, tell your parts it's okay to let you feel the pain of that disappearing.

Helen: It's really scary.

George: Yeah. Okay. And is all this emotion coming from the narrating part?

Helen: No.

George: No.

Helen: It's a part underneath it.

George: Underneath it. So, we just want to make it over with the narrating part. Ask if it's okay if we give some attention to the part that attacks.

Helen: Yes, it is. It's been waiting for years.

George: Okay, good. That's great.

Helen: I'm sorry. Yeah, it's like it's stepping back.

George: Good. Good, good. So, just see if there's any other part that's afraid to let us be with this disappearing part.

Helen: Yeah, there's a part that's kind of hovering here, and it's just this dark, dark energy.

George: Okay, so let's get to know it first a little bit. Ask what it's doing there and if indeed it's afraid to let us go to the pain of that disappearing part.

Helen: It's not talking — it's just kind of hovering here. It's very dark.

George: How do you feel toward it?

Helen: Curious.

George: So, let's try it again. Just ask if there's something it wants you to know.

Helen: It's not talking, but it's just conveying that it's like some cloaking device, it's like, just hangs there.

George: It's cloaking.

Helen: Yeah.

George: Cloaking another part or what is it… can you tell?

Helen: It's like it just kind of blanks, blanks out…

George: Yeah.

Helen: … my access somehow.

George: Got it. Alright, let me see if it will talk to me. Is that okay?

Helen: Yeah.

George: Alright. Are you there?

Helen: Yes.

George: And you're this dark, cloaking, blocking-out part?

Helen: Yes.

George: Helen, is that right?

Helen: Yes.

George: And have you been doing this for her a long time?

Helen: I've always been here.

George: You have, yes. Uh-huh, and what are you afraid would happen if you didn't do this for her?

Helen: I'm just here, I don't…

George: So, you just do this? It's your job and you just do it?

Helen: I just do it. I'm not afraid for her. I'm just in here, just do this.

George: Okay, but you just do this. Okay.

Helen: I've always been here from the beginning of her.

George: Do you like this job?

Helen: No.

George: No, right. Doesn't sound like it's much fun, really.

Helen: It's not — it's just who I am.

George: Yeah.

Helen: I don't, it's not even, it doesn't feel like a job, I just, I'm here.

George: Just what you do. Are you a part of Helen, or are you something else? Or do you know?

Helen: I'm not part of her.

George: You're not a part of her. Okay. Do you know how you got into her?

Helen: When she was about four months old.

George: You came in when she was about four months old?

Helen: Yeah.

George: Yeah. And you've been there ever since. And are you giving her this emotion, or is that somebody else?

Helen: I feel like I'm feeling it, not the part.

George: Okay, alright.

Helen: Or this thing.

George: Yeah, so the thing. I want to go back to the thing — we'll get to the part that was emotional about it. So, um, let me talk to you again. Yes, Helen. So you heard that conversation?

Helen: Yeah.

George: How do you feel toward this thing now?

Helen: I just feel like it's some dark energy. It's gotta go. It doesn't feel like it has a job, it just feels like it's...

George: Yeah, it has that feel to it. Um, do you feel at all afraid of it?

Helen: Yeah.

George: Okay.

Helen: I do.

George: So, let's get all the parts that fear it into a waiting room with the assurance that it has no power if you're not afraid of it. I promise. Okay. How do you feel toward it now?

Helen: Better, much better.

George: Good.

Helen: It's lighter.

George: It seems lighter?

Helen: Yeah.

George: Alright, so ask again if it's a part of you or not.

Helen: (shaking head)

George: It said no?

Helen: No.

George: Okay, so let it know we're gonna...

Helen: It's outside of me — it's not in me. It feels really different.

George: Okay, yeah. Let it know it doesn't really belong in you. We know it's been in you a long time, but it's not where it belongs, and we're gonna send it to where it belongs. Does it seem okay with that?

Helen: It's not talking, but…

George: It's not fighting it?

Helen: Yeah.

George: Alright. So, are you ready to send it out? So, typically, we bring in light to shine on it. You up for that? So, we'll do that. Bring in the light, have it shine on this thing, and tell me when it's in the light.

Helen: It's coming now.

George: Light coming in?

Helen: Mm-hmm.

George: Is it having any reaction to being in the light?

Helen: Yeah, it's breaking up.

George: It's breaking up? Okay. So, just ask the light to take it where it belongs, out of your system, and just watch until it's all gone, until it's not in there anymore. Okay?

Helen: (deep sigh)

George: Okay?

Helen: It's going. Yeah, it's going away. It's like breaking up, it's…

George: You're good. We're gonna wait till it's all the way out. So just keep watching. Okay? Good.

Helen: Yeah.

George: Okay.

Helen: It's lost its power. It's just like it's…

George: Good. So, let all your parts know now that it's gone and…

Helen: Sorry.

George: Let all your parts know and, yeah, you can move your body however you want to.

Helen: Yeah, it just feels like it's…

George: Yeah, good. What's the feeling?

Helen: It's, it's just so much relief. (Helen cries intensely.)

George: Yeah, that's great. It's great. Long time coming. That's great. Yeah. Lot of relief, and grief too, huh? Yeah.

Helen: Oh. Oh, gosh. I have this, uh, piercing pain.

George: Okay, let's check and see what that is. A piercing pain in the back of your head?

Helen: Yeah.

George: Just ask what that is.

At the end of this part of the session, Helen felt a piercing pain at the back of her head. It was a part of her that had been concealed by the unattached burden. When the therapist said, "Just ask what that is," this began a forty-five-minute session of classic IFS parts work. The unattached burden was gone — it was no longer part of the session, and it did not return.

The name "unattached burden" is rather awkward. Most people in the IFS world refer to them as UBs. Early on, Dick called them "critters," a name I preferred. That name helped people lose their fear of them, and this loss of fear is crucial in this work. Also, it reminded us that we do much better when we treat these beings as people rather than things. The name "unattached burdens" was chosen at a trainers' meeting, reportedly because the name "critter" seemed so disrespectful. My guess is that there was also the hope that the name "unattached burdens" might be easier for people to accept. In the UK, some IFS therapists call these "stray burdens." Many other names have been used for this phenomenon: intrusions, attachments, introjects, negativities, energies, entities, spirits, demons, jinn, dybbuks, ibburs, possessions, obsessions, infestations, archons, curses, lost souls, beings, spiritual presence experiences, incorporations, irradiations, residues, adhesions, incubi, and succubi, to name a few. Each one of these names has a slightly different definition and theoretical structure around it. Almost every culture and language has its own ways — often many ways — of referring to these types of things. We could learn a lot by studying them comparatively. I considered renaming them the "other within," or OWs. This is a more inclusive term, as it includes UBs, guides, legacy burdens, cultural burdens, and spiritual presence experiences in general. Distinguishing between these various categories is often a subtle and delicate task. So having a broader name, at least at the beginning, has advantages. But for now, I will just refer to them as UBs.

What in the World Is Going On Here?

You have very little chance of getting at the truth
if you know in advance what the truth ought to be.

—Robert B. Parker

Making assumptions is volunteering to be stupid.

—Andrew Vachss

How in the world could there be some psychic content in a person that is not part of them and is not an epigenetically transmitted legacy from their ancestors? This did not fit in with my worldview. I prided myself on how open I was, but it still didn't fit. It definitely didn't fit in the academic worldview. The topic is so far outside the range of what is considered possible that Dick did not like it being discussed as part of IFS. He would teach about unattached burdens in advanced classes, but he always cautioned people to talk about them with discretion because he didn't want this oddity to be used to discredit IFS.

Once when I was assisting in a Level 1 training, the lead trainer said in a staff meeting that there are two things he did not want us discussing with participants: legacy burdens and unattached burdens. Right after that staff meeting, he did a demonstration therapy session with one of the participants in front of the whole group. She had a huge, dramatic unattached burden that had been passed down through her family as a legacy. The lead trainer skillfully helped this participant get this unattached burden out of her system. Mike Elkin, another IFS lead trainer, often says half-jokingly that irony must be the driving force of the universe. Many IFS practitioners don't deal with this stuff at all. Some people are still also squeamish about legacy burdens, but much less so now that epigenetics and studies of the descendants of Holocaust survivors have provided a solid scientific basis for this.

The Invisible Gorilla

It seems we're not able to perceive things until we have a cognitive framework to put them in. There is a famous story about some Natives who were on an island when Columbus first approached. It is said that they couldn't see the ships even when they were close and clearly visible. They had no category for these ships. Some accounts say that the tribe's shamans could see the ships because their perceptual systems were much more open, but it is unclear to me how we could know this. The predictive processing models of perception can explain how we could make ourselves blind in this manner. We filter out raw data that our unconscious predictive filter systems do not think will have survival value. In some of these models, there are six or more levels where top-down predictions determine which bottom-up raw sensory data are allowed through.

In a very famous experiment conducted at Harvard in the late 1990s and first published by Daniel Simons and Christopher Chabris in 1999, the subjects viewed a film clip of less than ten people passing a basketball back and forth. They were asked to count the number of times people in white T-shirts passed the ball. In the middle of the video, a person in a gorilla suit walked through the center of the scene. Fifty percent of the subjects did not see the gorilla at all! Almost all of the subjects were Harvard undergrads — intelligent and sophisticated people. We only see what we're looking for. In 2010, the same authors published a book-length treatment of this subject.

Even closer to our concerns, a similar study was reported in 2013 called "The Invisible Gorilla Strikes Again." In this experiment, twenty-four highly trained radiologists were monitored as they examined CT scans of lungs, looking for the tiny nodules that indicate lung cancer. In one of the scans, an image of a gorilla approximately forty-eight times the size of the nodules was inserted. Twenty of the twenty-four radiologists did not see the gorilla! Here we have experienced medical professionals missing something grossly obvious right in front of their faces. This sobering result should make us doubt our certainties in our own areas of expertise. This also offers an explanation of why some therapists might never see UBs. In addition to this therapeutic blindness, clients with these experiences are often used to being ridiculed and called insane, so they are unlikely to mention UBs to a therapist until they believe that the therapist has an open mind in this area.

The *DSM*

In the mental health field, at least in the United States, we are supposed to consider the *Diagnostic and Statistical Manual of Mental Disorders*, which is published by the American Psychiatric Association, as our bible. So, I examined it first. It is a terribly flawed bible. Many, possibly most, clinicians routinely ignore it as much as they can. For insurance and reporting purposes, they are often required to use one of the diagnoses in the book. The *DSM*, as everyone in the field calls it, is in its fifth edition now. The first edition, back in the 1950s, was about thirty-eight pages long, and the fifth edition has nearly nine hundred pages. For each edition, committees are formed to review the diagnoses. Sadly, much of this seems to be about politics and academic territory building. The *DSM* is heavily influenced by the pharmaceutical industry and focuses on biological models for human mental distress. This is a very unpromising place to look for information about phenomena that look like possession. But starting in the *DSM-IV*, the writers did make an attempt. In Appendix B, which listed areas in need of further study, they introduced the idea of dissociative trance disorder. The criteria pointed to conditions that involve the alteration of the identity of the patient — in which the patient was completely taken over. They distinguished sharply between kinds of possession and trance behaviors that are culturally approved and therefore not considered pathology versus those behaviors not culturally approved and therefore considered pathology. The point that jumps out is that the same subjective experiences and behaviors are absolutely fine and valued in one cultural context, but in another culture they are considered disease and eradicated as much as possible. This seems to imply that the problem is in the cultural context, not the individual — the problem is in the attitudes and ideologies of the culture rather than in the person's experience. Therefore, the real healing would be in changing the cultural context and the ideologies of the healers. This possibility does not seem to have been discussed at all in either the *DSM-IV* or *DSM-V*, nor in the extensive articles that were published in many journals about this potential diagnosis. Of course, the psychological and psychiatric establishment would find it very difficult to welcome such ideas. It would mean they would have to question some of their most basic assumptions and perhaps even admit they had been wrong. As the anthropologist Janice Boddy wrote, "Coming to grips with the normality of possession requires us to abandon, or at least reevaluate, the western idea that in every culture a normal healthy self will be internally coherent and relatively well integrated" (Stephenson 2017, 78), but as IFS practitioners, we already know that the human personality is multiple. This recognition of multiple mind allows us to be open to phenomena that others are ideologically blind to.

Another issue is also very problematic. The *DSM* wants to use the criterion of whether or not an experience is distressing, painful, or unpleasant to determine pathology. This seems okay until you realize that in almost all cultures where possession is a valued experience, it often starts out being very painful, disorienting, and unwelcome. A classic example is the initiatory illness of shamans and various other traditional healers. Often the illness is so bad that it nearly kills them. This kind of extreme distress is also prevalent in the accounts of South American possession healers, for example, in Umbanda or Candomblé. In Korea, hardly anyone used to want to become a *mudang*, the Korean name for their shamanic healers. Until very recently, mudang were despised and viewed as about the equals of prostitutes. For much of Korea's history, their work was outlawed. They only became mudang because the distress inflicted upon them by the spirits possessing them was so intense that they had no choice. These are just a couple of examples, but they are enough for us to see that distress and difficulty are not useful criteria in distinguishing a disease process from a culturally valued norm. Another perhaps even more important point that seems to have been almost totally ignored by the powers that be is that other cultures have ways of transmuting these difficult, painful, and terrifying experiences into something of value for both the person and the society they live in. Isn't this exactly what we as therapists want to learn how to do?

The *DSM* seems to want to take the peculiarities of modern American practice and ideology, and call anything that doesn't fit this model a disease. The basic attitude is that anything outside our rather narrow view of what is natural is a disease with clear causes and sometimes cures. It universalizes our unique cultural experience. There are obvious economic and political motivations for the psychiatric establishment to maintain this position and to promote it worldwide as though it were a basic biological truth rather than a cultural artifact. Some people have even called these tendencies imperialistic. Many Indigenous healers here in the United States talk of decolonizing therapy. Roland Littlewood (2001, 2004b) makes the important suggestion that perhaps our attempt to view possession phenomena through the lens of a dissociative disorder disease model is backward. Perhaps we should look at what we called dissociative disorders through the larger lens of possession phenomena all over the world and throughout history.

The *DSM-IV*, which we've been reviewing, has a lot of problems, but the *DSM-V* seems even worse. It categorizes possession trance disorder as a type of dissociative identity disorder. DID almost always follows severe child abuse and tends to be chronic rather than episodic. The language in which this entire discussion is lodged is an almost impenetrable barrier. I feel as though I'm hacking my way through a jungle of jargon. Sometimes I wonder if that language is meant more to conceal than express. A humorist once said about an academic, "He must've studied for decades to learn to write that badly."

While we're on the subject of jargon, there are a couple of words I need to discuss: *emic* and *etic*. These terms originated in linguistics but have been used extensively in anthropology. The emic view or explanation of a phenomenon is the one adopted by the culture in which the phenomenon occurs. The etic view is the supposedly objective explanation offered by an outsider. The problem with the etic view is that in practice, it is usually the viewpoint of the anthropologist or academic, and it is assumed to represent some universal truth. It often seems to be a way to disrespect the views and beliefs of the people being studied. It seems to claim that we know better — that our currently fashionable academic interpretations are more important and valid than how the people hold their own behaviors and feelings. Our Western arrogance is especially damaging in the tender and vulnerable area of psychological diagnosis.

What academically respectable theories could account for UB phenomena? It seems that the standard perspectives of Western psychotherapy are sadly inadequate — we will have to look further afield. Part 2 will take up these issues in more detail.

Case Studies

First let's look at a few more case studies to get a good taste of how weird this stuff can be — as Zorba the Greek said, "the full catastrophe."

Sarah

Here is an example from a session that was done by a different IFS therapist, another prominent lead trainer. He was doing a demonstration in front of the group in a Level 2 training with around forty people present. (The client herself has edited and rewritten this account.) At first the client, Sarah, didn't know what she wanted to work on. She had vague fears about her mother's death (her mother was still alive) and also had concerns about the death of her father, who had died decades earlier. Then she noticed something in her inner world and said, "There's a big guy in the corner." A part told her that "it's a triangle — there's a third one involved here." She realized it had something to do with her dad's psychotic states. The "big guy" was very big, demon-like, and dripping with malevolence, and she had a hard time staying with the images that came up. The therapist asked her over and over again, "How do you feel toward this being?" She was scared.

(Note that perhaps the biggest rule in dealing with UBs is that when you're not scared of them, they lose all power. UBs only have power in a person's system when the person is scared of them. And the corollary of this is that UBs are really good at scaring people.)

Sarah asked all her other parts — all the scared parts — to leave and go somewhere safe so she and the therapist could deal with this. In her inner world, she saw the parts leaving almost like in a ceremony. Parts came up to her one at a time, nodded, and left respectfully. The therapist asked her if this malevolent being knew that she (her Self) was here, and she said, "Yes, it does now." But two parts of her refused to leave. They stood on either side of her, a male and a female. They wanted to stay and protect her, but the therapist insisted that they go. They didn't want to leave, she realized, because they love her. But the therapist insisted, so the parts talked to each other, then kissed her and left. The therapist reassured them, "We've got this." Absolute confidence.

After they left, the therapist said, "Look toward the big guy in the corner." And this woman, who was very polite and civilized, said, "What the fucking hell is that?" (There was actually real curiosity in that expression.) The big guy started calling her names, and she put up a hand in her inner world and said, "No. You don't get to speak anymore." The therapist asked the being to walk around her and check her out. It tried to scare her repeatedly and failed. Then the therapist said, "Okay, we're going to send it on its way." He said, "I'm sending it a lot of love from out here. Can you send it love, too?" From inside herself, she heard, "Turn on the metta." (*Metta* is the Buddhist word for loving kindness — an energy that can radiate through and out of the body.) This thing went around her faster and faster and faster. It turned into a white ball of energy, and shards of light from all around her inner world came into it. The therapist encouraged her to keep going. The thing started going so fast, in a ball of light, that it spiraled up and out of her. Then it was quiet, and it felt as though someone had left the stage.

(I do not use this idea of having the unattached burden circle the client in my sessions; it is unique to this session. I include it here to show that there are many ways to do this work.)

Then the therapist invited other parts back in. He asked, "How are the bodyguards?" One of them said it had been trying to contain this negative energy since Sarah was three or four, and this part sort of resented the therapist for not recognizing how fiercely it had worked to protect her. Other parts had long feared this fierce protector part. The other bodyguard was pleased but said it had not really been something to do with her. After this, the woman felt as though there was a celebration among all the parts inside of her.

After coming back "outside," Sarah — who'd had back problems for her entire life — suddenly realized that for the first time ever, she was able to lean all the way forward. She could bend. And ever since then, she's been much more flexible. However, a day or so after this powerful session, her whole system crashed. Having felt great, now she felt a growing panic inside, even a paranoia, and realized that somehow the unburdening experience had destabilized her system. She noticed fearful thoughts that perhaps she'd gotten rid of "the wrong one," the good one, and feared that the bad one was left in her and running her. Her own therapist became frightened, and one question seemed to keep arising in sessions — she needed to decide whether to go to the light energies or the dark energies inside her. She tried to get back in touch with the leader of her group, but he was too busy to help her. Then she found another experienced IFS therapist who was not afraid and offered to help.

In working with him, Sarah saw herself at the Grand Canyon, with dark energies behind her and the light on the other side. It felt as though she had to make a choice. At first she didn't know how to get across the chasm, but someone inside said, "You can just walk across." (Dick often talks about the difference between "inner physics" and those of the external world.) She was able to go across and join the light energies. After this, she felt big relief. This choice had given her new resolution and new peace. She also felt that she had lost contact with her parts, as though there was a thick black curtain blocking them off from her Self. In her next session, the IFS therapist offered compassion to the paranoid part and listened to it, then invited the bodyguards into the discussion, too. This helped the parts who had closed the curtain between Self and the parts to reopen it, reintegrating the system. This resolved her issues and settled her system into a different, Self-led, integrated configuration.

Sarah's father had been adopted at one year old and suffered all his life, becoming alcoholic and later psychotic. He often heard the voices of devils, as he called them, and more than once accused Sarah and her sisters of being devils. From a very early age, Sarah had developed the ability to appear very scary to other people and had realized she could use it to keep herself safe in dangerous situations. She came to believe that parts of her had developed the ability to call this negative energy forward, even while it was contained, so that other people would see and sense it and leave her alone. She also said that she'd had suicidal thoughts previous to this experience, many times thinking it would be better for everyone if she were dead, but after releasing the unattached burden, she no longer has these thoughts. It's also worth noting that before the first session of the IFS training, Sarah had never heard of unattached burdens and had no beliefs or thoughts about them.

Several people have mentioned that they find this particular case confusing, and it is. Confusion is common when dealing with unattached burdens. I have interviewed Sarah, the therapist who did the primary unburdening in the workshop, the therapist who did the follow-up work, and another participant in the workshop. Something very impactful for Sarah happened in this process. It does not fall into neat categories; there is something uncertain, perhaps even mysterious, about the process. When I asked the primary therapist why he had the UB circle her in that way, he said that was purely intuition and he trusted his intuition. It was not his normal way of working. The second therapist involved said he found the work with Sarah some of the most fascinating of his long career. The image of her needing to cross the Grand Canyon and make a decisive choice between good and evil was powerful. The other participant in the workshop said that he felt uncertain about what was happening during the process but had the sense that it was significant and strong. This is a wonderful example of returning to the calm and curious energies of Self, even when all the familiar road markers are gone. Later on, I came across a couple of other cases where this circling tornado-like process was used to remove the unattached burdens from someone's system, but it's not common. The confusion, however, is very common. UBs seem to love to spread confusion and uncertainty. When we can change fearful confusion into calm curiosity, this strategy of theirs backfires and actually helps us work with them.

Harry and Pat

This is a married couple with a long-term stable relationship. I will call them Harry and Pat. Both parties were experienced with IFS. The husband is an alcoholic in recovery with long-term sobriety. The wife is a very experienced IFS therapist who had approached me to set up the session. She told me that her husband had this suicidal part in him and that, for years, she'd told him that it had a good intention and that they could work with it. He'd said, "No — there is no good intention. It just wants me dead." She would not believe this because in IFS, all parts have good intention. Her husband went silent, figuring she just didn't understand. This is a classic example of why people do not see unattached burdens, even when they are right in front of them. She called and asked if I would do a session with him while she watched. I agreed.

It started with them sitting side by side in a sunny porch-like space in their house. When I started working with Harry, a concerned part came up right away who said, "You have no idea what you're doing at all." I thanked the part for being honest and direct, and then told it that it had no reason to trust me and that it was my job to earn its trust. Then I told the part that its distrust of me made sense. It said it didn't care. I told it that it was the boss and that I wanted to be totally transparent and direct with it and get its permission and approval for anything we did inside Harry's system. This was speaking its language. I told this part, "If you're ready, we could get this thing out." It said it didn't want to be the one to stand in the way.

Harry described this thing as being like three different colors of wax that had all melted together. Two of these were parts of him, and the third was something else. I asked, "How are you feeling toward the thing that is not you?" I was looking for fear. A whole group of young parts were somewhat frightened. They agreed to go someplace safe and comfortable and have a couple of representatives watch what we were doing. They said their fear would not inhibit them or cripple them, but it was normal, like before a big battle. Then we returned to "How do you feel toward this thing that's not part of your system?" When the fears were cleared, we worked with the two parts who were intertwined with it. One came out fairly easily, but the other one did not want to leave. The area where they were locked together now looked like a battlefield. The being turned into the most beautiful, sensual, sexual woman you could ever imagine. She and Harry both knew that if he went to her, she would stick a dagger in him and gut him. This being kept offering addictions. There was a vivid image of a needle full of heroin poised over a tied-off arm with bulging veins. I said to Harry, "Well, addictions work a little at first, but then they don't and there's a big price to pay." He roared at me and raged, "They don't work a little — they work a lot." He said calling it "a little" was disrespectful of all the addicts and their decision-making process. He was right about that, and Harry's comment has changed the way I talk to addicts. We kept working with his system, and when there was a space, I apologized. Harry then said, "There's no need to be delicate here — we're big boys." The part of him that was still attached to that thing that wasn't a part of him was afraid its life would be drained, dull, and gray without that being and all the excitement it brought.

I kept asking Harry how he felt toward the part of him that was still attached to the being. I wanted that part to turn toward the Self for connection. Eventually, the part took off the uniform of the unattached burden and put on the uniform of Harry and all his parts on the battlefield. Then the part came toward Harry and joined him. At some point, I asked him to surround the being with a ball or egg-shaped container of light and pull it out of his body to a good conversational distance in front of him. He reported back that the being did not like being contained. I asked him to look for any connections back from that ball of light to his body. There were many. Many parts gave back to the being things it had given them. The strings and connections fell away. Harry asked his wife to move away from where she was sitting next to him. She moved across the room. As the connections weakened between Harry and the being, the being yelled at his wife, "It's your fault — you loved him too much, you bitch." The being felt it would have gotten him completely if it weren't for his wife's steady love throughout his addictions. I told the being, "We're not here to punish you or judge you. We're sending you to a place where you too can heal and transform."

I then asked if any parts of him would miss the being when it was gone and we got this cleared. Then I suggested that he see the ball start to move upward toward the sky and eventually disappear into loving hands. His body started moving, and his hands shook very quickly. I encouraged him, saying, "Let your body move. Your body knows how to do this — it knows how to get rid of these things." There was more and more movement. He was stomping his feet, shaking, and moving around in his seat. The thing went up into the sky, and I had him tell it, "We know we need to respect your free will. Just as you could not stay here when there was no part of Harry that would allow you in, we do not get to determine where you go. You can go back to the darkness, or you can go to the healing realms." I also said, "All your slaves, minions, employees, and subordinates also have free will to make their own choices." Harry said this choice was easier.

Later, Harry said there was still one string connecting this being back to the dark. After we took care of it, we came back to Harry and his parts. Everyone seemed happy and good. I mentioned that at times like this, people often experience a higher power or guidance. I knew that Harry had participated in AA, and that's why I used the specific phrase "higher power," which is used in twelve-step programs. Harry took some time with this in silence. Later he reported that he felt a golden light coming down and connecting to him, and golden light from Earth coming up. This light spread out horizontally to the world around him. Later still, he said he had an auditorium in his inner world that he frequently saw, but he'd never before been able to see the audience. Now it was all light in there, and they were trying to put a robe and crown of gold on him onstage. At about this time, I said, "Well, I know we're all big boys here and maybe we're supposed to be tough, but I have tears in my eyes." He jokingly yelled at me, "You wimp!" He had a regular check-in process twice a day to stay in contact with his parts, so I didn't have to make arrangements for him to stay in touch internally.

At this point, his wife came back in and sat next to him again. She expressed a lot of gratitude. It was really sweet to watch the connection between them. He talked a little bit about when she had sort of tried to work with this and said he felt she didn't know what she was trying to do, and he had told her, "You don't know what the hell you're doing." This is big — many people do not want to work with this darkness. He said, "Bob, you must have paid in suffering for these skills." I briefly described my childhood. At one point in the session, he said he didn't want to have to be a perfectionist about this work, but what if he didn't get every little piece? I said, "That's fine — that'll just show us where we need to come back to and do more work later."

A UB in Me

Now I'll give an example from my own life. I have serious eye problems — wet macular degeneration, dry macular degeneration, and some others. Quite a few years ago, I was told that I was going blind and should prepare myself. I worked on this a lot with an IFS therapist, and when I directed my inner attention to my eyes, I had images of a spiderlike creature attacking the retinas, poking at them with what looked like a scorpion stinger. This would cause the blisters that then caused the bleeding, which was the wet macular degeneration. We were able to work with this spider being. It had my mother's energy in it, and we were able to get it out of my system and send it on. My mother was horribly abusive, and her betrayal always seemed deeper than my father's, even though she was not as sadistic as my father. You have to go very, very far back to find creatures where the mother will eat her children. Spiders do this, I believe. But for fathers, it's not so far back. Bear fathers will eat their own cubs, and the mothers have to protect them. So somehow, the betrayal from my mother felt like a much deeper betrayal, and that energy was attacking my eyes.

Since we got it out of my eyes, I have done much better than the doctors thought possible. I still have the problem, I still get it checked regularly, and when I need to, I get the injections or other medical care. I don't know what that energy was or what that vision of the spider was. Was it a maternal introject or what? I don't need to know. What I need to know is how to pragmatically deal with experiences like this in myself and clients. The way to do this is to find all the parts of me who were scared of it, connect to them with love, get them to a safe place, and then, after being absolutely sure this is not a part of me, get it out of my system. I can worry about what it is later.

Marsha

Another UB incident occurred with a long-term client I'll call Marsha. Marsha was very athletic, a triathlete, with the kind of blood pressure and heart rate you would expect from someone like that, 95/65 or something like that. She'd had an incident of a strong allergic reaction to a medication and had to go to the emergency room, where they put her on so many antihistamines and other drugs to control her allergic reaction that she became semiconscious for an extended period of time. She completely recovered from the allergic reaction, but after she came out of the hospital she felt weird, so she went to her regular doctor. He told her that her blood pressure was somewhat elevated — 110/90 — not bad but very high for her. She kept feeling weird, and her blood pressure kept going up and up: 120/100, 130/105, and so on. It was starting to be a medical issue. Her kidney numbers were not so good, either.

When we did a psychotherapy session around this, what she saw in her inner world was a very obese man lying down and struggling to breathe. She had never seen a part like this inside her before. As we interacted with it, it became clear it was not a part of her. We told it that it was lost and in the wrong place and that we were going to help it go to where it belonged. We helped it leave her system and move on. After this, her blood pressure started going back down and returning to the realm that was normal for her! Who knows what this was. The sort of obvious idea we might want to jump at is that perhaps a morbidly obese man had died in the emergency room next to her while she was comatose, and somehow their energies had become entangled, but we don't know. That kind of thing seems absolutely impossible by any kind of Western standard. But we do know that dealing with the thing in this way helped her. Really, that's all we need to know.

An Irish Experience

As it became known that I was interested in these phenomena, many people told me stories of their experience that they had kept secret because they feared ridicule or being diagnosed as insane. For example, a woman who is a very experienced non-IFS therapist told me of some events that had occurred many years earlier in Ireland. She was working there as a psychotherapist. One day while driving toward her supervisor's office, she felt an odd sensation. She felt terrified — it felt as though some malevolent energy had gotten into her and was moving around in her body. For the rest of the drive, she had powerful urges to drive her car off the road into a stone wall. She repeatedly had to wrestle the car back onto a safe course. When she got to her teacher's house and reported this to the teacher, the teacher said, "Something has gotten into you." She lay down on a table. The teacher told her to keep her eyes closed. She could sense the teacher moving around the table, sometimes talking and sometimes yelling. After a while, the teacher said, "I think it's out." The woman still felt the malevolence in one foot. The teacher worked on this, and afterward the woman felt free and back to normal. She was amazed that her teacher knew what to do. There were no more weird experiences driving the car. She has never had a recurrence of this strange phenomenon.

———

Dick frequently says that you have to follow the data no matter where they lead — follow the data. This simple directive is incredibly difficult to live up to. There's a similar quote with a similar message, an old saying that goes "The sailor who would discover new worlds must be willing to lose sight of the shore." With these cases, I had definitely lost sight of the shore. There's also a story that I believe was about Bertrand Russell and Alfred North Whitehead. Whitehead, the great philosopher, gave a lecture on the philosophical implications of quantum mechanics, and Sir Bertrand Russell was in the audience. At the time, this was the cutting edge of Western intellectual progress. As Russell came out after the lecture, a reporter asked him, "Sir, what did you think of the lecture?" Russell smiled and said, "Oh, it was a magnificent lecture — it left the vast darkness of the subject unobscured." That may be my goal with this book: to leave the vast darkness of this subject unobscured and not to pretend I know things I don't.

CHAPTER 4

Interesting People on a Winding Path

If you desire to reach what you do not know,
you must go where you know nothing.

—St. John of the Cross

If you are not willing to be a fool, you can never become wise.

—Anonymous

As I've started exploring the topic of UBs more and more, I've run into some amazing people. I've had to go into areas where I am an absolute beginner, and I've had to ask beginner's questions. I have had to be the innocent, the fool. My active interest in this stuff has definitely closed some doors to me, but it has opened many more, especially to non-Western cultures and parts of our own culture that we ignore and denigrate. This chapter is not strictly chronological, because all these investigations overlapped. My goal in this chapter is to bring you along as I felt my way into these strange waters and opened myself to areas of experience I used to ignore or dismiss. Meeting all these different people from different cultures gave me the feeling that I was circling my subject and getting to view it from many different vantage points. Each perspective had something of great value to offer. I worked to keep my figuring-out parts from prematurely creating grand theories. This was and is primarily data collection, and the great virtues here are curiosity and openness. The path was not straight, but it was frequently exciting. There was no curriculum to follow, no study guides.

Pakistan

I have worked in Pakistan teaching IFS. I haven't gone there — I've done all my work online, but through this work I've come in contact with some of the Pakistani community. Many of them believe in jinn, which are sort of like demons but not really, and they think people are affected by jinn possession. It should be obvious now that some of this unattached burden stuff looks like what was traditionally called spirit possession. One of the people I was working with in Pakistan had a relative who was a psychiatrist in New York City. She'd personally had experience with jinn possession in her family. We had a long talk about it and how disruptive it was. She and her religious leaders did get this jinn out, and her family was freed of it. It had been an arduous process, and she had to move to a new apartment with her family to help her escape from its influence. She worked in an emergency room doing psychiatric intake. I asked her, "Is it possible that some of the people being sent to you in the emergency room are actually suffering from something like jinn possession rather than a diagnosable psychiatric illness?" She said, "Yes, definitely." I asked, "How can you help them?" She said, "I can't — I'd lose my license. I can't." She cried a little, and we were both very sad. Then she said, "Bob, write your book — write your book."

Also through my Pakistani friends, I met Shaykh Muhammad, who is the imam of a mosque here in California. My wife and I went to visit him. He works quite a bit with jinn, removing these spirits from people. He works on Christians, Jews, and Muslims. Sometimes he just goes to a nearby hospital and works with whoever is ill, whoever wants help from him. He said that one of the things that made him become a religious man was an experience he'd had very early on. Shaykh Muhammad is a very large man. I'm six feet tall and two hundred pounds, and he is substantially bigger than me and powerfully built. He'd been a boxer as a young man. One time he was called to a neighbor's house, and there was a small woman there whom they said was possessed by a jinn. He could not hold her down. It took several people to hold her down while the local shaykh worked with her to get this jinn out of her. This incident made a deep impression on him. How could this possibly be?

Shaykh Muhammad performed a Ruqyah on me and my wife — a way to diagnose whether you have any jinn in you. It uses the exorcism method itself as a method of diagnosis. This same method, probably independently found, is sometimes used by modern Catholic exorcists. It is called diagnostic exorcism. He put his hand on my head and recited certain verses from the Quran. He said, "No, you're clear." Then he did the same with my wife's head. He put a cloth over her head before he touched her because it is improper for an imam to touch a woman. He said, "If there'd been a jinn in either of you, it either would have started speaking through me or you would have become unconscious." So neither my wife nor I had jinn in us, according to the imam.

Spiritism

Very early in my search for answers or at least parallels with what I was seeing, I came across Spiritism. Spiritism today is primarily a Brazilian phenomenon.

There are also Spiritists in the Philippines and, in fact, all over the world. The first resource I found was Emma Bragdon, PhD, who founded the Integrative Mental Health University in Vermont. She is deeply influenced by Spiritism and led groups down to Brazil to learn more. I found that most of the Spiritist groups in Northern California, where I live, only conduct their services in Portuguese; however, I found one about an hour away that held a service in English once a month. I was able to go to that several times. The building was an old office in a semi-industrial area. The people were incredibly welcoming, warm, and kind. There was a talk — very Christian, very Gospel-based — and then there were healings where a few people at a time would go into back rooms. Some of the people from the center would perform what they call *paseos*, or passes, which are very similar to Reiki energy healing. While you sat in a metal folding chair, they would take their hands, palms facing you, and slowly go down over your body without touching it, about six inches away, several times to clear the energy and clear spirits. This is the first level of Spiritist healing, and it seems that it's done or offered in most Spiritist healing meetings.

At this meeting, they were so pleased to have Western people showing interest that they made a point of introducing me to Dr. Kathleen Seaton, who, at the time, was completing her residency in psychiatry at Stanford. She was also very interested in Spiritism. Many times she and I carpooled about three hours away to Sacramento, where the only center in Northern California whose services were always entirely in English was located. This gave us a lot of hours coming and going to discuss Spiritism — how weird it was, how it didn't fit the Western medical view, and how, even so, it seemed to work. The Spiritist meetings at the Sacramento center also started with a talk, and then there would be paseos. After this, they would ask people who wanted more healing to come up and lay on massage tables they had set up behind screens. Two of their practitioners would work on those people. Several times I did that. One time, I said I thought there might be spirits bothering me, trying to attack me, and they said, "Yes, there are," and they gave me a green card to take to the leader of the center, which I guess was a code. He set up healing sessions to get those spirits removed from me. These sessions were remote; I was not present at the time. He told me when he would be conducting the sessions and suggested I meditate or pray during those times. I asked if the group who did the healing would give me information about the spirits they found in me, and he refused. He said, "No, if you knew more about these spirits, it might serve to reattach you, so we don't give any information."

Spiritist healers always work in teams, and there are usually at least three and often about six people on a team. They are mediums — they channel the spirits.

One person welcomes in the spirit who was in the client, and another person welcomes in a healing spirit. There's a dialogue between them until the spirit that was in the client is released. The Spiritists believe that the spirits in us are also suffering beings and need help. There is no big clash or battle as in the movie version of exorcism. I experienced three or four of these remote healing sessions. I'm not sure if anything happened. Several of the people at that center were very impressive to me. They were all humble, mostly blue-collar. Some of them embodied peace and joy. It was a very multiracial group with every color you can imagine. There was one very large Black woman who seemed to radiate kindness like a furnace on a cold day. One of the men who greeted people at the door had been burned horribly as a child; he had been blinded and had great difficulty breathing because his throat was burned. In desperation, after all Western medical treatments failed, his parents took him to the Philippines, where he was healed by Spiritists there. By talking with this man, I learned of this connection between the kind of healing in the Philippines and in Brazil. In the Philippines, Spiritist healing was outlawed, and for hundreds of years people were prosecuted for doing it, but they kept on with the work. To me, that indicates there must be something of great value in it for them. There were no Philippine Spiritist healing centers in Northern California, so this man worked at and participated in the Brazilian one.

The place itself was a storefront in a clean, unpretentious strip mall near a freeway. The average meeting had perhaps twenty attendees; thirty would be a big meeting. Many Spiritists believe that smoky quartz can contain and control negative spirits, and every Spiritist center I've been in has a big piece of smoky quartz. This place did as well. Ironically, Spiritism in Brazil is based on the work of a Frenchman, Allan Kardec. Between the 1840s and 1860s, he wrote some six big, fat books on this subject. He also published a newspaper and was very active in promoting what he had come to understand about spirits, the nature of the world, and healing. His method in writing his books was to create a list of questions and then ask those questions to a group of the best mediums he could find. He would compile the answers and unify them. His first, and generally considered most important, book is called *The Spirits' Book*. It consists of just over one thousand questions and the compiled responses of all these mediums. They reflect a fairly consistent worldview: The spirits of humans live on after death. We are reincarnated over and over and over again. We tend to reincarnate in spirit groups and work out our issues with each other over many generations. There are hierarchies of more and more healed spirits who can help us. We are composed of three layers — spirit, perispirit, and the physical body. The perispirit is halfway between spirit and the physical body; it is what is affected by these spirits who get attached to us and who operate in us. The work of Allan Kardec was so dominant in Brazil that one kind of Brazilian Spiritism is often called Kardecismo. It fits quite well with other Brazilian traditions of spirit possession and contact with the other world — Umbanda, Candomblé, and more. Kardecismo is the most European of these traditions. The others have stronger African and Indigenous influences.

One of the basic tenets of Spiritism is that no Spiritist should ever receive payment for their work, and as far as I know, they are all true to this today. There are about fifty psychiatric hospitals in Brazil that have Spiritist healing teams associated with them. This is the closest cooperation of modern mental health providers with blatantly spiritual healing that I know of. Spiritists believe that all the spirits that might inhabit us or bother us are the souls of deceased humans. They are lost and suffering and need help to move on to the realm where they can grow and learn and prepare to reincarnate. They are not enemies to be driven out and damned. No matter how much chaos and illness they have caused, they are lost, suffering souls who need our help. These assertions I'm making about Spiritism are big generalizations. There are a couple of Spiritist federations, but none have any real authority, and each center has its own practices and style.

Perhaps the most famous Spiritist of all time was Chico Xavier (1910–2002). He was a humble civil servant, a low-level postal clerk who never accepted a penny for any of his Spiritist work. He would do automatic writing, which the spiritists call psychography. He produced some 490 books and thousands of letters even though he only had a third-grade education and worked full time his whole life. He gave away all the royalty income from his books, which amounted to a huge sum of money. His most famous book is called *Nosso Lar* in Portuguese, which translated means "Our Home." It has been translated into many languages, including English, and has sold some thirty or forty million copies worldwide. However, because of our narrow Eurocentric view, very few of us have even heard of the book or him. *Nosso Lar* was also made into a movie that's available on the Internet with English subtitles. Oddly, it is titled *The Astral City*.

Chico, as he was called, also did readings for people who wanted to talk to deceased relatives. Most nights at his small home, there'd be a line of many people, often hundreds, wanting his help. He never accepted a penny. When a prominent magazine had a contest for most important Brazilian of the twentieth century, Chico was voted one of the top few, and yet very few outside of Brazil know anything about this remarkable man or have even heard of him. About a dozen of his books are available in English. They are very readable; they're sort of like Mexican telenovelas except that the dramatic interchanges between the people go on for generation after generation, lifetime after lifetime. A mother and son in one generation might be a married couple in another or a boss and an employee, and these relationships work through issues over many generations. *Nosso Lar* starts with the death of the hero and takes place entirely in the afterlife realm. At the end of the novel, he is preparing to be reborn. The more deeply I explored this subject, the more I realized how narrow and Eurocentric our views are. We focus only on what comes out of the Western intellectual tradition.

Cáli Ornelas is an IFS therapist who is originally from Brazil. She became an international personal growth and meditation teacher with centers in India and Europe, and is now a therapist residing in Europe. She told me of some experiences she had when she was a child back in Brazil that convinced her of the reality of these types of occurrences. She loved her mother's sister a great deal, but this aunt was deeply troubled and had psychotic episodes. The family got the aunt to a Spiritist healing center, and they found two malevolent entities in her. She was admitted to a clinic where she attempted suicide during the treatment, but she recovered. The healer who helped her aunt recognized Cáli's psychic abilities.

Cáli had had many encounters with entities from a very young age. The word used in Portuguese for these entities is *entidades*, and Cáli asked me to use *entity* for the English translation. She'd felt spirits getting into her dolls and felt that strange energies wanted to hang out around her. The healer told her that she was like a sponge for the spirits. Cáli wanted it shut down, and the healer did that for her. Her abilities stayed largely shut down for decades until she became deeply involved with meditation. At one point, a Tibetan Buddhist teacher worked to open her third eye. During this experience, she felt a burning sensation there for many days. Spirits started to get through to her again. At first this was too much, but now it only opens when she wants, and most of the time she gets information through her guides. When she is receiving information this way, she is careful to tell the client that this is not therapy.

When Cáli was in her teen years, she did many very dangerous things and took extreme risks, even by the standards of a wild youth. When she was fifteen, her mother went with one of her friends to visit a card reader. The mother returned home deeply scared. The reader described Cáli in great detail and said that they needed to protect her because there were entities in her that would get her in trouble and provoke sexual abuse unless they were removed. Cáli was very skeptical at first, but at her mother's insistence she went to the card reader without her. The card reader knew Cáli even though they had never met. This reader warned her that in seven to ten days, two men would try to abuse her. "They will be driving a red car. They will smell of alcohol." The reader also warned her, "The entities inside of you will make you forget things," but Cáli remembered the experience. It happened just as predicted a week later, but she was able to get away and ran home.

After this, she went to a healing ceremony to get the entities out of her. There were about a dozen people at the ceremony, which lasted all night. She was informed that the entities were passed on to her by family members and had been in the family for generations. There was drumming, dancing, and incense. People brought offerings, candles, flowers, and sweets. The healer let a spirit enter him, a *Prieto Velho*. These are the spirits of old, wise Black slaves who are kind and helpful. They usually smoke a pipe, and this one did. This spirit, working through the healer, found two spirits in Cáli. They were both *Pomba Giras* (also spelled *Pombajira*), which are the spirits of an African-derived goddess of love and sex. They are described as beautiful, insatiable, and dangerous. They are often full of wrath and are invoked in witchcraft. One of them wanted to use Cáli in order to have a lot of sex; the other one was just going along with the first. Cáli was frightened during the ceremony, and her body made involuntary movements for five to six hours while the Prieto Velho spirit in the healer negotiated with the Pomba Giras in Cáli until they agreed to leave her. These entities in her had also been causing her to do dangerous thrill-seeking behaviors.

Cáli said that every therapist should know about these entities. They are real, and they are indeed around. She recommends that therapists work with their parts who are afraid of them. She believes that we need to have respect; these entities have tentacles and a deep need to reconnect to the world via a living body. They can strongly influence thought processes and emotions. As all IFS practitioners who work with these entities are advised to do, Cáli emphasizes staying with the question "Is it a part or a UB?" These entities might make a feeble attempt to lie about this, but generally they will tell the truth and say they are not part of the person. Their pride and sense of their own importance make them vulnerable to manipulation by the therapist. They are often arrogant and disclose their need for malevolence. Cáli works a lot with the location in the body where they are lodged. She is careful to note if this location moves, and after one of them is gone, she spends time healing the physical place in the body where it had been located. Cáli and I had many conversations, and this discussion is just a synopsis of some of her points. Later I asked her to summarize the most important lessons about this topic, and she wrote the following:

I think there are two important factors from my story for others to hear:

First, I had no idea that I had a couple of them and that there was more than one UB lodged in me, as I was so young and just wanted to explore freedom. In my view, I was just a normal teenager; there was no suspicion on my side that some of the thoughts and impulses I was having had to do with their presence in me. When I look back on what this means, it is clear that one might be the "carrier/host" of these entities and not know it for a very long time. As I have repeatedly seen later in life, and in my practice, people can indeed learn to live with them and host them for years and years. It is very sad and very disrupting.

Second, some people have parts that are inclined to make alliances with UBs. One of the reasons could be that the parts have been so isolated from Self energy that they feel safer and more powerful in connection with a UB. It can be a repeated experience to pick them up if they are floating around. My running theory is that people with parts like this, which was for sure my case, need to be made aware to periodically check thoughts, emotions, fears, and nightmares to see if there is a new intensity or oddness that does not belong to their system.

Later in one of her emails, Cáli wrote, "The most helpful [knowledge] is that having one of these UBs removed from one's system is not as difficult or complicated as it is made out to be… and how much life can and will change when they are gone, but I think that's one of the core reasons you're writing your book anyway."

Tibetan Buddhism

As I was studying the Spiritists (and I still study them — it's a vast and deep field), I learned about an advanced Tibetan Buddhist practitioner. Since I was studying spirits, he suggested I read *The Spirits' Book* by Allan Kardec. He said there is an intermediate realm between spirit and the physical body and that Kardec and the Spiritists are the experts on that. The Spiritists talk of the perispirit, which is similar to the concept of an aura — "a subtle body that envelops the physical body and holds the blueprint of the body and the seeds of illness" (Bragdon 2012, 15). It is through this that other spirits can attach.

He also suggested that I read Terry Clifford's book *Tibetan Buddhist Medicine and Psychiatry* (1984), which the Dalai Lama endorsed. In the traditional Tibetan view, there are five causes of mental illness: (1) karma — the working out of intergenerational consequences of past behavior; (2) physical humoral imbalance between phlegm, bile, and wind; (3) physical poisons; (4) emotions; and (5) unseen demons. Despite being only one of the five classes, demon possession gets a great deal of attention. In studies of folk belief and shamanism in Tibet (e.g., Peters 2016), it predominates. Here we begin to see a phenomenon I have noticed in many cultures and historical eras. There is a vast gulf between the elite view of spirit possession and the folk view. Some anthropologists even view possession states and rites as ways the disempowered segments of a society gain voice and power.

In Buddhist language, Clifford echoes the IFS view that UBs lose all power when we do not fear them. "In this wisdom there is no hope or fear. Therefore even if a 'demon' appeared to rush towards one with a flaming dagger, the person… is immovable, adamantine, and no demon can harm him" (Clifford 1984, 161).

This fearlessness as the key to dealing with demons is also reflected in a story of one of Tibet's great holy men, Milarepa. He had been gone from his mountain meditation cave for an extended period of time. When he returned, he found it filled with demons. Many fled, but a few remained. He offered food, and some more left. Only the fiercest, angriest one remained. It had a huge, open mouth filled with long, sharp fangs. Milarepa went over to the demon and put his head inside its threatening mouth! The demon then disappeared. Another Tibetan idea that resonates with IFS is that compassion is the "supreme medicine and protection against ghosts and demons" (Clifford 1984, 163). Traditionally, people in Tibet believed that rudraksha seed necklaces could provide protection from spirits. Some people believe that certain other minerals or gems protect them.

I have also had the opportunity to interview a man who had traveled with this advanced practitioner for six years. He is now a licensed psychotherapist. He described how this practitioner lived guided by inspiration, visions, and his contacts in the spirit realms. It was impossible to plan in any conventional sense. He was constantly working with many people and their physical, psychological, and spiritual problems. The former companion said that most of the practitioner's healings had to do with spirits — with cutting our links to the lower realms — but he also worked with poorly formed psychic channels and damaged or blocked chakras. There is a field around us; the first step in healing is to brush this out so there are no leaks. This seems to be the same process as the Spiritist paseos. This practitioner felt that here in North America, black magic and curses are rare, but they are common in other parts of the world, and counteractive white magic is needed there. As they traveled together, the practitioner would comment on the spirits he saw almost everywhere: in shops, on streets, on the beach. There were many spirits on the sites of former battlefields.

This man had traveled with the advanced practitioner for six years after the practitioner had healed him of a physical problem. He had also removed a spirit from a friend of this man, and that removal changed the friend's life. When I asked him what his major lessons were from those years, he said, "This s**t is real." The companion also said that he now thinks schizophrenia is really a spiritual problem. (The practitioner did not believe in schizophrenia at all.) When I asked the companion about protection for practitioners, he said that every traditional Tibetan monastery had a monk who focused on protecting all the other monks, usually by embedding a protective spirit. He quoted the practitioner as saying, "You cannot turn on a light in the dark without attracting moths." These spirits or UBs tend to attack people who are doing healing work. When I was talking directly with the advanced practitioner, he told me that a sangha, a community, was a very important part of protection.

The Spiritists almost always worked in teams. In Western-style therapy, it is almost impossible to have four or six therapists working simultaneously on one client.

Judaism

An orthodox Jewish friend of mine introduced me to a rabbi who lives in Jerusalem. The three of us had several fascinating Zoom meetings. Possession and exorcism are actually quite common in Judaism. The Jewish name for an attaching spirit, *dybbuk*, is interesting; it is related to the word for "glue," which suggests how sticky these things can be. They also use another word, *ibbur*, which means "pregnant" and suggests one being contained within another. For me, this word is one of the many hints at the connection between sexuality and possession. Ibbur can be from either negative or positive beings. The kabbalistic tradition is particularly involved with spirit removal and exorcisms. Isaac Luria, the great kabbalist who lived in the 1500s, was definitely a believer in spirit possession and exorcism. He saw the spirits of the dead with his inner eyes and knew how and when they died and why they were being punished (Chajes in Goldish 2003, 124). An interesting thing is that in that period, many Christians went to Jews for exorcisms because they thought Jews understood it better, and Rabbi Luria's student Rabbi Vital actually went to a sheikh — ibn Iyob. It seems that people often think that outsiders or other cultures can do this work better than we can. We tend to look for this in the other — in strangers or in people of low and despised classes.

The rabbi let me know about the work of Rabbi Yehuda Fetaya and sent me some translations of parts of his work. Fetaya lived in Baghdad, Iran, and died in the 1940s. Some of his life's work involved removing bad spiritual influences. He left us a book called *Minhat Yehuda*, which contains accounts of many of these cases. A woman in this book stated, with Fetaya's approval, "If people would endeavor to rectify spirits, they would hasten the coming of the Messiah." Fetaya thought that spirits could only enter where there was sin. His book contains vivid descriptions of hell, paradise, and destroyers as well as vivid punishments, but all of these were meant to purify and cleanse the soul, not really to punish. Reincarnation, in his view, could happen in metal, vegetable, animal, and human forms. Spirits of the dead infested people and often required years of work with special prayers to be freed and helped. Fetaya personally witnessed that this work of unifications is very painful for the spirits. He was also an expert in writing prayers on paper that were then rolled up and worn as amulets to protect a person. This is rather like the mezuzah that Jewish people often place at the doors of their house. These may have originally been intended to keep out bad spirits.

Jewish possession beliefs are complex and multifaceted. Many of the exorcisms are reminiscent of Catholic ones. The traditions are very different, of course, but there are some similarities. The exorcist was seen as heroic, and the exorcism itself restored and healed the society as well as the possessed individual. The rituals were dramatic, even shocking. Many of these rituals were brutal, and people sometimes died while being exorcised. Fumigation — the use of incense or smoke to drive out the evil spirit — was common among both Jews and Catholics. Foul-smelling plants were often burned, sometimes suffocating the possessed. Much of this comes from academic sources, notably Gershom Scholem. The rabbi warned me strongly that "academia is extremely off in areas like this."

There also exist possessions that are very positive and sought after. This statement has unintentionally offended some of the Jewish people who helped me. They feel that the word *possession* is so tarred with negative connotations that it should never be applied to positive spiritual experience. I also offended some Koreans by using this same word in reference to their tradition. I do not mean to give offense, but there seems to be some basic structural similarity: having a spiritual being inside one's system. In individual cases, there was often much debate as to whether it was divine guidance or demonic interference. The anthropologist Tanya Luhrmann's phrase "spiritual presence experience" is cleaner. For example, people would lie on the grave of a holy man so that his spirit could possess them and speak through them. This is a clear example of a positive, sought after version of this dynamic. As in other cultures, there was a folk/elite divide. The elites tended to reject or discount possession; it was more prevalent in the backcountry and in the so-called low-class environments. It is probably obvious by now that my sympathies are primarily with the non-elite views.

This brings us to something of major importance that is crystal clear in Jewish traditions and occurs almost universally in more disguised forms. States of holiness, divine euphoria, possession, and madness are very similar in appearance and are often mistaken for each other. A *maggid* is a type of benevolent heavenly spirit who can possess worthy individuals. These possessions, or spiritual presence experiences, are intensely beneficial. There is a complex relationship between madness and prophecy. *Devekut*, the clinging to God or closeness of God, is often a deep trancelike state that can look similar to possession. Holy ones are often incomprehensible, as are the possessed. The prophets of the Old Testament could be seen as possessed by the spirit of God, and by the time of Jesus, belief in negative possession was common in Jewish communities. Even so, Gershom Scholem, whom some consider one of the greatest scholars of Jewish mysticism, and his followers have asserted that it was the idea of reincarnation, which only became prominent in the 1500s, that really opened the way for these experiences. When you believe that a soul can move from one life to another and inhabit a new body at birth, it is logical to think other souls could also move in this way. The close association between possession, holiness, and insanity occurs almost universally.

Swedenborgianism

One of the longest and deepest contacts I've developed in my search to understand this stuff is with the Reverend Rachel Rivers, a retired minister and pastoral counselor of a Swedenborgian Christian church. For more than five years, Rachel, Jim Sutherland (a now-retired IFS therapist), and I would have conference calls almost monthly on Swedenborg, IFS, and possession states. Many people have never even heard of Emanuel Swedenborg (1688–1772), a Swede. During his early life, he was one of Europe's foremost scientists. Swedenborg was a mining engineer who designed military devices and was a prominent member of the Swedish upper class. He produced books on many scientific topics. In his fifties, he started to have visions and was taken on what he described as guided tours of heaven and hell. With his scientist's detached, observing attitude, he recorded what he was shown in approximately thirty thick volumes. He wrote these in Latin, which was the scholarly language of his day. Those volumes are now all available in English. Toward the end of his life, there were many examples of his having developed clairvoyant abilities. For instance, he was at a party in a town several hundred miles from Stockholm and suddenly became very distressed and said, "Oh no, Stockholm is on fire." Then an hour or so later, he said, "Oh, the fire has stopped just short of burning my house." These events were proven a day or so later when messengers arrived and confirmed their occurrence. Swedenborg used his abilities to help the Queen of Sweden, but those events are not really relevant. More to the point, he saw that there are spirits all around us. He referred to them using the language of his day, calling them demons and angels. He said that they're constantly whispering to us, and that's where our thoughts come from. According to Swedenborg, our thoughts aren't really ours until we appropriate them and take them in. Only then do we become responsible for them.

Much of Swedenborg's writing was expressed as commentary on the Gospels and is very Christian in orientation. A church based on his teachings was founded in England, where he lived during the last years of his life. He was a major influence on William Blake, Robert Frost, Carl Jung, Jorge Luis Borges, Ralph Waldo Emerson, both William and Henry James, and W. B. Yeats, to name a few. Helen Keller was a Swedenborgian and used his teachings to guide her difficult life. D. T. Suzuki, the famous Japanese Buddhist, wrote a book about Swedenborg titled The Buddha of the North. There are many Swedenborgian churches throughout Europe and the United States.

As Swedenborg's visionary abilities increased toward the end of his life, he said he could see angels and demons as clearly as he saw the people around him.

At the beginning of his visionary years, he used breathing exercises and special postures to help him enter these states. Later he lived in both worlds simultaneously. He said there is no hell with locked gates after we die; our spirits go to whatever they truly loved, and if that was power, they go to a realm where people were striving for power. If it was sex, the spirit would go to a realm that was all about sex; if it was knowledge and love, the spirit would go to those realms. No being was ever locked in a hell realm; the doors were never closed. If a spirit turned and asked for help, they would be helped. Swedenborg saw the divine as characterized by two things — wisdom and love — and they're ultimately indistinguishable, but he would say that truth without love is not really true at all. So in some sense, love was the primary reality of the universe for him.

When I asked Rachel to sum up our years of conference calls, she said she felt Swedenborg would say the most important things to keep in mind to remove UBs are: (1) they are not part of you; (2) they are not trustworthy; don't believe what they tell you; and (3) don't fear or hate them; have compassion for them instead. When I asked Jim this same question, he came back to Swedenborg's core assertion that love and truth are the two sides of the divine nature and that truth, when expressed without love, is not ultimately true at all. Jim emphasizes that kindness and love are necessary even when — perhaps especially when — dealing with these dark forces.

Korea

My wife is Korean, and it is very common in Korea to believe in this spirit realm and the presence and existence of spirits. Koreans have a form of shamanism that is practiced by the mudang. They're mostly women. For many, many years, they were looked down upon and regarded as only slightly better than prostitutes. They were also outlawed for centuries, but they persisted despite the persecution. Again, this tells me that the people found something of great value in them. We should be curious about whatever it is that was so important to them that they would endure even in the face of this negativity and persecution. Christianity is spreading very fast in Korea. Some of the missionaries say it's the fastest Christianization of a country that has ever happened. However, the missionaries have noticed that when Confucianism, Taoism, and Buddhism entered Korea, they all were transformed into something essentially Korean and also essentially related to the deep shamanic tradition of Korea. There's fear among the Christians in Korea that this will also happen to Christianity there.

The mudangs recognized that spirits do get into people, and they have elaborate ceremonies to help these people. The ceremonies, called *gut*, often last for days. During them, the shamans allow various gods to enter their bodies. They sing and dance to loud, rhythmic music. Many of the people who are present often sing and dance along with them. I once made the mistake with a Korean expert of using the term *possession* when referring to entry of the gods into a mudang. He became somewhat upset with me and said, "No, no, no — it's an entirely different process," even though to me, it seems basically similar in allowing a spiritual entity to take over a person's body. One of the tests they have for the mudang in a gut to see if the god's spirit is in her is to stand barefoot on very sharp knife blades. In that position, riding the knives, she speaks as the god or spirit within her. In some videos of this test, right before the mudang mounts the knives, an assistant takes a silk scarf and runs it over the blades, which cut the silk easily. In Indonesia, there is a tradition of men dancing barefoot in trance on broken glass without having their feet cut. We are much more familiar with firewalking, which happens in many parts of the world and has been demonstrated in the West. Firewalking, standing on knives, and dancing on broken glass have absolutely no explanation in Western medicine. There are some rather pathetic attempts to explain them away, but they are beyond our science right now, so we mostly ignore them.

With my wife serving as a translator and helping me search the Internet in the Korean language, I was able to listen to recordings or watch exorcisms performed by a Buddhist monk, a Christian minister, and a mudang, all in Korea, as well as someone who called himself an independent scholar. They were all quite similar; there were more similarities than differences among these various rituals. In Korea, it's commonly believed that the negative spirits are staying because they have unresolved *han*. Han is an emotion that we don't have an exact equivalent for in English. It's a mix of anguish, pain, resentment, and a sense of injustice. It's not a desire for vengeance — that's a different emotion. The belief is that the spirits need to have their han witnessed before they can move on. This is amazingly similar to the witnessing phase in IFS. It's not catharsis — it's witnessing; these are different things. A very famous gut was performed by Kim Kum-Hwa after a ferryboat disaster in Korea. The boat had turned upside down with hundreds of school-aged kids trapped inside. The government refused to send divers in to try and rescue them, and they all died in the capsized boat. This was such a national dishonor and disgrace that the president eventually had to resign.

Kim Kum-Hwa was the premier mudang of Korea at that time, and she had many students, or daughters, as they call them. She performed a gut in which many of her daughters became possessed by the spirits of the dead children. One of the possessed mudang was yelling over and over, "I'm so cold, I'm so cold, I'm so cold." Other people came and wrapped her in blankets while she continued to express how cold she was. She had taken in the spirit of a dying child who died of cold. Another mudang was stuffing her face desperately with food; the spirit in her may have died of starvation under the boat. This gut was very public and was broadcast on TV. Videos of it are still available. The relatives of all the children who had died on the ferryboat watched the gut. It was an incredibly emotionally powerful event. These guts are accompanied by very loud, rhythmic music. The mudang dance, and many of the people there often do as well. The mudang often change their outer clothes and their hats according to the phase of the ritual and which god has come down into them. Once these spirits were witnessed, they were helped to move on.

While in Korea, I was able to interview, again with my wife translating, a Buddhist monk and a mudang on this subject. They both acknowledged that yes, possession happens, and it's an important part of spiritual experience. We met the monk at his mountain monastery. Like most Korean monasteries, it was a campus made up of multiple buildings spread over many acres. Statues and shrines lined the paths. The Buddhist monk said that many big monks do exorcisms but that he personally believed that this might not be appropriate because it might be an important part of a person's karma to deal with this spirit entity in them. The mudang described his own path in becoming a mudang. He'd had horrible neck pain that nothing would cure, and he had to give up his other job and study to start to become a mudang amid great loss of income and prestige. Now, in the past decade or so, being a mudang has become somewhat popular and is socially acceptable. One of the older gentlemen I talked to about this said, "Oh, 90 percent of them are fake now — it's not like the old days."

These ceremonies are impressive, and the music is strong, even harsh to Western ears. The emotion in the mudang and everyone present is often intense. These gut look and feel like powerful transformational events. Another gut we saw involved a bereaved mother whose teenaged son had recently died in a motorcycle accident. The mudang welcomed her spirit guides in, and then the deceased boy's spirit entered her. Surprisingly, he started by yelling at his mother, berating her for her failures in caring for him as a child. This shocked me. As soon as this was aired, as soon as this han was witnessed, the boy's spirit, still yelling through the mudang, was telling his mother, "You must live a long life to make up for my short one. Live well. Live long. Live long." He shouted this repeatedly. The tears and emotion in the mother and the mudang were strong, clear, and undeniable.

Again with my wife translating, I was able to interview and exchange emails with Lee Sunhwa, PhD, the past president of the Korean transpersonal psychology association and a prominent therapist there. She said that in Asia, spirit possession is generally common. The dead stay around; some parts may leave while other parts stay. Souls, like people, are made up of parts. In her case, she was aware of the loving spirit of her mother-in-law, who often helped her with very mundane things, for example, finding parking places. She felt that this experience of spirits taking care of a person was fairly common. When souls of people we knew come into us, they are usually helpful; it's the souls of people we did *not* know who can be more negative. Dr. Lee said that traditionally it's been religious leaders who do this work — mudang, monks, and ministers — but now many therapists are also able to help. She emphasized asking the name of the being, asking its purpose and why it came in, and asking about its pain and suffering. When a mudang takes in a spirit and witnesses it, it often leaves very gratefully. For Dr. Lee, it is important that the client get to decide whether the spirit stays or goes; there can be some profit in being possessed, a sense of power or confidence. She says that when she does get a spirit out of a person, she works to replace it with a larger, more beneficial spirit. She described a case of the woman who came to her with a stomachache. This woman had had an abortion, and it was the spirit of her unborn child. Much grief came up, after which the spirit was able to leave.

Dr. Lee repeatedly emphasized that spirit possession is a normal part of human life. She is able to see spirits, but she hid this for most of her life because she didn't want to seem odd. She said there are all kinds and levels of entities: spirits, animals, human and otherwise. Dr. Lee knows IFS well; she said that the recognition of multiplicity and IFS is vitally important and that the next step is the recognition of the other inside of us. She insists that spirits cannot be clearly sorted into good versus bad. Many ancestral spirits, which are so important to traditional Koreans, have this ambivalent nature. She emphasizes listening and comforting the spirits. For her, the process of working with the others inside of us should not be violent or confrontational. She believes intuition is crucial in this work. It is a different way of knowing. She says we can develop this by paying attention to our five senses so we can recognize the intuition before our thoughts are activated. "Thoughts come from ego; intuition comes from before ego," she says. When I asked Dr. Lee if she felt that negative spirits usually attacked people who were trying to bring light, she replied that both Jesus and Buddha became enlightened through such attacks by dark forces. The role of the dark spirits is to test us. She said that negative and positive spirits smell differently to her.

Tom Zinser

There are many modern American practitioners who deal with possession states whom I will discuss later, but I've only had the opportunity to meet one in person. Tom Zinser has written three books on Soul-Centered Healing. I met him in Michigan near his home in Grand Rapids. He is a conservative-looking man. He arrived in a newer, spotless SUV. He was well-groomed, short-haired, Midwestern polite, and soft-spoken — a gentleman. Nevertheless, his career has been one of the most adventurous and, I might add, courageous of all the therapists I've talked to. Early on, Zinser realized that some people had spirits in them or beings or entities, or whatever you want to call them. He had studied with John and Helen Watkins, as I had. The Watkinses were the developers of ego state therapy, a hypnotherapeutic form of parts work. Ego states are subpersonalities — what we call parts in IFS. Zinser realized that much suffering originates in difficulties at this level, and he also came to realize that there are things in us that are not ego states but rather spirits — what in IFS we would call UBs, things that are not a part of the person. He feels that the first therapeutic task is to help the client develop an "open and free" connection to their higher self. This is a close parallel with Dick Schwartz's assertion that Self leadership is the most important discovery of IFS. The higher self will know what is an ego state and what is not part of the client. Zinser was very clear; he called these things "spirits," and he did not want to compromise or fudge on this. He said it is time for a paradigm shift — that consciousness, not matter, is fundamental. He seemed to feel that beating around the bush and trying to adapt to the old merely delays the emergence of the new model.

Zinser reminds me of Michael Harner, the anthropologist turned shaman who, when he was in his late eighties, was asked to identify the most important learning of his long life. After a short pause, he replied in only three words, "Spirits are real." Zinser stayed with his hypnosis-based techniques. He explicitly induced trance and relied extensively on ideomotor signaling. This technique, which has been used in hypnotherapy for a long time, consists in getting the client's body to directly answer questions. One standard way is to ask one finger to lift if the answer is yes, and a different finger to lift if the answer is no. A huge number of signal systems can potentially be set up. This bypasses the conscious mind or dominant ego state, but it can be slow with only yes and no answers available.

Zinser also met with a channeler who channeled a guide named Gerod for him. He met with her once a week for fifteen years and after that occasionally. Almost all of this was to gain information about his clients; he felt that this allowed him to test how helpful the information from this channeled guide was. He did not conceal any of this, and it exposed him to ridicule and contempt. However, he was able to help a lot of people. As word of mouth spread, clients kept coming.

Many therapists know that this is part of their work. They know this stuff is real, but they hide it. Zinser said spirits are real, and this is the big paradigm transformation that's coming. We need to be courageous and state this clearly and strongly. He's done that his whole life. He's in his seventies now, retired from clinical practice but teaching and writing. We have stayed in contact on Zoom and email; he has always been kind and generous.

Mexico

More recently, thanks to the kindness of Laura Roel, I've met a couple of Mexican healers: Roberto and Adriana. Roberto holds a master's degree in Gestalt psychotherapy and has also trained in the Toltec shamanic tradition. Unfortunately, he knows no English, and I know no Spanish, so Laura translated for us. Roberto works a great deal with these spirit energies. He says they come in several varieties. One variety, which he calls "predators," hunt our energy and suck it. They're always around and hunting. The main door they enter through is anxiety and fear, but they can come in through any emotion. This is very similar to the IFS idea that fear is the main emotion we need to deal with to remove UBs safely. When you're not afraid of them, they lose power. The second major category Roberto describes is souls and energies of the dead. This is the kind of thing that the Spiritists thought all these beings were. He also says that witchcraft and curses are quite prominent. He says that ancestors can get into us, which would be the equivalent of IFS legacy burdens. He said that energies from our partners, especially sexual partners, can get broken off and stay in us. He calls some of these energies demonic. He says they're immensely powerful energies, but they need to feed on physical energies. He says they're not really good or bad energies; they just need to feed.

Another energy Roberto described he calls The All, in which nothing is lacking. If you can contact this energy, you get all knowledge and all the power you need. He says we're not just physical bodies — we're actually like luminous spheres or eggs. A luminous sphere or egg can get indentations, or weak spots. Roberto uses various herbs and other methods to bandage these weak spots and help them grow back. He described some of his cases to me. One was helping heal a child with severe deformities. I asked how he acquired his knowledge about these things, and he said that his grandmother knew these things and handed them down to him. As a young man, he had been very scientifically oriented and had not believed in any of this, but on a whim he went to a *santero*, a practitioner of the Santería religion. Like Candomblé and Umbanda in Brazil, Santería is one of the African diaspora religions, which grew up in the New World. This one developed in Cuba in the nineteenth century. It is a syncretism of the Yoruba religion, Spiritism, and Catholicism. The santero told Roberto that he had been given an ability from his grandmother and that he needed to develop those gifts. The meeting with the santero was powerful enough that it changed him from an atheistic rationalist into someone with a deep spiritual connection. He said that for me to be able to write my book, I needed to allow myself to be touched by life, all of life — the flying of a bird, the limping of a dog, everything — to reconnect me with deep life. I asked him what I should call the different types of people who work with these energies. He said a *curandero*, or healer, is often considered a low-level practitioner. A *hechicero* is a sorcerer. A *bruja* or *brujo* is a female or male witch. This last category is often employed to cast curses on others, but their knowledge is also needed to defend against curses. The name he preferred is "man or woman of knowledge." Then he said that the real answer would be "a pilgrim who walks his path picking the flowers that never wither — love and knowledge — and this pilgrim is only an apprentice of intent." Toward the end of our talk, he said, "They're pleased with your work." When I asked who "they" were, he just gestured impatiently to something behind him.

Adriana is a Mexican woman who now lives in France. One of her eyes is blind and milky, which gives her a rather eerie appearance. My two eyes are quite different due to an early accident, and I used to be shy and self-conscious about this, but I was told years ago that it is actually a sign of a shaman to have two different eyes. This is because a shaman sees in this world with one eye and in the other world with the other eye. This relieved my self-consciousness about my eyes. I have never considered myself a shaman; many times I wanted to be one but knew I wasn't. Now as I work with Indigenous people, I am glad I never claimed that title. Many First Nations people deeply resent white people using that title. When I told Adriana of my experiences with UBs, she said that these spiritual beings have always been around but are especially active now. Some of this is because pseudo-shamans have opened up portals as a result of not knowing what they were doing. Some of it is also due to all the war and violence. Mostly it's spirits of the dead who are trapped here; they don't know how to leave, so they possess the physical bodies of weak individuals. Some of them are fallen angels — beings of darkness trying to stop the evolution of humanity. This world, she asserted, is primarily spiritual energy at its essence, not material. The West has denied this truth, and certain beings have taken advantage of this willful blindness.

Adriana also told me about some cases of spirit possession she'd worked on. She, like Roberto, often uses candles when she works. She will say to the candle, "I sacrifice the candle to give light to the spirit." The flame will move and make noise, which gives her clues as to what's going on. It is a channel for her to learn about the spirit. In Adriana's view, the spirits don't know where to go — they don't see the pathway to leave — and that's why they cling so much. Also, they often expect punishment. She said she frequently yawns during her work and that this yawning is a manifestation of spirit moving. I've heard this from others who do this work, and I no longer suppress my yawns when I'm doing therapy. If a client yawns, I encourage that and tell them it often means that energy is moving in them. She has said that we need to remember that we don't really do this work; rather, spirit does it through us. She emphasized and repeated this statement. If we start thinking we are doing this work, we will get proud, and this pride will be our downfall. Very often, the possessed person needs to take a lesson from the spirits, and once the possessed person has taken the lesson, the spirit leaves much more easily. This reminds me of the Korean monk not wanting to remove spirits because they could help a person resolve their karma.

Adriana also said that many spirits are stuck here because they're thirsty for acknowledgment and want recognition. We need to give them recognition and witnessing so they can leave. This is very much like the mudang belief in Korea that we need to witness the han, the suffering, of the spirit. Adriana emphasized that we cannot do this on our own — we need to invite in spirit's presence to do it through us. She said it's not combat; love is the best medicine for these beings, who will often try to provoke us into hatred. She counseled me strongly against falling into that warfare. She said when the possessing spirits feel real love coming toward them, their armor starts to melt. I asked her how we can tell the demons from the angels, the bad spirits from the good. I really liked her answer. She said that first, it's a feeling in your body such as tingles going up and down your spine or a disturbance growling in your stomach — that's your first brain. Your second brain of discernment is in your mind; you must be mentally clear and think about the being. Then you can bring these two discernments together in your heart, which will bring peacefulness and certainty.

Sukyo Mahikari

I also want to mention another group I have had personal contact with: Sukyo Mahikari. This is one of the new religions of Japan that now has centers in more than a hundred countries worldwide. These new religions in Japan constitute the fastest-growing religious interest there. Despite strong missionary efforts, only about 1 percent of Japanese people are Christian, but over 15 percent have joined one of the new religions. There are many, and they focus on healing and deliverance. Sukyo Mahikari began when the founder had a visionary experience. This revelation is described in one of their pamphlets: "At five o'clock in the morning, February 27, 1959, Great Saint Kotama Okada, was revalated by God, the Creator: Rise up, name yourself Kotama (literally, Gem of Light). Hold your hand up and purify the world. The world will become more and more bitter and severe for the human being." Great Saint Kotama Okada started holding his hand over people soon after the revelation, and he found a dying man come to life again, paralyzed people start to walk, and blind people begin to see, just as Sakyamuni or Jesus Christ performed miracles. God ordered the saint, "Go and save human beings, distributing the light of God, and the power of Mahikari No Waza to everybody who wishes to obtain it" (MacNutt 1995; 2005, 61).

Another pamphlet contains the question "What would you think if you were told that your life is partially controlled by some invisible force?" There are also vivid descriptions of people being freed from the spirits of the dead.

My wife and I visited a Sukyo Mahikari center in San Francisco in 2022. It is a large, well-maintained building in a good area near a university. We both received the light. We each had a practitioner work on us individually for about forty minutes. They held their palms toward us and passed their hands over our bodies, first in a sitting position and then lying on a mat on the floor. This is very much like the paseos of the Brazilian Spiritists. This is similar to healing touch, Reiki, and other Western modalities. Several other people were receiving similar treatments in other parts of the large, sunny room. Some of the practitioners chanted in Japanese as they worked. The people seemed polite, civilized, and middle class. All races were present. I felt a mild glow, perhaps only the result of the peaceful environment; my wife found the experience pleasant but was unsure if anything more had really happened.

Father Tom

For several years, I had tried to interview a Roman Catholic exorcist. Understandably, many turned down my requests. I believe they feared that I would be another sensationalist or that I'd be a scoffing skeptic. Exorcists have not been respectfully received by most therapists and academics. A colleague named Justine Wiercimok in Poland found a Polish exorcist, Father Tom, who was willing to talk with me. She also acted as translator during our two interviews. In the first interview, he was quite cautious with me and stayed with rather cut-and-dried factual material. There are 120 priests in Poland who are pretty much full-time exorcists. They are all very busy. This is for a population of slightly less than forty million Poles.

Father Tom said there are two orders of things: the therapeutic and the religious. To distinguish the two, practitioners need to conduct meticulous interviews and precisely name what is happening. As many Catholics do, he cited Saint Ignatius of Loyola as the great expert on discernment, but he also stated that connection to the Holy Spirit is necessary for reliable discernment. He emphasized that bad spirits are often characterized by very strong desires; they help us commit sin without any discomfort and stimulate greed, sexual desire, ownership, and power. Bad spirits attack us and convince us we are wrong; they believe in lies. The devil is the father of lies. Bad spirits can twist truth into lies, stimulate shame, create low self-esteem, and deplete our life energy. Father Tom talked of ways to "put the lie into the light." Disagreeing with the IFS view, he believes that bad spirits can lie about whether they are a part of us. They search out and prey upon our weaknesses. However, he talked about the visible and invisible worlds in ways that fit very well with Dick's description of the outer and inner worlds. When discussing protection from demons, he talked about focusing on the light inside rather than creating some sort of boundary. This is an exact corollary of the kind of protection I discuss in detail in the basic clinical outline chapter.

Father Tom divides the ways bad spirits affect us into three basic categories: (1) obsessions, which include influences on our psyche, demonic visions, nightmares, hate, fear, and anxiety; (2) oppression, which includes external physical effects, accidents, animal attacks, and fires; and (3) possession itself, in which bad spirits take control of a person's mind and body. When possessed, people often have extraordinary strength, great knowledge, and extrasensory abilities. They are also repelled by religious objects and prayer. Father Tom says there are various percentages of possession, some much more complete than others.

By our second interview, Father Tom had decided he could trust me, so he was much more emotionally involved and forthcoming. As a Catholic, the first step for him was helping people believe in Christ. He also mentioned Viktor Frankl, meaning, and belief in beauty, truth, and goodness. Something good must come in; it could be any of those qualities. He emphasized that self-centeredness is a basic characteristic that lets in bad spirits and that in order to assist a possessed person, we need to get their attention off of themselves and onto others and God — "to open to the love flow." A major goal of the demons, according to Father Tom, is to prevent connections and lock us into isolation and a self-centered identity. This isolation creates a state in which demons can feed upon us and prevents us from receiving healing. Father Tom's profound understanding of the pervasive crippling effects of deep isolation is fundamentally important for all our work with UBs. He agreed that these things primarily get in during childhood and that children often perceive that these dark beings are the only ones who are interested in them. The demons promise the children whatever it is they want and get them to make agreements or sign contracts. I have seen a few of these contracts, but it is not a prominent feature in my experience.

I asked Father Tom about the reality of curses, which we hardly ever hear about here in the United States but which seem to be quite common in Mexico and Brazil. He said, "Yes, curses are definitely real." He said the strongest and most destructive curses occur when a parent curses their child. This was a chilling comment. He agreed that demons or bad spirits frequently attack healers. He said not to dialogue with them — that they are more intelligent than we are and are very tricky. He said the key to being safe is the absolute lack of consent in us to their presence. In his words, "I do not belong to them. I belong to God." He said we cannot do this work on our own; we need to have spirit with us — God, Jesus.

I believe that the IFS concept of Self can allow atheists to have this bigger presence with them as they do this work. The biggest point of divergence in our views is that Father Tom does not believe that demons can ever be taken to the light to heal. He says they have no interest and will not go.

Basic Themes

As you can see, this material quickly takes us into deep waters. I want to briefly introduce five major themes that will run throughout this book. The first I've already mentioned: radical pragmatism. When faced with this stuff, I've done what worked and sort of felt my way forward. It has been said that one good question is worth many good answers. The question I ask of these phenomena is "What helps — what relieves the person's suffering?" This leads to an entirely different domain than asking the obvious questions of what these experiences are and what UBs are. In the vast anthropological literature in this area, almost no one focuses on the practicalities of how to work with this stuff or how we modern Western psychotherapists can learn new ways of helping our clients by becoming students of the traditional ways of working with possession. I've also made use of whatever the client offered, whatever their worldview was, their ideology, their metaphors. Everyone has a mythology; everyone lives inside a story that gives their life form. We need to honor these and learn their language. Learn the client's language — do not make them learn yours.

Milton Erickson was perhaps the greatest master of using what the client presented. He called this the "utilization principle." He was a psychiatrist who worked in locked mental hospitals for much of his career. He encountered a man in a locked ward telling everyone that he was Jesus Christ. Erickson went up to him and started a conversation, and then he said, "I hear you're a pretty good carpenter." The guy said, "Yes." Then he got the guy down into the woodshop, and the guy started doing woodworking projects. Another case with Erickson involved a man who just stood in the hallway all day long, for years, and spoke word salad almost nonstop. Erickson went there and listened very carefully to the guy's word salad, actually transcribed a bunch of it, typed it up, and learned how to speak with approximately the same vocabulary, rhythm, and intonations. He went back and stood next to the guy and started speaking the man's word salad back to him. Erickson did this for several days. Then the guy turned to him one day and said, "Cut it out, Doc." He then turned back and started speaking his word salad again. Erickson had been able to establish a bridge to this man who had been totally isolated for years by using the man's language.

Another example comes from Erickson's childhood. He was raised on a dairy farm in the Midwest. One day, a big storm was coming, and his father was hurriedly trying to get all the cows into the barn, but one calf wouldn't budge. The more his father pulled the calf toward the barn, the more the calf dug in and pulled backward. Young Erickson started giggling at his father's trouble. His father angrily said, "Okay, you do it then." Erickson went behind the calf and pulled its tail away from the barn. The calf then ran into the barn. Later, in talking about this incident, Erickson said, "I used what the calf could do, which was resist." So, the utilization principle fits with radical pragmatism. We accept whatever worldview a client offers us and work with that. Some therapists refuse to do anything like this, claiming that it amounts to colluding with the client's delusional system. I think this is a bad error. It imposes our ideological structure on the client, which often hinders healing. This is very clear when dealing with people from other cultures who have a strong belief in possession. Even if this is beyond our ideology, we can help them if we work within their framework. To dismiss them out of hand is arrogant and Eurocentric.

A second major theme that will come up over and over again throughout this book is possession. Boy, is this ever a loaded topic. It's anathema to talk about it in modern therapy circles. I have no idea about the metaphysical realities behind it, but I think we can say with great certainty that possession and possession-related phenomena are one of the most widely distributed cultural characteristics, found in tribes and cultures all over the planet and as far back in history as we can trace. I think a reasonable hypothesis — and that's all it is at this point, a hypothesis — is that some biopsychological reality occurs in almost all human societies that has normally been described with metaphors of possession. This phenomenon can destroy people's lives, and it can also help them change in wonderful ways. It is psychologically important — this is abundantly clear. Because of this, I think it is incumbent upon us to take it seriously and study it, not just sneer and walk away. The fact that it is so widespread across almost all human societies gives me confidence that there's something real underlying it — some psychological reality that's important and significant and needs to be included when we work with deep healing.

A third theme that will run throughout this book, and perhaps it is the major theme of this book, is that our minds are porous. Our minds are surrounded by a semipermeable membrane, as are all living systems. Every cell is surrounded by a semipermeable membrane. We could not survive if we could not receive and expel. This is true biologically, and I also think it's true psychologically. If you start to consider this, I becomes obvious that it's true at some level. Porosity has profound implications. Dick's realization and explication of the fact that our mind is multiple actually changes almost everything about therapy. When you start to work out the implications of multiplicity, it makes us see the whole inner world very differently. I think this is also true of the idea of porosity of mind. At one level, it's obvious. We take in information, we get rid of old ideas, stuff like that. But I believe it's much deeper than that, and if we take it seriously, it changes the way we do therapy and the way we are in the world.

A fourth major theme in this book is the value and importance of inner experience. As a long-time therapist, I've taken this idea for granted, and most of the people I work with also take it for granted. But I realize that for many, it's still a departure. Our rationalist, materialist culture has devalued the subjective realm. It wasn't that long ago that the behaviorists dominated academic psychology and asserted that the only thing worth studying was observable behavior. They said the study of subjectivity was unscientific and without value. The study and understanding of the inner world is not a frill, not frosting we put on the cake, not something we occupy our time with when the real work is done. Not at all. A stark and dramatic example of this comes from the work of Viktor Frankl, a psychiatrist from Vienna who survived many years in Nazi concentration camps. After liberation, he wrote that it was the ability to make meaning from his experience that allowed him to survive. He said it was clear in the camp when someone had lost that ability. Those men died within days. Something subjective, something entirely unmeasurable and not observable, determined who would live or die, something in the inner world. It's from the subjective realm that our values, feelings, and life satisfaction come — all the things that are deeply important to us. Some forms of therapy, particularly some types of cognitive-behavioral therapy, just aim to put a bandage on people so they can go back out and engage with the external world. But all the depth therapies value inner experience. Human artistic creativity and spirituality also come from this realm. We need our visionaries and imaginative people to help illuminate the road ahead. Also, our value systems come from this inner world, and our value systems shape who we are, what we perceive, and how we act. Dick talks about there being two worlds: the inner world and the outer world. He says that just turning inward and having relationships with your parts — your little kid parts and all the others — takes you into this internal world. Dick insists that it is simple and natural to enter this world of the subjective; you do not need hypnotic inductions or elaborate meditative training. Just turn your attention inside.

The fifth core theme is personalism. This is the name of a school of philosophy or, more accurately, a trend in many philosophies that emphasizes the importance of the person. For our purposes in inner work, this comes up with the idea that we do much better if we treat our parts as whole people, unique individuals. We resist the tendency to reduce them to representatives of a type or, even worse, to things. An early and crucial discovery in the development of IFS was that this basic respect for parts dramatically facilitated healing. This is very hard for many rationalist materialists to swallow, but pragmatically it can be shown that this approach works better in therapy.

In Gestalt therapy, which is also a form of parts work, they have an adage, "You can talk to a part or as a part, but do not talk about a part." Old-school Gestalt therapists often used empty chairs. (Dick also did this early on.) They would say, for example, "Have that child part sit in that empty chair and talk to it." Then they might say, "Go sit in that chair and talk as the child. Do not talk about the child part; that's gossip, and no one likes being gossiped about." This process is quintessentially personalistic; it is respectful and relational. This is almost the opposite of psychoanalytic insight work, which involves talking about and developing theories about our inner experience. Dick now goes further than this when he talks about parts; he often says they are fully independent subpersonalities.

With UBs, as you can see from the case studies, we treat them as persons. They can talk to us. They take action. They seem to have wills of their own. People see them in their inner worlds as independent beings. Pragmatically, it works better if we operate this way. This much is clear from a decade of working with UBs and studying them. What UBs are — whether they are independent persons in some sense — is a question I'm not even going to attempt to answer now. Some people object to working with them as though they had personhood on the grounds that we are colluding with an illusion and encouraging a flight from reality. Was Erickson colluding with an illusion when he got the man who said he was Jesus to work in the woodshop? Did Gestalt therapists encourage a flight from reality when they had their clients sit in an empty chair and become a child? Should we discount the deep emotional and psychological growth great art produces in us because it is not real? Great art and these inner-world images and events have a reality of their own, a humanly important reality that is central to healing. Working with UBs as though they have some kind of personhood is effective and powerful.

To recap, these five themes will weave throughout this book: radical pragmatism, the metaphor of possession, the porosity of mind, the value of internal experience, and personalism.

CHAPTER 5

Interoception

What lies behind us and what lies before us are tiny matters
compared to what lies within us.

—Ralph Waldo Emerson

Worldly power means nothing.
Only the unsayable jeweled inner life matters.

—Rumi

We will now turn our attention more deeply to the value of the inner world because without an appreciation of it, everything else in this book will seem like nonsense. The first steps in this direction are fairly obvious and easy for most people to welcome nowadays. For example, the value of interoception — the perception of internal sensations — is well documented, as we will see below, but if we pursue the implications of this line of thinking, it takes us into some very deep waters. We are not yet completely free of what Bernardo Kastrup, the wonderful Dutch philosopher and computer scientist, refers to as the dark ages of materialism and behaviorism. Those dark ages were perhaps at their worst in the early decades of the twentieth century. Behaviorism, with its insistence that studying the subjective was an unscientific waste of time, ruled academic psychology. Logical positivism in all its sterile dryness ruled philosophy. Materialism still absolutely dominated the academic world. Quantum mechanics had not yet begun to erode materialism's foundation. A French priest of this time, Georges Bernanos, lamented, "You understand absolutely nothing about modern civilization unless you first admit that it is a universal conspiracy against the interior life."

In IFS we focus on this inner world, but Dick does not discuss it in terms of altered states of consciousness. He only asks people to turn their attention inward and pay attention to their parts. As clients get more and more used to this and more proficient, they enter states that look like deep hypnotic trance or other altered states of consciousness. Dick does not concern himself with this; he focuses on the quality of the connection between the person's Self and their parts.

Frequently when we first identify a part, we ask a person how it shows up in or around their body. This question brings them out of their rational, thinking brain and gets them paying attention to their sensations — to the subjective qualities of their experience. This is entering the inner world. Going to physical sensation first is very helpful because it is extremely hard for the rational, analytical brain to think its way through this point. William James understood this. He said that trying to use the scientific method for introspection is like trying to turn up the light fast enough to get a glimpse of how darkness looks. People actually have to open and become curious about their inner experience. This simple turning inward is crucial. It is a skill we can train and become better and better at.

Most people, perhaps 80 percent, primarily see their parts — they interact visually. For example, they might see themselves as a six-year-old, frightened and cowering in the corner. Then they can relate in a loving way with this inner child part of them. Between 10 and 20 percent of people almost never experience any internal visual imagery. Ironically, Dick is one of these people. All of the sense modalities are ways we can experience our inner world. People feel body sensations, hear voices and sounds, see things, and experience intuition beyond normal sensory modalities. Pretty much everybody is capable of experiencing this inner world except perhaps in cases of organic brain damage, and there I am uncertain.

This ability to perceive and act in the inner world is crucial for IFS therapy. Mindfulness meditation, for example, helps us become aware and sensitive to the inner world. IFS sees this as an important and necessary first step but not enough. We also need to learn how to *act* in the inner world. As in the example above of seeing the frightened six-year-old cowering in the corner in our mind's eye, not only do we perceive this but we also act. We offer that child compassion, curiosity, and care. We move toward it if it will welcome us closer. We offer help; simply observing but failing to act is not true compassion.

This insistence upon taking action in the inner world is very much like Jung's active imagination. He thought that we should not only enter our inner world and observe what we see there but should also interact with it. Jung stated that active imagination is where conscious and unconscious meet on equal terms. In Jung's view, this equal meeting gives rise to the transcendent function and then the emergence of the self. Dick clearly states that when we go into our inner world and interact with our parts, we are visiting realms that shamans have been visiting for tens of thousands of years. He is working on developing what he calls the laws of inner physics to help us navigate this terrain. The tools of materialism do not work here, but perhaps the most important reason our culture as a whole is reluctant to enter into this realm is that once we are aware of it, it quickly becomes undeniably clear that we are not the masters of our own house. There are parts or energies in our inner world that seem to have wills of their own. Jung called this "the autonomy of the psyche." This disconcerting revelation is, in fact, a beneficial portal to healing.

Interoception is the word psychologists use for this ability to know our inner experience. The concept was first introduced in 1906, but it wasn't until 2010 that much research was published in this area. Now there's a lot of research — hundreds of articles. Problems with interoception have been implicated in many psychological difficulties, including panic attacks, anxiety disorders, posttraumatic stress disorder, eating disorders, major depression, obsessive-compulsive disorder, and autism. Some people seem to be naturally more skilled at it than others, just as some have better vision or better hearing. Interoception is trainable; it can be learned, and good interoception skills can be made better. It is vitally important in many areas of functioning — emotional self-regulation, social participation, embodied cognition, self-care, and body awareness, to name a few.

Our subjective experience is very important, but until recently, science has largely tried to ignore this area. It should not surprise anyone that Western science, which strives with all its might to be objective and remove subjectivity from its research, is not very helpful when it comes to dealing with subjectivity itself. We need to learn how to navigate the inner world, to increase our interoception skills, and to move in the realms of subjectivity, not just to perceive but also to act there. As Viktor Frankl showed, not only does this realm where meaning comes from determine who lives and who dies, but it's also all we ever really experience directly. As the writer and addictions expert Ernest Kurtz wrote, "It is not the subjective that's merely subjective. The objective is merely objective—less than the full reality." We must strip away much nuance and savor from the subjective to reduce it to the objective. Early on when I was being trained to be a counselor, a supervisor told me that there was a quick way to see who would be a relatively easy client. Just ask them as they sat there if they could sense their own heartbeat without putting their hands on their body. If they could, they had some native interoception skill and would probably do fairly well in therapy. If they couldn't, it might be slower and harder.

There are many measures of our ability to become absorbed in our inner world. These include the Tellegen Absorption Scale, the Stanford Hypnotic Susceptibility Scale, various dissociation tests and scales, the Transliminality Scale, the Sensory Delight Scale, and the Schizotypy and Psychoticism Scales at the extreme end. In 1985, Richard Noll wrote a seminal article on mental imagery cultivation as a cultural phenomenon in which he showed that many religious traditions have a focus on developing these abilities. He analyzed shamanic training as a very clear example. This same kind of training is present in Tibetan Buddhism and in early Christian monasticism, and it is at least implicit in most religious practice.

How we pay attention to our internal world makes a big difference in how we can live. It can be very positive or very negative, but it should not be ignored. Even the extreme ranges of intensity and vividness of our internal world, as measured by the Schizotypy and Psychoticism Scales and which often look like mental illness, also correlate with creativity and spiritual experience. The research with these two scales is tending toward the conclusion that schizophrenia is not a separate disease but rather an extreme version of measurable qualities and abilities we all have. The ability to become absorbed in our internal experience is, like fire, a wonderful servant but a dangerous master. It is definitely worthy of study. Francis Weller said that if we approach our inner world with reverence, great things will approach us. George Washington Carver, in a very different field (agricultural science), said that if you love anything enough, it will reveal its secrets to you. There is also the old story of the gods wishing to hide a great treasure from humans. They wondered, should we put it on a mountaintop? No, they will go there. Put it on the bottom of the sea? No, they will go there. After considering many alternatives, they decided to hide it deep inside each person's mind since that's the last place they will look.

Luhrmann and Inner Sense Cultivation

Tanya Luhrmann, the Stanford anthropologist, is doing groundbreaking work in this area. She has produced a large body of work, most of which focuses on the areas of mental health and spirituality. She asks slightly different questions than most people have asked, and this changes her whole line of inquiry and makes it very powerful. As she says in the introduction to *How God Becomes Real* (2020), this is not an atheist's book, and it's not a believer's book — it's an anthropologist's book. She asks how God becomes real to people and how this experience changes people's lives and the cultures they live in. These are at least to a degree answerable questions, and they keep us away from the angry, obnoxious, and endless debates over theology.

Another one of my intellectual heroes, Mircea Eliade, made a similar shift in questions as he developed the field of the history of religions. He stopped arguing or debating about the reality of religious assertions; instead, he studied how they functioned in cultures, how they changed in history, and how they functioned within people and changed them. Again, these are answerable questions or at least ones we can move forward on. I am trying in this book to make a similar shift. Instead of arguing about the reality of UBs, I focus on how to work with them — how to relieve human suffering.

Luhrmann writes of inner sense cultivation. She says that people do not easily believe in unseen realities — the invisible other — gods or spirits. She says these must be made real for people by helping them focus on the inner world. This "real-making," as she calls it, changes people. It can change them profoundly. As therapists, our ears should perk up at this, as it is a clear example of human emotional and mental change that has worked in many cultures for millennia. This is what we are about: helping people change. Much of this change is very positive. Many studies now show that people with an active religious or spiritual life are physically healthier and live longer. The 2012 edition of the *Handbook of Religion and Health* reviewed almost three thousand of these quantitative studies, and they overwhelmingly supported this assertion (Koenig et al. 2012).

Luhrmann also points out that detailed stories help us develop our inner senses. Saint Ignatius's spiritual exercises are a clear example. He directs people to clearly imagine themselves in a biblical scene, including all their senses — the sights, the heat, the sounds, and the smells. This helps people create a vivid internal reality. This internal reality matters. Luhrmann writes about the "faith frame," which allows people to move beyond the bare world and to trust that there is more to the world than they can see. She compares this to Donald Winnicott's play frame. Winnicott, a psychoanalyst and pediatrician, showed the importance of play in the development of children's psyches and social abilities. The importance of play in psychosocial development is true for other species as well, not just humans. Dogs play, rats play, wolves play, many species play.

Jaak Panksepp, the developer of affective neuroscience, thought that seven primary affective systems exist in all mammals, and one of these is play. Panksepp studied play in rats. In one experiment, he put large rats in with smaller ones. They had play "fights." The large rat let the smaller one win about 30 percent of the time because if it did not, the smaller rat would no longer play, and play was important to both of them. Winnicott said that the illusions of play are a necessary and often healthy part of reality. There is an intermediate space between subjective and objective — a third experiential reality. This psychological continent (as clinical psychologist Charles Spezzano called it) and the internalized objects found there have profound effects on the individual. This growth-producing play frame in children is like the healing and growth that art and fiction can produce in adults; participating in "illusions" can help us grow. Entering into a faith frame or a play frame changes people, sometimes dramatically. Children who can't play with their peers don't develop well. These frames can be considered paracosms — alternative worlds we enter into. To enter them, we need what Luhrmann calls "attentional learning." We need to learn about how we pay attention, and we need new ways to do so. She says it is not a matter of belief or intellectual conviction; rather, it is a matter of experience. These experiences change people. One key to the potency of these experiences is that they are relationships, they are interactive. You interact with the spiritual beings in your faith frame. They have some autonomy, like characters in your dreams or like parts or UBs in IFS. These relational experiences are very significant in people's development.

Luhrmann's first fieldwork, which is reported in her *Persuasions of the Witch's Craft* (1989), involved working with and joining the witches' groups of the United Kingdom as they practice today. What really surprised her is that their practices worked. They had a meditation — an imagery practice — that involved building up an inner picture of a walled garden. After Luhrmann had worked with this for several months, she felt she had acquired new skills, and she knew that these skills could be taught and trained. She wrote, "And as I acquired those skills, the world became drenched in meaning" (2020, 63). This ought to tell us that these skills are very important in healing and therapy. We have already seen how Viktor Frankl saw meaning as the central factor in survival at Auschwitz. I believe it was the Canadian psychologist Jordan Peterson who said that meaning is the holy grail of psychotherapy, that the will to meaning is more important and more central than Freud's focus on sex and the will to pleasure or Nietzsche's will to power.

In addition to inner sense cultivation, Luhrmann points to one other factor that she believes is extremely important — our model of mind, or how we map and describe our thinking, feeling, intending, and desiring into a coherent culturally specific model. She calls our American model of mind the "citadel model." We tend to view our mind as our private fortress. Everything inside is ours; it's part of our identity, of who we are, and nothing gets in or out without our permission. We take this as an unexamined assumption; once we start examining it, it's obviously false. It also seems to correlate with poor results with mental illness. More on this will come later when I discuss porosity of mind in detail.

When you have some inner sense cultivation and at least a partially open model of mind, these practices of inner sense cultivation can create what Luhrmann calls "spiritual kindling." (Kindling is a relatively well-known concept in psychology that was first discussed in the development of seizures. Small electrical impulses in the brain could kindle a fire that later became a seizure. The more these pathways were developed, the quicker the movement became. This has also been used in analyzing bipolar disorder and other conditions. Positive outcomes can also be kindled.) This kindling actually changes the events as they are experienced by the person. Luhrmann uses the predictive coding model of perception to show how this works and how these changes can become stronger and stronger. Predictive coding suggests that our perception, and therefore our experience of the world, is a two-way street. Sensory data flow toward our brain bottom up. But at the same time, our predictions about the nature of our world and what's important in it are sent top down. These predictions are often described in six to ten layers that act as filters that therefore largely control the nature of our experience. When these predictions change, the nature of our experience changes, and this can kindle bigger and bigger effects. It can change who we are and how we behave.

One other point before we leave Luhrmann for now is her discussion of the "in between." She describes how some experiences are felt to be in between the external world and the internal world, in between subjective and objective. Dreams are a good example of this blurring of mine versus not mine and inner versus outer; they are clearly ours and yet they're autonomous. At first we rebel at this idea, but it is really another expression of the porous nature of mind. Luhrmann cites the philosopher David Abram, who talks about the entanglement of our senses with the world around us. She also mentions the anthropologist Lucien Lévy-Bruhl, who used the word *participation* to describe a way of being in the world. Many religions and spiritual traditions describe an intermediate, in-between realm like this. In classical Greece, they talked about the daimonic realm, a realm between the realms of the humans and the realms of the gods.

My favorite example of this is Socrates and his daimon. There is a delicious irony in the fact that Socrates, who is usually considered one of the most important sources of our Western rationality, talked with a daimon throughout his life and based many of his life decisions and much of his thought on it. He held conversations with a voice in his head! For example, one time he was leading a group of men up a trail to a house where they were to meet for an evening of conversation. He said that his daimon told him to turn back and take another trail. He did, and some of the men went with him. This group arrived at the house first. When the others arrived, they were all spattered with mud. They said they'd run into a big herd of pigs coming down the trail at them. Socrates also based many of his major life decisions on what the daimon told him. After he was tried and convicted for corrupting the minds of the youth of Athens, he could have either gone into exile or accepted the death sentence. His daimon told him to stay and drink the hemlock. He did and died there, with his students around him.

Daimons and Bernardo Kastrup

A modern example of the daimons at work comes from Bernardo Kastrup, who worked at the particle accelerator CERN, which we could call the greatest cathedral of modern physics. Kastrup has a PhD in computer science and another one in philosophy. He builds computers as a hobby to relax. He also was on the board of a major high-tech company, making a lot of money and doing exciting work. However, he kept feeling a push from what he refers to as his daimon to do philosophy instead. He struggled against this direction for five years. He described this daimon as telling him what nature wanted him to do, or what nature wanted to do through him. After about five years of struggling against this, Kastrup developed severe tinnitus. He said it was like hearing a dentist drill in each ear. He quit his big, powerful job and focused his intellect and powers on philosophy. He has since produced more than ten volumes arguing powerfully that the psyche — the subjective consciousness — is the real nature of the universe; the material world is secondary. The only real thing is the field of subjectivity.

In one of Kastrup's several recorded conversations with the psychologist Jeffrey Mishlove, he described a fantasy he'd had about this. He imagined some daimons with the project in mind of reintroducing idealism (the belief that consciousness is the only reality) as a respectable intellectual position. In his fantasy, the daimons went around looking for a good mind who could do this. When they found Kastrup, they thought, "Oh, this one has the tools we need," and they decided to get him to do the work. It seems they made a very good choice because not only is Kastrup brilliant, but he also loves to argue. He thinks strong opposition brings out the best in him since he is going against the dominant paradigm. Kastrup now says that after the decision was made, he realized it was a good one. He says his life is now rich in meaning, even if it's not so rich in money. He has said that the daimons' treatment of him has felt like tough love, but he's also said that it doesn't feel as though the daimons care about his well-being. He says he senses their feelings and thoughts but that they feel alien to him, "not me." He describes producing one of his daimon-inspired books as though he had a hot ball of iron in his throat that had to come out. Bernardo repeatedly uses the expression "I am the horse." The daimon is the rider. This is especially interesting because *horse* is exactly the word used in Haitian voodoo. When people there are possessed, they are the horse for the *loa*, the possessing spirit. We will delve deeper into Bernardo Kastrup's work later.

Patrick Harpur

Another modern thinker who deals deeply with the daimonic is Patrick Harpur. He has written some ten books. The most important for our purposes is *Daimonic*

Reality: A Field Guide to the Otherworld (1995). He traces the idea of the daimonic back to ancient Greece, where daimons were experienced as beings in the realm between humans and the gods. Some were helpful, like Socrates's daimon, and some were destructive. Often they were tricksters, shapeshifting and paradoxical. They are both spiritual and material. They are necessary intermediaries.

Plato famously asserted that the ordinary world is a shadow world that is a less perfect and less real version of the realm of Platonic ideas. Between these two worlds, there is the soul of the world, the anima mundi. This is where the daimons live. Like Jung's collective unconscious, the anima mundi is a whole autonomous realm — the source of myth, contact with divinity, creative inspiration, and the daimonic. As such, learning to contact and interact with it is important, both psychologically and spiritually. The Neoplatonists developed this thinking in great detail.

Harpur sees the next major expression of this reality in Western civilization as the Romantic poets' conception of the imagination. This is very different from our concept today, which dismisses imagination as referring to things that are false, phony, unreal — just imagined. This is an exact parallel to the way the word *myth* has been degraded. It now usually means something false, whereas the reality is that these stories contain great wisdom and depth. They provide the basis of our culture and civilization. It's often easier for us to see this when we look at foreign cultures, especially so-called tribal ones. The way their foundational stories shape their worldviews, values, sense of meaning, and therefore their whole culture is fairly visible. But in our arrogance, we somehow suppose that we are the exception. It happens everywhere else, but we are immune — we're above all that.

The undegraded concept of imagination that the Romantic poets expressed is that it is our most important mode of perception. As William Blake wrote, "This world of imagination is the world of eternity; it is the divine bosom into which we shall go after the death of the vegetated body. This world of imagination is infinite and eternal whereas the world of generation is finite and temporal" (1966, 604). For Blake, the imagination was the true mode of perception — where we go after death and a way to contact the divine and the source of all poetic inspiration and creativity. Coleridge, Keats, and Shelley shared similar views.

John Keats wrote of "negative capability." As schoolkids, we were taught that this meant the suspension of disbelief so we could enjoy fiction, but it goes much deeper. Keats (1899, 277) described it as "when a man is capable of being in uncertainty, mysteries, doubts, without any irritable reaching after fact and reason." In this state, a person can enter imagination and meet the daimonic. The rational ego's attitude can seem imperialistic, as though it wants to colonize the unconscious. In IFS, we know that the most necessary quality of Self for healing to proceed is open and nonjudgmental curiosity — "being in uncertainty, mysteries, and doubts," as Keats described it. W. H. Auden, the twentieth-century poet, referred to this imagination as "primary imagination" and the more ordinary kind as "secondary imagination." Yeats had similar views of the value and central importance of primary imagination.

Harpur sees a third major expression of the daimonic reality in Jung's concept of the collective unconscious. Jung insists in many places that the collective unconscious is autonomous, not under ego control. For example, he says, "There are things in the psyche which I do not produce, but which have a life of their own," and again, "There are higher things than the ego's will, and to these one must bow." Jung's encounter with the figures of the daimonic or collective unconscious is recorded in the *Red Book*. (His will stated that it was not to be published until fifty years after his death, but it was released earlier because fragmentary pirated versions were starting to circulate.) This encounter nearly cost Jung his sanity; he was in fear of psychosis because of the autonomous nature and great power of the images and beings he met. He said that all of his later work sprang from what he experienced and learned there. This encounter is the same as entering the daimonic, or at least it's isomorphic. He met beings — Philemon and others — who had intelligence and wills of their own. Some, wiser than Jung, guided and taught him. These encounters shook him to his foundation and affected him for the rest of his life. It is a sad commentary on our modern culture that he found it necessary to keep these crucial experiences secret.

One more point here. In Jung's active imagination, the figures we observe there soon become autonomous; they act on their own without a "let's make something up" attitude. This is a move from Auden's secondary imagination to his primary imagination; it involves entering the Romantic poets' imagination as a mode of perception. Once in this world, Jung insists that we need to act there — hence the term "active imagination." We interact with the figures who appear and hold conversations with the inner voices. This fits IFS's insistence that the locus of healing is in the inner relationship, in the interaction between Self and parts. Simply witnessing, as in mindfulness, is not fully compassionate. Jung entered this realm, which he called the "collective unconscious" — the realm of primary imagination or the daimonic — and he interacted with the beings he met there.

Henry Corbin

As with Plato and the Neoplatonists, the Romantic poets' understanding of imagination, the daimonic, and Jung's work, we have entered more deeply into giving the subjective the value it deserves. The stripping away of the subjective is clearly important and effective in dealing with material things, but it requires us to strip away all that is of real human value — the inwardness that gives our lives meaning and direction. We need to revalue the subjective.

Let's look at one more statement of the value of the inner world, this one from another culture. Henry Corbin (1903–1978) is one of those scholars whose knowledge and achievements boggle the mind. As a young man in his native France, he mastered Latin, Greek, and German. His German was so good and his knowledge of philosophy so strong that he was the first to translate Heidegger into French. For most academics, this work would be a whole career, but for Corbin it was only a start. He then became interested in Islamic thought and learned Persian, Arabic, Turkish, and Sanskrit! He taught at the Sorbonne, in Paris, and at a graduate school in Tehran, Iran. He was also deeply involved in the Eranos conferences. These meetings of great scholars from many fields centered on the psychology and work of Jung. Although Corbin remained a lifelong Protestant (he also wrote on Protestant theology), he became fascinated with the twelfth-century Persian mystic Suhrawardi. Most of Corbin's most famous work focuses on Islamic and Persian spirituality and philosophy.

Corbin invented the term "mundis imaginalis" to translate the Arabic and Persian concept Nā-Kojā-Ābād, which literally means the country or city of nowhere. He felt that this described "a very precise order of reality which corresponds to a precise mode of perception" (1972). In Persian gnostic traditions, there is an overarching theme of the stranger or captive aspiring to return home. We must escape our jailers, the world of the senses and sensory experience, and go beyond Mount Qaf, beyond the shackles of physical reality. Once beyond Mount Qaf, we enter the city of nowhere, the mundis imaginalis or, to use Harpur's term, the daimonic realm. Some of the Persian texts refer to this as the spiritual city; William Blake sometimes called this realm of the Romantic imagination the New Jerusalem. This realm has no space or time. Corbin compares space and time to the shell of an almond that conceals hidden inner realities. For the philosophers and mystics he studied, there are three worlds: the physical sensible world, the mundis imaginalis, and the world of pure archangelic intelligence. These correspond to body, soul, and mind. Each has its own perceptions: senses, imagination, and intellect. This intermediary world, the Alam Al-Mithal, is the world of the image, the mundis imaginalis. Corbin insists it is ontologically as real as the world of the senses or the world of the intellect. He sought throughout his life to preserve humankind's ancient spiritual heritage, which in this life is best met in visions and dreams, against the corrosions of modernity, secularism, and reductive materialism.

I started this chapter with the now well-established importance of interoception. I reviewed Luhrmann's understanding of cultivating inner senses. This discussion is also based on the IFS understanding that when we contact our parts, we are entering the same realities that shamans have been visiting for tens of thousands of years. I traced some other expressions of this same reality: the daimonic, the Romantic poets' primary imagination, and Corbin's mundis imaginalis. Even though this is a realm exiled from Western discourse, we can find it almost everywhere if we but open our eyes and look. The inner world is vast; it largely determines how we can live our lives, and we continue to ignore it at our peril. As Rumi said, "We rarely hear the inner music, but we are all dancing to it nonetheless."

Suryani and Stephen

Let's look at one more non-Western example of the importance of the inner world. Luh Ketut Suryani, a professor of psychiatry in Bali, and Michelle Stephen, an anthropologist and professor in Australia, have developed a body of work that emphasizes Stephen's concept of autonomous imagination. Stephen states that autonomous imagination is

> … a continuous stream of imagery thought taking place in the mind although mostly outside conscious awareness. At regular intervals, it spontaneously enters consciousness in the form of sleep dreams; and under certain conditions, which, like dreams are associated with high cortical arousal combined with low sensory input, it may result in waking visions and other hallucinations. Dreams and hallucinations are usually experienced as taking place independently of a person's conscious intention or will. But with special training, it becomes possible to deliberately access the continuous stream of imaginary thought, bring it into the conscious mind and even direct its unfolding, as we find occurring in the controlled trances of Shamanism and meditative practices, in Western hypnosis, Jungian active imagination, and many other Western imagery-based psychotherapies. This special imaginative mode possesses certain important qualities which not only distinguish it from thought and imagination controlled by ego-consciousness, but also suggest capacities beyond those normally available to consciousness. (Suryani and Stephen 2000, 26–27)

Suryani states that

> autonomous imagination is characterized by: A. being more freely and richly inventive than ordinary thought; B. emerging into conscious awareness in a form of vivid hallucinatory imagery which is experienced

as an external reality; C. possessing a more extensive access to memory; D. exhibiting a special sensitivity to external clues and direction which enables communication to and from deeper levels of the mind, while bypassing conscious awareness; and E. possessing a capacity to influence somatic and intrapsychic process usually beyond conscious control. (Suryani and Stephen 2000, 26–27)

These authors make no reference to Henry Corbin, the Romantic poets' concept of imagination, or the daimonic. They seem to have developed this concept independently. They do assert strongly that this is not Freudian primary process thinking.

The authors use this concept to explain the development of the Balian, the traditional healers of Bali. They argue convincingly that although the start of a Balian's career is often a dramatic change in their life, it is not a classic shamanic initiatory illness. Sometimes, this beginning is triggered by uninvited suffering, but often it is the result of intentional practices like fasting and prolonged prayer. Suryani and Stephen show that it is not the overcoming of the illness itself that makes a Balian; it is the development of a learned ability to control and act in the special mode of autonomous imagination. Perhaps this is also true of many other shamanic cultures. The authors also point out that a Balian's healing does not end this kind of experience but rather creates a new and beneficial relationship to it. These are very important points: the real value of initiation is learning to move in that other world instead of silencing it or shutting it off. These realms can help both the Balian and their society. The ability to touch and move in this realm without being overwhelmed by it seems to provide access to profound healing energies.

Perhaps we can apply this model to other shamanic initiations around the world. Categorizing shamanic initiations as illness is highly questionable. In working with Indigenous people here in North America, especially around the use of sacred plants, I've learned that one thing they often object to is the medicalization of this work. For many of them, it is primarily spiritual, and putting it in the Western framework of medicine and disease diminishes and disrespects inner work. This concept of autonomous imagination may provide a respectful bridge between cultures.

The Transliminal

The transliminal is a concept that can illuminate this point. It has been developed by Isabel Clarke, a clinical psychologist in the UK who works for the National Health Service in acute mental health, primarily with hospitalized patients. She is also an original and profound thinker who focuses on the relationship between spirituality and mental illness. Clarke finds that the terms *subconscious* and *unconscious* have a lot of built-in negative judgments. They contain the implication that our normal, daily ways of being and knowing are superior to what we might learn or experience in our depths. In IFS, we know that parts and Self, which are usually considered as residing in the unconscious, have their own kind of consciousness — their own memories, intelligence, and wisdom. They have great gifts, and calling them "sub" or "un" has never felt right. "Like the frogs in my pond, we are amphibians. We can either hop on the solid ground of ordinary logic and well-understood reality, or swim in the enticing, ever-shifting water of the transliminal" (Clarke 2008, 131). This concept of the transliminal has room for the transcendent spiritual experiences as well as the psychoses. It might be the same as Suryani and Stephen's autonomous imagination. Clarke sees seven signs of the transliminal at work:

(1) **Loss of boundaries.** This is in the very nature of the phenomenon — going across the doorway, which is a boundary. In a religious experience, this might be called piercing the veil or transcending ordinary reality.

(2) **Unshakable conviction.** This is one of the characteristics of both psychedelic experiences and classical mysticism. It is noetic. Realer than real. It is known with absolute certainty. This is valued in religious leaders and despised in those we judge as insane.

(3) **A sense of mission.** This again is often met with ambivalence and is either considered wonderful or terrible. Many of us long for deep purpose, yet we recoil from the fanatic.

(4) **Sensitivity to cosmic suffering.** This can create either saintly compassion or a turning away and curling inward in despair.

(5) **The numinous.** When we touch the transliminal, things seem sacred, holy. Rudolf Otto, who invented the term *numinous* to describe the sense of the sacred common to all religions, described it as "mysterium tremendum et fascinans" — an experience both fascinating and so frightening that it makes us tremble. Numinosity is also a two-edged sword.

(6) **Encounters with supernatural beings.** The transliminal seems to be home for these, and many reside there.

(7) **Both/and logic.** This is a logic of meaning in relationship and relationality. Things can be both true and false simultaneously. All seven of these signs of transliminality can describe transcendent spiritual experience or life-destroying psychosis. How any culture holds these kinds of experiences can profoundly affect the outcome of these openings.

We started with the simple, and by now I hope unassailable, proposition that increasing our interoception abilities can be beneficial. All the voluminous studies of mindfulness meditations and how healing they are for so many issues should put this basic proposition beyond doubt. As we pursue the exploration of subjectivity, it takes us into odder and odder realms. Jung noticed this, too. In his mapping of the psyche, we usually first meet complexes, which are the equivalent of IFS's parts. They are from our own personal life history. If we keep going, we start meeting archetypes. These are larger than our own lives. At first they are human in form and image. If we keep exploring, they become less and less human, more and more otherworldly, god- or demonlike. Where do we choose to stop?

CHAPTER 6

A Basic Outline of
Dealing with Unattached Burdens

This outline is a general suggestion of direction rather than a precise method. Few of my case studies follow this outline closely, and some don't follow it at all. The general approach is to follow the client. Follow their beliefs and imagery and myths. Follow their inner world, their system. Welcome flexibility and openness. Stay curious.

You can consider these steps as broad brushstrokes that indicate tasks to be accomplished or areas of concern to be visited.

Clinical Outline

Step 1: The role of fear — UBs are best removed while in Self

We need our basic IFS skills to be sure that we and our clients have a critical mass of Self. Our first rule or guideline is that UBs only have power if you're afraid of them. They lose all power when you're not scared. This is one of Dick's laws of inner physics. He says that when we're not scared of anything in the inner world, it loses its power. Here is a quote about Self-presence that he wrote in *Internal Family Systems,* 2nd ed. (2020, 278):

> Keep in mind as well that Self can handle anything in the inner world. When trauma survivors face a very scary part, I often tell them, "Nothing inside has power over you when you're not afraid of it, and your Self will not be afraid."
>
> This crucial law has never been violated in my decades of doing IFS, and I have encountered many scary parts who engage in nasty behaviors. As a result, parts who seem all-powerful and dangerous become approachable and can be unburdened of their jobs when they are ready. I am filled with awe every time I see one of these inner monsters melt and transform in the presence of Self energy.

This law applies not only to parts but also to things that are not parts, including legacy burdens and the unattached burdens we're dealing with here.

The first step is to find your parts who find this scary. If you, as the therapist, are frightened of these phenomena, you can't work with clients who have UBs. You can't power through these inner fears, either. You can't bulldoze them; you can't just muscle up and push through. The process is basically the same for the therapist working with their own scared parts and for the client working with theirs. As therapists, we need to do this work with our own therapist before any sessions with the client. If, even after we have done this preparation, a scared part comes up in us as the therapist during a session with a client, we ask that part to unblend and step back to a safe, protected space and let us complete the work from Self. There is no need to conceal this process from the client; it is really good modeling for them to see us handle our own fearful parts. After the session, we need to be sure to go back to this part and help it with its fears. If we don't, the part will be less willing to step back the next time.

The IFS way to help fearful parts is to find the parts who carry the fear, un-blend from them and welcome them with love, and develop a warm and strong Self-to-part relationship with them. This sounds relatively straightforward, but it's one of those things in IFS that's very simple but not easy. Once you get unblended from a part who's holding fear of these unattached burdens, there are two basic paths available. The better path is to work with the Self-to-part relationship with that part until it's very comfortably attached to your Self and no longer has any fear. The other way is to get this part who holds the fear to a safe, comfortable, enclosed, and protected space behind the client and you so it can let you work with the UB. If you do this, it's necessary to come back and help this part later.

These fear parts in us and in our clients are not a problem. They're actually the goal. They hold treasure because working with these fearful parts, reconnect-ing with them, and holding them close are the royal road to our deep healing. So, we don't want to push them aside and disrespect them; rather, we want to welcome them wholeheartedly. Working with them is a portal to transformation of our whole system. It's also how we grow deeply as therapists.

There's a quote I like that goes, "What's in the way is the way." One of the great gifts of doing this work at the outer edges of therapy is that it will scare and trigger many of our parts; it will help us get to know them and welcome them in more quickly than we would have if it weren't for these strange stimuli. There's another saying with the same basic meaning: "The only difference between a stumbling block and a stepping stone is your attitude toward it."

We need to have a loving, welcoming, patient attitude toward the parts of us who hold fear. We need to be in Self with them. They offer us a healing path to becoming better therapists, more comfortable human beings, and deeper spiritual beings. This is true of therapists, and it's even truer of clients. So once you, as the therapist, have worked with your frightened parts, are not scared of what's going on in your client in any way, and can be in Self with the eight Cs with them, you can start to do this kind of work. You do not need all eight Cs 100 percent; you need a critical mass of Self — enough Self so that Self can do the session.

Of the eight Cs, curiosity is the most important. You can't proceed without it. If I'm not curious about a client, I stop the session and ask them to give me a few minutes to help my parts step back and get back in Self. Curiosity is that important. You may have more than one part who holds fear or anxiety about doing this kind of work. It's very important to work with all of them who do. Treat them with love, welcome them, help them. If you're holding fear and trying to muscle past it, you won't really be able to do good work.

Once you have dealt with your fearful parts, you ask the client, "How do you feel toward the unattached burden? How do you feel toward that presence in you that's not a part of you?" If the answer is fear or anxiety, or anything like that, you do regular IFS with those parts. You welcome them, help the client unblend from them, get to know them, and help the client relate to them from Self and love them up. The other alternative, just as in working with yourself, is asking the client to have these parts go to a safe place behind them so you can complete the work with the unattached burden. It's best, in working with UBs, if they can be removed when the client is in Self. If there's any fear, you need to work with that first. That's the number one rule — that's how UBs gain power. Anger can also keep people connected to UBs. It's very understandable that people can have parts who are absolutely enraged at them. UBs often appear in a person's system as angry, sneering, contemptuous, threatening, and doing all sorts of nasty stuff. Anger is a natural response and in many ways is healthy, but it can become something that keeps people connected to the unattached burden.

Years ago when I was working with Pia Mellody, I learned an important lesson about justified anger. We'd been working together for a long time, and she knew me very well. In a small-group setting, she said, "Bob, today I'm going to tell you about your character defects," which is a phrase that's frequently used in twelve-step environments. She said she'd come up with a list of six, and I wasn't to take notes — somebody else would do that for me. I was just supposed to listen and understand. She started with, "Bob, you're arrogant." She gave examples of how I'd been arrogant and gone one up on other people, and she was totally accurate and devastatingly right. Next, she talked about my sarcasm and how I'd caused pain with it, and again, she was right on the mark. After she'd gone through all six, I felt like a puddle on the floor. Pia said, "Okay, Bob, you got that?" I said, "Yes, I do." She said, "Now we're going to do the hard part. I know your father raped and beat you and tormented you throughout your childhood, but your anger is now something that keeps you connected to his spirit. It's like a spear you hold in him, and it keeps you two connected. To break that connection, you're going to put his spirit in that empty chair over there, put him in that empty chair over there, and you're going to tell him how much he hurt you without getting angry. How close do you want the chair?" I started swearing and yelling at the top of my lungs, screaming every four-letter word I could think of. "That's the stupidest thing I've ever heard of," I shouted. While this was going on, she just had a little smile on her face. When I ran out of breath, she said, "Okay, Bob, how close do you want that chair?" Eventually I did what she said, with the chair as far away as it was possible to get it in that house. It did make a difference. It broke a connection between me and the spirit of my father.

This same kind of connection can form between people and unattached burdens who have been tormenting them for a long time in their inner world. UBs often seem to be doing everything they can to provoke a fight, to provoke anger. This keeps the person connected to them. The lack of anger and combativeness is a huge difference between IFS UB work and exorcism. UBs like the fight, and they love to provoke us into our protector energies. It is a standard idea in IFS that protector parts usually create in the outside world exactly what they are trying to protect against. It is the same with UBs. Don't let your protectors fight them. It might even be that UBs feed off of this protector energy coming at them.

It's necessary to deal with all the fear-holding parts before you do this work, and it's also important to clear anger, at least substantially, or it will keep the person connected to the UB. That's the most important thing about doing this; they only get power when you're afraid of them. Sometime I tell people that any being who would gain power by scaring child parts is not really powerful at all. UBs often become enraged at me for this assertion. It is actually a good development because the client can see that I am totally unafraid and that the UB can't harm me at all. As a corollary, UBs are quite good at scaring people. But this actually has a benefit: it reveals tender parts who need more attention and care. I think it's rather like ants in the kitchen. The ants obviously don't have any good intentions to help, but they unerringly show where food is spilled. Unattached burdens show people the weak, tender, frightened parts who need help. In this way, they can actually be a well-disguised blessing.

Step 2. Assume it's a part until proven otherwise

The second basic piece of working with unattached burdens is that you need to assume this thing is a part of the person's system and not something from outside the system. Do this over and over and over again until it is absolutely clear that it's not a part of the system. There's a great price to pay if you try to amputate a part of the system. The whole system won't trust you anymore because you've tried to expel a part of it, and this can take a long time to repair.

One of the great advances of IFS is the realization that parts are not their burdens. At their core, all of them are well-intentioned and have great gifts to give once their burdens can be released. Most other therapies before IFS would try to amputate parts or at least lock them in a soundproof dungeon deep in the psyche so they wouldn't be heard from again. This is not helpful.

I've helped train the staff in some eating disorder clinics, and they obviously need to get people who are anorexic to eat because they'll die if they don't. We do need to control the eating disorder part, but we do it from a place of compassion and respect, knowing that it is doing this destructive behavior for what it sees as good and important reasons. As Dick colorfully says, "If you get in a battle with ED [eating disorders], ED will kick your ass."

With alcoholism, we want to befriend and help the part who wants to drink — we don't want to shame and imprison it. This IFS approach is often revolutionary in a person's system. It requires time and care to build internal trust. Therefore, if you attempt to amputate and expel a part, thinking it's a UB, you can undo a lot of valuable work and cause a great deal of damage. So, assume it's a part, assume it's a part, assume it's a part. There's a saying that almost every medical student has heard when being taught diagnosis: "When you hear hoofbeats, don't think of zebras." You don't go to the weird, exotic thing first — you stay with horses or mules or donkeys. You go with those first, and parts are the familiar thing in a person's system. Many people never have any unattached burdens or legacy burdens that they're aware of, and they can do powerful and life-transforming therapy without going to those areas.

The first thing about checking to see if it's a part is to ask about its intention. If you look deeply enough, parts always have a good intention. Suicidal parts are an excellent example. Most people have them; most people have thought of killing themselves at some point in their life. If you ask a suicidal part, "Why do you want to kill this person?" they might say, "Well, then they wouldn't be on the planet anymore." Then you ask, "What's good about not being on the planet anymore?" Then they might say, "They wouldn't suffer anymore." There's your good intention. Sometimes you have to drill down many layers because the good intention isn't clear, but if it's a part, eventually there will be a good intention.

If it was an unattached burden that was trying to get the person to kill themselves, you could ask the same question. "What would be good about you killing them?" It would say something like, "They wouldn't be on the planet anymore." You could then ask, "Well, what would be good about that?" They might say something like, "Well, then it means I would have won." There's no good intention in that, which means it might be an unattached burden. You need to keep asking, "What's good about that? " or "And then?" over and over. Drill deep when you look for intentions; they can be well hidden.

A slightly different way to approach the same issue is to ask about and look for a productive function. This slightly different line of questioning can add clarity. UBs can be very intimidating and have serious deleterious effects on a person. Suppose one of them had ruined a relationship. You would still need to know more. Did it ruin the relationship with what it thought was a destructive partner? Then it's a part. Or did it ruin the relationship to isolate the person to make them more vulnerable and pliable? Then it might be an unattached burden. UBs are purely malevolent. Stay in Self, stay curious, take your time, and it will become clear.

There is a particular kind of part that needs special attention here: perpetrator introjects. Think of a child who is being abused. Who has all the power in the room when that's going on? The perpetrator, clearly. Very often a protective part takes on some of the perpetrator's energy and beliefs in its efforts to protect the child. These protective parts then do battle with the perpetrator. Mostly they are hated by all the other parts because they have qualities of the perpetrator. These parts are tragic heroes who have sacrificed everything in their attempts to keep the system alive. They are usually hostile and defensive when we first meet them, so it is very easy to mistake them for UBs of some kind. This is a terrible error; these parts are already horribly isolated in their struggle to help the system survive. If we try to send them out of the system, believing they are UBs, we compound this damage. In doing this work, we need to be especially careful and sensitive about any perpetrator introjects in the system. They deserve a hero's welcome home.

There is another diagnostic question to ask as well. When the being expresses a belief or opinion, ask where it got that belief. For example, if it says, "It would be better if she were dead," ask where and when it took on that belief. We use this question often with parts. When a part answers, it begins the process of deconstructing the belief — helping the part start to disidentify from the burden. The part realizes that this is a belief it took on at a certain point in time, not a reality or part of its identity. UBs typically can't or won't answer this question. If they do, their answer often reveals what they are.

Once you've very carefully explored for good intentions, the next thing to do is to ask this thing directly, "Are you a part of her?" Even better, have the client ask it: "Are you a part of me — are you a part of my system?" It's very important to ask the thing itself and not let any other parts speak up. Almost everyone has polarizations in their system, for example, one part that wants to eat ice cream after dinner and another part that's saying, "No, you're already a few pounds over-weight." Very often those polarized parts will point at each other and say, "Hey, that one's not a part. Get rid of that one." You have to ask the thing itself, "Are you a part?" Very often they'll refuse to answer at first. This happened, for example, in the case that changed my life that was described in Chapter 3. The thing didn't want to answer that question, but if you just keep asking calmly and clearly, even-tually they usually will. Be persistent until you get a clear answer.

Dick has said that these things can't lie about this, even though they seem to be masters of lying and dissimulation in many other areas. I've heard some replies that are almost lies, but they seem to be very rare. Sometimes UBs are still blended with or attached to a part and can still say they're a part until all the parts who were attached to them let them go. I was teaching about this point once, and one of the students, a powerful woman from Nigeria, interrupted and said forcefully, almost yelling, "They lie!" When I got past my surprise, I was so grateful that she spoke and gave us some insight into another culture's views. She also said that in her tradition, many UBs were believed to be the spirits of deceased people, some of whom had been dead for so long that they forgot who they really were and came to believe they were parts of the person.

The following are the two most foundational and important things about dealing with unattached burdens, or anything inside a person's system that doesn't seem to be part of them:

- no fear in you, the therapist, and no fear in the client (or at least having any fear-holding parts in a safe, contained space)
- sure knowledge that this thing is not a part of the person's system

You can't really go on unless these two are in place. If you're in doubt, keep working them. Just working these two steps can make an incredible difference for people because the young, tender parts of them that held all the fears can be welcomed and unburdened, and they will get clearer and clearer about what is them and what is not. These steps seem fairly universal in doing this work. All the other steps are much more a reflection of the person's ideology and their own internal imagery, mythology, and metaphors. The other steps can diverge much more widely, but these two are pretty solid and need to happen at the beginning.

I am going to repeat this information about dealing with unattached bur-dens because it is fundamentally important. First, UBs lose all power when you're not afraid of them. This is very simple and also very difficult. It goes against much of the Hollywood version of exorcisms. It takes a lot of the drama out of it, but it's really important and profoundly true. Second, assume it's part of the person's system until proven otherwise. This is another error that many exorcists and deliverance ministers have made. They have tried to amputate parts of a person. This always fails, and it always causes deep damage. It may look as though it succeeds for a while, but the part will come roaring back, and it will be angry and in no mood to cooperate because it's already been betrayed once.

The parts work model is a huge advance over old ways of dealing with these kinds of issues because it allows us to own, accept, and welcome parts of us and get out of our system what is not ours. Terrible damage has been done by well-meaning people who have tried to amputate and banish parts in the name of exorcism. These parts were often the very parts who had taken on the heaviest burdens in order to save the person.

Step 3. Create some distance between the person and the UB

UBs are often as sneering and obnoxious as they can possibly be, but we do not have to respond or engage with them at that level. We do not need a confrontation or a fight. UBs will do what they can to provoke us into power struggles and hatred. Anytime our protectors get triggered and we relate to a UB from protector energy, the UB is fed by this and becomes stronger. UBs love the conflict. Remember the old IFS adage that protectors tend to provoke whatever it is they most fear in the outside world. This is even truer in the inner realms. There is no need to fight these beings; don't do it.

Very often, unattached burdens are bullies. They are contemptuous and sneering, and they say things like, "I'll never go — you can't make me." This is a lie; in truth, when all parts of a person's system are ready to let a UB go, it can't stay. In the deliverance ministries, they say that there has to be "ground" for what they would call a demon to stay in a person, and they often think of this ground in terms of sin, which I think is a sad and limiting way to view it. The reason these things can get into a person and stay there is because some part is allowing them to attach. Dick has said in the past that in his belief, all of these things promise power to the powerless. The vast majority do. It's very easy to imagine a young child who has been hurt and traumatized to look for any kind of power it might get, and then something offers it power or, more accurately, the illusion of power. That would be an irresistible temptation. There's also another motivation for children taking in these kinds of external energies: they offer companionship to the lonely. Abandoned children need companionship, and they can be so desperate that they will do anything to get it. Remember that isolation *is* a mortal threat for young children. They will die if abandoned, and their bodies seem to know this. It is biologically hardwired in us.

If it is impossible to get any degree of separation from the unattached burden, this is not a disaster. It just means we need to find the parts who are letting it stay so close. Ask the client to find the parts. Ask how they feel toward the parts. Once your client is in Self in relation to these parts (and this often may require getting other frustrated parts to step back), have them offer those parts compassion and care. This is standard, classic IFS. With steady presence, a strong Self-to-part relationship will form. This is much more secure, warm, and loving than any relationship with unattached burdens. When all is said and done, UBs always drain the parts they are attached to as well as the entire system. They are parasites. In contrast, Self's presence makes the whole system stronger. Therefore, you can be confident that the Self-to-part relationship will ultimately be much more rewarding to the part. Just patiently work with every part who is unwilling to get any distance from the unattached burden.

Once all these parts have been worked with, you and the client will be able to get some separation. My favorite metaphor for this is to use light. I'll say something like, "Surround this thing in a ball or egg-shaped container of light, and pull it out of your body to a good conversational distance, perhaps six or eight feet away from you." Or sometimes I say, "Surround yourself and this thing in you in a ball of light, and then back out of the ball of light, leaving the thing in the light." Light is definitely the most popular metaphor for this. Dick uses it all the time. Orthodox Christians talk about the uncreated light, and Buddhists talk about the clear light or basic luminosity. There are all sorts of phrases that fit different traditions. However, some people find this light metaphor repellent: "Oh, that New Age bullshit." I've also used the metaphor of a magnetic field and talked about how if you have iron filings mixed with sand, the job of separating them looks impossible, but a magnet does this easily and quickly. Another metaphor I've used is combing it out. I watched a film about Mongolian shamans who do this. They spread their fingers wide and comb the air around the person they're working on to heal them. I'll ask the client what metaphor works for them, such as washing or whatever metaphor they suggest. If at any point a client's metaphor differs from my preferred metaphors, I drop mine and go with the client's. We want to use the images that are the most powerful for the client. We need to be able to put our belief system on hold, to bracket it, so it doesn't interfere with the client's process. I believe we can really make a difference in the client's system, in how the client experiences their world, and in their emotional well-being by doing these kinds of processes. We need to use the client's language, culture, and worldview as much as possible.

As we will see later, meeting beings like these UBs is very common in psychedelic work. Stan Grof, a great pioneer in this field, developed his own way of dealing with them. He would challenge UBs, asking, "You do not really know who you are, do you?" When they stumbled with this, which they almost always did, he would press the point by asking them more questions, such as "Where do you come from?" This would often disorient them and shake their confidence, but it is dangerous to do anything with protector energy in it. UBs grow stronger when they meet protector energy. Paths like this can make the removal of the being more traumatic than it needs to be.

Once the unattached burden is in a ball of light, or whatever container works for the client, and at a conversational distance, I ask the client to notice if there are any attachments of any kind coming back from that being to them or their body — any cords, tubes, lines of smoke, anything. Many people immediately want to cut these connections. I say, "No, no, no, no, please don't." These things are very valuable diagnostic indicators. I ask the client, "Where do these things touch your body?" This shows the place in the client's body where the part who still has some attachment to this thing lives. Then it's back to classic IFS with the part attached to the UB. "How do you feel toward that part?" We keep working until the client reaches compassion or at least curiosity. Curiosity is the Self quality they can't proceed without.

Extend curiosity toward the part, see how it responds, and work to develop the relationship, slowly and patiently, until that part, of its own accord, turns toward Self and lets go of this other thing, the unattached burden.

Step 4. Detach from the unattached burden

You continue doing this until all the attachments extending from the UB in the ball of light fall away and none are coming back to the client's body. A very useful question here is: "Ask inside if there are any parts of you who will miss this thing when it's gone." We do not want parts who will miss it hiding in shame or fear. Therefore, I often add that it makes sense that parts might miss it since it's been here a long time and is familiar. It's crucial to carefully and lovingly find all parts who had attached to that UB. Then it won't be able to stay or reenter and will leave without rupture or violence. This question is carefully phrased. "Who will miss it when it's gone?" contains the presupposition that the UB will leave the system. It's only a matter of when.

IFS therapist Michi Rose developed a series of statements that can be very useful during this phase of the process. She would have the client say to the UB, "You are no longer welcome in my body. You are no longer welcome in my emotions. You are no longer welcome in my thinking. You are no longer welcome in my beliefs. You are no longer welcome in my spirit." At first when I tried this, I was only using it as a ritualized way of marking an end. Several times, UBs popped up and said things like, "Well, that other stuff might be true, but I'm still here in her thinking." Now when I use this protocol, I watch the client very carefully looking for "tells," as poker players call them — physical signs that give away the information that something is still going on in the area I've just mentioned. This has been so useful that I have added to Michi's list. Now I also say, "You are no longer welcome in my exiles. You are no longer welcome in my managers. You are no longer welcome in my firefighters."

If any physical difficulty or illness has been associated with the UB, I also mention the body parts involved. For example, "You are no longer welcome in my stomach" or whatever areas have had problems. In this list, beliefs are often especially significant. One belief that UBs almost always work to implant is that the person does not deserve love. We need to look for this belief. It prevents parts from letting go of the UB because they've been brainwashed into believing that no one else will ever be there for them. In the context of the external world, Marshall Rosenberg, the creator of Nonviolent Communication (NVC), said that the most dangerous word in the English language is *deserve*. This may also be true in the inner world.

In Step 3, we got the UB out of the client's body. Now we are sending it off entirely. These are imagistic-imaginative ideas, obviously, but they can have great emotional power. Very often these steps are intermingled rather than separate. I typically address the energy in that ball of light (the UB) and give it these messages throughout the process: "We're not doing this to punish you or judge you. You're lost, you're in the wrong place, and you can no longer stay here. Even though you pretend to be tough and strong, we know that you too suffer. We're going to send you to where you can transform and grow and get real nourishment and healing."

More and more, I am telling the UBs, "When you go to the healing realms, you'll get real power, not this fake, small stuff you have been fooling around with." This is very, very different from a traditional exorcism. A group of neo-shamans centered in Seattle talk about compassionate dispossession, and it's very much like this. Also, the Spiritists of Brazil believe that all of these things that get into people, no matter how horrendous, devil-like, mean, and terrifying they appear, are really just lost souls in the wrong place. They are very frightened and are suffering deeply, too. Some Spiritists actually seem to believe that it becomes our job to help them, almost as much as helping our client. In Tibet, there is a long tradition of befriending demons that is exemplified in the Chod rituals. Tsultrim Allione has adapted the Chod rites for Western use and published a book (*Feeding Your Demons*, 2008) explaining this in detail.

Typically a UB says, "I'm not going; you can't make me." It snarls, rages, hisses, and often utters a lot of very colorful swear words. It seems that we have some kind of basic free will and that these things cannot stay in us when no part of us wants them in any way anymore. There is no longer any "ground" for them in us. But the UBs also seem to have some kind of free will. I would like to send them all to the healing realms, but some of them seem to want to scurry back into the darkness, and I don't have choice over that. I can only encourage.

These unattached burdens seem to be uniformly miserable, even if they pretend to love what they're doing. What they're doing is not actually pleasant, and it's left them in a starving or semi-starving state. One of the major reasons they won't leave is that they fear punishment or they believe that a good realm would never welcome them because they've done so many terrible things. I keep working to reassure them, "You will be welcomed there. There will be a feast like for the prodigal son. All you need to do is turn and look, and you'll see kind beings leaning down to help you." I've started using imagery from near-death experiences (NDEs), telling the UBs, "If you look upward, you'll very likely see a tunnel and light at the end of the tunnel, and you might see those kind beings there." Adopting NDE imagery for this work is very promising. There are now more and more studies of NDEs and many vivid descriptions of imagery you can offer. NDE expert Dr. Bruce Greyson and others have made lists of the most frequent images that you can work from. I tell the UBs they'll be feasting in celebration when they return to their true home. Still, many of them don't believe this and won't go. Most of these UBs seem strongly focused on power, so I remind them and tempt them by telling them that if they go to the healing realms, they will find real power, not the cheap counterfeit power they have been using here.

Dr. William Baldwin, the founder of Spirit Releasement Therapy, did two things at this point. I have no idea where he got these ideas, but pragmatically, they often seem helpful. He would say to these beings, "You have been lied to and deceived about your nature and the nature of your world, and I can prove it to you. The first lie is that light will hurt you and cause immense pain. This is not true; take one finger and touch the light that surrounds you, and you'll see." Very often, these beings will refuse; they'll bluster and give all sorts of reasons. But once they do touch the light, it almost always feels good to them, at least warm and definitely not painful. When Dick used to work with these things with light, they would be hurt by the light, and if they came into contact with anything that was like light, they'd be screaming and flailing in pain. I think it was actually their fear, their terror of light, that was hurting them, not the light itself. They resisted being forced through their terror.

The second lie that Baldwin would tell these things they'd been told was that if they looked inside themselves, there was nothing but dark, and that they were mortal beings who would die. He would tell these things, "Look inside yourself and you will see a spark of light." They would often balk at this task, too, and bluster and huff and puff. But every time they have done it, when they looked inside, they did see a spark of light. When they realized that the light didn't hurt them and that they had a spark of light deep inside them, they were much more willing to take the risk of going up into the light, into a realm of healing. These beings are uniformly proud, or perhaps I should say, I haven't met one yet who is not proud. This can be used to manipulate them, and I'm perfectly willing to be quite confrontational with them. I'll say things like, "A powerful, proud being like you is too frightened to touch the light with one fingertip? Or are you really a coward or weakling?" I also issue other challenges very much like that. I'm not really hostile when I do this — I'm trying to get them to do something that I believe will help them and help them transform. I behave with UBs in ways I never would behave with a part.

As the unattached burden becomes more and more ready to leave the person, it's important to make sure that it's taking all its parts, employees, minions, objects — anything of that sort that it left in the person. We don't want any residues left in the client. Some UBs are devious and intelligent in their strategies. One, for example, gave a twelve-year-old boy part a pocketknife in the imaginal, internal world, and the boy did not want to let go of it. It was a treasure for him, but if it had stayed in his system, it would have functioned as a way back in for this UB energy. It's important to check for any things or parts of slaves or employees left behind. If one of these things is especially resistant to going to the healing realms, when it's out there at the conversational distance, I will say, "Yes, you have free will, but so do all of your slaves, employees, minions, underlings, whatever words you want to use, and they can all go to the healing realms now." Several times people have reported that they see UBs getting smaller and smaller and looking more frightened and concerned as their army melts away.

Another reason these things sometimes won't go is that they're frightened. They've been sent there by some other being that they consider more important or more powerful than either themselves or us. UBs are often organized into local hierarchies with bosses and underlings. If a UB is recalcitrant, I'll say something like, "It seems like you're an underling. Let me talk to your boss." Sometimes there is a boss who sent them, in which case the procedure is the same. If you're not afraid of it, it has no power. Very often the unattached burdens are terrified of this boss, and that's how these bosses get power. For a UB to see you standing up to a boss makes all the difference in the world. You can do the same entire procedure with this boss. Surround it in some type of containing field, move it out, make sure all the connections back to the person are gone, and then send it away. Some therapists find it scary to ask for the boss, and it's important to work with any scared parts before doing this.

Even if you've done all this, some unattached burdens will still be snarling and contemptuous, spewing hate and scorn, and vowing to destroy both you and the person they've been in. In truth, they don't have that power, and if you have no fear of them, they have no power whatsoever. I just remind them that they can't stay here anymore; we can't force them to go to the healing realms, but they have to leave. I acknowledge that they, like the client, have free will. I tell them that all their slaves, soldiers, and underlings also have free will. I encourage them to go to the light and tell them they can safely make the transition now. Often once one underling has gone to the healing realms, many others witness this and follow. Sometimes the major UB will follow, too, when it sees the greeting all its underlings receive and when it realizes it has lost its army. Some do not; instead, they return to the darkness. I don't like letting them go back there, but I don't have control over that. I think it's bad for them, and I also have concerns that they'll harass others. As a UB leaves the person's system, especially when it is going toward healing, there are some valuable questions to ask: "Have you left any parts of yourself or objects in the person?" "Are there any other beings like you still in them?" UBs seem to know about the presence of others who may be trying to hide so they can stay in the person. The anthropologist Tom Csordas pointed out that hidden possessing spirits — hidden demons, to use his language — are often the most powerful. The strongest sacrifice their underlings and try to hide. It is good to check.

These UBs seem to be some kind of parasite. One group of people I know who work with them calls them "the feeders," based on the belief that they feed on the negative emotions and pain of humans. This would seem to be a fair description of how they have appeared in my clients. As I said before, they often get into a person by promising power. Power to the powerless — what a seductive offer. They might give the appearance of power or at least enough power to give the person the illusion that they have more power, but they actually cripple the person. They keep people weak, dependent, and powerless in order feed off of them. Very often, people with unattached burdens in them are terrified for much of their lives. They don't know where the fear comes from, and it seems irrational. When a UB offers companionship to the lonely and abandoned child, what it really does is increase the isolation of that person so the person becomes more dependent, more isolated, and more in need of the energies of the unattached burden.

Sometimes the unattached burdens come in offering numbness when there is great pain, and then they cause pain in order to create the need for numbness.

All of these parasitic behaviors are offers of a solution that actually makes things worse. This is very reminiscent of the addiction process. For example, alcohol promises conviviality and confidence but actually leads a person down a path to loneliness and ever-increasing dependence on the alcohol, and more is always needed. There's a very odd parallel here. When the UB is leaving, it is good to ask the client to watch it until it disappears completely. Several have reported that it went through a hole in the sky and was totally gone. If it balks and turns back at the last minute, do not get discouraged. This is valuable information. It means that parts of the client are still holding on to it or allowing it to hold on to them. The poet Charles Upton once said that the devil is an opportunistic infection. These things can't help but show us where we need to heal. The parts where the UBs attach need our care and love. Removing UBs can help us find deeply hidden parts and inadvertently facilitate the client's healing.

Step 5. Rebalance the system

The UB is now entirely gone, and the client is welcoming back all their parts. After the unattached burden has moved on, hopefully to the light but perhaps back into the darkness, it's very important to check with all the parts in the client's system to see if they're all okay with its absence. UBs have often been in people for decades. It has been very familiar to have this external energy in them, and it can be disorienting and odd to have it gone. I like to use a metaphor to explain this. I tell people it's like when a very heavy person gets out of a canoe; the canoe will tend to bobble and rock in the water. This is to be expected. We need to check with all the parts who detached from the UB to make sure everybody's okay and well connected with Self.

If we did help any parts to step back and go into a safe room, it's vital to bring them all out and have them look around and see and feel how things are without the UB in the system. Most of the time, people feel good when the UB is gone. Even then, we need to look for any parts who are uncomfortable, frightened, disoriented, or otherwise troubled and take time to reconnect with them in a positive way. Sometimes when UBs have left, they immediately turn around and offer to come back as guides or protectors. Do not trust this. I do believe there are energies we can connect to that are guides and protectors, and these are very valuable and wonderful for a client to connect to, but it's a very dangerous idea to allow a UB to return in that guise right away. Usually, it's just a front, a pretense. They still want to do damage. Even if they want to do good, they haven't had a chance to receive any healings themselves. I discourage this intensely when it's proposed to a client, even though it's a very seductive offer. In other cultures, we see this direct transformation of a negative intrusion into a positive force. For example, shamanic initiation transforms a dangerous spirit illness into a source of power. The Zār spirits, which are found throughout North Africa, do not leave the person, but the relationship is improved so it is neutral or beneficial. In voodoo, lifelong relationships are often formed between the possessing loa and the possessed person. I sometimes wonder if my reluctance to let UBs return as helpers might be more about my limitations and the fact that our culture has no established ways to work with this stuff rather than something structurally necessary.

Quite often, as these things leave, they apologize and say something like, "I am so sorry — I didn't realize how much damage I was doing. I was lost. Please forgive me." Sometimes people are sad to see them go, and the parting is poignant and filled with grief. Even so, it needs to happen. There is another phenomenon that can also happen. Sometimes parts, especially deep exiles, have been hiding behind the UB and all the ruckus it caused. It's good to inquire gently at this point to see if any parts are feeling exposed or pulled out of their hiding place. If there are any parts like this, offer them a new, more comfortable hiding place and let them know you will be coming back to help them fully join the system.

It seems that Westerners almost always want to send UBs upward — that the healing realms are imagined as being above us. I think this is very deep in our history. It's in almost all of our mythologies, but it's not necessarily the only option. Our mythologies indicate an upward direction and light, but it's also perfectly possible for these things to go down — to sink into the earth or into the primeval waters. Again, go with the person's mythology, religious orientation, metaphors, and worldview. Michael Harner, the great anthropologist of shamanism and a shaman himself, divided the spirit world into three realms: the upper world, the middle world where we live, and the lower world. I think this model is useful, at least to open our symbolic systems so we are not upset or bothered by the idea of sending things down into the waters or down into the earth. Harner and his school also say that you can find real guides on any of these levels, but it's much better and safer to look in the upper world or the lower world because many of the beings in this middle world where we live are tricksters and are not reliable. They might well fool us.

Many people who work with UBs are aware of the cords, connections, and ties coming back to a person, and they cut them rather than work with the parts they're attached to. As I've said before, I don't like this practice very much because I think it loses something of value. UBs actually do us a service by showing us where in the client there are frightened parts who need our love and attention, and we should make use of that precious information. There's often been a high price paid for that knowledge; tuition is high at this school. If you feel you need to cut these cords, there are ways. There is a shamanic method called the "jaguar breath." When the client is seeing the cords, have them purse their lips and blow downward — three strong exhales — moving their head from side to side with each exhale and visualizing each breath cutting across one of the cords. Have the client do three breaths with each cord. This ritual does seem to be helpful for some people.

As part of cleaning up, it's often necessary, or at least a good idea, to find out how the UB got in in the first place. Sometimes UBs are passed down as legacy burdens from our ancestors. However, when this is not the case, they usually get in when, in one way or another, we weren't in our body. Very often these things get in through rape, and the place they got in was the place that was raped. Trauma of all kinds lets UBs in. Sometimes they get in when someone is under anesthesia. If there is concern about the presence of UBs, it is good to ask about childhood surgeries. Sometimes they get in through betrayal, and I've noticed that very often, betrayal entry is in the back of the heart. You can ask the client to look around for any sense of where this thing got in.

Now, there are many different kinds of visualization and other methods to stay safe. The most basic and sure rule is that when you're not afraid of a UB, it loses all power. This absence of fear is the real power. I generally hesitate to use other methods because they can be fear-based, but I do sometimes offer others. Very often, people build some kind of boundary around themselves or have imagery about that. This feels powerful to them, so I go with what the client wants and their imagery and mythology. But I prefer an approach that I've heard in many meditative traditions, which is building up inner light inside that fills the whole body and whole person more and more so there is no way the person can be penetrated. This is imagistically as well as energetically different from creating a shell around something.

William Baldwin described a meditation he called the "sealing light meditation" to establish safety. He would tell people to look inside themselves, and deep inside they would find a spark of light. As they focus on that spark of light, slowly and calmly, they notice it growing. The more attention they put on the spark of light, the more it grows. Then they have the light grow until it fills their entire body, all the way to their skin. From an IFS perspective, I would add that they should notice if there are any shadowy areas, constrictions, or places where the light does not penetrate. If they find any, I recommend they not fight or blame them but instead welcome and befriend them. These are trailheads that guide us to where we need to focus next; they're very important clues about the direction of our future work. Then Baldwin would say, when the body is entirely full of this light, let it burst forth and extend a foot or two beyond you in every direction.

I also have people look in the area around their body for any clouds, obstructions, or dents. The idea is that in this state, no external energy can get into you — there is no room for it. Baldwin suggested practicing this meditation. It might take a half hour or more to do it thoroughly at first, but after a while it becomes so automatic that you can do it in a breath or two. Once it has become that automatic, it can be very useful in real time during a session. You can use it yourself, and you can also train clients in it if they're open to this sort of thing.

I've heard several people who work in this area say that it's extremely rare for the same unattached burden to return. This is also my experience. Some say that it never happens. But once there's an opening in a person, other UBs might come in because they'll see an inviting door. So it's a good practice to check with the person and look for any openings, any access points, and work with them.

Step 6. Invite guidance and guides

Now that the unattached burden is out of the person, the place where it got in has been addressed and sealed, filled, or dealt with in some way, and all the parts who stepped back or who had been connected to this thing in any way have been reconnected with and reassured, there's still work to do. This is very much like the phase called the "invitation" in regular IFS after we've gotten a regular burden out of a person. In regular IFS, we ask the client to ask the part to welcome in any qualities it may need in the future, and that's basically what we do here as well. We encourage all the parts in the system to welcome in any qualities that will feel good. Very often it's just light or warmth or something of that nature that comes in. Sometimes it's courage, excitement, playfulness, or any of the eight Cs. I ask the person to say aloud the qualities they want to welcome in if they're willing to. This filling process is sort of like the sealing light meditation. We don't want to leave a big, empty space in that person's system, in their imaginal field.

Now, some energies that get in from outside are benign, benevolent, wonderful, and important. Self sometimes is experienced as coming in from outside when it's experienced as part of a wave. The twelve steps talk about a higher power. Almost every religion talks about contact with Spirit, the Holy Spirit, or whatever they call it. This kind of experience has been happening to people throughout history and often changes their lives dramatically. In IFS, we call these energies guides because this term seems to offend the smallest number of people. It still offends some. The word *guidance* is even more inoffensive. Use whatever term is okay with your client. Many more IFS therapists are willing to talk about these kinds of energies, which we tend to call guides, than they are willing to talk about dark energies — the unattached burdens. This is very understandable, but I think it's quite unfortunate. This period after an unattached burden has been removed from the person's system is an excellent time to see if any guides are around.

One of the things about IFS that is central and important is that it's a constraint-release model. Basically, we are Self and we are curious, compassionate, courageous, connected, calm, clear, all those wonderful qualities, and the reason Self doesn't shine forth all the time is that there are constraints, or things blocking it. Our path to healing is the removal of these constraints rather than the building up of some kind of muscle or resourcing. In IFS, we view even the most damaged person, and even the person who's done horrendous things, as having a fundamental Self that cannot be damaged or even tarnished. We need to remove the constraints so it will shine forth. When there is a huge storm, the sky is black, and there can be mudslides, trees blown down, and our house destroyed. When the storm is over and the clouds part, the sun is there, undamaged, unblemished, not affected in the slightest. IFS says Self is like an inner sun no matter how bad the trauma. This is a tremendously liberating and positive idea for people who have suffered big T trauma or addiction. I also think it's a tremendously liberating idea for pretty much everybody.

With this constraint-release model, it makes sense that we would need to focus on these unattached burden energies first. They're huge constraints. The idea is that when enough of these constraints are removed, Self and guides will appear. Just as with Self, guides are always there, and we don't experience them all the time only because of constraints and things blocking them. The constraint-release model is a model of subtraction, not addition. It's based on the fundamental belief that we are good and whole, and that Self — the goodness and wholeness — is who we really are. It is absolutely undamaged even in the most traumatic and depraved lives.

This constraint-removal model of psychospiritual growth has a very long history. It's found in many religions. Perhaps every religion has people within it who practice this way. The theological name for this is *kenosis*, which is the removal of obstacles from our path to God, to holiness. The *Cloud of Unknowing*, by an anonymous British monk of the late medieval era, is a classic example. This text teaches that we approach the divine by progressively shedding more and more of our thoughts and ideas, including all our concepts of God and holiness. William Johnston, an Irish Jesuit priest who lived, worked, and taught in Japan for over forty years, has written brilliantly about kenosis in Christianity and Buddhism (2006). A related term is *apophaticism*. The narrow meaning of this word is the attempt to describe God or the divine by what it is not. This again is our constraint-release paradigm. Apophatic texts are found in all religions. We will revisit this subject in more detail in Part 2.

Even though we have worked hard to prevent this, one question I am sure to ask again in the later stages of this work is: "Are any parts missing this unattached burden?" We really need to make room for this, and we really need to ask this question in a way that's not shaming. It may even be helpful to preface it with "It's okay and understandable if you are — it was around for a long time. Are any of you missing this?" We need to check for this in all phases of this work. We don't want these parts to feel they have to hide from the rest of the system; we want to bring them forward and love them. This is our real safety: the loving connection between Self and parts — all the parts. Also, even though the UB was a very negative presence, having something big removed can be a trauma in itself, just as a healing medical operation is a trauma. This too can require room and time.

Once it's clear that no parts are still missing the unattached burden and that all the other work has been done thoroughly, you can see if the client wants to invite in guides or invite awareness of guides at this time. Again, follow the client's mythology, worldview, metaphor system, or religious orientation. Don't impose anything, and make all statements in a very permissive, open-ended way, not as commands. You might say something like, "Some people, at times like this when they're clear and open, can feel a presence of some kind of guidance or guides. Let's just take a few moments here to see if anything like that occurs for you." I use the word *guidance* first because it is the one that people are least likely to react to. It's important to be open and nondirective. If I know about the client's spiritual orientation, I will gently suggest that language. For example, with a twelve-step person, I might say, "Some people at this time feel a strong connection with their higher power. Let's pause and see if anything like that happens now." We will talk more about this later, but Dick has said that the only really safe time to ask for guides is when you're in Self — when there's a critical mass of Self available. Very often, at this stage of this process, a lot of Self is radiating throughout the system, and that's why I often use this as an opportunity to see if the client wants to open to guide energy.

Step 7. Cleanup

The last phase of these sessions is usually what I would call cleanup. The presence of a UB in a person's system often causes a lot of damage that appears as regular burdens carried by parts. For example, if someone is seeing vivid imagery of a negative being inside themselves and they share that information, others are likely to think of them as insane, which may prompt them to start hiding their experience and doubting their sanity. So, a whole bunch of parts in that person's system may be full of shame and may doubt their sanity and feel a need to hide. Those parts will need a regular IFS unburdening process to be freed from where they're stuck in the past. There are also many other ways that the presence of these external energies can damage a person, especially when they're young. There's what I call the "developmental cascade." Let's say, for example, that the UB's presence caused the person to isolate because they felt weird and strange and didn't know how to relate to others. That isolation can cause all sorts of social difficulty, deprivation, and loneliness. The existence of a UB can create many other normal burdens that then need to be witnessed, unburdened, and grieved.

Dick has said many times that he considers our world a school and that it's a very, very tough school, and that our guides are proud of us for having chosen such a tough and challenging education. He sees the burdens we had to take on as children as being the curriculum, the great teachers, as difficult as they are. I think unattached burdens are also teachers. Unintentionally, they can do us a lot of good and can give us a great deal of knowledge when we change our attitude from fear to curiosity. I've already mentioned comparing them to ants in the kitchen. There are several spiritual traditions that present a similar idea. The Kabbalists talk about "the opponent" in reference to the Devil or the evil one. There are all sorts of different names for it. The idea is that without the opponent, we couldn't really grow. We can't grow strong unless we wrestle with something strong. The Jungians and other psychological-philosophical traditions talk about how there is no light without darkness, how the existence of evil is what allows good, that we can't have one without the other, all that sort of stuff. I want to stay at a very practical, pragmatic level and not go off into those enticing philosophical discussions. I distrust going up into my head, where I can take the light and speculation and never need to do the hard emotional work. There's a saying from the twelve steps that I really like: "When I'm in my mind, I know I'm in a dangerous neighborhood."

CHAPTER 7

Cheat Sheet

Here is the same basic pragmatic outline in the form of a cheat sheet for easy reference. It's a basic set of suggestions so you have an orientation and direction, a sense of where you're going, and the general flow.

Follow the client — follow their imagery, their spiritual orientation, their mythology. Listen deeply. The most important thing is that you, the therapist, stay in Self. If you lose your curiosity, stop the session and work with your own parts until you are genuinely curious about the client and the client's process again.

Step 1: Work with fear

When you are not afraid of UBs, they lose all their power.

Work with your own fear first, as the therapist. Then work with the client's fear.

Two basic methods:

—Find each part who is frightened and do classic IFS with it until there is a strong Self-to-part relationship and the part feels secure.

—Help the scared parts go to a safe, contained space until the UB is out.

Step 2: Assume it's a part until proven otherwise

"When you hear hoofbeats, don't think of zebras."

Two basic steps:

—Explore the intention. Look for a good intention or positive function. If the initial answers seem negative, ask what's good about that and drill down for the deeper underlying intention.

—Have the client ask the being directly, "Are you a part of me?" Don't let other parts answer. Be calm and persistent. The being might resist answering, but UBs don't seem to lie about this.

Step 3: Create some distance between the person and the UB

—A good conversational distance is best. If the client has trouble creating this distance, help them get in Self by asking how they feel toward the UB.

—It is often good to use the light or a ball of light to pull the UB away from the person.

Have the client notice if there are any connections, cords, or strings of any kind coming back from the UB to their body.

Have the client look inside their body where the cord connects and find the part of them that is allowing the attachment. Develop a Self-to-part relationship with that part until it willingly lets go of the UB. Do this with each connection.

Step 4: Offer healing to the UB

Tell it, "We are not here to punish or judge you; we want to send you to a place where you can heal." It has to leave the client now that no part is allowing it to stay.

Make sure it takes all of it soldiers, employees, underlings, and objects with it.

Sometimes UBs balk at this stage because they fear punishment by a boss. Call out that boss and deal with it in the same way you've dealt with the UB.

Send the UB out and watch it until it's completely gone.

Step 5: Rebalance the system

Ask if all the client's parts are glad it's gone. Ask, "Does anyone miss it for any reason?" Be kind and nonjudgmental. Having the UB in the system often felt very familiar, and some parts might have a reaction to its absence.

Clients can feel disoriented with this energy out of them. Help them rebalance.

Be sure the UB is gone from the body, emotions, mind, beliefs, and spirit — and also gone from the exiles, managers, and firefighters. Going through each of these, look for where and how the UB got in and close that entry point.

Being fearless and in Self is the best protection. You can also teach the sealing light meditation now.

Step 6: Invite guidance and guides

Invite in new energies, perhaps a guide. Fill the empty space.

Step 7: Cleanup

Having had a UB in the system will most likely have caused damage to the system.

Use classic IFS to work with any hurt parts and their burdens.

CHAPTER 8

More Cases

These cases are how I learn this material. As I stay present and curious with whatever is real for the client, they always teach me. For healers, I believe that these reports are important, but if you are more of a general-interest reader, please feel free to skim them or skip them entirely.

We will start with a case I did in a consultation group. The five participants were all highly experienced IFS therapists. I structure most of my groups so that each participant has a full hour with me of whatever kind of session they want, and then we have thirty minutes for debriefing and didactic.

Mary's session

We will start with excerpts from an email this client sent me shortly before the session.

Hi Bob,

It is my turn this Wednesday night to have a demo with you. While I am honored to have the opportunity to have a session with you, there are parts that are also very nervous about it. So we agreed that I would give you a little background ahead of our demo so you can perhaps manage my system better than I can.

I have a history of child sexual abuse. This has resulted in complete dissociation from the events. I was abused by two brothers who lived close to my home. With the exception of the first time this happened (which was really only being touched sexually by them), I have no memory of what happened each time I was forced to attend their house. I believe the abuse started at about age 4 and continued until I was about 13 years old, but I honestly don't remember when it stopped. I do have one or two memories about trying to escape from their house (unsuccessfully), but other than this, it is pretty much a blank. The extent of the abuse is a total mystery to me, but my parts regularly allude to the fact that it might have been way more severe than I think.

I did your workshop back in May. When we did some of the meditations, it was clear that my young parts trust the UBs much more than Self. The UBs have much more to offer them than I do...things like protection, safety, and I get the sense that they feel that the UBs are much stronger than Self. In fact, the idea of Self is often met with disgust in my system. I have done some other meditations, and I have a strong sense that Self was in fact pushed out of my body, but if it was, there is also a sense that the parts are not very interested in having it back.

I have IFS sessions regularly, and with my therapist we have discovered that my UB, or UBs, because I think I have a few, try to keep me prisoner because what they say internally is so appalling that they know that I won't repeat it out loud to anyone. It is always of a very sexual nature, so in anticipation of our session, I am hearing the UB saying that it will ask you about sexual stuff and if you would like me to do sexual stuff. They know that this kind of thing is absolutely unacceptable to me. I am very happily married, and so any kind of disloyalty is a complete NO-NO for me (disloyalty is thinking or even mentioning anything sexual with another man). They also use very vulgar language and curse and swear A LOT. Again, this is something I will not repeat, so in this way, they keep me shut down a lot when I am with my therapist. I don't want to allow them to have this power over me anymore, and so I believe in warning you ahead of our session that it might take their power away.

I have worked with my parts, and there are no longer parts that are scared of the UBs, but there are parts that don't want them to go. Again my polarization is around sexuality. There are parts that believe that my UBs have injected me with some kind of serum that makes me appealing and sexually attractive to men and this has enabled me to be successful in life and get what I want, and they fear that if this goes, I will be an old, useless woman who can't achieve anything. The other groups of parts know that this sexual serum is what has made my life very, very difficult. Once the sexual abuse stopped, I was stalked by another man from age 13/14 until I left home. My parents had to get a restraining order against the man because he believed I was his and he physically assaulted me when I was 15 by punching me in the face at a local nightclub when I refused to dance with him. I have had several incidents of being assaulted/followed/threatened by men my whole life, so it makes much more sense to me that this apparent serum has not served me well at all and does not give me any power either.

Finally, my UBs seem to be very tricky and can lead me down a path that ends nowhere or doesn't make sense. They have done this several times with my current therapist, and I am a little concerned that they will do this with you also. For example, the last time we interfaced with one of my UBs, it started by saying it came from my abusers into my system, and when it was time to ask them (notice that whether it is singular or plural keeps changing; we are still uncertain whether it is one or many) to leave, it turned into a crying little child who was really afraid, and so my parts did not want to ask it to leave because the child was crying uncontrollably and asking me not to get rid of it. This was a ploy by the UB because it knows me so well and knows that I would not abandon a helpless, crying child. I didn't ask it to leave and gave it *permission to stay, but since then I have realized that this was just another ploy for the UBs to stay in my system.*

After that session, I have a very vivid dream about the Master UB who showed up. He was really sexy also and very appealing to my parts, and it was all going well until he revealed his head, which was like a goat/sheep head with lots of eyes and very scary. The message was very clear: he is the boss of my system, and I will do as he commands.

Anyway, I hope this gives you some insight into what goes on internally for me. Knowing my session is on this Wednesday, they are extremely active and they are really trying to make me terrified about having a session. I wish to apologize in advance for anything they say internally, as I intend to say it out loud — otherwise I know we won't make progress. I know you have seen it all, but I am equally quite conscious of the other therapists in the group, and they may be very appalled by my session. I am sincerely hoping that we can do something meaningful for these UBs and direct them home, but I am not expecting miracles in an hour either.

Anyhow, please let me know if you have received this email and if you have any further questions. I look forward to working with you Wednesday night.

Kind regards,
Mary

The session itself

Bob: Okay. So, ready to go?

Mary: No.

Bob: Do you want something from your colleagues here before we start?

Mary: No, they've been very supportive already. So in our weekly meeting, I kind of said what I needed, and I know that they're going to deliver it, and I just am going to trust and go with it.

Bob: Great, great. So, I read your letter twice, actually.

Mary: That makes me feel, oh yeah, it had to be read twice. Oh no. Um, yeah.

Bob: And I know you want to fool yourself into thinking it's just us, but the Self energy of the group really makes a difference and can really help us.

Mary: That's true. I think it's my shamed parts that — I've lots of shame in my system. So I think it's not really got anything to do with the wonderful group, it's just that if I open my eyes and see somebody else, they kind of let me know about it.

Bob: Yeah, I got that. And I want to say something about foul language. I've worked construction most of my life. There is no way you can offend or surprise me, and it's absolutely fine with me. I know it might not be fine with you, but any of that stuff is absolutely okay with me.

Mary: I think that for me, what I've tried to do for myself, to give myself the gift, is to just say that ahead of time so that if I don't speak, that's how they keep me preserved. If I don't speak what I hear, then they've got me all the time, I'm in this cycle of saying, "I can't say that, I can't say this, and I can't say that," and then they win and I lose.

Bob: Yeah. So I want to encourage you to say whatever. You're not gonna blow me out of the water.

Mary: Okay.

Bob: Once I had a gang of Hells Angels get into one of my rentals, and I had to evict them. You would not believe the creative swearing. I don't think you and any entities in you can rise to that level of foulness.

Mary: That sounds good. They might give you a run for your money, Bob, but…

Bob: Okay. So, are they here now?

Mary: Yeah, they've been here pretty much all week. They're here all the time actually, to be fair. I shouldn't say they're always here, but in the last hour, because I can feel myself really nervous. The best way to show you is… if you can see my neck, it's just, they are…

Bob: Red.

Mary: Perfectly alive and, I'm not scared of them…

Bob: Great.

Mary: … but it is, it is, they are really probably quite furious that I'm here.

Bob: Mm-hmm. Yeah, okay. So, how are you feeling toward them?

Mary: I really am… how do I feel toward them? I…

Bob: Yeah, right now.

Mary: Yeah, I don't like them. I don't want them to be in my system anymore, I want them to go to where they need to go. And I regularly do try to say to them, "Look, you're not supposed to be here," and I go with the notion that "Look, if you can go back to your families — you're going to be happy," but I don't really get very far with that kind of discussion with them. So, you know.

Bob: So right now there are no parts of you in there who are afraid of them?

Mary: Eh, no. They're afraid of what they will say that I will have to say out loud, but they're not actually afraid of the UBs.

Bob: Okay, great. And is anybody in your system gonna miss them when they're gone? Is anybody relying on them for power or anything like that?

Mary: Yes, yes.

Bob: Okay.

Mary: It feels to me that there are a number of parts that would be very concerned if they left.

Bob: Okay, those are the ones we need to get to know.

Mary: Okay.

Bob: Okay. So can you find them? Do they come as a group, or do we need to work with them one at a time?

Mary: No, they are a group, but they're a group that, like when we talk about polarization in IFS, they are polarized. They trust the UB, they don't trust me. They don't like Self, they don't like niceness, they don't like compassion, they hate all that stuff, and it's wishy-washy shit to them, and they really would prefer if I went to their side if there was a way of doing that, you know.

Bob: Yeah.

Mary: And then it would be much easier, and we'd all be on the same team.

Bob: Yeah, okay. Great. So, now how are you feeling toward them? I know they don't like compassion, but is curiosity okay with them?

Mary: Em, no. They don't want anything at all from me that does not involve me going and joining. I think one of the problems for me as well is they know too much about IFS, if that makes any sense. So now I kind of feel like I'm between the Devil and the deep blue sea. So if I say I'm curious, they're going, "You're not curious — you just want to get rid of us."

Bob: Okay. How would it be if I talked to them directly?

Mary: Eh, if they will talk to you, yes. People have tried, but they normally just go quiet, but we can try.

Bob: Okay. Hello in there. Can you talk to me directly?

Mary: No, they're giving me the F-bombs to say to you, so…

Bob: Oh, that's fine. That is talking to me directly, and if you can, please repeat that. So, I guess you're swearing at me, and that's fine. Can you tell me why you are angry at me?

Mary: Yeah, actually, just to, they're not, I never realized this before, but they are not speaking to you. They were saying to me — "Tell him to F off." So they weren't actually speaking to you.

Bob: Okay.

Mary: And when I went in and you said, "Oh, you're speaking to me," they're actually quite afraid to speak to you, actually.

Bob: Okay. Ask them, "What are you afraid would happen if you spoke to me?"

Mary: Yeah, they'd be punished, they'd be punished by the UB.

Bob: By the UB, okay. Tell them that UB will have absolutely no power over them.

Mary: Yeah, they don't buy that at all.

Bob: Okay. So they're still frightened of the UB.

Mary: Yeah, they are. It's almost like they're looking up at the UB as if to ask, "Do we have permission to speak or not permission to speak?"

Bob: Okay.

Mary: And they don't have permission to speak.

Bob: Okay. Ask this group, "What's your intention — what do you want to have happen? What's your goal?"

Mary: They want me to take on the UB's energy.

Bob: Okay, ask them this: "Are you parts of me?"

Mary: They are, yeah.

Bob: Okay, okay.

Mary: They don't really care about being a part of me, but they are a part of me, but they're not, they're not the UB's actually — they work, they're like under the UB's control. They're on his side.

Bob: Okay. Ask them, "Would you like to be free of anyone's control?"

Mary: No, they quite like... they're not really afraid of the UB. Well, they are, and they're not. They like what the UB offers them.

Bob: Okay. "What is it you like about what the UB offers you? What's good about this?"

Mary: Well, they like that they're safe with him, and they like that he's powerful.

Bob: Okay. They're not really safe with him, and he is making them weak and dependent on him. He's not making them free. This is not power; this is dependency and slavery. "The UB has turned you into slaves."

Mary: Yeah, they don't believe that, Bob.

Bob: Okay.

Mary: And what they're saying is that before the UB, they were really slaves then.

Bob: Okay. What happened before the UB that was so terrible?

Mary: You see, before that, it was just abuse.

Bob: Is that when, is that when the sexual abuse happened? Yeah, yeah. That was really terrible. And tell them, "We cannot change history, but we can go back and get the parts who are still trapped back there in those terrible times of abuse, get them out, help them unburden all of that pain, and then, they can take on new qualities and be free. We can do that."

Mary: They really just don't trust that. It's just as simple as, they're very kind of… they don't believe they can be free because when they were free, they got in trouble.

Bob: Mm-hmm.

Mary: Their freedom, their innocence, their, you know, their willingness, maybe, is the word, didn't work so well for them.

Bob: No, it didn't. They're really trapped.

Mary: Mm-hmm.

Bob: Do they know they're trapped in a terrible place?

Mary: Yeah, they do know they're trapped, but they don't… they think that they have the best of two options, and they just…

Bob: Oh, okay. That's really important. There are not just two options — there are many, many, many options. And the UB keeps them blind because the UB is actually a parasite feeding off of their distress. And like all parasites, it makes them weak, and they could have a much bigger, more joy-filled life.

Mary: They're interested suddenly. They just want to know, they want to know what the other options are.

Bob: Okay. Well, there are many. The biggest one is, you can send that UB where it belongs, where it can heal, and then you'll be free of that influence, and once that happens, you'll be able to be received with love and be able to unburden all of those beliefs and terrible feelings you had to take on back then. And then you can dream. Ask these parts of you, "Have you ever had the chance to really dream of what you would love to be if you were free and didn't have to struggle with all this dark stuff?" Dream big. Yeah. They've never had that chance, have they? In the abuse before and now with the UB, that's never been open to them. That can open to them. They can dream and imagine the most wonderful, fulfilling, deep, and creative lives. And probably, each one has a slightly different life, a different dream. How are they feeling about that?

Mary: They're like real small, little children, and they're looking at the UB to see how the UB is reacting. The UB is getting more furious as you're talking.

Bob: Yeah.

Mary: They're not particularly… they're listening, but they're not… they don't feel they have permission to take that in.

Bob: Yeah. Tell them this: "The UB will never give you permission because this is how it keeps you enslaved. The UB is a lost, confused, and suffering being, and in its desperation, it is clinging to you all and feeding off of you. This is not healthy for you, and it's not healthy for the UB. We're not here to judge or punish the UB — we're actually here to help it go where it can get the healing and nourishment and care it needs." What do they think of that?

Mary: I get a sense… they're not saying anything, but I get a sense that they, they really like that, but they're really afraid that if they believe you and it's not true, then what are the consequences for them after?

Bob: Okay, that's a great question. I'd be willing to take any consequences from that UB, and the UB can blame me for anything it doesn't like. And this does take some trust in you, from all these parts of you. They have to trust that there's some light somewhere, that their dreams are valid and real. I have something they could try if they want, to sort of test this out.

Mary: Just first, when you say you can take the consequences, what do you mean?

Bob: I'll get between them and the UB. I'll invite the UB to get angry at me. I'll show them that the UB doesn't really have power, that it's blustering and scared and weak itself.

Mary: You're really getting him quite irritated, and he wants me to let you know that you're no match for him.

Bob: Yeah, well, I am.

Mary: He just wants me to tell you that he knows all about you.

Bob: Great. Great, that's fine. What I'm interested in now is not so much in his threats and bragging — I'm interested in these parts of you who are scared little kids. Are they getting to understand that this UB is a bully? It's not really powerful.

Mary: They think he's powerful now because he stood up to you.

Bob: Well, he just threatened and mouthed off.

Mary: Yeah, and they feel that you backed down and that you backed away from it, so now they're going, "No, he's more powerful."

Bob: Well, I don't want to fight with this being. This is sort of like, um, perhaps a rabid dog. You don't want to fight with it, but you don't let it rule the street.

Mary: I'm just gonna say what I hear, Bob, 'cause otherwise…

Bob: Yeah, good, good.

Mary: He's just saying, "How dare you compare me to a dog."

Bob: "Well, your behavior is pretty bad. And telling these little kids this… a truly powerful being would not spend its energies terrifying children, would it? That's not the actions of a powerful being. That's the actions of a coward, and a weak coward." They know that's true, and the UB knows that's true.

Mary: The UB does not believe that. The UB is there and it's really strong and it's saying, "I'm not frightening them — I'm protecting them," and he's saying, he's contradicting you internally, and he's saying, "They know I protect them, and I provided safety when there was none."

Bob: Ask the UB, "What's your long-term intention for them? Why don't you release them so they can live their dreams?"

Mary: He needs some of their energy, not all.

Bob: "Yeah, you're feeding off of them."

Mary: Yeah, he's also saying that to me again — he's saying that this is what they do. They recruit parts, and then those parts can go into other people. That's what they do.

Bob: Mm-hmm. Yeah, yeah. So, he's feeding off of them, he's admitted he's feeding off of them. He's a parasite.

Mary: He's saying he's training them; he's not feeding off them.

Bob: Well, he said he's eating their energy. That's feeding. This UB isn't so important — what's important are your parts who are still scared of him. Ask them if they would be willing to go behind you and behind me into a safe, enclosed room and let me deal with the UB. Are they ready to let it go?

Mary: Yeah, they'd like that as long as there are some guarantees that you… I mean, they're nearly afraid to admit it, but I feel like they want to scuttle quickly into the room before…

Bob: Yeah. Go ahead, tell them to get into the safe room. Now here's what we're gonna do. Surround the UB in a ball or egg-shaped container of light and pull it out maybe six feet in front of you, a good conversational distance. And let me know how that goes.

Mary: I can't do it. I can't get it.

Bob: Excuse me?

Mary: I can't do it. I can't get it to create the distance.

Bob: Is it contained in the light?

Mary: No.

Bob: Okay, where is it? How is it appearing?

Mary: It's not appearing. It's like I got a bit distracted by making sure, because I felt like there are lots of, lots of young parts that were trying to scuttle into the room...

Bob: They fled behind you. Okay. And the UB has gone into hiding?

Mary: Yeah, he's not there now.

Bob: Okay. "Hey UB, I thought you were this big, powerful being. Don't go hide — come on back. You were bragging about how you're way stronger than me, and now you're running from me. Come back. You're so proud, you're almost arrogant, and now you're running. We're here to help you, not to punish you and not to judge you. You are in the wrong place."

Ask this UB this... It can still hear us even if it hides...

Mary: I just... sorry, I've just had an image of it, so...

Bob: Okay, great.

Mary: In his armchair.

Bob: He's sitting in an armchair.

Mary: Kind of (inaudible) sitting back with a cigar, laughing as if to say...

Bob: Yeah, surround that image with light.

Mary: Every time I try and do that, it's gone, just goes.

Bob: Mm-hmm, okay. "Hey there, mister cigar-smoking, laughing being, is the reason you're too scared to talk with me because you're afraid of your boss who sent you? It seems like you're an underling, an employee, a slave yourself."

Mary: It's saying it's not, it's not any of those. And it knows what we're going to try and do, and it doesn't buy the fact that we can make something nice for it, and it doesn't want to go. It simply doesn't want to go.

Bob: Yeah, I get that it doesn't want to go. "You have been lied to and manipulated yourself, Mr. UB, and I can prove that to you if you have the courage. This light that you keep fleeing, you've almost certainly been told that it will hurt you horribly, so gather up your courage and touch it, maybe just with one finger and see what happens to you."

Mary: He's saying he's not afraid of the light.

Bob: "Well, then touch it. Does it feel good, or does it actually hurt?"

Mary: Just neither. He's like going, yeah, okay, bring on the next trick.

Bob: "It's not a trick. You have been lied to. You were told the light would hurt you horribly, weren't you?"

Mary: He's not afraid of the light, he's not afraid. He wasn't told it would hurt him — he just needs to do what he's supposed to do.

Bob: "Well, you can't do it here anymore, and you know that. None of her parts are welcoming you anymore, so you can't stay here. Now it's true you also have free will and can go where you want, but so do all of your soldiers — they all have free will, and they can start leaving you now and safely go to the light on their own. You no longer have control over any of the employees, slaves, soldiers, minions, or underlings. They can all leave now very safely. Another lie you've almost certainly been told is that you're nothing but darkness through and through. Look inside yourself and you will see that deep inside you at your center, there's a spark of light."

Mary: He doesn't want that light.

Bob: "Well, it's there, isn't it?"

Mary: He doesn't even want to look. He's like, "I don't want that."

Bob: "Well, you're scared of it. Have some courage and look. For all your bragging, your life has been miserable. There are some moments of a little buzz, like snorting cocaine, but your life has been miserable. You know that's true. Who you are at your core is light. Look and see. Then you'll know of your own experience what the truth is, and you'll know you've been lied to and used."

Mary: He wants you to listen to him carefully. He's saying he doesn't want to leave, he enjoys living in my body, he enjoys putting me through misery as much as he can — that's entertainment for him — and he doesn't want to look at any fucking light as you're asking him to, as any time he ever looked at a light it brought him pain.

Bob: "Yeah, try it now."

Mary: He wants you to listen to him. "Stop pretending that I have somewhere to go that's gonna help me because there's nowhere to go. I'm staying here."

Bob: "No, you're wrong. You're just point-blank wrong, and you're frightened. Try it. You touched the light; it did not bring you pain."

Mary: "It didn't do anything. It didn't bring me pain, it didn't bring me ease, it brought me nothing."

Bob: "Yeah. Look inside — you'll know this is who you really are. You might already be feeling your soldiers and employees leaving safely, making you weaker and smaller."

Mary: "No, they will do as I ask them."

Bob: "No they won't."

Mary: "Yeah, they will."

Bob: "They can see, they can see the light, they know better. They're not as frightened as you are. Despite all your claims of power, you're too frightened to look inside yourself and see the light. And everyone inside you and around you sees your fear and smallness. It's obvious to all now, including you. And you do have somewhere to go — that's not a lie. If you look up, you'll see kind beings leaning down to help you, and they will celebrate when you arrive like the prodigal son. You have been trapped in a terrible, terrible place, and you've suffered immensely for a very long time, I think. And now you can be free if you can gather the courage. And all your soldiers and employees see how you're paralyzed with fear, and they're no longer afraid of you, and they're leaving safely. Can you see the welcome they received? The same welcome is waiting for you. If you look up, most of the time beings like you see something like a tunnel, and at the end of the tunnel there's a warm light, and there are many beings leaning down to help. It's time for you to go. You have suffered long enough. She has suffered long enough. This part's over, and you get a choice as to whether you want to go to the light where you can heal and get real strength, instead of this fake stuff you've been fooling around with, or you can go back to the darkness, but you cannot stay here anymore."

Mary: He wants to know if he can heal in me.

Bob: Excuse me?

Mary: He wants to know if he can heal where he is, in me.

Bob: No, he can't have anything more to do with you — he just has to go. "We will help Mary heal"; he needs healing himself. He can go and receive that healing and the feast and the real power that await him. Is he going up to those beings who are reaching down to help him?

Mary: He doesn't want to go to the light.

Bob: I know he doesn't — he's frightened. It's very sad. Can he see the beings leaning down to help him? He probably will recognize some of them if he just looks up, and he will see the real care in their eyes. There will be no punishment, there will be no judgment. There will be celebration at his return. And he probably can feel all the employees and parts of him going up to the light, and he can go, too. And he can see how they are greeted there with care. And there's real power in the light; the power of the darkness is fake.

Mary: I get a sense from him that he doesn't want to go to the darkness; he doesn't want to go back there.

Bob: No, good. That's very intelligent. So tell him it's time to go. "Look at the beings who want to help you — look up, look up."

Mary: He wants you to tell him what's there before he looks up. He's afraid to look up. He wants you to say what he... where he is gonna go.

Bob: Okay. It's different for many people, but for many, they see hands reaching down to help them, like, pull them up the ladder, and then they see friends and people they've known before, and they're welcomed and hugged and then fed, because he's been starving. You know, for a being to feed off the misery of children, that's a starving being. So he'll go up there, and he'll get real food. Sometimes beings like him are so hurt that they have to be carried off in a cot or a litter. He might be able to walk on his own, or maybe he'll need a wheelchair to take him to the places where he can really heal.

Mary: He's saying that he... um, he doesn't have any friends up there.

Bob: He does. All he has to do is look and go.

Mary: He wants to know if this is a trick.

Bob: Not at all. Not at all. Tell him to test it out. Look up, see the hands, maybe take one of those hands and touch it and feel what comes through that hand, and feel the care of those beings who want to help him.

Mary: I'll say what he's saying to me. He's saying if he looks up, if somebody tries to blind him, then they'll... they're gonna... then he can't see, and then he'll be grabbed, he'll be brought somewhere bad.

Bob: Yeah. He's had experiences like that. Well, tell him to look up through his fingers and take a little peek. They will modulate the light so that it doesn't hurt him. They so want to welcome him home... that's his true home, and he has wandered and been lost far too long. Encourage him. "Move up a little and see if it feels better the closer you get to those realms. See if you feel stronger and lighter as you move up. Try it and you will know from your own experience." Is he finding the courage to move up a little bit at a time so that he can sense what's happening? Great. Wonderful, wonderful.

Mary: He's reached his hand up and just... I can just sense again from him that he felt a bit of warmth there, which he's not used to, you know.

Bob: Yeah, yeah.

Mary: He wants to know if it's not what you say, can he come back?

Bob: He can always go to the darkness, but he can never come back into you. He can't do that no matter what.

Mary: That's a huge risk for him, a huge risk that it's either that or the darkness. I guess it's the same thing, isn't it?

Bob: Yeah, well, he can't stay here. We want to do everything we can to help him to go to the best of all possible places. He put his hand up and felt the warmth. Tell him, "Follow that — follow your own experience. You will feel stronger and better." Is he going?

Mary: Yeah, I'm getting a sense that he's really afraid, but he's trying it out almost, that he's…

Bob: Great, great. Very courageous of him — he's showing real courage now. (At this point, birds started singing outside of my window quite loudly.)

Mary: The birds that you have in the background, that you can hear… he's like going, that's what, there would be birds in that land that he would go to. It's like he's softened or something.

Bob: Yeah. "I've only explored the very entries of that land, but everything I have seen has been beautiful. I do not know what happens when you go deeply in, but I have seen and felt the emotions of the reconnection that happen when people like you, when beings like you, return there." Is he beginning to feel them welcoming him? Yeah. Great, great. If it feels right for you, just tell this being, "Go in peace, go in peace," and then watch until he's completely welcomed there and gone.

Mary: I can see them pulling him up. It feels like as he's moving up, he's becoming more human.

Bob: Yeah, yeah. Yeah.

Mary: And he's absolutely exhausted.

Bob: Yep. Is he feeling the kindness in their welcome? Can you tell? Yeah, yeah.

Mary: He's just a person like the rest of us.

Bob: Huh?

Mary: He's just a person like the rest of us.

Bob: Mm-hmm, yeah.

Mary: A bit damaged.

Bob: Yeah, really damaged. He suffered a long time. And let me know when all that's disappeared and gone, if there are any last things… Wave goodbye, go in peace. Any last things to end.

Mary: I want to tell him that I just don't hold any badness toward him.

Bob: Great, yeah.

Mary: A bad feeling or…

Bob: Mm-hmm. Yeah, you can see his terrible suffering. Okay. Is that… has he disappeared completely and that realm closed off?

Mary: Just a little sense from me that there's almost, not a fear, I don't even want to say fear or anything, but just a sadness of saying goodbye to him, but not really, but you know it's like…

Bob: Yeah. It was really familiar.

Mary: Yeah.

Bob: It's gone, and there's always a sadness even if what was familiar was unpleasant. Does it feel right to you to welcome all those kids back from the safe room?

Mary: I just want to make sure that, it feels like it's a hole, and I just want to make sure it's perfectly closed.

Bob: Okay, great. Wonderful, wonderful.

Mary: I don't know if it's right, Bob, but I almost feel I want to say goodbye to him. He feels like slightly unconscious as they've brought him up.

Bob: Yeah, yeah.

Mary: I just, I kinda want to say goodbye to him.

Bob: Yeah. Do you want to say that out loud or just in your inner world?

Mary: In my inner world.

Bob: Okay.

Mary: Please.

Bob: I wanna encourage you to just remind him, "You can never come back here — you have to continue your journey. Go in peace."

Mary: He wants to know if he can watch over me.

Bob: I don't think that's a good idea for now. He needs all his energy for his own healing. Maybe after a fair amount of time has passed, if he still wants to do that, then that's something you two could talk about. But right now, no — no more connections. He needs all his energy for his own healing.

Mary: I said farewell to him. He said, "We'll see ya when ya get here."

Bob: Yeah.

Mary: In a nice way, not in a bad way.

Bob: Yeah.

Mary: Okay.

Bob: Okay. Some people, sometimes they see something they describe as a hole in the sky.

Mary: Yeah, that's exactly…

Bob: It opens up and then it closes.

Mary: Yeah, that's exactly what I saw. Like they were the hands of angels is what it felt like to me. You know, a bit like what you'd see in a Michelangelo painting, and it's just, it's like he's… yeah, that's exactly what I saw.

Bob: Okay.

Mary: And then it all closed up and it's…

Bob: Great, great. Let's invite the kids out of that room where they've been safe. How are they all doing? Could they all watch from in there? Did they all see everything?

Mary: God, yeah.

Bob: Yeah. How are they doing?

Mary: They're just like little children, they're so excited. They're like…

Bob: Yeah, yeah.

Mary: They're kind of looking at each other and kinda saying, "Did you see that?" They were kinda a bit dumbfounded when they were watching; they weren't speaking to each other, and they feel light and free and…

Bob: Yeah, yeah.

Mary: Not scared anymore.

Bob: No. Yeah, that's lifted off. Are they all good? Is there anybody in there who's scared or tired or…

Mary: No, they're just full of energy — they're like jumping around…

Bob: Yeah, and there won't be anything draining your energy anymore. So you're gonna have lots of energy. And I want to encourage you again to dream big. Dream about what you really want as your most fulfilling and exciting and deep and wonderful lives. And you might want to take your time to dream on that so it gets clear. Is that okay with them? Yeah. Do any of them wanna say anything?

Mary: Thank you.

Bob: Mm-hmm, they're so welcome. They're so welcome. Such a pleasure to meet them, and I'm so sorry they suffered for so long. And I know you know this, but I just wanna remind you and them once again, we can come in there, even back to the horrible times of abuse, and get them all out of there and get all those terrible feelings and beliefs and energies out of them so they're really completely free. We can do that, no doubt, when they're ready. They've done plenty for one day.

Mary: They're kind of saying to you that if this is as good as it gets, this is fantastic already. They can dream big and then you add healing onto it, they're like, hold on a minute, like, have we just won the lottery here or what, you know?

Bob: In a way, yes. Okay, ask everybody else in your system to come forward. How is everybody doing? Anybody scared or angry or anything? Is everybody okay?

Mary: Everybody's great, yeah.

Bob: Yeah.

Mary: Yeah. It feels great.

Bob: Okay.

Mary: There's one part that says, "Oh my god, there'll be no more cursing internally. There's no more cursing." You know, this is the part that always hated the cursing, you know.

Bob: Yeah. They don't have to hear that anymore. Now, very often, when we get stuff like this out, there are a couple more things we could do now in our last few minutes here. One is sometimes there's like dirt or something left behind. Do you have any sense of that, or is your system all clean? Is there anything that needs to come out to be washed away?

Mary: No, I don't think so.

Bob: Okay, great. Yeah, I'm just being extra careful checking stuff. Now, you might notice like, sort of at the edges of your body and all around your body, are there any holes or anything where this thing came in or might have come in? Are there any places that we need to fill up? There might not be.

Mary: It's very rude, and I'm just going to say it… they're saying, "How this came into me was through the sexual abuse," and then there's quite a comedian part in here, Bob, and it's saying, "Well, we can't really fill that hole up — that might not work, you know." A bit of a laugh about that and, you know.

Bob: Yeah, good. Yeah, this is, most sexual abuse injects beings like this into people. And you don't want to fill that hole up.

Mary: No.

Bob: But you can sort of, from the inside out, just find that light energy deep inside of you and just let it grow so that there's light energy coming out through your genitals, through your sex organs, and then beings like this will not approach there, cannot approach there. Only beings of love can approach.

Mary: They like that a lot.

Bob: Okay. Now, I'm gonna take… we're about to shift to the group, but I would like to, if it seems right to you, I would like to take you and the group through a short meditation that people often use around this stuff. Would you like to do that?

Mary: That would be lovely.

Bob: Okay. Just sort of focus inside in your inner world, and as you focus down, there's a point of light and warmth. Some people find it in their hearts, some find it in their stomachs, some between their eyes. I don't know where you'll find it, but there's always this point of light and warmth and life force energy. And as you focus on that and bring it your attention, it grows. When we focus on things in the inner world, they grow and change — they can't remain the same.

And just feel this light as it starts filling your whole body moving through all your tissues, filling up all those spaces until it fills your whole body all the way to your skin. And notice carefully if there are any shadowy areas or darker areas or congested areas. Don't fight these — it's really important information about where you need to come back and love and help. That means there's some part who's still distressed there in that area of your body. So make a note if there are any trailheads like that for you to follow later. And then, with this light energy, warmth energy all the way to your skin, then let it sort of go out beyond your skin. Maybe about a foot out all the way around you. Feeling that light and warmth pulsing through you and around you.

And then, when you're ready, just bringing yourself back to this external world in a gentle way. And you know, many people find a few deep breaths bring them back in a sweet, easy, pleasant way to this external world. And I want to invite everybody else to turn their videos back on. You had a whole team here helping you. Would you be open to hearing comments and questions from your peer group?

Mary: Yes. I had asked them not to, but I feel so elated and so light and so amazed that you did what you did in an hour. I didn't expect it, I really didn't. I didn't expect this at all.

Bob: Good.

Mary: So yeah, absolutely.

Bob: Okay. (To the group) Now, you know, gang, first round from your heart. What happened inside your heart with your parts, stuff like that, and then if we have time at the end you can ask more technical or process questions, okay.

Participant 1: Very moved. I got the sense that no matter how bad or difficult a life is, there is always hope.

Participant 3: Also deeply moved. When the birds started singing, she felt a tingling in her body, and that was calling the UB home.

Mary: Yeah, that's right. Yeah, they were. As he was going up, he said, "Let them know that there are birds up here, too." And that, I didn't say it, but that's what he said.

Bob: Yeah, you know, the Sufis say birdsong is the voice of God.

Mary: There you go.

Participant 4: Mary, I'm delighted for you.

Mary: Thank you, thank you. I'm ready to dance again. And again I want to say, thank you all for being there because I could feel it. I could feel it. When I felt like I was wavering myself inside because there were moments where I was going, "Aw, this is not gonna happen," but I was kind of not resolute, but just trying to stay with it, and I could feel your energy. I really could.

Bob: I could feel your energy, the other four of you. It really makes a difference. I don't have a theory that would explain how that's possible here on different parts of the planet connected by the Internet, but it really makes a difference.

Mary: I've never done a demo before, ever — this is my first ever demo — but it was always this notion, and of course, this is the one I pick, like, but it was always this notion that seeing people, like I never got a sense of that holding, so I never knew what that felt like, but it's really important.

Bob: You're doing great. Are there any sort of process questions or stuff like that?

(A participant asked if she could do this work since she didn't have the confidence or experience in these realms that I have.)

Bob: That's a good question, and my answer is I don't know. But this was an extremely well-embedded one. It had long-established, intricate ways of attaching to her system, so it was not typical — most of them are much easier. Many of them, most of them, are sort of almost like cardboard, two-dimensional things. They'll just say something like, "She's an idiot; she should die." And you say, "Well, why do you think that?" "Because she's an idiot; she should die." That's like all they've got. And those are typically very easy, and you know, you do a bunch of those and with each one, you learn a little more.

Participant 1: Bob, it seems like you implanted a lot of little suggestions, almost like a hypnotist.

Bob: Well, there is a general principle here. These things are often full of pride, and you can use their pride to manipulate them. *Manipulate* is a bad word because it has bad connotations — let's say to help them go where they're going to be happier. But it is a little manipulative. And I did study Ericksonian hypnotherapy early on, a lot, a lot. I do think it's okay to use their pride to sort of, you know, say, "Hey, you're claiming to be a big, powerful being, and you're running away from me." Stuff like that. That's directly appealing to its pride and using its pride to try and channel its behavior. Is that what you're talking about?

Participant 1: Yeah, yeah, but it felt like almost every sentence that you said held an aspect of that in it. You were just straight in there doing that.

Bob: Yeah, pretty much. With the thing, yeah, but with her parts, I hope I was a lot gentler.

Participant 1: Yeah, yeah, yeah, for sure. And obviously it worked. I did notice in me, very early on, that I had a… it really changed during the process, but very early on I had a part that was angry at the UB. I'm just curious about you and your system, if you maybe don't experience that anymore or if you do…

Bob: Sometimes I still get angry at the UBs, but hardly ever. The metaphor I like to use for that, because people are often enraged at them, and I say, your rage is now a spear that keeps you connected to that being, and it doesn't matter how justified or righteous your rage is — it still keeps you connected to that being. Do you want to be connected to that being? And I just try and work with it on that pragmatic basis. Because fear is the number one glue, and rage might be number two, you know, in terms of being hard to let go of. But it's fear that lets it in. So the number one question is, "Are there any parts in you who are afraid of it?" Over and over. You get all those parts safe and usually well enough attached to the Self so that the attachment to the Self is more powerful than any attachment the UB can offer, and then the attachment from the UB just falls away. You don't even have to talk to the UB — you just work with the person's parts. Yeah.

Participant 1: Thanks.

Participant 3: Bob, just curious to know, well, I suppose two things. So, do you not experience any fear?

Bob: No, none, basically. Not in these sessions.

Participant 3: So then, I'll still ask the question… so how is your system after a session? Like, um, you know, do you notice any sort of release or…?

Bob: Sometimes. Today I felt emotional. There were tears at the end of the session, tears of gratitude, gratitude for Mary. Gratitude for that being, but even more for the ones who were reaching down to help it. You know, "Aw, man, I couldn't do anything down here without you." I'm just like a bit player, you know, waving things on. You know, so there was that kind of gratitude, and there were tears, and sometimes I'm quite tired, and sometimes these things can jump into you, but because I'm not afraid of them, that's no longer such a huge thing. Like oh, I got one of these things in me — I can get that out.

Mary: I found when the UB was leaving, I felt quite emotional. Almost like it had been there for my entire life and there was, I don't really even feel there were parts. I felt like when you were having to speak to it and speak to it, I felt like there was a wall of parts around me, holding me strong, you know almost to kind of stay steady…. when it said to me, "I don't wanna go to the dark," then I knew we were okay.

Bob: Yeah, me too.

Mary: When he was going up there and I saw him, literally it felt like he went from being this dark, awful-looking thing as he was going up, and turning into this human being, I felt sad. I felt saddened, and there was a real sense that he has been through what I have been through. The real sense that he is no different, you know what I'm saying, that he has had that. And I wonder, do people report that kind of sense of sadness almost, like a… you realize it's not as much of an enemy as you think.

Bob: This kind of sadness is not uncommon, and it's just the familiarity. This thing has been around, you know, most of your life. You know, like even if you lived in a horrible house for fifteen years, when you leave it there'll be sadness.

Mary: Yeah.

Bob: I want to say, the nature of these things, even this one that looked pretty dark, turned out to be what is usually called a "lost soul" — you know, something human that was misguided and in the wrong place and was a suffering being. But I do know that they can't stay in someone once there's no ground for them anymore, and that means no part is afraid of them and no part will miss them when they're gone. So, the real work is classic, traditional IFS. You're working with those scared parts and the ones who will miss it when it's gone. When that's all done, the rest is not so much, really. I mean, there's stuff to it, but maybe if we hadn't worked so hard with that thing, it would have gone back to the darkness and tried to attack some other person. Maybe — who knows?

Participant 4: I may have gotten this wrong, that the darkness's intention was to recruit the young children and train them to send them into other people.

Bob: It said that, but it also admitted that when I said something about "You're feeding off of them." It said, "Oh, I just need some of their energy."

Participant 4: Yeah.

Bob: And there are some people who refer to these beings as the "feeders." They feed off of human misery, and that's what they're doing — they create human misery. They sort of farm it, and then they can feed off it. So, I think that other thing happens — they recruit parts of people to send into others, but I think the more fundamental dynamic is this feeding thing.

In our last minutes here, no skeptical parts? You know, "This is the weirdest woo-woo horseshit I've ever seen"? (None of the participants had skeptical parts.) Yeah, well, the emotional power was so blatant that it's hard to stay skeptical. I want to say, about skepticism, that I don't know in the sense of ontology or a reasoned worldview what these things are or how the other world operates. There's no methodology that would allow me certainty about those kinds of questions. However, I can ask, "What helps relieve the human suffering of the person in front of me?" That I can gain experience with. Every time I do something like this, I gain experience with that. And while I don't have statistical analysis, I can have a very firm sense of when we treat it this way, it's very, very likely to relieve her suffering. And to me, that's radical pragmatism, radical empiricism. What works? What works is what's real. My goal here is to relieve human suffering; it's not to do academic research.

Participant 4: Just wondering how you are, Mary.

Mary: I feel amazing. I feel amazing, yeah. And I know that it's just going to get better — that's the most exciting part for me. Like, there are parts of me that, as you're talking, I was thinking, I might sleep tonight, you know, because I don't sleep well. I'm thinking we might sleep tonight; nobody might interfere with our sleep because a lot of the time there are lots of bumps in the night in my house, so there's, it feels like there's lots of energy, and I'm thinking what if, maybe they will, you know… anyway, I don't know. I don't want to make any assumptions, but I just feel, I truly did not expect this tonight. I just didn't. I thought, no, this is going to be too much of an ask — we've only got an hour, you know, and I'm, I'm just flabbergasted really. I just did not, I just, I just did not think that that was gonna happen for me. I didn't think it was available to me, and that is the power that is Bob. Yeah, you know, and you guys, too. Hats off to you guys because it's a chain reaction, and it's a group effort, and I feel amazing.

Bob: Yeah. I wanna say, if I was working with you, Mary, on an ongoing basis, in the next session I'd want to ask you about your sense of guides, guidance, higher power, spiritual connection. These things seem to have to block spiritual connection in order to keep their place, so very often when they're out of a person's system, the person is open to receiving a whole new kind of spiritual energy, and so I like to check up about that later. Because sometimes these things will try and pretend to be spiritual energy when they're not and try and sneak back in that way. They usually are not very good at it. But, I mean, look at how much damage has been done in the name of churches, so they do succeed sometimes. So that would be something that I would… that would be my follow-up if we were ongoing — that, and checking with all the kids who had been closest to them. Make sure everybody feels well connected, nobody's lonely or anything.

Mary: I'll check in with them a lot over the week because they did run out of the room like to me, like little, you know as if, it's just wonderful. They just, just were full of life really, and they just … amazing, yeah, it was amazing.

Bob: Yeah, so hopefully you'll spend time with them every day next week, couple of weeks.

Mary: I will.

Bob: Okay, everyone. Take care. Blessings.

———

The following are some excerpts from Mary's emails after the session.

Hi Bob,

… I have felt profoundly healed since our session. It has been truly life-changing for me and my parts… Also, I thought you might like to know that I did my first UB unburdening today with a client of mine. It was magic, and I felt I could really understand what might be going on for the client…

In another email about a week later, she wrote:

Since I was a very young child, I have lived with this UB. While I count myself a very lucky and fortunate person generally, what was happening on the inside was crushing me. When I first heard about UBs I got it immediately, and the thought that this might be a solution for my internal suffering was nearly too good to comprehend. Trust me, internally it was putting up an enormous fight last week, but your confidence and your willingness to sacrifice yourself for me and my system still makes me emotional. I had met it before through therapy with my therapist, but she was no match for him. I am happy to stand behind you in any way I can, and if you need me to support you with any testimonials or in any way in bringing forward how important this work is and how unbelievably life-changing it has been for me, I am certainly happy to do this. I believe people have a lot more UBs than the IFS Institute is willing to admit, and it saddens me that we cannot be more open about this. (About doing more sessions) I don't feel the need, as I can't imagine feeling much better than I do right now.

(Mary's session is presented here verbatim. The feedback and questions were heavily edited.)

This kind of feedback is wonderful and dangerous. Pride is the greatest danger to a therapist doing this work. If I get proud, I believe I will lose any abilities I access now, and it will damage my own growth and spirit. I need to remember that something greater than me does this work through me. It is necessary for me to get my therapist parts and managers to step aside so this larger energy can flow. We can call this energy Self or spirit or whatever we like as long as we resist the temptation to take personal credit. Also, notice in this case that what I did was fairly simple and direct, nothing fancy. These are easily learnable skills. The hardest part is dealing with our parts who carry fear of the unknown. Yet this woman had suffered for most of her lifetime because no therapist would touch this. The avoidance of this work is mostly because it does not easily fit in our existing paradigm. Which is more important: the paradigm or relieving human suffering?

Charlie & Hank

The following session was done by a prominent IFS trainer whom I will call Charlie. He recorded the session and used it to help train other therapists in this work. (Again, the session itself is verbatim, but the feedback and comments are edited.)

Charlie's introductory comments:

So today, I wanted to introduce a new topic, really. It's maybe not new to some of you, but I think it probably is to a lot of you, and it's a topic that I talk about with some reluctance. You'll realize why shortly. It is a topic that is important, especially for those of you who work with people who have had a lot of trauma or a lot of addiction kinds of issues, or sometimes people who have had a lot of operations — people who have spent a lot of time out of their bodies where their Self isn't in their body tend to pick up these things that we're gonna call "unattached burdens." I just thought it was time that we talked about it, and I actually have a nice video to show demonstrating my working with a guy who had one. So that's the topic today.

So, if you do enough work with that population, on occasion you'll run into something that seems purely malevolent and, it turns out, *is* purely malevolent. Initially, because I didn't know what these things were, I assumed they were parts. I would spend a lot of time interviewing them about trying to find some kind of protective function, unsuccessfully. I would ask if they were a part of that person, and they… for whatever reason, they don't lie. So they would say, "No, I'm not a part. I'm something else." And sometimes they'd be very intimidating and often had had a really deleterious effect on the client and had ruined relationships or had prompted the client to do things, sometimes sort of evil things that they didn't want to do. Inside the client, they often could be intimidating. They could look like monsters or devils or things like that.

So just staying curious about them and trying to figure out how to deal with them, I hypothesized, and it turned out to be true, that they couldn't have any power over a client if the client was in Self. And so I tried to get myself in Self and then get my client in Self by getting the scared parts to step back, and I found that indeed, these things would often try to intimidate more when that happened but weren't successful, and we actually could just send them out of the system as if they were burdens, just like we do with burdens. But in this case, they weren't attached to a part, hence the name "unattached burdens."

So anyway, it's good to know about this. Now, there are parts that will present in that same way initially, so it's important to interview whatever it is for a while until you really get a sense of whether it's one of these UBs — unattached burdens — or a part carrying some kind of nasty burden. 'Cause we don't want to send that out of the system.

So just to illustrate this, I'm gonna start a video with a guy named Hank who was at a Level 2 training some time ago. I'm very grateful to Hank for letting us watch this.

Charlie & Hank's session

Charlie: Okay. Okay, Hank. So you said you think you might have an unattached burden. Maybe you could describe why you think that and what it's like.

Hank: It, it's a thing that comes. It just doesn't feel like it fits with anything that is in my work and my system. It comes in these momentary flashes of wanting to cause pain to people. Like, the ways I get it is sometimes if I'm just talking with someone and I'm holding a hot coffee in my hand, I'll have this flash of throwing the coffee in their face. And I, you know, my system just goes poof. I just ignore it. You know, it doesn't feel like it's gonna take over my body, but it feels like there's just this flash, this impulse in my body to do that. My system, you know, I guess my other parts in my system just kind of push it away — "I don't know what that was" — and just move on.

The most disturbing time it comes is… it's around my dog.

Charlie: Mm-hmm (affirmative)

Hank: I love my dog. I have a tiny little dog, Mr. Shoes.

Charlie: Mr. What?

Hank: Mr. Shoes, Mr. Shoes. Once in a while, it comes to… like, I take him for walks all the time. There was this bridge and I was walking him, and there it came. Just, "Throw him over the bridge."

Charlie: Yeah.

Hank: You know, it's come in thoughts of throwing him in the fire, you know? I'll see a fire and think about throwing him in the fire, and there'll be a few seconds of how much pain he would be in. And of course, all my parts react, "Oh my god, no! I don't want to, I don't want to see that." And then my system just pushes it away, and I just go about my life. And you know, it's not something that really intrudes in my life. It doesn't fit in with anything else that I ever experience. My managers have been able to kind of manage it just by pushing it away.

Charlie: Right.

Hank: But when you said that and I thought about that, I've thought about that. Like, "What the heck? What the fuck is that?" Sorry. What is that, you know? And it's something I never talk about, 'cause it's so …

Charlie: Shameful.

Hank: So shameful, yeah. It's so shameful. Don't want anyone to know.

Charlie: Well, I appreciate your bringing it here. So are you up for finding out what it is?

Hank: I'm scared.

Charlie: What's the fear?

Hank: I have two fears. I have a fear of some malevolent presence inside me and a fear of that coming out and being seen, and maybe being misinterpreted as me.

Charlie: Mm-hmm (affirmative)

Hank: And the other fear is that some part of me is making it up or something like that. So I don't know what it is. I don't know if it's a part of me or if it's outside of me, and there's a part that's just afraid of that unclarity. Like, I don't know. It's just a lot of fear of that.

Charlie: Okay, well, let me say a couple things. I mean, it does sound like it is there. It's not like you're making it up.

Hank: Right, yeah.

Charlie: And it's one of the... one of two possibilities. Either it is something that came into you from the outside, or it is a part of you, neither of which are shameful.

Hank: Yeah, but they both make me cringe. I heard you say that. Like, either option was "Oh, oh no." You know, just in a...

Charlie: Yeah, but just to the parts that are cringing. You know, it's just something. We all have parts we gotta deal with, and this is yours, and we will. But they need to just give us a little space.

Hank: Right.

Charlie: Just see if they're willing to maybe go into a waiting room until we're done... just let you and me get to know this thing and see what it is.

Hank: Wow, they're like... I can sense, they're like, "Really, are you sure?" You know, like, willing to, willing to go off to separate room, but even as they start to recede, feel...

Charlie: Just tell them this rule that there's nothing inside of you that can ever hurt you if you're not afraid of it. I promise.

Hank: The words that are coming to me... It's like, and I don't know if this is a part or what, but it's like, it takes a lot of trust.

Charlie: It does.

Hank: Trust in you, trust in that.

Charlie: That is true.

Hank: That's what came up in me.

Charlie: That is true.

Hank: This takes a lot of trust.

Charlie: It does take a lot of trust. And they don't have to do it, but the opportunity is here. If they, if they don't want to keep having this inside of you, there is this opportunity to get it to change. But they do have to trust.

Hank: Okay.

Charlie: Okay, they're willing?

Hank: Yeah.

Charlie: So how, how does it feel to you now, to pursue this part, whatever it is?

Hank: I feel more, more presence, more confidence.

Charlie: Great. Okay, so maybe just invite it to come forward, or just focus on that voice you got, and we'll just track it down.

Hank: Yeah, I am. Yeah, it comes in a voice that says, it says, "I want to kill that fucking dog." And, and I can even just picture impulses. If I look at you, that impulse of throwing boiling water at you or something hot, or something. Yeah.

Charlie: Okay. Okay, good. So I'm glad we found it, and tell me how you're feeling toward it now as you notice that. And is there a place in your body you feel it the most?

Hank: I don't think I have a bodily sense of it. It seems to just be more of these images or the words that come along with it.

Charlie: That's fine. How are you feeling toward it?

Hank: I'm angry, I'm angry at it. I feel it's definitely a part that's, you know, I want to tell it to fuck off. I feel very protective of my dog.

Charlie: Yeah, yeah, yeah… of course.

Hank: You know, that's, that's what comes up first.

Charlie: Yeah, so let's get that angry, protective part. Let him know we get why he would want to do that, but it's not necessary, and he can trust you and me to handle this thing.

Hank: Oh, he's so angry.

Charlie: It's okay.

Hank: He, he's like… He's got my dad's energy of rage, and he wants to break… he wants to kill that thing inside me. He wants to rip it out.

Charlie: Yeah, of course. But we are gonna ask him to go into a waiting room, too, and let you and me handle this.

Hank: He's like, "Okay. Well, if you need me, I'll be over here."

Charlie: That's fine. We'll call on him if we need him.

Hank: Yeah.

Charlie: How do you feel toward this thing now, Hank?

Hank: I don't know. It's like… the words that are coming are "Why?"

Charlie: Why, out of curiosity, or…?

Hank: It's curious. It's also got a pain to it almost. It's like a… there's compassion, there's curiosity, and there's a kind of pain to it. Like, "Why? Why would you… why would you want to do that?"

Charlie: Alright. So the one who's got the pain also needs to step out. We're getting there, but we want to do it from Self.

Hank: Yeah. Okay.

Charlie: So now how do you feel toward it?

Hank: More neutral and curious.

Charlie: Yeah, good. So ask it why, or whatever question comes to you.

Hank: It's saying, "I hate people. I hate cute, cuddly things."

Charlie: Okay. Ask it why it hates all that.

Hank: It's saying, "'Cause it's not… since it's not me," it says it's not… It hurts it. It stings.

Charlie: What hurts it and stings?

Hank: The love.

Charlie: The love from cuddly things or from people hurts this part? Is that what it's saying?

Hank: Yeah. I can… I get the feeling of it, like, recoiling, like that.

Charlie: Yeah. Ask it about that. Why does it do that? Why does it sting so much when people are loving?

Hank: It says it's like acid.

Charlie: Okay. And how are you feeling toward this part now, Hank?

Hank: Curious. You know, I feel curious.

Charlie: Okay. So just keep encouraging it to let you know why all this feel so, so hurtful to it.

Hank: I just want to name a part so you can help me separate it. I have a part of me that's going, "Is this a part of me or is this…?" You know, I have that.

Charlie: We don't need to know at this point.

Hank: Right.

Charlie: So just tell that part to go away, to chill.

Hank: Yeah. Yeah, I have a more clear sense of this thing. It's, 'cause it's singing. It totally feels like it revels in wanting to hurt.

Charlie: Right.

Hank: And it does feel, I've been kind of… I don't know. The image I'm getting of it, is a somewhat demonic image that's coming now.

Charlie: So like a devil image, or what? What's it look like?

Hank: Like a, like a beast. Like a…

Charlie: Uh-huh.

Hank: Like a man shape, but kind of snarly teeth, kind of you know, some type of man/animal/beast.

Charlie: Okay. And how are you feeling the more that you see it there?

Hank: I'm not scared of it. I feel, I wouldn't say I feel compassionate toward it. Curious.

Charlie: Yeah.

Hank: You know, it's a little caution. I wouldn't say fear, but there's a little, "Hm. Alright, this is here."

Charlie: My feeling is we're in good shape with it, so… So just ask it if there's more it wants you to know about itself.

Hank: Oh, it says it fucking hates me.

Charlie: Ask it about that.

Hank: It says it's gonna destroy me.

Charlie: But why, why does he want to destroy you?

Hank: It says 'cause I'm healing, 'cause I'm, 'cause I have, I'm bringing light, it wants to destroy me.

Charlie: Yeah. So why does it want to destroy light and healing and that kind of thing?

Hank: It says I'm the problem — the light and healing are the problem. Like… He's saying he has the truth. Viciousness, killing, hate, that's the truth.

Charlie: Okay. Where did this truth come from? Ask him where he got these beliefs.

Hank: At first, he was showing a little bit of my dad, but he was very clear. "Your dad was clued into it, or carried some of the energy." But he's more showing me killing, like, animals killing, this ripping of guts and… Yeah. I can, I'm seeing lions killing, and the weaker animals kind of dying and getting their throats eaten open.

Charlie: Yeah. So he's showing all that.

Hank: "This is true," he says.

Charlie: But yeah. I'm still not clear why he thinks that's true. I mean, I get the images. I don't get where he got the belief that that was truth rather than love or whatever he hates so much, or light.

Hank: I… Should I ask him something directly? I'm a little, I'm lost.

Charlie: Yeah. Just ask him again where he got this belief that that kind of violence is the truth.

Hank: He says he didn't get it from anywhere, and he says, "Look." He wants me to look at him to see, "I'll show you the truth. Look, look at my teeth. Look at… I will kill you. That is where I get this truth."

Charlie: No, that isn't where he got it. That's really not an answer. He got it someplace, these beliefs. Did he get it from a person? Did he get it from some experience? Some being gave it to him?

Hank: It's getting pretty riled and seems to be getting very aggravated and angry.

Charlie: He doesn't like this line of questioning.

Hank: No, he's trying to attack me, but it's not doing anything.

Charlie: Yeah, he can't hurt you now.

Hank: Right, yeah. But he's getting more, he's getting more energized at trying to attack me, and I can feel him trying to scrape his claws and teeth into me, but it's not doing anything.

Charlie: Yeah. Alright, so tell him we won't aggravate him with this line of questioning anymore. You can relax a little bit.

Hank: Yikes. He's calmed down a little bit. He's kind of pacing, and he's a little bit more on all fours now and pacing, and kind of snarling.

Charlie: Yeah.

Hank: He looks a little distempered, like a wild animal a little bit.

Charlie: Earlier, you said that love is painful to him, something like that. Was that him saying that, or was that somebody else?

Hank: Yeah, it's him. He's… this whole thing is very painful to him.

Charlie: You being nice to him or listening to him is painful to him? Or, what's painful to him?

Hank: The light. Your light, my light.

Charlie: Yeah, okay. Alright. Can he say anything more about why it's so painful? Why he wants to destroy it?

Hank: Saying he doesn't belong here.

Charlie: That may be true, that might be true. And we might be able to send him some place where he belongs. We would just need to know him better first.

Hank: I'm feeling more compassion for him because he seems… he seems kind of lost, actually.

Charlie: He's lost, yeah. So extend that compassion to him, even though it might be painful to him.

Hank: Yeah, it hurts him.

Charlie: It hurts him, doesn't it?

Hank: Yeah, he's recoiling. He hisses and wants to attack me more when I do that.

Charlie: Yeah, but let's do it anyway.

Hank: Okay.

Charlie: Yeah.

Hank: It's hard to do. He's screaming, "No!" And it's so hard to not see the direct causal impact of the pain.

Charlie: Alright, so we'll back off a little bit. We don't want to torture him. Hank, ask him if he's a part of you or if he's something else.

Hank: He's really… that question really made him want to attack me more. It's not doing any good, though. Let me, let me ask him again.

Charlie: Ask him again.

Hank: How did you phrase it exactly? Is he a part of me or something else?

Charlie: Yeah, exactly.

Hank: He said, "Fuck you, you want to get rid of me. And you're not gonna get rid of me." That's what he said.

Charlie: Well, tell him he doesn't really have a choice in all this. But if he is a part of you, then we don't want to send him someplace. But if he isn't, we'll send him to where he belongs and he'll be much happier, and he'll be able to transform. I'm still not sure which it is, so if he would enlighten us, that would help a lot.

Hank: He wants to stay, is what he says.

Charlie: Okay. Why is that?

Hank: 'Cause he wants to hurt me, and if he stays, he can hurt me.

Charlie: Okay. So he's not interested in going somewhere where he'll be transformed into something good?

Hank: He doesn't believe that.

Charlie: Okay. Well, it's true. If it were true, would he be interested?

Hank: He's struggling, 'cause he's saying, "You're gonna transform me into something good and light, which is painful for me. How could that be good? That will be painful."

Charlie: Yeah. Alright, so we gotta work…

Hank: He doesn't quite get that.

Charlie: We gotta work that out. So, so my past experience is that we transform it into something good and it's no longer painful. It just likes it. This is how people do it.

Hank: He's trying to strangle me and cover my mouth.

Charlie: Okay.

Hank: Which is funny, though, 'cause I can just feel that it has no impact or effect on me.

Charlie: That's fine. Let's just try it again. Ask him, 'cause generally, they can't lie about that. So he hasn't really answered the question yet. Just see if he'll answer if he came into you from somewhere.

Hank: Begrudgingly, he's saying he's not a part of me.

Charlie: Yeah, he's not. Ask him how he got into your system.

Hank: My uncle.

Charlie: So he was in your uncle and he jumped into you?

Hank: My uncle invited some evil into the family.

Charlie: Okay.

Hank: So, he's kind of showing that.

Charlie: Okay. Thank him for showing you that and everything he wants you to get about that.

Hank: I, I just have a feeling of the energy of my family in him, like, in his arms as he tries to choke me.

Charlie: The energy of your family?

Hank: Yeah, of my uncle and all… my uncle was carrying the pain and all the blackness in the family.

Charlie: Oh, okay.

Hank: My uncle practiced black magic.

Charlie: Okay.

Hank: So it's all connected.

Charlie: Yeah. So let him know this all makes sense.

Hank: He, he doesn't… he's determined. He doesn't stop with the "I hate you, I'll get you," to me, you know. Just… he's like, "And this guy too — fuck this guy. I'll get him."

Charlie: Yeah.

Hank: Yeah, he doesn't stop, regardless of how ineffective it seems.

Charlie: Okay. Well, let him know we get that he's really afraid of getting hurt by the light and that he's doing a lot of this out of fear.

Hank: There is a softening.

Charlie: Yeah. And we're gonna try and work it out so that the light doesn't hurt him, so that he can willingly go to the light and be transformed. 'Cause we actually want to help him, 'cause what he's doing, he can't really love that much.

Hank: Yeah, there… It's like he's just focused on kill, harm, kill.

Charlie: Yeah, right.

Hank: It's like this… he's stuck in that. And this squeezing energy, which is him trying to kill and harm — it's all he has.

Charlie: That is all he has right now.

Hank: Yeah.

Charlie: But we can, we can change that. So, so Hank. Ask if there are any guides, for lack of a better word, around who can help us with this dilemma of his getting hurt by the light.

Hank: Yeah. I have a few guides. One of them has this beautiful energy of… she drips light — little balls of light kind of drop off her, and she can cover people in that. But she also has a really… I'm getting the sense she has this ability to kind of titrate that, and she's saying she can make it so that he won't… It's almost like anesthesia, like it will start so slowly that he will begin to not feel the pain of it, and slowly increase it. By the time the light actually hits him, he won't, he won't feel it.

Charlie: Okay, so ask her to do that, to start that process.

Hank: Something is confusing me. Do we even ask for its permission? You know, that it… we're just gonna do it? Do we ask if it wants that?

Charlie: No, no, we don't ask permission. No. He won't, it won't want it.

Hank: It's gone.

Charlie: The thing is gone? Or, what's happening?

Hank: Well the… Spirit was kind of doing that. It's slowly a low-level light that kind of anesthetized it and… And it was almost like it was raging, but then falling asleep and losing consciousness. And then as that happened, the light began to increase, increase, until a blinding, a blinding white space. But there was no screaming or pain or anything.

Charlie: Good.

Hank: I mean, I have flashes of what that thing looked like, but it doesn't feel like it's here. It just feels like my memory of it.

Charlie: Okay. Just check to be sure. Or if there are traces of it still.

Hank: There are traces. I asked, "Are you still here?" And it replied, "Only in your memory." It still came from its voice, though, so it feels like a trace of it, but…

Charlie: So let's ask the light to take the trace of it, too.

Hank: I have another guide that's a dragon.

Charlie: Mm-hmm (affirmative)

Hank: Red dragon, and it's kind of burning out the rest.

Charlie: Perfect.

Hank: Yeah, no… feels pretty clean.

Charlie: Okay, good. You can ask this angel and the dragon what's gonna happen to it. If they know. They may not.

Hank: Says its energy is being recycled back into animal energy where it belongs.

Charlie: Okay, good. Just see if there's anything more they want you to know.

Hank: They said they're very proud of me.

Charlie: Mm-hmm (affirmative), that's great.

Hank: That they're here for me.

Charlie: They're here for you?

Hank: Yeah.

Charlie: That's right.

Hank: They're here for others, too.

Charlie: Uh-huh. For others, the people you work with? Or who do they mean?

Hank: Mm-hmm (affirmative), yeah. They mean people I come in contact with. They're willing to serve in any way that might help other people as well.

Charlie: Okay, good. So thank them for helping us today. And then let's go back to your parts and just to the one that hated this guy and one that feared him. Just tell them the coast is clear — they can all come out and check it out.

Hank: The angry one, the one that was very rageful, seems a little disappointed. He doesn't quite know what to do with his anger and his rage.

Charlie: Okay.

Hank: He got kinda worked up about that guy, and he doesn't get the opportunity to get worked up all that often, so he's a little frustrated, I guess. Yeah.

Charlie: He mentioned that he carries your father's energy. Is that right?

Hank: Yeah.

Charlie: Does he like having to carry that?

This is the end of the part of the session that removed the unattached burden. They go on to do standard IFS work to help the part who took on his father's rage unburden that rage. As in this case, the UB often blocks inner work that had been needing attention for a long time. Once the UB is out of the way, the work can proceed smoothly.

Charlie's comments on the session:

A couple of things I wanted to highlight. One is this rule, this law of inner physics, that if you can get somebody in Self, there's nothing inside of them that has any power or can hurt them. I've been doing this work for many years and have worked with lots of scary inner beings and various other things, and that law has never been violated. As soon as I get somebody in Self, beasts like that no longer have any power, and the client relates to them in the way that Hank did. So you know, that was a great thing to be able to show. And then, you know, I am an empiricist, phenomenologist, and I'm just reporting the data. And so the data has led me down these, these roads that are pretty far away from the scientific kind of education that I had, and involve things that call themselves spiritual. I don't know exactly what to make of it except that it seems to be very useful to people. So things like guides and these unattached burdens seem to come from other places, other kinds of realms. Shamans for centuries have been playing around with that stuff, and there's something about it that kind of makes sense that it would show up as we do IFS, too. So initially, I was very, very skeptical. It wasn't until I'd run into the phenomena many times that I started to actually learn more acceptance. It's something that I — I mentioned this earlier — I share reluctantly because I'm very afraid of IFS being written off as New Age or something like that, and so it's not something that we do routinely at all.

If you work with these populations, you will run into these phenomena, and it's just good to know that it's not a part, that it's something you can actually send out of the system. You don't have to do it in a harsh way. You can do it with compassion, as we did, and with reassurance that it's gonna like where it's going. And you know, it's very common that they don't like the light, that they get hurt by the light. That's all very common. So as I say, they're often inside of people who have been out of their bodies a lot.

Student: Is it good to get to know the UB? Or do you have to be cautious?

Charlie: No, it is good to get to know them, and particularly in the beginning when you're just doing this. And as you could tell, it was only about halfway through the session that I actually concluded that it wasn't a part. So I give parts a lot of leeway, or these UBs, to let me see what they really are.

Student: Asking permission from a part or UB versus just doing it. Can you expand on that?

Charlie: My experience with UBs is you can't ask permission for them to leave 'cause they never will. They don't want to, they're afraid to, and they just try to intimidate. So at some point, you just have to say, "You don't belong here, and we're gonna do this. And you'll be glad we did, although you'll fight it until we... until you're out of here."

Student: This went so quick, I'm wondering if I am doing something wrong in my practice.

Charlie: Yes, it went quickly. Hank is a Level 2 trainee; Hank knows his parts well. They kind of trust his Self, so we could move pretty quickly, and that isn't true with a lot of clients in the beginning, so I wouldn't worry too much.

Student: What do you use if the client does not have guides?

Charlie: We just use his Self energy, and we would just keep brainstorming and experimenting until we found the right way to make it so that UB could leave without pain.

Student: I was very interested in how you very persistently pushed the part to reveal where it got its ideas. If it had related that to an event or person, would you have suggested it was a part and not a UB?

Charlie: Yes. That's what I was doing. It was a kind of a test. 'Cause at that point, I wasn't sure what it was, and so I was doing what I typically do with a part that has an extreme belief. You know, whenever they say, "This is true," and it's something extreme, I'll always ask, "Where did you get this belief?" which is called *deconstruction* in other systems literature. So you're challenging assumed truth. Usually, parts will respond to that by telling you where they got the belief. After they fight it for a while, at some point, the part will confess that it's… it really is a belief it got from some person or some event. So that helped me realize this was probably not a part.

Student: You mentioned that if the client is in Self, nothing bad can happen. What if I as a therapist think my client is in Self, but it's actually a Self-like part?

Charlie: It just won't work. You will not be able to get it to leave. You know, the scary thing will be able to continue to intimidate.

Student: What was your clue that it was an unattached burden? What can help us identify them?

Charlie: The first clue was that it really just wanted to wreak havoc and hurt his dog and him. So that primes me to think maybe it is, but I run into parts that do that, too. So then I keep an open mind. I interview the thing until I can get enough from it that I really get a sense that that's what it is.

Student: I've had this experience with clients who struggle with schizophrenia. I think this is what is going on with that group. What are your thoughts? Also, criminals say "the devil made me do it." This could be true for them?

Charlie: You know, I've worked with schizophrenics who didn't have any of these. I think I worked with maybe one that did, so I wouldn't make that generalization. And with criminals, yes. I have, in the years that I worked with sex offenders, for example, we found a bunch of them. So I do think that in that population, you're likely to find more.

Student: I was really impressed with Hank's ability to stay in his own Self.

Charlie: Me, too. You know, it took a while for us to get the scared parts to step back, but it's just such a beautiful example of how once you get the client in Self, how everything's okay. Everything works.

Student: I had a question about a UB. I had a client who had a UB that we thought we got out of her system, but she later felt that it left residue behind. That residue then began to torture her with nightmares.

Charlie: You know, and Hank implied there might be some residue, so if that's true, you go back to it and you send that out, too. I actually saw Hank last week; he was at a Level 3 training here. So, he's had no more recurrence with this thing. The only reason they come into people, and they're in me occasionally, is because they want something. Like, this one hated the light, and they're drawn to people who carry a lot of light partly 'cause they want to attack the light. Sometimes, 'cause they want to sort of parasitically draw from it.

Student: Is there a risk of the UB jumping on the therapist?

Charlie: Yes, there is. And that's why when I'm working with somebody who might have one, I'm very careful to be sure I'm fully in my body during the whole time. And I mean in my Self and in my body.

I have followed up with Hank for several years after this session. The UB has never returned, his fantasies of hurting his dog are gone completely, and he feels ongoing relief.

Brief Cases

Sessions with Eric

These sessions were profoundly moving for me. I'd been working with Eric for most of a year, and these sessions were in many ways the culmination and conclusion of all that work. Eric is an Indigenous man who lives on a reservation and works to help his people and other First Nations groups. He is deeply connected to his culture and is conversational in its language.

June 25, 2020

We reviewed a previous session where we had worked with a lot of trauma from age three to seven. There's a boy who had been taken up into the spirit realms but came back down. The spirits kept a part of his spirit up there so he could survive. This week, that boy was happily playing and running around outside of Eric. All of his spirit was back in him. This boy would check in with Eric every once in a while. Eric talked of a female entity that he knew was not part of him. He also mentioned that, while doing a pipe ceremony, he had noticed a dark shadow moving quickly across the weeds. I felt that we had stopped the story of his childhood trauma at age seven last week and wondered if we should move forward with that. He wanted to work with the female energy. When I asked him to go inside and review all these possible focuses, he and his guides chose to work with the darkness. It is so important that we follow the client's wisdom. We focused on this. It was very familiar to him. I looked for any part of him that might be afraid of it. There were none. The three- to seven-year-old part had held some fear, but he was fine now.

I mentioned that beings who are not part of us usually offer power as a way to get in. He described how he felt very uncomfortable when being in positions of power. We asked the darkness, "Who are you?" It said, "I have been here from creation. Most of the universe is dark. I balance the light." I asked Eric to find his guides, the ancient ones. He did, and we talked with them. They told us that the darkness thrives on fear, ego, power, the quest for power, and anger. It's everywhere in the world now. He saw it in hospitals swirling around those near death who were alone and frightened. The ancient ones told him to acknowledge and respect it, and to walk lightly on Mother Earth's back. The darkness is like a snake; it can strike at any time. The way to be safe from it is to be in Self, in my IFS language. He said some words in his Native language that translated roughly as "I have the Great Spirit in me in a good way." He was told to honor each moment of life; it can change on a dime. Offer food when you eat, especially to water. This was repeated. The darkness is the force in volcanoes; there is much fire in it. It is a necessary balance to light; it's been here since creation. Eric's being able to see it is a blessing and a warning. Most of the healing ceremonies require darkness. He talked of light spirits coming into him in a dark healing space. The spirits do not like the body; it's a smelly thing; they don't like to be around it.

Then we went back to the female spirit, who now tried to choke him and sat on his chest. With the help of the ancient ones, we addressed her respectfully. She said it is not enough that you are respectful — you must also help others be respectful. He talked of all the Indigenous teenage girls who were raped and murdered and how the white police would not investigate. The spirit said it is helping him create his healing center. He wondered if he needs to focus on this more personal stuff and not be distracted by all the other work. The female spirit said that we are not to judge the girls who are promiscuous. She addressed me and wondered why I focused on men and did not offer my healing to women. It knew me enough to truthfully say, "You have been raped like women, and so you could help." I got defensive and said many of these abused women prefer to work with women; the spirit answered me calmly and said yes, but this healing across sexes is especially powerful. We asked if the female spirit could communicate with Eric in other ways so she would not have to choke him. She seemed to say yes. I was thankful that she'd given me some attention. I mentioned that the mystic swims in the sea where the mad man drowns. And I told Eric that I've met one other person who had this darkness in him and that that person was drowning. So his being able to see the darkness is a dangerous blessing. At the end, we thanked the ancient ones, the darkness, and the female spirit.

September 21, 2020

Eric started the session by describing some preliminary work he'd done since our last meeting. He realized that there were many, many spirits all around him and attached to him and in him. He said he felt ready to let them all go. This felt like a milestone and a watershed. We started by imagining him in a very large ball of light with all the spirits who had bad intentions for him in there, too. Then he slowly moved away from the ball of light, and it slowly moved away from him. He could see many of them in there, pounding on the inside of the ball and trying to get out. I asked, "Are there any cords or tubes or connections back to you from the ball?" He said yes — there were a bunch of them back to his stomach. I asked, "What do they connect to? Who is in there?" He first saw a bunch of his relatives. They were all relatives who had died. I asked if they knew that they were dead. They did not. Somewhere early on in the session, he let me know that we had missed a step. For his Plains Indians tribe (I imagine that using the word *Indian* will bother some people, but it is the word he suggested I use, and I am going to honor his wish), it was the wolves who led the souls of the dead to the Milky Way. We had not invited them. He invited them.

Eric informed the deceased relatives that they had died and let them know that the wolves were there waiting to guide them on. They started leaving. Then there were many, many, many more. Hundreds. Maybe thousands. They included the souls of women and children who had been herded into stockades by the cavalry and who were nearly starving to death. They had picked through horseshit for kernels of corn in order to survive. Many, many more ancestor souls. Beside them, there were their dogs, which were part wolf, pulling the poles that carried their belongings. It was a huge group of ancestors, moving in the traditional way. We spent a long time in silence watching this column as it proceeded. It was a very long line. It went up to the Milky Way, which is the home for spirits.

When the last soul had gone, Eric said, "I have a slight headache." I said, "Ask the headache why it's here." After a pause he said, "All the tears, all the crying, all the grief" — his and his ancestors'. The spirit of a warrior came and brushed him off with an eagle feather. The warrior told him, "You do not have to carry that anymore." We focused back on the ball of light with all those spirits in there who did not have good intentions for him. The wolves escorted this ball of light full of spirits up to a mountaintop. Eric said he knew that when they went up to the mountaintop, the wolves would run around and around the ball, which would form a tornado-like energy that would lift it off of Earth and up and away. He also said that even with these spirits gone, he knew there were residues in his body. I told him he had the wisdom and asked which one of these we should focus on — the residues or the spirits. He said he wanted to spend more time watching the ball of light and the wolves on the mountain. As he watched, he saw many other animals emerge; bear came first, I think, then bobcat came and coyote and deer and more. There was a small mountain stream there, and spirits of the water came out and watched. All these animals ran around with the wolves. The tornado spiral became strong.

Then this ball of spirits ascended. Someone in it said, "You know we're all one, don't you?" Eric said, "Yes, we will meet again soon." Eric talked of the significance of the Big Dipper and how it is relevant to his tribe's lifeways. He also mentioned the significance of some other stars. An old man spirit said, "You know, your voice will be weaker now." (I felt annoyed by this, but I kept my mouth shut and did not contradict this spirit.)

Then we returned to Eric's body, and the residues were already falling away from it. Some fell into the earth, some to water, some to fire, some to air. After encouraging this process, I said that at times like this, we can often invite in Great Spirit and other benevolent spirits. Spirits came. A circle formed around him of seven spirits, I believe, who held the values deeply treasured by his group: courage, humility, wisdom, being in truth, and more. I said it was my belief that these benevolent energies would never enter us without an invitation. I asked him if he wanted to invite the energies of these spirits into his body, into every organ of his body, and into every cell of every organ of his body. I said that every moment we spend with these energies in us is profoundly healing for us, for the people around us, for our ancestors, and for our descendants.

I asked if any parts of him were frightened by this energy and not ready to welcome it. I said many times young child parts are easily scared by this. He said, "No, they are grabbing it." I told them that the best way to hold onto this energy is to give it away. I said this might be very hard to believe, and I asked if some of them would just try it just a little to see if it was true. I mentioned that he might check the soles of his feet because often some of that residue comes out down there. He told me he'd already noticed it coming out down there. I asked if there was anything more that should happen inside for this to be as complete and healing as possible. Eric said no; it felt complete.

When he reoriented to this daily reality, he said that his hands were wet with sweat. This almost never happened to him. I said, "Spirit and energy often move through our palms." The soles of his feet also felt different. I felt moved to ask that he focus on his dreams over the next few days. He replied that that's where he's gotten most of his direction and guidance. Repeatedly, I had the image of a sweat lodge, but I didn't want to say it out loud because this is his realm, not mine. But as the image kept coming, I did say this aloud, and he said he thought he would do a sweat in the next week or so.

Tears were running down my face for much of the session. I lost all track of time, but I had decided early on that I would stay with this as long as it took.

Amazingly, it only took an hour. I had entered altered time. Sub specie aeternitatis. Especially when the long columns of his ancestors were being guided onward toward the Milky Way, I too left this world.

It almost feels sacrilegious to add comments, but there is one aspect of this that I want to point to — the spiral movement of the wolves and other animals that lifted the bad spirits up off of this world. I saw this once before when a therapist followed his intuition. A European therapist once told me that he has seen an uncannily similar spiral of wolves lift negative spirits off a client from northern Norway. In modern Wicca, some practitioners use this spiral motion in two ways: counterclockwise movement to remove bad spirits and clockwise circles to draw down the gods. The earliest form of religious ceremony and prayer was almost certainly circle dances. Is this some archetype we can tap into in our work?

Pat's session

Pat started by describing how hurt she'd been by a colleague's insensitive comment about a case she was presenting in a supervision group. She said she'd been crying a lot all week. I kept working to keep the focus on the part of her who held the sadness. We did get to the part and she got in Self with it. It was attached to a couple of places in the past, and I asked her to let her system choose where we should go. She said, "Back to this time when I was three years old, but I've worked on that so much." She'd been born with an eye problem that required surgical correction and had gone into the hospital for eye surgery at age three. After the surgery, she was standing in the crib in the hospital with a bandage over her eyes. She was holding the railings on the crib and listening intently to steps as they came down the hall, hoping it would be her mother, but her mother never came. Several times Pat protested that she had worked on this so much already. I took this to mean that something important must have been missed.

Knowing that unattached burdens often get in during childhood hospital stays, I started exploring this. I had her ask the three-year-old, "Did you let somebody into you when you were so lonely when your mother didn't come?" This did not really get a response, and I regretted the question because it didn't allow for an unattached burden getting in when she was having the surgery under anesthesia. So I rephrased the question in a way that would also allow for this possibility: "Did some other beings get into you there in the hospital?" This also did not get a response. She said that her mother had not come to the hospital because of her mother's high level of fear, which she always hid under a veneer of control. Knowing that children often pick up unexpressed emotions like sponges and that this is a way legacy burdens can be transmitted, I asked her to ask the little girl if she had taken in some of her mother's stuff. This didn't get a response either.

Knowing that it didn't really matter whether it was an unattached burden or a legacy burden, I switched to a broader question. I asked Pat to ask the three-year-old, "What percentage of this is yours from your lifetime, and what percentage comes from somewhere else, anywhere else?" She said 70 percent. I misunderstood and started asking her if she wanted to unburden the 30 percent that wasn't hers. She said, "Oh no, it's the 70 percent that's not mine." I asked her if she wanted to unburden that, and she said yes. She started unburdening it, and some things started happening in her throat. She looked very distressed, almost choking. She brought her hands up in front of her throat and made a gesture of something coming down in. I asked her to use the light to remove it, but she said, "It's too big — the light can't get around it." She was choking, but she courageously stayed with it, and we found it was intertwined with something else inside her. There seemed to be a six-year-old part of her who'd had to go to the hospital for tonsil removal. That part got somewhat freed, and still there were problems getting this thing out. But we persisted and completely surrounded it with light and got it out. A bird came and took this bundle and flew away with it.

Pat watched for a long time as it flew away into the distance, becoming very tiny and then disappearing entirely. We went back to the three-year-old to see how she was doing, and she seemed good and relieved. I said, "Sometimes when there's a big unburdening like this, guides or guidance can come in; let's see if that happens for you." The bird returned from far away in the sky, this time not carrying anything. Pat welcomed it. I was wanting to be careful, so I asked Pat to notice if it respected her free will — if it only came in when she asked it. It did. I was relieved. She invited it more deeply into her. She realized that she will also need to work more with the six-year-old who had her tonsils removed. She may be able to do this on her own, or it may be in another session we do together. There was powerful physiological expression in her throat; there is so much in her throat about learning to sing and having a voice and much, much more. Notice that it didn't matter whether this stuff was a legacy burden or an unattached burden. My being too specific in my questions slowed the process. We only needed to know that it was not part of her.

Lisa's session

Lisa came specifically to work with a UB. A curandera (a folk healer from Lisa's homeland of Puerto Rico) had sensed dark energy in Lisa that she could not remove. We looked for parts of Lisa that were afraid of it. "If you are not afraid, it loses all power." We found a three-year-old who was very frightened. In getting to know her, we realized that she was protecting even more tender parts behind her. Even very young parts can be protectors. The three-year-old let us go to a part who was frozen in terror. Lisa got in a good Self-to-part relationship with this frozen part. It turned to her Self and no longer wanted the dark energy in her. We used light to pull the dark energy out of her to a conversational distance. It said, "You are not getting rid of me so easily." I asked if there were any connections coming back to her body from this being. Yes, there were some to the right side of her body and head.

Lisa experienced confusion... "Is this connection to me?? or... my family??" We asked, "Is this from the ancestors?" Yes. We did a multigenerational legacy unburdening. She passed the burdens back up through the generations of ancestors to the first ancestors in her lineage, who took them in. We then asked those first ancestors to send the burdens up into the light, where the burdens could be transformed. When the old burdens had completely disappeared, we asked those first ancestors to invite in new qualities they would like. I shared that often it is just light and warmth that come in at times like this. We invited the ancestors to fill with this until they overflowed. The overflow came down the generations, each generation filling and then overflowing. It filled Lisa and her parts to overflowing. She offered it out into the world. She was now part of a stream, a river. I told her that the only way to hold on to this energy was to give it away. Lisa was glowing. Although the session only lasted fifty-five minutes, she said it felt like four hours. Lisa told me at the end that many of her ancestors were healers of many kinds.

Lisa's response to my session notes:

I'm doing great. Thank you for following up with me! The shift has been subtle, but quite profound in the sense that I've noticed that the darkness/fogginess is no longer present. There were a few moments that really stood out to me as being incredibly helpful in preparation to work with this being. By focusing on my fearful parts first, I felt like Self energy was so much easier to access — I think I had expected to go directly to the being, but it dawned on me as we were working that the fear was being protective by keeping me away from the being. I was also very moved to "witness" the joy and celebration of my ancestors and to feel the presence of a being who was regal, strong, and grounded. After our session, what was clear to me about this other being was that it was genderless. Another thing I noticed was a somatic shift in my body — a lightness along the right side of my body where there had been a sense of stagnant energy/heaviness. Lastly, the part, where we trapped the dark entity in light and removed it from my body in that way, came with powerful imagery and somatic features. It felt as though something was being pulled out of me that did not want to go. The remaining tendrils that we ferreted out, which were really holding fast out of the fear that it would return, felt like bands of heaviness that snapped when the worry was released. To be honest, I wish I had thought to record our session because some of the things you said during the unburdening were so helpful. I think my Self energy hung around that day because subsequent sessions with clients that day were so lovely and effortless.

Amy's session

The client, Amy, is herself a therapist who had spent years working with a very disturbed client with a history of attachment-related wounding, including abandonment by her mother, multiple friends, romantic partners, and previous mental health providers. This client became very upset with Amy and behaved in an aggressive manner and then abruptly terminated their therapeutic relationship. Amy felt that she went way beyond the call of duty in caring for this client. She was aware of a part of her that held some anger towards this ex-client. Two weeks prior to our session, she had been using an IFS-related meditative exercise to begin to work with this angry part when she noticed the presence of a rubbery white figure inside her system that seemed to be related to her client in some way. This figure had no features. It was about the size of a tall, thin eight-year-old girl. Amy saw a visual image of this figure lying in her arms across her lap with its head resting on the right side of her chest. As this figure did not feel like part of her system, Amy sought out my assistance to work with it.

We began the session focused on the part of Amy that held some anger toward the ex-client. Once this part felt welcomed and understood, it stepped back to reveal the part that was hurt by the client's behavior. Amy had cared very deeply for this client and had invested a great deal of time and energy in her. As this part relaxed back, we were able to focus attention on the rubbery-looking white being in Amy's lap. Amy was not afraid of it and was able to look at its face with some compassion. As she did this, she began to feel the presence of the Virgin Mary. She felt that both she and Mary were looking into this being's face through her eyes. Amy had a strong connection to the Virgin Mary before this session. The being opened and closed its mouth, which was very vague in form, but it did not speak. It became clear to Amy that this was not part of her system. As I suggested that she bring light to surround us and the being and to draw it out of her system, the being threw its thin arms around her neck and clung more tightly to her with what seemed like a sense of desperation.

Amy was able to maintain a caring presence with this being as it clung to her, and I spoke to the whole system, letting the being know that we would be able to help it get to a place where it could receive the care it truly needed. We reassure it that there was no judgment and no punishment and that it was in the wrong place and could not get what it needed here with Amy. Amy and the Virgin Mary were able to bring in a healing light and surround the being in a cocoon of light. As the being was too weak to be upright, it was lying in this cocoon as though the cocoon were some sort of bedding made of light. When I suggested that Amy and the being could say goodbye before it went off to receive its own care and healing, Amy became very emotional. She reported later that she experienced a wave of emotion regarding the ending of the therapeutic relationship with her client, as there had been no formal termination experience. She was getting the sense that she had been caring for this being because of the connection to her client. So she was essentially saying goodbye to them both.

As the wave of emotion resolved, all the parts in Amy's system that had responded to this being's neediness and desperation for care were able to release their attachment to the being and allow it to leave. Amy felt ready to see the being off to its destination. As the cocoon of light began to ascend, Amy noticed that it could not move beyond a certain height, as there was a thick rubber cord attaching its back to something inside the body of her ex-client. I let Amy know that while parts of the client might or might not be ready to let this being go, the being could choose to let go of any attachment to the ex-client's system if that was what was keeping it stuck. Amy looked at the cord and saw that it was being clawed at by small black entities inside her client's abdomen as they grasped at the cord, trying to keep the being tethered to them. The rubber of the cord began to develop holes and became weaker. Amy got the distinct sense that something within the ex-client's body had been using this being as a method of infiltrating the systems of those caring for others to keep them attached to her, almost as though a hook had been inserted inside of them.

When the being heard from me that it could choose to go to be welcomed by others of its kind and receive healing, the golden light that surrounded it began to glow very strongly until it severed the cord, freeing the cocoon to continue its ascent. The cocoon ascended past several figures who were welcoming it. Amy was very emotional at this time, but she was not experiencing any pain or suffering. She was very moved by the welcome that the being received. As she continued to watch the rubbery being, it began to transform as though a spark of golden light within it expanded to transcend the boundaries. The rubbery shell transformed into a golden light so that the being became a spark of light within a much larger field of light. We then returned to Amy's system. Her attention returned to her felt sense of connection with the Virgin Mary, and she further welcomed the Virgin Mary's energy into her. Even though I wanted to pursue the black things in the ex-client, this was not appropriate. After some minor cleanup, everything seemed complete, and at this point we ended the session. Amy let me know later that she realized this being could only get into her because it seemed so hurt and needy. She was vulnerable to neediness, not to fear.

In a session Amy and I had done months before, we had found another similar UB energy. It looked like a small sort of sad and pathetic spider. Its legs moved around ineffectually. Once again, it had gained access to her system by appearing weak and needy. This one came out fairly easily, and it did not appear to have done much damage, but as soon as it was out, Amy began experiencing the presence of the Virgin Mary. Amy's head turned slightly to the right and down, almost as though she was looking at a child in her arms. Her eyes were closed. There was a sense of peace in the room that grew and grew. Her face took on an expression of exquisite tenderness and seemed to fill with a soft inner light. Tears came down her cheeks quietly, and mine, too. I felt so blessed to be present at such a moment. This UB had appeared helpless and small; it had not done much damage directly, but it had blocked an important realm of experience. Removing a UB can often reveal parts who need our connection or the possibility of connection with guides and spirit. Amy told me much later that this earlier experience had helped her reconnect with her family's religious tradition and with her father and ancestors.

I've also worked with other people who had a UB get in by appearing weak and needy. A male client took in an energy that was not part of his system that appeared to him as a stray dog needing at home. He was reluctant to release this energy, but when he came to believe that this being would also be better off moving on, he let it go. It is so appropriate that in the UK, some people call these "stray burdens."

In my own inner life, I've had a very similar experience. I got several UBs out, but more kept coming in as quickly as I could get them out. So, with my therapist's help, we went to look for what part of me was letting them in. What I saw in my inner world was a child part of me sitting on the back steps of my house, welcoming in all the stray dogs in the neighborhood. He himself felt like a stray dog, completely unwanted. This part of me resolutely refused to stop helping the strays. He was sitting on the back steps of the house with the door into the house behind him open, and he let all the strays come into his house. They made a mess in the house, which I took to represent my life and my personality structure. At this impasse, we negotiated with him and set up a hospital for the strays in a garage out in the backyard. This way, he could continue to offer them care, and they would not enter the house and be destructive. Most of the time, fear is the point of vulnerability that allows UBs to enter, and it may also be anger or loneliness. These energies can get into our systems in many ways.

Julie's session
Julie had been a client of another therapist who removed a UB from her about two years before I interviewed her. Julie had a very narcissistic mother who was

a medical doctor. In the session with the other therapist, they were working on a three-year-old part who was afraid to make any noise that might wake up her mom. They got this three-year-old part up to the present with Julie, but it still had a lot of fear. Julie looked inside her and asked her three-year-old part to show her what was scary. It showed her a blood-red cave with a large black blob inside. The blob would not move or respond. They put it in a bubble and sent it up to the light. Then they did the same with the mom, but as they were doing this, the mom morphed into a terrifying being with huge teeth. It seemed to be alien, sometimes black, sometimes with green slime… terrifying, hard to look at, and creepy, but Julie also had a part that almost wanted to laugh. They put this thing in a bubble and sent it to the light, too. It went without a fight. The cave turned into a light-filled bright room. At this point, the therapist explained to Julie what a UB was.

After this experience, Julie felt quite transformed. She hadn't even really realized it, but she'd always been sort of depressed, and now that lifted. She'd had a lot of dark thoughts and sometimes thought of suicide, but all this stopped and never returned. One of her inner voices had told her over and over again, "You are worthless and shouldn't even be here." This voice also stopped completely. Julie was so grateful that this thing was gone but felt as though she had to keep it a secret because it was so weird. She was grateful to talk to me; she felt less isolated with this experience. This is a good example of how our culture's narrow-minded attitudes toward these experiences can increase the suffering and isolation of people who have them. Clients will keep these experiences secret until they trust our open-mindedness.

George's session
George started with how agitated and upset he got when thinking about meeting with his father or even when getting an email from his father. George had plans to meet with his father, who had always been abusive, that afternoon and terminate all contact. This meeting looked as though it would be a watershed in his emotional life. I had assumed that our session would be a traditional one in which I would help him get ready for this meeting with his father. We located the part who got so upset in George's body; he found it in his solar plexus. It was an odd feeling, hard to describe, but one he knew well. It left him feeling weak in the extremities. I asked how he felt toward this part, and he found some curiosity, but it immediately blended with him and he felt all its feelings. I asked it to unblend to a good conversational distance so we could get to know it. It did, and George was surprised by the change in his feelings and body.

We asked if the part was stuck in a particular scene in the past, and it showed him an infant in a crib. Other parts distrusted this, but we got them to step back.

The infant was terribly alone and frightened. I asked George, "How do you feel toward the infant?" He replied that he felt caring and parental. As we asked the infant to let us know more, its head split open, and this red-and-black raging being came out. It was snarling and writhing. George felt disgust for it. I looked for any parts that were afraid of it; there were none. I got the part who held the disgust to step back. Then we used a ball of light to draw this being out of the baby. We got it separated. The baby was pleased, relieved, happy. He seemed surrounded by light. I asked if there were any strings or cords or connections of any sort between the being and the baby. There were none.

I started addressing the being, and when I got to telling it that we were sending it to a place where there was no punishment or judgment, an angry part of George came up. It wanted that being punished. I welcomed this angry part and said how glad I was that it was showing up. I also told it that its anger was a spear that kept it connected to the being — that this was a trick these beings often use to stay in someone's system. The angry one agreed to step back. George checked and now there was a thin thread like a cord connecting the being with the arch of the baby's left foot. We worked with the baby until it no longer wanted this connection, and the cord dropped away. Then I again addressed the being. I told it that it had been lied to and had almost certainly been told that the light surrounding it would hurt it. I said to the being, "I challenge you to touch the light." It did, and the light did not hurt. I challenged the being to look inside, telling it that it would find light there even though it had been told there was none. It looked and there was light. I told the being again that it had been lied to. I told it we were going to send it to a place where it could heal and grow and find relief. It was willing to go. I told it to take all its employees, minions, slaves, subordinates, and others like it with it. I asked the being to look up and asked what it saw. It said portals of light. Then I asked George to watch until the being and all the others disappeared. They went.

Then we returned to the baby, completed the witnessing, and retrieved it to a safe place in the present time. (It wanted to go to a childhood place, but I encouraged it to come all the way away.) The baby did a huge unburdening. Green slime came out of its body, and stuff came out of its throat. Black tar came out of its feet. The unburdening was long and detailed and thorough. I noticed again how the presence of the UB had prevented a needed process from occurring. Then we invited new qualities to fill the baby.

Then I said, "At times like this after a deep unburdening, there is often an opening for a guide to appear. If it feels right, look for one now." George did and was surprised to see something. He described it as an armored griffin. This made me suspicious — an armored guide? I asked him to ask the griffin's intent. He said it wanted to remove fear from him. More questions followed, and, surprisingly, the griffin appeared to be a real guide. It offered some deep guidance. Then we started working a little with the angry part, but even though George really wanted to continue since that part was present, he was too tired, so we stopped. I talked with him about maintaining contact with the baby and the angry part and about having all his good protectors up for his meeting with his father later that afternoon. We arranged another meeting soon after.

This is some of George's email back to me the next day:

Bob, these notes are great. Thank you so much for yesterday's session. Wow. About 30 minutes before my dad showed up, the land owner where I live, who has gone off the deep end and is addicted to drugs, showed up at my door screaming obscenities at me for no reason. I was able to handle it with total calm and then stayed firmly seated in Self during the whole encounter with my father. After I finished, I went straight to talk to the land owner, who essentially told me that she is preparing for WWIII and that if I am not on board, then I will be considered an adversary. Again, I stayed totally calm and in Self. I finished the conversation and went on a long walk in the woods…. I have never felt so little fear with so much intensity being channeled at me. Our session was truly a godsend. I can only pray that I am able to stay in this state of Self… it feels so good to not be afraid of things. Thank you, Bob, thank you so much for helping me.

Christine's session

Christine's metastatic breast cancer has been bad. She's been having problems with deep vein thrombosis — extreme swelling of her right arm and more. The tumors had returned and were growing in different places. She felt near despair at the start of our session. We went to her image of spirit, which is a small flame; she could find it, but it was still very small. I asked her to focus on it and invite it in. It became bigger and stronger. Then it turned blue, which it had done before. It became a cooling flame.

She had previously mentioned that she thought there was something inside of her that was not part of her system. I asked her to look for that. She had an idea about a child who had died young and was angry about it. We looked and there was this very heavy rock on her right shoulder pushing her forward where the cancers were. I asked her to ask if it was a part of her. It was both a part and not a part. We found a tiny part in there, a very small version of Christine, who was anxious to be rescued; we got it out, and it stood on Christine's palm. Then we asked if there were more parts in there. There were! Many of her parts lived inside the rock. We invited them all out, and they came as she offered them love. We took them out, or she took them into a forest where a big banquet table was set up. They said, "We are free!"

Then we went back to the rock. There were no more of her parts in it. I asked her to surround the rock in a ball of light, get it off of her shoulder, and pull it around in front of her to a good conversational distance. She did this and then wrapped it even more securely in light. I reminded her that these things only have power if they can scare us and that when we're not scared of them, they lose all power. I asked her if there were any cords or connections coming back to her body, and there were. She said, "I'm snipping them." I said, "Oh, please don't. Notice where they touch your body and connect to you." She said, "This is weird, but they seem to attach wherever I have a tumor." I said, "This is not weird. See if there are any parts holding onto this or if everyone is willing to let this go." Her parts said they would be so happy to let this go. So we had them let it go, and all these cords went back into the ball of light. Then we told the being in the ball of light that this was not about punishment or judgment. It was lost and in the wrong place, and we were going to send it to where it could heal. I asked the being to look up and it would see helping beings leaning down. It did. Then I told it to test the light and see if it really hurt or helped. It helped. When we sent the being the rest of the way, it just dissolved. After this, we had her go gather all the kids in from the forest and bring them into their comfortable home. Several times during the session, we had the blue flame light come in and help us. We did this when we were helping those lines detach from the tumor sites.

The next week Christine had a legacy unburdening. This is her account:

I just had the most incredible session with Bob. There was a sense of a fight between light and dark in my body, the dark being on the right and the light being on the left. I thought the anger that was behind the screen on the left was something to be frightened of or that it was dangerous, but in fact I found that it was a source of creativity and strength and life force. As we gave the screen permission to open and the fire to come out, we assured it that it was safe and welcome and that we didn't view it as something bad but something powerful and good. It shone more and more brightly and filled up across the top of my head like a canopy on the left. Then it got stuck as if the dark wouldn't let it go further than the center line because the right was so dark. The darkness on the right felt like a volcanic moving mass of black and gray gurgling away. I emptied it out of my arm. I had to stand up to do this, and I felt like a teapot! It poured out into a golden egg-shaped receptacle.

Bob invited me to allow anything that wasn't mine into the receptacle — any pain or fear or uncertainty that wasn't mine, that was my ancestors' or my parents' or anyone else's — to go into that receptacle. I had stood up at this point, and he invited me to turn around and pass it back to my parents and that they in turn could then pass it back to theirs and to theirs and to theirs right up through the ancestral line right back as far as it went. I had a sense that there were many, many people in the line; they had suffered — some were children and some were soldiers. There had been a lot of war and poverty on both sides of the family and a lot of fear about cold and darkness. They kept on passing it back and back and back and then up into the light above. I took some deep breaths, as did all of us, in this empty state. Then we allowed the light to cascade down from above like a tidal wave, down and down and down through all of us, filling us with warmth and courage and joy. It felt beautiful.

As this happened, I was moving my body and so allowing the golden light to flow through all of my bones and tissues and cells. I went this way and that and folded down through my spine as the golden light poured down my spine; and then I opened my arms so that it could come into my body through my arms, and it came up through from my fingertips (where the darkness had left from) and filled up my heart and my center, and it seemed to join with the fire that I had thought was anger. I described it as awesome in the beginning in the real sense of the word. I felt humbled in its presence. It turns out it was awesome, truly. It joined with the light from above, as it was somehow all the same thing. It was life force, it was energy, it was spirit, it was life, and it was beautiful and eternal. It became easier and easier to move my body in the places that have been so uncomfortable and tight for so long, and it went from the top of my head and the tips of my fingers, right through my body and to the soles of my feet and into the earth. It felt magical and peaceful, and I am so grateful for this experience.

Here is my reply to her account:

Yes, Christine, this seems like a wonderful description. The one point that is missing is the role of the blue flame. I believe we started the session by focusing on this and looking for any part who did not want to welcome it… I'm not sure of this next part, but I believe a part came up who was fearful of the blue flame, and the anger part came up in response to that.

After these two sessions, Christine went to a family gathering, and everyone there remarked on how pleasant it was to be with her and how unusual this family gathering was. She was also feeling much better physically and able to cut her pain meds way down.

Kathy's session

Kathy was a regular client. She started one session by telling me how she had been getting all this feedback that she was too much in her head, too masculine, too domineering, and too controlling. She identified these feelings as coming from a part. We looked for where this part lived in her body. She was aware of it as pressure on her head, like a cap on top of her head or brain. There were hints that it wasn't a part; Kathy used the word *parasite*. When she asked, "Are you a part of me?" it replied, "You wish." There was much more prevarication. Finally after we said, "We don't want to judge you, and we don't want to punish you," it said that no, it wasn't a part. We got a ball of light and pulled the thing out of Kathy's body. She was shocked. It was a woman who had been a supervisor of hers at another job who was very mean, pushy, and narcissistic. She got away with it because she was having an affair with the CEO. This thing was a part of the ex-supervisor. It had been a truly terrible work situation.

This being started lying to us, so we stopped talking with it. I suggested that Kathy pull the light holding the being a little farther away and to look for any connections back to her. There was one to her throat and one under her ribs on the left side of her body. We focused first on the part in her throat. We asked to meet whatever part it was attached to. Kathy extended love toward this part, and it turned to her and released the ex-supervisor. The part on the left side of her ribs looked like a scab with tendrils over most of the left side of the trunk of her body. We got it to lift off. At that point, no connections were still visible.

I asked, "Is anybody in there going to miss this thing when it's gone?" Three or four parts came up. One hated the smell of male genitals and semen; this one came from Kathy's childhood abuse. We promised to come back to this one, and it released the intrusion. Then there was a very angry part. At first I thought this was actually a fragment of the intrusion, but it wasn't. It was a raging part, and it said, "I needed this energy, as I could not protect myself as a child." The part apologized to Kathy, explaining how helpless and trapped it felt. Kathy apologized to it for not being able to protect it back then. I let them both know that this is a classic way that unattached burdens get in: they offer power to the powerless. Then they feed off of them, making them weaker rather than stronger. All her parts were now ready and comfortable letting it go. I said we could send it back to the woman it came from, but it would probably cause much pain in the world. Or we could send it up to the light and healing realms. Kathy knew that this women had two children, so she wanted to send it up. It started going up and wanted to go up, but the woman resisted; she wanted to keep it. It appeared that it would get free of her, but this was not our battle.

Kathy is now entirely free of this being. Many of the parts who had been attached to this being had taken in the belief during their abuse that they could not be beautiful because it would only attract more abuse. With the unattached burden gone, they were willing to get rid of this toxic belief. This took a while. We promised to return to the one who was bothered by the smell of male genitals in our next session.

Donna's session

Donna specifically came to work on a critter. This is the original name for UBs in IFS, and it's the word Donna used. We need to use whatever language the client prefers. The critter first appeared behind bars with his hand on the bars, shaking them hard. He seemed threatening and big. We looked for any parts that were frightened of it and found a part in her neck that had choking sensations. This part felt that the critter was attached to it by suction cups, one on the front of her chest and one on the back. She felt immobilized by this. We looked inside to see how this was attached and whom it was attached to. When we met these parts, we asked them how old they thought Donna was. They said nineteen. We had her update them. After they realized that Donna was an adult, they trusted her enough to release the suction cups. Then we pulled the critter out of her body and surrounded it in light. We told it that this was not about punishment or judgment in any way but that it was in the wrong place and we were going to help it go where it needed to be. The critter expressed regret and remorse that it had attached to her and had done her damage. It was ready to go. Donna said, "Can it be this easy? I was expecting a real shit show." We ask the critter to take all of its employees, minions, subordinates, and allies with it. It was sort of dubious and shrugged.

Donna had the correct intuition and knew there was something more. As we sent this one away up to the light and healing, we asked, "Who sent you?" There was a big, dark energy. We focused on this, surrounding it in light and moving the light away from her body. I asked if there were any cords connecting this to her. There were some cords, but they all fell short and didn't touch her. Some part of her was concerned about this being's leaving, but we developed a good relationship between this part and Donna's Self. When we asked this part, it thought she was twelve years old. When updated to her real, fully adult, status, this part attached to her and was willing to let the critter go.

As this critter went off, another appeared. Once again, Donna had parts that were attached to it. This time they were afraid they would be so alone without it. She remembered a time in her childhood when there were no other children around to play with. Her family had lived isolated way out in the woods. When we asked this part how old it thought Donna was, it said eight. When we updated it, it could develop trust in Donna's Self, and it became willing to cheerfully let go of this critter. This one went up to the healing realms. When asked to scan her system again for anything that was not part of her, Donna found a little tiny one. Again with really good intuition, she knew it was important to get this one out, too. Very often some tiny thing like this is left behind to allow an opening back into the system for the others. We got this little one up into the healing realms, too.

Then I asked her if she could breathe her Self bigger than the three parts she had met who had connected to the critters and asked if all three would unblend from her for a little while. I asked her how she felt toward all three of them. She felt much love and care. With all of this Self on board, I told her that very often this was a good time to invite in guides. She met a guide she had not met before. This guide was a woman of love, almost a flower child. I asked about guides partially because it often helps to fill the empty spaces in someone's system with positive guidance or good qualities. This helps prevent any return of the critters.

Donna wrote me an email the next day. "Thank you so much for our session, it was mind-boggling, fantastic, shocking, exciting, and very settling." One interesting sidenote here is that as we went deeper and deeper into her system, her parts thought she was younger and younger. This is fairly typical, and as usual when the parts were updated to her real age, it was much easier for them to trust her.

I really wish I had written up this session right away, but I didn't have time. I enter such a dreamlike state doing these sessions that my memory is often compromised if I don't record them immediately. Donna said that she would send me copies of her notes and that I could use this material in classes or in writing later.

Donna's notes:

The first part I noticed was incredibly afraid and stuck — like it couldn't go forward or backward or left or right. The suction cups certainly felt like they were not part of the part — kind of like when you ask how much of this is yours and how much is a legacy. It was 100% not the part's.

Worry and concern around letting the suction cups go, but the more I was able to have the part turn to me, the quieter it got. Once the UB showed up and felt badly and remorseful, it was even easier for the UB to go to the light. It shot up there like Mighty Mouse — quick and with vigor! It was the only UB that did that so quickly. (I think this part below was not mentioned in your notes.)

The second part is a part that feels so much tension and fear that it turns to food. It was very frustrated by its own responses but was unaware there were other options. It felt stuck in this loop of fear, tension, worry, and then some sort of minor relief with grabbing a snack. We listened to this part and had it feel into me for reassurance, and also the being surrounded by light seemed quite a bit less daunting to this part. This UB was released up to the sky, surrounded by light.

The third part was shaking due to the intensity of this UB. Bob had asked the previous UB, "Who sent you?" This UB showed up these past few weeks shaking and clamoring at these metal bars to "release itself." It was furious and scary. Once we had Self there and surrounded it with light, the part it attached to settled a bit, and I gave it comfort and support, this UB apologized for being so difficult.

The fourth part told a story of being a latchkey kid for a LONG time. Our family house was out in nature with no neighbors for at least half a mile or so. This part had attached to the UB, which was a small, hot, red burning sensation in the left side of my throat — many of the UBs were in my throat. We surrounded it in light and slowed the process down, and had the seven- or eight-year-old say goodbye to the UB and send it up to the sky. This took longer than the other three. It felt as though this part had minions and staff, etc., with it for sure. This UB shrugged its shoulders, kind of like "It is what it is, and it ain't my fault." The process was hard for the part that had attached to it, but the part realized that it could be with me and other parts — it just wanted to know someone saw it and knew that it was there and wished to be with other parts, which we had happen. Compared to Mighty Mouse, this was SSLLLLOOOWWW motion.

CHAPTER 9

Other Modern Therapies

I have already mentioned how many modern therapists have felt the need to conceal the spiritual nature of their work. Jung and Assagioli, even though far more courageous than their contemporaries, kept much back. If spirituality in general has been difficult for professional therapy, the stuff we are working with — UBs and guides — is the third rail of the field, an area better left ignored. The increasing globalization of psychotherapy is having an unintended positive effect here. As we Westerners work more and more with non-Westerners (for example, Islamic immigrants to England who consider jinn possession to be a major cause of mental illness), we are forced to make at least a little room for these ideas. As Stafford Betty wrote, "Much of the world is mystified by the West's refusal to acknowledge the existence of spirits and takes a dim view of any therapy that excludes spiritual healing from the picture. It is possible that the West took a backward step long ago when, under the spell of scientific materialism, it dogmatically refused to give spirits their due. Millions of us might have been harmed by this refusal" (Betty 2005, 25). I work with some people in Mexico, and one educated woman there said she didn't know why we Yankees were so uptight about this. In her words, "Down here, these are as common as tacos."

Most Western academics assumed that as our "advanced" culture spread, possession cults would die out. There was even a feeling among anthropologists that they needed to rush to study them before the last of them were gone. But this has proven to be dead wrong. The numbers and vitalities of these possession-based religions are growing worldwide! Therefore, this is not some quaint and curious relic of "primitive" peoples that is only of interest to the antiquarian — it is a living, growing, vibrant reality for many people all over the world. As uncomfortable and disturbing as it may be, it is not something to be ignored or swept aside lightly.

Carl Jung, MD

Let's start with Carl Jung, probably the most overtly spiritual of any of the big-name psychotherapists in the last several hundred years and, not coincidentally, still the least taught in colleges and graduate schools. The *Red Book*, which he took steps to keep from publication until long after his death, is the key here.

Right after his break from Freud, Jung turned inward, and by his own account, what he discovered there was so powerful that he feared for his sanity. He said it was only the regularity of his life — family, work, responsibility — that kept him sane. In his inner world, he met many beings who were conscious, had a will and an agency of their own, and often had access to deeper wisdom than anything he knew. He dialogued and interacted with these beings, and these relationships had great emotional and spiritual power. He said that all the rest of his life's work sprang from these visions.

Jung crafted the *Red Book* starting in 1915 and ending perhaps as late as 1930. He died in 1961. Therefore, all of his mature work, which is what has earned him fame and respect, comes from these visionary experiences that emerged from his inner world — the collective unconscious, the daimonic, primary imagination, mundis imaginalis, the transliminal, the spirit realm, or whatever we choose to call it. Jung wrote toward the end of his life that "I prefer the term 'unconscious,' knowing that I might equally speak of God or daimon…" (quoted in Voss and Rowlandson 2013, 377). It is significant that he formed relationships with these denizens of his mind. He had conversations with them, he interacted with them, and he experienced them as autonomous. He did not analyze or think about them; rather, he related to them. Hillman suggested that Jung's great contribution to self-knowledge is to reanimate the possibility of dialogue with daimons (1983, 55). This took him to a realm that offered wisdom and health but also threatened insanity and psychosis. In IFS terms, we could describe these experiences in terms of UBs and guides.

Jung's psychology clearly recognized the multiplicity of mind. What he called complexes are analogous to what IFS calls parts. They are fragments — subpersonalities that can take over a person and cause them to think and act differently. One person who was at the Jung Institute in Zurich reported that students there would often accuse each other, "You are in your complex." This semi-hostile confrontation is similar to IFS's recognition that we all get hijacked by parts. This fundamental dynamic — the person being taken over by a part — is the same as the fundamental dynamic of possession.

Craig Stephenson, a prominent and well-respected Jungian, has written an entire book forcefully arguing that Jung's understanding of possession is the basis of all of his psychology — the linchpin of his thinking. "Possession is the ubiquitous concept with which he formulates ideas about this dynamic between an ego-consciousness and autonomous unconscious, and it allows him, in turn, to convey phenomenologically the power of neurotic and psychotic symptoms (Stephenson 2017). In denying this reality, our culture pathologizes the ordinary. Our ideology makes us fragile and ill. In IFS we know, and work daily with, the fact that people are made up of parts, which are often at war with each other, so perhaps we are more open to these realities than most. Roland Littlewood (2004b) proposes that instead of trying to analyze non-Western experiences of possession in terms of dissociative disorders, we should turn this around and seek to understand dissociative disorders in terms of the broader cross-cultural understanding of possession. This feels like a positive example of what Indigenous psychotherapists refer to as decolonizing therapy.

Jung wrote of a troubled patient, "Instead of allowing himself to be convinced once more that the daimon is an illusion, he ought to experience once more the reality of this illusion. He should learn to acknowledge these psychic forces anew and not wait until his moods, nervous states, and delusions make it clear in the most powerful way that he is not the only master in his house. His dissociative tendencies are actual psychic personalities… they are real…" (quoted in Stephenson 2017, 124).

Jung often chose deliberately ambiguous and equivocal language to stay respectable. He thought that "the unconscious" was "too neutral and rational a term," but he wouldn't use "daimon" or "God" because that would provoke too much controversy (ibid., 103). Denying the reality of possession makes us more brittle and more vulnerable. Jung noted that the work with these autonomous contents is often in dialogue form — it is relational. He recognized that there are at least two levels from which we must be dispossessed: the personal with its shadow, and beings of the collective unconscious who are somehow outside, beyond, or greater than us.

The following long quote from Jung illustrates how pervasive the idea of possession was in his thinking and describes his feelings about Freud after Freud's death:

> In the course of the personal friendship which bound me to Freud for many years, I was permitted a deep glimpse into the mind of this remarkable man. He was a man possessed by a daemon —a man who had been vouchsafed an overwhelming revelation that took possession of his soul and never let him go. It was the encounter with Charcot's ideas that called awake in him that primal image of a soul in the grip of a daemon, and kindled that passion for knowledge which was to lay open a dark continent to his gaze. He felt he had the key to the murky abysses of the possessed psyche. He wanted to unmask as illusion what the "absurd superstition" of the past took to be a devilish incubus, to whip away the disguises worn by the evil spirit and turn him back into

a harmless poodle — in a word, reduce him to a "psychological formula." He believed in the power of the intellect; no Faustian shutterings tempered the hubris of his undertaking. He once said to me, "I only wonder what neurotics will do in the future when all their symbols have been unmasked. It will then be impossible to have a neurosis." He expected enlightenment to do everything — his favorite quotation was Voltaire's "Crush the Monster." From this sentiment there grew up his astonishing knowledge and understanding of any morbid psychic material, which he smelled out under a hundred disguises and was able to bring to light with truly unending patience. Ludwig Klages' saying that "the spirit is the adversary of the soul" might serve as a cautionary motto for the way Freud approached the possessed psyche. Whenever he could he dethroned the spirit as the possessing and repressing agent by reducing it to a "psychological formula." Spirit, for him, was just a "nothing but." In a crucial talk with him I once tried to get him to understand the admonition: "Try the spirits whether they are of God" (1 John 4:1). In vain. Thus fate had to take its course. For one can fall victim to possession if one does not understand betimes why one is possessed. One should ask oneself for once: why has this idea taken possession of me? What does that mean in regard to myself? A modest doubt like this can save us from falling headfirst into the idea and vanishing forever. Freud's "psychological formula" is only an apparent substitute for the demonically vital thing that causes a neurosis. In reality only the spirit can cast out the "spirits" — not the intellect, which is at best a minor assistant. (Jung 1966, 48–49)

Paul Levy is a modern student of Jungian thought who has developed this work by focusing on *wetiko*. This is the name of an evil spirit recognized by many Indigenous peoples here in North America, for example, the Cree and Ojibwe. This name has been transliterated into English in at least twenty different ways; *wendigo* might be the most common spelling. It is mainly found in Eastern forest peoples up around the Great Lakes and out into the Northern Plains. The wetiko spirit has a stinking, gaunt, human form and is often seen as a giant with a heart of ice. It has insatiable hunger and greed, and is cannibalistic. Like Buddhist hungry ghosts, it could never feel full. This spirit most often appeared in late winter, when famine and starvation were common for many of these tribes. People who were possessed by wetiko would no longer share anything. They would eat everything and kill others to eat them. Mostly, this possession was considered incurable, and the possessed person was killed. We know this is real because court records date back to the late 1800s in Canada in which medicine men accused of murder defended themselves unsuccessfully by saying they had to murder the person because that person had wetiko. Jack Forbes, in his 1978 book *Columbus and Other Cannibals*, suggested that the entire white race was possessed by wetiko. Forbes's ideas were influential for many First Nations peoples.

There is a very interesting parallel to this in the Andes, in South America — the *pishtaco*. This creature is an evil, fat-sucking being who is always seen as being a foreigner, a stranger, an outsider. There are no records of stories or myths about pishtacos from before the Spanish conquest, so this may well be a symbolization of cultural trauma. It is often depicted as a white male with facial hair and a lamprey-like appendage on its mouth to help it suck human fat. The Natives accused the conquistadors of harvesting human fat to grease their weapons. Factory owners were later accused of being pishtacos and harvesting human fat to grease their machines. Like the wetiko, the pishtaco is characterized by unending greed and hunger. We will meet a similar being, the phii pob, when we talk about spirit possession in Thailand.

Paul Levy interprets this idea that our culture is possessed by wetiko through the lens of Jungian thought and Tibetan Buddhism. Levy himself was hospitalized for psychosis but now, for many years, has been productive, healthy, and not taking any medications. Some people tend to discredit anyone with this kind of history, but I believe we should listen even more closely; he has been on the front lines, has been in the belly of the beast and walked the edge. Levy points out that in Jung's thought, autonomous complexes, and even more so archetypes, have a luminous quality; they appear sacred. They feel like spirits or daimons. They also behave like autonomous foreign bodies. He points out that people can be possessed by ideas, singularly or as a group. Millions have been killed for ideas. He says this kind of possession happens to all of us; therefore, we need these words back in our vocabulary. Psychologist Rollo May called the daimonic "any natural function which has the power to take over the whole person." Many believe this can be creative or destructive and can happen to a person, a group, or a nation.

Levy says that wetiko is a contagious psychospiritual disease of the soul, a parasite of the mind, a virus of the mind, a vampire. Repeatedly, he emphasizes that it is our refusal to see this being that gives it power. This echoes the old idea that evil's greatest triumph is to make people believe that it does not exist. This underscores the importance of our opening our minds to consider these possession states. He also states that once you are aware of wetiko, it loses power. Fear is its base of operation. This closely echoes IFS's first step in dealing with UBs: helping the parts who held fear to feel safe. Levy also says that wetiko can only thrive where there is a strong sense of separateness of each person. This echoes the Polish exorcist Father Tom's emphasis on the power of isolation and separation in creating victims for possession. When we realize the dreamlike nature of reality, the non-local field in which we are contained, and that all is relational, interdependent existence, wetiko cannot take root. This echoes my belief that we need a much more porous model of mind for resilient mental health. Refusing to see wetiko or evil feeds them. As Jung said, making the darkness conscious, not focusing on beings of light, is the way to enlightenment. This echoes the kenotic process of IFS (I will discuss kenosis in detail later).

More positively, Levy points out that wetiko and possession can be great teachers. Encoded in the dark is the real light. Jesus confronted the devil for forty days. Buddha had to confront Mara. Both of these great awakenings came out of direct experience of evil. Rudolph Steiner said that for the Christ to reincarnate in our era, we must first encounter radical evil, which he called the Beast. The dynamic or metaphor of possession and the necessity of facing evil and our own shadow are essential for Jung and his followers.

Wilson Van Dusen, PhD, and Jerry Marzinsky, EdM

Wilson Van Dusen (1923–2005) is another modern thinker who worked in this area. He was a PhD clinical psychologist who mainly worked with hospitalized psychotic people. He was a deep student of Swedenborg's work and a mentor and teacher to my friend and teacher the Reverend Rachel Rivers, whom I mentioned earlier. Van Dusen had the revolutionary idea of holding conversations with the voices his psychotic patients heard. Most people in the academic and professional hierarchy considered this taboo. They saw it as colluding with and encouraging patients' delusions. Therapists could lose their jobs and licenses through this kind of behavior, but Van Dusen was relatively secure because he held a senior position at a big state hospital with long-term patients. As he dialogued with these voices, he came to divide them into two categories, which he at first called lower- and higher-order hallucinations. This was perhaps based on his desire to remain at least somewhat academically acceptable. Later, he called them lower- and higher-order spirits.

This division echoes IFS's separation of UBs and guides. It also validates the utility of Isabel Clarke's use of the term *transliminal*. Once we cross that threshold, we are open to a vast array of influences, both negative and positive. Swedenborg, in his highly religious seventeenth-century language, called these beings demons and angels. By dialoguing and interacting with these hallucinations — spirits — Van Dusen was able to help severely disturbed people find some peace. The patients often knew that if they discussed these voices with most professionals, they would be even further stigmatized, so they kept quiet. They were left to struggle with these very difficult and often overwhelming inner relationships by themselves. Van Dusen's ideas were ahead of his time, and sadly, as is the case with many pioneers, his work has not gotten the recognition and study it deserves.

One person who picked up on the work of Van Dusen is Jerry Marzinsky, a licensed psychotherapist with about thirty-five years of experience working with psychosis. Marzinsky cites the *Wiley-Blackwell Handbook of Transpersonal Psychology* in support of his claim that interest in traditional transpersonal psychology is waning, but interest in spiritual psychotherapy (which focuses more on spiritual contact experiences) is rising. Marzinsky, while working in a mental institution, started dialoguing with the voices in his clients' heads. He came to the attention of his superiors because he was getting results. They were appalled by what he was doing and ordered him to stop. He quit that position and then began working in a prison for people who were criminally insane. Here no one interfered with his work because, as he said, they did not care much about his clients — the prisoners. Marzinsky went further than Van Dusen in print; he said that the voices were real and that they were conscious parasitic entities that feed on peoples' energies, especially their emotional distress.

Marzinsky's method of working with these negative forces was the first to show over and over again that they were unmitigated liars. Most of his patients had tried at first to just ignore the voices, but the voices would only get louder. He advised them not to block out the voices but rather to watch the thoughts from a distance. He stated that the probability of recovery depended most heavily on each patient's interpretation of these voices. He broke these interpretations down into three groups. The first group, which had the best prognosis, concluded that the voices did not belong to them and instead were invaders. The second group suspected the voices did not belong to them but had a hard time believing it. (This idea does go against almost everything our culture tells us.) The third group, which was the least likely to recover, could not distinguish outside voices. These patients believed that every thought in their head was theirs. As Marzinsky says, "Unfortunately, this debilitating, hopeless, and destructive interpretation was the only one psychiatry insisted was the truth" (2019, 121). Radical pragmatism points us clearly to the first of these beliefs. If it helps our patients, we should encourage it, even if it is very uncomfortable and disconcerting for us. We are in the midst of a mental health epidemic; our mental health care system is an expensive failure. These stark facts should help us open our minds to radically new approaches. Here is an example from among the Zulu: "The shaman does not view the patient's state of mind as being detached from reality, but rather as a reflection of an internal spiritual crisis requiring as much respect and acknowledgment as physiological illness. If you bar the way to the Itongo [ancestral spirits that cause the spiritual sickness], you will be killing the patient. For he will not be an in-yanga [diviner-shaman], neither will he be a man again; he will become delicate and become a fool and he will be unable to understand anything" (Rojas 2021). The Zulu description of what happens when you block access to the inner voices certainly looks like the fate of people we label "mentally ill." Doesn't it?

Mad Pride and Hearing Voices

Marzinsky's negative attitude toward the mental health establishment leads us to another area that we can only briefly discuss: the psychiatric survivors, Mad Pride, and Hearing Voices movements. The psychiatric survivors movement was strong in the early seventies, but by the late nineties it was largely succeeded by the Mad Pride movement. The word *insane* is one of the most pejorative terms in the English language. One anthropologist compared the diagnosis of schizophrenia to a traditional tribal curse. The diagnosis tells someone that their brain is broken, there is no hope of recovery, and their suffering is meaningless. If the patient accepts this label, which, after all, comes from a trusted medical authority figure, it has the same effect as a traditional curse. It robs them of hope, meaning, and a good life. The Mad Pride writers insist that they have a right to be different from others, to hear voices and see visions no one else sees, and to interact with spirit beings. Some insist that those who are mad are superior to ordinary people. We already know that those who score high on the Schizotypy and Psychoticism Scales are also more creative. R. D. Laing, back in the sixties, said that these people were often more sensitive and spiritually aware. These attitudes find a cross-cultural echo in Morocco. Stefania Pandolfo (2018) describes how a young Moroccan with a severe mental disorder is caught between modern psychiatric logic and a culture that is in agony. She suggests that those who are mad may be the mourners of this culture, and the madness may be a form of deep witnessing. Islam takes the idea of *al-gayb*, the invisible world, very seriously. Pandolfo does not try to reduce "the other" to something familiar and unthreatening. There is a term, *hala*, which means both mental illness and an altered mystical state. She talks of this as an organ of active perception of super-sensible realities. The visionaries — those who are mad — have messages if we could only learn to listen to them.

Seth Farber (2012) reminds us that homosexuality was considered a diagnosable mental illness until the 1970s. Many of the spiritual presence experiences now diagnosed as mad are actually "dangerous gifts" that deserve respect. This change in attitude will help people find meaning in their experience and lead useful lives. It would also help society welcome their creativity and visionary capacities. We need to learn how to welcome and learn from these non-ordinary experiences instead of pretending they don't exist or are just the result of a broken brain. Farber (ibid., 120) quotes R. D. Laing, "The condition of alienation, of being asleep, of being unconscious, of being out of one's mind is the condition of the normal man. Society highly values its normal man. It educates children to lose themselves and to become absurd, and thus to be normal. Normal men have killed perhaps 100,000,000 of their fellow normal men in the last fifty years." So who is insane? "Psychosis" and spiritual experience are very close. As Joseph Campbell has been quoted as saying, the mystic swims in the water where the mad man drowns. (This quote appears in many different forms and is attributed to many different thinkers.) We need to broaden our very narrow range of what are considered acceptable and potentially valued psychological experiences. Just as our culture used to judge and diagnose homosexuality as a mental illness, we now judge and diagnose whole ranges of visionary and spiritual contact experiences that many other cultures value despite their difficulty. This needs to stop.

The Hearing Voices Movement is similar and overlaps in many ways. They rightly insist that hearing voices is not an indicator of mental illness; many normal people hear voices, and some greatly value these interactions. Between 3 and 10 percent of the general population hears voices fairly regularly, and about 75 percent of the general population has experienced hearing voices at least once in their life. Socrates led his life based on what the voice in his head — his daimon — told him. Many people, when grieving, hear the voices of their deceased loved ones and treasure these experiences. Visionaries and prophets throughout history and across cultures hear voices, and often what the voices tell them changes history dramatically. Think of Muhammad or Jesus or Moses or Joan of Arc or many, many others. It can be a difficult experience to hear voices no one else hears, but it also can be a wonderful, life-transforming experience.

The Hearing Voices Movement was started by Professor Marius Romme, a Dutch psychiatrist, back in the late 1980s. There are now active groups in over twenty countries. The groups do not impose any theory about what the voices are; they focus on helping people live well with the voices. This is a parallel with the expectation in many traditional cultures that once someone is possessed by a spirit, this will continue for their whole life. They do not get rid of this contact; instead, they learn how to manage and work with it so it is beneficial or at the very least neutral. This is true, for example, in the Zār cults of North Africa, voodoo in Haiti, and Umbanda in Brazil. The research to date indicates that many people who attend Hearing Voices groups have fewer rehospitalizations and better outcomes than those who don't. Our rigid Western insistence that we silence or ignore these voices causes suffering. When they are accepted and interacted with, this suffering can be lessened.

William James, PhD

Let's go back a little in time to William James (1842–1910), whose ideas of radical pragmatism and radical empiricism have inspired my basic approach to all this material. James founded the psychology department at Harvard and is one of the great thinkers in American philosophy and psychology. Perhaps this gravitas will help even the most skeptical to pause and consider his words. His great classic book *The Varieties of Religious Experience* consisted of his written version of the Gifford lectures, which he delivered in 1901 and 1902 in Edinburgh, Scotland. He gave another series of lectures, the Lowell lectures of 1896, in his native Boston; these are titled "On Exceptional Mental States." James never produced a written version of these, but in 1982, Eugene Taylor and a team of mostly Harvard scholars published a reconstruction of the lectures based on notes, reviews, and other materials. Some people find James's formal, nineteenth-century academic language in the Edinburgh lectures a barrier to his thought. Taylor's reconstruction is in clear, concise, readable, modern English and gives us an easier place to be introduced to the thought of this great man. One of these eight lectures was titled "On Possession." James said, "But the obsolescence of the public belief in possession by demons is a very strange thing in Christian lands when one considers that it is one of the most articulately expressed doctrines of both testaments and… it reigned for 1,700 years hardly challenged in all the churches. Every land and every age has exhibited the fact on which this belief was founded. China, India, Egypt, Africa, Polynesia, Greece, Rome, and all of Medieval Europe believed that certain nervous disorders were of supernatural origin, inspired by Gods and the sacred; or by demons" (Taylor 1982, 94).

According to Taylor's research and reconstruction, the main point of James's lectures was that the demon possession of old has been transformed into modern mediumship; that which was seen as a diabolical cause of psychopathology is now seen as a gateway for personal growth, healing, and spiritual or philosophical knowledge. James strongly underlines this idea — that this transformation is in large part due to the fact that these experiences are now viewed less alarmingly and with optimism. He is pointing to an important theme for us: the way a culture or era holds this kind of experience — the belief structure around it — determines in large part whether it is healing or harmful.

James thought the most important impact his lectures could have would be to change the medical establishment's attitude. "The first thing is to start the medical profession out of its idiotically *conceited ignorance* of all such matters — matters which have everywhere and at all times played a vital part in human history" (Taylor 1982, 110). This is a direct quote from a letter James wrote in

1897, and the italics are his. Sadly, medical attitudes have perhaps gotten even worse since his day. James also wrote, "The refusal of the modern enlightenment to treat possession as a hypothesis to be spoken of even as possible in spite of the massive human tradition based on the concrete experience in its favor, has always seemed to me a curious example of the power of fashion in things scientific. That the demon theory will have its innings again is to my mind absolutely certain" (quoted in Baldwin 1992, 24).

James was much impressed by the work of the Reverend John Nevius, DDiv, which was published in 1892 (Nevius 2020). Nevius was a protestant missionary to China for many years and was fluent in spoken and written Chinese. Nevius did not believe in possession when he arrived in China, but he soon became aware that many of the Chinese Christians were using the Bible and the Christian religion to cast demons out from other Chinese people and were thereby winning many new converts. This was disconcerting to him, to say the least, and he investigated and saw that it often seemed to work and to relieve human suffering. After experiencing casting out demons himself, he sent circular letters to all the other missionaries in China, almost all of whom had similar experiences. Seventy percent of them had come to believe in possession and reevaluate their faith. After all, there are many accounts of Jesus casting out demons in the New Testament. The remaining thirty percent did not change their opinions. Nevius also compiled accounts of possessions from missionaries all over Asia, many of which make for very dramatic reading.

Some thirty or forty years later, Dr. R. Kenneth McAll had a similar experience. Many years later, he wrote,

> In the 1930s when I was a missionary surgeon in the interior of China, devil possession was not uncommon, though the diagnosis could sometimes have been in question. The only treatment offered to those possessed was death by stoning unless the case occurred within reach of a Christian community, in which case villagers would send for the highly trained and extraordinarily fearless bible woman who would lay hands on the victim, pray and release him. The effect was always immediate. At the time, I was afraid of the whole subject, dismissing it as primitive. However, over the next few years, during which I spent varying periods of time in communist and later Japanese hands [he was imprisoned before and during the Second World War in horrendous conditions], I found myself quite shaken by the transformation of some of these people who were obviously in the grip of evil and by the fact that it was our prayers which had initiated the cure. (Montgomery 1975, 268–69)

Later, when McAll was back in England, he worked as a psychiatrist for many years. To his surprise, he discovered cases that involved possession and hauntings, and was able to work with them successfully. McAll is most remembered for his work with intergenerational trauma and healing the family tree. His work with possessions has largely been ignored.

James was also fascinated by mass possessions and how this phenomenon is contagious. He cites one that occurred in the Italian town of Monte Verzegnis in 1878. It started with a woman who had a severe convulsive crisis. Soon, more than forty people were experiencing these crises. After many exorcisms, it finally subsided. James also cites a case of imitative cholera among a group of soldiers in a hospital suffering from wounds during the American Civil War. Perhaps this was an early example of PTSD. Another case was the epidemic of Morzine, which started when one young girl saw another young girl die by drowning and developed convulsive seizures. Many other young girls were afflicted, and then adults had the seizures as well. It went on for over a decade, and there were well over a hundred clearly recognized and documented cases. We will return to this subject of mass possession and the contagious nature of these experiences later.

One more point before we leave James. He describes the fox cult in Japan at some length. This is a possession cult; fox spirits would take a person, and special treatment was required to remove them. There are similar fox cults in China and Korea. In China, they have been illegal and intermittently suppressed for a thousand years. It's cheap and easy to sniff and sneer at these "primitive superstitions," but this arrogance prevents us from learning anything. Why would people persist in doing something that exposed them to persecution for hundreds and hundreds of years? There must be something of great value in it for them. Our reflexive contempt precludes us from understanding the real significance of these patterns. In addition to the outright religious approaches of exorcism and deliverance, which have continued unabated, a few isolated therapists have consistently worked with possession states and developed their own unique ways of handling them. For example, Carl Wickland, MD, published a book in 1924 describing his thirty years of working with spirits.

Multiple Personality Disorder

The next major expression of interest from psychotherapy professionals came from some of the doctors who courageously explored and treated multiple personality disorder and trauma in the 1970s and 1980s. It's almost hard to conceive now, but back then the major graduate schools that trained therapists taught that child sexual abuse almost never happened and was not significant. They ignored all trauma as a cause of psychological distress. It took a few rebellious psychiatrists and therapists to shake the medical establishment awake. I'm old enough to remember this era and the scorn and contempt that were poured on the therapists who were courageous enough to believe what their clients told them. Even the diagnosis of PTSD was vehemently resisted by the academy and only got into the *Diagnostic and Statistical Manual of Mental Disorders* because of the political pressure that came out of the Vietnam veterans' rap groups. One psychiatrist, Dr. Robert Jay Lifton, believed these men and helped organize this effort. The academics understandably want this shameful era and how spectacularly wrong they were to be forgotten or at least downplayed. Perhaps it was the contentious nature of the times and the fact that many therapists completely lost faith in the field's experts and professors that opened the door so these pioneers could also consider the subject of possession.

Ralph Allison, MD, is perhaps the clearest and most explicit example (Allison 1980). He is most famous for his work on trauma, dissociation, and multiple personality disorder (now known as dissociative identity disorder), but he clearly believed in possession. He described five grades of it. Grade 1 is usually described in psychiatric terms as obsessive-compulsive disorder or addictions. Grade 2 is the result of the person being under the influence of a negative alter personality, a negative part of an MPD's system. Allison rightly points out that many of these cases would have been treated as an evil spirit invasion, and he shows how much better it is to help the patient reintegrate the alter. Grade 3 possession occurs "when the controlling influence seems to be the mind of another living human being" (1980, 198). This could be what traditional societies view as witchcraft. Grade 4 possession is control by the spirit of a dead human. This seems equivalent to Dr. Tramont's earthbound spirits — the souls of dead people who have lost their way. These will be discussed more later. Grade 5 is control by a spirit who has never had a life of its own and who often identifies as an agent of evil.

Allison states that these beings are not parts or alters of people with multiple personality disorder. Alters have a purpose — they handle an emotion or situation, and they were created at a specific time, which is not the case with these spirits. Allison, like almost all of these moderns, relies on radical pragmatism. "I can only reiterate my own belief that an effective doctor must use whatever methods benefit the patient most. In my own cases, this has often entailed the utilization of techniques that are bizarre, unorthodox, and even religious in nature. But these methods have successfully cured many patients, and the patient's welfare must be the only concern" (1980, 200).

Allison is perhaps the most courageous and explicit in print, but many doctors and therapists back then thought and wrote about possession. An entire issue of *Dissociation*, the official journal of the International Society for the Study of Trauma and Dissociation (Volume VI, December 4, 1993) was devoted to possession. The impressive array of scholars (more degrees than a thermometer!) agree with much that we have already seen: (1) possession-like phenomena occur all over the world and in all areas of history; (2) possession states are a psychobiological capacity available in all societies; (3) possession states are desirable and normal or pathologized and scorned, which reflects whether the society values them or marginalizes them; and (4) nineteenth-century mediumship and twentieth-century channeling are in the tradition of possession.

What is original in this volume of the journal is two studies reporting on the use of exorcism with MPD patients. Both studies had terrible results. Elizabeth Bowmann, MD, reviewed nineteen MPD patients who were exorcised. There was an 80 percent negative response and nine hospitalizations after the exorcisms. George Frazer, MD, had seven patients who were exorcised, all with negative outcomes. Two comments here: (1) The first rule in the IFS approach to unattached burdens is to make certain that it is not a part, or an alter in the case of a DID/MPD patient, as a mistake here can cause disaster. (2) Exorcism, which is often confrontative, hostile, and violent, is not a good way to deal with this, even when one is sure there is something in a client's system that does not belong to them. All of these authors knew they were treading on taboo ground; they were careful to document and footnote their work. So many therapists today have seen evidence of something like possession but keep their mouths shut out of fear of seeming weird or gullible as well as fear of being shunned. It is good to see that sometimes this unspoken prohibition is defied. As it became known that I was interested in this topic, many therapists approached me with their stories but asked me fearfully not to mention their names.

William Baldwin, DDS, PhD

Now let's turn to more modern researchers and healers who have none of James's academic position and power. William Baldwin was a dentist (yes, a dentist) in Southern California in the 1970s who learned hypnosis in part for pain control in his dental practice. He began to run into strange and fascinating things. Baldwin gave up dentistry, went back to graduate school, and got a doctorate in psychology. He developed what he called Spirit Releasement Therapy. He has left us two books, one an account of his work and the other a training manual. He has also left us some hard-to-find recordings of some of his workshops. The spirit release forum, based in England, developed out of this work. They used to hold annual conferences, but COVID has derailed this. They do offer online trainings, however. The work of David Furlong, Terence Palmer, Alan Sanderson, and Sue Allen is in this tradition.

Baldwin, like William James and like me, practices radical pragmatism. He wrote, "The therapist must work with whatever material, energies, whatever memories, and images are presented by the client. The map is not the territory; the description is not the experience. ... As the client perceives the therapist as safe and accepting in the face of disclosing such improbable information, deeper subconscious material will surface for processing" (Baldwin 1993, 53). "The conscious mind often judges the subconscious material as unbelievable and censors the narrative. This interferes with the therapeutic process" (ibid., 69). "The therapist must work within the paradigm which emerges as if it were real. At some level of consciousness, it is real for the client." "As a therapist, I am sensitive to the client's feelings, memories, and experiences no matter how far from consensus reality the stories range. I have seen and listened to human pain; it is real... A large part of human experience lies outside the parameters of the scientific method" (2003, xxiii).

Baldwin divided his work into three areas: past-life therapy, spirit releasement therapy, and recovery of soul fragments. The soul fragment work is like IFS's basic parts work, and spirit releasement is like IFS's UB work. Just as IFS relies on the client's Self as the center of healing, Baldwin works with what he calls the client's higher self. He is more radically spiritual. In his words, "The basics for spirit releasement therapy is the certainty that all God created — all God-created beings — contain the eternal, indestructible spark of light. All else is illusion and transitory" (2003, 86). This is different language for IFS's assertion that everyone, no matter how traumatized, has a Self that is undamaged and undirtied. Baldwin also names many guides as universal — the archangel Michael, warrior angels of light, and more. Much of his material is way beyond my belief structure and most likely yours as well. However, let's apply radical pragmatism and see what we can learn from him by bracketing our disbelief. He had a large following in his day and many clients who were grateful for his work. Many other therapists and healers have learned from him, which suggests that there must be something of real value here. I have tried some of his techniques many times, and they've worked. For example, he suggests dialoguing extensively with a UB because it is likely to know of others in the person's system and can help us find them. He said that UBs frequently come in groups.

Two of Baldwin's weirdest ideas that are consistently helpful are the two interventions he makes when a spirit is reluctant to leave. He tells the spirit that it has been lied to and told that light will hurt it terribly; then he challenges the spirit to touch the light and see for itself. When the spirit, often with a lot of goading, does touch the light, it finds it to be neutral or pleasant. I have tried this often with clients, and it works. This is important because it shifts what could have been a hostile exorcism type of experience into something that can be cooperative. This stunned me at first. It was way beyond my worldview or comprehension, and yet it consistently worked. The other intervention was also about light. He would ask the spirit to look inside itself and would assure it that it would find a spark of light there, too. This also helps the spirit leave without hostility. It also leaves me dumbfounded.

Baldwin has developed a detailed geography of the spirit world. He delineates four planes of being above ours and speaks of source. He separates out many types of possessing entities and parasitic attachments: earthbound spirits (entities who were once human), alters of multiple-personality people, mind fragments of another living person, walk-ins (spirits who were allowed to take over the life of a person), past-life personalities, thought forms, inspirational possession (creative, positive beings), nonhuman entities, substance spirits (like Mother Ayahuasca or Castaneda's Mescalito), little people, extraterrestrials, implants, spirit guides, electronic devices, dark thought forms, the demonic, and more. He traces the demonic through many cultures and with all the different names and characteristics. It seems to be a natural human response to try and get our bearings in this odd terrain of the inner world by creating maps and taxonomies of the flora and fauna found there. But I think we are too ignorant for this. Almost every religion has maps and hierarchies of angels and deities and elaborate demonologies of hell. Perhaps there could be, in the future, a comparative cartography of the inner world. But for now, our ignorance is too vast, and the danger of our categories limiting our view is too real. I find it is best to approach each person fresh and to open to what they have experienced without the filters or blinders that any theory brings. In the antipodes of the mind, our sure safety is the fearlessness of being in Self with all our parts unblended. Our best guide is an open heart.

Baldwin's work has much that is valuable. His books contain many suggestive case studies. He did his homework. He knew the work of others who had done this work before. He was fearless and unconcerned by what academics thought of him. Perhaps because he came from dentistry, he did not have the baggage — the indoctrination, jargon, and territoriality — that traditional professional education gives most therapists. His books are all worth reading; they will take you far outside your comfort zone. His openness allowed him to see and work with phenomena that most of us routinely ignore. He relieved human suffering.

Edith Fiore, PhD

Another modern therapist who did this work is Edith Fiore, PhD. Early in her career, she used hypnosis to access unconscious material. She knew and worked with ego state therapy, the kind of parts work developed by Jack and Helen Watkins.

She understood traditional parts work, but when her patients started reporting past-life experiences, she had the courage to work with what they brought her. Then she discovered that there were also other beings inside her patients. She had some of these leave one of her patients and got great results, so she switched from her ego state and MPD model. Like William James's attitude of radical pragmatism, Fiore did not care much about theory; if it worked, she used it. These ideas are not scientifically accepted, but they are sociologically and anthropologically validated. She said her expertise is what to do to help people, and that's where she focused. She noted that Sai Baba, the Hindu teacher, taught that spirits are coming and going through us all the time. Fiore felt that possession is common and that most of us are possessed at some time in our lives. Her general method is friendly, not combative or hostile at all. She, like the Spiritists, believes the therapist has an opportunity to help the possessing spirit itself. She convinces the possessing spirit of several truths so it can leave peacefully. She lets the spirit know that its own body has died, that there is no hell, that loved ones are coming from the spirit world to help it, and that there are spirit guides here to help. In her clients, 90 percent of the spirits go easily.

Fiore has a generalized depossession format that she uses sometimes while monitoring the response of the client. It gives us a good taste of her work. Note that it is entirely addressing the possessing spirit, not the client. Here is a summary and paraphrase:

> You have been with the client, but you're not him, are you? It must be hard for you to be in there. You don't get to do what you want. I want you to think of the last time you were in your own body. Then your body died, but you did not. You should have gone to the light, but you made a mistake. You stayed here in the material world instead of joining loved ones. You became a lost soul. At some point, you entered the client, and now you're hurting both of you. It's bad for you and bad for him. Fortunately, there's help. Someone has come from the spirit world with big smiles and is greeting you. You can feel their love. In a few moments, when you leave the client, you'll go into the light over there, and you'll find yourself in a beautiful body of your own — your rightful body. There is no such thing as hell, and I've called in a spiritual teacher to help you understand… You can look around and remove others who are ready to go. Hand them to the healers. I bless you as you go in peace and light and love.

I believe Dr. Fiore lost her license because she dared to work so far beyond the current paradigm.

Shakuntala Modi, MD

Shakuntala Modi, MD, is another modern practitioner who does this work. She used hypnosis early on in her work but quit using any kind of formal induction. A key inquiry for her is to focus on the symptom and to ask the patient to go back to the source of the problem or symptom. This occurs over and over again in her case reports. Like Fiore, she first encounters past-life stuff. Modi states strongly that the patient does not need to believe. What is needed is the patient's willingness to undergo the experiences provided by their unconscious mind. This is a significant observation — that the theory or interpretation does not matter much; what matters is the emotional/imagistic/somatic experience. This fact of psychological functioning is very difficult for most academics since they have devoted their entire lives to the theories.

Modi clearly understands parts and multiplicity of mind. She refers to these as soul fragments. She says spirits get deep into people because they are missing soul parts and that soul parts can leave the body but remain attached by a silver thread. She believes bad spirits can capture a split-off fragment and use it to get into the person. Also, she states that soul fragments can leave and enter into other people as possessing spirits. Like William Baldwin, she would ask a spirit to look down inside itself, where it would find a spark of light. Baldwin used this to show the spirit that it had been lied to and misinformed, but Modi instead works to keep the spirit focused on the spark of light. She says that if the spirit stays focused on this spark, it will be transformed by its own light.

There are many others I could discuss, but we'll only look at few more moderns.

Charles Tramont, MD

For thirty-two years, Charles Tramont, MD, was an OB-GYN surgeon in Ohio. He was also a flight surgeon in the U.S. Air Force and a full colonel. One of the things he said he was proudest of was his repeated election as the head of surgery at his hospital because this meant that the other surgeons respected him. This is almost as conservative and respected a background as can be imagined — a very practical medical professional in the hospital and military in a conservative part of the country. Then Dr. Tramont started studying hypnosis, in part for pain control, then past-life experiences, then spirit possession phenomena. He researched past lives and found that Dr. Ian Stevenson and colleagues at the University of Virginia had investigated and verified over a thousand cases of reincarnation.

This groundbreaking body of research deserves to be better known. The research team would find children who claimed knowledge of a previous life and would then locate the family and village where the child said they had lived before. This way, they could check the accuracy of the child's memories of their previous life (Stevenson 1966). If our culture were not so willfully and stubbornly blind, this data alone would change our worldview. Stevenson's 1966 book-length report is modestly titled *Twenty Cases Suggestive of Reincarnation*. The research continues to this day, piling up more and more evidence. Now there are over 1,500 "proved cases" — that is, cases where the researchers went to the location where the child said they had died in a previous lifetime and interviewed the people there to confirm the child's account. Stevenson was a professor of psychiatry for some fifty years and head of that department in the medical school. He has all the scientific medical credentials one could want. And still, this work is ignored or ridiculed.

Back to Dr. Tramont. He studied with William Baldwin but developed his own way of working. It's not surprising, considering his military background, that much of his work is more confrontational and more like traditional exorcisms. He calls on spirit guides and teams of helper spirits to encapsulate and immobilize the foreign energies and then has these beings take it away. He also makes use of his patients' guides. He wrote that there are three basic varieties of foreign energies: dark forces who never were human, earthbounds who are the souls of dead humans, and extraterrestrials. He says that the worst are what he called "demonic reptilians." When asked if he believed in this stuff, he said absolutely because it has cured so many people. Many of Dr. Tramont's ideas and terms seem incredible, but he makes one point that fits perfectly with IFS. He says fear is the key; fear is how they get in, and fear is how they stay.

Much of the above is way beyond our modern belief structures. You might well be scratching your head and wondering how such well-educated and accomplished people can believe such stuff. The answer they give is consistently because it works, because people heal, because suffering is reduced. They all put this pragmatic result ahead of ideas and theories. They stick with this even though they know it exposes them to almost universal ridicule and is likely to destroy their careers. I already mentioned Tom Zinser in the section on interesting people I've met studying this stuff. He also endured isolation, ridicule, and ostracism because he stuck with what he experienced as helpful to his patients.

M. Scott Peck, MD

Another modern example is M. Scott Peck, MD, probably the most famous of the lot. Peck (1936–2005) was a psychiatrist and the medical director of a facility, and he also had a private practice in Connecticut. He was educated at Harvard and Case Western and, like Dr. Tramont, became a colonel in the military. His first book, *The Road Less Traveled* (1978), became a bestseller, and he lectured widely.

His second book, *People of the Lie* (1998), took him into less popularly acceptable grounds: the recognition and study of evil. As a society, we tend to ignore evil; it's such an unpleasant subject. The cost of this is to make it easier for evil to flourish in our world. Peck's understandings are valuable. He called evil "malignant narcissism" and said it lives in human weakness. It consistently lies to others so it can deceive itself. It projects onto scapegoats. It hates with the pretense of love and maintains respectability.

Peck followed his inquiry into even less popular areas — possession and exorcism. He believed that evil is prevalent and possession is rare, but he definitely believed it was real. Even though Peck was not Catholic, he was heavily influenced by Father Malachi Martin, who wrote very dramatic accounts of modern Catholic exorcisms. Both Peck and Father Martin recognized that the possessing demon got in because some part of the person allowed or welcomed it. They speculated that loneliness might be a necessary precondition for possession. They both said that we healers never see the cases of perfect possession because those people never seek treatment. We only see the imperfect possessions. Peck described four stages of exorcism: pretense (the spirit hiding), presence (the evil spirit revealing itself), clash (the exorcist and spirit fighting), and expulsion. Like Catholic exorcisms, Peck's work was full of violent conflicts, and it put the exorcist in a seductively heroic role. Peck's exorcisms included a team of assistants and often lasted for days. He only did a few, but they left him 100 percent convinced of the reality of Satan. He also said that demons came in tightly organized hierarchies and that centuries of demonologies have described them. He stated that "despite the triumphs of modern science… the world remains utterly mysterious… explanation represents falsity, whereas mystery represents truth" (2005, 52). Along these lines, he pointed out that humility is the real basis of all scientific work.

"Explanation is falsity; mystery is truth." I want to have that engraved over the door to my house, but still I have this ceaseless urge to explain. It seems that the farther we go with our explanations, the deeper the mystery becomes. Astronomy has explained the universe all the way back to the big bang, but what a colossal, stupefying, and majestic mystery that is. It seems as though this may also be true as we pursue the nature of our subjective experience deeper and deeper.

Richard Gallagher, MD

Richard Gallagher, MD, is a psychiatrist with impeccable academic credentials. He is a full professor of psychiatry at New York Medical and a psychoanalyst on the faculty of Columbia University. He graduated from Princeton with a Phi Beta Kappa in classics and trained as a resident in psychiatry at Yale University School of Medicine. Joseph English, MD, a past president of the American

Psychiatric Association, recommends Gallagher as a superbly credentialed academic physician and a man of sound judgment and unimpeachable integrity. Gallagher believes in the reality of possession and exorcism. For more than twenty-five years, he has evaluated people who had approached the Catholic Church for exorcisms. He has also evaluated people for Protestant, Islamic, and Jewish groups. He makes it clear that his role has been to rule out any physical, psychiatric, or psychological causes in the person being evaluated; the actual diagnosis of possession he has left in the hands of the religious professionals. He thought that many of the people he saw had psychopathology, but in his supremely well-educated view, some of these cases did not have medical causation. He personally observed many exorcisms and witnessed many phenomena that we consider impossible: a person levitating for half an hour, people speaking languages they had never been trained in, bruises and scratches appearing spontaneously, superhuman strength in possessed people, knowledge of hidden things, for example, personal history of the exorcists, and more. I have seen some strange things in my clients but nothing like this. My hypothesis now is that the cases I see are not full possession — they are probably what Gallagher would call obsession.

Professor Stafford Betty has also called attention to the many reliable reports of extreme phenomena like this associated with possession states worldwide. In his article arguing that psychiatry needs to take possession seriously, Betty (2005) states that the well-attested existence of these "supernatural" physical phenomena alone indicates the importance of studying this subject. Gallagher makes many interesting comments in *Demonic Foes*, his 2020 book on this subject. One of the most useful is his emphasis on the fact that one of the first goals of a possessing demon is confusion. They love to create confusion. This is important because in IFS, we know that curiosity is a characteristic of Self — perhaps the most crucial Self quality. We can work to shift the confusion into curiosity; this is often much easier than trying to banish confusion outright. Gallagher believes that all of the possessing agents are really demons; he thinks they claim to be dead souls or ancestors to sow confusion. As noted earlier, the Spiritists of Brazil believe that all the possessing agents are the lost souls of dead people; this is almost the exact opposite of the view of Catholicism and Gallagher. I must respectfully disagree with Gallagher's view here. He deals with the extreme cases; however, in the more ordinary ones that I have seen, I think there are likely many different kinds of possessing agents. He does insist that the possessing agents are real entities — distinct spirits with personalities and intelligences of their own. Gallagher is a Catholic and has worked for a long time in association with the Catholic exorcists. He has lectured to the International Association of Exorcists, which was founded in Rome in the early 1990s; they provide education and support worldwide for the priests doing this work.

Neo-Shamanic Compassionate Depossession

I want to touch on two more subjects in this brief overview of modern therapists' attempts to work with possession states: neo-shamanic compassionate depossession and DMT entities. *Neo-shamanism* is an umbrella term for many modern practitioners who do some kind of psychological-spiritual healing work that is not part of any traditional lineage. For example, there are many modern dance and movement teachers (Gabrielle Roth and Ya'Acov Khan come to mind) who claim the title "shaman." Their classes often create intense and powerful experiences for many. Here I will focus only on those neo-shamans who do explicit work with possession states.

Dr. Michael Harner was a respected academic anthropologist who did field-work in South America. He became so fascinated with shamanism that he abandoned his academic career and became a shaman. Many Indigenous peoples are repelled when white people call themselves shamans. Harner was very careful to call his work "core shamanism" and not to appropriate any specific culture's tools or concepts. Shamanism or something like it (there are an incredible number of academic articles arguing about its definition and characteristics) is found all over the world, largely but not exclusively in hunter-gatherer societies. It's probably our oldest form of spirituality. After Harner quit academia, he devoted the rest of his long life to training modern Westerners on how to go on a shamanic journey to the other worlds and how to do healing work there. I had the great pleasure of working with him personally many years ago. He was an impressive man, completely unpretentious, with sparkling eyes and a great sense of humor. He and his wife, Sandra, created the Foundation for Shamanic Studies, which supports their work and helps honor and support traditional shamans in many cultures. In an interview slightly before his death, he was asked if he could sum up his entire life's work. I thought this question was out of place, but he considered it for a moment and then replied with only three words: "Spirits are real."

Harner and now his successors teach about removing possessing spirits, but for them this is advanced work. Training in this is only available near the end of the three-year program they offer. Before you can learn about it, you need to master the basics of their system. Shamanism is a science of the spirit — a methodology — not a belief system. People can learn to journey in the inner world and to explore non-ordinary realities. Harner's school insists that this subjective realm is a reality and that the spirits we meet there are real. They train people to form a relationship with an advanced spirit, often a power animal. This way, the student becomes a power-filled person and develops a spiritual immune system. Harner's school recognizes that there can be unwanted influence in the non-ordinary. Some are "negative energetic processes" and are removed and often sent into a large body of water. They call this extraction. Other influences are spirits with a will and mind of their own. With these, they do depossession and guide the beings to where they truly belong. They warn that this work must be done when the shaman is merged with their compassionate helping spirit. This reminds me of IFS's insistence that this work should be done from Self. Exorcism, according to Harner's school, only casts the spirit out and fails to heal it. There used to be shamanic "sucking doctors" who would literally suck these entities out of people with their mouths, but this is no longer done. Unlike IFS, Harner's school does not focus on light as the primary tool to remove these beings. The individual spirit teaches how this is done. Harner did not mix shamanism and therapy; he was strongly opposed to this. He felt that you had to be a master, which for him meant at least nine years of work in each method before even attempting to combine them.

I discussed this with Narrye Caldwell, a shamanic practitioner of their tradition, and she emphasized not doing this work unless you are filled with power and your spirit guides. Sing and rattle and journey until you are filled before you begin. She described the work with possessing spirits in terms of being a psychopomp, a term from ancient Greece that refers to a guide of souls after the body dies. We, or rather our spirit guides, help the attaching spirit go on to its true home.

Another modern Western shamanic group that does this work centers around Betsy Bergstrom, a neo-shaman in the Pacific Northwest. She calls her work "compassionate depossession," which distinguishes it sharply from the hostile and combative tradition of demonic exorcisms. Bergstrom's work is not adversarial. She received Buddhist training and sometimes does the *chöd* practice, which is a traditional Tibetan practice of feeding and helping demons move on. She sees most of the possessing spirits as earthbounds — souls of dead people who lost their way. She said there are so many of these now because we no longer have psychopomps to help spirits after death. Interestingly, she says some of these beings are the gods of other religions we have demonized. One of Bergstrom's students, Kriket, starts her depossession work by asking where this energy is most intense in a person's body and what color it is. These are the same kinds of questions IFS uses to get to know a part or a UB. Many other people are doing this kind of work as well. Some websites claim over a hundred thousand people helped. However, my experience is that most people doing this are isolated by the stigma attached to this area. Most seem to work alone with no advertisement or fanfare, relying only on word of mouth.

There is another interesting parallel here between neo-shamanism and IFS. Many modern Western shamans do a lot of extraction work, pulling negative energies out of a person. This is akin to IFS's unburdening process, which all IFS therapists learn. The neo-shamanic process of depossession is much rarer and is usually limited to advanced students. It parallels IFS's work with unattached burdens, which is also usually limited to advanced students. Both groups recognize a similar dichotomy.

DMT Entities

There is one more area we need to touch on, which is DMT entities. As the psychedelic renaissance progresses, it has become undeniably clear that the majority of the people who are given high doses of DMT-containing plants (ayahuasca, psilocybin, DMT itself, and more) meet intelligent beings of some kind during their experiences. This has deeply upset many researchers in the field.

A new study (Lawrence et al. 2022) was just published by Roland Griffiths and his team at Johns Hopkins. It states that 45.5 percent of those who had taken DMT-containing medicines in a sample of 3,778 cases reported encountering entities, and most of these encounters were positive. David Luke (2017) says that with high doses, we can reliably produce entity encounters. A total of 34 out of 36 people in his study met entities. Rick Strassman, the psychiatrist who ran the DMT research at the University of New Mexico and supervised over four hundred sessions, reported slightly over 50 percent of his subjects meeting sentient beings. After these meetings, 60 percent reported desirable alterations in their view of reality, while only 1 percent reported negative alterations. Roland Griffiths's team (Davis et al. 2020), with their usual scientific and statistical rigor, reported on a survey of 2,561 individuals who experienced entities. The most common labels for the entities were *guide*, *spirit*, *alien*, and *helper*. An overwhelming 99 percent had an emotional response to this meeting; 41 percent reported fear, but the most prominent emotions were love, kindness, and joy. Most of the entities were conscious (96 percent) and intelligent (96 percent). More than half of the subjects who had been atheists before these meetings were no longer atheists after.

These experiences were rated as some of the most meaningful in the people's lives, and they reported positive changes in life satisfaction and meaningfulness afterward. These entity encounters are often described as hyper-real — more real than ordinary life. There are some very vivid descriptions of these beings. Terence McKenna saw bejeweled self-dribbling basketballs and machine elves. Praying mantis–like figures are often reported. Ayahuasca users often meet Mother Ayahuasca herself or jaguars and pythons. A major international invitational conference at Tyringham Hall in England in 2017 focused on DMT entities and resulted in a book on the subject (Luke and Spowers 2021), and another conference is scheduled.

Strassman described these entity encounters as interactive, dynamic, relational experiences with intelligent beings. When he started his research with DMT, he'd expected something like Zen enlightenment or a type of near-death experience, but this is not what he got. He ended up going back to his roots and modeling his understanding of DMT entities on Old Testament prophecy. He defined prophecy not as the prediction of the future, but as experiencing the spiritual world directly. For our purpose, the most important thing about these encounters is that people reported pervasive, ongoing, positive changes in their psychological well-being. This is what matters for the radical pragmatist. These experiences help people, so who are we to judge them? But of course, I cannot resist trying to assess DMT entity experiences.

The most extreme interpretation I've seen is based on the fact that DMT quiets the default mode network in our brain and lessens brain activity globally rather than increasing it. Some thinkers have combined this with the theory that our brain functions primarily as a filter, screening out information that is not relevant to our survival and reproduction. If all this is true, DMT could be opening us up to perceive other dimensions or levels of reality that are just as real as our ordinary ones. The least extreme interpretation comes, surprisingly, from Terence McKenna, who is famous for pushing the edge. He wrote, "We are alienated, so alienated the self must disguise itself as an extraterrestrial in order not to alarm us with the truly bizarre dimension that it encompasses. When we can love the alien, then we will have begun to heal the psychic discontinuity that plagues us" (quoted in Luke 2017, 97).

Researchers at the Imperial College London have recently devised a way to create a long-lasting DMT experience by controlled intravenous administration. It appears that people are witnessing a fairly consistent geography of the other world as well as fairly consistent descriptions of the types of beings found there. This might allow us to create maps and taxonomies of the other world. This work is not yet published, and I only have anecdotal accounts.

Many modern Westerners have worked with something equivalent to UBs and guides. I have not even mentioned all the channelers and mediums. I've shown the statistics about how common belief in something like this is, even in the modern Western world. There is overwhelming evidence that working with this stuff can have profound and long-lasting positive effects on people. And yet, the professional therapy world taboos the whole subject. Most of the people who have worked with this have been shunned, ridiculed, and marginalized, but they did not stop. They kept going because they saw that the work could benefit people.

PART 2

This Changes Everything

CHAPTER 10

Other Cultures & Anthropology:
Non-Western Examples

There is a basic biopsychological process found in pretty much every culture and all eras of history. This process can have profound, life-changing effects for good or ill. It can cause disease or cure it. The most frequent metaphor used to describe this experience is possession. This phenomenon is worthy of study. That much seems unarguable, a solid ground we can build on. We, in our Western arrogance, have looked down at people who have these kinds of experiences; we used to call them primitives and savages, and now we tend to diagnose them and label them as having some form of psychopathology. This is only a slightly more sophisticated way of discounting, disrespecting, and denigrating them. We consider them either uncivilized primitives or insane.

Earlier in the book, I discussed the emic-etic dichotomy with its presupposition that we in the West know better and can provide an objectively real and culture-free understanding of human emotional and spiritual experiences. This is absolutely false. Our ideas are also culture-bound. In mathematics and the hard sciences, we can hope to escape this, but in understanding people's subjective experience, we cannot. The very concept of psychological illness is a product of our culture. Anthropologists often use the phrase "idiom of distress" to avoid imposing our category of mental illness on others. All the Western authorities predicted confidently that possession-based religions (*cults* was the pejorative term usually used) and possession-based healing ceremonies would die off as our obviously superior civilization spread. This was dead wrong. Possession-based "cults" and healings are expanding worldwide. In many places around the world, for example, Korea and China, possession-based practices have been suppressed for centuries, and yet they have endured. These two facts — that these practices endured even when suppressed and that they are expanding now, even though the dominant Western worldview holds them in contempt — should inform us that people find something of great value in them. Sneering at the "superstitions of the primitives" is not science and is not helpful. Discounting it as psychopathology is no better. What if these people were onto something of real value? What if we studied them in hopes of finding out how they can inform our own clinical practice and help us deal with the current epidemic of mental illness? Early on, we ignored the witch doctors gathering their weeds and twigs, but now there is a sophisticated science of ethnobotany, which is learning a great deal by studying traditional ways of plant medicine with respect. We need to do the same with possession practices.

Not only are we not listening to other cultures' ways of healing, but we are actively exporting our own concepts of mental illness, our diagnoses, and our drug-based treatments. We intentionally replace Native metaphors with experience-distancing jargon. Eighty percent of the world is non-Western, but because it does not have an opportunity to publish much, it is not heard in our world. Two big World Health Organization studies over twenty-five years showed that people diagnosed with schizophrenia living in India, Nigeria, and Colombia had less severe problems than those living in the United States, Denmark, or Taiwan (Watters 2011, 137). Those third-world countries have no social safety nets and spend much less than we do. And they get better results. Shouldn't we become their students?

In Zanzibar, they also get better results with schizophrenia than we do. The idiom of distress there is jinn possession. *Jinn* is the Islamic name for a class of spirits. This explanation decreases shame and blame. Everyone there expects to have entities in their heads sometimes. As one of the investigators there said, "When humans do not assume they have rather complete control of their experience, they do not so deeply fear those who appear to have lost it" (quoted in Waller 2009, 159). How we name a condition and how a culture holds it have a huge influence on how damaging or beneficial it is. The greater the belief in a biomedical model, the more stigma is attached to the sufferer and the more others want social distance from them.

There is a chilling chapter in investigative journalist Ethan Watters's book (2010) in which he details how the idea of depression as an illness was sold to the Japanese people. Drug companies collaborated on this and paid academics large fees to help them. Japanese traditional culture valued melancholy and sadness as ways to create deep beauty and to appreciate the transitory nature of life. Deep sadness had social and moral meanings. States of sadness, *yuutsu*, were often idealized and prized. They were seen as *yibyo*, personal hardship, which could build character, create moral meaning, and enhance self-understanding. All of this much more helpful way of holding so-called depression had to be undermined and invalidated before our ideology of mental illness and our drugs could be sold to the Japanese. There is much we could learn from the traditional Japanese ways of being with melancholy that would relieve suffering in the West.

How a culture conceives of a mental state has a huge influence on how destructive it is. Our way of holding many of these states creates and exacerbates human suffering. After spending years studying spirit possession religions in Brazil, the noted anthropologist Rebecca Seligman wrote that in one of them, Candomblé, dissociation is not a pathological experience but rather a therapeutic mechanism. We need to make a 180-degree shift in our approach to studying these non-Western ways of conceptualizing and handling mental distress. We need to get off our high horse and become their students. The need for this transformation is especially acute when it comes to meeting the other within us — the guides, the visionary states, the spiritual presence experiences, or whatever you want to call them. Let's focus now on possession from this new perspective. There is a vast library of research on possession. This chapter, like many others, should be a multivolume book in itself, but I offer here a brief outline and some hints as to how this study can help modern clinical practice.

Possession is found in every major world religion: Christianity, Islam, Hinduism, Buddhism, and Judaism. Erika Bourguignon, an expert in this field, did a study of spirit possession prevalence in 488 societies worldwide back in 1969, sponsored by the National Institute of Mental Health. She said, "If we speak in very general terms… the behavior is probably universal and occurs in all societies; however, it should not properly be referred to as possession states" (Bourguignon 1976). She found explicit possession belief in 74 percent of her sample (ibid., 31). Tremendous academic controversy exists over what counts as possession and what doesn't. For example, the question of whether or not shamanism involves possession has caused huge arguments that have gone on for more than fifty years. Some argue that because shamans are in control of their spirit allies, it is not possession; others insist it is the same phenomenon. These extensive and often vehement debates are not important for our purpose, which is learning what we can that will help modern psychotherapists reduce human suffering. I much prefer Tanya Luhrmann's broader term "spiritual presence experiences." It opens us all to consider benign experience as well, and it avoids all the stale controversies, but it is not widely used, and you can't use it to search the literature.

Let's briefly look at possession in the major world religions. We will look at Judaism and Christianity in the next chapter, which focuses on Western culture. An important distinction here is the vast difference between the folk and elite versions of religion. The people who write about religions tend to be scholars, academics, and teachers, so they see religion in terms of beliefs, doctrines, and texts. It is said that doctrine is the corpse of revelation. In less religious terms, this means that belief structures are the residue of experience. For the vast majority of those who practice, however, religion is a matter of experience, ritual, and emotion, not some dry cognitive material. It is a vibrant lived experience, a framework of meaning and relationship that is felt and enacted. The Princeton readings in religions, a wonderful series that comprises some fifteen volumes, focuses on what people actually say and do. Each volume contains "in practice" in the title: *Buddhism in Practice*, *Religions of Japan in Practice*, *Tantra in Practice*, and so on. This series highlights the vast gulf between what people do and how they are as religious beings versus what scholars theorize about it. Even in this wonderful series, there is not much about possession. This difference between the elite and folk views is especially deep and significant when it comes to possession issues. In the United States today, the academic elite scoff at and ridicule this subject, yet well over half of the population believes in it. In many cultures, possession cults have been a way for marginalized, disempowered, and downtrodden people, especially women, to gain respect and power. Possession complexes are often outlawed yet persist underground. The eruption of psychic energies into a society that occurs in possession cults is often destabilizing. There is a wildness to it. It has sometimes triggered civil wars, for example, in China's Taiping and Boxer Rebellions. This parallels the way in which individuals are both enlivened and destabilized when there are major new openings from the unconscious into their lives.

Hinduism

Let's start with Hinduism. Here we encounter a magisterial work, Frederick M. Smith's *The Self Possessed*. The word *magisterial* has a special meaning for me; it implies a work that is so thorough and complete that any serious scholar in the field will have to refer to it. There are only a few such works of this size that I have found: Ellenberger's *The Discovery of the Unconscious*, Eliade's *Shamanism*, and McGilchrist's *The Master and His Emissary*. It is a delight to discover such authoritative texts. Smith is a Sanskrit scholar who uses and explains the Sanskrit terms, knows the literature, and provides fresh translations. His book is not an easy read, but it is deeply rewarding. Smith says that possession in South Asia is not just one thing — it has become perhaps the region's most widespread form of spiritual experience (2006, 597). It is a "vibrant presence" in public and private spirituality. I want to repeat this sentence ten times to counteract the elite version of the serene meditator as the emblem of Indian spirituality.

In India and South Asia in general, there is a sharp divide between positive possession and disease-producing possession. The two only rarely converge. Both forms of possession have a moral basis. Negative possession comes from pollution, weakness, or contact with evil, while positive possession comes from virtuous actions, devotional practice, or divine grace. Possession does not follow a single prototype. There are many kinds and many different terms to differentiate them. Possession is always disruptive to some extent. There is a violence to it. It is out of ordinary human control. There has always been an acceptance of the reality of spirits in South Asia, as in almost all non-Western cultures. Just as elsewhere, the established elites do not much like this. The most orthodox Brahmins have sometimes tried to contain or limit possession beliefs, but their efforts have largely failed. Smith points out that although possession has an especially vigorous presence in women's religious practices, it is found in both sexes and all classes, casts, and linguistic groups. It is so pervasive, "very multi vocal and ubiquitous… it is inadvisable to offer a grand theory" (Smith 2006, 598).

Instead of being seen as pathological, dissociation in this worldview is normal and has exalted potential. Smith describes how the pain of possession is caused by trying to fit something big, frightening, wild, powerful, awesome, unfamiliar, and beautiful into a small, limited, and culturally reconditioned enclave: the self (Smith 2006, 154). He clearly states that possession is not acceptable in the West because it "opposes the assumption of normalcy of an inviolable and unitary self on which this Western biomedical system is founded" (ibid., 44). Here we have Luhrmann's citadel model of mind once again, found by a different scholar in a different field. The tantric texts give precise, detailed instructions on inviting in the deities. They divide this into four phases: attracting, entering, fixing, and pleasing. Each phase has its own mantras and prayers. Smith sees "the concept of a multi-faceted and multiform self… a complex and permeable self," which underlies tantra, as opening the practitioner to nurture the other within. This meeting of the other within often dissolves the small social self, and this may be a key to the subversive and destabilizing nature of possession. Nearly every disease could be personified and experienced as possession. Also, the sattvas, the personality attributes, correspond to the descriptions of the grahas, the possessing agents. The lines between possession and disease on one hand, and possession and character traits on the other, are variable. The traditional South Asian attitude is that individuals are not fully autonomous; we are porous, and others can enter us. People in the Vedic tradition are not fractured by possession. This Vedic way of seeing is the opposite of what has been called the Western monotheism of consciousness. In the very last sentence of the book, Smith says that the most difficult and perhaps irreconcilable problem for us Westerners in understanding possession is the acceptance of our own multi-vocality (ibid., 602).

Many temples in India are devoted to healing mental illness. A 2002 study by Dr. R. Raguram published in the *British Medical Journal* reported that a stay at the Muthuswamy Temple was at least as good as antipsychotic medications (Raguram 2002). It is sad but predictable that despite these good results, the temples are being attacked. Anubha Sood (2016) reported that the state's disapproving stance toward traditional healing had turned into vehement condemnation. The state denounced the temples as backward and harmful to the people. This occurred in the face of growing acceptance of alternative mental health care in the West. Sood reported that this condemnation especially damaged the Balaji Temple in Rajasthan, from which a number of the key healing rituals have disappeared.

Smith has given us a detailed description of the activities at this temple from a few years earlier. He's not only studied and translated the available texts but has also visited the temple for fieldwork. Balaji is one of the names for the god Hanuman. The temple has general offerings and kirtans, which are open to all. The exorcisms themselves are not standardized; many practitioners are in and around the temple, and they each have their own ways. When a pilgrim arrives, they are usually accompanied by a relative; they settle in, attend the distributions of Prasad (blessed food), and kirtans (sacred chants). The pilgrim (isn't this a much better and more respectful name than patient?) often connects with an exorcist. A few days later during the kirtan, the pilgrim and the exorcist usually fall into a trance together. They chant and clap rhythmically with the music. As their consciousness alters, a swaying begins in their head and upper body. This becomes more and more intense. The hair is loosened so it flies about freely, the head and body whirl violently, and the movements become chaotic, often with eyes locked or rolled back. It is believed that a double possession is occurring. Both the negative spirit, who has been bothering the pilgrim, and the spirit of the temple god are now in them. Often both the pilgrim and the exorcist are now possessed. There is a battle between the gods and spirits. Pilgrims' low backs are often pummeled with fists to drive the spirit up and out. The spirit is interviewed and forced to confess. This benefits both the spirit and its victims. Spirits are not called evil. Smith never found the word *evil* used to describe them. They are instead called unhappy. Converting criminal gods and demons into devotees is a major theme. After this ritual, pilgrims may stay on for a while longer. Later they are sent home with advice, especially about diet. Some pilgrims stay and become attendants at the temple or even exorcists themselves.

Each temple has its own deities and saints as well as its own theoretical system, so generalizations are vague and tenuous or impossible. In Southern India at the Chottanikkara Temple, they say mental illness has three possible causes: (1) Paedi (fear and anxiety); (2) Cheeta (bad thoughts, guilt, or physical cause); and (3) Pretham or Thullal (spirit possession). This may be a fairly typical understanding. Practices at other temples can be very different from Balaji. The Muthuswamy, for example, primarily provides a safe refuge without traumatic rituals. People often come accompanied by a relative and stay for weeks. They are asked to do chores and help in the functioning of the temple. India is so huge, and the religious practices so varied, that any generalization will be only partially correct at best.

Islam

Islam has also recognized possession and its role in illness from its beginnings when the angel Jibril (Gabriel) dictated the Quran to Muhammad. Many other angels are also mentioned in the Quran. In addition, the Quran mentions jinn — the beings responsible for most human possession. Jinns can be good or bad; some are devout Muslims. They are beings who were created from smokeless fire. We humans were created of mud. We live in the same world as jinns. They can perceive us, but we cannot perceive them. The concept of Al-Ghayb, the Unseen World, is central in Islam. Arabic literature professor Amira El-Zein (2009, 6) states that there are three basic realms: the terrestrial or material realm where we live, the intermediate world of fire where the jinn live, and the celestial realm of angels and light. Above these three is the infinite Divine. The intermediate realm is what the great French Islamic scholar Henry Corbin called the imaginal. For Islam, the Al-Ghayb is the world that really exists. It is ontologically as real as the world of the senses or intellect. In the Quran as well as in other fundamental religious texts, the difference between the outward Zahir and the inward Batin is emphasized. The etymology of these two words is significant. Zahir refers to the back, while Batin refers to the belly or front. So Islam places the hidden, esoteric world in the front (Hanegraff and Kripal 2011, 49). In addition to the angels and jinn, there are also other orders of beings, including Marrid, Shaitan, satanic beings, Bhut, and evil spirits (Dein and Illaiee 2013), but it's the jinn who are seen as responsible for most mental illness. In the Middle East, there's an ancient belief in spirits causing illness. The Sumerians believed the diseases of the body and mind were caused by sickness demons, the Giddim. The belief in jinn antedates Muhammad. The Quran states that since Muhammad's Revelation, the jinn were no longer allowed access to the angels, something they had previously enjoyed. Jinn are a major cause of mental illness, but they also bring inspiration to poets and artists. There is a tricksterish kind of ambiguity that is reminiscent of the diamons of ancient Greece.

Certain types of jinn possession are clearly seen as harmful and causing mental illness. The word for insane in Arabic, *majnun*, literally means "to be possessed by a jinn." The human body was often viewed in the ancient Near East as the locus of fights between good and evil spirits. There are a variety of religious interventions to remove pernicious jinn; Ruqyah (reciting specific verses from the Koran over the possessed) seems to be the most common, at least among Islamic people living in the UK today. There's also Dhikr (remembrance and chanting invocations of Allah), reading the Quran over water and having the person drink it, and Dua (a prayer of supplication). Some say that jinn can only enter if someone is in an extreme state of anger, fear, heedlessness, or desire. Other accounts say it can be more random. You might unintentionally disturb them, or they might dislike you or even lust after you. In one tradition, sexual intercourse and marriage between jinn and humans is possible. In North Africa, especially Morocco, there is a tradition of men being seduced by 'Aisha, a powerful goddess who takes many forms. These men often lead very diminished lives and are incapable of having relations with human women. Vincent Crapanzano, the famous anthropologist, wrote a book-length biography of one such man, Tuhami (Crapanzano 1985).

As strange and incomprehensible as all this may sound to our ears, these curative methods work for some people. In the UK, more therapists and caregivers are collaborating with Islamic exorcists because it helps some of their Islamic patients. Kemal Irmak, MD, PhD, in an article in the *Journal of Religion in Health* (2014, 773–777), proposed that some schizophrenia might actually be spirit possession. Dr. Irmak is a colonel in the Turkish army and a professor at a military medical school. He has published over eighty articles in medical biochemistry, which is his specialty. He is a hardheaded scientist; it is not easy to dismiss him out of hand. In his words, "Demonic possession can manifest with a range of bizarre behaviors which could be interpreted as a number of different psychotic disorders… a local faith healer in our region helps patients with schizophrenia. His method of treatment seems to be successful because his patients become symptom-free after three months. Therefore, it would be useful for medical professionals to work together with faith healers to define better treatment pathways for schizophrenia" (ibid., 773). This proposal set off a firestorm of negative comments, of course, and I don't believe anyone has studied or learned from the successful village faith healers.

This brief glimpse into Islamic practices with possession, and its connection to mental illness, indicates that the practices are deeply embedded in the religion. In the Middle East, these beliefs and practices are ancient, and they have endured. Today in the UK and all over the world, modern Islamic versions of them are helping people heal. Nevertheless, our culture mostly continues to either ridicule or ignore all of this instead of learning from it.

Buddhism

In Buddhism, we find the same dynamic: spirit possession is pervasive, ancient, and widespread. Its prominence and popularity are growing today, not shrinking. Perspectives on spirit possession are ambivalent; sometimes it is sought out and valued, and sometimes it is seen as the cause of illness and troubles. Buddhism is often divided into three main groupings: Mahayana (the Great

Vehicle), Theravada (the Way of the Elders), and Vajrayana (the Diamond Path). Sometimes Vajrayana is considered a type of Mahayana. All three recognize and work with spirit possession. As Lama Govinda wrote, "…animism permeates all Buddhist texts, wherein every tree and grove, and every locality, is held to have its own peculiar deities; and the Buddha is represented as discoursing with gods and other spiritual beings inhabiting the earth and the realms beyond as if it were a most natural procedure. Only a completely intellectualized and Westernized Buddhism which attempts to separate the thought content of Buddhism from its equally profound mythological elements, can deny this animistic background and with it the metaphysical foundations of Buddhism" (Govinda 1960, lvii).

It is perhaps easiest to see this in Vajrayana, which is epitomized by Tibetan Buddhism. The Dalai Lama wrote, "Basically we can say that there are different worlds, different experiences; human life is just one of them. What we usually call spirits are some different form of life, beings who have a different body and mentality. Within the desire realm, and more specifically within the environment inhabited by human beings, there is quite a variety of other entities… And they are all cohabiting with us right here" (quoted in Varela 1997, 141). We have already met this in Clifford's great work on Tibetan psychiatry. Spirit possession, for Tibetan Buddhists, is one of the main causes of mental illness. Spirit possession can also be a great blessing, and it is viewed this way, both with folk healers and at the highest levels of Tibetan Buddhism.

Let's focus now on the Tibetan State Oracle, the most prominent, prestigious, and honored example. The tradition of exorcism and subduing of spirits goes back to Padmasambhava, the Indian monk who brought Buddhism to Tibet in the eighth century. Earlier efforts to bring Buddhism had been blocked by the fierce Indigenous deities and demons. Padmasambhava subdued them and turned them into Protectors of the Dharma. He tamed the wrathful gods and spirits and connected them to the sangha, the Buddhist community. One of the most powerful of the subdued and converted protectors is Pehar, who became the state Oracle of Tibet. The word *oracle* here refers to the god who possesses the human, who is only a mouthpiece for that deity. Padmasambhava is not the first to subdue demons; the Buddha himself subdued Mara, fire-breathing Nagas, and other members of the Hindu pantheon. As the Dalai Lama explained, "The word Oracle is itself highly misleading, it implies that there are people who possess oracular powers. This is wrong. In the Tibetan tradition, there are merely certain men and women who act as mediums between the natural and Spiritual Realm, the name for them is *Kuten*, which means literally the physical basis. Also, I should point out that whilst it is usual for people to speak of oracles as if they were people, this is done for convenience. More accurately, they can be described as spirits which are associated with particular things (for example, a statue, people and places)" (Dalai Lama 1999: 232–233). This Oracle has had a huge impact on Tibetan statecraft, both historically and today. It was on the advice of the Oracle that the Dalai Lama fled Tibet just in time to escape safely after the Chinese invaded. The human who was then the vehicle for the Oracle, known as the Kuten, accompanied the Dalai Lama into exile. This oracle is called the Nechung Oracle because the subdued God Pehar resides at the Nechung Monastery.

When the Kuten — the human vehicle — dies, there is a search for a new one. When one is found, the person must go into retreat for extended training. In the actual ceremony, when the Kuten is possessed by Pehar, many monks chant and play cymbals, drums, and horns. The Kuten wears a huge costume that weighs well over seventy pounds. It is so heavy and cumbersome that he needs help to walk into the ritual hall. After being seated, the spirit starts to enter. The Kuten often has mild convulsions and emits hissing sounds. As he fully enters trance, a massive headdress weighing over thirty pounds is strapped on his head. When the god takes over, the transformation is extremely forceful, and initially the Kuten's assistants need to restrain him. Then the Kuten almost unbelievably gets up and dances, also often waving swords. The Dalai Lama describes this (1999, 233): "… the volcanic energy of the deity can barely be contained within the Earthly Frailty of the Kuten who moves and gestures as if his body were made of rubber and driven by a coiled spring of enormous power." In this profoundly altered state, the Oracle responds to the questions put to it. As the Oracle Spirit leaves, the Kuten's body collapses. His attendants remove the hat and carry his unconscious body from the hall to a recovery room. The genuineness of the trance is thought to be proved by the Kuten's superhuman strength when possessed. Kutens often die fairly young; this is attributed to the strenuous nature of being possessed.

Afterward, the Kuten remembers nothing of what happened during the trance. The current Kuten, Thupten Ngodup, has described what all this feels like in a series of YouTube interviews. The onset of trance he describes as "unimaginably intense. It is both distressful and exhilarating." Sometimes he experiences something like a lightning flash or a flash of red. Then he completely loses consciousness, which he regains only in the recovery room. Sometimes he's left with a headache, but afterward he feels very happy. In one interview, he says with a big smile that he thinks he may be the happiest person alive.

I've chosen to give a detailed description of this possession ceremony, out of the myriad of similar descriptions of equally dramatic possessions that are available, for two major reasons. We need to have a detailed example. This example is explicitly approved and endorsed by the Dalai Lama. His Holiness has said repeatedly that if modern science and religions disagree, we need to examine the religious belief and question it. His Holiness has convened many meetings with leading Western scientists. He continues to use and value this Oracle. The conclusion is inevitable: he does not believe there is anything in modern science that invalidates this possession. In his brilliant and profound mind, he must have found a way to reconcile these two worlds. This is also an important example because the Dalai Lama is so honored by Western academics. Perhaps the deep respect in which he is held can help some closed minds open.

Mahayana Buddhism is the most popular and widespread form of Buddhism. It's found in China, Korea, Japan, Mongolia, Central Asia, Taiwan, Singapore, and more. Mayahana emphasizes the concept of Bodhisattva — saintlike beings who have vowed to continue returning to these worlds until all sentient beings are free. Theravada, which is also known as Hinayana, the ancient way, focuses on each individual achieving freedom on their own. It tends to be more austere and focuses on monks who devote their lives to Liberation. Mayahana is more flexible and has blended with and absorbed many of the native traditions and the cultures where it has thrived. China, Korea, Japan, and Central Asia all had ancient traditions of possession, both as causing illness and as positive spiritual experience. This is such a vast subject. Whole libraries are devoted to each of these four traditions. The most I can do is hint at some outlines to give you a deeper sense of the ubiquity of possession.

China

China has a long history of suppressing possession cults. The Confucian emphasis on social order and filial piety is antithetical to possession, possession cults, and visionary experience in general. Also, possession has been associated with great rebellions in the relatively recent past. The Taiping Rebellion, which lasted from 1850 to 1864 with some remote rebel armies surviving until 1871, is the bloodiest civil war in human history with over twenty million dead. This rebellion was led by Hong Xiuquan. He was severely ill at one point and, while in a coma, may have had a near-death experience during which he had visions of being taken to heaven and meeting Jesus, Mary, and God. He was recognized as Jesus's younger brother and returned to Earth feeling he had a divine mandate to overthrow the devil demons, the ruling Manchu Dynasty. At the height of his power, he ruled much of South China from his capital at Nanjing. He sought to upend the entire moral and social structure of China. Several other leaders of rebellious forces at the same time claimed to be able to go into trance and speak to the Heavenly family. The rebels called themselves the God worshippers.

More recently, from 1899 to 1900, the Boxer Rebellion tried to throw all foreigners out of China. The Fists of Righteous Harmony, as they called themselves, were based in martial arts schools in Northwest China, which was a poor but relatively egalitarian area. In the south of China at that time, to become a shaman and to become God's friend required a teacher. But in the north, an individual could become possessed by learning a few incantations and employing charms or amulets. The Boxers attacked Christian converts and burned churches. They used ceremonies to induce mass possessions among the warriors. Largely teenagers, the warriors would twirl swords violently, chant incantations, and prostrate themselves repeatedly to achieve trance. There were many different folk religious societies and many different martial arts schools, so there was little cohesion. It was widely believed that the millions of soldiers from previous times could come down from the heavens and join in the fighting. Once again, the enemy forces were called devils — foreign devils this time. There are records of arguments over who was more truly possessed. They were possessed by many spirits and gods, but they especially worshipped and valued possession by Guan Di, a warrior god. With no central leadership, the rebellion spread like wildfire but collapsed very quickly.

Robert Weller, a professor of anthropology at Boston University, in describing this rebellion, said that "uncontrolled spirit possession, more easily than other forms of religious communication, undercuts authority of all kinds." Opinions about this uprising vary widely. Mark Twain and Leo Tolstoy praised the Boxers as real patriots seeking freedom, while other Westerners saw them as crazed savages. Opinions are also varied in China, but it is easy to see how this history would make a centralized authoritarian government in China leery of all religious sects, especially when they involve possession. Expectedly, the current Chinese government keeps a tight lid on all possession cults, but among Chinese people overseas, especially in Taiwan and Singapore, there is a vibrant flowering of spirit possession phenomena. These are some of the regions where the modern growth of spirit possession is most obvious and robust.

Korea

In Korea, there is a five-thousand-year history of the unique Korean form of shamanism, the mudang. The mudang have been mentioned before, and I want to go into a little more detail here. Because my wife is a native Korean, I have a deep affection and connection with this culture. Korea has much larger and more powerful neighbors on both sides, China on one side and Japan on the other. It has managed to survive for five thousand years by developing a strong and vibrant cultural core, which has formed around its shamanic traditions. All the foreign traditions that have been imported to Korea — Buddhism, Taoism, Confucianism, and now Christianity — have been absorbed and adjusted to such an extent that they've become fundamentally Korean. Christian missionaries are aware of this process and actively work to prevent it from overtaking Christianity. Koreans have a very ambivalent attitude toward the mudang, their shamans. These mudang are mostly women. There are a few male mudang, but they usually dress as women and wear makeup when doing the rituals. Historically, the mudang were looked down upon and despised; they were put in the same class as prostitutes. But almost everyone went to them when in need. This was illegal for centuries, but it endured. Today it is legal and flowering, and there are many mudang competing for clients.

The mudang perform complex ceremonies called *gut*, which often last several days. These ceremonies include very strong trance-inducing percussive music. The mudang sings and dances, putting on many different prescribed sets of clothes as the various gods descend and enter her. She changes clothes at different phases of the ceremony. When the gods are in her, she answers questions and resolves the issues that were brought to her. Often when a god is in her and she is deep in trance, she will stand barefoot on very sharp knife blades and let the gods speak through her from there. Sometimes the mudang climbs stairways made of knives to speak from the top. Not only do gods' spirits enter her, but also dead people's spirits, ancestor spirits, or suffering souls. This standing on knives is similar to the much more common phenomenon of fire walking. Trance fire walking occurs in many cultures and has been documented many, many times. Our current worldview has no explanation for this, or for standing on blades without being cut, so we just ignore it. Once I made the mistake of referring to the gods being in a mudang as possessing the mudang when I was talking with a Korean expert with my wife translating. He was upset — I had unintentionally offended him. He told me that in Korea, two different words were used for spirit possession and the presence of gods within a mudang. They do not consider this as negative or as positive forms of possession; they see it as two totally different processes.

The Korean mudang also recognize and work with the possession of ordinary people by spirits, usually those of dead people who died with some unresolved issues that need to be witnessed before the spirit can move on. Koreans recognize an emotion we don't: *han*, which is sort of a mixture of anguish, resentment, regret, and a sense of injustice. It is usually han that needs witnessing. Korean Buddhism, which is a form of Mahayana Buddhism, has totally absorbed the mudang's attitudes and methods. I have seen many video recordings of Buddhist and shamanic exorcisms, and they appear very similar. When I interviewed a Buddhist monk at his mountain monastery in Korea, again with my wife translating, he acknowledged that many big monks routinely performed exorcisms. He said that he and a few others refused to do them because he felt the possessing spirit was there as part of the person's karma; therefore, the person needed to struggle with the spirit to grow spiritually. Even "negative" possession can have value. This is a significant point for Western therapy. Often when an unattached burden is in a person, it does us the totally unintentional favor of helping us find the tender parts of the person who needs our care. In this way, they help the person resolve their karma. The witnessing of the spirit's han that happens during the gut ceremony is also intriguingly similar to the IFS witnessing process on a spiritual plane. In summary, possession and allowing the gods to enter both have important roles in traditional Korean spirituality.

Japan

Japan also has an ancient and widespread tradition of possession. Percival Lowell, in 1894, wrote the book *Occult Japan*. He wrote that the Japanese people are easily possessed. He said there were a surprising number of forms of possession. People could be possessed by animals, evil spirits, or gods. Lowell was a world traveler, and he said that the quality and quantity of possessions was unparalleled in other modern nations. Unlike most of his contemporaries, he maintained a curious and polite but skeptical viewpoint. Possessions, known as *kamigakari*, were found in both Shinto and Buddhism. Both positive and negative possession existed, and vengeful spirits of angry dead were responsible for many negative possessions. Demons, including oni, as well as gods, both Shinto kami and Buddhist devas, could possess. Among other texts, two great classics of Japanese literature, the *Kojiki* and the *Tales of Genji,* contain vivid accounts of possessions.

In the Japanese context, harmful spirits are not seen as permanently evil. They can harm sometimes and help at other times. This is reminiscent of the Indian temple of the Balaji, where they called them unhappy spirits rather than evil ones. A good example of this in Japan is the case of Sugawara no Michizane, a state official in the ninth century who died in exile. His spirit returned and killed those who had caused him to be exiled from the court. To tame and pacify his enraged spirit, he was deified and became a protector god who since then has become especially favored as the protector of students. Many kinds of mediums — oracular mediums, healing mediums, and exorcist mediums — used their contact with the spirits to help others. A vast variety of people performed exorcisms, from Buddhist monks to solitary mountain ascetics. The belief in and use of possession states pervaded traditional Japanese culture.

Southeast Asia

In the Southeast Asian countries of Laos, Cambodia, Myanmar, and Thailand, Theravada, the ancient path of Buddhism, dominates. Many Westerners consider this the pure form of Buddhism and see it as closer to the Buddha's original atheistic teaching. Its emphasis is on monks who work intensely to achieve their own liberation. As a result, one would expect less possession and less interaction with spirits, but this is not the case.

Erick White, an independent scholar who has done extensive research in Thailand, divides Western attitudes toward Southeast Asian possession into four phases (de la Perrière 2022, 292ff). Before 1965, possession was ignored; it was marginalized and viewed as a primitive relic that was not really part of the civilization. All the Western scholarly attention was on the respectable mainstream Buddhist doctrines, texts, and literary sources. Between 1965 and 1985, anthropologists started considering possession but saw it as constrained and dominated by Buddhism. It was seen as marginal and peripheral. The possession complex focused on illness and healing, not on spiritual liberation. Monks and mediums were mostly separate and did not interact. More recent scholars disagree with these early characterizations.

A new wave of understanding in the West occurred between 1985 and 2005. Possession was now seen as a religious innovation. There was a change in Southeast Asia and in this scholarship as well. With the great rural-to-urban migration and the increasing percentage of the population who lived in cities, urban possession mediums became prominent. They developed followings, students, and lineages, and became more and more professionalized, a process that continues today. Now there are more possession mediums. All classes are involved, from elite members of the neoliberal global culture to the middle classes, working classes, and the rural poor. New spirits have been imported from India and China as well as new rituals and techniques. Ties are now forming with Buddhist monks, with some monks performing exorcisms and some mediums becoming monks.

From 2005 to the present, White sees all these trends continuing. Possession now is an alternative piety. The Buddhist domination of spirituality is fading, and the possession complex is growing in numbers of mediums, variety of practices, and kinds of spirits found. It is also growing in social influence. This is more than a resurgence of old ways; rather than being a return, something new is emerging. In both socialist Vietnam and capitalist Thailand, the governments, out of their desire to become rapidly modernized, attempted to suppress possession cults as uncivilized superstition that held the country back. Both governments failed and have now given up these policies. Many of the scholars in this area discuss Max

Weber's famous prediction that modern Western knowledge would inevitably lead to a disenchantment of the world. The opposite is happening in Southeast Asia; as its economies gain strength and join the globalized culture, their world is becoming ever more enchanted and is recognizing the spirit world more and more.

If we take the idea of porosity of mind seriously, it can help us here. In the jargon of the anthropologists who are studying this, if we focus on the human as being a dividual rather than an individual (anthropologists are divided in perceiving people as dividuals characterized by multiplicity and porous boundaries versus as individuals, more like our Western view), or on the new animism, we realize that within these ways of being a person, we only become complete through the establishment of mutual two-way relationships with nonhumans as well as the humans around us. The nonhuman persons are seen as sources of potency and help. Baumann (quoted in de la Perrière 2022, 253–291) says the possession complex forms "multiple mutualities of being either temporary or lasting, loathed or desired." Here, as in many other cultures, the medium's first encounter with the spirits is often a period of sickness or insanity. The relationship needs to be cultivated to turn into an asset, a friendship, a beneficial mutuality.

White, in his 2014 doctoral dissertation for Cornell University, points to five different traditions of possession in Thailand: (1) malevolent possession requiring exorcism; (2) possession as playful entertainment; (3) possession by guardian spirits; (4) possession by empowered teachers; and (5) possession by virtuous deities. His suggestion that this typology seems to be expanding and diversifying even further is noteworthy in that the majority of these possessions are beneficial.

There is one minor point I want to mention before we move on. Kanya Wattanagun focused her 2016 doctoral dissertation for Indiana University on *phii pob*, which are evil spirits that live inside a living human. They are ravenous and endlessly hungry; they eat the flesh of living people. They come out from their human hosts and attack other humans. Wattanagun points out that in Burma, similar ravenous spirits are called *tasei* or *thaye*. I mention this because it is such an astonishing parallel to the wetiko spirit of the North American Plains peoples. Another parallel is that in both places, once people were believed to be inhabited by the phii pob or the wetiko spirit, they were considered incurable. Sometimes they were killed to limit their damage. Wattanagun reports the chilling case of a mother killing her thirteen-year-old daughter whom she believed was possessed by a phii pob. As mentioned earlier, Paul Levy has written extensively about his belief that this ravenous spirit possession is a chillingly apt description of our current mainstream Western culture.

Vietnam

The study of Vietnam's spirit possession complex has been "siloed," to use the currently popular academic jargon. It is unique in many ways. Vietnam has more than forty ethnic groups as well as powerful long-term Chinese influence and a vibrant native mother goddess religion. Unlike Laos, Cambodia, Thailand, and Myanmar, Vietnam's Buddhism is primarily Mahayana rather than Theravada. There is a powerful and growing spirit possession complex, both in Vietnam and among Vietnamese people overseas. Traditionally, illnesses with a more or less biological cause are called Yang illnesses and are treated in a variety of ways. In contrast, Yin diseases are caused by spirits; since they have a supernatural cause, they require supernatural treatment. Simple home remedies include being beaten with a mulberry branch to drive the spirits out and the use of talismans. But if these fail, people can go to a spirit priest who operates in a Buddhist temple. The exorcisms performed by these priests are notoriously violent and bullying of the spirits.

The last resort for most people is going to a spirit medium. These mediums do not fight the spirits; instead, they create dialogue and allow spirits to speak through them. (Here we have another iteration of the elite Buddhist versus folk medium dichotomy.) Very often, a spirit gives the possessed person and their family a list of demands in order for it to leave. Retrieval and proper burial of the spirit's physical remains are a frequent demand as well as regular offerings on the family altar and more. The medium is mounted by a spirit and goes into a trance to find healing for illness. These mediums often use the metaphor of becoming a seat for the gods to sit upon. Possession by a negative spirit is the same process that happens involuntarily to a sick client. Vietnam has a strong folk tradition of spirits seeking a medium looking for someone who "has been damaged in some way." The damage is thought to open doors that people who are healthy in mind, body, and heart keep closed (Gustafsson 2009, 111). Learning to cope with personal traumas at least in part gave mediums the power to channel spirits and help others. This is similar to the initiatory illnesses so common among shamans as well as the worldwide presence of the wounded healer archetype.

The war in Vietnam left over five million people dead, many of them not properly buried or mourned. This is a tidal wave of angry spirits. The demand for help with spirit possession illness has soared. A similar phenomenon occurred in China after the millions of deaths in Mao's Cultural Revolution. This was especially prominent in the 1990s in Southwest China. It was called "the age of the wild ghosts." The ghosts were said to be responsible for possessions, violence, and revenge killings (Mueggler 2001).

The communist government of Vietnam outlawed mediums because it saw the complex as a backward superstition with no place in a modern communist world. The mediums continued their work underground, risking severe punishment. However, by the mid-1990s, the government recognized that the public health menace posed by all the angry ghosts was so severe that they began sponsoring the mediums, supporting them financially and otherwise. What a turnaround! By 1997, seven women were operating as state-sponsored mediums in Hanoi (Gustafsson 2009, 121). One of them located the remains of so many dead soldiers that she was given an award by the state. Gustafsson met with almost 190 people in Vietnam suffering from possession, and almost all of them found relief with the mediums. She writes, "I will give no explanation for what ailed the Vietnamese I worked with... beyond what they offered themselves. To do otherwise would denigrate their years of suffering, give the lie to what I witnessed and imply that they were not sound of mind" (ibid., 10). "Existing spirit possession theories simply do not apply and are generally dismissive of the subjects' experiences and beliefs" (ibid., 130). I wish more researchers were so respectful. The ability to enter trance involuntarily for the possessed and voluntarily for the mediums has been called "a psychobiological heritage of mankind" by Suryani and Jensen, the scholars who studied possession in Bali. As modern Western psychotherapy is realizing the effectiveness of psychedelically induced altered states of consciousness in healing PTSD and major depression, perhaps we can open our minds to the healing potential of possession trance.

As in the rest of Southeast Asia, the spiritual possession complex is becoming more powerful in Vietnam. There's also gender fluidity here. Barley Norton (2006) refers to "hot-tempered women and effeminate men." Spirit possession involves special music, as is true all over the world. Reporting on Vietnam's mediums in California's Silicon Valley, Karen Fjelstad and Lisa Maiffret (quoted in Fjelstad and Hien 2006, 111–126) say the mediums report that their lives improved dramatically when they became mediums. They felt stronger, happier, and healthier. They develop increasing awareness of the spirit world.

Becoming a medium is a life-transforming event. Here in the United States, as in Vietnam, the number and variety of mediums is increasing. If one fails to respond to the call to become a medium, the person or their family suffer. This belief is found in many cultures. Mediums gain reputation and prestige only when they can successfully cure Yin diseases, especially mental illness. In the Silicon Valley temples, some mediums talk of percentages of possession. Sometimes the spirit takes over completely — a 100 percent possession — and sometimes less than half — 40 percent or so. The Vietnamese possession complex is in many ways unique, but it also shares many of the more universal features. People report real relief from distress, especially from mental illness. A person often becomes a medium in response to their own illness or trauma. Special music accompanies the healings. There is a predominance of women and some gender fluidity. The complex is growing rapidly, and new forms are evolving.

Gender issues are very significant in studying possession. Every source I have studied agrees that it's predominantly women who are possessed. This seems to hold worldwide. This very basic fact seems clear; there are all kinds of theories to explain it, but none seem convincing. Another fact is that gender fluidity seems prominent in possession complexes. This is not nearly as universal a phenomenon as the predominance of women, but it is very widespread. Many of the spirit mediums of Myanmar are beautiful, extravagantly gay men. One of these mediums said, "So many of us are gay because we can better embody both male and female spirits." The spirits like powerful mediums because they help make the spirit famous and popular. In Thailand, the mediums used to be almost all women, but now more and more gay men and transvestites are mediums. Again, there is no convincing explanation, but possession has very often had something antiauthoritarian and transgressive about it. It makes sense. It could be a home for those who have been marginalized.

Anthropology

Separating anthropology from the material on non-Western civilizations is totally arbitrary. Eighty percent of the world's population is non-Western. One commentator objected to the phrase "third world" and suggested instead that we should refer to Western culture as WEIRD: white, educated, industrialized, rich, and developed. We are so blind, narrow-minded, and arrogant that we have seriously proposed that other cultures are primitive and even pathological when they disagree with our culture's views and assumptions. As we have seen, possession is one of the most ubiquitous human experiences and is recognized by a vast majority of the world's cultures and people. The anthropological literature on this subject is huge. Janice Boddy, the great authority on the Zār cult of North Africa, said over a quarter of a century ago that studies of possession in Africa alone were more than any one research scholar could review in a lifetime. Many more studies have been published since then. Boddy (1994) notes that much of this seems to be an attempt to tame possession — to reduce its reality, often by medicalizing it. Governments, especially colonizing powers, see possession as subversive. Even Indigenous power structures often view it with distrust. It is wild, uncontrolled, and unpredictable.

Extraordinary states of mind are not essentially pathological. They are frequently intentionally evoked for healing, often with music and dance. The vast majority of the world knows this, and hopefully even here in our WEIRD culture it is becoming acceptable to state this: altered states of consciousness, anomalous experiences, non-ordinary realities — whatever you choose to call this whole domain — can be immensely valuable and healing for individuals and the cultures they live in. The incredibly positive and now rigorously researched and documented results that psychedelic-assisted psychotherapy is getting with PTSD, major depression, and more should open even the most fossilized skeptic's mind, but they probably won't. As the great physicist Max Planck said when quantum mechanics was being introduced, "Physics progresses funeral by funeral." Scholars can be incredibly rigid and territorial.

Some anthropologists divide cultures into monophasic and polyphasic. Monophasic cultures (which is basically the modern West) only value one way of knowing, one state of being. Polyphasic cultures value two or more states of consciousness as sources of knowledge. Many of you were probably already polyphasic in your thinking; hopefully after reading about Isabel Clarke's propositional and implicational cognitive systems and Vervaeke's four ways of knowing, many more of you will be questioning the monophasic assumptions our educations were largely built on. In some Australian Aboriginal groups, they say that we humans have four brains: a story brain (which handles the myths and thinking), a family brain (which handles relationships and emotions), a country brain (which handles environment, nature, and navigating trails), and a body brain (which handles physical sensation and movement). This is a beautiful polyphasic system, and it fits very well with modern evolutionary psychology's descriptions of mental modules that evolved for special purposes. Iain McGilchrist describes three ways of knowing: the rational, the irrational, and the transrational. He cites music as an example of the transrational that everyone has experienced. There is meaning and power in music, but it is not merely rational. McGilchrist is much more famous for his discussions of left- and right-brain function. In recent interviews, he warns that our civilization itself is in danger now because we have become almost totally monophasic, with the left brain's way of knowing entirely dominating our world.

In possession complexes, the possessed person often leaves the social world and enters the Wilderness, either literally or metaphorically or both. They spend time in this liminal realm interacting with the spirits, and then they return to their culture. This roughly follows the pattern laid out in Joseph Campbell's hero's journey and in Arnold van Gennep's analysis of initiation rituals and other rites of passage. Entering this liminal realm is a de-automatization process, a disruption of the habits and patterns of a lifetime. This is parallel to the emphasis at the Harvard and Massachusetts General Hospital's Center for the Neuroscience of

Psychedelics on the fact that psychedelics downregulate the default mode network (the neurological system that generates our ordinary reality) and disrupt rumination, repetitive ideas, and thought loops. The hypothesis is that this new flexibility is what creates the psychedelic healings. In Plato's *Phaedrus*, Socrates insists that "our greatest blessings come to us by way of Madness. Provided it is given by Divine gift." He cites poetic, prophetic, erotic, cathartic, and initiatory madnesses. The fountainhead of Western philosophy clearly states that there is great value and knowledge in non-ordinary states of being. Both Plato and Socrates were polyphasic thinkers.

The spirit possession complex relieves human suffering. In many ways, Indigenous healers get better results with mental-emotional distress than we do. "Possession is a form of knowledge," Michael Lambek stated after studying it on Mayotte, an island off the east coast of Africa, back in the '80s and '90s. Alexander Moreira-Almeida, MD, a psychiatrist in Brazil, has developed the idea that possession is actually a form of anomalous information. Gregory Dawes said spirit possession provides access to "unconscious cognition." Michael Winkelman stated that altered states of consciousness in general "increase our access to novel information." Winkelman believes the altered states of consciousness in possession can release ancient brain structures to have their say. He suggests that the paleomammalian brain had access to innate healing states and that possession can access these states. There is an entire field of neuroanthropology, which suggests that spirit possession experiences can enhance neuroplasticity.

Jack Hunter (2020) points out that voluntary desired possession is much more common worldwide than illness-causing possession. Dissociation, instead of being seen as pathology, is viewed as a very valuable skill. The ability to become possessed helps the medium; it help her clients and, even more, it can be deeply healing for the group as well as the culture. In Brazil, Vietnam, and other cultures, it has been noted how mediums' lives often involve a passage from suffering to well-being. In Brazil, this initiatory period in a medium's development is often called *fazer o santo*, which means "to make a saint." I have noted before how close the experience of religious revelation and insanity can be. Have Brazilian practitioners found methods that can help move these experiences into the positive realm?

William James famously wrote about conversion experiences — single events, usually framed as religious, that allow people to transform their lives. We therapists have largely ignored this class of phenomena, perhaps in part because we cannot induce them, and their existence painfully reminds us of the shortcomings of our profession. Dissociative capacities we pathologize become resources for the medium and her community. A revealing study was done by Stolovy et al. in 2015 in Israel. They studied 150 women with similar trauma histories who were divided into two groups. One group were channelers who had and who cultivated contact with spirits, while the other group were not. All of the women were given the same five psychological assessment measures. The channelers scored significantly higher on dissociation, which should have predicted more pathology, but it didn't. The channelers also scored significantly higher on psychological health. The lesson, I believe, is that dissociation in and of itself is not bad. It is only harmful because of the way our culture and mental health system relate to it. Institutionalized inductions of altered states of consciousness exist in 90 percent of the world's cultures, but not our own. Dr. Roberto Lewis-Fernández, during the debate on possession in the *DSM-IV* and *DSM-V*, pointed out that most societies have patterned dissociation — patterned major discontinuities of consciousness, memory, identity, and behavior — that are culturally structured so they benefit the individual and the people near them. We lack these patterned forms.

Scholars have tried to fit different kinds of possession into different systems of categories and types. Michael Lambek emphasizes that we need to respect the unique and individual nature of the complex in each culture. Our attempts to fit possession complexes into systems will always obscure something of great value. This seems very respectful to me, but nonetheless I feel we can learn from the types these experiences seem to fall into. I. M. Lewis's *Ecstatic Religion* (1971) is one of the most famous books in this field. He proposes that possession could be divided into central and peripheral. Central possessions are orthodox and highly structured and support the domination structures of the culture. The Nechung State Oracle of Tibet, discussed earlier in some detail, is a classic example. Peripheral possessions include organized groups that are independent of the central culture as well as the individual, unwanted, sickness-producing possessions. Raymond Firth, a famous anthropologist of an earlier generation, proposed two categories: spirit possession, which is uncontrolled, and spirit mediumship, which is controlled, sought after, and valued. He distinguished both of these from shamanism. A similar distinction is involuntary versus induced possessions. T. K. Oesterreich, whose hundred-year-old book, *Possession*, is still a valued classic, distinguished between somnambulistic possessions states (in which the possessed has complete amnesia for all events) and lucid ones (in which there is continuous awareness).

Maya Deren, in her 1953 classic *Divine Horsemen: The Living Gods of Haiti*, described her entry into full somnambulistic trance during a ceremony as being engulfed in the White Darkness. As the drums beat louder and stronger, the

White Darkness starts to shoot up. The Whiteness is glory, and the Darkness is terror; the terror is stronger, and when she feels her foot rooting to the ground, "I wrenched my foot free, but the effort catapults me across what seems a vast vast distance, and I come to rest upon a firmness of arms and bodies which would hold me up." She feels that her sense of self doubles "as in a mirror." Straining every muscle, she pulls loose again; and after she frees herself, her leg roots again. So it goes, the leg fixed, then wrenched loose, the long fall across space, the rooting of the leg again, for how long, how many times she does not know. "My skull is a drum, each great drum beat drives the leg like a point of a stake into the ground." Later the great spirit mounts. "The White Darkness moves up the veins with great force, which I cannot sustain, or contain, which surely will burst my skin. It is too much too bright too white for me. This is its Darkness. Mercy I scream within me. I hear it echoed by the voices shrill and unearthly: Erzulie! The bright Darkness floods up through my body, reaches my head, engulfs me and I am sucked down and exploded upward at once" (1953, 259–260). Erzulie is the name of one of the spirits who descend and possess the humans. She is the goddess of love. After this, Deren remembered absolutely nothing until Erzulie left her near the end of the ceremony. Deren is a superb writer, and her books are a pleasure to read and an eloquent introduction to possession.

Rebecca Basso (2006) proposed three classes of possessions: pathological, curative, and neutral. Rahardanto and Subandi (2012) proposed four types: pathological, curative, religious, and entertainment. Are your eyes starting to glaze over with all these classifications? There are more. These are all Eurocentric classifications. Each culture in which the possession complex is active has its own system and categories. They are the real experts we should be listening to, but to even start to enter this area is beyond the scope of this book. This may seem like a hopeless, bottomless morass, but just noticing all the different ways that scholars have tried to slice up the pie is instructive. It gives us a sense of the size of the subject, its great variety, and the scholarly squabbles it has provoked.

One of the most appealing and seemingly simple classifications is involuntary versus voluntary, but this conceals something extremely important. Most spirit mediums and shamans started with involuntary possessions that were extremely distressing and totally unwanted. They learned through an apprenticeship and initiation period of training to convert these into wanted, invited, and salutary experiences. This could provide a model for healing that we have no parallel for in the West. The Hearing Voices Movement makes room for people previously diagnosed as psychotic to dialogue with and relate to their voices. This seems vaguely analogous to shamans learning to relate to their spirits. The social

anthropologist Luc de Heusch proposed in 1962 that while much distressing possession was met with exorcism or removal of the spirit, there is another way, which
he named adorcism. In these practices, the possessing spirit is placated or accom-
modated, which often involves initiation into a spirit cult. Forming a lifelong relationship with the spirit converts an often painful and overwhelming experience
into a voluntary, controlled, desired, and curative possession. Other scholars have
discussed this same thing as two varieties of exorcism: permanent exorcism — the
removal of the spirit — and transformational exorcism — forming an ongoing
relationship with it. In IFS, we know that various parts of our system often feel
foreign to us when we first meet them. We can easily experience them as foreign
intrusions, but we also know that trying to amputate any part of ourselves only
makes things worse. Are adorcisms and transformational exorcisms other names
for this aspect of parts work? Or do they also indicate something more?

There are many paths and patterns in possession complexes. I want to highlight three. A person can experience an unwanted possession and go to some
religious practitioner to have it removed. A person with an unwanted possession
can have it transformed and tamed into a desirable and controlled form, which
often involves membership in the group. A person who experiences intrusive possession can undergo training and initiation to become a healer who then helps
others with the same issue. The first of these three looks like the kind of person
who comes to therapy for relief for a specific symptom. The second looks like the
suffering people who have something like William James's conversion experiences
and join a twelve-step group or a spiritual or religious organization. The third
looks like those of us who pursue our own healing, become wounded healers, and
work with others. This reminds me of the old joke that therapists are people who
need thirty hours of therapy a week.

There is so much rich and fascinating material I want to describe, but I need
to limit myself severely. Hopefully you're intrigued enough to pick one culture
with a strong possession complex and study it in detail, if you have not already
done so. This will expand your view of what it can mean to be human. For example, spirit possession often gives the possessed physical abilities that are not explainable. We have seen some instances of superhuman strength, for example, and
walking on fire is common. There is no scientific explanation for how this could
be possible, yet it happens all over the world. In Korea, shamans stand barefoot
on very sharp blades with no damage. In Tamil rituals, people are pierced through
with steel and do not bleed or exhibit symptoms of pain. In Java, men dance barefoot on broken glass with no injury. Stafford Betty, a professor in the University
of California University system, has pointed out the ubiquity of these physical

phenomena and says these examples alone make the area worthy of focused study. Since these visible, undeniable, and unexplained physical changes happen worldwide, shouldn't we be more curious about their claims of physical healings? Isn't it possible that these states could also have an effect on physical disease, as is so often claimed? The psychiatrist Roland Littlewood (2002, xii) wrote, "Western illness can only be understood in the context of a wider look at psychological distress in other societies… Rather than follow psychiatrists in labeling spirit possession as hysteria, we can approach hysteria through the idiom of spirit possession." He goes on to question our assumption that Europeans' symptoms are assumed to be more real and less culture-bound. We have judged all the other world cultures and eras and found them wanting. This is Eurocentric arrogance. Dr. Littlewood reminds us that psychiatry and imperialism historically developed simultaneously. Both assume that our view is the real one, and both objectify other people. Littlewood asserts, and I agree wholeheartedly, that all mental illness is culture-bound and socially constructed in profound ways.

The anthropologist Rebecca Seligman (2014) has applied the philosopher Ian Hacking's (1999) idea of biolooping to possession cults. Hacking states that there is a circular relationship between bodily processes and sociocultural meanings. Body interacts with cultural meaning systems, which create behavior patterns, which create body experiences, and round it goes in a circle. There is a feed-forward interaction among experience, physiological response, and meaning. In Seligman's words, "One of the most noteworthy aspects of this biolooping model then is the idea that some bodily qualities that fed the negative loop prior to initiation [as a Candomblé medium] also feed forward into a positive loop that is established through religious involvement" (2014, 130). This model doesn't just describe the healing effects of becoming a medium; Hacking also argues on a larger scale that the social construction of mental disorders becomes real through this same biolooping process.

Can we somehow intervene in this cultural biolooping process to reduce human suffering? For me, this is always the underlying question. I believe the answer is yes, but the how is not yet clear. Seligman gives us another important clue with her distinction between bounded and unbounded models. She draws on the work of the cognitive anthropologist Claudia Strauss (1992). Bounded models are typically learned explicitly; oftentimes we claim these ideas but don't necessarily act on them. Unbounded models are absorbed through experience and modeling; they are assumed to be true and often cannot be expressed. Both kinds of models are usually socially shared. Bounded models are easier to change but don't have much effect. Unbounded models are much harder and slower to change, but when they do, the effects are pervasive. Okay, then the question is: can we change the unbounded models that undergird our biolooping around mental illness? Too much jargon? My apologies.

Let me try one more time. A human has an anomalous experience, which is often frightening or difficult at first. This gets fed into the culture, in our case, especially into the mental health system. The culture can interpret or bioloop this experience back as a pathology or as a gift. It makes a critical difference how the culture holds it. Many other cultures do much better at this than ours. One last point from our survey of non-Western possession complexes: notice how many of them have some kind of befriending of the spirit. We are used to thinking of exorcisms as some sort of heroic battle with raw evil using violence and force. This is not so common. In India, they call them unhappy spirits, not evil ones. In Korea, the mudang often help the spirit to have its suffering witnessed so it can leave in peace. In the Zār cult, the women form lifelong relationships with the Zār spirits. The Spiritists of Brazil believe that an intrusive spirit needs our help as much as the client does. In Malaysia, when spirits of the land are assaulting people, small spirit homes are built for them to live in peacefully. In shamanism, the tormenting spirit that threatened madness often becomes a trusted and valued ally. We can learn from this great befriending.

Many anthropologists separate shamanism from spirit possession. In possession complexes, the spirits often take over completely, while the shaman learns how to control their spirit helpers. In possession, the spirit comes to the person, while the shaman often leaves their body, and their soul travels to the spirit ground. Possession complexes tend to occur in larger, more hierarchical and organized societies, while shamans tend to be associated with smaller and more egalitarian hunter-gatherer bands. There has been a tremendous amount of scholarly disputation on this distinction, but for our purposes it's not so important. Both make contact with the other inside, usually called spirits of some kind, for healing and transformation. Both have much to teach us about relieving the human suffering of what we call mental illness.

CHAPTER 11

A Totally Eurocentric View:
Spiritual Presence Experiences in the West

Despite my best efforts and decades of study, I know that every word I've written in this book is Eurocentric. There are no value-free perceptions in a field like this. Much of the structure of values and categories of perception come from our culture; we absorb them with our mother's milk; they are bred in the bone. All this is far beneath our normal conscious awareness and experience of the world. It actually creates the way we experience the world. "We see the world not as it is, but as we are," Anais Nin said, but I believe similar ideas were expressed by some ancient Jewish rabbis.

Having acknowledged this, there are two changes that I believe can help us loosen the hold of our unexamined assumptions. One is starting to use the concept and word *transliminal* instead of *unconscious* or *subconscious*. *Transliminal* means "across the threshold," whereas *unconscious* and *subconscious* imply a spatial relationship and an inferiority. They also carry the huge burden of all the theories and history that are embedded in them. In IFS, Dick usually only asks people to "go inside." He does not refer to altered states of consciousness or trance — just "go inside." Pretty much everybody knows what this means and is able to do it. In some of his writings, Dick describes the laws of inner physics in order to explain the dynamics of the subjective world. I think this inside/outside dichotomy is much more helpful than the conscious/unconscious one, and I feel it is even more helpful, especially given the topic we are exploring, to use the even less structured term *transliminal*. When we go inside, for example, we get to realms where the inside/outside distinction loses meaning. In the past, Dick has not agreed with me on this point. When someone hears the voice of a dead loved one, is it inside or outside of them? When someone experiences possession? When a mystic experiences the divine in all its effulgence and glory? When the deep Jungian archetypes emerge, where do they come from? Does the inside/outside distinction apply? The people who experience these things often insist that they come from something and somewhere way more powerful and vast than they are. Do we really want to use terms that invalidate their experience — and, in the very act of naming, push their experience into the realm of delusion and pathology? Actually, this inside/

outside issue is an ancient theological question: is God immanent (inside) or transcendent (outside)? A vast amount has been written on this debate. My favorite answer comes from a teacher who, when asked this question, just said yes. Then after a long pause, he said both. The inside/outside language is a great first approximation. It is useful and easily understood. Like Newtonian physics, it can become limiting when we explore the further realms.

Another problem with the terms *unconscious* and *subconscious* is that they imply that everything we find there has no consciousness. This is very misleading. In IFS, we recognize that all parts have consciousness of their own. They also have agency and will and intention. It also does not fit to call the great archetypes and guides that Jung discovered "unconscious." They were often wise, capable of dialogue, and deeply aware. The term *transliminal* can be liberating. Much of my thinking here is based on the work of Isabel Clarke. I want to acknowledge my debt to her but do not want her blamed if I have gone too far.

The concept of the transliminal is one freeing change, and the other is the concept of spiritual presence experiences, which I believe originated with Tanya Luhrmann. The word *possession* carries so much baggage. A person may have a visionary experience that they find deeply meaningful, only to have others denigrate it by calling it evil possession. I noted that in Korea, it is insulting to use the word *possession* when the mudang receives the god. When Pentecostal Christians feel the Holy Spirit enter them, would they be offended if we called it possession? In Europe, people have been burned at the stake when their visions were judged to be possessions. What do we say when an artist, poet, or mystic receives inspiration? We could try to dust off and clean up the word *possession*, but I fear this may be a hopeless task.

The phrase "spiritual presence experience" avoids all this; it points to a person's experience without judgment as to its reality or benevolence. This phrase could free us from many of our limiting presuppositions. Actually, I prefer the phrase "the other within" or "the others within." So many people these days are allergic to the word *spiritual* that I hesitate to use it. Like "spiritual presence experience," the phrase "the others within" is also nonjudgmental. A big problem with the IFS nomenclature of "unattached burdens" and "guides" is that it makes us sort out these phenomena into good or bad right from the start. This is not helpful. It would be better if we had language that could help us reserve judgment. We often do not know what these beings are or whether they are benevolent or negative for quite a while. Some seem to be ambivalent and capable of both roles. Despite all of these points, I'll mostly continue to use the more familiar terms. I do not want to introduce more jargon into an already overcrowded field. I hope we can hold the old names in this larger, more open frame.

Judaism

Let's start with the Jewish tradition. In the Old Testament, there is very little explicit reference to negative possession, but there are a substantial number of references to positive possession or spiritual presence experiences. For example, when many of the Jews started to question the wisdom of fleeing Egypt, God commanded Moses to gather seventy of the elders. Then, "the Lord came down in the cloud and spoke to him, and took some of the spirit that was upon him and put it upon the seventy elders; and when the spirit rested upon them, they prophesied" (Numbers 11:25). Ritually induced ecstatic possession was accepted. Once God sent Samuel to meet "a band of prophets [who were coming down from the mountains] with harp, tambourine, flute and lyre before them prophesying." Samuel would be "overcome with the spirit of the Lord… and be turned into another man" (1 Samuel 10:5–6). What impresses me most about this is that no surprise was expressed at there being bands of male ecstatics in the mountains. Does this imply that it was an accepted practice? Perhaps the most cited Old Testament text about this is Joel 2:28: "And it shall come to pass afterward, that I will pour out my spirit on all flesh; your sons and your daughters shall prophesy, your old men shall dream dreams, and your young men shall see visions." This text was used centuries later by many spirit-possessed Christians as biblical validation of their experience.

The only event that clearly looks like negative possession in the Old Testament happened to Saul, the first King of Israel. He disobeyed God's command, and an evil spirit of God came to him. He was troubled by the spirit but not completely taken over. David soothed him by playing his lyre, an interesting echo of the importance of music in possession complexes worldwide. Positive possession is more in evidence. Writing of Jesus's time, David Hill summarized the prevailing views of scholars: "Within Judaism of the time, possession of the Holy Spirit, the Spirit of God was regarded as the mark of prophecy" (Hill 1979, 58). R. Wilson, quoted in the *Harper's Bible Dictionary* (1985), says, "Israelites thought of the prophetic experience as one that occurred when people were possessed by the spirit of God." Examples include "The hand of the Lord" fell upon them (1 Kings 18:46, Jeremiah 15:17, and others) and the spirit of God "rested on them" (Numbers 11: 25–26) or "clothed itself" with them (Judges 6:34). "In these situations they were no longer in control over their actions and words, but were completely dominated by God." Ezekiel's visions were possession states: "A spirit entered into me" (2:2). He also reported spirit travel and ecstatic trance (Samuel 10:9–13 and 19:18–24). Isaiah, Jeremiah, and Amos all had these experiences. Some scholars assert that the Old Testament prophets were "ecstatic, trance possessed prophets" (Jonathan Seidel, quoted in Goldish 2003, 77).

Here are the words of Philo of Alexandria, a Jewish Platonist who worked to combine Judaism with Greek philosophy and an approximate contemporary of Jesus:

> So long as our mind pouring as it were, noonday light into the whole soul, shines about us and encompasses us, we are in ourselves. And we are not possessed. But when this light reaches its setting, then, as might be expected, ecstasy and divine possession and madness fall upon us. For when the divine light shines, the human sets, and when it sets, then the other rises and shines, and this is want to happen to the prophetic kind. The mind that is in us is banished at the coming of the divine spirit, and at its departure returns home... For the prophet, even when he appears to speak, is in truth silent, and another uses his organs of speech, his mouth and his tongue, to declare whatsoever he wills. (quoted in Davies 2014, 85)

In Jesus's time, the situation is much clearer. Abundant evidence exists in Greek, Roman, and New Testament sources that possession — both by demons and souls of dead sinners — and exorcism were common. There is no evidence that these beliefs went away. But accounts of possessions and exorcisms were relatively rare throughout the Middle Ages. In both Jewish and Christian traditions, the number of accounts of possession exploded again in the fifteenth and sixteenth centuries. This has been called the Golden Age of the Demonic.

The most common name now used for a possession spirit in Judaism is *dybbuk*. The entry of a dybbuk into a person is also often described as a rape. *Dybbuk* is a Yiddish word that comes from the same root as the word for glue. This feels accurate considering how sticky some of these UBs can be. They seem to always be negative. There is also the word *ibbur*, which can mean "impregnate," either in a negative or positive sense. A *maggid* is always a positive being, a heavenly mentor granted only to holy people.

Dybbuk possession seems to always involve souls of the dead rather than demons. The symptoms have been reported consistently for four hundred years, from sixteenth-century Palestine to nineteenth-century Poland. These possessions and exorcisms are strongly associated with kabbalism. Rabbi Isaac Luria, his chief disciple, Rabbi Hayyim Vital, and their followers, who settled in Safed in the late 1500s, created a school of kabbalism and a tradition of study of possession and exorcism. Luria was reported by Vital to be able to see the souls of dead people with his own eyes. "Many of the Jewish exorcisms were dramatic and sometimes shocking" (Yoram Bilu, quoted in Goldish 2003, 62). They were sometimes so violent that the subject of the exorcism died! It was a heroic conflict between the exorcist and the possessing spirit. Exorcism could be seen as something that supported social control; it exalted the status of the old rabbis. Some of the major big-city rabbis would not allow exorcistic healing because they saw it as lower-class backcountry stuff. Once again, here is the elite versus folk dichotomy. Fumigation — the use of incense or smoke from burning plants — as well as rigorous interrogation of the possessing spirit, whipping the possessed to drive the spirit out, and the blowing of the shofar (a ram's horn trumpet) were all common in exorcisms.

In the Jewish tradition, it has long been recognized that dybbuk possession and devekut, divine euphoria, can look alike. Often, mad people were believed to be able to perceive the hidden sins of those around them. "The possessed person acts mad whether the spirit within is evil or holy… There was a preexisting belief that the external manifestations of Dybbuk and Devekut states were identical since the phenomena themselves are similar" (Zvi Mark, quoted in Goldish 2003, 269). "It appears that the existence of possessions that were positively valued and even viewed as religious achievement or ideal was reflected as well in the positive attitudes toward the insane" (ibid., 287). Isn't this something we should emulate? People at the outer edges of what humans can experience still deserve our kindness and respect. They may have gifts for us, perhaps new ways of seeing.

The Greeks and Romans

Just as Jewish thinking recognized the similarities between divine prophetic contact and madness, so did the ancient Greeks. Their word *mania* is often translated as madness. But as archaeologist Yulia Ustinova points out (2018, 2–29), this is inadequate. Mania refers to any deviation from baseline ordinary consciousness; it can be a godsent blessing, great love, or insanity. It could be "superhuman or deranged" (ibid., 3). This is much closer to the expression "spiritual presence experience" than our normal word *possession*. The Greek word *kakodaimonan* means both to be possessed by an evil spirit and to be mad, insane. Possession was seen as a major cause of insanity. Divine vengeance was another recognized cause of madness. Florid psychosis was a common expression of God's wrath. Even though there were evil spirits, daimons in general were often benevolent (remember Socrates's experience) or neutral. The daimons were a class of beings between us and the gods and were necessary for us to communicate with the divine.

The Oracle at Delphi and many other ancient oracles depended on possession. This oracle was in operation for at least 1,200 years until the church shut it down around 400 AD. It was the most respected oracle of the Greco-Roman world. A female priest, the *pythia*, would sit on a three-legged stool over a crack in the rock where the fumes emerged in a cave. She would respond to questions in trance or, perhaps more accurately, the spirit responded through her. She was seen as possessed by a god. Sometimes she spoke in poetry, and sometimes her words seemed nonsensical. They were interpreted for the questioner by a male priest.

As we have noted before, elites often suppressed the possession complex in all its forms. Ustinova analyzed this in relationship to prophecy in the classical world. "The entire phenomena is difficult to manage and control. The most natural way to overcome the difficulty is to suppress ecstatic soothsaying... The more rigid and ubiquitous the state and or priestly authority, the less place is left for open-ended ecstatic prophecy" (Ustinova 2018, 86–87). She notes that Egypt, the most rigidly stratified society of the ancient world, would not tolerate any prophecy unless it was performed in the official temples. Perhaps one reason the Oracle of Delphi was so influential for so long is that it had struck a balance. The wild, direct, and uncontrolled voice of the god spoke through the female pythia and was filtered through the interpretation of a male priest.

Euripides's great play *The Bacchae* is one of the West's most important and profound explorations of this tension. It was first performed in 405 BC, shortly after Euripides's death. Greek theater was a religious ritual; it was not considered entertainment. The citizens of Athens were required to attend dramatic performances as part of their civic duty. The actor became the character; in a sense, they were possessed. This theme comes up in acting all over the world. Modern method acting echoes this theme. In ancient India, actors sometimes became so possessed by their roles that they actually killed the actors playing their enemies in the play.

As the play begins, the god Dionysus announces that he will go to Thebes and prove to the city and its king, Pentheus, that he is indeed born a god. He inspires and leads the women of Thebes in revelry and ecstasy in the wilderness. King Pentheus hears of this and has his guards bring Dionysus in. Then he interrogates the god in a scene that has been compared to Pontius Pilate interrogating Jesus. Pentheus is annoyed by the god's cryptic answers and has his guards take him out. But now Dionysius comes out of his disguise, reveals his power, breaks free, destroys the palace, and leaves the city. Later, Pentheus is told that there are more bands of ecstatic women up on the mountains. They tear cattle apart with their bare hands and raid villages. Dionysius, in disguise, persuades Pentheus to dress up as a celebrant and go up on the mountains to spy on the women. The ecstatic women discover the spy and tear him apart. Pentheus's own mother, not recognizing him in her god-maddened state, puts his severed head on a stick and returns proudly to Thebes. Her ecstasy vanishes when she sees what she has done. She and her sisters are exiled. Pentheus's parents are turned into snakes, and Dionysus leads barbarian hordes to plunder the countryside. This play is so violent and shocking that it was not considered fit for public performance in Europe until the end of the nineteenth century.

We see the overwhelming ecstatic power of the god and his terrible vengeance when it is denied or suppressed. "Mortals, who eagerly surrender to the divinely inflicted madness, will find in it the greatest joy and return to normality relieved of their grief; Those unwilling to succumb will be maddened, but with disastrous consequences: Dionysus is most terrible and most gentle to men" (Ustinova 2018, 197). R. S. Kraemer, classicist, feminist, and professor at Brown University, quipped, "It is insane to be sane, sane to be insane." This divine bliss, when not resisted, was a purification and liberation that created inner peace and harmony. For the Greeks, it was an experience of *enthousiasmos* — attaining unity with the god.

In Rome, which had stronger centralized authority than Greece, only possession fury on the battlefield and **poetic** inspiration were welcomed. Other possessions and ecstasies were marginalized. In the Roman Empire, mystery cults flourished intermittently, but they were only tolerated at best and never seen as truly Roman.

Before we leave the Greco-Roman classical world, one more subject needs our attention: theurgy. This is a system of rituals and contemplative practices developed by the Neoplatonists in the first few centuries of our era. It has been dismissed as magic, but it has had an enduring influence on esoteric Christianity and occultists ever since. Iamblichus (c. 242–325 AD), a Syrian, is usually seen as its most important thinker. He stated, "It is not pure thought that unites theurgists to the gods" (quoted in Kupperman 2014, 174). The word *theurgy* comes from two Greek words meaning "gods" and "action." It involves rituals and actions. Its goal was henosis — becoming one with God. Iamblichus described it as "raised up to union with the highest power," "To assume the mantle of the gods," "as much as possible... in union with God" (ibid., 177–8). It is clear that this state is not exactly possession, but it is related.

Professor Wouter Hanegraaff is a Dutch classicist who has studied this area extensively. He has also demonstrated that the Western intellectuals have banned entire areas of knowledge. He refers to this as the systematic pathologization of entheogenic practice and entire cultures, especially the mystery religions, hermetic traditions, theurgy, and the spirituality of ancient Egypt. These have only survived in the occult, the esoteric, and hidden traditions. The theurgists often referred to *phantasia*, which is usually translated as "imagination," but this is a very different concept from what we are used to. It refers to a sensory modality, like sight or hearing, that allows us to perceive the gods. This is very close to Henry Corbin's concept of the imaginal, but almost two thousand years earlier.

In Hanegraaff's view, theurgist rituals were twofold. They invited the gods down to enter the worshipper, which is positive possession, and while this was taking place, the worshipper soul was freed to ascend to heaven. This looks like shamanic soul journey with both traditions occurring simultaneously. The rituals often included music, dance, shouting, and involuntary movements. They were intense and emotional, and they looked like possession rituals. The focus and intent were on healing both physical and emotional distress. Iamblichus insisted that our human role is to bring the divine beauty down into this realm. The gods are everywhere — in plants and rocks, in animals, in temples, and in us. This recalls a type of animism in which everything has spirit and personhood. It is our task to embody the divine beauty here, not to escape into a noetic realm. Here the theurgists are clearly more like the Mahayana Buddhists than the Hinayana. Hanegraaff's meticulous scholarship has given a picture of theurgy, a native Western tradition that combines possession and shamanic soul flight in service of healing. He has also shown how this has been suppressed and pathologized for many centuries (Hanegraaff 2012, 2013). The conflict between the wildness and uncontrollable nature of spiritual presence experiences and the dominant culture and power structures has taken many forms.

For the theurgists, the major pathway to this union is working with your personal daimon, the semi-divine spirit that can connect you to the divine realm. Iamblichus states that the divine is superrational; therefore, we cannot expect to reach it by reason. This union requires action. Much of the work with personal daimons looks more like familiar possession states. The theurgists were often ecstatic and inspired. Action and emotion were important. They had one practice that seems especially bizarre to us: sometimes, instead of inviting a daimon or god down into themselves, they would invite it down into an object, usually a statue of a divine being. Then they would have dialogues with the statue. There is a similar practice in India: *murti*. A god's spirit is invited into a statue so that it can be worshipped there. In the possession rites of Tonga, the spirit would be invited into a shell or a bowl that became the god's canoe (Mills, quoted in Blythe 2021, 74–91). The priest then became the anchor of the god's canoe in this world. Sometimes objects can mediate possession states. The theurgists were working to unify the most sophisticated rational philosophy of the ancient world with the felt reality of spiritual presence experiences. We could learn much.

Christianity

Now we come to the subject of possession in Christianity, the core of the Western tradition, the world's most widespread religion and something many people have very strong feelings about. It's unfortunate that the word *possession* has such unpleasant connotations for many. I do not want to offend anyone, so if it helps you, you're welcome to mentally substitute the phrase "spiritual presence experience" or "the other within" for the word *possession* as you read.

Jesus was a spirit-possessed healer. He exorcised demons from people. When he was baptized by John the Baptist, the Holy Dove came down and entered him. If we were reading this as an account of a spiritual leader in another culture, we would immediately think of spirit possession and the spiritual authority this brings. His forty days in the desert being tempted by Satan recall accounts of a shamanic initiation in which the shaman was able to convert the life-shattering intrusion of spirit into something of great value for themselves and their people. Mark's description, which is generally considered the oldest, is the most vividly shamanic. There was a "tearing open of the heavens" at the start of the descent of the Spirit. Mark said the spirit descended like a dove and entered into Jesus (*Eis*). Matthew and Luke softened this word to the spirit descended upon (*epi*) him. In Mark's version, the Spirit threw or drove (*ekballei*) Jesus into the wilderness. The verb implies harsh force, while in Luke and Matthew he is passively led there. The baptism of Jesus shows a lot of the characteristics of a shamanic initiation.

Jesus was known as a successful exorcist. The three synoptic gospels — Mark, Matthew, and Luke — described seven of Jesus's exorcisms in detail. But they were excluded from the Gospel of John, perhaps for theological reasons and perhaps as the earliest Christian example of the repression of the possession complex. In addition to the seven detailed exorcism descriptions, others are mentioned in passing, and there are references to other Jewish exorcists of the time. It seems that possession and exorcism were part of the normal experience of people of that time, including Jesus and his disciples.

Jesus was accused of being possessed by the demon Beelzebub and using power from this demon to cast out other demons. The early Christians and their founder were accused of practicing sorcery. Mark's gospel also reports that Jesus's family tried to restrain him from his ecstatic states because people were saying he had lost his mind. John's gospel, which omitted all the exorcisms, does report that Jesus was accused of being possessed by demons and of being insane. Here again, as in so many other cultures, we see that people having spiritual presence experiences are often seen as mentally ill or negatively possessed, and the accusations are used to discredit them and their work.

Jesus is presented as an authority in control of the unclean spirits. He typically rebuked and commanded them. He relied on the spirit of God and did not use charms or talismans or magical papyri, which were common in his day. He sent out his disciples, clearly stating that he gave them the authority and power to control demons. Even the skeptical researchers looking for the historical Jesus admit that if anything can be known with certainty about him, it's that he was a healer and an exorcist.

The Pentecost, looked at from an anthropological, cross-cultural perspective, appears to be a mass visionary possession event. "They were all in one place together. And suddenly there came from the sky, a noise like a strong driving wind, and it filled the entire house in which they were. Then there appeared to them tongues as of fire, which parted and came to rest on each of them. And they were all filled with the Holy Spirit..." (Acts 2:1–4). This receiving of the Holy Spirit became the requirement for becoming a Christian. It was not espousing a belief — it was having a certain powerful experience that changed people's lives. The purity of this reliance on direct spiritual presence experience had already begun to die down after a generation or two. As soon as there were church authorities, they feared the wildness of direct experience and wanted to control it.

This language will be distressing to some. We have loaded the word *possession* with all sorts of negative baggage. Davies (2014, 22) states it bluntly: "The Holy Spirit is a form of experience that falls under the general category of spirit possession. It is a form of experience that is probably available to any human being given the right cultural setting." In no way do I want to denigrate or downplay the great value of this experience by classing it with other possessions. Rather, I hope it will lead us to remove the negative connotations from the word *possessed*. There is linguistic evidence that early Christians grouped the two experiences together. The same Greek verb, *ĕcho*, is used for a person who has the Holy Spirit and for a person who has an unclean spirit. The word *enoikeo* is used for the presence of the Holy Spirit: the spirit is "in house" or ensconced within us. People are filled with the force of the spirit.

Neuroscientist Patrick McNamara writes, "Positive possession enhances self-control, dignity, autonomy as well as holiness and compassion for others (2011, 136). Demonic possession is associated with loss of control, slavishness to the appetites, being hated of others and violent passionate emotions. Jesus thought that negative forms of possession could only be prevented by positive forms of possession. There was no neutral state." This is farther than I want to go, but if we close ourselves off to all possessions, all spiritual presence experiences, we become very brittle, fragile, small, and impoverished.

The domination structures of the early church started working to kill off these positive possession experiences very early. But they did not die easily. We have seen this conflict repeatedly now. If we cut off all contact with the depths, if we invalidate spiritual presence experience totally, we become dry, brittle husks.

But if we totally open our behavior, we can be seen as insane, and we lose touch with consensus reality. This conflict is often played out in society, with the central authorities and elite suppressing any openness and the common people and outsiders welcoming it. It does not ever really die off; it only goes into hiding and reemerges in more difficult forms. Euripides's *The Bacchae* gives us a foundational myth for this dynamic.

In the early church, this welcoming of spiritual presence experiences — of possession by the Holy Spirit — had a resurgence with the followers of Montanus. Montanus was a Christian who lived in the second century AD in Phrygia, which is in Asia Minor. In 156 AD, he fell into an ecstatic trance and prophesied under the Holy Spirit. Soon he was joined by two women, Priscilla and Maximilla, who also entered into ecstasy and prophesied. They were called "The Three." The main church called them Montanists, but they called their way the "New Prophecy." Many of their followers entered into ecstatic trance and prophesied. These trances were evidently quite dramatic. Eusebius, a contemporary, said they would go into "a frenzy or ecstasy, babble and rave strange things." When Montanus was in possession states, he spoke in the first person as God: "Lo, the man is as a lyre and I fly over him as a pick, the man sleepeth" … "I am the father and the son and the Holy Spirit" (quoted in Tabberaee, 2009). This clearly looks like complete possession. The main church did not question the reality of the possession but said it was demons, not the Holy Spirit. They tried unsuccessfully to exorcise him of these demons. The Montanists thought they were receiving new material from the Holy Spirit. Montanus and his followers were excommunicated in 177, but the church did not have the power to stamp them out. It wasn't until the sixth century that Emperor Justinian was able to crush all their organized centers. They probably survived for another two or three hundred years in the rural and small-town areas that had always been their strongholds. Tertullian, the Great Church father from Carthage, in North Africa, was the most famous convert to the New Prophecy. This movement had rigorous moral standards — far more stringent than the Catholics of the day. This is what Tertullian admired. Today, many also admire the fact that women had a prominent place and were welcome as bishops and leaders. This was the last time for a while that vivid possession-like states would be prominent in the Christian West. It does not seem that anyone at the time questioned the reality of the possessions. The arguments were about who was doing the possessions — the Holy Spirit or demons.

Exorcism stayed a part of the church. All new Christian converts had to be exorcised as part of their being welcomed into the community. Baptism rights contained an exorcism within them and still do in many churches. Church officials were entitled to exorcise demons, though which officials were allowed to changed over the ensuing centuries. Christians had succeeded in turning all the Greco-Roman gods and the daimons who had been their intermediaries into demons who were purely negative. In terms of spiritual presence experiences and possession states, it was largely a quiet time until around the twelfth century. There were exceptions, of course, especially on the margins. The desert fathers — men and a few women who had fled deep into the deserts of Egypt — maintained this living contact. The temptations of Saint Anthony, one of the greatest of the desert fathers, are famously portrayed as dozens of demons surrounding the holy man and attacking him. There is evidence that the folk and village culture maintained these traditions, but the church disallowed individual inspiration.

The return of the possession complex to prominence started around the year 1000. A new form of religious experience or an old form returning started to emerge, mainly among women. This new old form was "… deeply **ascetic,** highly ecstatic and devoted to meditation upon the events of Jesus's life on Earth… identification with the suffering body of the human Christ… immobile and insensible trances, reception of the stigmata or uncontrollable fits of crying [the gift of tears] were commonly reported…" (Caciola 2003, 15). This is also the period when extreme fasting became more prominent among the women mystics. Rudolph Bell (1987) wrote a book-length study of this called *Holy Anorexia*. Again, we see the close proximity of spirituality and mental illness. What was held then as a potentially deeply meaningful spiritual practice is now seen only as pathology. The most extreme form of holy anorexia I have encountered is in the Jain religion of India. Many Jain holy people literally starve themselves to death slowly over long periods of time.

The Middle Ages and Beyond

Thomas Aquinas wrote about trance possession states. He called them "abstraction." "Abstraction… can occur from three causes: first, from a bodily cause… second, through the power of demons as seen in those who are possessed. Third, from the divine power. It is in this sense that we speak of ecstasy when one is elevated to a supernatural level by the divine spirit, with abstraction from the senses" (quoted in Caciola 2003, 33). Aquinas was well acquainted with these states. He also distinguished between ecstasy and rapture as the more extreme and violent form of the experience. Both kinds of abstraction, from demons or God, were attended with spectacular abilities: knowing the future, prophecy, understanding the supernatural, special knowledge, and more. Hildegard of Bingen (1098?–1179) is a good exemplar of this new age. She was the head of one monastery and founded more. She composed music, painted, wrote books, and was an expert in herbal medicine. As a child as well as throughout her life, she had powerful visions. She had kept these secret, but when she was a nun, she heard a command to write them down. She refused. She became more and more physically ill and eventually wrote her visionary experiences down. When she did this, her illness left her. This is so like the way of shamans and mediums all over the world. When they resist the calling, they become ill.

Divine possession had not been claimed in the West since the times of Montanus, but there had been a continuous tradition of demonic possession. There were many Latin words for demonic possession (for example, *possessio*, *obsessio*, *daemoniaci*, *energumeni*, *vexati*) but none for divine possession. These possession states were not subtle. Sometimes they looked like catatonic trance, even temporary death. The woman's body would become rigid and completely insensible, not responding to pinpricks or other stimuli. One woman would fall into trance with her eyes partially opened and remain immobile even when flies walked on her eyeballs (ibid., 65). Sometimes the possessed were writhing, screaming, and disheveled. Clamors, or uncontrollable shouting, were frequent.

Divine and demonic possession looked identical. The external signs were the same; both involved incorporating a very powerful foreign energy into the body. The issue of discernment came to the forefront. How can divine and demonic possession be distinguished and separated? The Eucharist could be considered a form of divine possession. Just as the Holy Spirit descended into the bread and wine, it descended into the heart of the woman devotee. It is interesting to note that here, near the center of Christian religious tradition, we have divine spirit entering material objects, a practice that seemed so odd when we encountered it in theurgy or in the Indian practice of murti.

You probably can guess that this eruption of spiritual energy into the culture would not end well. It was overwhelmingly female, it came up from the experience of the people rather than down from the authorities, and, as always, it was disruptive. Early in this era, it seemed that there was a genuine interest in these experiences and a sincere and sustained attempt to distinguish the divine from the demonic. Some of these ecstatic women were recognized as deeply holy and were honored. Exorcism later gained prominence. Whereas before, exorcism was often improvised at a saint's tomb or performed by a village woman, now it became formalized and something male literate clergy did to illiterate lay women. Once again it is the elite versus folk traditions. The elite church version was that all the possessing spirits were demons, and all possessed people had sinned. The folk version saw people as sometimes being possessed by chance, and the possessing agents could be nature spirits, souls of the dead, or demons. Also, a new idea started emerging among the elites that the real spiritual presence experiences were not the intense, high-arousal, anomalous states of possession and inspiration but rather were calm and serene meditative conditions. This devaluing of high-arousal spiritual experience has continued and grown until now, in our day, most Western intellectuals act as though the only valid spirituality is found in total stillness and silence. We take this for granted so much that even calling it into question may seem odd, and yet historically this is very much a minority point of view.

The possessions and exorcisms had sexual overtones. Sometimes a possessed woman was stripped naked in a public exorcism. The exorcist would go from one body part to another, expelling demons from the eyes, ears, necks, bones, arms, veins, and so on. A model for expelling demons from the body was God expelling Lucifer from heaven. Within a few hundred years, exorcisms became part of the church's attempt to exert control and domination. We can understand why possession is so difficult for the authorities. It is an interiorized spiritual practice — an embodied encounter with the supernatural — and is not accessible to external scrutiny or evaluation. Holiness was increasingly defined to exclude ecstatic states. Trance, visions, convulsions, tears, frenzies, and extreme fasting were all now seen as coming from demons. Exorcisms and demonic possessions reached epidemic proportions before and during the Protestant Reformation; attitudes about possession were the kindling that started a wildfire of hate during the witch hunt craze that killed many of the remaining folk healers and shamans of Europe. The witch hunts were an incredibly effective way to silence all claims of spiritual presence experience. In a few hundred years, we had changed from curious inquiry about people who had these experiences to burning them at the stake.

Sluhovsky (2007) argues convincingly that up until the sixteenth century, folk and official exorcisms practiced side by side. Exorcisms were a common part of local healing practice, but this changed in the second half of the sixteenth century. The church started working to suppress folk healers, calling them superstitious magicians and witches. In 1614, the church published the *Rituale Romanum*, an official handbook of how exorcisms are to be performed. Now exorcists could only be male priests who could read Latin.

Quietism and Loudun

Another issue arises now that is deeply significant. This is the time of the emergence of quietism — a new, or newly rediscovered, form of spirituality. The basic idea of quietism is that what is needed is radical spiritual passivity, openness, and receptivity. We need intellectual stillness, not vocal prayer. We need to abandon our will and leave behind all our ideas about spirituality and God. Miguel de

Molinos, a Spanish priest and one of the most prominent quietists, was tried by the Inquisition and found guilty of heresy. He died in prison. In France, Madame Guyon was jailed and then exiled for her beliefs.

A radical implication of this doctrine is that once a person has this interior connection to the divine, they no longer need the church, its rites, or its doctrines. Therefore, the church crushed them. Saint Teresa of Avila and Saint John of the Cross are often called pre-quietists or proto-quietists. They managed to stay in the church's favor. There was no official thing called quietism; the name was invented by opponents of this kind of spirituality. This trend or flavor of quietism can be found in all religions. Later this type of spirituality was developed by the Protestant Pietists. The absolute passivity and radical unknowing that are espoused as the road to the divine are an interiorized spirituality that is fundamentally anti-authoritarian. This thoroughgoing receptivity opens the soul to all influences, both positive and negative.

As quietest tendencies in Catholic spirituality spread among the nuns, there were more than fifty mass possessions in female religious houses (Sluhovsky 2007, 235ff). There were hundreds of cases of possession among nuns who practiced quietist spirituality. Only a few of them became famous; mass possession seemed to be accepted as relatively unexceptional. Nuns exhibited the classic signs of possession: supernatural physical strength, aversion to holy objects, fainting, vomiting, fits of paralysis, convulsions, and contortions. There are reports of suicide attempts. One of these mass possessions has become especially famous, and Aldous Huxley wrote an excellent book on it. Two nuns encountered a spirit in a convent at Loudun, France, on September 22, 1632. Two days later, a large black ball went through the dining room, pushing some nuns to the ground. A human skeleton was seen walking. The nuns saw the spirit clearly as the local priest Urbain Grandier. Many nuns were possessed, heard voices, and were attacked. Others laughed uncontrollably. Some had superhuman strength, screamed, cried, fainted, or exposed themselves. Seizures and convulsions were common. An exorcism ritual was conducted, and some of the nuns accused Father Grandier of making a pact with the devil and causing these events. He was tried, found guilty, and burned at the stake.

Here we have a vivid demonstration of how possession and exorcism transformed into witch killings. During the possessions, people traveled from all over France as well as from England and Italy to witness these events, which were recorded in great detail. After the burning of Grandier, much of the possession died down, but the Mother Superior had seven different demons in her. A prominent Jesuit, Jean-Joseph Surin, arrived from Paris to help exorcise her, but instead the demons got into him. He deteriorated badly, having visions, hallucinations, seizures, and temporary paralysis as well as losing his ability to speak. He spent most of the rest of his life in this state. The Mother Superior, on the other hand, flourished. Images of Mary and Jesus miraculously appeared on her left arm. She traveled around France, showing these markings to many, including the king and queen and Cardinal Richelieu. Then she returned to her nunnery, where she became a mystic, communicating with the guardian angels and having visions. She became a conduit for the divine.

This is an astounding and well-documented series of events. Despite the drama and fascination, I want to return to our concern here: what can we learn from this possession, perhaps the most famous in Western history, that can help us today with clients who feel something alien in their system? (1) Certain types of spiritual practice, such as radical openness, can make us more vulnerable. Perhaps there is only one doorway to spiritual experience, both positive and negative. (2) These possession states can be contagious — very contagious. (3) They have profound physical effects that defy easy explanations and might also be harnessed for healing. (4) The negative energy, unattached burden, belief complex, behavior pattern, whatever you want to call it, can jump from one person into those trying to help. (5) This point is less certain, but I believe that these events show the inadvisability of the hostile, combative, warlike way that exorcisms were performed at the time. Just knowing that these events and many more like them took place among our ancestors not so long ago might jar us out of our complacency and open our minds at least a little. We have all been profoundly indoctrinated into a Eurocentric worldview. Perhaps seeing this in our own tradition will be harder to dismiss than when it happens in Thailand, Korea, Africa, or Brazil.

The Camisards

Even during the height of the Enlightenment era — the alleged triumph of rationalism — these kinds of ecstatic events continued to occur. As we look a little deeper, they are common, though they seem to be routinely ignored by most historians, perhaps because they write from a perspective that is based on the values of the Enlightenment. Let's look briefly at the Camisards. They were a group of Huguenots (French Protestants) in southeastern France. After Louis XIV revoked the Edict of Nantes, making Protestantism illegal, these people rebelled. By 1702, it was open war. Eventually the revolt was crushed and the remaining Camisards, who were given safe passage, left France and spread throughout Europe, including England.

What is significant from my point of view is that the Camisards were led by prophets who were clearly possessed. An early prophet was Gabriel Astier. In the 1680s and '90s, he traveled throughout the mountains and valleys of south-eastern France, preaching to those who assembled to hear him speak. Typically after beginning to speak, he would fall to the ground and be carried to a bed. There he would have convulsions and begin to speak from the spirit. The audience would gather around the bed on their knees. At one of these gatherings, a local seigneur tried to get the assembly to disperse, but two of the prophets came up to him and hugged him, trying to infuse him with the spirit. After singing some psalms, these two fell to the ground, and one of them cried out in ecstasy, "I see the heavens opened! oh, how lovely the angels are" (Clarke, G., 1987, 26ff). Two more prophets described their visions, and then, according to one account, all of those assembled fell on the ground as though they were dead, without action or movement. The aftermath of these meetings was often a general feeling of emo-tional catharsis and the experience that angels were all around. There were many of these prophets, both male and female. They were often adolescents. Sometimes they were also military leaders of the rebel bands. After the rebellion was quashed, the prophets dispersed throughout Europe. They were very influential among the German Pietists and in England, where they were greeted with great curiosity. One of those who went to England, Durand Fage, has left us an account of his first possession. After witnessing the possession of an eleven-year-old girl, he was "surprised with a shivering all over... and a sense of agitation... [his] lips and tongue were of a sudden forced to pronounce words with vehemence... [that he was] amazed to hear, having forethought nothing and in no ways intending to speak" (ibid., 40). Many other similar possession trance–type religious experi-ences also occurred during this era.

The early Methodist meetings often had behaviors like these. Wesley quick-ly accepted the trances, ecstasies, and convulsions as manifestations of the su-pernatural. The famous preacher George Whitefield wrote to Wesley, "There is some thing of God in it but the devil... interposes. I think it will encourage the French prophets, take people from the written word, and make them depend on visions, convulsions, etc." (Clarke, G., 1987, 83). Wesley encouraged people not to believe every spirit but instead to test them to see if they were of God. He performed an exorcism in at least one instance (ibid., 86). There is so much more of this possession-based spirituality that is ignored in most histories. There were the jumpers of Wales, and there were women who would sleep and preach in their sleep. The Moravians also had these types of experiences in their meetings. One critic described this by saying he was "alarmed and almost terror stricken at hearing their sighing and groaning, their whining and howling, which strange proceeding they call the demonstration of the spirit and of power" (ibid., 89). Much more evidence exists along these lines, but perhaps I've already given too much detail. Religion in the 1700s often had dramatic possession experiences. Events like these were common in the early meetings of what are now mainline conservative and staid Protestant groups. The German Pietists and separatists; the English Moravians, Methodists, and evangelicals; the awakened Presbyterians of Scotland; and in the Americas the "new lights," the Strict Congregationalists, and the Baptists of New England all shared similar convictions and experiences. They believed that a powerful emotional experience of personal conversion was central to human spirituality.

The Convulsionnaires

Let's not leave the Catholics out of our description of possession experiences in the religions of the 1700s. After the suppression of the quietists, the most dramatic spiritual presence experiences were probably those of the Jansenist convulsionnaires. The Jansenists were a group that emphasized original sin, human depravity, and the need for salvation. Starting in early 1727, groups of Jansenists would gather at the grave of one of their deacons, François de Paris. He had been born into a wealthy family but gave all he had to poor people. He lived an extremely ascetic life, living without heat and wearing chains and hair shirts. Toward the end of his short life, he started whipping himself until he bled. Many considered him a saint. They went to his grave in the Saint-Medard cemetery, and there they would go into convulsions. Usually one or two people would start, and then it would spread through the whole crowd. There were reports of many miraculous healings. Blindness and cancer were reportedly healed. David Hume, the great Scottish Enlightenment philosopher who is often called the father of empiricism, said, "There surely never was a greater number of miracles ascribed to one person than those which were lately said to have been wrought in France upon the tomb of François de Paris, the famous Jansenist deacon... many of the miracles were immediately proved upon the spot, before judges of unquestioned integrity, attested by witnesses of credit and distinction, in a learned age" (Hume 1777, 84). Many would be writhing and convulsing on the ground, believing they were possessed by the Holy Spirit.

This became so popular and regular a phenomenon that crowds gathered to watch. There were even some enterprising small businessmen who brought chairs and rented them out so spectators could be comfortable while watching. The authorities closed the cemetery in an attempt to stop this practice, but the closure backfired, as the meetings continued in private homes, which allowed the practice to disperse more widely. Besides healing physical illness, many other features we have seen in other possession complex groups were also present. These groups were largely antiauthoritarian; they disliked both the state and the church. Women were prominent, as were lay preachers. Class distinctions were ignored. Millenarianism and apocalypticism were strong themes. The world was about to end.

Given the fact that these people were persecuted and many of their meetings were secret, it's hard to know when these practices ended, but they persisted at least into the 1760s. As the years went by, their behaviors became even more extreme. Some of them practiced real crucifixion using nails. This group also used "secours," which were violent and often erotic tortures. This started with the practice of beating the person who was convulsing in order to free them from that state, but it seemed to become almost sadomasochism. The Enlightenment thinkers of the time attacked these people. Voltaire was especially critical, but he never wrote about the fact that his brother participated in these meetings. In an early example of using medical diagnosis to pathologize and discredit possession experience, the authorities gathered a group of doctors who declared that this was an illness, not a spiritual experience. What are we to make of this? At its start, it looked like a genuine spiritual phenomenon, but it seems to have degenerated badly. If the culture of the time could have provided some kind of container or holding, would the outcome have been different? If we could safeguard our visionaries and ecstatics, could these experiences benefit them and the whole culture?

The medicalization of mental-emotional distress gained power at this time. While it had always been recognized that some of what we today call mental illness had purely bodily causes, much of it was treated as a spiritual problem with a spiritual solution. More and more cases were moved from the realm of spirituality and meaning into a biological dimension. Ironically, a major early contributor to this was Saint Teresa of Avila. She herself experienced visions, ecstasies, and reportedly some supernatural physical effects, and so did some of her nuns. This worried her, as it was very dangerous to have signs like these. Enemies could claim the nuns were demon-possessed and destroy them and perhaps the entire reform movement she was leading. Saint Teresa ascribed these symptoms to physical disease as a way to protect her nuns from the Inquisition and attacks by her numerous enemies. It seems to have been a successful strategy, but it also came to be a watershed in the secularization of the healing of human distress, an outcome she would not have wanted.

Mesmer and Gassner

The Protestant Reformation and later the Enlightenment thinkers took their toll on the Catholic Church's authority. Possession, ecstasies, and exorcisms, with their vivid, dramatic and hyperemotional expressions, seemed especially hateful to the Enlightenment thinkers. It is hard for most of us today to imagine the vehemence and hostility of this war between the Enlightenment and religion. This more global war found expression in the increasing secularization of the understanding and care for mental-emotional distress and an increasing denial of the impact of anything spiritual on the human mind. Another milestone in this secularization was the conflict between Franz Anton Mesmer (1734–1815) and Father Johann Joseph Gassner (1727–1779). Mesmer's name is probably familiar to many readers as the founder of hypnotism, even though the word *hypnotism* was not coined until well after his death. Mesmer was a figure of the Enlightenment who had a medical degree. He married a rich noblewoman, lived in a luxurious estate in Vienna, and treated very rich people. He believed he had discovered a special fluid that he called "animal magnetism," which could be accumulated and given to patients. He did heal many people, but his work was extremely controversial. He claimed that this subtle fluid filled the universe and was also in people. Diseases were blocks to this fluid's movement. As a child of the Enlightenment, Mesmer claimed that this was all rational, and he rejected any mystical implications.

Gassner was a priest in a small village in Germany. He performed many exorcisms successfully. His miraculous healings attracted crowds. He exorcised and healed some prominent noblemen and was catapulted to international fame. He used a technique he called "trial exorcism." With the patient kneeling before him, he would command the spirit to produce the symptoms. If they appeared, he concluded it was possession. If they did not appear, he sent the patient to a regular doctor. The Enlightenment thinkers hated his success and fame. This became one of the most heated disputes of the day. The Enlightenment thinkers organized an investigative commission in Munich in 1775. The commission had Mesmer attend, and he was able to replicate Gassner's effects of inducing and dispelling symptoms without reference to spirits or possession on the allegedly purely rational basis of the universal fluid of animal magnetism. Gassner was not present and did not get a chance to respond. No one at any time doubted the reality of Gassner's cures. Mesmer said that Gassner unknowingly used the animal magnetism fluids. What was denied was the spiritual nature of Gassner's work. Gassner had an unblemished reputation for humility, piety, and generosity. He was sent to a small parish and ordered by the pope to stop performing exorcisms. He lived out his life in obscurity. As psychiatrist Henri Ellenberger (1970, 57) wrote, "Curing the sick is not enough; One must cure them with methods accepted by the community." Of course, today Mesmer's theories seem as irrational and mystical as anything Gassner proposed.

Gottlieben Dittus and Johann Blumhardt

Another case of exorcism received a great deal of attention in its day. Johann Blumhardt was a German Lutheran pastor in a small town. In the fall of 1841, he was called to help Gottlieben Dittus, a relatively poor young woman in his village.

This began a two-year battle that, for the rest of his life, he simply referred to as "the fight." Blumhardt was a careful man; he never met with Gottlieben without other people present, usually the town mayor or church elders. She exhibited all sorts of severe symptoms, including seizures, fainting, copious bleeding, vomiting nails, other objects coming out of her body, and more. Once again, we see allegedly possessed people exhibiting physical phenomena beyond what is considered possible. Because this exorcism was so prolonged, many people came to witness and study these events. Gottlieben was very close to suicide several times. The events of her possession were dramatic and extreme, but they were witnessed by many people over the two-year struggle. In the end, Blumhardt and Gottlieben came to believe that while there had been hordes of demons in her, there were two major demons as well as the soul of a dead woman who had murdered her two children and buried them in a field.

Blumhardt wrote an extensive account of this for his supervisors in the Lutheran Church, who seemed embarrassed by these events. Many people came from surrounding towns for healing, and they were frequently healed. These events sparked a revival, and Christian renewal in the area increased strongly. At one point, the Lutheran authorities forbade Blumhardt from healing people from outside his parish. He complied. Later they relented and allowed him to move to the hot springs around Bad Boll, where he established a retreat center in 1853. He worked there, focusing on healing, until his death in 1880. Some modern Protestant writers see him as an important forerunner of the twentieth-century healing ministries. His son Christoph also became a minister and founded Bruderhof, a group of Christian communal living centers that continue today.

These three events — the Loudun mass possession, the Gassner-Mesmer affair, and the exorcism of Gottlieben Dittus — share some characteristics. They were all well witnessed by skeptical and hostile observers as well as by sympathetic ones. They all included events that modern science had no explanation for it. Copious records exist from all viewpoints. Seriously considering these events and not just dismissing them because they're uncomfortable and bizarre can help us open our minds and realize that things occur that our current medical-scientific paradigm completely fails to explain.

Spiritism and Spiritualism

While the heirs of the Enlightenment, with their rejection of spirituality, increased their domination of the centers of learning and the elites, there was still a vibrant and widespread belief in spirits and spirit possessions. In the nineteenth century, perhaps the two biggest examples of this were Spiritualism and Spiritism. Spiritualism is the belief that the spirits of the dead can be contacted and have knowledge and wisdom we don't. These sought-after contacts usually occur through mediums. In 1848, the two Fox sisters from upstate New York claimed contact with the spirit of a dead person who had been murdered and buried in the basement of their house. The case attracted great attention and sparked an investigation. They both went on to make careers of being mediums, and later in life one of the sisters claimed to have faked it. But their notoriety sparked a wave of interest that spread across the United States and into Europe. Having spiritualistic seances became a fad, and mediums became celebrities. Even though some of these mediums were frauds, some seemed very real.

Sir Arthur Conan Doyle, a medical doctor who is much more famous as the author of the Sherlock Holmes novels, was an ardent believer and has left us a long book on the history of Spiritualism. William James investigated this subject painstakingly. Leonora Piper (1857–1950) was a prim, proper, and shy Bostonian who was also a gifted medium. James investigated her for many years. "If I may be allowed the language of the professional logic shop, a universal proposition can be made untrue by a particular instance. If you wish to upset the law that all crows are black, you must not seek to show that no crows are black. It is enough if you prove one single crow to be white. My own white crow is Mrs. Piper. In the trances of this medium, I cannot resist conviction that knowledge appears, which she has never gained by the ordinary waking use of her eyes and ears and wits" (1894 speech on becoming president of the Society for Psychical Research).

Spiritism is different from Spiritualism, or perhaps it is best considered a type of Spiritualism. Spiritism started with the work of Allan Kardec and his followers in France. Kardec gathered a group of reliable mediums, submitted thousands of questions to them, and then published the collated results in many fat volumes. He also published a newspaper. He is discussed earlier in this book, in Chapter 4, because his work is so influential in Brazil. He made a serious, diligent, well-organized, and rational attempt to understand these phenomena. Spiritualism reached its peak in the late nineteenth century and persisted into the twentieth. It has not disappeared. It has morphed a little and continues under the name of channeling. It still has the basic theme of voluntary, sought-after communication with spirits.

The Presence of the Holy Spirit

Another major intrusion of spirit into the Western world in the twentieth century was the birth of Pentecostalism, which has grown from nothing in 1906 to approximately five hundred million people worldwide today. Not only has Pentecostalism grown dramatically, but it has also sparked the charismatic revival of old-line denominations and churches. Now, many of these faithful expect miracles, healing, and being filled with the spirit to be part of their spiritual lives. Pentecostalism should get far more scholarly attention than it does, but as we get to know the post-Enlightenment, rationalist, materialist prejudices of our elites, this should be understandable and perhaps expected. On April 9, 1906, a Black preacher named William J. Seymour was praying with a group of men. Six or seven of them (accounts vary) were knocked from their seats as though by lightning and fell to the floor, speaking in tongues and shouting praises of God. A few days later, Seymour himself received the spirit. Neighbors overheard, and participants brought their families. Soon crowds gathered around the little home. Many received the spirit. Diseases were healed. They got a bigger building on Azusa Street that had most recently been used as a stable and storage space. These experiences continued to happen. The fact that Reverend Seymour headed an interracial group was unheard of in 1906. In addition, there were women in leadership, which was also unheard of then. The revival continued, with almost round-the-clock church services going on for three years. There were extremely intense experiences; many would shout praises and scream, fall to the floor, shake all over, or fall unconscious. Diseases were healed. A proud, educated minister came to scoff but ended up on the floor, screaming and begging forgiveness. A young boy came and said he didn't understand it, but the hair stood on end all over his body. There were no ads or announcements, but people came. Later it was reported across the United States and around the world.

If we use the phrase "spiritual presence experience," we will be less likely to offend anyone. These events look a lot like the voluntary, sought-after group ecstatic possessions we have seen in other cultures and other eras. As stated earlier, a basic biopsychological process seems to be available to all humans in all cultures and ages. It can have profound effects for good or for ill. The most common metaphor to describe this is possession. The regrettable fact that our elites do what they can to ignore or suppress this process does not stop it from continuing to emerge. My focus is on relieving human suffering. Therefore, I do not need to consider or debate the reality or identity of the possessing agents. This would lead me far astray and surely offend many, no matter what I said. If I keep my focus on the process and how to work with it, there is much to learn. Some people found physical healing at Azusa Street. Some people changed the entire course of their lives. To use William James's image, these are white crow events.

The Azusa Street Revival was far from the first in the United States. One called the First Great Awakening occurred in the 1730s and '40s, a Second Great Awakening in the 1820s and '30s, and some scholars claim a Third Great Awakening in the late 1800s. The two most famous preachers in the First Great Awakening were Jonathan Edwards and George Whitefield. Edwards was famous, or infamous, as a puritanical fire-and-brimstone, stiff-necked man. His most famous/

infamous sermon was "Sinners in the hands of an angry God." He mostly stayed in his Northampton, Massachusetts, home church, but the emotional intensity of his religion was contagious and spread throughout the colonies. Whitefield was an itinerant minister who came from England and delivered over 350 sermons throughout the colonies. He emphasized direct personal experience of the divine. He was one of the first to also preach to Indigenous people, slaves, and the rejected. Benjamin Franklin, a lifelong skeptic, heard Whitefield speak and was so impressed with the man that the two became friends.

This First Great Awakening also had a huge impact on the colonies. The older denominations lost influence, and the ones emphasizing spiritual presence experiences grew. Some historians say this series of events paved the way for a national identity and provided a spiritual basis for the Revolutionary War. The Second Great Awakening started in regions of Western and Central New York State that had seen so many waves of contagious spirituality that it was called "the burned-over district." Again, this awakening emphasized direct spiritual experience of the divine. There was wild excitement as well as criticism and revulsion. This awakening is one of the origins of the anti-slavery movement, the beginning of calls for women's rights, and the breeding ground for many utopian social experiments. This is also the region where, in 1820, a farm boy named Joseph Smith had his first vision, which led to the founding of Mormonism. Right at the start of Smith's ministry, he performed a dramatic exorcism on Newel Knight. Knight experienced an inability to pray, followed by more severe symptoms. He levitated and his body contorted. Smith was able to grasp his hands and exorcize the demons. Mormons believe in the devil and perform exorcisms, but it is kept quiet. Taysom (2017) reports that the Mormons believe that demons possess us because they want our bodies, our tabernacles. They had been refused bodies as a punishment.

Almost all the modern Protestant denominations began with breakthroughs of powerful spiritual presence experience. These were tamed, domesticated, and then ignored or denigrated as churches became established. This pattern is ubiquitous, perhaps inevitable. The wildness of the intense spiritual presence experiences may be inherently too unstable to be institutionalized in a society.

The Welsh Revival

I want to talk about one more revival, which started before Azusa Street. It is not so well known, but it is very instructive. This is the Welsh revival of 1904. A young man, Evan Roberts, was a student who experienced an emotional-spiritual crisis in September 1904 that gave him the conviction that he should go preach in Wales. He did, and within a week it was clear that something dramatic was happening. The little parish church in Loughor where he was preaching was filled beyond capacity, and crowds gathered outside to listen to him preach. They prayed and sang enthusiastically. The meetings lasted for many hours. Roberts began an itinerant ministry, and in two months over thirty thousand people were converted. There were also other preachers working in this revival. Roberts experienced a breakdown of his physical health, and his behavior became increasingly erratic and unpredictable. This Welsh revival, like the others, focused on direct spiritual presence experience, in their language, the "baptism in the Holy Spirit." Jessie Penn-Lewis was a well-known preacher at this time. She befriended Roberts, and when he suffered a complete breakdown in the spring of 1906, she took him into her family house. He became a recluse there, devoting himself to a private life of prayer. The two of them wrote a book, *War on the Saints* (1912). In it, they expressed their belief that while baptism in the Holy Spirit is beneficial, it also opens people to the spiritual realms and therefore to evil spirits. "Evil spirit possession has followed and checked every single revival throughout the centuries since Pentecost, and evil spirit possession must now be understood and dealt with if the church is to advance" (Penn-Lewis, quoted in Collins 2009, 116).

This revival is significant because it emphasizes three important principles: (1) A clear association exists between powerful spiritual experience and mental illness or instability. Roberts had some form of charismatic power; he inspired many very quickly, and then he broke down and needed a private, protected environment for the rest of his life. (2) Once the gates have been opened, once we have more access to the transliminal, once the veil has been lifted, we are available to both benign and malevolent energies. This is also a lesson that seems inherent in the history of quietism. (3) These emotional spiritual states are wildly contagious; they do not stay neatly confined in one mind. This may be another piece of evidence for the porosity of mind.

Now let's briefly look at modern Western Christianity's ways of dealing with the possession complex and spiritual presence experiences. The positive side of this — the direct personal experience of the indwelling Holy Spirit — seems to have penetrated almost all Christian groups. The charismatic movement emphasizes spiritual presence experiences and healing. It is not about beliefs — it's about intense spiritual, emotional experience with enough force to heal disease and change the course of people's lives. There are charismatic Catholics, Anglicans, Methodists, Presbyterians, Baptists, and more. Of course, the Pentecostals are all fundamentally charismatic.

Deliverance and Exorcism

Along with this great opening to spirit in our age, which has an entire library of research documenting and explaining it, there is also the dark side — the pressure of unwanted and pernicious possession states. It may be that it is not possible to open the doors to spiritual presence experience selectively and that when we become sensitive to this inner world, all of its denizens have access to us. Whether or not this hypothesis is true, it seems that there has also been a growth in exorcisms and deliverance ministries. It needs to be crystal clear that there are some fundamental differences between these practices and what I and IFS are proposing. Exorcists and deliverance ministers almost universally do not try to help the spirit that is in the person. They get it out believing it is condemned to hell. This creates a very confrontational and combative atmosphere. Also, these ministries by and large do not understand parts and multiplicity of mind, so they often try to remove and amputate parts of the person.

A very large percentage of people believe in possession; in most studies, a majority of people do. Professor Joseph Laycock referred to a 2012 poll reporting that 57 percent of Americans believe in demonic possession. A 2007 Baylor University study said 48 percent of the respondents strongly agree that demonic possession exists. A 2007 Pew Research Survey showed that 68 percent believe in demons and angels. YouGovAmerica.com reported a 2021 poll showing that 51 percent of Americans believe possession is possible, 28 percent say no, and 20 percent do not know. In 2017, Public Policy Polling reported a study of young Americans aged eighteen to twenty-nine; 63 percent of the sample believes that "invisible noncorporeal entities can take partial control of humans." The 1998 New York Times/CBS Poll reported that 63 percent believe in demonic possession "not explainable by modern medicine or psychiatry." Multiple Pew surveys indicate that American belief in ghosts is up about 400 percent since the early 1970s. There are many more surveys, all worded slightly differently, all with slightly different results, but the major trends are clear. At least half of us believe in possession. The belief in possession and spirits, and their importance, is growing, not shrinking. This is in line with what we have seen in other cultures and around the world. It goes directly against Max Weber's famous secularization narrative. Remember, he predicted that the disenchantment of the world would cause all of these beliefs to die off and wither away as Western rational materialism spread. This is not even true here in the very center of this ideology. For Western psychiatry to pathologize these states that more than half the population believes in seems to be the height of arrogance. If something doesn't fit your ideology and worldview, you declare it a disease. Also, for academics to sneer at what the "uneducated" believe reeks of smug elitism. We need the basic respect to take these people's experiences seriously.

The Catholic Church has always recognized possession and performed exorcisms. Until very recently, they used the Roman Rite of 1614 as the guide. This has been revised. In 2014, the Catholic Church formally recognized the International Association of Exorcists. Most dioceses have an exorcist, and there are fairly strict rules. There must be psychiatric screening and approval of the bishop before exorcisms can proceed. The Catholic exorcisms that I have been able to gather information about are highly confrontational. The heroic exorcist is locked in a battle with the forces of evil and wins through the power of God. This is not a model I have found useful, but in fairness to the Catholics, they seem to be dealing with more complete takeovers of a person. They discuss levels of demonic activity. For example, Sister Mary Margaret Funk cites temptations as the demons' basic activity. She says there are four levels of more intense demonic interference. The first level is infestation, which pertains mainly to objects and locations. The second level she calls oppression, which is physical attack. The third level is obsession, which involves persistent, intense suggestions to the mind that can become a fixation, both when awake and dreaming. The fourth level is possession itself, where the demon takes control of a person's speech and behavior. Perhaps everything I have seen clinically falls short of full possession. Of course, a full 100 percent possession would never appear to a priest or a therapist because the person would not want help. There would be no conflict left within them.

In the cases I have seen, the UBs or demons, or whatever you call them, seem to love conflict. They want to provoke a battle, and they gain strength and energy from it. They also love argument, disputes, sneering, and contempt. When we allow ourselves to be sucked into a "war with the forces of evil," we may feel like heroic crusaders, but it does damage to us and to our client, and, I believe, to the UB.

The Protestants in recent American history also have a strong tradition of working with demons. They usually call it deliverance rather than exorcism. Despite the name change, they frequently seem to share the combative/confrontational style of the Catholics. Father Michael Perry (1987), an Anglican, uses the same four levels of involvement as Sister Funk. The Exeter report, published in 1972, summarized the official views of the Anglicans at that time: they recognize spirit possession and the usefulness of exorcism. Since that time, they have adopted the word *deliverance* as a broader category that only occasionally requires exorcism. Perry uses the phrase "spiritual bacilli," which reminds us of Dawkins's memes. These are infectious diseases of the mind.

There is one more Anglican we need to discuss. T. Craig Isaacs, PhD, is a clinical psychologist and an Anglican priest who works in Marin County, in Northern California. He is the author of five books, two of which focus on possession. He writes, "The existence of the possession state in the human condition is not a matter of faith, it is a phenomenon that demands explanation… it appears that even though we may have witnessed the removal of the belief in demonic possession from our diagnostic categories, the phenomenon that once was described with attributes of the demonic is still with us" (Isaacs 2018, 1–2). He points out that mysticism in general, with its concept of the complete surrender of self to the divine, can be seen as a possession state. In his analysis of the development of the soul, he points to its mediating function between the body and the pure spirit. This is the realm of conscious experience and the imagination. This is an internal version of the Greek image of the daimonic as a mediating realm between gods and humans. Isaacs discusses the Hebrew concept of soul — *nephesh* — which is not a self-contained unity but rather very much a part of the group one is living in.

This model fits very well with the idea of porosity of mind and gives a framework in which possession seems natural. Citing Eliade and Harner, Isaacs points out that shamans require two separate kinds of knowledge to become healers: (1) direct ecstatic experience in dreams and trances; and (2) traditional forms from the culture: names and functions of spirits, mythology, and more. We no longer have much of this second category. What we did have has been mocked, ridiculed, and largely discarded by the Western elites. The first kind of shamanic knowing is also discredited as unscientific.

Dr. Isaacs points out that possession is a much less devastating diagnosis than mental illness. It wards off the cognitive dissociation and feelings of being broken and defective by giving a culturally accepted framework in which to hold the experiences. It also lessens the perceptual disorganization because this experience of the afflicted persons is validated by the culture (Isaacs 2018, 109). Isaacs's two major influences in this work are Rollo May and Carl Jung. May felt that the Greek concept of the daimonic was important: "The daimonic is a fundamental human experience. It cannot be said to be part of the self… the daimonic does not derive out of the ego, the self, or any portion of the psyche…" (ibid, 143). He saw that the daimonic has the potential for good and evil. He divided these into symbolic — thrown together — and diabolic — thrown apart. The roots of these words actually mean "thrown together" and "thrown apart." The symbolic integrates the individual into the whole and leads to creativity. The diabolic tears the individual apart and isolates them from themselves, their society, and the environment. May also clearly understood that the violence and negativity of possession were often caused by our negative repression and rejecting attitude toward the daimonic. He acknowledged that a classic response to possession was to cast out the spirit, but he also saw that there needs to be an integration and welcoming of the daimonic.

Jung was an even larger influence on Isaacs than May. We have already discussed the work of Craig Stephenson, the Jungian who insists that possession is the central image and metaphor in all of Jung's work. Isaacs has come to a very similar conclusion, but surprisingly, the two do not seem to know of each other's work; they do not refer to each other or list each other's work in their bibliographies. Isaacs asserts the centrality of possession forcefully: "For the Jungian, all forms of psychopathology are the result of some form of possession, either due to a soul complex or a spirit complex. That is, process is related either to the ego and the personal feel of the individual or it is related to the self and that area of functioning general to the whole human species" (Isaacs 2018, 163). In IFS language, the soul complex possession refers to being taken over or hijacked by one of our own parts; the spirit complex possession means being taken over by an unattached burden. Other Jungians have discussed this as the difference between being taken over by a complex or an archetype. The fundamental dynamic of something hijacking our minds may be the same. The more unconscious we are of any of this stuff, whether part or UB, complex or archetype, the more freedom it has and therefore the more ability to take us over. Isaacs makes a strong case for possession needing treatment on both the transpersonal and personal levels.

One of the best-known modern-day Protestant deliverance ministries is the work of Frank and Ida Mae Hammond, a husband-and-wife team. They are Texas Southern Baptists, a group that is very conservative and fundamentalist. They hold views that are offensive to liberals and can be difficult for many of us to abide. However, if you read their works and listen to their talks, their basic goodness and healing intentions shine through. Early on in the growth of IFS, Dick was invited to teach at a seminary in the Deep South that did not emphasize deliverance but was run by people very much like the Hammonds. Dick had to set aside his ideology and politics to interact with these people. One professor there, a minister, was hostile from the beginning, but as the training was nearing completion, he came up to Dick and told him that he was finally getting what IFS teaches. For him, IFS was doing what Jesus did. In the outer world, Jesus went to all the rejected and scorned, the prostitutes and tax collectors and publicans. The minister said, "Dick, you are doing the same thing in the inner world. You help people go to the scorned and rejected parts of themselves with love." That school is still teaching IFS now, some twenty years later. I tell this story because it illustrates that there's great value in setting aside our politics and ideology, and meeting people at deeper levels. Sadly, this ability seems to be getting lost more and more.

The Hammonds had a lot of experience with deliverance. Their book *Pigs in the Parlor* (1990) has over one and a half million copies in print in eighteen languages. Despite this, it is totally ignored by academics and mainstream media. The Hammonds believed the demons usually came in groups. In one speech, Frank Hammond joked that his critics said he saw a demon behind every bush. He said. "That's not true — I see six demons behind every bush." These groups of demons are usually led by a "strongman." The Hammonds named demons by the qualities they evoked, for example, demons of anger, bitterness, alcohol, control, cruelty, phobias, and so on. In their book, the list of these demons and their common groupings is three and a half pages long. They stated bluntly that they believe everyone needs deliverance. Demons are persons — beings — not just energies. They enter through "open doors." The vast majority enter during childhood and are trauma-related. This fits perfectly with psychotherapy's emphasis on childhood experiences. Many enter through sin. Many are legacies from our families. The Hammonds did their deliverance work as part of a team of two to six people. Husband-and-wife pairs are the best foundation for a team. They stated clearly that demons cannot exist if they are surrounded by love. Love "heaps coal upon their heads" — that is, purifies their minds (ibid, 77).

This typically plain-spoken and graphic language reminds me of a very different case I had. A woman went to an ayahuasca ceremony that involved a large group of people taking high-dose ayahuasca with poor supervision. Returning home, she had a mental breakdown and ended up being confined in a mental hospital. Her family came and got her and drove her to her original home halfway across the country. During that trip, she became so distraught and out of control that they had to stop three more times to have her hospitalized again. They finally got her safely home. She would have periods of lucidity followed by periods of psychosis. A cousin who was sort of psychic told her that the next time the darkness came, she should just say, "There is nothing here for you but love." The cousin suggested she repeat this statement over and over like a mantra. The next time the darkness came, she did this and it worked! The disturbances stopped. I was called in after this to help her integrate these strange events. She could not decide why the mantra worked. She thought that maybe it was just coming to realize deeply that this energy was not a part of her. She also thought it might be that these energies are allergic to love. I've never heard of anyone else doing this, but it did get her out of a terrible situation. She is stable now and has a productive life. This possibility that love itself might be enough to get the disturbances to leave should underline the inadvisability of entering into combative relationships attempting to judge or punish or be hateful toward these energies or beings.

The Hammonds believed that demons most often reside in the lower abdomen and that they are best expelled through the mouth using forceful exhales, coughing, and spitting. This emphasis on using breath to expel demons is echoed by many other modern Protestant deliverance ministers. It is something that can pragmatically help our clinical practice. These deliverance ministers often encourage people to exhale forcefully or cough voluntarily. Because I believe the real healing power is within the client and not in me, I stay less directive and usually only say things like "Let your breath and body do anything they want. They have access to deep knowledge." Yawning can also be significant. Some healers say it indicates a deep movement of spirit and should never be repressed in a client or a therapist during sessions. The New Testament uses the word *pneuma*, which means "breath," for spirit. In stoic philosophy, there were two basic realities: matter and logos, which is divine knowledge. The two were only able to interact with each other through pneuma. So *pneuma* comes to mean something intermediary between the divine and humans, very much like the daimonic earlier. For the Gnostics, the pneumatikos were the highest level of humans. All of this only scratches the surface, pointing out the ancient and profound connection between breath and spirit, which we might be able to more actively engage as we do this kind of work.

In prayer, Ida Mae Hammond was given a series of visions that gave her a complex understanding of schizophrenia as possession. She explained these by giving detailed diagrammatic outlines of two hands with each part of the hand showing some aspect of the invasion or its cure. If you read their folksy and unpretentious book or watch Frank's talks on YouTube, it's obvious they are sincere and well-intentioned people. No matter how much we may dislike their ideology, it behooves us to learn from their work and its lasting popularity and impact. There are many other prominent deliverance ministries in our era as well. Derek Prince and Francis MacNutt stand out. Prince was a classics scholar who knew Greek, Latin, and Hebrew and who taught at Cambridge. Later, as his religious calling grew, he was a minister in London, then Kenya, and then the United States. He developed a radio ministry and focused on deliverance. He insisted that demons are persons, "persons without bodies" — not things, not parts of us, but other distinct people. He said that guiding a suffering person to this understanding is 80 percent of the work of deliverance. Once the possessed person accepts this, most of the work is accomplished. This idea is usually the most difficult and repellent part of this field for rationalists, and Prince insists that it is absolutely central. From a clinical perspective, this is a crucial point. We do not have to go as far as Prince does; all we need is the realization that from a pragmatic standpoint, the healing goes better if we treat these things as people. With experience, this pragmatic result is something we can know with reasonable certainty. In IFS, we already know that therapy is much more powerful when we treat our own parts as full-spectrum people. We need to extend this pragmatic realization to the others within us.

Prince had a dry sense of humor. For example, in one sermon he remarked calmly that demons were very comfortable in many churches. He himself was healed from very serious cancer when he was in his seventies when another minister removed a demon from him. He felt that all addictions are demonic. He listed the characteristic behaviors of demons as: entice, harass, torment, compel, enslave, defile, and deceive. This list is more detailed and nuanced than the Catholic one described by Sister Funk, but they both indicate a progression from mild irritation to life-changing event.

Francis MacNutt, PhD, is a former Catholic priest who left the church, married, and formed a healing ministry. If you read his books, you may not agree with him, but you will have to admit that he's educated, reasonable, and thoughtful. He has studied possession states in many parts of the world, including South America and Japan. He makes many points that are already familiar to us. Deliverance or exorcism is central to the New Testament, not something peripheral that can be discarded because it makes us uncomfortable. All early Christians cast out spirits. At the end of Mark's gospel, there is a list of the five signs of a real believer. The first of these is "in my name they will drive out demons" (Mark 16:17). Like Prince, MacNutt notes that demons often come out through the mouth, and coughing and vomiting often occur. He echoes our emphasis on the elite versus folk views in discussing how legalism, the elite's program, has overtaken the church. He quotes Prince: "Theology will be exalted above revelation… psychology above discernment; program above believing in the holy spirit; laws above love" (MacNutt 2009, 119). Like the Hammonds, he recognizes what he calls "spirits of trauma." He says these account for 75 percent of the possessions he sees and that he recognizes the need for healing as well as deliverance. Frequently, this healing must occur first. He states that when healing has occurred, the spirits must leave. This is promising because it opens a path that could lead us to a way for the two usually mutually antagonistic fields of psychotherapy and deliverance to cooperate.

Certain core beliefs and methods are shared by many of these Protestant deliverance ministers. The demon or UB or spirit must have a "ground" within a person. Most often, this is identified as an unconfessed sin. One preacher said there are "sin handles" that demons can grab. In IFS, we hold that UBs cannot stay in a person's system once all the parts in the system no longer want it there. The basic dynamic is the same. There is something within the person we can change that will make it necessary for the negativity to leave. Many of these deliverance ministers write of binding the spirits as a first step. Sometimes they describe this with vivid, almost sadistic language. They bind and tie it very tightly so it feels the restraint. In my work, I often use a ball or egg-shaped container of light to contain the intrusion, but this is done with kindness, not combativeness. Many of the deliverance ministers emphasize that spirits most often leave through the mouth. Many state that the gift of discernment is needed and that it is a God-given grace and cannot be explained. IFS's ability to help us distinguish between parts and UBs does much of this work, and we will talk more about the important topic of discernment in the next chapter. Just throwing up our hands helplessly and saying that this only comes as a God-given grace feels inadequate; it is at least in large part a learnable skill. The Hammonds said that self-deliverance is possible. People can often become aware of demons in themselves and get them out on their own. Several deliverance ministers insist that every Christian has the power to do this work. This does seem to be what the bible says.

Neopagans

We will now look at a very different group of people. Neopagans and Wiccans highly value possession states. Drawing down the spirit, drawing down the moon, or drawing down the gods is prominent in their rituals. (Of course, these groups are decentralized, with no unified ideology or practices, so any generalization will only be partly true.) In the sources I've found, voluntary sought-after possession is the main focus. There is the recognition of danger, even in divine possession. "Once you begin to work with the Gods and spirits who are real and not just mental constructs, you soon realize that they are dangerous. They can turn your life upside down on a whim. They can have you dressing in sackcloth and ashes, or decide you need to spend the rest of your life living a different gender. They can break up your relationships, cost you your health, home, and job, or drive you bug fuck nutty insane. And that includes all the Gods, not just the ones you've heard described as 'evil'" (Filan and Kaldera 2009, 36).

There are many metaphors for deity possession, such as being God's spouse or slave or horse. These people have ways of working to guide possession into certain times and places. These are mainly group rituals, something we've seen all over the world and something that is extremely difficult or impossible to replicate in a psychotherapeutic setting. Filan and Kaldera (ibid., 133–137) separate out seven levels of deity possession: enchantment, inspiration, integration, aspecting, shadowing, channeling, and possession. They put substantial energy into their categorizations, then say something I deeply appreciate, "Nailing down the Gods is like trying to squeeze water, or sunlight, or shadow: one may fool oneself into believing one has done it, but one's hands remain empty" (ibid., 137). If we try to force this vast and multiform reality of spiritual presence experiences into neat boxes of theory, our hands will remain empty.

Tanya Luhrmann's first major study (Luhrmann 1989) focused on ritual magic among neopagans in modern England. As anthropologists often do, she operated as a participant-observer, attending groups, studying books, and doing the practices and rituals. Some astonishing things happened to her. One morning after waking up, she looked over to her window and saw eight druids standing there. At other times, she felt power flows of unexplainable energy in her body. One time she was working with an energy that interfered with electronic devices. She felt it in her body, and her watch stopped. There were more incidents like these. Luhrmann avoided the two most obvious responses. She did not pretend that these events had never happened and keep them secret and hidden. Neither did she abandon anthropology and the Western intellectual tradition and become a full-on neopagan magician. She had the courage, integrity, and strength of mind to choose a third way. She respectfully studied what the modern magicians did that created the potential for such experiences.

It took Luhrmann about thirty years to gain enough of an answer to publish her book *How God Becomes Real* (2020). I discussed some of her conclusions back in the section on interoception. Here I want to emphasize her respectful attitude and choice of questions. People who have these types of experiences are not un-educated primitives or diagnosably pathological. Most people all over the planet throughout history have had similar experiences. These experiences are powerful. They can be very valuable or devastating. They can also help us fathom some profound and obscure areas of our consciousness. They have great therapeutic significance. For us to harvest these benefits, we need to stop disrespecting and discrediting the experience of others because it does not fit in our worldview. We also need to ask new questions, as Luhrmann does. Mostly, these are "how" questions, not "why" questions, and not "what is it?" The how question I've been focused on is how can we work with all of this to relieve human suffering. If the clash between these types of psychological events and our Western worldview is jarring for us clinicians sitting with people who have these experiences, imagine how much more jarring and sometimes shattering it is for those who experience this directly. We can change the way we and our culture receive these experiences, which will vastly decrease human suffering.

Egregores

Egregores are a concept that comes out of the Western occult, esoteric, and magi-cal traditions. Not only are we going into spiritual-religious realms that violate the rules of rationalist materialism, but now we're going into the realms that even mainstream religion considers weird and unacceptable. Ironically, we discover here a concept that's quite close to memes and memeplexes that come from an extreme reductionistic rationalist. An egregore is a phenomenon of group minds and crowd behavior. Here are two definitions: "Autonomous psychic entities composed of and influencing the thoughts of groups of people" (from wikidictionary.org) or "A collective entity such as a nation-state or religion and their adherents... they have physical bodies... and also astral and mental ones" (Stavisk 2018, 4). The Nazis and communists are prime examples of the collective demonic. These energies can be manipulated and structured, as Hitler and his propagandists did with their mass rallies and Mao did with the Cultural Revolution. Egregores can be beneficial or harmful. In the classical world, some cities and towns would create psychic entities for defense — gods of the polis. Odd as they are, egregores are important for our exploration because they illustrate two important principles. First, emotionally toned thought complexes are highly contagious. They can take over whole groups, even nations. This contagion is powerful evidence for the porosity of mind. Second, the process by which egregores influence people seems to be a possession-type event. People's minds are overtaken by something external.

Back at the beginning of the twentieth century, the theosophists created the idea of thought-forms, which has since passed into general usage. It's very similar to egregores: when a group of people share thoughts and attitudes, especially ones that are emotionally highly charged, the thoughts gain an autonomy that in turn influences people. The French sociologist Gustav LeBon noticed something similar in his famous 1895 book *The Crowd*. He said people in a crowd are in a special state of fascination that he likened to hypnosis. From our perspective, you could also frame this as a possession phenomenon — possession by the spirit of the crowd or its egregore or thought-form. Crowds have no reason; people in them often do things they would never do on their own. The concept of an egregore takes this basic recognition and extends it over time; these systems of thought and emotion can persist for years or centuries. All this sounds bizarre and extreme, but it is very close to evolutionary biologist Richard Dawkins's hyperscientific thinking about memeplexes and how they are contagious and infect people like viruses of the mind. An egregore might be an epidemic of memes.

The concept of thought-forms was used by anthropologist Walter Evans-Wentz in his groundbreaking 1927 translation of *The Tibetan Book of the Dead*. In Tibetan Buddhism, there are many elaborate visualizations. Powerful thoughts can eventually have effects in our bodies and in the world. One of the most extreme forms of this concept is *tulpas*. These are beings created by advanced practitioners in their meditations that can go out into the world and perform tasks, including influencing or controlling other people. Madame Alexandra David-Néel, the intrepid early explorer who snuck into Tibet while it was still illegal to study the religions there, said that the creation of tulpas was fairly common. She reported that she herself had created one and that it got out of control and had to be destroyed. Not surprisingly, there's a lot of scholarly debate about the reality and scope of this phenomenon in Tibet. Surprisingly, there are now groups of people in the West, known as tulpamancers, who create tulpas for themselves as imaginary friends, helpers, and companions. Many report that the tulpas take on a certain autonomy. One of their techniques is to talk to someone in their mind until that being starts talking back. They call this "forcing." When a tulpa can take a person over, they say that the person is now plural. They call this "fronting" for a person. They also sometimes call the tulpa their "head mate." One person reported that his tulpa had saved him from suicide as a teenager and then later dissolved itself. Many involved in this hide it for fear of being diagnosed and stigmatized. The neuroscientist Michael Lifshitz commented on this topic, saying, "The thing that's clear is that tulpamancy helps people… we're interested in how we could use it for developing better treatments for… DID or psychosis" (quoted in Luhrmann 2013).

Dr. Samuel Veissière, an anthropologist and professor of psychiatry at McGill University, has studied the people involved in tulpamancy. They're mostly young, urban, and educated. A total of 93 percent report that working with tulpas improved their overall well-being, and 76 percent think this has a psychological or neurological cause — that it is not a spiritual phenomenon. This reminds me of studies showing that children who have imaginary friends tend to grow up to become happier and more socially connected than children who don't. These results are significant because they clearly show that imaginal actions can improve subjective well-being and can reduce human suffering. We can learn from this if we can open our minds and resist the temptation to sneer. Moreover, over three-quarters of these people gained these results without having to abandon their Western scientific frame. They viewed it as a psychological/neurological phenomenon. Veissière also emphasized that the ability to create these beings is trainable.

DMT Entities

There is one last subject we need to cover in this brief survey: DMT entities. DMT is the active ingredient in many psychedelic medicines: psilocybin, ayahuasca, and, of course, 5meo-DMT and nn-DMT. When people are given high doses of DMT, approximately 50 percent meet entities. When given very high doses of DMT, this percentage goes up to the high 90s. These entities are conscious, intelligent beings with intention and agency of their own. Sometimes these beings are wise teachers and guides. With ayahuasca, many report meeting the plant spirit herself as Mother Ayahuasca, who teaches them. Sometimes the entities are more elf-like or humorous. Terrence McKenna famously reported meeting intelligent bejeweled self-dribbling basketballs.

This finding is very well attested. Roland Griffiths's team (Davis et al. 2020) reported in the *Journal of Psychopharmacology* about a study in which they surveyed 2,561 individuals with nn-DMT experience who had met entities. Even though the most common descriptors checked were *benign, guide, being, spirit, alien,* and *helper,* and the most common attitudes attributed to the entities were love, kindness, and joy, 41 percent still felt fear during at least part of the encounter. Of the subjects, 69 percent reported receiving a message. Many report this meeting as one of the most significant events of their lives. More than half of those who reported having been an atheist before the meeting were no longer atheists afterward. As Griffiths's team put it, these encounters produced profound and enduring changes in the people's worldview. An even more recent report from Griffiths's team (Lawrence et al. 2022) confirms the prevalence of entity encounters. Rick Strassman, the University of New Mexico psychiatrist who did extensive work with DMT, found these encounters so upsetting that they were a major factor in his pausing his work and reconsidering his orientation. He was expecting a Zen Buddhist–type enlightenment experience, but that's not what he got at all. This turned him back to his Jewish roots, and he came to understand psychedelics in terms of prophecy and a prophetic state of consciousness. A total of 60 percent of Strassman's more than four hundred cases reported a desirable alteration in their view of reality. Only 1 percent reported a negative shift.

These phenomena are so prominent that an entire invitational conference was held at Tyringham Hall in 2017. A book with some of the papers and discussions has been published (Luke and Spowers 2021). Another conference will be held soon. This subject makes even psychedelic researchers, who tend to be extremely open-minded, uncomfortable. It definitely does not fit in a Western worldview, but it keeps recurring in people's psychedelic experiences all over the world. The explanations suggested at the conference range from scientific (it's a hyperactive agency-detection mental module that we evolved as hunter-gatherers) to the mystical occult. It's like Rudolph Steiner's demons, Lucifer and Ahriman. Or it's like the Renaissance Neoplatonist philosopher Marsilio Ficino's ideas of the demonic realm of half-fire and half-material beings who mediate between us and the gods.

Luis Eduardo Luna is a very experienced ayahuasquero originally from Columbia who now lives in Brazil. At the 2017 Tyringham Hall conference, he discussed the art of Pablo Amaringo, who gave us many images of the entities. Luna has a new way of speaking about the daimonic realm. He reminds us that Descartes divided the world into two categories; *res cogitans* (thoughts and mental processes) and *res extensa* (material things, which extend in space). Luna says we need a third category to mediate between these two, which he calls *res fantastica*. It is very refreshing that these psychedelic researchers, instead of fleeing from this subject because it's so bizarre and unsettling, are turning toward it with curiosity and bringing the light of awareness to this dark and ignored field. People have been having experiences of something "other" within their minds for as long as we have records and in every culture on the planet. It's high time we look at this without the usual dismissal of it as primitive or psychopathological. Spiritual presence experiences are a common part of our humanity and often have profound impacts on those who have them.

CHAPTER 12

The Porosity of Mind

Our minds are porous — they have to be. All living beings are surrounded by a semipermeable membrane. In this chapter, I will provide evidence from many different areas to demonstrate this basic principle: the porosity of mind. To some of you, this may appear self-evident, but much of our culture is based on the assumption that our minds are our own and are private and inviolable. Those of us in IFS know that accepting the multiplicity of mind — an idea that, like porosity, is obvious when you examine the subject — changes everything. When we take multiplicity of mind and the existence of parts seriously and explore the consequences, it radically transforms psychotherapy. I propose that as we examine porosity and its implications, it will offer a further transformation and deepening of psychological healing. We will look at the work of Tanya Luhrmann and Isabel Clarke, measures of porosity, the neuroscience, Dawkins's memes, distributed cognition theory, Bateson's cybernetic model of mind, Charles Taylor on the buffered self, animism and neo-animism, cross-cultural studies, and more. All living systems are permeable. When it comes to our minds, we have tended to ignore this because it has such uncomfortable implications.

Tanya Luhrmann

Let's start with the work of Tanya Luhrmann. Even though I've never met her, she is one of my intellectual heroes. Her work is opening new ground and shining light on old issues from new directions. In 2015, the *British Journal of Psychiatry* published an article by her and others that described the results of a study she organized doing in-depth interviews with sixty psychotic people, twenty each in San Mateo, California; Accra, Ghana; and Chennai, India. These people all had psychosis and heard voices. Broadly speaking, the voices were similarly experienced in all locations. Many reported good and bad voices and whispering; some said God spoke to them, while others experienced the voices as assaultive. But there were also major differences. Many in Accra and Chennai insisted that the voices were predominantly or entirely positive. Not a single American reported this. In Ghana and Chennai, many saw the voices as people and seemed to have real human relationships with them. This was rare in San Mateo, where the encounters were remarkably more violent, harsh, and hated.

One of the most robust observations in psychological anthropology is that we Westerners imagine ourselves as individuals. As Clifford Geertz famously put it, "A bounded, unique, more or less integrated, motivational, and cognitive universe; a dynamic center of awareness, emotions, and judgment organized into a distinct whole and set contrastively against other such wholes" (quoted in Luhrmann et al. 2015, 43). This individual model of self is contrasted with the dividual model of Self, which is seen as emphasizing the interwoven nature of identity. We are intrinsically and necessarily connected in a web of relationships. The very word *consciousness* comes from roots that mean "to know with." Consciousness develops with others, not individually. Babies learn who they are through others.

This more porous model of mind allows for a much more benign experience of voices and psychosis in general. In Chennai, people tended to hear the voices like the voices of relatives. It could be chiding or encouraging, but there was more playfulness and even an emphasis on sex. In Accra, the voices were often spirits or the dominant voice of God. One could speculate that in India, the definition of Self was more sociocentric, and in Ghana more cosmocentric, or centered on the spiritual world. However we gloss this, the fact is that with their more porous views of the mind, they had more benign outcomes with schizophrenia than we see in the West. There's been a lot of follow-up research, especially in India, and the findings stay strong. I want to suggest that the rigid and brittle nature of our implicit view of mind makes us more psychologically vulnerable.

Elsewhere in her interviews, Luhrmann has discussed this Western idea as the citadel model of mind. We don't think through, model, and choose it; instead, it's one of the underlying presuppositions of our culture. We absorb this through-out our childhoods and education almost viscerally. I hope by the time you finish this chapter, you will join me in concluding that it is both wrong and pernicious. At the very least, I hope you become aware of this unconscious presupposition and start to have serious reservations about it.

Isabel Clarke

Isabel Clarke, whom I've mentioned earlier, is a psychologist in the United Kingdom who works primarily with hospitalized people diagnosed as psychotic. She is coming from a very different background but has reached a very similar view of our Western model of mind. She calls it the "billiard ball theory of mind," which is a nice parallel with the Luhrmann citadel image. Clarke also sees this Western assumption of the impermeability of mind as problematic and contributing to the suffering of her patients. I have an adolescent part who likes to call this the "bowl-ing ball theory of mind" or even the "blockhead theory of mind." Like many adolescents, this part of me is both disrespectful and humorous. He is also truly angry at this unspoken theory — a presupposition, really — because it precludes us from working in ways that can relieve human suffering.

Clarke uses the conclusions of cognitive science — specifically, interactive cognitive subsystems, or ICS, theory as developed by Teasdale and Barnard (1995) — to loosen our certainties about the indivisibility of mind. This body of theory, which is quite similar to McGilchrist's work on the hemispheric process, states that we have two separate ways of knowing, two separate meaning-making systems. One is rational and verbal; the other they call the implicational. The rational one is fairly obvious; it's the one the Western worldview tells us we should live in exclusively. The implicational one makes meaning by relationship, not analysis. The logic of the first is either/or, while that of the second is both-and. This distinction between the two logics is illustrated by something the great physicist Max Planck said: that the opposite of a small truth is a falsehood, but the opposite of a great spiritual truth is often another great spiritual truth.

Clarke notes that when the two meaning-making systems become separated from each other, we become open to many non-ordinary experiences. She also describes how these states and the depths of the implicational mind have been sought after by humans for centuries with religious ritual, in healing ceremonies, and for creativity. When these states emerge in uncontrolled ways and there is no easy return to the everyday state, we call it psychosis. Notice how the implicational way of making meaning through affect and relationship is inherently porous — the meaning of who we are is in our web of relations, not inside some billiard-ball identity. This porosity becomes even more extreme when the two ways of knowing desynchronize.

Clarke states, "Once we accept that we are porous and that this has dangers as well as potential, we can start to learn how to deal with it" (Clarke 2014, 46). This change allows us to validate the spiritually framed experiences at the same time that we discuss their dangers. This helps us form a collaborative and respectful alliance with our clients instead of telling them that their experiences are meaningless. We can normalize their experience and help them navigate the threshold between our shared reality and their implicational world. Is the implicational world the doorway to Corbin's mundus imaginalis, the daimonic, the collective unconscious, the autonomous imagination, the other world of the shamans?

Clarke notes that adding argument and confusion are unhelpful when people are seeking help with disturbing experiences. If we base our view of ourselves on a model of mind that is porous and acknowledge that anomalous experiences are a normal part of human life in all cultures and all eras of history, we can reduce human suffering.

John Vervaeke of the University of Toronto has proposed a more nuanced cognitive architecture that can build on Clarke's use of ICS. He proposes not two but four kinds of knowledge or meaning-making systems. He calls these the four Ps: propositional (knowledge about, which gives us theories and corresponds to ICS's rational knowledge); procedural (knowledge of how, which gives us power to do things in the world, like walk or ride a bicycle); perspectival (knowledge of perception, which states that our value systems determine what we attend to and therefore what we perceive; this is a subtle interactive dance); and participatory (knowledge or experience of relationship, being in relationships, and being changed by them). As we explore this model, it becomes clear that our minds are porous and exist only in many-leveled interrelationships with our environment. Much of Vervaeke's work is about the crisis in meaning that he sees resulting from pervasive alienation. The citadel–billiard ball unconscious presupposition about mind that our culture holds necessarily produces alienation and profound isolation.

Clarke also discusses dominant and subjugated ways of knowing. In many other cultures, implicational knowing, especially in its more extreme visionary modes, is accorded higher status than ordinary knowing. The increasingly multicultural environment she works in, in the United Kingdom, makes this impossible to ignore. In the Western academic world, all modes are subjugated to the propositional, to use Vervaeke's term. Many of the Indigenous therapists I work with here in the United States talk and write about decolonizing therapy and decolonizing trauma work. Have we subjugated and colonized their more honored ways of knowing? Have we subjugated and colonized large areas of our own experiencing?

Clarke (2010, 111) cites Richard Warner's 1994 book *Recovery from Schizophrenia*, which shows that societies that value religious or mystical experiences have a far better outcome with schizophrenia than we do. We have an illiteracy, a blind spot for this meaning-making system. She quotes the anthropologist R. H. Prince, "Highly similar mental and behavioral states may be designated psychiatric disorders in some cultural settings and religious experiences in others" (Clarke 2001, 206). Cultures that value these experiences often get better results with people who undergo them. Comprehensive literature reviews show that religion contributes to positive outcomes from psychiatric disorders (ibid., 207). Clarke argues convincingly that we need to give people in crisis a positive context for their experience. We have largely given up our anthropomorphic language to describe the world and have moved into a mechanomorphic system. She states that we need a new language for psychosis and other extreme states. It needs to be more multivalent and open. The limits of our language are the limits of our world.

Clarke is a fascinating clinician and thinker. Sadly, she is not well known on this side of the Atlantic. She started out as a historian specializing in medieval Europe. When a friend of hers had a psychotic episode, Clarke was appalled at the care she received, so she retrained and changed careers. Perhaps this beginning gave her more compassion than most. She describes how we are in webs of relationships: primary caregiver, family, wider groups, the culture, nonhuman, environment, spiritual. We are both constituted by and contained in these multiple webs. Self is a process, not a thing, and without these webs, self, mind, the person, and identity are unstable and incomplete. The widest of these webs, the spiritual, is also the deepest. Even though it is beyond verbal processing, it is nonetheless real and powerful.

The Measurement of Porosity

Back in the chapter on interoception, I reviewed some of the measures that had been used: the Tellegen Absorption Scale, the Stanford Hypnotic Susceptibility Scale, the Sensory Delight Scale, the Schizotypy and Psychoticism Scales, Hartmann's Boundaries in the Mind questionnaire, and the Transliminality Scale. While many of these are not exactly on target as measures of porosity, they all can be construed as probing dimensions of this larger issue.

We do not need to review all of them, but there are two I want to go into a little deeper: schizotypy and transliminality. The work on schizotypy has been led by Gordon Claridge and his colleagues in the United Kingdom. This study has been his life's work. The team started out focused on vulnerability to psychopathology, but their focus has morphed into establishing openness to wonder and newness as a universal human dimension. This is important clinically, sometimes crucial. When we share the understanding with clients that high schizotypy has benefits — more creativity and spiritual experience, for example — this more hopeful and respectful view of their situation can be a key to gaining their collaboration. Some researchers have talked about a distinction between pathogenic and healthy schizotypy. The emotional tone seems to predict a positive or negative outcome; anhedonia predicts pathology, while positive affectivity predicts religious experience and creativity. Therefore, shouldn't we as care providers offer as hopeful and positive a framework for these experiences as possible? How a culture holds our experience has a major role in determining whether it is benign or destructive, and much of the difficulty and suffering experienced by our psychotic patients may be exacerbated by our current attitudes and beliefs. High schizotypy does not equate with a broken brain. The trait can be a blessing or a curse.

Transliminality is another measure of porosity with important and wide-ranging implications that Clarke has developed and expanded. The term was originally coined by two British scientists in 1909 who were writing about psychic phenomena. Michael Thalbourne, a professor in Australia, has done a lot of work on this topic and has developed a reliable instrument to measure it. People with high transliminality are susceptible to and aware of high volumes of imagery, ideas, perceptions, and affect originating in the unconscious or the external world. These people often have mystical experiences, high creativity, and belief in and experience with paranormal phenomena. They are fantasy-prone and fascinated by dreams. They are also more vulnerable to psychosis. In a phrase that's popular with the researchers, they display "openness to anomalous experiencing." As mentioned earlier, Clarke proposes using the word *transliminal* to replace *unconscious* or *subconscious*. We do not need more jargon, but this idea appeals to me. It is a vastly more accurate term. In IFS, we know that our parts have their own consciousness, and much within us that is not in our awareness is conscious. We speak of going inside to the inner world that shamans have been visiting for tens of thousands of years — a world that has its own laws of inner physics and reality. To call it "sub" or "un" is disrespectful and can cause us to overlook the healing potential and wisdom that can be found within. Transliminal, which means "across a threshold," seems much more helpful and accurate.

I want to connect this concept with the work of anthropologists Victor Turner, Mary Douglas, and Edith Turner, even though none of the other researchers I know of do this. The three of them seemed to develop these ideas together, but because Victor Turner published a famous book on ritual (*The Ritual Process*, 1960), he is the one usually cited. The three analyzed rituals in terms of liminality. In initiations, for example, a phase of the ritual involves taking the initiate out of the ordinary social realm and into the liminal — the world of the spirits, the wild, outside of culture. Certain actions could be performed there that transform the initiate in ways not available in ordinary reality. The last phase of the ritual process helps the changed and newborn initiate back across the threshold, the limen, and into the world of the culture. Strong beliefs exist that the liminal is powerful and dangerous. It offers huge life-transforming gifts. This same concept of the liminal is used to describe healing rituals. Can we become more aware of this threshold? Can we learn to help people cross it and return mindfully? Can we help those lost or stranded on the other side of this threshold to have hope that their suffering may have meaning and healing potential?

A Little Neuroscience

Let's briefly look at some neuroscience. Interpersonal neurobiology (IPNB) is a field that was pioneered by Daniel Siegel, a Harvard-trained MD. In the 1990s, he brought together a multidisciplinary team at UCLA, where he taught. Some of the sociologists, anthropologists, and linguists argued that the mind is not just in the brain but also happens between us. This was ridiculed and sneered at by some neuroscientists and physicians. Dr. Siegel gathered a team (including, notably, the renowned neuroscientist-clinician Allan Schore) and for years worked on this issue. They started with the well-accepted fact that early attachment interactions with the primary caregivers profoundly impact the child's mind, personality, and identity. This is no longer in dispute. So at least at this stage, mind is undeniably porous. Siegel added to this new discoveries about neuroplasticity showing that the brain continues to grow and change throughout life. This suggests that the earlier porosity endures. Like Clarke, he came to define mind as a process, not a thing. According to Siegel, mind is an embodied and relational process that regulates the flow of energy and information. He developed what he calls the "triangle of well-being," which is composed of brain, mind, and relationships. These three interact to create psychological health. One of the points that Siegel emphasizes in his talks is that our primary way to regulate our internal states is through relationships with others. This is an example of porosity. This is crystal clear with infants and their mothers, and it is often also true for adults. There are over forty-eight books published about IPNB, with cumulative sales of well over a million and a half. This is a well-established therapy model and is based on a recognition of the porosity of mind.

In his more recent work (Siegel 2023), he goes even further. He states that the idea of a "solo-self" (his phrase, which parallels Luhrmann's citadel model of mind as well as Taylor's buffered self, described later in this chapter) is at the root of our modern disasters. It is a pandemic that was once Western but has now spread globally. In Siegel's words, "An excessively differentiated self in modern culture may be at the root of our most pressing challenges today" (2023, 57). He calls this solo-self "self as a noun" and equates it with top-down processing; he says self is really a verb and is more like bottom-up processing or, even better, the interaction of the two. He quotes an Aboriginal elder, Tyson Yunkaporta, who said, "Look beyond the things and focus on the connections between them. Then look beyond the connections and see the pattern they make… Systems are heterarchical — composed of equal parts interacting together. Imposing a hierarchical model of the top down control can only destroy them" (ibid., 37).

For the title of his new book, Siegel felt he had to invent new words because the old solo-self concept is so deeply embedded in our language. He calls the book *Intraconnected MWe (Me + We)*. He is right; this model of mind has become such a deep assumption of our culture that it's almost impossible even to discuss without inventing new words. Our old words keep looping us back into the old theory. DeCicco and Stroink (2007) coined the term "metapersonal self-construal" to describe the kind of self that feels its interrelationship to all of humanity and nature. They developed a scale to measure this and subsequently reported that higher scores on the scale predicted emotional well-being and emotional health. In some of Siegel's talks, he is much more blunt, saying we have been living a lie and it will destroy us… the lie of the separate self. He compares living from the solo-self to a cancer cell that's only concerned about its own well-being. He also uses a metaphor that I prefer, saying this solo-self idea is an autoimmune disease of the mind. We are nodes in a vast system, not independent beings at war with the world. Siegel states that Indigenous peoples and mystics have known this for a very long time. When we come to live this way, it can have a profound and pervasive healing impact on us and all those around us.

There is also an impressive body of hard science (meaning machines and statistics) that is now backing this up and yielding powerful evidence for porosity. This is the field of hyperscanning. This is a generic term for studies in which two or more people are simultaneously monitored using an fMRI, EEG, MEG, or another measure of brain activity. The machines are so powerful, light, and portable that assessment of neurological activity during real-time social interactions is possible. As of 2020, there were at least 20 major studies and over 140 peer-reviewed published studies in the literature. Some conclusions: brain waves and activity synchronize when people interact. The existence of brain-to-brain entrainment is real. Even in strangers in a first conversation separated by a screen, brain waves synchronize. Experimenters could tell when two people were in conversation from their brain wave recordings (Perez 2017). Eye contact increases the entrainment of brain waves. Uri Hassan of Princeton noted in studying a group of people listening to a story that the greater coupling of the listener's brain waves to the storyteller's, the greater the comprehension and recall of the story. He said, "Your brain as an individual is really determined by the brains you are connected to" (Hassan 2019). The more you like the person, the more your brain waves synchronize. Vikaas Sohal, MD, PhD, at UC San Francisco has done research showing that out-of-sync brain waves play a role in schizophrenia (Sohal 2020). As Anna Valencia and Tom Froese (2020) state, "These findings challenge the standard view of human consciousness as essentially first person, singular, and private." Human consciousness and cognition are interactive.

This phase synchronization is also known to be important within a person's brain as they think, feel, and decide. Many theorists have proposed that consciousness itself depends on the large-scale synchronization of neural oscillatory activity. This was first proposed by Sir Francis Crick, who is usually credited as the discoverer of DNA, back in 1990. The idea has been developed by Rodolfo Llinas of NYU and many others. Llinas has based valuable treatments for Parkinson's and other maladies on this idea. McFadden (2020) is developing the CEMI theory, which holds that the synchronization of the brain's global electromagnetic fields is what binds consciousness together.

There is also a field called resonance therapy, pioneered by Jonathan Schooler, a professor of psychology at the University of California, Santa Barbara, the mathematician Stephen Strogatz, and the neurophysiologist Pascal Fries. They are coming to similar conclusions. There are more as well. Now it appears that this phase synchronization is similarly significant outside the individual brain. This interactive nature of mental function is leading researchers to describe "second-person neuroscience" and to discuss consciousness as a social phenomenon not contained inside a single brain.

All of this challenges the individual notion of the human mind. "The boundaries that distinguish self from others instead of being fixed …are under constant renegotiation" (Valencia and Froese 2020). The properties of consciousness and mind are not reducible to the individual. Some researchers call this the second-person perspective, and some call it the "we" perspective, but the implications are clear: to understand mind and consciousness, we need to move beyond the first-person, private, citadel mind model.

Memes

Richard Dawkins has given us another lens through which to view this permeability of mind. This is significant because Dawkins is one of the most vehemently anti-spiritual atheists of our era. For example, he's working on a children's book to prevent kids from becoming religious, tentatively titled *Outgrowing God*. In 1976, Dawkins proposed the idea of memes in his book *The Selfish Gene*. This idea is modeled on the gene and is its mental equivalent — a virus of the mind that can be transmitted from mind to mind and replicate itself. Dawkins also described memeplexes, or complexes of memes, that could be transmitted and replicated as a group unit.

Nicholas Humphrey, another prominent British scientist-intellectual-atheist, proposed that memes should be considered living structures, not just metaphors, and that they physically reside in the brain. Dawkins welcomed these ideas. It was Humphrey who first suggested to Dawkins that religions are a mental virus, and this infectious process explains their persistence and spread. Daniel Dennett, the philosopher of consciousness, also embraced the concept of memes. He called them "information packets with an attitude." I believe it was Dennett who made it clear that memes that would destroy their hosts could also exist. For example, there is an idea meme that suicide bombers go to heaven. Dawkins and the others have largely used this concept of memes to attack religion and spirituality, so it

is wonderfully ironic that their work clearly demonstrates the porosity of self —
and that it can even more significantly provide a hyperrational theory to explain
the subjective experience of spirit possession! When you savor the implications of
Humphrey's ideas that there are living structures and Dennett's assumption that
they can have attitude, they start to look a lot like conscious, intelligent entities.
Dawkins would probably be appalled by these ideas.

As long as we're talking about biology, let me add another point. Stress is
contagious. Tony Buchanan at St. Louis University has done several studies showing that it is contagious among people. When people are hooked up to moni-
tors and exposed to images of stressed people, their stress markers go up. Jaideep
Bains at the University of Calgary has shown that this also happens in animals.
My twelve-year-old part finds one of his results hilarious: in mice, stress is com-
municated by a pheromone that is emitted from their anal glands. Jens Pruessner
at McGill University has shown that stress is contagious among many different
kinds of animals at very different levels of complexity.

Distributed Cognition

In our whirlwind tour of the evidence that mind is necessarily porous, let's look at
another realm that is rational, practical, and non-spiritual: distributed cognition
theory. This work has been applied, for example, to the study of air traffic control
systems. This area is hyperrational and results-driven; with so much human life
at stake, there is no room for sloppy thinking or sentimentality. Think of a pilot
being guided to land their plane at a busy airport. Where is the cognition — the
intelligence? Is it in the pilot's brain? Is it in the instruments in the cockpit? Is it in
the air traffic controller's brain? Is it in their instrument panel? Is it in the remote
radar installation that tracks everything? Well, none of these. It is in the entire
system. The cognition is distributed, and to improve air traffic control, the whole
system must be considered as a unit. This same method of analysis is being applied
to the command structures on naval vessels. Is the cognition in the captain's head?
The radar and sensors? The other officers and crew? I was once describing this
to a man who'd been in the navy for a long time. He started laughing and said,
"Well, we all knew it definitely wasn't in the captain's head!" The point is clear:
in areas where precision and freedom from error are vital, distributed cognition
is important. The New Agey soft thinkers who speak of extended mind and one
mind and the like have not been interested in this work, and vice versa. It's time
these separate worlds laid down their prejudices and came together.

There are two very important topics in this field that I need to mention.
First, distributed cognition is distributed in at least three domains: one, among
people and their social and cultural environment; two, in things; and three, across

time. Our assumed citadel model of mind is way too small in many directions. We are only considering cognition, the most cut-and-dry function. When we consider emotion, intuition, and imagination, the concept of the distributed mind is even more powerful and vast. The second point is that mental real estate is biologically very expensive. Our unmoving three-pound brain consumes about 20 percent of our body's energies, so we off-load every function we can. You can consider the use of pencil and paper as an off-loading strategy. Consciousness itself is perhaps the most expensive real estate in the brain. We continuously, and often against our will, off-load material from consciousness. A familiar example is learning how to ride a bicycle. This off-loading of things from consciousness is incredibly valuable, but it can get out of hand. Colin Wilson called this the robot. He wrote that when he realized one night that the robot was making love to his wife, he knew he had to take this process in hand. Margaret Wilson (2002), no relation, wrote: "The information flowed between mind and the world is so dense and continuous that for scientists studying the nature of cognitive activity, the mind alone is not a meaningful unit of analysis." I'll repeat that: "the mind alone is not a meaningful unit of analysis."

Relational Systems Intelligence and Actor-Network Theory

It may now seem totally obvious to you that the mind is porous, but I'm going to explore this more because the implications of this realization are far-reaching, and the opposite belief is deeply and often unconsciously embedded in us. Two more areas where this stuff shows up are relational systems intelligence (RSI) and actor-network theory. RSI is a group that provides training and consulting for businesses internationally. When I last checked, they were active in twenty-two countries. They focus on the team and redirect focus from the individuals to the team itself. The team needs a strong identity. They have five core principles: (1) access the team as an entity; (2) hear, see, and feel the team; (3) the team has the answers; (4) roles of individuals belong to the team; and (5) change is constant.

The actor-network theory was developed in the French high-tech industry to understand innovation. It asserts that nothing exists outside the complex web of constantly shifting relationships and networks in the social and natural worlds. Therefore, the objects, ideas, and other factors involved are as important as the humans. Actor-network theory is perhaps most helpful in increasing our sensitivity to our unexplored assumptions and presuppositions, and the limits they impose. This is the kind of sensitivity I assert that we need around our beliefs about the nature of mind. Both of these groups are pragmatic consultants working to produce better results in the business world, and both seem to place the real intelligence outside of the individual's mind and instead in the group interaction system.

Gregory Bateson

Another thinker who needs to at least be mentioned here is Gregory Bateson. He was an anthropologist and one of the early cybernetic systems thinkers. He's stimulating and likable but also immensely frustrating to study. Sometimes he issues Delphic pronouncements, and he seems to delight in a trickster's way in refusing to give a simple rational response. He forces us to think outside our boxes. Bateson straddled two worlds; he was academically respected, and he participated in a great deal of nontraditional teaching at the Esalen Institute and other places.

In his book *Mind and Nature* (1979), Bateson insisted that mind and nature evolved together and are completely interlinked. One cannot be studied without the other. It is the interaction, the interrelationship, that is crucial. Bateson wrote about the ecology of mind. He asserted that most of the project of the modern Western intellectual tradition involves cutting up the vibrant living system and analyzing bits of it one at a time. This can only provide a very limited and often misleading understanding of the mind.

Charles Taylor

Charles Taylor is an emeritus professor of philosophy at McGill University who has given us a detailed and sophisticated philosophical and historical understanding of the importance of the boundaries of self. Starting with his 1989 book *Sources of the Self: The Making of Modern Identity* and culminating perhaps in his 2007 *A Secular Age*, he has described the modern "buffered self," how it developed historically, and its ramifications and problems. He emphasizes that this change is not mere subtraction, the removal of old, superseded ideas. It is a remaking, a "change in sensibility." This is not a matter of theory or belief but rather a fact of experience. We have lost a way of experiencing the world. Taylor traces this back to the Protestant Reformation and Catholic Counter-Reformation. Max Weber, the great German sociologist, wrote about the disenchantment of the modern world beginning in the same era. There have been many attempts to re-enchant the world. Taylor said the whole Romantic movement engaged in this. For example, Schiller depicted the Newtonian universe as a dead one, shorn of the life it used to have. To Taylor, it is clear that even the poetry of Wordsworth, Novalis, or Rilke cannot come close to recreating the experience of porous self that we used to live in naturally. Taylor describes how we make a sharp distinction between inner and outer, what is mind and what is world, even between mind and body. This modern "buffered self" sees itself as invulnerable and as a master of meanings.

For Taylor, the porous self was vulnerable to spirits, demons, the divine, and cosmic forces; the buffered self has removed these fears. I would say it has only buried them, but Taylor might not agree with this. Many people look back on the world of the porous self and experience this creation of a thick emotional boundary as a loss. This change is a change in our experience, in how we are in the world. It is not a theory. If we have a porous self, we live in an enchanted, living world, whereas if we have a buffered self, our universe is disenchanted, dead. Taylor also underlines the fact that this is not an intrapsychic issue; it is about the felt boundaries of the psyche. With the porous self, we live embodied in our flesh, embedded in society, embedded in the world, and embedded in the divine. Taylor sees deism — the doctrine that emerged in the late 1700s that God issued a set of laws and then stepped back, and therefore it is not useful to relate to him as a person — as crucial in this transition. He points to the emphasis on discipline in the Protestant Reformation and Catholic Counter-Reformation. This valuation of discipline creates a disciplined society that controls rowdiness, poor people, and nonconformists; tames aristocrats; and moves toward a centralized bureaucratic state. This is pure work and control, no more carnival. Max Weber also famously proposed that it was the Protestant ethic — this discipline Taylor writes of — that created the ground for the rise of modern capitalism. This buffered self creates a new moral order based on the idea that humans are rational, and the only valuable knowledge comes from detached investigation, reason, and moralism. This change in the experience of self from the porous to the buffered changes almost everything. Taylor mentions culture, art, philosophy, and the economy explicitly. This change also definitely and decisively changes our view of mental health and psychotherapy.

Taylor is a nuanced and careful thinker; this brief overview of a major portion of his life work does not do him justice. It is unfortunate that psychotherapists rarely read him, but many anthropologists, in their studies of self and personhood across cultures, make reference to his work. The idea that the experience of self varies in different societies is one of the most consistent and recurring themes in anthropology. If you ask whether the experience of self varies cross-culturally, there is widespread consensus — the answer is a loud, resounding, unequivocal yes. But if you ask what the differences are, things quickly become murky, undecided, and disputatious. There are many ways to slice this pie: hierarchical personhood in India versus Western egalitarianism, wholism versus individualism, sociocentric versus egocentric persons, relativism versus individualism, and many others.

Perhaps the most prominent of these dichotomies is the distinction between a dividual and an individual. This has a long history dating back at least to the 1950s, but it seems that anthropologist Marilyn Strathern's use of it to differentiate between Western and Melanesian concepts of persons is the most cited.

The individual is Taylor's buffered self; the dividual is sociocentric, ecocentric, cosmocentric, permeable, and relational. It is not disenchanted but still lives as part of a living world. There is a big problem with much of this analysis. It posits a Western standard view of person/self and compares all other views to it. This is very misleading; there very well may be a greater difference between, for example, Indian, African, and Melanesian views than there is between any one of them and our Western experience. Many anthropologists seem to see an inevitable progression toward an individual experience of self. Taylor is a salutary correction to this, as he points out how historically specific the rise of this position is and how, while it has given us much, it has also created great losses. In IFS, we know that we are multiple; therefore, we already have half of the dividual understanding. Dividuals are divisible, comprising a complex of separable parts. The other major feature of dividuals, that they are permeable and porous, has not yet been fully accepted by IFS. To be permeable and porous means we exist as completely embedded, inexorably engaged parts of a relational web with particular people, particular places, and particular things. N. E. Spiro noted correctly that this other experience of self creates a mental reality, and "such a condition (according to modern psychiatry) is a sign of rather severe psychopathology" (quoted in K. Smith 2012, 54). I want to reemphasize that it is the lived experience of people, not some theory or belief or idea, that matters.

Taylor argues that the self is constructed by narratives that answer the question *Who am I?* in three dimensions: temporal, spatial, and social. These narratives are always dialogic. They are constructed in interactions and relationship to others, first with caregivers and significant others but later with a more generalized other of society and culture. Ironically, even the independent individual buffered self is created in and by relationship. The disengaged stance of the buffered self has methodological advantages for the natural sciences, but it grossly misrepresents how humans are in the world. We can only become socialized into a buffered self because we are intrinsically porous, relational people. The recognition of this permeability is important for the culture in general, as Taylor describes, but it is even more crucial and necessary for psychological healing.

Animism

Another angle on the appreciation of human psychological permeability comes from the study of animism. *Animism* is a term invented by a different Taylor: E. B. Taylor (1832–1917). This Taylor was one of the fathers of British anthropology, and unfortunately most of his work is permeated with a colonialist and even imperialist attitude. Animism is roughly the belief that everything is alive and has a spirit. I prefer these two more sympathetic ways of describing animism:

(1) it is an embodied and re-souled existential understanding of being in the world, or (2) it is a relational epistemology that asserts that we know things most deeply by relating to them and not by analyzing them. Taylor saw this as a primitive phase of religion that culture evolved out of. Most later anthropologists found this kind of attitude quite distasteful and rebelled against it. In this reaction to the unsavory aspects of Taylor's work, the word *animism* and the phenomena it refers to were largely ignored, but now the topic is again an acceptable one, often referred to as the "new animism."

Back in 1942, Irving Hallowell declared, "No one is more aware than the ethnologist that human beings always live in a meaningful universe, not a world of bare physical objects and events" (quoted in Astor-Aguilera and Harvey 2018, 2). We have never been rational Cartesians; we continue to relate to beloved animals, special things, and natural processes as though they were more than just purely things. Hallowell came up with the happy phrase "other-than-human persons" to describe it. We know this world by relating to it, not by analyzing it, and many Indigenous peoples use kinship terms for nonhumans. Remember the classic American prayer "to all my relations." Our Western attempt to deny this is built into our language, which separates nature from culture, spirit from world, and human from nonhuman.

Animism is not a curious, outdated belief system; it is a vibrant way of being in the world, a way of experiencing reality that is thoroughgoingly relational. With our Western, modern project of human separation and aggrandizement, which is a purity system, we create individuals and "buffered self" individuals, and then we create nation-states. A group of Indigenous scholars are working to develop Indigenous research methodologies that respect and make room for this permeable and relational way of being. Indigenous scholar Shawn Wilson is one of these. In *Research Is Ceremony* (2008, 73), he writes, "An object or thing is not as important as one's relationship to it. This idea could be farther expanded to saying that reality is relationships or sets of relationships. There is no one definite reality, but rather different sets of relationships that make up an indigenous ontology, therefore, reality is not an object but a process of relationships..." Therefore, relational accountability and attending to one's relationships are important values. Other-than-human persons are not things; they have life, agency, intentionality, and social relations. Agency is viewed as variable. Powerful medicine men and women have more agency than normal people. Some objects have less agency than humans. Spirits have more. In a world experienced this way, it is only fitting that contents of the psyche are also viewed as persons. To know them, we do not dissect or analyze them — we relate to them. Wilson, who considered research a form of ceremony, wrote, "The purpose of any ceremony is to build strategic relationships or bridge the distance between our cosmos and us" (ibid., 137). We are nodes in a network of living agents. We learn by tending these relationships and strengthening them.

We need to consider another anthropologist on this topic of the porous mind as well. Lucien Levy-Bruhl (1875–1939) wasn't actually an anthropologist at all; he was a professor of philosophy at the Sorbonne for more than twenty-five years, but most of his work focused on "primitive mentality." Like the work of E. B. Taylor, the early British anthropologist who coined the term *animism*, Levy-Bruhl's work is seen as very flawed at best. When I was an undergraduate, his ideas were ridiculed, but as with Taylor's idea of animism, it contains valuable insights. Levy-Bruhl wrote extensively about "participation mystique," the idea that "the primitive" has a different way of thinking, of being in the world, and therefore values a different kind of knowledge. According to him, the native way participates in the world almost in a mystical union. In his notebooks from late in life, he acknowledged that the two ways of thinking — modern rational and participation mystique — were both still used today. He hinted that he didn't want to discuss this for fear of offending religious people. He also developed Emile Durkheim's idea of collective representations. This is the concept that be-liefs, ideas, categories, and values exist that are elaborated by the collective and not reducible to an individual. They are richer than an individual's thoughts, and they become autonomous. They often create a sense of the meaning of the world. Both of these core ideas of Levy-Bruhl's became important influences on the work of C. G. Jung. They both also reflect the fundamental porosity of mind. For the modern as well as the primitive, one of the major ways of knowing the world is by participating in it. This requires very open or even temporarily nonexistent boundaries of the mind. The collective representation concept shows that much of "our thought" is really something much bigger than our minds, more ancient, more vast, and in many ways autonomous.

We have glanced at many ways in which cultures create a sense of self, Strathern's dividual/individual distinction, and talk of relational versus sociocen-tric selves. One of the clearest might be Lawrence Kirmayer's four selves: sociocen-tric defined by the group, ecocentric defined in relationship to nature, egocentric defined as individual, and cosmocentric defined in relation to the all, the divine. Only an extreme form of the egocentric model can give us the citadel model of mind that is the underlying assumption of the Western way of being. It is a very narrow and limited vision.

Mass Psychogenic Illness

Another indicator of the extent and power of the porosity of the human mind is the existence of mass psychogenic illness, also known as both MPI and mass sociogenic illness. My personal favorite example of this is the dancing epidemic of 1518 in Strasburg. It started with one woman dancing uncontrollably all day and into the night. She couldn't stop and kept dancing even though her feet were bleeding until finally she collapsed in exhaustion. At least fifty people also danced involuntarily for long periods of time; some accounts put the number at over four hundred. Some people danced themselves to death. John Waller (2009) claims over a hundred died in this way. This outbreak continued from July until September, when it seemed to fade away.

Several other dancing epidemics also occurred throughout Europe. Perhaps the most famous is tarantism. This was at its peak in the sixteenth and seventeenth centuries, but it persisted well into the twentieth century. The great Italian anthropologist Ernesto de Martino (2005) has given us a book-length account of the dance as it occurred in 1959. The dance gets its name from the dancers' belief that it was caused by the bite of a tarantula spider. These epidemics of dancing spread from village to village. There have been dancing epidemics in France, Germany, the Netherlands, and Switzerland. It is generally agreed that the dancers were not able to control themselves and were in an unconscious or altered state of consciousness.

There are many other kinds of MPIs as well. Most are associated with physical symptoms, including headache, dizziness, nausea, fatigue, and pain. They are also often associated with behaviors and emotions such as fainting, screaming, inability to think, anxiety, paralysis, and so on. Especially in the fifteenth century but persisting into the nineteenth century, there are many instances of this in the nunneries of Europe. They were most often attributed to mass possession.

Six of the outbreaks of MPI that occurred in factories in Singapore between 1973 and 1978 have been extensively investigated. They were characterized by seizures, screaming, violent movements, trance states, numbness, and panic. The workers attributed these to jinn (spirits). Bomoh (medicine men) were often called in to help. Similar mass outbreaks have occurred in the US, England, Russia, France, Germany, and Africa. These events have also occurred in schools. A contagious laughter epidemic took place in Tanzania in 1962. More than fourteen different schools and over a thousand students were affected. In 2011, there was an outbreak of Tourette's syndrome–like tics and sounds in Upstate New York. Even though there are well over two hundred published accounts, the experts in the area of mass psychogenic illness say it is underappreciated and severely underreported. This is sadly predictable; we tend to ignore phenomena we do not have a conceptual framework for. A deep understanding of mental porosity would make MPIs comprehensible and even expectable. It might also lead to ways to work with these events because some contagious outbreaks have positive effects.

Barbara Ehrenreich

Barbara Ehrenreich (2006) has written a history of collective joy that gives deep insight into psychic contagion and porosity of mind from a very different angle. Ehrenreich has a PhD in cellular immunology and is a lifelong atheist, so it's hard to accuse her of being woo-woo or soft-headed. She has also forged an independent career outside of academia as a writer. This, I believe, contributes to her openness to new ideas and ways of seeing. She points out that as Europeans spread over the globe, one thing they were consistently repelled by was the group dances of the "primitives." These dances were nearly universal. Colonizers and missionaries found festivals and rituals involving rhythmic group movement almost everywhere, from Australia and Tahiti to the Americas to Africa to the Middle East and beyond. Depictions of group dance are found in prehistoric rock art as well as in the art of Mesopotamia, India, China, and Palestine. The Old Testament makes it clear that a tradition of collective ecstasy existed among the Hebrews, but it was hardly officially appreciated. There's also evidence that early Christians danced in worship. The missionaries expressed disgust, repulsion, and severe judgment, often saving their most hate-filled denunciations for this "deviltry and savagery." "The existence of widespread European campaign against indigenous ritual is beyond dispute" (Ehrenreich 2006, 157). These colonizers prided themselves in never having sunk to this level of primitiveness, but about this they were absolutely wrong. For example, in Paris in the 1730s, there were the Catholic convulsionnaires, whom I have already mentioned and whose worship was just as wild as any ecstatic tribal dance. "While the assembled company redoubled their prayers and collectively reached extreme heights of religious enthusiasm, at last, one of their number would suddenly lapse into uncontrolled motor activity… They thrashed about on the floor in a state of frenzy, screaming, roaring, trembling, and twitching… The excitement and the disordered movements, which might last for several hours, usually proved highly contagious, with certain convulsionnaires apparently serving as catalysts for the onset of various bodily agitations in others" (Robert Kreiser, quoted in Ehrenreich 2006, 7–8).

More significantly than this colorful description, the Western tradition of ecstatic group dance and its repression goes back at least to the Dionysian rites of ancient Greece. The elites almost never liked these festivals. The festivals and rituals melt boundaries, abandon social hierarchy, and give unity and strength to the people. The rituals involve music and dance, feasts and wine, costuming, body painting, and masks. Very often there's transvestitism, a king of fools, and mockery of the elite. All differences and roles are broken down. Hierarchy does not like this but sometimes seems to tolerate it as a safety valve. The culmination of these rites is not orgiastic sex, as the missionaries suppose, but ecstatic trance where the dancers are possessed by their gods. These rituals and festivals were not some uncontrollable outbreak — they were carefully planned, with weeks or months of preparation. Even in the most intense parts of the ritual, there was structure. The possessions tended to follow culturally approved forms and occurred at appropriate times in the ritual. If people were possessed outside of this socially approved framework, they were often helped back to ordinary consciousness.

These rituals presupposed a different lived experience of self. The group dance actualizes a bigger self; transcendence is involved. Suryani and Jensen (1993, 173) write, "The sense of being in control of one's self is prominent and highly valued in Western personality and thought. This trait is not characteristic of the Balinese, whose lives have been in the main controlled by their family, their ancestors, and the supernatural."

Our Western psychology and therapy focus on the individual self and do not look for healing in melting that self into something larger. We tend to bolster and fortify the citadel of mind. We tend to assume that the desire for self-loss, for an experience of permeability, must be the result of antisocial and regressive drives. But for many other cultures and in many other periods of our own history, healing was found precisely in these moments of self-transcendence in group ritual. With the emergence of a state-supported monotheism, this was largely lost. The old "biotechnology of danced ritual" (Ehrenreich 2006, 254) could no longer help the formation of groups, induce ecstasy, heal the afflicted, or reunite the isolated. Nature became dead, and joy was postponed until the afterlife. The Roman Empire did its best to kill this off, but it kept reemerging, often in the churches themselves as ritual. Then it was driven out of the churches and reemerged as carnival and festivities. The hierarchies and elites were fairly consistent in their hostility. According to Ehrenreich, the real death blow didn't come until the Reformation and Counter-Reformation. This is the same period that Charles Taylor (oddly, Taylor and Ehrenreich do not seem aware of each other's work; neither one references the other) pointed to as the origin of our concept of a "buffered self," isolated, independent, and alone. Something happened then that was the end of rituals and festivities of renewal and communal joy as well as the birth of the citadel experience of self as private and inviolable. I also want to call to mind the fact that one of the primary ways of healing sickness-producing possession was to have large, communal dances for the afflicted person. Rhythm, song, and ecstatic dance can heal.

Ehrenreich provides extensive evidence that this period was also the beginning of an epidemic of depression that continues to this day. Many books on melancholia, which is the old word for depression, started appearing. Many of the intellectuals of the day wrote of their struggle with melancholy. There is evidence that suicide rates increased dramatically and that rates among Protestants were close to twice as high as among Catholics. As evidence of this change in the concept of self, Ehrenreich points to the fact that autobiography first became common in this era and that mirrors became an important part of peoples' homes. She seems to attribute most of these effects to the loss of the rituals and festivities of group dance and communal joy. But I feel that the development of the isolated, cut-off model of self is more fundamental. Ehrenreich quotes author Lionel Trilling as saying, "Historians of European culture are in substantial agreement that in the late 16th and early 17th centuries, something like a mutation in human nature took place" (Trilling, quoted in Ehrenreich 2006, 137). There was a great new emphasis on disengagement, self-consciousness, individuality, and personal autonomy. While this sounds great to Western ears, it also creates isolation, loneliness, and a sense of loss of belonging and meaning — in short, alienation and anomie.

These old tendencies and ways have not died — they keep reemerging. Ehrenreich cites rock 'n' roll music, the Burning Man Festival, all-night raves, and similar events. I would add the ecstatic and conscious dance movements, which have grown like mushrooms after rain in recent years. She describes how sports events have come to be more participatory with rhythmic movement of the fans, for example, the wave, costumes, face paint, and revelry. There's a dark side to group bonding as well; it has been used by fascists and other totalitarian governments to great effect.

Ehrenreich's work is deep and rich. I've not done it justice. For our purposes, what is important is that dance rituals all over the planet and throughout history, back into the Stone Age, have helped humans melt their little selves and bond with other humans, with their gods, and with the spirits of their ancestors. These rituals heal. When the definition of the self in the West became rigid and impermeable during the Reformation, it triggered a centuries-long epidemic of depression and anxiety that continues. The refusal to acknowledge and honor the porosity of self has baleful consequences. When we once again welcome this porosity, we should expect people to experience things in their minds that are not part of their own personal history. In IFS, we call these legacy burdens, unattached burdens, and guides. Many other traditions speak of possession states or spiritual experiences. Some people hear voices in their heads. They are sometimes considered insane and sometimes considered prophets. Whatever language and cognitive framework we use, if we take seriously the porosity of mind, we should expect these things as part of the normal range of human experience.

Interbeing

It may feel as though this idea of porosity — permeability of self or mind — has been hammered home, but I will go a little further with it because: (1) the citadel model of mind is deeply embedded in us and hard to remove, even when we know it is inadequate; and (2) the ramifications of porosity are so manifold and vast that we need many angles of approach to appreciate how thoroughgoing a change this involves. An entire book, or an entire library, really, could be written about the spiritual implications of this concept. In IFS, we talk about Self as a particle and also as a wave or field. Our Self — the curious, compassionate, creative, clear, light-filled being that we really are — is a particle, and this particle is also part of a wave or field of Self that is far larger and wiser than we are. The idea of Self as both particle and wave, particle and field, is mainstream IFS, and if we start to follow its implications, it leads to deep waters indeed.

For now, in order to show the depths to which this idea of porosity and interpenetration can lead, let's discuss the Hindu and Buddhist concept of Pratityas-amutpada. This is translated variously as dependent arising, dependent origination, or interdependent co-arising. This is the idea that all things arise together, come up at once. It's found in the Vedas and became a core belief of almost all Buddhist traditions. Here's a poetic description from Thich Nhat Hanh, the Vietnamese monk:

> For a table to exist we need wood, a carpenter, time, skillfulness, and many other causes. And each of these causes need other causes to be. The wood needs the forest, the sunshine, the rain, and so on. The carpenter needs his parents, breakfast, fresh air, and so on. And each of those things in turn has to be brought about by other conditions. If we continue to look at it in this way, we will see that nothing has been left out... Looking deeply at the sunshine, the leaves of the tree, and the clouds, we can also see the table. The one can be seen in the all, and the all can be seen in the one.

If this is true of the grossly material things like a table, it must be even more true of our minds, our thoughts, our emotions, and ourselves.

A classic image of this is Indra's Net. It dates back to the Vedas and is also found in Buddhism and Hinduism. In the heavenly abode of Indra is a great net that is infinite in all directions. At each knot of the net, there are jewels, infinite in number. Each of these jewels reflects on its polished surfaces all the other jewels in the net, infinite in number. Also, each of these reflected jewels reflects the infinite number of other jewels. An infinity of infinities, interpenetrating and inter-being in infinite ways. This is the idea of interbeing. Charles Eisenstein (2007, xvii) wrote, "We are not just a skin-encapsulated ego, a soul encased in flesh. We are each other and we are the world." We inter-are. In a YouTube interview with Deepak Chopra, neuroscientist Chris Neibauer said, "Perhaps the reason we can't find the self in the human brain is because it is not there." The poet e e cummings wrote in one of his poems, "I am, through you, so I."

William James had a wonderful image for this that is much less jarring than these full-on ideas of interbeing. He said we are each an island in a vast sea, and our physical, social, and seemingly private selves all arise from and are part of the same seafloor. Iain McGilchrist, the great scholar of hemispheric brain function, wrote in many places of the "betweenness," and it is this that tells you who you really are. The relationship, resonant and bidirectional, is prior to the relata. He also has pointed out that there are no isolated things; even a great mountain, seen from the perspective of geological time, is merely a process. In the Xhosa language of South Africa, the word *ubuntu* means a person is a person through other persons; we are only human among others. Stan Grof talks of his field theory of mind, saying it extends beyond us, just as gravity extends beyond Earth. He says our bodies are really antennas.

Charles Eisenstein and Johann Hari

There are two modern theorists on this issue of isolation and connection that I want to discuss in a little more detail: Charles Eisenstein and Johann Hari. Eisenstein's 2007 book *The Ascent of Humanity* proposes that we live in the age of separation, which began way back in prehistory and is at its apex now. It is poisoning us. He proposes that we need to enter into an age of reunion. He writes, "This book proposes a conception of self that is not a distinct, separate entity but an emergent property of complex interactions, encompassing not just the brain but the entire body and the environment too, both physical and social. To pretend otherwise is to cut ourselves off from most of what we are" (Eisenstein 2007, 151). This is an easier-to-digest version of McGilchrist's often-repeated saying "The relationship is prior to the relata." The self emerges from, and is created by, the relationships between the person, the environment, and the society. It is porous and interdependent. Eisenstein encapsulates his whole argument in his introduction. He says, "… [there is] a common root underneath all the diverse crises of the modern age. Underlying this vast swath of ruin our civilization has caused is not human nature but the opposite: human nature denied. This denial of human nature rests in turn upon an illusion, a misconception of self and the world. We have defined ourselves as other than what we are, as discrete subjects separate from each other and separate from the world around us" (ibid., xvii).

Eisenstein maintains that this illusion of the separate self is so deeply intertwined with our cultural-political structures, technologies, and society that it is very difficult for us to extricate ourselves from it. This illusion of separate self is Luhrmann's citadel model of mind. Her work has shown us how this misunderstanding makes us brittle and psychologically vulnerable. Eisenstein shows us how this same way of thinking and experiencing on a bigger scale can poison the planet and cripple civilizations.

Johann Hari also writes and speaks eloquently about separation. He states that the opposite of addiction is not sobriety — it's human connection. Addictions are not caused by some addictive chemical but rather by a failure of connection. In a very famous series of experiments, Bruce Alexander and a team of experimenters (Alexander et al. 1981; Alexander 2001) put rats in individual cages and gave them water laced with heroin or cocaine that the rats could get when they wanted. Many of the rats took the drugs until they died. The scientists declared that they had proven that the substances themselves were addictive. Bruce Alexander realized the glaring flaw in those experiments. He created big cages with many rats and rat toys for them to play with. He put the drugged water in there as well. Almost no rats became addicted and none died. It was the isolation that caused the addiction, not the chemicals. This may be one of the big reasons the twelve-step movement continues to get better results with addiction than most therapists. Twelve-step meetings provide connection, get addicts out of their self-centered isolation, and get them helping other addicts. In short, the meetings get them connected.

In Hari's book *Lost Connections* (2019), he describes in detail our disconnection from meaningful work, other people, meaningful values, childhood trauma, status and respect, the natural world, and a hopeful future. I believe that underlying all of these disconnections is the disconnection from everything and everyone that we create when we take on the citadel model of mind — when we absorb our culture's belief that each of us is an impenetrable, private, contained, and independent self. This is the underlying separation. There are many others I could mention as well. Rupert Sheldrake describes how mind extends in space (vision and perception), time (memory and planning), and spirit (all religions began in this experience). Melody Hayes, MD, says illness is not in the body of the patient but in the community or the failure of community, and that healing should be in **done in** circles. Daniel Foor works with how our identity extends back into our ancestors. Ernest Hartmann evaluates psychopathology by the condition of the boundaries of the mind; if it is too thin, it's psychosis, and if it is too thick, it's obsessive-compulsive disorder.

The Big Picture

I want to come back to where we started: meeting unattached burdens and guides. If you accept the porous nature of mind and self, these phenomena are to be expected — they're not weird at all. UBs and guides are part of the subjective experience of porosity. Tanya Luhrmann's phrase "spiritual presence experiences" is useful here. Throughout most of our history as well as in other cultures, when people become aware of these things or beings entering the porous membranes surrounding them, they have interpreted this as spiritual — as angels and demons or spirit possessions or contact with the gods. Now, in Western academia, we discount the reality of all these experiences and call them all psychopathology. This is a significant loss. No matter what your views on the ontology of the situation, pragmatically this is a disaster. We in the West are experiencing a long-standing epidemic of mental illness that only seems to be getting worse. The citadel model of mind or billiard ball model of mind or "buffered self" model of mind creates isolation and brittleness, and is a big part of the problem.

This brief chapter, which really should have been a multivolume book, should convince you that self is not an inviolable fortress or should, at the very least, call this belief into grave doubt. The problem is that this is not just a cognitive belief; it is a way of experiencing the world. It is deeply embedded in our culture and unexamined assumptions. It takes more than a new intellectual conviction to change.

IFS has an important part to play here. Dick does not agree with much of my thinking, and I do not want him blamed or held accountable if you find my ideas weird or objectionable. IFS has given us a model of the human mind that is multiple; we are made up of many parts who are relatively encapsulated subpersonalities and are sparsely interlinked. IFS also knows that a person's whole system is often hijacked by one of these parts. This Self and multiplicity of parts is a model of the human mind that is new and revolutionary in many ways but has become well established and respected. IFS is certified as evidence-based therapy. It is taught all over the world, and thousands of therapists are using it with excellent results. There are huge waiting lists for all the IFS trainings. What I am proposing is a step beyond all this, and I do not want my work to be used to attack mainstream IFS.

The model of multiplicity of parts who are sparsely interconnected holographically can also be applied to us as people in our culture and in nature. As Dick has shown, each part within a person has this same structure, too; each part has parts and a Self, and this same structure repeats itself on different levels. One big aspect of our subjective experience of being sparsely interconnected is UBs and guides. The porous nature of mind allows for these sparse interconnections. When we recognize this as a healthy part of our being, we can learn to work with the energies that get into us from outside without a **brittle** shattering of who we are. We can also learn how to make our semipermeable selves more supple and flexible as well as how to control this threshold in more selective and life-giving ways.

One more point before we leave this subject. I want to make clear how I see the big-picture thinkers, especially Charles Taylor, Charles Eisenstein, and Barbara Ehrenreich, fitting together here. Taylor sees the Reformation as the era that really gave birth to the "buffered self," the isolated mind theory. This is Max Weber's disenchantment of the world. Ehrenreich sees the same age as the beginning of the epidemic of depression, called melancholy then, which continues into our own times. She also sees during this era a major increase in the suppression of communal rites of joy and connection. Eisenstein sees this era as a smaller but very significant part of the story of separation that he traces all the way back into prehistory. These three fit together to create a picture of a decisive move occurring in the West some five hundred years ago that gave us the isolated, encapsulated self as a way of experiencing the world. It also opened the door to technological and scientific progress at an unheard-of rate. It began a centuries-long epidemic of mental illness that continues and accelerates now. Eisenstein calls for an age of reunion. Some radical shift seems needed, but perhaps it is more like Hegel's model of thesis, antithesis, and synthesis. We had the animistic thesis that everything is alive, everything is conscious, everything is a person — and the antithesis, which is that it's all a great machine. We need not a return to the thesis but rather a new concept that contains and transcends both.

D. H. Lawrence expressed this porosity vividly:

This is what I believe: that I am I. That my soul is a dark forest. That my known self will never be more than a little clearing in the forest. That gods, strange gods, come forth from the forest into the clearing of my known self, and then go back. That I must have the courage to let them come and go. That I will never let mankind put anything over me, but that I will try always to recognize and submit to the gods in me and the gods in other men and women. There is my creed.

CHAPTER 13

Personalism

All knowledge is personal.
—Michael Polanyi

Thoughts are personal powers. It is impossible to
do them justice as long as one tries to be impersonal.
—Friedrich Neitzsche

If you see things as "thous" it will change your ego.
—Joseph Campbell

The movement from porosity of mind to personalism may seem like a big, random jump, but there is a method to my madness. If you put these two ideas together, they describe an experience that looks like spirit possession. Stuff comes in and out of our porous minds, and it is most useful if we consider all mental contents as persons. So, we have persons coming in and out of our minds — possession and exorcism in another language?

One of the most challenging ideas in IFS for many people is Dick's insistence that we need to treat parts as people — full-spectrum personalities. They, like many areas in the unconscious, are autonomous. Very early on, Dick realized that these inner personalities had a life of their own and could not simply be imagined. At first he viewed them as unidimensional mental states, each designed for a specific role. As he became more familiar with parts, they taught him that they are multidimensional; "each part has a full range of feelings, needs, and desires… just like external people" (Goulding and Schwartz 1995, 130). The mind's natural multiplicity is hard enough to accept; the idea that the parts have full-range personalities is even more jarring for the Western scientific worldview. It is easier to think of parts as impersonal mental states, but there's a cost.

If a therapist sees it as just a mental state, the therapist will be less interested in helping the part discover the best role for itself, based on its feelings, talents and desires. Thus if the therapist views parts simply as mental states or as introjected images, he or she will relate to them differently than the therapist who sees them as people. It is possible to view them as people while one works with the internal system, but to think about them in other ways that are less disconcerting when one is theorizing. The important thing is that when one is relating to them, this personhood must be respected. (ibid., 131)

This is a practical, pragmatic position. Listening to clients and their parts has repeatedly shown that therapy works best when the parts are treated as people. This is one of the causes of IFS's phenomenal success. Science values the objective and depersonalized, and rejects some ideas as "merely" subjective. In reality, it is the objective that is merely objective. Much has to be carved away and thrown out to get there. As Nietzsche said, "The impersonal is merely the personal weakened, something feeble" (quoted in Parkes 1996, 303). For emotional work, we need the full power of the personal. If this is difficult to accept and pragmatically use with parts, it is even more challenging with the others within. This flies in the face of the Western worldview, but if we can demonstrate that a personalistic approach is the most potent and effective way to work with UBs and guides, their ontological status is not our present concern. Radical pragmatism tells us that what works is what's real.

The behaviorists were extreme impersonalists. They refused to deal with consciousness or subjectivity at all on any level. Freud and his followers also take an impersonal approach. It is important to remember that in the original German, Freud did not use the Latin word *ego* or *id* or the hybrid *superego*. He used the plain German words: the *I*, the *it*, and the *over-I*. This clearly labels the unconscious as an it, a thing, not in any sense a person. For all Freudians until very recently, the unconscious has not been considered a being, or group of beings, with whom one can form a relationship. It has been viewed as a collection of impersonal drives and forces that must be carefully managed, as an engineer would manage a machine that used hydraulic pressure to function. Jung and most of his heirs are personalistic in their conception of the unconscious. Jung himself had dialogues and relationships with some of the beings he met there.

James Hillman

James Hillman was very explicit about treating psychic contents as persons. He wanted to dethrone the dominant fantasy ruling our world — the heroic ego fantasy (Hillman 1991, 32–33) He saw this model as creating a mind that is a military barracks ruled by ego. He held that modern psychology itself is ill.

Diagnosis and the medical model are an insult to the soul. In working with Indigenous peoples, I have discovered that many Indigenous therapists and others talk and write about decolonizing psychotherapy and decolonizing trauma work. They reject the medicalization of human misery because it downplays the reality of their suffering. Sometimes the ego or rational materialist mind appears to me as an imperialist force that is colonizing the unconscious, which creates a stunning isomorphism between the inner and outer worlds. We need a paradigm shift that will re-embrace subjectivity and personhood as important. "Personifying is the soul's answer to egocentricity… we are imagining the psyche's basic structure to be *an inscape of personified images*. The full consequences of this structure imply that the psyche presents its own imaginal dimensions, operates freely without words, and is constituted of multiple personalities" (Hillman 1991, 48; emphasis in the original).

Hillman writes extensively about personifying, but he's very clear that this process is restoring something that has been lost, not adding something new. "Both the world out there and in here have gone through the same process of depersonification. We have all been de-souled" (Hillman 1975, 2–3). He traces the history of this process in the West over the last five hundred years. Hillman stresses the importance of the sense of personhood both in his own thought and in Jung's. "In Jungian practice the words Shadow, Self, Ego, Anima, and the like refer to the structural components of the personality. These basic structures are always imagined to be partial personalities… rather than a field of forces, we are each a field of internal personal relationships…" (ibid., 22). He also quotes Jung: "It is not we who personify them; they have a very personal nature from the very beginning" (Jung 1967, 42). Hillman is painstakingly clear about the personal nature of our parts and how vitally important this is for psychology. It is also clear that he and Jung think of all the contents of the psyche as persons — beings you can form a relationship with, not objects or forces to be manipulated and controlled.

Mary Watkins is another Jungian who makes this point using the word *image*, not *person*. She states that concepts, not images, are the reduction. Images have a living quality, and whenever we've translated one into a rational knowing of what it's about, we need to apologize to it. Joseph Campbell emphasizes that living myths and symbols have a direct emotional effect on us and change us. Interpretation is after the fact and almost beside the point. The image-symbol-myth is more like a living being than a thing. We can have a valuable personal relationship with it, whereas analyzing and depersonalizing it weaken it and impoverish us.

Other psychotherapies and even individual therapists within traditions can be placed on a continuum from fully personalistic to completely impersonal. John

Beahrs, MD, is a retired forensic psychiatrist and student of Ericksonian hypno-therapy. He asserts that parts of the psyche are never mechanisms; they are always "actually experiencing beings" and therefore deserve respect. He also reminds us that internal dialogue is a universal human experience, and dialogue occurs be-tween persons, not things. Psychosynthesis and Voice Dialogue are person-based. The inner child movement is person-based. Focusing is quite personalistic, despite its use of the word *something* instead of *someone* inside. However, it does con-sider these "somethings" to be blocked processes, not independent beings. Jeffrey Young's Schema Therapy is quite personalistic. Most other cognitive behavioral therapy is less so.

Martin Buber's Personalism

The most important form of personalism for our work is what is called "dialogical personalism," and the towering figure here is Martin Buber. Dick is not so fond of Buber, and I am going beyond IFS here. Buber is often called a philosopher, but he disliked being referred to as a philosopher or a theologian. His major state-ment of personalism is his dense and poetic 1923 book *I & Thou*. Buber says it was written in a "creative ecstasy" that was "… impelled by an inward necessity." He says, "This clarity was so manifestly suprapersonal in its nature that I at once knew I had to bear witness to it" (quoted in Kramer 2004, 6).

Buber states that for humans, the world is twofold because we can only speak two primary words; these are not single worlds but word pairs: I-Thou (this was Smith's translation; Kaufmann translated it I-You) and I-It. We relate to everything either as an object or a person. We live on a continuum between these two stances. I-It is objective and monological; I-Thou is immediate, mutual, and dialogical. Buber asserts that there is no I taken by itself; I is relational. All real living is a meeting, an encounter. Everything can be related to as a person, even a tree or a rock. We are unable to sustain this. All our Thous become Its (with one exception: Buber indicated that God, The Eternal Thou, is the only being who can never be an it). I-Thou relationships are wholly personal and present. I-It knowledge is objective. The majority of human discourse is I-It. Buber says we are born relating to the entire world as Thou. We learn to use the I-It mode. This inborn Thou continues throughout life to seek genuine meeting. We cannot live without I-It, but we are not fully human without I-Thou. Buber discovered the "between" — the living mutuality in I-Thou dialogue. He describes how these two modes function in the three realms: with nature, with humans, and with spirit. (In the postscript, written thirty-five years later, he expanded this to four realms, separating out the Eternal Thou.) He talks of the way of turning, the "holy insecurity" (ibid., 157) of surrendering to the unfathomable, giving up the false self-asserting self without giving up the I (ibid., 158). This turning opens the unreserved spontaneity and immediacy of mutuality. Buber originally held that all evil originates in I-It relations, but after the Holocaust he modified this view.

Here we have a thinker who sees the degree to which we take the other as fully a person as the major determinant of the quality of our existence. When we apply this to the inner world of parts, the importance of treating them as Thous is underscored. This is also true of the other within. Surprisingly, not many psychotherapists (Carl Rogers is the exception) have pointed to Buber as a major influence. Another dialogical personalist, John Macmurray, has been cited as an influence by Guntrip and Laing. For Buber, the I-Thou relationship is a necessary precondition of deep inner work. For technological and material control, we need I-It relationships, but to work with psychological depths and spirituality, we need to be grounded in dialogical I-Thou relationships. This is also true for IFS and for work with parts and the others within.

Nikolai Berdyaev is also a dialogical personalist and is a theologian. He argues that the fall of Adam and Eve occurred when they started seeing their bodies as objects and forgot that they were persons. "Objectification is always antipersonalistic, hostile to personality and signifies estrangement of personality (Berdyaev 2009, 1). If the depersonalization of Adam and Eve caused the fall, what does it do to parts and the others within when we objectify them?

What Is a Person?

What is this concept of "person"? What's the defining difference between a person and a thing? This is one of those ideas, like consciousness and subjectivity, that seem obvious and self-explanatory at first glance but are extremely subtle and difficult when we examine them closely. Most modern neuroscientists, when they talk about "the hard problem," are referring to the nature of consciousness and how it could be generated by matter. Antonio Damasio states that the real hard problem is the nature of self and how this subjectivity, this personhood, could arise. Perhaps we should call consciousness the semi-hard problem. The really hard problem is what constitutes a person, what creates a Thou.

The difficulty and even mystery of the concept of a person is spotlighted by IFS's concept of parts and the concept of unattached burdens. How are parts contained and separate? They have parts, too. We are parts of larger things. Do personhood and identity arise at all levels? Does identity depend on the level of analysis? How are these boundaries formed? All living beings are encapsulated in semipermeable membranes; this is obvious with single-celled organisms. Life begins with this encapsulation, this formation of a Thou that is separate from the world around it. And yet the boundary is, of necessity, semipermeable; it ingests and excretes.

This is obvious physically, and it is also true psychologically. An impervious being is a dead being in either realm. There is something mysterious about how these persons and subpersons form, separate, and have agency and identity.

Just as the behaviorists ignored consciousness because it was so awkward, much of the modern scientific and philosophical world ignores the question of personhood. However, there is a substantial but often neglected body of work on the subject in modern Western thought. Throughout the 1800s, there were strong reactions against the depersonalization inherent in Enlightenment rationalism, and by the early 1900s the term *personalism* was adapted as the name for some philosophical schools. One of the earliest uses of the term in the United States is in an 1868 essay by Walt Whitman. His poetry embodies personalist principles. The New England transcendentalist Bronson Alcott was also an early proponent. The central idea here is that the concept of personhood is at the core of understanding our world and ourselves. Personhood is the ultimate explanatory and ontological principle, not something that is an embarrassing add-on to an otherwise efficient and mathematically precise clockwork universe. Personhood is the foundation that gives meaning to reality and constitutes the ultimate, highest value. The concept is not reducible to anything else. Much earlier, Immanuel Kant stated that things have price, but persons have dignity, which cannot be priced. No one is dispensable or interchangeable. Each is unique, a singularity. As we will see, this has led some personalists to take strong and distinctive ethical stances.

Brother David Steindl-Rast is a Benedictine monk who has studied Buddhism extensively. He approaches the problem from the opposite direction. He relates (personal communication) a story he got from a Zen teacher. When asked about personhood, the Zen teacher replied that we individuals are all like waves on the ocean, and we feel we are persons. Where could we get this quality if the ocean itself didn't have it? If the ocean itself did not feel it was a person?

We often encounter the personalist ontology in religions. We are probably the most impersonalist culture in history, and yet a 2008 Pew survey of American religious belief showed that 92 percent of the population believed in God, 60 percent in a personal God, 25 percent in an impersonal God, and 7 percent didn't know which. A 2010 Gallup poll was even stronger: 80 percent believed in a personal God, 12 percent in a Universal Spirit. Staretz Silouan (1866–1938) was a Russian Eastern Orthodox Christian monk on Mount Athos who has been sainted in the Orthodox church (Sophrony 2021). He taught that "What is truth?" is the wrong question. The question should be "Who is truth?" He also said that life itself is a person to be related to, not an object to be studied. We need a personal, face-to-face meeting with life and truth. In Islam, one of the most used of the ninety-nine names of God is al-Haqq, the truth. The truth is Allah — a person, not a thing. Bede Griffiths was a Benedictine monk who spent most of his life in India studying Hinduism. In his later books, he came to view the non-dual (*advaita*) absolute as the supreme Person incarnate in all humanity and all matter (Griffiths 2001). These issues of personalist ontology may seem esoteric, but they underscore how powerful this idea can be. What IFS found to be a practical, pragmatic help in doing effective therapy — treating parts as full persons — has some surprising echoes. As we treat unattached burdens and guides as persons, we are following these traditions. Pragmatically, we do this because it works.

Modern Personalists

Even though sometimes it seems that the Western intellectual tradition (TWIT for short) is doing its best to ignore personalism, there have been major schools of personalism in American academia. In this, as in so many other things, William James was ahead of his time. He wrote that a religious attitude means that we take the universe as a Thou, not an It (James 1956, 278). This personal nature of religious thought is "the one fundamental fact" about religion (ibid., 480–81). He stated that the person is always present in psychology, and the tendency of scientists to ignore this in their search for objectivity is a mistake (James 1950, 221). He argued that a real radical empiricism must include subjectivity as well as objectivity, both the personal and impersonal, because both are present in all our experience.

Personalism has been important to many prominent people, including Pope John Paul II, Gordon Allport, R. D. Laing, and Martin Luther King Jr. King studied at Boston University, which was the center of personalism in the United States for many years. The Boston personalist tradition was begun by Borden Parker Bowne, a minister and theologian, who asserted that ultimately only persons are real. Edgar Brightman (King's teacher) and Albert Knudson were major figures in the second generation of personalists at Boston University. George Howison and Ralph Flewelling were major figures in California personalism at University of California, Berkeley, and the University of Southern California.

King acknowledged how deeply personalism influenced him both in his belief in a personal God and in the origins of his nonviolent civil rights movement. The concept of a unique, irreplaceable dignity in each person is central to his ethics and his life. In his sermons, he did not use the philosophical language that he knew well, but instead talked of each person's "somebodyness." This idea of personhood is oddly powerful. Everyone deserves basic respect because they have their own "somebodyness," a basic dignity. Each person without exception is unique and of great value; no one is dispensable or interchangeable. People cannot be reduced to something smaller or only seen as valuable when thought of as a member of a larger group. Personalist views are diametrically opposed to totalitarianism and collectivism. Some of the earliest objections to slavery on moral grounds came out of this kind of thinking, and we can see how Martin Luther King Jr.'s work grew out of this basic attitude.

Gordon Allport, the famous Harvard professor, was also a personalist. He met regularly with Edgar Brightman and other Boston University personalists. Abraham Maslow and Carl Rogers both acknowledged Allport's formative influence. Humanistic psychology grew out of this nexus. Karol Wojtyla, before he became Pope John Paul II, was a prominent personalist who wrote two books of personalist philosophy. There is a strong personalist strain in modern Catholicism. Jacques Maritan is another major figure. As in the case of Martin Luther King Jr., personalism for John Paul II was a deep source of his ethics and belief.

The West does seem to have a uniquely developed tradition of thinking about personhood. Much of this grew out of early attempts to clarify the idea of the Trinity. How could there be three persons in one God? Bishop Kallistos Ware (1995, 27) of the Orthodox Church explains: "The Christian God is not just a unit but a union, not just unity but community. There is in God something analogous to 'society.' He is not a single person, loving himself alone, not a self-contained monad or 'The One.' He is triunity: three equal persons, each one dwelling in the other two by virtue of an unceasing movement of mutual love." Since we humans are made as an image of God, we are also a multiplicity, a unity of persons. Gregory of Nyssa was a theologian who was active around 350 AD. He was one of the very first people to argue that slavery is morally wrong, and he based his thinking, as Martin Luther King Jr. did, on personalism. Taking personalism seriously has deep effects on people and their behavior, just as taking the idea that parts and unattached burdens are persons has deep effects on psychotherapy.

Personhood and Agency

In working with the parts of a person's system, we see that personhood and agency are intertwined. We need the agency of parts — the independent action of subsystems — for large systems to function well. This encapsulation is the core of personhood. Is this a necessary illusion or a deep reality? Pragmatically, we do not need to solve this mystery; we only need to know that we can relieve more human suffering if we act as if the parts and the others within are full-spectrum persons with their own agency, their own will, and their own consciousness. This echoes Jung's insistence that much of what is in the unconscious is autonomous. This also fits well with Suryani and Jensen's description of the autonomous imagination as a key to shamanic healing abilities.

I started with IFS's pragmatic finding that therapy is more effective when we treat parts as full-spectrum people. This has led to seeing how shifts along the Thou-It person-thing continuum have far-reaching implications for a wide variety of thinkers. As Hillman pointed out in his discussion of personifying, he was not adding something; rather, he was restoring something that had been cut away. This is important. We naturally experience other humans and the world as persons; it has to be trained out of us. Our minds may go along with this indoctrination into cultural norms, but our hearts and emotions often do not follow. When we work with emotions, we need to meet them where they are: in the I-Thou of a personalistic relationship. The vast majority of people and cultures are personalistic. This is clearly seen in religious studies. Almost all religious people are theistic — they relate to the sacred as a person. Even in Buddhism, which is theoretically nontheistic, most practitioners worship Quan Yin or some other bodhisattva, some personal embodiment of the divine. For a long time, TWIT tried to ignore consciousness because its existence is so challenging for the physicalist "scientific" ideology. The reality of persons and subjectivity is even more difficult for that worldview. But it is crucial for emotional healing and health.

Evolutionary Psychology

There is one other major argument to support the practice of relating to the contents of our inner subjective world as persons. It comes from evolutionary psychology. This may be the most important point for the hard-core rationalist if any of you have gotten this far in this book. It is clear now that when we are born, our minds are not a kind of tabula rasa, a blank slate. Most academics used to believe that there was nothing in the mind that was not first in the senses — that our life experience taught us everything. This is wrong. We are born with many specialized modules. Some are basic and almost mechanistic — facial recognition, for example. Newborn babies will orient toward schematic line drawings of a human face and not to similar drawings with the same lines in different positions. Some of these modules, in contrast, are amazingly complex. For example, Noam Chomsky has described what he calls the "deep grammar" underlying all human language. It seems that we have a language learning module that turns on at around one year old and then turns off or weakens at about the age of ten.

Many other modules also evolved: social interaction, tool use, toolmaking, animal behavior and hunting, spatial orientation, and many others. John Tooby and Leda Cosmides at the University of California, Santa Barbara, and their students have done extensive research in this area. Now, if you think back to our earliest hunter-gatherer existence (which is more than 90 percent of our species' history), what is by far the most dangerous and most numerous animal around?

It's other people. Also, if you think of humans in these hunter-gatherer bands, we are rather pathetic creatures. We can't run fast. Our teeth and claws are weak. We stand upright and are easily seen. Our vital organs are not shielded from attack. Our most significant survival skill is our ability to form groups and work together. Therefore our social module — our personalistic, relational skills — are extremely well developed. Perhaps they are our greatest intelligence.

Now add to this the idea of exaptation, a concept that comes from evolutionary biology. It names the process by which a trait that evolved for one purpose is used for an unrelated one. For example, feathers evolved for insulation; they were used for flight. The tongue evolved to move food around the mouth; it is used for speech.

Our relating to parts and to the others within as persons could be an exaptation of our highly evolved human relations module so that we could use this powerful mental resource in our inner worlds. I have come to believe far more deeply in the personhood of beings in our inner world, but this exaptation by itself is enough to justify the pragmatic use of relating to psychic contents as independent, full-spectrum persons.

Much of my thinking about psychological exaptation was inspired by archaeologist Steve Mithen, who attempts to explain the Upper Paleolithic revolution. Humans had had very little biological change in about five hundred thousand years, but between sixty and thirty thousand years ago there were vast cultural changes reflected in the artifacts we've been able to find: art, toolmaking, burials, and personal adornment all changed radically. The brain did not change in size; as a matter of fact, it shrank slightly in the preceding hundred thousand years. It was not a hardware upgrade but rather a change in the software. Mithen (1996) proposes that this explosion of growth was due to the fact that humans had developed the ability to exapt their specialized modules of intelligence and use them in other areas. The modules and skills we had developed for social relations could now be applied to hunting, making tools, and more — and vice versa. This increased our functional intelligence manyfold. Many scholars see psychological exaptation as a significant factor in the development of modern humanity. It can also be important in the development of the inner work of psychotherapy.

For many people, the most difficult aspect of working with unattached burdens and guides is treating them as persons, agents, beings with their own intelligence and wills. This perspective is totally unacceptable in academia, sniffed at as primitive superstitions at best. But I believe I have shown that from a radically pragmatic point of view, working with psychic contents from this personalistic stance is useful in relieving human suffering. At the very least, it should be one tool in our toolbox.

CHAPTER 14

Guides & Discernment

There is some kiss we want with our whole lives,
the touch of spirit on the body.

—Rumi

It is a good idea to go looking for God,
before he comes looking for you.

—Chris Rock

Now we finally come to the subject of guides, also known as positive spirit possession or spiritual contact experience or contact with Holy Spirit, inspiration or channeling or mediumship, or connecting with a power animal, the muse or the wisdom of the archetypes. Or whatever you want to call it. Inside people's psyche, there often is valued and positive contact with someone who feels benevolent and wiser than we are. Sometimes these experiences are so powerful that they suddenly and totally change the course of a person's life. Sometimes they are subtle and gentle. A tremendous amount of effort in every religion and meditative tradition has been devoted to eliciting and maintaining these connections. It seems odd to me that perhaps in our "dark age of scientism" (as James Tunney calls it), I need to say something about the search for inner wisdom. So many scoff at this pursuit. Why would anyone think that science, which has striven so hard to be values-free, could tell us anything about values? We need values to guide our lives. Why would someone think that science, which has worked so hard to remove the subjective from its studies and to be purely objective, could teach us about our subjectivity?

There's a wonderful story about Mulla Nasrudin. One evening, neighbors saw him outside his house on his hands and knees under a streetlight, looking for something. They asked him, "What's wrong?" He replied that he'd lost his house key. They gathered and helped search. After a while, they had scoured the area.

Someone asked, "We've looked everywhere; are you sure you lost it here?" Nasrudin replied, "Oh, no, I lost it down the street; but the light is so much better here." The methods of rational materialist science, which work so magnificently in the external world where the streetlight is, fail in the shadowed internal world, and we need other ways of knowing. We need to look in the unlit parts of the street. There is overwhelming evidence now that these other ways of knowing work. Many studies show that people with some religious or spiritual orientation have better mental and physical health. The Mayo Clinic concluded, "Most studies have shown that religious involvement and spirituality are associated with better health outcomes, including greater longevity, coping skills… and less anxiety, depression, and suicide. Several studies have shown that addressing the spiritual needs of the patient may enhance recovery from illness" (Roberts 2019). Some 80 percent of the studies on religion, spirituality, and health focus on mental illness. The connection seems even stronger there. If the relief of human suffering is truly our goal, we need to include the spiritual.

Our language itself makes talking about this topic far more difficult than it needs to be. Luhrmann's phrase "spiritual presence experiences" is so helpful here — it is broad enough as well as nonjudgmental. Clarke's use of the word *transliminal* is also freeing. When we leave shared reality, we have anomalous experiences that shape our lives for good or ill. As I have studied this field intensively, I have come to believe that the sought-after, positive, and highly valued experiences are more common than the damaging possessions, which are relatively rare. This is probably not quantifiable. Negative possessions have gotten more attention, probably because they are so dramatic and arresting.

Why have I focused so much of this book on the damaging contact with the other within? (1) Being a therapist, people come to me with their problems. (2) By the end of the classical Greco-Roman world, Christians had turned all the other gods and the daimons into demons. (3) Our culture treats spiritual presence experiences, hearing voices, and seeing visions with hostility, fear, hate, and contempt. So of course, most of these encounters would be experienced as difficult and conflicted. (4) We have not had many social and cognitive structures to welcome these experiences into. Without these in place, even potentially positive encounters may well become damaging. (5) I have also adopted the IFS constraint-release model of psychological healing. This last point is significant and needs to be developed at some length.

Constraint-Release Models

Constraint release is a basic underlying concept for IFS therapists. Self, with all its eight Cs — curiosity, compassion, clarity, connectedness, calm, creativity, courage, and confidence — is always there. It cannot be damaged or even dirtied. It's like the sun; even the worst storm that destroys your home and floods your city cannot touch the sun. When the storm ends and the clouds part, the sun is there, totally undisturbed, not damaged, not even dirtied. We are that sun. This is our real identity. This is a basic tenet of IFS, and it goes against many other therapeutic ideas, especially some forms of attachment theory. This concept was crucial for me and many other people who have experienced severe childhood trauma; it meant that we were not damaged goods condemned to a second-rate life. Based on this, healing becomes a task of constraint release — getting the clouds to move back and helping hurt parts unblend. Healing is about removing obstacles and burdens rather than adding anything. It is a subtraction process, not an addition process. This model leads us to focus on removing the negative, so of course I would initially focus on the UBs, the negative spiritual experiences, rather than on guides, which IFS calls positive encounters.

Kenosis

This approach echoes spiritual traditions that are truly ancient — thousands and thousands of years old. Kenosis, apophaticism, and the via negativa are some formal names. These are three distinct phenomena in the history of religions, but they share much common ground. For our purposes, I have focused on this common ground and the similarities to IFS. There are many things in IFS and in the ideas I'm proposing that the classical proponents of these traditions would find repellent, but all three point to a spirituality of constraint release. Rumi, as usual, has a beautiful way of expressing this concept. "Your task is not to seek for love, but merely to seek and find all the barriers within yourself that you have built against it." The via negativa is both a type of theology and a method of spiritual practice — not just a philosophy, but a way of life. Apophaticism also has this dual meaning, but it is most often used to describe the type of theology.

These words define a tendency that is found in most, if not all, major religions. This is the preference for describing God or the divine by who it is not rather than who it is. We often hear descriptions of the holy or God as great, compassionate, omnipotent, all-knowing, and much more. The apophatic tradition holds that any description is ultimately too small and therefore constricting and misleading. The divine is ineffable and nonconceptual. The divine, like the Self, is approached by unblending, by separating off all the characteristics we think we know. Plotinus, the Neoplatonist philosopher, used the image of a sculptor chipping away the stone to reveal what is already there. In Hinduism, there is the tradition of "neti, neti," which literally means "not this, not that." This is a key element of jnana yoga and is characteristic of Vedic inquiry. Therefore, it is found in some of the most ancient religious texts on our planet. All worldly experiences and names are negated until all that remains is Self. In Advaita Vedanta, this form of Brahman is call Nirguna: without qualities.

These kenotic traditions are based on the belief that the divine is present right here, right now. All we need to do is help any frightened parts so they will allow us the experience. This is completely isomorphic with IFS's conception of Self; it is always here, right here, right now. There is an Islamic expression of this that is very vivid: that Allah is closer to us than our jugular vein. Swedenborg beautifully made a similar point. He said that many consider the spirit to be like a rare and exotic bird of paradise who lives in some faraway place. Actually, the bird is right here, and its wing tips gently brush your eyelids, wanting to be seen.

Taoism states that the Tao that can be named is not the real Tao. Brother David Steindl-Rast has said (personal communication) that our image of God is often our biggest and most subtle block to the experience of God. Just as we do not have to build up or develop Self, apophaticism asserts that we do not and should not build up images and descriptions of the divine. Unblending from and separating off our old descriptions and ways of relating are what is needed. In describing the Self using the eight Cs, we are in some ways trying to "eff the ineffable." Some apophatic traditions hold that while we can't speak of the divine itself, we can point to the kinds of relationships it forms. All the eight C qualities can be read as relational terms. They describe how the Self interacts with other persons. What we need in our present frame is a way of relating to the possessions, not a definition of what they are.

Kenosis is the closely related concept of emptying. Kenosis has a dual meaning. It refers to the spiritual discipline of self-emptying to make room for the holy, and it also refers to God's self-emptying. In the second meaning, it is controversial and has even been called a heresy in Christianity. The question is how infinite God could become Jesus, a human. Kenosis, a process of self-emptying, has been proposed as the answer. More kenosis, more giving up of powers, more emptying is behind the sacrifice of crucifixion and death. This kind of thinking has been called a heresy because it can be seen as denying Christ's full godhood. This somewhat arcane bit of theology is important for us because God's kenosis became a pattern to be imitated by many in the West who used kenosis as their spiritual path. In the Jewish tradition, there is a similar idea of God's kenosis. God had to contract his infinite light to make room for creation. This self-restriction, concealment, or even divine exile is called *tsimtsum*.

Kenosis as a spiritual path is what concerns us most here. This self-emptying to reveal the immanent God is a method very much like unblending from parts to reveal Self. The language of kenosis is religious and often mystical, which is difficult for many, but the underlying processes are deeply similar. The way to find guides and guidance kenotically is to first remove the UBs.

There is a long tradition of kenosis in Christianity; Gregory of Nyssa, Pseudo-Dionysius, John Scottus Eriugena, Meister Eckhart, Nicholas of Cusa, and St. John of the Cross are some major representatives. It is interesting that Gregory of Nyssa, who was also an early personalist and opponent of slavery, should also be an early exponent of kenosis. There may well be a deep interrelationship between these two ways of thinking, but this thesis is beyond the scope of this book.

The Pseudo-Dionysius, also known as Dionysius the Areopagite, sometimes erroneously called St. Denis, was thought until recently to have been the disciple of St. Paul mentioned in the New Testament and as such was considered immensely authoritative. St. Thomas Aquinas quotes him some seventeen hundred times, more than any other author. He is now believed to have been a Syrian monk whose words were written down around 500 AD. Dionysius brought together Neoplatonist thinking and Christian theology. Luther hated his work because it was so influenced by Plato. Dionysius asserted that the higher we climb, the more language falters. We have to enter the divine darkness of unknowing, which is out of reach of easy rational processes. This darkness is also light. The distinction between the unity of godhood and the multiplicity of names parallels the unity of Self and the multiplicity of parts. Dionysius often dealt with this by using the Greek prefix *hyper-*, meaning "over-," in front of descriptive terms: the hyper-good, the hyper-alive, the hyper-being. He liked to use "dissimilar similarities," for example, the psalm that compares God to a worm, because these are likely to break up our normal ways of thinking.

Dionysius's writings are dialogic and intersubjective. They are usually written as dialogues. The in-betweenness, the intersubjectivity, is emphasized by his Neoplatonic preference for triads. Whatever the opposition, there is a third in-between element that relates them. This again is Corbin's mundus imaginalis, or the Greek demonic realm between the gods and humans, or the autonomous imagination. Besides Dionysius's massive influence on Christianity, his work has been taken up by postmodern thinkers, notably Jacques Derrida and Jean-Luc Marion. Dionysius's emphasis on agnosia or unknowingness, his self-emptying kenosis, and his concern with finding the One among the many are all themes that IFS takes up fifteen hundred years later in nonreligious language. The kenosis and agnosia are especially close to unblending. All we need is constraint release.

Father Stephen Freeman, a priest of the Orthodox Church, writes, "Humility and kenosis are not the loss of self but the gaining of a true self" (Glory to

God for All Things, n.d.) He speaks of how we must get free of false selves to do this. Brother David Steindl-Rast makes a similar point; there are innumerable "I"s and only one Self. Self is united with all, so it is never lonely; it is not in time. It is the observer who is not observed, the Christ Self, the Buddha Nature. Brother David honors the apophatic truth that God can't be named or fixed in place by saying his favorite name for God is Surprise. He also calls this observing Self the "pregnant nothing" (personal communication). The spiritual claim that by imitating the radical kenosis of Jesus, our self-emptying humility will lead us to salvation and becoming godlike is mirrored on the earthly level by IFS's statement that by unblending from our parts and emptying ourselves, Self manifests. This also seems true in our area of focus; the shortest path to finding true guidance is to remove the blocks — UBs and others. To paraphrase Matthew 16:25: "He who loses himself finds himself." In no way do I want to reduce these spiritual texts to IFS or to explain them away; I merely want to point to a deep structural similarity of method.

The Cloud of Unknowing, an anonymous fourteenth-century text written in Middle English, is a great monument to the apophatic-kenotic approach. It insists that as we ascend toward God, we must leave behind our intellect; in IFS language, as we move into Self, we must unblend from all our managers and figuring-out parts. Intellect and imagination started the ascent; we proceed further by apophatic methods: unblending and unknowing. We rise through love, not knowledge. The text (Gallacher 1997, lines 2007ff) is very clear that we separate from the old knowledge — the parts — but we do not throw them out. The author uses the image of a cup after you have gotten a drink. You would be foolish to break it. You do not destroy a tree after you have eaten its fruit.

St. John of the Cross, Meister Eckhart, and many other great Western mystics are in this tradition of kenosis. Rick Johnson puts this into a psychological language that many of us are far more comfortable with: "Individuals need… to empty themselves of their self-identifications and experience the fullness and energy of their Real Self. It may sound like an oxymoron — emptying oneself as a way to experience fullness" (Johnson 2013, 158).

Two Modern Kenotic Religious Thinkers
Modern spiritual writers who embody kenosis include Maggie Ross and William Johnston. Ross is an Anglican who spent many years living as a solitary hermit in the Alaskan wilderness. She has written five books, all of which have this kenotic element. Perhaps her strongest statement is in her 1987 book *The Fire and the Furnace*. This volume focuses on the essential role of tears in spirituality. "The whole point of the journey into the fiery love of God is *self-forgetfulness*" (Ross 1987, 23;

emphasis in the original). Again, "In giving up self, self is found" (ibid., 29). Willing powerlessness, the kenotic-chosen small death leads to exaltation. God can only come to me through the window of tears, and tears are part of kenosis. Theology is killing God. We must live in the radical insecurity of kenosis. We must "fall through despair into the hands of God. Kenosis is the opposite of the need to control and it is our real potency" (ibid., 139). This is very close to the quietists, whose methods opened the doors to both negative and positive spiritual presence experience.

Ross compares our quotidian personalities to a house of cards (ibid., 121ff), which, if we are lucky, is easily blown away. But often we lie and glue the cards together and spend more and more of our lives keeping these closed systems in place. In her words, "There are people who have spent all their lives managing problems so that they do not have to go through the pain of solving them… creating lifestyles that mask the terror…" (ibid., 123). Her solution is kenosis, to willingly empty ourselves — to unblend, in IFS language. This is the little death that allows greater life. She writes that we are always neophytes and must continually empty ourselves. This is an imitation, a reflection, of Jesus's kenosis. There is a natural kenosis of God and humanity. She quotes Rabbi Lawrence Kushner, who says, "All genuine creation must originate in the darkness. All transformation must commence during the night at the price of the 'old ego' and its organization" (ibid., 193). Using metaphors that can be read as describing parts as sets of clothing, she writes, "We seek the realm of tears in order to be stripped of all that is not God, of all that keeps us in the shabby costumes we substitute for the clothing of the children of God" (ibid., 223). And again, "We have been stopped in our tracks by astonishment and have let fall the rags we clutch about our selves" (ibid., 293). Truly meeting guides requires at least a movement in this direction; perhaps this is why these meetings are rare.

William Johnston was a very different figure, but kenosis was also central for him. Johnston was an Irish Jesuit priest who lived for fifty years in Japan, where he taught at Sophia University. He was also a longtime student of Zen and Japanese culture. He wrote eleven books and translated several volumes from the Japanese. He was a deep student of Christian kenosis. His PhD dissertation and first published book were on *The Cloud of Unknowing*. "Knowing by unknowing! These words echo through the apophatic tradition from the time of Dionysius… They mean that to know with divine wisdom one must abandon ordinary knowing… One must un-know." Johnston points out that Dionysius was not just some coolly rational Neoplatonic philosopher arising into pure form. He also entered an ecstasy based on love. St. John of the Cross, another major influence on Johnston, wrote,

"To come to the knowledge of all, desire the knowledge of nothing.

To come to possess all, desire the possession of nothing.

To arrive at being all, desire to be nothing."

(Johnston 1998, 122)

When it was still a great insult in the Christian world, other Catholic authors described St. John of the Cross as Buddhist (ibid., 115). Johnston saw this intended insult as a valuable insight. The Japanese Buddhist scholar Masao Abe suggests that sunyata, the emptiness that is the ultimate ground of reality in Buddhism, is the same reality that kenosis leads to. The Buddhist concept of nothingness is not nihilistic. For example, there is an old Japanese Buddhist saying *ku soku jihi*, which translates as "emptiness equals compassion." This emptiness is akin to Christian humility (Johnston 1996, 114). In Japanese, the word *mu* is usually used for "emptiness" and is often inscribed over temple gates. The phrases *mu-shin*, "no mind," and *mu-ga*, "no self," are central to martial arts, the tea ceremony, and calligraphy. This mu, this emptiness, allows chi energy to move from its base in the stomach.

The Buddhist concept of Prajnaparamita takes kenosis all the way to the letting go of all concepts, of everything, including Buddhist doctrine itself. Pema Chödrön's repeated instructions to the meditator to learn to live with "groundlessness" are a practical help in living kenosis. This same kenotic emptiness (the IFS state of not being blended with parts) is also found in the Taoist concept of *wu-wei*, the non-action that accomplishes everything. Johnston described wu-wei as "the mental state of one who submerges his ego or little self in order that the forces of life may begin to work within" (Johnston 1996, 109). In his last published article, Johnston noted how Meister Eckhart also refers to this void when he says that God pours himself into the person who is empty. IFS sees the Self as taking leadership when the parts are unblended. I am reminded of Engler and Fulton's insight (in Germer and Siegel 2014, 176–188) that Buddhist no-self and IFS Self point to the same thing. To welcome guides and guidance requires some movement in this direction, though thankfully not the thoroughgoing kenosis that these giants of the spiritual life developed. We need some openness inside for the guides to enter. Dealing with any UBs in the system is an important part of this kenosis.

Inviting Guides

The work of inviting guides and getting in contact with them is mostly kenosis — clearing and cleaning our interior world to make welcoming room for them in us. There are at least two levels of this emptying: unblending from parts and removing UBs. This distinction between parts and spirits is perhaps the greatest contribution that IFS makes to deliverance work. We know that we need to welcome all parts and not expel them. IFS teaches how to unblend from parts and then help them unburden the difficult and often toxic burdens they were carrying. We know that parts are not their burdens. This knowledge allows us to welcome them joyfully into our system. This basic understanding, along with the tools to distinguish parts from UBs and guides, prevents so much unintentional damage. Other deliverance workers have unintentionally tried to get rid of parts.

Dick says that the only safe time to ask for guides is when there is a critical mass of Self present. This is kenosis; we can meet guides when the parts are unblended, emptied. After the witnessing, retrieval, and unburdening of an exile, a vibrant Self-to-part connection is usually present. At this point, I often say something gentle like "Some people at times like this have a sense of guidance or a guide. Let's just pause a little here and see if something like that happens now." It surprises many people that deep wisdom is let into their system by very young parts. We expect to receive wisdom from wise, mature-looking ones. I remind some people of the biblical saying that unless you become as little children, you cannot enter the Kingdom of Heaven.

When someone's system is strongly Self-led, I often pause and see if there's guidance or guides around. Asking for guidance when there's a lot of Self is the safest way to find inner guidance, but I do not believe that is sufficient. In the twelve steps, for example, people usually find their higher power only when they have hit bottom — when they are broken and accept their powerlessness. This is when they are able to turn to guide energy. This is not a sweet Self-filled moment in any way. The phrase "higher power," which plays such an important part in all of the twelve-step traditions, is very significant; it allows people to have what is an essentially spiritual experience in language that is totally acceptable to a rationalist, materialist, atheistic worldview. Everyone, even the most thoroughgoing atheist, will have to admit that there are things bigger than they are. Maybe it's the twelve-step group itself or the ocean or a forest. This cracks open the door to receiving understanding and guidance. It seems we need new language and methods that help people have deeply spiritual experiences without challenging the dominant ideology. It's almost like you have to sneak it in to avoid offending the materialists. The word *guidance* is easier for many people than the word *guide*. Most everyone can recognize that the depths of their mind sometimes contain wisdom. So I offer the word *guidance* first. The connotations of personhood in the word *guide* are difficult for many materialists.

Discernment

Whatever method or path we have used that has led us to meeting a guide, how can we tell if it is truly benevolent? This is a difficult question; it is so easy to delude ourselves in these matters. Let me remind you that most of the greatest crimes in human history were committed by people convinced of their righteousness. Thomas Merton wrote, "When one is firmly convinced of his own righteousness and goodness, he can without qualms perpetrate the most appalling evil." Mao Tse Tung believed he was fundamentally transforming society, and his regime resulted in the greatest mass murder in human history. Hitler was stridently self-righteous and seemed to deeply believe in the purity and goodness of what he was doing. Pol Pot was trained by the most prominent French leftist academics of his day when he studied at the Sorbonne. He went home to Cambodia, put these idealist ideas into practice, and killed something like one-quarter of his people. Great criminal acts have been performed by churches in the name of God. It's a very long list. As Rumi said, "The Veil of Light which is the barrier brought about by self-righteousness is more dangerous than the Veil of Darkness produced in the mind by vice." We are not somehow superior to all these people; we too can delude and deceive ourselves easily and profoundly.

Terrence, the Roman playwright, wrote, "Homo sum: humani nihil a me alienum puto." ("I am human, nothing human is beyond me.") Terrence was a slave brought to Rome from North Africa. His owner recognized his intelligence and ability, and freed him. Maya Angelou has written that this saying is usually taken to mean that there's no human crime I could not commit, and it definitely does mean this. It also means that the great and heroic acts of humans are not alien to us either. This attitude opens us up to the heights and depths of human experience and shines a spotlight on the need for discernment. We are also capable of extreme self-delusion.

This should also remind us that the seemingly bizarre experiences of possession states are fundamentally human and are therefore not alien to us either. Aleksandr Solzhenitsyn also knows the need for discernment. "The line separating good and evil passes, not through states, not between classes nor between political parties either — but right through every human heart — and through all human hearts. This line shifts. Inside us, it oscillates with the years." It would have been easy for Solzhenitsyn to cast blame; after all, he fought the Nazis and then was a prisoner in the communist Siberian labor camps. But he did not blame. Instead, he looked for the evil in his own and every human heart.

This is a verse from Thich Nhat Hanh's long poem "Please Call Me by My True Names":

"I am the twelve-year-old girl,

Refugee on a small boat,

Who throws herself into the ocean

After being raped by a sea pirate.

And I am the pirate,

My heart not yet capable,

Of seeing and loving."

Another piece of evidence of the difficulty and subtlety of this art of discernment is the Buddhist concept of near enemies. This is such a pragmatically helpful tool. Every great virtue has a far enemy — an opposite that's usually fairly easy to spot. Each great virtue also has a near enemy: something that appears very much like the virtue itself. For example, let's take the four immeasurables. These are often considered the four greatest Buddhist virtues: equanimity, loving kindness, compassion, and sympathetic joy. Long treatises have been written about the nature of each of these. The far enemies are fairly obvious. Equanimity's far enemies are instability and agitation. The others are loving kindness versus hate and ill will, compassion versus cruelty, sympathetic joy versus jealousy and envy. The near enemies are trickier: equanimity versus indifference or numbness, loving kindness versus sentimentality or codependency, compassion versus pity, sympathetic joy versus hypocrisy and phoniness. These can be very hard to discern in others and even harder in ourselves. One clue offered in some Buddhist discussions is that the near enemies all separate us in some very subtle ways, while the four immeasurables always unite us with others. Discernment is not easy, and once we have achieved the first levels of discernment of the far enemies, more and more subtle levels are revealed to us. The continuum between separation and connection may be an important indicator.

Real-Time Discernment Tools

So how do we distinguish? How do we know? The biblical answers are "by their fruits you shall know them" and to take any guidance or revelation you receive to trusted spiritual elders. However, trusted spiritual elders are kind of hard to come by these days. Knowing the nature of an idea or attitude by its fruits is the gold standard, the ultimate test, but it only works in hindsight. Can we develop real-time discernment tools? How do we evaluate a spiritual presence experience? In IFS language, how do we tell a guide from a UB? Let's explore three basic ways we might do this.

The first method is perhaps the most vivid and immediate. How does the spiritual presence respond to your fearful parts? We have seen how UBs use fear as their primary way of gaining power and staying in a person's system. When they sense fear in a person, they focus on it and push on it and do everything in their power to increase the underlying fear. Sometimes they offer bogus protection, but they always work on increasing the fear so the person becomes more and more dependent on them for bogus protection. Guides never do this. If they sense that their presence is scaring someone, they respectfully back off and wait. They so honor our autonomy that they usually require an invitation, often repeated invitations, to enter us. UBs' voices will be loud, domineering, and aggressive. Guides' voices will be still and quiet. With this understanding, it makes sense that most of what we hear in our world will be dominated by negative energies. Even though this is a good indicator, it is not always true. The initiatory illnesses of shamans are a clear example of spirit breaking in despite being unwelcome and inducing fear, pain, and illness.

This guidance about fear comes out of the work of Wilson Van Dusen, who was previously mentioned in Chapter 9. He was a psychologist at one of the huge long-term California mental hospitals that used to exist before it became standard to put patients out on the streets with heavy medication. Van Dusen did something that was radical; he started listening to his patients and then dialoguing with the voices the patients heard in their heads. He soon realized that some of these voices were negative and damaging, while others were positive, wise, and helpful. Because he wanted to keep his job, at first he called these voices lower-order hallucinations and higher-order hallucinations. Later, he explicitly identified these voices with Swedenborg's demons and angels. He found Swedenborg's description of the geographies of heaven and hell very much like what his patients experienced, expressed in old-fashioned religious language. The Reverend Rachel Rivers (personal communication) has compiled a summary of Van Dusen's conclusions, which makes a very useful discernment tool.

Lower Order:

(1) Persistent will to destroy

(2) Teases and torments

(3) Gangs up on one's weaknesses

(4) Bragging and argumentative

(5) Insulting, threatening, attacking, cruel

(6) Works against one's will

(7) Speaks to one's fears

(8) Malevolent; seeks to undermine us in every conceivable way

(9) Cannot accurately see the higher order but may know of its presence

(10) Can be extremely verbal and uses trickery, cajoling, intruding, threatening; seeks to cause harm

(11) Causes pain, anxiety; lies; goes against higher value; seeks to destroy our conscience

(12) Opposes love and truth and the desire to do good

Higher Order:

(1) Creative

(2) Withdraws if we become frightened

(3) Wise, loving, humble

(4) Gently leads and leaves us in freedom

(5) Generally richer than our normal experiences

(6) Can broaden our values

(7) Likely to be highly symbolic

(8) Usually supportive and genuinely instructive

(9) Usually communicates directly with our inner thoughts and feelings

(10) Can touch deep emotions and carry an almost inexpressible ring of truth

(11) Can see through the lower-order lies

(12) One thought from the higher order can cover thousands of thoughts in our usual mode

This is an important list. It is distilled from many years of work talking with the voices in schizophrenics' heads. Each point is helpful. From this, it seems that the most obvious sign is how the voice or presence responds to the person's fear.

Our second discernment tool is a pair of questions: Does contact with this other within make you feel better than other people? Does it make you feel less than other people? The first of these questions is usually more significant because the sugarcoating of feeling better than others, superior, and one-up makes it almost irresistible to many. Witness how much of our society is organized by people competing with each other to feel better, higher, and more than others. This is a deep hunger, for many an addiction. Many traditions consider pride to be the greatest spiritual danger. Humility has ceased to be held as a spiritual virtue and is often seen as almost a flaw. As Winston Churchill joked about a political rival, "Chamberlain is a humble man, and has much to be humble about." Pia Mellody, whom I got this understanding from, called this "riding in the one-up position." She stated that we are all precious, but none of us are special.

The element of comparison is the core of the problem. Our worth and value should not be at stake at all in relationships with others. If an attitude or message you get from a spiritual presence, UB, guide, or inner voice makes you feel superior, beware. In the more extreme forms, this leads to what the Jungians refer to as inflation. Jung saw this as the greatest danger of contact with the archetypes: that we would become puffed up with those great energies even to the point of believing that we were the new messiahs. These messianic feeling are an especially great danger in psychedelic-assisted therapy.

If a message from your inner world makes you feel one-up in relation to others, it is almost certainly not a guide. The opposite of this is also true: if it makes you feel less than others, it is also not a guide. This is not a message our conscious minds want, but most of us have young exile parts who took in a belief about their worthlessness and fundamentally flawed nature very, very early, often with their mother's milk. These one-down messages are easier to spot because they sting when they go in. Pia Mellody said that if we do not generate our sense of value and self-esteem internally, we are condemned to steal it from others. The poison here stems from the impossible attempt to generate our sense of value from others. It cannot reliably come from comparison. If any message from your inner world makes you feel less than others, it is not true guidance either.

The third real-time discernment rule has to do with love. In some ways, this is the only and most basic criteria, but I've shied away from using it because the word *love* is so misused and so many lies are told about it. This virtue has many near enemies. How many times have you heard someone justify atrocious and harmful behavior by saying, "It's because I love them"? Or people invading other countries and killing people because they love their country? It is so easy to delude ourselves with this word. And yet, it is the most fundamental thing.

Going to back William James's radical pragmatism, I've experimented to find a way to approach this that is a real-time discernment tool. What I've come to is this: notice the effect the presence from your internal world has on your polarizations. These are parts who are at war with each other. I love my partner versus I want to be alone again. This job is necessary versus I need to quit. My mother was so mean that I hate her versus I need to care for her as she ages. Polarizations are an important part of IFS; we all have them, and at times much of our life energy is locked up in these internal battles. If the other within lowers the amount of hate and intensity in these inner fights, it's likely a guide. It is even better if the two sides can become compassionate toward each other, even if they do not change their positions one iota. If your inner polarizations are more intense and hostile, it is more likely UB energy.

There is also another way we can use the concept of love pragmatically for discernment. If there is some presence in your inner awareness, offer it a free gift of light and love. Carefully observe its reaction. If it accepts it easily and warmly, it's more likely a guide. If it reacts with disgust, distrust, revulsion, or disdain, it is very likely a UB. Even hesitation can be a giveaway. This idea and approach comes from Dr. Charles Tramont.

So, our three basic real-time discernments are: (1) How does the being react to your fear? (2) Does it make you feel one-up or one-down? (3) What effect does it have on your preexisting polarizations?

This is very much a work in progress. Perhaps it would be more accurate to call this notes toward real-time discernment. The real test is the fruits of the guidance. If they are not sweet, you will know that you need to change course.

Can Discernment Be Learned?

I want to remind you of what Adriana, the one-eyed Mexican bruja, said about discernment. She said, first, it's a feeling in your body, in your stomach; it might be tingles going up and down your spine or some disturbance growling in your stomach. That's your first brain. Your second brain of discernment is in your mind; you have to be mentally clear and think about this. Then you can bring these two discernments together in your heart, and then there will be peacefulness and certainty.

Many of the modern deliverance ministries say that discernment is a God-given grace that cannot be learned or taught. One prominent Anglican deliverance priest, Israel Martin, would pray over a coin and then flip it to reach a decision. Even if our discernment methods are tentative and uncertain, we need guidelines. IFS makes a big contribution here. The first level of discernment is: "Is it a part of the system or not?" I described in detail how to do this in the clinical outline chapter. If deliverance ministers knew about parts and the natural multiplicity of mind, they could avoid many negative outcomes. Trying to amputate a part may provide big drama and look like relief for a short time, but it always backfires, often very painfully. This is why we need to assume that an inner presence is a part of the person from their personal experience in this lifetime until it is clearly demonstrated that it is not. Only after this first level of discernment is clear do the other discernment tools become relevant and useful.

In late medieval times, many people, mainly women, were having intense internal experiences, some of which seemed to be genuine spiritual contact, and some were judged to be possession by demons. At first, there was much concern about how to distinguish the genuine divine inspirations, but by the fourteenth century the church began condemning almost all of these unauthorized experiences as possession. This became fodder for the Inquisition and then fed the witchcraft persecution mania. This effectively eradicated all of the remaining European shamans and most of the village folk healers. With the burning of witches in the background, medicalizing the entire issue was a mercy, even though it invalidated peoples' experience. We are heirs of this, and many still pathologize every experience of others within us.

It takes intellectual discipline to stay with radical pragmatism here. Regardless of our theories about the reality of these events, people suffer less when they have an experience of inner wisdom and guidance that they can rest into. In the IFS world, there are questions and debates about the difference, if any, between Self and guides. Ontologically, I do not know. Experientially, guides are felt as something that is not part of the Self. Following the client, we work with their way of experiencing their depths.

When people come specifically asking for help in establishing or increasing their connection with guides, kenosis and constraint-release are the keys. Ask the client if they can find any parts who do not want connection to the guides. Typically, they will be hiding because they've been attacked by parts who do want the connection. Some initial shame-reduction work might be called for at this point, for example, telling these parts that their reactions are perfectly natural. Many parts are afraid of guides and do not want anything to do with them. It can be helpful to reassure them with statements such as "You are not bad or wrong. We are not going to force you to do anything. You can be honest and direct with us about your concerns." Basic IFS skills are called for with these parts.

The Path Meditation

The classic IFS way to establish contact with guides is a meditation Dick developed called "The Path." Please do this meditation and don't just read it through; it cannot be understood from the outside. There are recorded versions of this meditation available on the IFS Institute's website. The version I will give you here is one that I have elaborated and changed a little from Dick's version.

The meditation begins by asking the person to be with all their parts in a meadow somewhere out in nature. Then gently ask all the parts if they would be willing to step back and stay in the meadow and let Self go off for a short time alone. If any parts refuse this, it's okay. Stay with the parts with curiosity and compassion and work with them. For many of us, this will occur many times before our parts will let us go off and leave them, even briefly. There can be much healing in these interactions. For me, it took many tries before all my parts would let me go.

When all the parts agree, let Self go off alone. This deep unblending is kenotic. With the clouds parted, the sun can shine forth, and we can begin to be aware of the depth and vastness of the sky around it. Now we ask Self to go to one end of the meadow, where it will find three trailheads it can choose from. One trail might go up a hill or mountain; another trail stays approximately level; and the third trail goes down, perhaps toward water. Tell Self that it can choose any of these trails, but the one that's on the same level often leads to trickster-like beings who do not make the most reliable guides. Encourage Self to follow the trail that goes up or down, all the while noticing its surroundings. As Self is going on the trail, ask the person if they see it walking on the trail. This would mean that it is not really Self because Self is always the witness — the one who is seeing. If they do see this part walking up the trail for them, have them thank it and ask it to step back and let them do this themselves.

Ask the person's Self to keep going until it finds what it feels is a good place to stop. Ask Self to settle there and to invite in guides and guidance, or whatever words the client uses for these deep knowings. Invite them to wait with all their senses open, noticing all details available to them. Most of us are visual, but be sure to ask if they hear any sounds, songs, music, or words. Also ask if they feel wind on their skin or perhaps cool fog or the heat of the sun. Work with them to open all sensory modalities. Ask them not to reject anything, and tell them that sometimes the most trivial and mundane-seeming image can have great import if welcomed.

Then, when the time seems right, ask Self to express thanks for whatever was given and then return down the trail to the waiting parts. Be sure they reunite well. It's usually best to have people write about this or share about it immediately after. Often, if people believe they have received nothing, when you ask them about details of their experience, there were things they had discounted, like a tree over them offering welcome shade, a beam of sunlight coming in at an angle, or birds in the distance, or the sound of the wind. Thousands of people have done this meditation now, so there's a great deal of information about potential stuck places and the ways to deal with them, but it's best to stay with the client's experience, language, and mythology.

Several other internal imagery patterns can be helpful here. First, ask the person about their images and use these as much as possible. One generic version starts with asking the person to imagine a stream of guide energy coming down from above and entering them. Ask them to be especially aware of any blockages, constrictions, or obstructions. Tell them not to fight these but instead to just notice the details with curiosity and feel the energy flow all the way through. You can also ask them to have the energy connect up from the earth or to have both energies enter and merge. We can also use the imagery of a mountain stream here. The important thing now is the constrictions, the blockages. We need to meet these with curiosity and welcome, not with combative energy. This again is basic IFS. Focusing on blockages and helping them dissolve is a kenotic process. When these blockages are lessened, there will be more awareness of the guide's energies. Some blocks may not dissolve, in which case you can suggest that they can become like boulders in a stream. Once the client's stream starts flowing, it tends to clear and deepen its own path just as streams do in the external world.

After this exercise, I like to offer the client a blank outline of the human body, both front and back. I ask them to make marks on this outline wherever they experienced blockages. If possible, I prefer that people use colored pencils or crayons. The unconscious loves bright colors. When no benign energy is found, this exercise is very valuable because it shows us somatically where the blockages are, which puts us in a good position to relate to them with compassion and curiosity.

In the modern West, we have damaged our internal capacity to have positive spiritual presence experiences. They're there waiting for us if only we remove the obstacles we've put in place. These experiences are important. We've already had a glimpse of the mountain of data showing that people with religious or spiritual orientations enjoy better physical and emotional health. I want to add two more bits of evidence about the importance of these experiences, the Bill Wilson–Carl Jung letters and Roland Griffiths's research on mystical experience.

The Bill Wilson–Carl Jung Letters

The twelve steps are a very effective way of dealing with addictions, and they are fundamentally spiritual. Many professional therapists have been pooh-poohing the twelve steps for decades, but the research shows that they are more effective than most therapy. The first three steps are about recognizing a higher power and turning our lives over to it. This is spiritual work, and the neutral phrase "higher power" disguises it enough to allow rationalist-materialist atheists to have spiritual experiences. Bill Wilson, the founder of AA, wrote to Carl Jung in 1961. Shortly before Jung died, he replied that he had to be exceedingly careful about writing about spiritual things because he found that he was "misunderstood in every possible way." But he did write frankly to Wilson about Roland H., an alcoholic he had treated. Jung wrote, "His craving for alcohol was the equivalent, on a low level, of the spiritual thirst of our being for wholeness, expressed in medieval language: the union with God." Jung added a footnote here quoting Psalm 42:1, "as the hart panteth after the water brooks, so panteth my soul after thee, O God."

The last section of the letter is:

I am strongly convinced that the evil principle prevailing in this world leads the unrecognized spiritual need into perdition if it is not counteracted either by real religious insight or by the protecting wall of the human community. An ordinary man not protected by an action from above and isolated in society cannot resist the power of evil which is called, very aptly, The Devil. But the use of such words arouses so many mistakes that one can only keep away from them as much as possible. These are the reasons why I could not give a full and sufficient explanation to Roland H. but I am risking it with you because I conclude from your very decent and honest letter that you have acquired a point of view above the misleading platitudes one usually hears about alcoholism. You see, alcohol in Latin is *spiritus* and you use the same word for the highest religious experiences as well as for the most depraving poison. The helpful formula, therefore, is: *spiritus contra spiritum* [the spirit against alcoholic spirits].

Jung could only be this honest very near the end of his life. Bill Wilson wrote him back almost immediately, but Jung died before he could respond. Spirituality — connection to a higher power, to the archetypal depths, to God, to something bigger than our isolated personal lives — is crucial for our health. Our society largely undermines and denies this.

Roland Griffiths's Theory

Roland Griffiths is the head of the Johns Hopkins Center for Research on Psychedelic Healing and a professor of psychiatry there. He is a careful research scientist who uses all of the most sophisticated statistical methods in his work. His research has been ongoing since 1999 and includes more than 375 participants and over 700 sessions with psilocybin. In studying the amazing success of psilocybin treatment for various conditions, he came to believe that a certain type of experience was largely responsible for the positive change. He settled on the name "mystical experience" but realized that there were many others, including "rapid conversion," "religious," "peak," "transcendental," "epiphany," and "transforming."

Being a scientist, Griffiths operationalized his definition of mystical experience so he could study it statistically. He used six descriptors. The first three are the core ones: (1) an experience of unity, pure consciousness, all is one; (2) an experience of the preciousness of each moment, reverence, sacredness; (3) noetic — the sense that this is real, more real than ordinary experience. The next three are: (4) positive affect, love, joy, and peace; (5) transcendence of time and space, which no longer apply; (6) ineffable — words cannot express it. With this detailed definition in place, Griffiths and his team could score people on how complete their mystical experience was. They found that more complete mystical experiences predicted more complete healing. In other words, intense spiritual experience predicts healing. This can be shown in highly quantifiable ways; it is measurable. Spirituality matters; contact with the other within — with UBs, with guides, with higher powers, with all that messy, "unscientific" stuff — is vitally important if your goal and measuring stick are the reduction of human suffering.

Written Dialogues with Guides

This is a practice that I learned from IFS senior trainer Kay Gardner, who said she learned it from psychotherapist Ira Progoff, but it is far older than that. As I mentioned in writing about the Brazilian Spiritists, they often use what they call "psychography," which is allowing one of the spirits to take control of their hand and write messages. Several of the Spiritists have written many books this way, and many other mediums and channels have used similar methods. Some people use the nondominant hand for this kind of writing. What I learned is very simple: I just write out dialogue. Usually I just start with the word *hello*. Then I wait and see if some words come into my head, and I write them down. This begins a dialogue. Amazingly, very often stuff comes out that I did not expect at all. Often this material seems wiser than I am. This has become a regular practice for me. At the very least, it gives my inner world the message that I am listening, that I want to communicate, that I want to be in relationship with whoever and whatever is deep inside me. When I started, this practice seemed so trivial that I almost didn't do it. I only went ahead because I like Kay and respect her a great deal. I'm grateful that my skeptical parts stepped back and let this happen. Now I do this simple practice almost every morning, and I have more than eleven volumes of these dialogues.

Case Studies

The following case study is one of the relatively few in which the client specifically came in wanting increased contact with guides. Most often, the appearance of guides comes in the course of other work. The client, a relatively young woman, lives in North Africa. Her therapist was also on the call but remained silent through almost all of it.

Bob and Amelia

Bob: So, Amelia, do you want to be seeing your therapist, too, or would you rather just we see each other?

Amelia: I'd rather see only you.

Jean: I will turn off my camera if you…

Amelia: Okay.

Bob: Yep. Okay, great. So, you wanted to work on a connection to spirit, is that right?

Amelia: Yeah, that's right.

Bob: So, tell me about how that's been for you. There's been some frustration around it or… tell me about this.

Amelia: Yeah, actually I realized that it was really a burden for me not to be, not to believe in something after death, so I wish I could believe, and if I did, life would be really easier for me. I worked with my therapist around this thing, and I realized that the part, there are many parts of me that wouldn't even exist if I believed in God. Actually, I do believe in something more powerful, I mean, something greater than us when I see nature, for instance, when I see something very beautiful in nature. I'm really oh, and I do, I mean, I admit there must be a creator, but I don't see him in day-to-day life, and also, I don't believe in religion and especially not in life after death, and this is the… the thing that brings anxiety in me is what's going on after all this and what's the meaning also of all this.

Bob: First thing I want to say about belief: there was recently a group called the Bigelow Foundation that gave $2 million in prizes for the best essays proving rationally that there is life after death, and you can find all those essays online, and they're amazing.

Amelia: Okay. Like, you mean they did it, they proved life after death?

Bob: Well…

Amelia: Not scientifically, I assume.

Bob: But there's incredible overwhelming evidence that something goes on. So, Bigelow Foundation… I don't know the exact name, but it's easily available on the Internet.

Amelia: Okay, I will look it up.

Bob: For your rational parts.

Amelia: Yeah.

Bob: Now, what I think we can do is help you have an experience of spirit rather than anything about belief.

Amelia: Mm-hmm.

Bob: So let's… why don't you go inside, and we want to find the parts in you that are afraid or don't want this. Okay. And we want to welcome them — we don't want to pick a fight with them.

Amelia: The parts of me that don't want to do this experimentation with you?

Bob: Parts of you who don't like the idea of there being a spirit connection.

Amelia: Oh, okay.

Bob: … who are going, "This is, no, this is all garbage."

Amelia: Hmm, okay.

Bob: Okay.

Amelia: Yeah.

Bob: Can you find them?

Amelia: Yeah.

Bob: Okay. How do they show up? Is it a plural "them" or is it single? Do you have a sense right off?

Amelia: There is at least one, a big one.

Bob: Okay, that's, a big one.

Amelia: Yeah.

Bob: How does that show up in your body? When that's present, what happens in your body to let you know it's there?

Amelia: I can't really tell.

Bob: You can't really say?

Amelia: No, I can't really tell.

Bob: Okay, well, just go inside and look for a while. Think of a time this thing has been really big in you, that doesn't want this experience, and then, just as you're thinking of that time, notice what goes on in your body, how your body feels.

Amelia: I would say in my solar plexus.

Bob: In your solar plexus. Okay, great. I'm going to ask you to get even more curious about this. There's some sensation in your solar plexus. Open all your senses to whatever is going on in your solar plexus and notice. Is this perhaps heavy or light?

Amelia: It's like a radiation. It's something that radiates.

Bob: Radiates, okay.

Amelia: Yeah, radiates.

Bob: Is it like radiating heat or cold, or do you have a sense… just get real curious.

Amelia: I'd say it's like, you know there is an epicenter and there are like waves, vibrations. Like, you know when you throw a stone in the water or something.

Bob: Yes. Okay, great, great. And open your curiosity to this. Are there any other characteristics you notice about it? Does it have a color perhaps or anything else? Any sounds or anything come?

Amelia: I would say it looks like, you know, stagnant water, a small lake or… and just dark.

Bob: They're dark. Okay, great. Dark, radiating circles from throwing stones in the water… stagnant, small lake. Great. So how are you feeling toward the part of you that shows up this way?

Amelia: Feeling empathy.

Bob: Great, great. So offer that empathy and see how it responds. Can it notice you?

Amelia: A little.

Bob: A little… well, that's good. That's a good start. And how is it as it's noticing you? Is it frightened, or does it like you being there… how is it?

Amelia: It's separated, so it's like two distinct parts.

Bob: Oh, there's two parts there now.

Amelia: I mean, they're not connected, actually. I mean this radiation thing, it's like it's as if it was always, you know, these small waves and this, whatever, I mean, it won't stop.

Bob: That's okay, we're not asking it to stop right now. Just how is it. Ask it, "How is it for you that I'm noticing you and curious and empathetic toward you… how does that feel?" And see how it responds.

Amelia: It doesn't matter to him.

Bob: It doesn't at all?

Amelia: No.

Bob: Okay. Wow. And it's a "him," huh?

Amelia: Seems like.

Bob: Yeah. Let this part know that you'd like to have a different kind of relationship with it, and ask it, "Is there anything you want me to know right at the beginning of this new relationship?"

Amelia: Well, it's like, this radiation, the message that it gave me that the shape of it can be determined by whoever wants to, I mean, it's like this image of the stone thrown in water, so it's shapeable, you know.

Bob: Mm-hmm, yeah. Is this part interested in forming a new relationship with you? It sounds as though it's not in the happiest place. Maybe we could help it get to a better one.

Amelia: Yeah.

Bob: Okay. Is that true, that it could use, that I… okay. Can you ask it to tell us, "Are you stuck somewhere in the past… is there someplace you're stuck that we could help free you from?"

Amelia: I don't know.

Bob: It doesn't know?

Amelia: No.

Bob: Okay, okay. Ask it, "Are you…"

Amelia: At least, I feel resistance, actually. I don't know if this part doesn't know or if this part doesn't want to tell.

Bob: Okay. Tell this part, "It's perfectly alright, and you get to say, 'I don't want to say.' You… we don't want you feeling we're like pushing at you — you get to say no anytime you need to." And see what the part says about that, how that is for the part.

Amelia: It's okay.

Bob: Okay. And just check, "Is everybody else inside of me okay with us getting to know this part, or has somebody else come up and is blocking communication?"

Amelia: There's a part that is interfering, and it's a skeptical part of, you know…

Bob: Mm-hmm. "Hi there, skeptic part. Welcome."

Amelia: Hi.

Bob: "Good to meet you. You know, skeptic, sometimes we just need to do data collection and not have theories, and if we have theories, it messes up the data collection." Ask the skeptic what it thinks of that idea.

Amelia: The idea of doing what, doing collection?

Bob: We just need to gather data at some…

Amelia: Yeah, gathering data is fine. Gathering data is okay for the skeptic part.

Bob: Great, great. So thank it. Ask it to step back and give us room, and maybe it could even help us by increasing curiosity and our ability to notice detail.

Amelia: Yeah.

Bob: Okay. So let's go back to this one that looks like a pebble in a pond and ask this one, "It seemed like you're the one who doesn't want any kind of connection with spirituality or anything like that, is that right?"

Amelia: Yeah, that's right.

Bob: Okay. Would you ask this one, "What are you afraid would happen if Amelia had that kind of connection?"

Amelia: I can't access… I don't know.

Bob: Okay. Ask it, "Would you be willing to tell us what you're afraid might happen? You get to say yes or no — either one's okay."

Amelia: Yeah.

Bob: It would be willing to tell us?

Amelia: It is, but it's not able to know what's behind the fear of, I mean, what's…

Bob: Mm-hmm.

Amelia: What would happen if, I mean…

Bob: Okay. So ask this part, "Would you yourself be willing, as an experiment today, to let her open to an experience of spirit or whatever, whatever we're going to call it?"

Amelia: Yeah.

Bob: And ask this one, "Do you know of any other parts in her system who are not… who are scared of this, or who don't want to do this?"

Amelia: The main one.

Bob: Okay, great. So ask it again, "Are you okay as an experiment if she opens to an experience of spirit now?"

Amelia: Yeah, I'm okay.

Bob: "Thank you so much." Now, Amelia, ask all your parts, including this one, if they'll just all unblend from you a little bit.

Amelia: Yeah.

Bob: … so that you can have a lot of Self, and think of times when you really felt like full of Self and compassion and curiosity even, that warm, loving feeling that's so confident and easy, and ask all your parts to just step back a little bit because this is how we get to that state. Is everybody willing to do that, or is anyone clinging to you?

Amelia: There is one. Yeah, this one is clinging, but I will unblend, yeah. I will ask it to, I will ask it to step back, yeah.

Bob: Yeah, and if it can't, that's fine... we'll just help it.

Amelia: Well, it did it, it stepped back, but I struggle to connect with the Self, actually. I'm not sure I find...

Bob: Okay. Well, let me suggest something: please stop struggling to connect with it. That sort of prevents it from showing up. Or like, if you just ask everybody to step back, it's there, like the sun on a cloudy day when the clouds part. If we struggle to get it, it sort of prevents its coming. So just ask everybody who's blended with you, including those parts who want to struggle who are so helpful, ask them all to just step back and make room and allow spaciousness and openness, and see how that is. It's fine if they say no — we'll just help them. How's that going in there? Everybody opening up for you?

Amelia: I think so.

Bob: Okay, great. So from this place — this calm, spacious, curious place — just gently open yourself and say, "I'd like a sensation of guidance or guides" and just listen. And get very curious, open all your sensory modalities. It comes in very strange ways; sometimes it's music or a feeling of light or an image. And how is it inside you right now, Amelia?

Amelia: How is it inside... I'm feeling good. I'm calm. But I don't know, there's still, I mean, I'm not sure I could access...

Bob: Okay, okay. Ask your figuring-out parts to stay back. We're definitely in data collection now.

Amelia: Yeah.

Bob: It's way too early for any kind of theories. So ask everybody to stay back, and go back to that calm, centered place, and then notice detail, even if all you perceive at the beginning is blackness. Blackness is never absolutely the same everywhere — it has detail. And anything you pay attention to with curiosity in the inner world changes and moves and grows. One thing some people like to do is they look for areas in the inner world where it's a little lighter, a little brighter, and they move toward that or toward warmth. Curious, noticing details, opening all your senses. My experience is that benevolent energies will never enter us unless we invite them because they respect who we are so much.

Amelia: Which energies?

Bob: Benevolent, kind energies.

Amelia: Kind.

Bob: Yeah, they don't enter us unless we invite them. So you might want to issue a welcome. The nasty energies will try and push their way in. That's how you can tell who's who. "So, is there anybody there for me today? Welcome, I've missed you. I want to be able to touch that feeling I've had at the ocean or out in nature where I know deeply there's something much bigger than me. Right here, right now with me. Welcome, come in, come in." No effort, effortless, like becoming part of a river.

Amelia: The thing I saw was this initial lake with... a lotus flower appeared in it. I mean, it's beautiful, but I don't know if it's a...

Bob: Okay, you don't know. If you can, pay attention to the lotus flower. Notice every detail. Not like Sherlock Holmes or some investigator, but sort of resting back and opening yourself. Especially notice if anything happens in your heart, if the lotus flower starts to resonate with your heart and bring out emotion, deep feeling. Have you ever had that experience when you've seen something so beautiful it brought tears to your eyes?

Amelia: Yeah, a birth.

Bob: Mm-hmm.

Amelia: When a baby comes to life, it's beautiful.

Bob: Good, yeah. And a lotus flower was just born inside of you, so focus back on that, and as much as you can, allow your heart to open. It's an effortless thing. The way it opened when you saw the birth, the miracle. Yeah, and just keep welcoming, Amelia. These energies need to be invited in. "Come in, great energy, come in. I welcome you; I've missed you, please come in." And your breath knows how to welcome these energies much better than our minds do... it's way smarter than we are, Amelia. And your body is smarter than we are, too. Your body and breath can help you welcome this energy.

Amelia: Are they energy or guides? Are they energies or guides?

Bob: I don't know, and let's not try and figure it out — let's just stay with whatever your experience is. I don't think the names we put on this are so important.

Amelia: I mean, it's the same, so I mean, I invite whatever good energy.

Bob: Yeah, whatever it is there. Focusing on what you're given, this lotus. Noticing its color, its texture. You might notice if there's fragrance. Allowing yourself to just be immersed in that inner world. Are any parts of you frightened or concerned about this experience, about welcoming in this lotus energy?

Amelia: No.

Bob: Okay, good.

Amelia: No, no, but I always have to push gently aside some parts.

Bob: Okay, let's try something else, Amelia.

Amelia: Mm-hmm.

Bob: Those parts you've been pushing gently aside, ask them, "Can you welcome this energy — can you also welcome the lotus?" and see what happens. They don't have to; they get to choose. Maybe say to them, "Taste a little and see if it's good, just a little, and then you'll know from your own experience, and you won't have to trust us." And your breath can keep helping you. Are they able to taste a little?

Amelia: Um, I was.

Bob: Oh, great, great. Do you have a sense of how far away from this lotus you are?

Amelia: Um, close.

Bob: Great.

Amelia: And I felt kind of a presence.

Bob: Great. Again, let's not try and figure anything out, not for a while yet. Okay. Open all your senses as tenderly as you can. The same attention you would give a newborn baby, a newborn baby inside. Sometimes things are so beautiful, they make us cry. Sometimes things are so sad, they break our hearts open, and there's a joy in that, a deep, deep connection. And just keep welcoming these energies. "Welcome into me. You're welcome in every organ of my body." Invite all your parts, taste, "Welcome, this is good. Maybe just take a drop in your mouth and see." And as you stay focused in a gentle way on that lotus and the presence around it, the more attention you pay to it in a gentle way, the more it changes and grows and shows you things, and the presence gets clearer, too. Sometimes the quality of light changes in the inside world, sometimes the temperature becomes warm, sometimes there are very sweet odors. I don't know if any of that will happen for you.

If any parts of you are in pain or distressed or frightened, invite them to come in so they can be held and loved and know they're related to something much bigger, much more powerful. Like your breath, your breath has been around for billions of years. It's way wiser than we are, and it's right there every moment. Yeah. Sometimes it's just like basking in the sun after a cold stretch. Yeah. It is so good to be in these energies. I think every moment we can spend connected to these energies is profoundly healing. And there's a secret about these energies that you probably already know, but I'm going to say it aloud anyway. You can't grasp them; you can't hang onto them. The only way you can do that is to give them away. The more you give those energies away, the more comes. So maybe just see if that works for you if that happens. The closer you get to that lotus energy and that presence, the more it can flow through you and you can give it away to your loved ones and all those around you, and then it floods in more and more and more. Just see if that happens inside. Like the warmth of the sun after being cold for too long. Yeah, I think your breath is helping more and more. Great. And if you want, you might focus on the sense of presence you have. The presence you're feeling around that lotus flower. And if you want, you can direct any of these questions that have been bothering you and just say, "Presence, can you help, can you guide me?" Sometimes what comes when we ask questions like that is totally unexpected and seems completely inappropriate, but don't throw anything away. Even the most bizarre image. I asked about my spiritual purpose on the planet once, and I was shown a sponge, and I thought that was absolutely ridiculous, but it became very important for me, very significant. So don't throw anything away, Amelia, no matter how bizarre or irrelevant it seems. And just be receptive, observe, welcome. Welcome, welcome, welcome. How's that going for you in there, Amelia?

Amelia: Um, connecting with the lotus. The main thing I'm getting is, the image I'm having is as if he has roots — a big, large root that is connected to my heart — and I saw it, it's just an image again, but I saw it pulsing like the umbilical cord, and I just have this image stuck and nothing else.

Bob: Great.

Amelia: And it's beautiful, but I have no other, I mean, I just feel it.

Bob: Great. That's a lot. So you see the root of the lotus as an umbilical cord going down into your heart, and you sense the beating and the pulsing in that umbilical cord.

Amelia: Yeah.

Bob: Okay. If you're willing, focus back there. Feeling this beating, this connection of your heart to the lotus. I believe that when we can connect to these energies, we connect to life forces and a flow of energy that's been going on for billions of years on this planet, and it's very, very deep and ancient, and it doesn't fit into words usually. But there's a connection here that's involved with birth, and it touches your heart. If it feels good to you, notice how it connects to your heart and just how that connection occurs. And again, if it feels right, open up that connection so that the flow through the umbilicus can be unobstructed and clear and strong. And each pulse in that umbilicus can help. You might also notice, are there any constricted or narrowed or congested places in the umbilicus? And don't fight them, if there are. They're very important markers as to where it might be good to focus later and to help those parts that are constricting. So if you can, welcome the constrictions, too. It usually is a really scared part. These energies do scare parts sometimes. Realizing how big and vast and ancient these energies are can make some of our parts feel very small and fragile and weak, and we need to offer them our love and welcome them, too. And maybe if there are any constricted areas or even sometimes there's scar tissue on the umbilicus or where it hits the heart, this scar tissue or objects, anything like that, notice that very kindly and with concern. We don't want to fight that or try and cut it out right now — we just want to notice it and get curious and welcoming. Oh, something must have really hurt here. And your breath can continue to guide the whole process. I know it's smarter than me.

And sometimes, as we enter these realms, we can sense the interior of our bodies, the subjective world inside, in much more depth. And there may be beings who emerge from the shadows and come toward this connection that's growing in you, beings you'll want to know. Helpers, allies, friends. Yeah, you're doing great. Welcome, open curiosity, all your senses; hearing, sight, body sensation. There's one esoteric school in Australia that insists we actually have twenty-seven different sensory modalities. I don't know about that, but I know we've got more than five. So ask all your sensory modalities to open, even the ones you're not really clear about yet. And if it feels right again, "Welcome, welcome, welcome. I want connection with this higher power, energy, being, spirit…" Whatever the words are. "I want this deep connection to the life force that's been flowing on this planet for at least 3.6 billion years, and probably a lot more. I'm part of that — I'm part of this great river, and it's absolutely effortless, and I want to feel that flowing through my body and my veins. Welcome, welcome, welcome."

Ask the presence and any other allies who've appeared if there's anything they specifically want you to know now. They've already given you a lot, Amelia, but see if there's anything more. Yeah. And if it feels right, Amelia… we're coming, we're coming, we're getting toward the end of our hour together… Ask them, if you want, "How can I find my way back to you? How can I make this the beginning of a whole new kind of relationship for us? I want to be part of this vast, effortless river. I know that's who I really am." There are so many ways they could offer you to come back to them. I have no idea what's right for you at all,

I have no idea. But I know that deep inside you know. You have that wisdom in you, deep in there. Now if it feels right, very gently start coming back. Find a way to say goodbye for now to the lotus and to the umbilical cord leading to your heart, to the connections to your heart. And remembering any and all places of scar tissue or congestion or constriction so that you can come back and love them and help them. Very slowly, and if it feels right, tell them, "I'm coming back." Slowly and gently, and all your parts, many of them might have tasted these waters, too, check on them. "How are you all doing?" And some may not have wanted to do this today, checking on them, too. "How's everybody, you all okay? This was pretty weird, huh?" Now, there are a couple more things we need to do carefully here. See how everybody's doing and, you know, take time, welcome them in. And then we need to come back to that part we started with, the pebble in the pond. Let this one know, I'm really clearly aware that we couldn't have done anything without its permission and I'm grateful, and I want to know if it feels that we honored it in how we went on today, and how's it doing now?

Amelia: It's feeling very curious.

Bob: Great, great. Does it need anything from you or from us? Can we help it in any way?

Amelia: Um, yeah from me — not to give up on the quest.

Bob: Okay, and what do you say to it?

Amelia: That I won't.

Bob: And does it believe you?

Amelia: Yeah.

Bob: Okay. Good, good. Real honor to meet this part today. Is it, does it feel complete?

Amelia: Yeah.

Bob: Okay. Now the skeptic. "Hi there, skeptic."

Amelia: Hi.

Bob: "Welcome. Thank you. You gave us a lot of room. How are you doing? Did you take any notes that we missed?"

Amelia: Yeah, I left you space, but I'm always taking a lot of space, this part. I will always be present anyway.

Bob: "Yeah, good." My skeptic has a clipboard and a pen and is always making notes like this about everything. It's a very valuable part. "Skeptic, do you have anything to say about what went on in the inner world now?"

Amelia: That I'm ready to challenge my thoughts and I'm ready to learn.

Bob: "Okay, great. Wonderful. And do you have any questions or specific things that are bugging you or bothering you in any way?"

Amelia: No, I don't.

Bob: Okay, wonderful. Now maybe just sink back inside, and I have one more question that I want you to ask in the inner world and that's "Is there anything else that should happen inside of me today for this to be as healing as possible?" And then just wait and listen and see if there's something. And you can keep it private if you want. What's important is that you get the messages, not me. (long pause) Okay. And a lot of people find a few deep breaths sort of help them come back to this external world in a gentle and sweet and easy way. And there's something I want to say when you feel like reoriented and back to more normal reality. (another pause)

If this inner world is important to you, the best way to stay in touch with it is daily. It doesn't have to be a lot, like, like five minutes a day seems to be more important than three hours twice a week. There's something about steadiness and regularity, and then your parts come to trust, and these inner presences come to trust. This is a whole new relationship, it's a whole new way of being, it's not some great big explosion and then everything is back to the way it was before. So really steady. Do you have some regular practice that you could, you know, check in with these realities and these parts, something you do every day?

Amelia: No, I don't. Are you asking me if I'm doing it? No, I don't, but I will. I do realize how important it is.

Bob: Yeah, and there's another way to build this into your life. A lot of people I know do it when they shower because that fresh, warm water hits their face and it reminds them in a very physical way. Another thing that might really work for you is a lot of people will go out and find a pebble or a seashell. It reminds them of the inner world, and then they just carry that around in their pocket. Or you know, an image or whatever it is. I mean, you have the creative resources within you to find a way to make this an ongoing, steady new way of being.

Amelia: Yeah.

Bob: Okay. Do you want to invite Jean your therapist back in?

Amelia: Sure.

Jean: I'm here.

Bob: And if it's okay, Amelia, here's what I'd like to ask. If he wants to say, Jean Batiste, if you want to say anything, would you just start with what happened in your heart or how that touched you and your parts so very… not like thinking stuff, right, to start, okay.

Jean: I also had some similar journey, something very deep.

Bob: Great.

Jean: So thank you for sharing this with me. Yeah, it's a big gift for me to be with you today.

Bob: I deeply believe we're part of this flow or whatever you want to call it — words don't matter — and I think the beliefs are almost inconsequential. What matters is the experience. Do we experience this in our hearts, in our bodies, you know, in our interior universe? That's what matters. And the words we put on it and the belief structures… meh, not so important. Okay, either one of you, we've got like a couple minutes left. Are there any, like, burning questions or things you really want to say or ask or…?

Amelia: I had one last question, if you don't mind. Before this session, I was very looking forward to it, very impressed also, of course, and one hour before, my body started aching, like my arms started hurting very much and shaking and shivering, and I really couldn't understand because it wasn't about meeting you, I mean, it was something really deeper. Would you have any idea, I mean, what does it suggest?

Bob: Get really curious. "Hi there, who's in my body? I really want to get to know you. You must be a really important part of me because you're able to have a big effect on my body. Please come to me — don't go hide. I'd really like to get to know you. I'm not going to use force on you."

Amelia: Okay.

Bob: Okay.

Amelia: Okay. Thank you both.

Bob: It was a pleasure meeting both of you.

A More Typical Case

The following case is more typical in that we didn't focus on guides — they emerged organically in the session. The client is a mature female therapist who was in a supervision group I led. She presented two separate issues, either one of which would have been plenty for an entire course of therapy. The first issue was that she always felt she lived her life from a few inches back, that she wasn't really in her life somehow. Associated with this was the fact that she could only remember negative things from her past clearly. For example, about being a mother who raised two boys to adulthood, she could only remember the errors and things she regretted. The second issue she mentioned as a possible focus is that she had never felt welcomed on the planet. Starting in the womb even before she was born, she did not feel welcomed. Her mother's pregnancy with her had been a surprise, not planned. Her mother was fairly profoundly depressed, and this only got worse after her birth. Her father was not there emotionally either. She did not feel welcomed into life.

Then she turned her attention inward and went into her inner world, her subjective experience. We let her system choose what to focus on, and it focused on her feeling of being somewhat separated from life, of living a few inches back from her body. As she focused, she saw a somewhat grayish but transparent film between her and her life. We got her parts who judged this film to step back until she was genuinely curious about it. When she extended this curiosity, the grayish film developed those shimmering colors that light has when reflecting off of bubble. As she got to know this layer, it was clear it was there to protect her, to keep her safe. We asked when it had first come in, and it replied that it came in in the womb. It came in before she was really even a fetus — while she was still just two and then four and then eight dividing cells. It had surrounded her closely. It told her that she really was meant to be born and really was needed on the planet even though her parents could not receive her. So this presence came in and kept her safe so that she could live. It was emotional for her to deeply feel that she did belong on the planet, that her life was needed and planned.

Then we came back to the present and focused on that film again. It had rainbows, like the reflections off of a bubble, and it was no longer gray. We asked her to look back at her life now and see if she still remembered it the same way. She said something had changed. She said, "When I'm gone, my sons will think, 'We had a kind mom. A kind mom.'" This was moving for all of us — the client, the whole supervision group, and me. In communicating with this film, she realized it was meant for her specifically; it fit her precisely.

She did not want to lose this being. I asked if maybe it could change to a new role now that things were somewhat different. It agreed, and the film transformed and became a robe that she wore. The robe also had the glittering rainbows like a bubble. It let her know that it was a badge of office or an official robe. Much of this session was deeply moving in a very quiet and dignified way. I felt grateful to have been a part of it. After one of the other participants asked, "What was that thing? What was that film?" I said we need to ask the client. When we did, she said somewhat shyly that in her Christian tradition they were called angels.

A week or so later, this client and I exchanged emails. She wrote, *You summarized it very well… The beautiful angel/robe has stayed with me, and I've been back to connect with it again several times, and it continues to be profoundly moving. I saw it again like the aurora borealis, huge dancing lights all around. It said that it was "God's yes." I experience more and more of God's life and vitality in mine...* "God's yes" to her life — what a beautiful phrase, what a beautiful welcome onto this planet.

Fernanda's Session

Bob: So, as we were chatting before we started, you have some little bit nervous parts?

Fernanda: Yes, I do, definitely. I didn't have a good night; I couldn't sleep much. Yes, I'm nervous but, you know, I'm here and I want to get this done.

Bob: Should we talk to the nervous parts, or is there something else we should focus on?

Fernanda: No, I guess I just want to go straight in.

Bob: Oh, okay.

Fernanda: Because I need to take some time to explain like, the whole background.

Bob: Mm-hmm.

Fernanda: So, what I want to look at, Bob, is something that I feel is a family curse. Mm-hmm. And, um, forty-five years ago, my father was minister of foreign affairs in South America, and he was a lawyer, an honest lawyer, and very idealistic, very rational. My mother was a psychoanalyst, one of the first ones in South America, also very rational. And so, they didn't believe in any of this hocus-pocus stuff. But at that time, the president's wife was very into magic and basically, I think, black magic. You know, my father worked for the president. So one day she decided that she wanted to bring in some shamans — not shamans; I would say witch doctors — from Haiti. And for that, she asked my father to give her the official government jet to bring them over. And of course my father said absolutely not. He would not allow that, and he said that the airplane was just for official visits. She got angry, but he was very proud of what he had done, and he told us and we supported him. But three days after that at a state dinner, the president's wife came up to my father and threatened him. And she said, you know...

Bob: What did she do to him? I didn't hear the word.

Fernanda: She threatened him.

Bob: Threatened him, okay.

Fernanda: Yeah. She came up to him, and she said, "Very soon, I will see you cry." Okay. So a week after that, my father was fired, fired from the job. He was three years into the six-year period.

Bob: Mm-hmm.

Fernanda: And the news the next day all over the headlines was that he was fired for the good of the nation. Okay. So, it was terrible for him; he did cry because of the shame and the honor, and he had to keep quiet. But not only that, the problem was… started happening a year after that. We are four siblings. I have two older sisters and one younger brother. So my two older sisters get pregnant. All this family curse has to do with maternity and stuff. The first sister, she has a baby girl, it's okay. My second sister at twenty-five, she has a Down syndrome baby. It was a shock to the family, especially in a family where the values are the intellect, it was really a shock. The second child she had, he has cerebral palsy. Mm-hmm.

Then, eight years after that, I get pregnant with triplets. And a very high-risk pregnancy. I go, you know, I have to have an emergency C-section at seven months because we were all dying. And so, I had clinical death during the surgery, and my three daughters were born very, very, um, weighing two pounds, in the IC unit, and the next day one of them died. Her name was Rebecca, by the way. Yeah. And so the other two survived; you know, they stayed two months in the IC unit. And the doctors told me, you know, they were on one side of the hospital dying, I was on the other side of the hospital dying. They stayed there two months, and the doctor said, you have to wait four years to see if they're normal, if they can see, hear, whatever. So I did wait four years. Fortunately, they're fine. They're beautiful, fine, healthy. After this, I got a divorce at four years.

Then, my brother and his wife have one child who is okay, but the next one, when she was born, there was a meningitis epidemic at the hospital. Most of the babies died, but she made it. But, when she was a teenager studying in France, she had like a psychotic breakdown, and she has not been well ever since, not well at all. I have the feeling there is something else going on, like she has entities or something.

So when I start looking at this, I think that it's not a coincidence, so I look into it, and I believe that this woman, the president's wife, and her witch doctors did a curse. And I felt that it was a curse… So for six years I traveled all around the world, Nepal, India, all of South America, all of Europe, Southeast Asia, you know, Scotland, Ireland, doing a lot of offerings, special offerings for the Earth, you know. I did this with a Peruvian shaman, and I thought that it was okay, you know, that it was gone. And because I have this rule that if you see it, you fix it. And I was the one that believed in all this, and I thought that was the thing. But this last year, obviously, my twins are terrified of having children, you know, and all of the rest of the nephews. So finally, one of my twins gets pregnant with a lot of tests; she was tested every month and everything was fine, blah, blah, blah. And at seven months, just this past February, the baby's heart stopped. So, it, this brought all of this back to me, and I do need to say that I had a preparation, that's sort of a preparation session with my IFS very wonderful therapist. Two weeks' preparation for this, and I think she did a great job; we went all the way. But still, I just want to check if there's you know, something left on another level.

Bob: Okay, great, great. Thank you, very clear. So, you know the path into your inner world. You ready to go in? Yeah. Are any parts of you afraid to meet anything that's left of this curse? And it's okay if they are — it would be understandable.

Fernanda: No.

Bob: Okay, great. So look around in your inner world and see if there's anything in there that's not from your own personal history, your own lifetime.

Fernanda: I see and feel this um, like, redness in my womb.

Bob: Mm-hmm, okay.

Fernanda: And it's painful.

Bob: Painful redness in your womb.

Fernanda: Mm-hmm.

Bob: How are you feeling toward this painful redness in your womb?

Fernanda: Curious.

Bob: Okay, great. And you know this, Fernanda, but say anything, whatever's real. Four-letter words, cussing, yelling, that's all fine, whatever comes up. Okay.

Fernanda: That would have to be in Spanish, but okay.

Bob: That's fine, I understand. I know enough Spanish to curse a little bit.

Fernanda: Okay. I was hoping you wouldn't understand, but okay.

Bob: Okay. Extend the curiosity toward this being and see how it responds.

Fernanda: It's sort of... it turned into like a fetus.

Bob: Mm-hmm.

Fernanda: You know, like, on my left ovary.

Bob: Mm-hmm, okay. And can it feel your curiosity coming toward it? Just check and see. No? Okay. So open up all your sensory modalities to this fetus-being on your left ovary. Sight, hearing, sound, any smell, taste, your other sensory modalities, too. And notice detail, all the detail that shows up.

Fernanda: At first it was like a white fetus, but now it's like spread and it's, um, it's like, doing like this (she made twisting gestures), I don't know the word…

Bob: Contorting, twisting?

Fernanda: Yeah.

Bob: Okay.

Fernanda: And it's painful.

Bob: It's painful. Is experiencing the pain okay with you — can you tolerate it?

Fernanda: Mm-hmm.

Bob: Okay. So again, gently extend your curiosity toward this one and let it know. "Why are you here? We want to help you, whoever or whatever you are."

Fernanda: It seems to be connected, um, outwardly, to all the other, you know, to all the other children or people that got hurt with this. It's like, um, like a net.

Bob: Yeah.

Fernanda: Um, like veins, red veins.

Bob: Mm-hmm, mm-hmm, okay. Ask it this: "Are you a part of me?"

Fernanda: It's saying like um, like, "Then all of the others would have to be part of you."

Bob: Okay, so that's a no, okay. So, if it feels right, Fernanda, surround this thing, flood the area around your uterus with light, surround this one with light, and just pull it out of you to a good conversational distance in front of you. And how's that going for you?

Fernanda: It's going.

Bob: Mm-hmm.

Fernanda: This part comes in and, you know, it reminds me that I have lost so much faith.

Bob: Yeah, of course, of course. How are you feeling toward that part that reminds you of your losses of faith? Kinda makes sense, doesn't it? Yeah, let it know that and see how it responds.

Fernanda: It wants to have faith.

Bob: Yeah. Let this part know, if it's true for you, that's one of the tricks these kinds of being play on us: they damage our faith. And ask this one who came up with the loss of faith, "Has any of this external being gotten into you that has helped make you lose your faith?" Just ask it to look and check. We don't know yet. It will know.

Fernanda: I think not.

Bob: Okay, great. Thank it for that. Okay, check inside… are there any parts of you who've still got any connection left to this being or who are gonna miss it in any way?

Fernanda: No.

Bob: Okay, real clear, real clean, great. Okay, focusing on this being out there contained in the ball of light, can you see it now?

Fernanda: Mm-hmm.

Bob: Ask it this: "You were sent here, weren't you? By somebody more powerful than you."

Fernanda: Um, I don't know how much consciousness it has because it's like a malformed fetus, like maybe like in a bottle, I don't know.

Bob: Mm-hmm, okay. Okay, so just, if you're ready, Fernanda, just call out, "Whoever sent this one and all the other ones in my family, stop hiding, come forward." And let me know what happens.

Fernanda: Yeah, I see two, like two witch doctors.

Bob: Mm-hmm, okay.

Fernanda: And the woman, the president's wife.

Bob: Yeah. Okay, great. How do you feel toward them? Are any parts of you scared of them?

Fernanda: No.

Bob: Okay. Are all your parts ready to have this go, have them go?

Fernanda: Definitely.

Bob: Okay. Surround this, surround the three of them with a ball or egg-shaped container of light. And tell them, "It's time for you to go and to remove all the objects you've implanted in all of my family — my children, my sisters, their children, my brother. It's time for all of that to go."

Fernanda: You know, Bob, my father is sort of saying, "I need to come in."

Bob: What does he want to say?

Fernanda: He wants to be a part of it because it was through him.

Bob: Okay. Is he still alive, Fernanda?

Fernanda: No.

Bob: Okay. So how does it feel… how are you feeling toward his spirit as it comes in? Is it good to see him?

Fernanda: It is… he's, um, he's sort of apologizing because he didn't believe in all this, and he was only concerned with his honor and stuff but not with this part — that what he did would affect all of us on another level, so he's, um…

Bob: Yeah. What do you say to him about that, Fernanda?

Fernanda: That he did the best he could… he didn't know.

Bob: Yeah. And as you tell him that, how does he respond?

Fernanda: Yeah, he's grateful, but he still wants to, um, he was a fighter, so he kind of wants to, wants to fight, or yell at these beings.

Bob: Okay. Yeah, that makes sense. Tell him this, this is one of the tricks of beings like this. They stay connected to us by making us angry at them. And your anger can become a spear that keeps you connected to them. The thing you can do, which may be extremely difficult for you, but this is what you can do for your family, is to put down that spear and send these beings away. And even, if you can, say, "Go in peace" or "Vaya con Dios."

Fernanda: Oh, he didn't believe in God, but okay.

Bob: Okay, don't let me…

Fernanda: No God.

Bob: No God, okay, sorry.

Fernanda: Well, maybe he does now, I don't know.

Bob: Yeah, well, you could just ask. Can he say one of those with his heart, from his heart?

Fernanda: You know, when you said this thing about the spear, he, um, he sort of, um, produced a spear of light.

Bob: Okay, great.

Fernanda: But he's kind of saying that, that he would like to have the cooperation of all of us, all of the affected ones.

Bob: Mm-hmm.

Fernanda: First, we can forgive him, no?

Bob: Yeah.

Fernanda: And, and then to, you know, to unite.

Bob: Yeah, yeah. Well, can you do that, Fernanda, from your heart, wholeheartedly? "I forgive you, Father."

Fernanda: Mm-hmm.

Bob: Yeah.

Fernanda: Mm-hmm. I'm sort of laughing because he never believed in my hocus-pocus. No, he always, you know, he wanted me to be a doctor or a lawyer, or something else.

Bob: Mm-hmm, yeah. And maybe that blind spot made him extra vulnerable.

Fernanda: He's saying that I was the one who helped him, you know, in the transition of death, and that now he believes me.

Bob: Great. If this is right for you, Fernanda, ask him, "Do you now have allies and guides up there who could help us do this in a good way?"

Fernanda: I don't know if I'm making this up, Bob, okay…

Bob: Mm-hmm.

Fernanda: But when he died, I did, you know, Poa, the Tibetan ritual, and I called in Padmasambhava, one of the…

Bob: Yeah, I know.

Fernanda: Okay. Of course, he didn't believe in any of that, but I did. And then I got messages from him after death. And so, I'm seeing Padmasambhava on top of him, and I don't know if I'm making it up.

Bob: This is wonderful, Fernanda. A fact about Padmasambhava and his career is that when he went to Tibet to introduce Buddhism, they were all the native gods of Bon, the native shamanism, and they resisted him. And he subdued them and converted them all to the Dharma.

Fernanda: Yes.

Bob: So we couldn't have a more perfect person to do this work.

Fernanda: I haven't seen him in a long time.

Bob: If it feels right, thank him for coming.

Fernanda: You know, I cremated my father with one of those little Padmasambhava stamps, you know, so, okay.

Bob: The perfect one.

Fernanda: Yeah.

Bob: Now, if you hear any advice from Padmasambhava, follow him, ignore me, okay? Here's what I think, if your dad and if Padmasambhava are ready, go gather from all your relatives who've been afflicted, gather the nasty parts that have been put in them. And gather them into that ball of light with the two witch doctors and the president's wife. And let me know how that goes for you.

Fernanda: Um, it's like with his trident, he's um, taking all of that.

Bob: Mm-hmm.

Fernanda: And um, and yes, putting it in a huge ball.

Bob: Great, great.

Fernanda: But…

Bob: Yes?

Fernanda: Something like um, like, there's, there's poison left in like the blood, you know, in the bloodline.

Bob: Okay, so just have him help you pull that out, too. All that poison can come out, and it can go into that ball with the others. And as he's doing this, there's something I want to say to all those beings who are going into that ball now. They can leave safely; they no longer have to obey those witch doctors or the president's wife. They can all go safely to the healing realms, where they'll be free and they'll be welcomed, and they will be received with joy, and they will be able to heal, too. So they can start leaving the witch doctors even as the poison keeps coming out of your blood and your family's blood.

Fernanda: They are all going because they're like, um, not even minions, you know, they're just formless. They're all, you know, going happily.

Bob: Great.

Fernanda: But the witch doctors are scared.

Bob: Yeah. Tell the witch doctors, "We're not here to punish you, we're not here to judge you. You too can go to places where you can heal, but you cannot stay here any longer. And none of your agents can stay here any longer." Are the poisons out of your blood and your family's blood, Fernanda?

Fernanda: I think so.

Bob: Okay, just check one more time, and ask Padmasambhava to help.

Fernanda: He's, um, he's sort of pouring, like, this elixir of life.

Bob: Great.

Fernanda: Into the, um…

Bob: Yeah. Okay, great. I want you to focus on those two witch doctors now, and I want you to just say some things with me, okay? "You and your minions are no longer welcome in my body in any way... You and your minions are no longer welcome in my emotions in any way... You and your minions are no longer welcome in my thoughts in any way... You and your minions are no longer welcome in my protectors, my managers, my exiles in any way... You and your minions are no longer welcome in my beliefs in any way... And you're no longer welcome in my spirit in any way. It's time for you to go."

Fernanda: And I add, nor in my daughters.

Bob: Yes, or your whole family, yes. Great, wonderful, Fernanda. Not in my daughters, not in my family, not in our blood. You have to go completely. And maybe Padmasambhava will want to add to that or modify it.

Fernanda: And the future generations.

Bob: And the future generations, great, great. Really good.

Fernanda: It's like the other ones are gone, but the witch doctors are like stuck to the ground, I don't know how.

Bob: Okay. Tell them this: "It's true, you get choice, just as I have choice and my family has choice, you have choice. You can choose to stay in the darkness, but you know that without all those slaves and soldiers you had, you know what's going to happen to you when you go back to the darkness. Or you can go to the light, where you'll be welcomed and healed; they won't punish you either. And if you have the courage, just look up. You might see something like a tunnel, and at the far end of that, there will be light and a bunch of kind beings leaning down to help you. If you have the courage, you can go there. But you cannot stay here." And ask Padmasambhava if he wants to deal with this now.

Fernanda: He, um, when you were speaking, he showed them an image of what it would be like if they, you know, they decided to stay on the dark side, and they were sort of scared.

Bob: Yeah.

Fernanda: Um, so now they have their backs toward us, and one of them is starting to look up.

Bob: Great.

Fernanda: Fearful.

Bob: Mm-hmm, yeah.

Fernanda: Like, they feel they are betraying all of their beliefs.

Bob: And tell them, if they need us to, we can go and talk to whatever forces have bossed them around and deal with those, too.

Fernanda: Padmasambhava is kind of happy, you know, about that. He's like saying, "You know, bring it on."

Bob: Yeah.

Fernanda: He likes you.

Bob: Oh, I'm honored.

Fernanda: "You're both brave," he says. Um, those guys are scared of bringing the boss.

Bob: Okay. Well, tell them they can just go to the light if they want and they will be safe, and there's nothing the boss can do about it. And tell them to notice that their big boss is scared to come. He's hiding in the dark. Powerful beings don't hide in the dark.

Fernanda: Oh, you got to its pride.

Bob: Well, it can stay hidden if it needs to, or it can come forward.

Fernanda: Oh, you know, he's not stupid — he's scared.

Bob: Okay, tell him we mean him no harm. We're not going to punish him or judge him. He can change now and he will be forgiven and loved, but he doesn't need to. He does need to leave you, your family, and your lineage totally alone. That's over.

Fernanda: Um, he shows himself as like a dark ball.

Bob: Mm-hmm.

Fernanda: And I have the feeling that it goes back to Africa.

Bob: Yeah, okay. Tell him this, the same thing: "If you wish, if you have the courage, look up. And you will see kind beings, ones you loved all the way back in Africa, calling you home. You've been in exile way too long."

Fernanda: He's kind of, you know, he has an eye toward Padmasambhava, who is with the, you know, with the trident, like that, and trying to look up with this one, trying to believe you.

Bob: Yeah. Tell him this: "I'm pretty sure Padmasambhava will not hurt you as long as you're looking up, and you can even ask Padmasambhava that."

Fernanda: Will not what? I'm sorry, I coughed and…

Bob: "Hurt you, as long as you're looking up."

Fernanda: Well, you know, he has a trident toward, okay, but…

Bob: Can this one look up despite its fear of Padmasambhava?

Fernanda: It's like it has no choice because if he stays, it knows that Padmasambhava will, I don't know what, burst the bubble with his thing.

Bob: Yeah.

Fernanda: So it just sort of has no choice. The other ones ran, the other two.

Bob: Okay, did they go up to the light?

Fernanda: I don't know, they went, maybe.

Bob: Well, we'll deal with them later. Let's get this one.

Fernanda: He's sort of in awe, looking a little bit up.

Bob: And what does he see?

Fernanda: White, and he's black.

Bob: Yeah.

Fernanda: Like a gnome.

Bob: Yeah. Can he see the kind beings, his ancestors, leaning down to help him?

Fernanda: Oh, yes.

Bob: They have been missing him.

Fernanda: Yes.

Bob: Can he feel that?

Fernanda: Whoa, yes.

Bob: They want him home. Can he feel that? Ask him, "Can you go now?" Yeah. And if you and your father and your whole lineage can say this with your whole heart, say, "Go in peace."

Fernanda: No God.

Bob: No God. Didn't mention God — just "Go in peace."

Fernanda: Yeah.

Bob: Yeah. And let me know when that dark ball has disappeared entirely, back to its ancestors.

Fernanda: It's gone. (many tears)

Bob: Okay. Great. Real good. The emotions are great, Fernanda. If it's okay with you, let them flow. And did the other two, the ones who this big one had sent, did they go up there to the ancestors, too?

Fernanda: They followed. They had to run off, but they followed.

Bob: Yeah.

Fernanda: Yeah.

Bob: Yeah, great. Ask Padmasambhava, maybe thank him, bow to him a little.

Fernanda: Yeah.

Bob: Yeah. And he was pouring an elixir before into you and maybe into your whole family and all your descendants. Let's just take the time to let that come in. And if he has other ideas, listen to him, not me. Okay, Fernanda. Does this elixir feel good? Yeah. You need to keep inviting it in and welcoming it. These good beings will not come in without an invitation.

Fernanda: I had forgotten to ask so much.

Bob: Yeah.

Fernanda: I had lost faith.

Bob: Yeah. Welcome, welcome, welcome. Ask the part of you whose faith was so damaged by these beings, "Can you welcome this elixir, too?"

Fernanda: Yeah.

Bob: Ask all of your parts, "Can you welcome this elixir?" Invite everyone in there, drink and drink and drink until they start overflowing. And when they're overflowing, let the overflow run down through you and into your descendants — the ones who are alive now and the ones who are as yet unborn. And let the overflow also run out to your siblings and their children and their descendants. And ask Padmasambhava to bless this, bless you and your whole family, and ask him if there are any directions or things we missed or should do. Is there any word, does he have any word for us?

You're doing great, Fernanda. Keep inviting the elixir in. "Welcome, welcome, I'm so glad you're here. I've needed you for so long. Welcome. Come into every organ of my body, come into my womb, come into all the places where those bad energies got in. Wash through, cleanse my family, fill me up."

Fernanda: He's just saying thank you and that he's glad that I could make the time.

Bob: Yeah, yeah.

Fernanda: That he has proven time and time again that he was there and that I know it, because I like confirmation, so he has given me quite a few.

Bob: Yeah.

Fernanda: So I'm waiting for one.

Bob: And maybe tell him this, only if it's true for you — if not, throw it out. Say, "I am so sorry that those beings damaged my faith in you. That was one of the worst wounds they gave me." And as this elixir, this energy, is flowing through every organ of your body, every part of you, and overflowing into your descendants and all your relatives, you know, you can't hang onto this, Fernanda. The way to get more is to give it away. The more you give it away, the more it comes in.

Fernanda: Yes.

Bob: And it becomes like a river. It's completely effortless. And as it flows through you and your family, it can wash away any remaining stuff. And it might reveal new treasures, you know, the way streams sometimes reveal what was buried under them. Crystals and gems, I don't know. And ask Padmasambhava if there's anything else he wants today.

Fernanda: He's, um, no, he says it's done and, um, just that when I do my practices, he will make sure that these, whatever energies, because they come near when I do practice, he will make sure that they stay away in a protective circle. They're not allowed to come in, so, um, and he's saying we did a great job. You too, Bob, and all of the ones that are hiding there behind.

Bob: And I'm very much aware I could have done nothing without him and his energy. I'm a fool, but I'm not enough of a fool to think I really did this at all.

Fernanda: But you have been the bridge. Thank you.

Bob: Okay, take your time. Take your time. Yeah, it's okay, just keep letting that emotion flow. And you know that elixir, that golden fluid, can keep flowing into you, whether it's in your awareness or not, and it can flow through you to all those you come in contact with. I'm nasty enough to sort of wish it didn't have to go to the people I don't like, but it seems to have to.

Fernanda: Oh, maybe they can stay outside the circle.

Bob: Yeah. No, it just, I think it just has to go to everybody.

Fernanda: I know, I know.

Bob: Okay. Gently coming back, take your time. A few deep, easy breaths to help you just come back in a sweet, gentle way. No need to rush, nothing jarring. Okay, good. Really good.

Fernanda: Thank you.

Bob: Thank you and thank Padmasambhava.

Fernanda: He has scared me a few times, you know. In a good way. Once I was in the Himalayas, and I spent a night in one of the caves where he had been meditating, and, uh, and I was doing his mantra and praying and praying that he show up, and then I thought no, no, please don't show up because there was a… you know, how can I say… his presence was on top of this cave, and then it was all the way into the cave. I said, "Please don't show up like that because, you know, you might scare me." But he showed up very nicely, gently, and gave me some information, so he's been there.

Bob: Yeah. Great.

Fernanda: Thank you.

Bob: You're very welcome.

Fernanda: Thank you.

Bob: Do you know about… there's a particular kind of seed that grows in the Himalayas that they make malas out of that's supposed to protect you from bad spirits… rudraksha, I think. I could get the exact name if you…

Fernanda: Rudraksha, rudraksha. I have some, yes, Bob. I have a mala made of that. And I have one special one, which is just, yeah.

Bob: For people who like that kind of thing, those and the smoky quartz are favorite protection items, but I don't think you need that. You have Padmasambhava on the inside — you don't need the seeds or the quartz.

Fernanda: Yeah. Little by little I have been getting rid of my ritual objects, but I'd rather have him inside or around.

Bob: Yeah, and I don't think the ritual objects are bad. I love them, but I don't use them very much.

Fernanda: I don't either anymore — just a little.

Bob: Should we call back your friends?

Fernanda: Yes, please.

Bob: Please join us, everybody. Are you open to some feedback, Fernanda?

Fernanda: Yeah, sure.

Feedback and Questions

Bob: Okay, You guys know, heart first.

Kerri: I am so overjoyed, Fernanda, for you. Just so overjoyed. Reconnecting with your guide has been a theme, and I'm just honored to have witnessed it. I'm just so, so overjoyed for you. Really, really beautiful.

Gina: I could feel the waves of love and healing going out to your two daughters and to the future, like generation upon generation. Can feel it so strongly like it's still happening, so yeah, beautiful. So powerful and beautiful.

Jackie: It was such a gorgeous demonstration of the connections through the generations back, and then it was beautiful to watch you wash it forward. It was such a... the scope was so big and just... you could feel the power of it all the way. I'm very far away from you, but it was palpable. Thank you so much. It is... it will stay with me forever, and I feel really, really, really honored. Thank you.

Bob: Great. Do you want to say anything now, Fernanda? Or I've got a bunch of comments I wanna make.

Fernanda: Go ahead, Bob, I can't speak. I've said enough.

Bob: Okay. I had the intuition, insight, fantasy, whatever you want to call it, that the poisons the two witch doctors carried were actually the hatred and vengeance and misery of generations and generations of slaves who were ripped out of Africa and brought over here. And that's where they got their power — by distilling and concentrating and focusing that hatred and that immense pain. It's like an ocean of pain, a reservoir of toxins.

Fernanda: You know what, Bob, what really, I don't know, struck me or made me very emotional was when you said to this, the dark ball, "Just look at your ancestors waiting for you." It was so touching because he was, you know, couldn't believe it. It was a beautiful moment.

Bob: Yeah. And I said that precisely because I just got this sort of intuition that this is the hatred and loneliness and unbelievable pain of millions of Black people ripped out of their environment and disconnected from all that.

Fernanda: And the distortion because their original religion or beliefs might not be, you know, dark, no, but when they brought them over, they had to do it to defend themselves from everything. So, yes, yes, thank you.

In Nepal, I've seen them [the oracles]. And it's really, I mean, amazing what they do, like you say, with those heavy things. There are a lot of oracles up there, and they get possessed. Last time I went there to the Himalayas, I got very sick with the altitude, and so I went to see the oracle of Lei. She was an old woman dressed in this Tibetan thing, and yes, she dances, and she does things, and then she took out... I had a terrible headache for a week because of the altitude, so she took out like a wooden straw and she put it on my head, and she sucked out blood. And that was it. I was great for the next two months when I was up there, perfect. So they do very strange things, yes. I know the oracles up there.

And you know, I had two things that I thought of working on during this session. One was this family curse, and the other was my obstacle to faith, exactly, but they're totally linked, and so we did two in one.

Bob: Yep, very often when you've got two issues, somebody says, "I've got two issues," they're actually the same.

Fernanda: So, thank you so much.

Bob: That's one of the classic things these UBs attack is your faith or connection. Another one of their classic things is you don't deserve love, you're so bad and nasty, you don't deserve love. Which is also sort of an oblique attack on faith, connection, love, owning, all of that.

Jackie: I was wondering, I think my… so I had a question about… I noticed she had a part that came in, and you did address that, but there weren't a lot of other parts, so is that just because she was so clear and you had a sense of it, so you didn't check?

Bob: When these things come in as curses, there's usually a lot less attachment to them.

Jackie: Okay, that makes sense, that makes sense. Because she didn't seem very attached to it — she just had the effects of it. That makes so much sense. Okay.

Bob: Yeah, but I did check a couple times. Are there any parts in there who it's still attached to… you know, check again… anybody gonna miss it? She was real strong and clear: "No, no." And if she'd even been a little bit hesitant about that, I would have stopped and done more.

Fernanda: And also, I have been trying to clear this for many years, and the session I did a couple of weeks ago with my therapist was, you know, also gave me a lot of light, so…

Bob: Mm-hmm. Yeah, I think it felt obvious that there'd been a lot of clearing away before I got here. A whole lot of clearing away of stuff. Mm-hmm, Kerri?

Kerri: Um, I have a question… this is just a nuanced… and it might be cultural, but um, before witnessing this, Fernanda, I didn't know the difference between a curse and a legacy burden, and this seems more like a curse, and is that right, Bob, you wouldn't call this a legacy burden?

Bob: Yeah, yeah, it could be. And very often, UBs get handed down as legacies. So are they a legacy burden or a UB? I let the client use whatever language they want to use.

Kerri: Okay.

Bob: And a lot of times, people are so uncomfortable with the whole idea of UBs, they'll want to call all UBs legacy burdens. I'm fine with that, no problem. If you want to call it pasta, I'll call it pasta — it doesn't matter.

Kerri: I just wasn't sure if one was just an IFS term and *curse* is more cultural, that's all. But yeah, it's whatever…

Bob: I think they're different things.

Kerri: Oh, okay.

Bob: The curse… actually, someone from the outside intentionally put nasty stuff into Fernanda's family system and into Fernanda.

Kerri: Yeah, and that's different.

Bob: A lot of legacy burdens are not like that. Sometimes they are, but…

Kerri: Now I understand.

Bob: I'm just thinking of this very odd thing. There's a series of novels, and this is fiction, but this guy wrote three novels, and the basic premise of them all is that WWI and WWII were caused by a bunch of shamans in Africa as revenge for colonialism.

Fernanda: Okay. So a curse would be put intentionally, while a legacy burden might just come out of emotions?

Bob: Yeah, all sorts of other stuff. Child abuse, abortion, all kinds of stuff. But sometimes… I've worked with a lot of Eastern European Jewish people, and they have big legacy burdens. Scarcity, don't shine, hide, all that kind of stuff. But some of their stuff was also like a curse that came in from the Cossacks, who were the Russian group that was really big on terrorizing and annihilating them. They'd ride into the shtetl on horses and slice everybody up, but they were also radiating all this hatred and the idea that you're not human, you're just vermin. So some of these people picked that up from the Cossacks. Now that's sort of a curse, but does the line matter? Is this a curse or a legacy burden or…? Does this matter? I think almost all these words are just sort of helpful trail markers for us therapists. They don't capture anything of the essence, and they're not even necessary. I think that's also true with the names "firefighter," "manager," "exile." I don't even discuss that stuff with clients unless they ask, and then I usually… the first thing I say is just hold this really lightly.

Bob: When your dad's spirit came in wanting to fight, the session could have gone into a bad direction then.

Fernanda: Mm-hmm.

Bob: It could have gone into hate and fighting, which beings like... those two witch doctors, they love that.

Fernanda: Yeah.

Bob: They love that.

Fernanda: Yeah. When I think about it, how stupid, no, I mean, just because they were not allowed to fly in privately and they had to fly commercial and all of this, I mean, it's really stupid.

Bob: Yeah, I think the stupidity belongs to the president's wife.

Fernanda: Absolutely, I have no doubt. I have no doubt.

Bob: But there's plenty of stupidity to go around. (laughter)

Fernanda: Yeah. I mean, a lot of ignorance, but it's really scary how because of all this ignorance, so many generations and so many people can get affected.

Bob: Yeah. The thing I'm going to be thinking and pondering more is the sense of this reservoir of hatred and pain.

Fernanda: Mm-hmm. Yes, because if we could get to that, and clear that more instead of individual things, it would help so much.

Bob: Instead of exploiting it and using it to damage others.

Fernanda: Yes.

Bob: You know, this guy Martin Prechtl is Mayan from one of the small tribes in Guatemala who came to the US, was sort of a shaman, and he has this idea that grieving is a necessary thing we do for the souls of the dead that helps them pass over. He says the tears create an ocean they can paddle their canoes across, and the power of our grief is their paddles, and without that they can't go. He was up here giving a class to a bunch of white guys at a men's gathering, and he started laughing. He said, "You and your families have not grieved your ancestors for two hundred years. When they are not grieved, they don't go — they become ghosts." He said, "There's enough work in this room to keep me busy for my whole lifetime." He's the guy who wrote that book *The Smell of Rain on Dust*.

Jackie: Can I ask, so, um, the visual in my mind was the two shamans standing on the earth and, but I also had the president's wife, um, can I ask where she went?

Fernanda: I just saw the two of them, the two witch doctors, they're not even shamans.

Bob: Mm-hmm.

Fernanda: Um, I really didn't pay attention to her. I don't know.

Bob: Yeah.

Fernanda: Well, her karma, I don't know where she went. It will be taken care of.

Bob: Yeah, and if she shows up again, we can deal with her easily.

Fernanda: I don't think she will.

Bob: I don't either.

Gina: A little comment.

Bob: Mm-hmm.

Gina: Um, yeah, I just noticed, Bob, when you were inviting Fernanda to kinda stay with you, um, I guess I'll call an invocation where you say, "You nor your minions are no longer welcome in my body in any way" and you went through. You added, right, "My protectors, managers, my exiles," and I'm like ooh, I like the sound of that. There's something about it that, I didn't, I'm like, I think he added that, I don't know for sure. But it struck me that, to me it felt new and I liked it, but maybe you've always said it, but I just heard it for the first time.

Bob: Nope, no, I started adding that, and I only do it with people who know IFS quite well. And what I'm really doing with that inventory is I'm looking to see if there are any parts of her, any aspects of her, where any of this is still stuck.

Gina: Yeah.

Bob: Because if there are, there'll be a reaction in her body. I was watching her very closely, looking for any physical reactions.

Gina: Oh yeah.

Bob: There wasn't — they were all clear.

Gina: Right.

Bob: I've even had in other people this… you know, I'd go through this whole thing and say, "You're no longer welcome in my beliefs," and the UB couldn't resist it, because it's so proud, says, "I'm still in her beliefs."

Fernanda: Outspoken.

Bob: Yeah, yeah, it was like, "Ah, no I'm not." So, that's why I do that — it's sort of a checking through. And you're right, I did, I am adding the parts now there, too.

Fernanda: I liked that part very much, that adding, because it went also to the part of me too that had lost its faith, so, mm-hmm.

Bob: Mm-hmm.

Fernanda: Yeah.

Kerri: Can I ask a general question about post-care?

Bob: Sure.

Kerri: Um, I don't mean to shift the topic, but perhaps as we've gone through this it'll help other people, but is it common or possible that you can subconsciously begin to put into place what used to be there because it used to be comfortable?

Bob: Yeah, yeah. And there's several things we did to prevent that. It sort of started… happened very organically, and I didn't even have to ask for them. Primarily it was the golden fluid that Padmasambhava started pouring in. There were no empty spaces left in Fernanda to be filled up with the old patterns. And very often I will ask some questions about stuff like that. Now, I happen to know Fernanda well enough to know that she has a regular practice of checking in with her parts and, you know, a daily sort of inner work practice. So if I didn't know that, I would be very careful to encourage her, "You need to stay in touch with these parts on a daily basis, especially the one who felt it lost its faith." I would have gone through a whole bunch of stuff like that, but because I know Fernanda's already got that down, I didn't do it. So you didn't see me doing that because it sort of happened all on its own.

And there is… one thing I'm using more and more is when people have gotten rid of a big thing of this, I ask them to notice if there are any indentations or emptinesses or hollownesses in or around their body anywhere, and if nothing came through for when I did the open space for guides, I'll just say, "Can you look inside and focus on your… you'll find a spark of light in there, or you may experience it as warmth or vibrations, the center of your life force. And just focus on that and open up to all the details, and as you know, anything you focus on in the inner world will grow. And just keep focusing and, you know, watch it grow and see as it grows and fills your whole body. And notice from the inside out, it fills those indentations. Notice if there are any dark areas or obstructions as it fills your body, and don't fight with them — we'll just make notes and come back to them. And then have it go, when it's filled your whole body, have it go poof, out of your body to a couple feet all around you. See if there are any holes or things in that area all around you. And that way, you've filled from the inside out. You haven't tried to make a border because that's always sort of vulnerable… no matter how big that border is, it's always sort of a pain in the ass and has to be maintained. But if you fill from the inside, from the core out, it isn't vulnerable in that same way. And it's always diagnostic — it tells you where your next sessions have to go. So that's what I've been doing that now because I think it does a lot more than just create borders. But yeah, there is a lot of aftercare stuff, and with Fernanda it sort of just all happened on its own. Or with Padmasambhava.

Fernanda: I'm so glad you know him, Bob, because, you know, it did help a lot the way you were guiding me about him.

Bob: Any questions in our last few minutes?

Fernanda: I'm just really… no, I'm sure, I'm sure that this is gone.

Bob: Great.

Fernanda: And um, I'm just very grateful, Bob.

Bob: Yeah, and I'm very honored to have been allowed to help here.

Fernanda: Two in one, but don't charge me more, okay. (laughter)

Bob: And you know, if there are little bits of this left somewhere in your lineage, we can get them out. It's not a problem, nothing to be scared of. It's like when you sweep the house — oh, I missed that corner, you go back. I don't think there is either, but if there is, it's not a big deal.

Fernanda: We would have to wait and see, you know. Everybody is so scared of having children.

Bob: Yeah. Maybe some of that fear can go too now.

Fernanda: And my niece that has Down syndrome, she now has Alzheimer's also, so she's dying. She's dying. So, you know. It's really good that this thing is gone.

Bob: Yeah, really good.

Fernanda: Yeah. Thank you so much.

Bob: Thank you, Fernanda. Thank you all.

Fernanda: Thank you.

Gina: And Padmasambhava.

Fernanda: Yeah.

CHAPTER 15

Advanced Cases

Bob and Luke

Luke is a very experienced IFS therapist. He had an extremely disturbing dream about an insect-like creature.

Luke: Thank you. Okay, so I go inside.

Bob: Mm-hmm, and focus on that image.

Luke: Yes.

Bob: The insect.

Luke: I can see it.

Bob: Okay.

Luke: And I can also see the leg of the table where it was coming from, the hole in it.

Bob: Mm-hmm.

Luke: And I can get this creepy feeling from the insect.

Bob: Okay.

Luke: And this extremely strong feeling of discomfort — it's so incredibly discomforting for me.

Bob: Okay. So let's find the part of you who feels this incredible discomfort. Can you find that one, Luke?

Luke: Yeah, it's coming from my lower abdomen.

Bob: Mm-hmm.

Luke: It's like a wave coming up like that.

Bob: Mm-hmm.

Luke: From there. There's definitely a very young part there that feels almost nauseous.

Bob: How are you feeling toward it?

Luke: I'm curious. And funnily enough, I'm a little worried about this part — is it too much for it, and has it been too much for it to be in this kind of energy for so long.

Bob: Okay. Ask that worried part if it could relax back and let us just be with the young part from Self and see. If it can't, that's okay, too.

Luke: It really doesn't want to.

Bob: Okay. Welcome, welcome. Ask the worried part, "What are you afraid would happen if we go to this young one who's been in this weird energy for so long?"

Luke: It says, "Secrets will be revealed."

Bob: Oh, and what's bad about secrets being revealed?

Luke: I think it's afraid that it could be something sexual. It could also have this kind of connection to my mother imposing this sexuality very early in that kind of emotional sense. It seems that there is a real concern about discovering something about her.

Bob: Okay, okay. So, suppose you discover something really nasty about your mom, what's the worst thing about that?

Luke: It would be a relief.

Bob: It would be a relief?

Luke: Yeah.

Bob: Yeah.

Luke: Yeah. And when I look at it from that angle, I don't think it would be so terrible either. I think it's more about her psychological condition. I don't think she has been doing anything sexual in that sense toward me, but it's more like this feeling of weight of her needs or desires or longing and this feeling of much too much.

Bob: Mm-hmm.

Luke: Being suffocated and feeling un-fresh in a way.

Bob: Yeah, let this part know that's why we wanna go in there — to get all this stuff out of your system. And see if it's willing to give us room to do that or not. It gets to say no, absolutely.

Luke: It really would love us to do that now.

Bob: Okay. Thank it so much for showing up and telling us about its concerns.

Luke: Yes. It's really feeling heard.

Bob: Good, good. So focusing back on that part that was down in your stomach that felt the repulsion the most, the nausea about this insect, how are you feeling toward that one now?

Luke: I'm curious.

Bob: Great.

Luke: Yeah.

Bob: Offer it your curiosity and see how it responds.

Luke: I feel a real surge of compassion for it because it seems to be so miserable, it's incredible. It's misery upon misery. It's like it's crawling around, and it's like it's been abandoned.

Bob: Mm-hmm.

Luke: A real little child, and it seems to be crawling around in feces or something like that.

Bob: Yeah. Extend the wave of compassion very gently. This being may never have experienced compassion in its whole existence. So real gentle and slow, Luke.

Luke: Yes.

Bob: Offer it some compassion and see how it responds to you.

Luke: It's very surprised. It's sort of looking around… Where is this wave of compassion coming from? What is it? It's not like it's frightened — it's really… it's a tough little one also. It doesn't expect anything.

Bob: Yeah.

Luke: Yeah.

Bob: Mm-hmm.

Luke: And it starts to enjoy the sort of a breeze of compassion that's coming to it. Oh, this feels nice. And also like it… it didn't know that something could feel nice.

Bob: Yeah, great. Great.

Luke: Yeah.

Bob: And ask it, "Would it be okay if I got a little closer so that you could see me?" And let it know that it has control now.

Luke: It would be okay.

Bob: Great. So get as close as it wants and let it decide what the best distance between the two of you is.

Luke: Yeah, it's surprised at how big I am, how tall I am.

Bob: Mm-hmm.

Luke: And it's a very small baby; it's much smaller than a normal baby would be also, or at least it perceives me in that way, that I am extremely big.

Bob: Mm-hmm.

Luke: But it's totally trusting toward me. It actually would like me to get so close that it can touch me and crawl up my leg.

Bob: Mm-hmm, is that okay with you, Luke?

Luke: Yeah, totally. It wants to crawl up my right leg. It's doing it now, it's at the knee now. But what is weird now is that it's sort of changing more and more into a grasshopper or an insect.

Bob: Okay. Why don't you ask it this: "Did you take on any energies that weren't really part of you in order to survive back then?"

Luke: I think that it is afraid of admitting it because it's afraid if there are any repercussions about it. It's not total shame — it's on its way to shame, but it's more like it feels guilty. It's really afraid of being punished, and it says yes. Since then, I can see that, it has done that — it gives it strength.

Bob: Yeah.

Luke: Yeah.

Bob: Tell it this: "It's perfectly natural that you would take on other energies. This might well have saved your life and Luke's life." See how it responds to that.

Luke: It really likes what you're saying, and at the same time, it is sort of looking down at itself and also looking back and saying, "But I knew it was wrong — I knew it was wrong energy."

Bob: Mm-hmm.

Luke: But I needed it.

Bob: Yeah.

Luke: Yeah.

Bob: Yeah. How do you feel toward it as it tells you that, Luke?

Luke: I still feel very compassionate and even a kind of understanding compassion because I can see how important it was for this little creature to survive and to do that.

Bob: Yeah.

Luke: Yeah.

Bob: It may have actually been a matter of life or death.

Luke: Yeah.

Bob: So offer it your compassion and ask it, "Can you take in, taste, a drop or two of my compassion? Maybe take it on your fingertip and put it to your lips. Then you'll know it's real. Your own body will tell you."

Luke: It's… that little baby is very curious, yeah, it's like a tingle on the lips of it, and it says that it can't have both. And it means that it can't have the UB energy and compassion at the same time because they are opposite.

Bob: Mm-hmm. There's some truth in there. Tell the little baby, "Here's our plan, here's what we want… We want you to come and connect to Luke and let go of that UB energy and say goodbye, because that UB energy actually drained you and kept you weak even though it offered you something you needed to survive. It's not really good for you, and it's not really good for the UB to stay with you either. It's also a lost and suffering being we need to help get on to where it belongs. But with Luke, you'll have a whole new kind of relationship that will get deeper and will make you stronger and stronger," and see what the baby says about this.

Luke: The first reaction was that it is scared of letting go of the UB energy because that's all it knows, and then when you said that it was also beneficial for the UB to, or the baby to let go of the UB energy, something shifted and it was like the baby became a little bit more mature and a little bit more conscious in a way.

Bob: Mm-hmm.

Luke: It has started to crawl up my leg now again and going much higher into the torso. It wants to go to my heart.

Bob: Wonderful.

Luke: And it wants to let go of that UB energy, and now the insect is becoming active.

Bob: Okay. Okay. So surround the insect in a ball or egg-shaped container of light and just slowly and gently pull it out of your body to a good conversational distance in front of you.

Luke: Yeah, it's there now.

Bob: Okay. And tell it, "We don't want to judge you, we don't want to punish you. You are a lost and suffering being… even though you may pretend to be strong and proud and all those things, we know you're suffering. We're going to help you go to where you can find what you really need, the support and healing you should have had all along." And how does the insect respond to all of that?

Luke: It's furious.

Bob: Okay.

Luke: It's sort of trying to send some kind of explosive energy toward me, but the glass is stopping it. It doesn't have that much power, but it's really furious.

Bob: Yeah, that's fine.

Luke: Yeah.

Bob: Yeah. Okay. Just check and see, are there any tubes, cords, connections, anything like that coming from that glass container that get and touch your body, Luke?

Luke: There could be, because the other end of the container was open, the end mostly away from me.

Bob: Yeah.

Luke: So it's like a little bit of a jellyfish also coming… there's some black coming out that wants to grab me.

Bob: Yeah, the key thing is, Luke, are they touching your body?

Luke: There's one going into my umbilical cord.

Bob: Okay, that's really important. Thank you. Look inside there, Luke, and see what part of you is still connected to this.

Luke: It's a very dark part. It's like the umbilical cord is full of ashes, and there's a room inside my belly where there's also a lot of ashes, and in there is a part that is creepy, very creepy. It is sadistic, and it wants to kill things.

Bob: Mm-hmm.

Luke: And very negative.

Bob: Okay.

Luke: Yeah.

Bob: Ask this one, "Are you a part of me?"

Luke: No.

Bob: Okay.

Luke: Absolutely not.

Bob: Okay. Find whatever part of you has let this in.

Luke: It's a scared boy.

Bob: Yeah, yeah. Looked like power back then, didn't it?

Luke: Yeah, and he knows that he has been doing something wrong, or at least he realizes now when he feels my consciousness. And he felt that he was doing the right thing at the moment.

Bob: Mm-hmm. And he might have needed that energy to survive back then.

Luke: Yeah.

Bob: He really might have. How are you feeling toward him right now, Luke?

Luke: I just feel a lot of compassion, and I also feel that he's very justified.

Bob: Yeah. Offer him your compassion and see if he can take it in. Gentle and slow… he's probably never had compassion in his whole existence.

Luke: He is really exiled.

Bob: Yeah.

Luke: In a way, he's more lonely than the first little baby because this little baby was pretty strong. He's sort of been tangled in a spiderweb.

Bob: Yeah.

Luke: He's been in a horrible place full of spiderwebs, and he is… he's more conscious because he's about four years old. And because of that, he also knows much more about his own situation. It's much more reflective, and he is… he has something that was in my family that I was always feeling that I was doing the wrong things. And I never understood what it was that I was doing that it was so wrong, but I was punished for it.

Bob: Yeah.

Luke: And he's very sort of attentive and expecting me to punish him, and he's also ready to be punished even though he doesn't know what he could have done that could be bad.

Bob: Great. And as you offer him the compassion, can he take it in, even a drop?

Luke: Yeah, he can.

Bob: And ask him, "Does this compassion make you stronger?"

Luke: It does, but he does not think that he deserves to be stronger.

Bob: Okay. Tell him that is a classic lie the dark powers tell people and parts, that they don't deserve love and compassion. That's a way they try and keep others enslaved.

Luke: That really goes deep into him. Really deep. And that is something to do with the spiderweb.

Bob: Mm-hmm.

Luke: He can see now that he has been in a kind of spell.

Bob: Yeah.

Luke: That he has been tricked into believing things that were not true.

Bob: Mm-hmm.

Luke: And the funny thing is that he's even been tricked into believing that his parents did not show him love.

Bob: Yeah.

Luke: And this drop of compassion is almost like a guide showing him how it really feels.

Bob: Mm-hmm.

Luke: He still does not feel worthy of love because now he says, "But I have been messing up things so strongly by being ensnared by this unattached burden. So do I really deserve to be taken back now?" And he also feels that he's tainted.

Bob: Yeah. Tell him he's not tainted. And just let him see how you're feeling toward him, Luke. Open your heart.

Luke: Yeah, he's afraid that he will enter my system with the disease of evilness — that's what he calls it.

Bob: Mm-hmm. Tell him, "No, we can get that all out — that's not who you are."

Luke: Now he is reaching out his hand to take my hand.

Bob: Wonderful.

Luke: Yeah.

Bob: That's courage, Luke… that's real courage, I think.

Luke: I can see how his heart is tainted by the unattached burden energy and that he has it there. He's stepping into me now. He's sort of leaving his place and going into nature.

Bob: Mm-hmm, great.

Luke: Yeah.

Bob: Tell him, "We'll get the unattached burden out of you and out of Luke's system entirely, and then if there are any residues left, we can help you unburden them later."

Luke: Yeah. He loves that.

Bob: Yeah.

Luke: He's very aware of, like his skin, how it is a border, and he has never felt rain or wind, or somehow he has never felt nature around him before because he has been in that dreadful place for so long.

Bob: Mm-hmm.

Luke: Death almost. The unattached burden feels like death.

Bob: Yes.

Luke: It's been totally a nightmare.

Bob: Mm-hmm. I'm so glad he survived.

Luke: Yeah, yeah. He is saying something about that he hopes that at least his experiences can be helpful in the system because he feels that he's coming so empty-handed and asking for so much.

Bob: Yeah. How are you feeling toward him?

Luke: I feel that I have a very big heart for him.

Bob: Great. Offer him that really gently and let him know that only beings like him who've lived in the deep hell realms can help others heal from there. And it's a terrible, terrible tuition he has paid for this knowledge, but it's very, very valuable.

Luke: He really likes to hear that. And he asks that he can... he asks for water because he wants to clean the dust off now.

Bob: Great.

Luke: Yeah. He's been so dirty.

Bob: Mm-hmm.

Luke: All this dusty feeling of these caves.

Bob: Mm-hmm. Yeah, so give him... he could have a whole river or an ocean if he wants.

Luke: Yeah, yeah. He wants me to pour water over him, and I'll do that, and it has to be very clean spring water. Very sparkling water and also going through his clothes and everything and yeah, like, his skin is starting to breathe again. The sun is not up yet, and I think that's a good thing because I think the sun would have been too much in the early stages of his return. I can feel it's the morning, and the dew is also in the fields, and everything is... it's a promising morning.

Bob: Mm-hmm.

Luke: And I'm really washing him. In the corners of his eyes, there's a lot of dust, and his nostrils. And I also guess that all his cells will have to let go of the dust over the next days or something like that. I think there's lots to clean out in that sense.

Bob: Yeah.

Luke: And then there is this dark stamp inside his heart that is the UB image, and it doesn't go away. It's very dark.

Bob: Okay.

Luke: Yeah.

Bob: Tell him, when he is completely done with that UB energy, it has to leave his system — it can no longer stay. And then he can heal anything that's left after that. He can heal… he can unburden, just as he's been cleaning the dust.

Luke: He definitely wants it out now.

Bob: Okay, great. So a lot of people use light, again, to sort of comb it out. Anything that's not his can just be removed from his heart and his body and go into that ball of light with that UB. You can comb through your whole body; any last little attachments can go back out there into the ball or egg-shaped container of light, and that thing can become a complete container.

Luke: I feel that there is a light being extending its hands into my heart.

Bob: Hmm.

Luke: And taking the black dirt out, and somehow, this black spot is connected to lizard energy.

Bob: Mm-hmm.

Luke: I get a feeling of a lizard somehow. It's also like an alien or something like that.

Bob: Mm-hmm.

Luke: And it's been there for a very long time.

Bob: Yeah.

Luke: And I'm seeing something very strange now. There was like, like a globe that turned, and then I saw… I see it lying down, and now it's coming up to standing, and I think what I'm looking at is a kind of ritual. It could be a ritual where I got the UB energy into me, or it could be a ritual that the boy has seen. It's not very satanic or something like that… a little bit, but it's not scary, but it's like, it's not in the service of good, definitely. It's more like this is what the unattached burdens do because they want to survive or spread or whatever. And there are some humans that seems to be helping them.

Bob: Yes.

Luke: I have not seen that before.

Bob: Mm-hmm.

Luke: But it makes a lot of sense, and they have a kind of cauldron with a liquid in it that they make people drink, and I think they become possessed by drinking this kind of fluid or whatever it is. It's very cloudy.

Bob: Mm-hmm.

Luke: Yeah it's just standing there. I can't make it collapse.

Bob: Let's go back to that. Are there any connections left from that creature stuck in the ball of light back to your body?

Luke: Yes.

Bob: Okay. Where do they touch your body?

Luke: They go through my chest into my heart still.

Bob: Oh, okay.

Luke: There are some black strings going in there.

Bob: Let's trace those down, Luke.

Luke: Yeah.

Bob: And see who the parts are who are still entangled with this energy.

Luke: There is a boy floating in a dream state. He's unconscious.

Bob: Mm-hmm.

Luke: He seems like he has been brought into this state where… oh, they have access to my system through his dream state.

Bob: Yep.

Luke: So it's important for them that he never comes out of it.

Bob: Yep.

Luke: He's like a portal.

Bob: Yeah, yeah.

Luke: He's lying in some kind of fluid, so that he can just be lying there forever in a sense. I think there is nourishment in that fluid, too.

Bob: Mm-hmm.

Luke: And they have really set it up in there in an interesting way, a supporting way for them. And the water is full of creeps. Not creeps. They're crawling on the backside of the boy, they're eating him from below. There's a lot of them, small and big and on each other. But this fluid is full of it.

Bob: Yeah, yeah. And very often, there are vast fields of boys like that trapped in the fluid.

Luke: Yeah, I can see that.

Bob: Yeah. Kept there and they're being fed off of.

Luke: Yeah, yeah.

Bob: The fluid might give them a little nutrient, but it takes more than it gives, it always does.

Luke: It's so interesting because on the front part, he looks normal. But then when you look from below, he's eaten up.

Bob: Mm-hmm, yeah. Luke, this is where you need to take control here. I'm going to make some suggestions, and you find what seems right.

Luke: Yeah.

Bob: Sometimes you can call to a boy like this in this coma-like dream state… call or sing to him, and he can wake up. Sometimes you can put your hand on his chest. Sometimes you can just send him waves of compassion. I don't know what's going to work best for you at this point, but I know he can wake up and he can get free.

Luke: I can call him. I can definitely call him. He's waking up when I say his name. And I have to admit that I would not like to touch him right now because I feel that he is so slimy and full of all this stuff.

Bob: Mm-hmm.

Luke: He is starting to sit up now in this liquid.

Bob: Great.

Luke: He is very much like a doll or a machine. He's very mechanic.

Bob: Mm-hmm.

Luke: Baring his brain, too, I can see that.

Bob: Yeah.

Luke: Yeah.

Bob: Luke, ask the part of you who feels the repulsion if it can step back and go somewhere safe and comfortable and let us do this.

Luke: It would love to do that, yeah.

Bob: Yeah, it doesn't have to see any of this.

Luke: No.

Bob: And when from Self, from your center, you put a hand on this boy, all that slime disappears. It just goes away.

Luke: Yeah, it does. Yeah.

Bob: And he comes alive again.

Luke: Yeah. I am putting one… my left hand on his shoulder, and my right hand on his forehead, and it's almost like I can push him back to life or something like that. Shake him back to life. Now he's opening his eyes. When he opened his eyes, I could see all these small, dark creatures floating around, and then when the lights come in, they disappear. They flee, so to speak.

Bob: Yeah.

Luke: He's still sitting in this water. He wants to get out of it.

Bob: Yeah.

Luke: So I'm helping him to step out of it, and I can see how they're trying to sort of attack me or spread to me, but the light in me is simply stopping them. They die when they try to.

Bob: Yeah.

Luke: They sort of die in the light. And now he's coming to standing. He's not that small. He's a little wobbly.

Bob: Yeah, of course. Reassure him — let him know he's doing great.

Luke: Yeah. And I can actually shower his back with water.

Bob: Great.

Luke: And there are some almost fishlike things sticking out that I can grab and throw back into the water, the dirty water.

Bob: Yeah.

Luke: All the infected water. They have been taking turns to splash from behind.

Bob: Yeah.

Luke: They're not really, how to say it, they're not demonic creatures in that sense — they're more like, yeah, fish and insects, like a lower class of beings.

Bob: Parasites perhaps.

Luke: Parasites, yeah. Parasites, yeah.

Bob: When you let your light and warmth and compassion shine on him, I believe it will drive all of these things out of him. He will no longer be food for them.

Luke: Yeah.

Bob: He will taste bad to them, and they will flee.

Luke: Incredible amounts of these creatures are streaming out of his back now… they're fleeing. There's so much that it's incredible. It just continues. I think, speaking of the other boys also, he is sort of dragging all these creatures out of the walls and out of these bathtubs, you could call them, and he's just, he's walking forward, and behind him there is just a big pile of these creatures. Now not in water any longer, and I don't think they can survive without their water.

Bob: Yeah.

Luke: And he's walking toward the light.

Bob: Great. Yeah, and very often, when a being who's been trapped like this is freed, it clears an entire area of those wards where all these beings were kept.

Luke: That's what is happening now. He feels really proud about that. They're zombies, but they're starting to wake up. They come out of these bathtubs now and they start to walk, and the closer they walk to the light, the more clear they also become.

Bob: Mm-hmm.

Luke: From Self, it's really easy to be there. I can see how scary it must be for a part to be here because they look like zombies and then they start to become more and more human.

Bob: Yeah.

Luke: And the boy, now there is something in his back — it's the last one screaming because of the light.

Bob: Okay. Tell that one, "What's hurting you is your fear of the light. The light itself with not hurt you. Touch it with one part of your body and you will see that it doesn't actually hurt. You too have been lied to all these years."

Luke: It touches the light with its tail, and it's true that there is no pain. It's slowly being sucked into the light now. It's like it's being sucked from the inside, like the molecules are being slowly sucked, and I can feel how everything remaining is being dragged out of the back of the boy and is really clearing now.

Bob: Great.

Luke: And also from his brain.

Bob: Yeah, and let all the other reptilians, fishlike, insect beings know that they've been lied to about the light, and they saw their brother touch the light and be transformed. As many as want can also do that now. It will not hurt them.

Luke: They are disappearing into the light, and then there was a different kind of boy lying on the floor. He's in a space suit somehow.

Bob: Mm-hmm.

Luke: And he also woke up now, like he really needs help.

Bob: Mm-hmm.

Luke: I think also that he has been lied to. I think that he has been told that the air is toxic — he won't take off his helmet. And he's almost just a skeleton. He has almost been eaten totally now.

Bob: Mm-hmm.

Luke: There is life in him still, but he's really just like a skeleton almost.

Bob: And how do you feel toward him, Luke?

Luke: I'm here for him.

Bob: Great. Let him know, offer him that, and see if he can receive it. It's a huge act of courage if he can receive it.

Luke: Yeah, he can.

Bob: Great, great.

Luke: He even starts to feel just a slight hint of hope. And he's sort of striving forward to get to the light also.

Bob: Mm-hmm.

Luke: And it's like when he is going forward there are sort of, kind of, hard to describe it, like sound waves in the air.

Bob: Mm-hmm.

Luke: Every step he's taking, something's happening to the energy. It's dangerous for the UB energy, I think.

Bob: Yes.

Luke: That they're making these waves in terror or shock or something like that. I think that he's sort of the source of everything in this room from the human side. And he's sort of getting more and more fleshy the closer he gets to the light.

Bob: Great. Is that space suit off of him completely?

Luke: He has the boots on still. I'll have to take that off.

Bob: Yeah.

Luke: Yeah, now he's walking barefoot, and his underwear is being stripped now, so he's totally naked, and there's a strong wind coming. It's a good wind.

Bob: Yes.

Luke: But very forward. He's walking bent over, and I think the wind is sort of stripping him of the energy. I'm reaching out and grabbing his hand, and I'm putting my arm around him and helping him forward.

Bob: Mm-hmm. Just if I can, just as you're leaving that area, remind the UBs, "Those vibrations… if you allow light in, it will not really hurt you. It's your fear that hurts you. You too can be transformed now. Any of you who want can safely go to the healing realms now. You do not have to stay in these hell realms where you have lived for so long."

Luke: Then I suddenly see a lot of scared parts or UBs.

Bob: Mm-hmm.

Luke: That sort of look… suddenly peek back and see the eyes. And is that really true? Can we leave these hellish realms?

Bob: Yes, notice the ones who've already gone and how they were received.

Luke: Now they are marching toward the light, and there is like, there is a feeling in my system that this dungeon has to close. It will just… there's nobody walking there… it doesn't matter if it takes a little time, but this is going to close, and it's going to be closed or even disappear.

Bob: Yes, yes. Wonderful, brilliant.

Luke: And they are walking toward the light, and they are very humble now.

Bob: Mm-hmm.

Luke: And I can sort of see that they have been doing what they thought they should do to survive. It's not like… yeah, they are one species, in a sense, that wants to survive, and they survive, among other things, by feasting on humans.

Bob: Yeah. Ask them, can they see kind beings leaning down to help them?

Luke: Yeah.

Bob: Ah, great. Great.

Luke: Yeah, they can. Oh, and something about "We are in contact with something that is as ancient as time." I can sense earth spirits.

Bob: Mm-hmm.

Luke: … who has this energy and has been trapping in people for centuries, and they are there but, and they sort of… in a way they accept their defeat, let's call it that.

Bob: Mm-hmm.

Luke: They are okay with it in a sense. They also enjoyed the dungeon with all that was going on in there, but they, in a sense, they also feel a kind of relief.

Bob: Mm-hmm. And let them know they too can go to the light, and they will be received with celebration.

Luke: And that was exactly it because they realized that they would also love to go back to God.

Bob: Yeah. Tell them, "You can go safely now."

Luke: They were so full of hopelessness, and suddenly it's like, okay, now they can go back.

Bob: Yeah.

Luke: And with them, the desert goes back. Whatever that means.

Bob: Mm-hmm.

Luke: We are back to Christ and the thornbush in the desert, and there are desert spirits that were tempting him. It's the same, like we are in contact with now. And in a sense, they didn't want to tempt him. They wanted, that was also because they didn't think they could go back to God.

Bob: Mm-hmm.

Luke: And now they are slowly starting to march, and I'll make sure that we get everyone.

Bob: Mm-hmm.

Luke: And I was wondering, is the devil or something behind, but I don't think that there is.

Bob: Mm-hmm.

Luke: They're sort of, they have been, they have strayed into a wrong territory, they have gotten lost. And now they're returning to the source.

Bob: Great.

Luke: And they are sort of melting into the source.

Bob: Wonderful.

Luke: And disappearing.

Bob: Mm-hmm.

Luke: Now the last ones are coming.

Bob: Yeah, let your body do anything it wants, Luke… your body and your breath.

Luke: Yeah.

Bob: Deep wisdom there.

Luke: Yeah. Something is finished now.

Bob: Okay, great. Let's go back to that being in the ball of light in front of you, if it feels like it's ready for that. Is that being still there?

Luke: Yes.

Bob: Okay. Are there any connections of any kind coming back from that being to your body?

Luke: It seems that the connection to my umbilical cord has been severed. It's slowly disappearing like, like when you smoke a cigarette, you can see the ashes.

Bob: Mm-hmm.

Luke: It's going toward this ball of light.

Bob: Mm-hmm.

Luke: And it's really disappearing now, and I can feel this creature inside the ball of light is giving up. It knows that it can't, it can't reach me any longer. It was so safe with this umbilical cord thing going on, it felt that it wouldn't be beaten or how to say it, it would win. But now it doesn't feel that anymore. And now, the insect that I dreamed about is coming crawling. It's sort of leaving the... leaving my body because it's not a good place for it to live any longer. And there's something happening deep inside my diaphragm. Oh, man. There was a big opening in my diaphragm, and I felt that there were intestines that suddenly created space and sort of gone a little bit forward that have sort of been pressed into the body cave. And this insect is slowly crawling to the one in the light, and now they are both of them into this light ball.

Bob: Okay.

Luke: And how would you say it, they're actually enjoying being there.

Bob: Yeah.

Luke: They think that the energy is tickling them in a funny way, and they like it. And now the big light is suddenly behind them, I think because they're ready for it. The light ball is slowly moving them toward the light so that the light will get them at the back end first.

Bob: Okay. Ask them this: "Have you taken everything, every possession, every little thing out of my body? Nothing can stay in me anymore. Take all of your stuff, all of your allies, your employees, your slaves, it all can go now. Take it all with you."

Luke: They said that they had left a stick up in my heart and that was the black spot that I have seen, and they have taken it now. It's on its way out of my body. And they say to me, "You know now you are without our protection."

Bob: Mm-hmm, okay. So to some degree, they're still lying and manipulating.

Luke: Yeah.

Bob: So tell them this, tell them, "You might choose to go back to the darkness — we have no power over that. You have free will just as I do."

Luke: Yeah.

Bob: "But all of your slaves, all of your soldiers, all of your parts, they can all choose to go to the healing realms now. They can safely leave your darkness and go to the light."

Luke: They really feel exposed now in their lie. It was like, damn, how did he know that? And I can see sort of a, a crowd of slaves or whatever… they are going to the light and also letting go of the chains that they have been in. And these slaves have also discovered that they were not actually tied — they just believed that they were tied up.

Bob: Yes!

Luke: Just let go of the ropes, and then there is no being slaves anymore. They can just leave if they want to.

Bob: Yes. Totally safely. And the light actually feels good — it doesn't hurt.

Luke: Yeah, exactly.

Bob: That was all a lie.

Luke: Yeah. And now these two creatures in the light ball are pretty pissed in a sense. And they know they can't do anything, but they just… "Aw, damn."

Bob: Yeah. Tell them, "You can do that, too. Look at the reception all those beings are getting. They're being celebrated and given feasts. You've been missed there. Many, many relatives will welcome you, and it's your choice."

Luke: They say two things. First of all, that God would not accept them back, they fear. And secondly, that if they go, a lot of constructions they have created will fall, and not only in me but in others.

Bob: Okay. Tell them this, and this is really important, Luke. God gives his biggest welcome to the biggest sinners — the ones who've done the most damage. When they return, there's incredible celebration in the healing realms. And I think they know this is true in their bones.

Luke: They do, and at the same time they can almost not believe it.

Bob: Okay.

Luke: But now I would say that God is reaching out his hand through the light and inviting them in — he's grabbing them. Sort of in a welcoming way… they cannot believe it. They don't want to, and now it's those two creatures that have to have the courage to actually grab God's hand.

Bob: Mm-hmm. And maybe ask, "Maybe one of you has a little more courage, and that one can go first and show the way."

Luke: Yeah, it does now. It's the insect that is left now, and it's saying something about, "Oh man, all this work for nothing. We've been building these constructions in humans and on Earth for so long, and now we can just go back, and we could have gone back ages ago."

Bob: Yes. "And now you can go."

Luke: "Are you really sure?" it says.

Bob: "Yeah. Look at your friend who just left. Look at all the others who've gone and been welcomed. You, too, will be welcomed with great joy and celebration and great healing and peace. The natural great peace will come upon you."

Luke: It is intending to do so now, but it's also telling me that it will be so embarrassing for it because it actually has a human form in the realm of light. So, it has been a human once that has been degraded to an insect. And to sort of dare to go back to being a human after being an insect, it's a big step.

Bob: Yes, yes. Suggest to it, "If you breathe deeply a few times in the natural great peace, your sense of humiliation or embarrassment can turn into humility, which opens you to great love."

Luke: It says it does that, and then it says something about "I want to serve God." It's crawling slowly into the light, one pair of legs after the next. And then it's transforming in there, becoming a person.

Bob: Hmm.

Luke: And there is something about cleaning the light of that person, or cleaning the brain of that person with light because it has been so used now for ages to thinking like an insect.

Bob: Yes, yes. So important.

Luke: And it's almost letting go now. There's this wave I talked about in the beginning coming from my lower abdomen, it's just back to love… now it's stretching. And now I've let go.

Bob: Ahhhh.

Luke: Yeah. No need for a contraction there any longer. And something is very changed. It's very different. And there is a feeling that I'm allowed to be here now in my own body, and somehow my system knows that this boy being stuck in the bathtub is not going on any longer, so there's no reason to, to try to hide that or to repress that or something like that. It's not there any longer. So there's no secret to be afraid of or hide or use energy on.

Bob: Yeah. I'm having a sense of the fresh breezes at dawn that gently come and caress your skin.

Luke: Yeah. And I can also feel that my system is clean but still shaken.

Bob: Mm-hmm.

Luke: A little time just to, in a way, just to realize how bad it was, and then to sort of just slide into being healthy again.

Bob: Yeah. And there may be some grieving, too.

Luke: Yeah.

Bob: So see if anyone wants to wash, shower or, or have the breeze blow over them or anything like that.

Luke: There is a need to clean the inside of the heart with water.

Bob: Great.

Luke: And it's still like I can grab something out of the heart.

Bob: Mm-hmm.

Luke: There was a little sort of cave in the heart, full of dust, but also something else. And I'm collecting it, and I really need to get that out. It's... a lot is coming out of there.

Bob: Mm-hmm.

Luke: Like chunks of earth.

Bob: Yeah.

Luke: And my heart let go. But it doesn't seem to be... this earth doesn't seem to be so dangerous — it just shouldn't be there.

Bob: Yeah.

Luke: I think I, yeah.

Bob: This might be more like your own scar tissue rather than something foreign. Does that seem right?

Luke: Yeah, yeah. And I think that it would be good to put it into a river.

Bob: Mm-hmm, great.

Luke: And just let it spread in there, and just let it float away.

Bob: And let all your parts know they can put stuff in the river, too, if they want.

Luke: Hmm.

Bob: Any dirt that got stuck to them from all of this. This was a lot, and I think it went on many centuries, not just one lifetime.

Luke: Hmm, yeah. Yeah. They're throwing things into the river now, and they are doing that. They are sitting in the trees like monkeys, and they are doing it. They are really enjoying it.

Bob: Yeah, it sounds like a lot of fun.

Luke: Yeah, it is. And actually, as you say, it's like boys come from many centuries to meet here at the river to do that. And there's a feeling of strength and health. And now, I get in contact with a man who was probably a king… he has a crown on. He has a red robe on. But he's just sitting very quietly. I think that he's just sort of satisfied with what has been done.

Bob: Okay.

Luke: He's very old, I think… he's an ancient king, and finally he can sort of relax.

Bob: Okay. Maybe ask him, "Have we done well? Is there anything more we should do now?"

Luke: He says, "Pray to God and thank God."

Bob: Mm-hmm.

Luke: And sort of rejoice in the power of God.

Bob: Rejoice in the power of God.

Luke: Yeah. In the healing force of God, that God, the light of God is capable of holding all this and transforming it. It's a miracle, it's a wonder. And then he says something about human hearts. I think that he says something about the human heart is an incredible, what to call it, feature in us. It's unpreceded by anything else because it has this capacity for love. Animals can love, too, and he says, "Yeah, but human love is at a different level because it has a transforming power."

Bob: Mm-hmm.

Luke: And then he's, I think he's ready to leave. He's come… he wants to leave now. He was sort of watching this spectacle. He was sort of watching what was going on, and now he's seen that things have closed down, he's ready to leave. And I think that's a good sign also.

Bob: Okay. As he leaves, maybe thank him for his presence and ask him for his blessing as he goes.

Luke: Yeah. He said something about that I should be the one blessing him.

Bob: Ahh, can you offer him a blessing, Luke?

Luke: Yeah, I can. Because I achieved what he couldn't do.

Bob: Hmm.

Luke: And he says something about now he's revealing himself as an ancestor.

Bob: Ahhh.

Luke: Yeah.

Bob: Ah.

Luke: He says we will stay in contact, but he has been worried for centuries, I think also. And one of the boys in the bathtub was really worrying to him, and he couldn't do anything about it. And he says also that we will have to be prepared that even though I'm clean now, there will always be unattached burdens attacking us humans.

Bob: Mm-hmm.

Luke: Of course it's different now. Somehow it feels good that he says that. So he said we still have to be alert, but something is easier. Also because I think that it's harder to get in now for the unattached burdens, but also something like my system knows how it feels if they were trying to get in, so it will be easier to stop them before they go too far.

Bob: I also think… Luke, see if this feels true to you… having all that going on inside you drained a tremendous amount of life energy and light out of you, and now that's going to fill you more and more and radiate out through you, and the unattached burdens can't swim against that tide.

Luke: Yeah. When you say that, I can see a lot of boredom that had happened in my life and the bitterness that I had for a long time is really also created by the unattached burdens, and they didn't want me to feel well in life.

Bob: Mm-hmm.

Luke: They wanted me to feel like it was a miserable life.

Bob: Yeah. They feed on you then.

Luke: Yeah. Because then they have the power.

Bob: Mm-hmm.

Luke: And now, Jesus is coming. He is making a cross at my forehead, and he's giving me a blessing. I even think that he's washing my feet.

Bob: Hmm. He's been known to do that.

Luke: Yeah. He has. And he is opening a door and inviting me in, or out. It's not into another room, it's not like into a house, it's another universe in a sense, and he says something about being clean enough to go there now.

Bob: Ah, wonderful.

Luke: It's an invitation, and he says we can look at the night sky together.

Bob: Hmm.

Luke: Look at the stars… we will just sit there and watch the stars. And the universe. Yeah. And now it stops.

Bob: Okay.

Luke: I just feel the turn of the Earth. I can just feel how it's rotating.

Bob: Open to very deep, slow, sort of cosmic rhythms.

Luke: Yeah, exactly.

Bob: Planetary rhythms.

Luke: Yeah, yeah. Find the balance. I know it's like… this is very old, and all the human worries and things like that, it's just like nothing compared to this old, slow rhythm.

Bob: Mm-hmm.

Luke: Yeah. And there is something, maybe Jesus, I'm not quite sure, but there is someone or something just wanting to express a great thank-you to you, Bob. It says that it is someone you know. That you have been in contact many times. They just want you to know that it's very grateful for what you did for me.

Bob: Great, what an honor.

Luke: Yeah. I feel ready to go back.

Bob: Okay. Well, maybe thank everybody.

Luke: Yeah.

Bob: And all your courageous parts and Jesus, and all of those wonderful energies and the light, and all of that. And then when that feels complete, maybe just call out, "Everybody okay? Anybody need some last little thing?" We covered a whole lot of ground today.

Luke: Yeah. There's… it's funny because there's a space suit… it is dissolving now, it's being destroyed by the light. One last look if anything was left… the space suit was there, and it's really disintegrating now.

Bob: Great.

Luke: Yeah. Yeah.

Bob: I'm getting the idea that the space suit is a very powerful image of fundamental isolation.

Luke: Could be, yeah. Oh, wow. Whoa, thank you so much, Bob. Thank you.

Bob: You're very welcome, Luke.

Luke: I could not have done this without you.

Bob: Yeah.

Luke: And I don't know who else could have gone there with me. And what feels so strong in me is also this feeling of this boy who was eaten from behind. It's, yeah… To get him out of there was incredible.

Bob: Yeah. I call that kind of area he was stuck in the "coma wards" because they really keep beings suspended in sort of a coma state between life and death.

Luke: Yeah, yeah. That's exactly how it felt. And it was also surprising how well you knew that realm.

Bob: Yeah, I paid a price for that knowledge.

Luke: Yeah, yeah. I guess you have been there, too.

Bob: Yeah, and that's what I was trying to tell that boy when he thought he didn't have anything to offer. He's paid an incredible price, and he has learned things that can help others.

Luke: Yes, yes. Wow. Oh my God. Yeah. I'm really grateful that you offered to do that session with me.

Bob: Yeah. You're so welcome. This is why I do this work, Luke.

Luke: Yes.

Bob: It's like I can get to help people like this.

Luke: Yeah, it's just incredible. Wow.

Bob and Jessie

The following session is from a supervision group.

Bob: Okay, you got it. Okay, we're off.

Jessie: Okay, awesome.

Bob: So, this has been up a lot lately?

Jessie: Yeah, it's been up a lot, and I actually did some work with it yesterday with my therapist, and so I feel like I have a part that wants to give some history. So the first… well, my anxiety often makes me feel like I can't breathe, so that isn't a new sensation. There it is. And, during my Level 1 IFS training, I was having a lot of sensation in my throat, and then I was just sort of allowing myself to feel it, just you know… I'm on zoom, it was probably some big teaching part… and I'm feeling like I can't breathe. And then my breath starts to get really ragged, and instantly I was reminded of my mom when she was dying in the hospital, how her breath sounded. And part of me got really anxious and afraid, like oh, this isn't me, she's stuck in there, right. So I, as much as I remember because I had taken your training, but also I was still in Level 1 training, so you know, my understanding was what it was, and I was by myself. So I did what I could to like, you know… I didn't check in very much with other parts, I just was like "Out, out with you, get out of me." And I felt like I got some relief from it.

A couple months later, again I'm working with a part with my therapist… she helped me kind of discuss it. Didn't seem like it was me. She helped me kind of walk through the steps of like, having it leave again, right. I don't know that it's ever gone away, or I just get kind of… it comes back and I have this intense sensation. So, yesterday, over the weekend, I've had it, here. And also, I have Graves' disease, which attacks your thyroid right here, which is also an autoimmune disease that my mom had. And I have really similar… I have chronic health issues that are really similar to the ones that my mom had; however, she was an alcoholic and a drug addict, and so, her health issues were a result of that. I am neither, but I still have the same sort of health issues.

Bob: Okay.

Jessie: So then, yesterday, I had a therapy session because I felt this in my throat all weekend, like I can't breathe. It was confusing because when I would go inside and try to interact with it, I would hear "I can't breathe — I'm dying and I can't breathe," but then I would get pain, and what the pain would do is activate other parts that are scared there is something wrong. I have also parts that carry a lot of health anxiety like "Oh, I have a tumor," you know. And so,

I worked with the parts with my therapist, the ones that were scared by the pain, right, to get them to kind of chill out. And then when I went back here, with those parts calm, I had a really small image, because it really was just kind of fuzzy, I had a small image of, I don't know, a portion of something with a little hand reaching out. Oh, because she said, "Can you give it drops of Self energy?" because I've done that before, and that has helped, and it was batting them away.

Bob: Okay.

Jessie: And she said, "Well, could Self energy shine like the sun so it doesn't have to accept it?" And when I did that, the little hand was reaching out from underneath what was covered in black tar. And when I saw the little hand reaching out, I got this snarl, like a snarl literally came on my face, and I've had that before, like that tremor before, but it's definitely 100 percent a snarl.

Bob: Okay.

Jessie: Oh, that's so interesting.

Bob: Mm-hmm.

Jessie: Unfortunately, we were really close to the end of my session.

Bob: Yep, of course.

Jessie: Of course. And so I thought, oh wow, so all weekend I can't breathe and then it's giving me these mixed signals of "look away," "I'm dying," or "look away," "pay attention to those people." And then the snarl at the end, and I thought, maybe I can work with Bob.

Bob: Okay. Great. Thanks for all the background. So, first thing I want to say to all your parts is that these things only get power in us by scaring us. When we're no longer scared of them, they lose all power. And they can be really, really good at scaring us. They know the tender, little parts they can get to, which can actually be really helpful because then we know where those tender, little parts are, and we can help them heal. Okay. So, let's go in, and there are at least three things that I want you to bring into your mind as you go into your inner world.

Jessie: Okay.

Bob: One is the difficulty breathing, which seems like how it's been coming up a lot. And then, there's also the hand reaching out from under that black stuff. And then there's also the snarl. So just focus. Open yourself, go in your inner world. Decompress, let your breath help, and see which one of those you're drawn to focus on first, which one's our doorway. And if you're not drawn to one in particular, I can always offer some suggestions.

Jessie: So, I'm feeling the sensation of not being able to breathe.

Bob: Okay, so focusing on that, how are you feeling toward that right now?

Jessie: I don't like it.

Bob: Of course. "Hi there, part who doesn't like it. Welcome." This part makes sense to you, doesn't it, Jessie?

Jessie: Yeah.

Bob: Let the part know, "You really make sense" and see how it responds to that.

Jessie: It's not really responding — it's just like, "I know what you're trying to do."

Bob: Oh, it knows. Would you ask it, "What are we trying to do?"

Jessie: I mean, "Do so much parts work," it knows, like, "You're trying to, you know, I know you want me to go away."

Bob: Yeah.

Jessie: Yeah.

Bob: Okay. Say, "You're right, again, and can you give us the room, or do you need the attention? And either one is okay."

Jessie: "You don't know how hard this is."

Bob: Okay.

Jessie: There's a lot of emotion behind it.

Bob: Yeah, yeah, okay. "Would you like to tell us how hard it is? Would you like us to know… would that help?"

Jessie: No.

Bob: No. Okay. How are you feeling toward this part as you see how it's trapped and suffering?

Jessie: I mean, I feel sorry for it, but I also feel like surprised at how much I think I'm blended with it, you know?

Bob: Okay. So offer your sorry, your compassion, and see if it can receive any of that.

Jessie: I scooted it along the ground… my compassion drops. It picked them up and put them in its pockets.

Bob: Great, that's great. Now ask it this: "Can you, and are you willing to, un-blend from me and let us go to this sensation and help it so that it doesn't bother you so much anymore?" And it gets to say yes or no — either answer is fine.

Jessie: It says, don't forget that it's dangerous.

Bob: Okay, okay. And remind it of this: it may think I'm a complete idiot, but when we're not scared of these things, they lose all power and they're no longer really dangerous. But that's pretty hard to do sometimes. And thank it for…

Jessie: It's like, well that's 'cause you're not in here.

Bob: Okay. Fair enough — it has a point. But it's willing to give us some room?

Jessie: Yeah, but it's gonna stand there like this.

Bob: Okay, great. Okay. So how are you feeling toward that stuff in your throat now, that difficulty breathing?

Jessie: I have a little curiosity about where it's at because it was in a different place yesterday.

Bob: Mm-hmm. Okay. Extend that curiosity to it and see how it responds.

Jessie: It bounced it back like a balloon.

Bob: Mm-hmm. Okay. Why don't you ask the part this: "Why are you doing this… what's your intention in here? What would you like… what do you want?"

Jessie: I literally hear screaming.

Bob: Screaming. Okay. "Are you in pain?"

Jessie: "I'm dying," it says.

Bob: "You're dying," okay. Ask it, "Are you a part of my system, or are you from somewhere else?"

Jessie: Oh my goodness. It turned to face me, but it turned to face me with a scary face. I've seen scary things in my system before, so I'm letting my body know like, "We've seen scary things in our system before, and they have never hurt us."

Bob: Yeah, and sometimes they get very big and make lots of noise and look as scary as they can. That's really to cover their weakness. So ask it again, calm, and steady, "Are you a part of me?"

Jessie: So, it's tightening its grip and it's like a beetle, like its legs are holding on to either side of my throat, and it's just not responding.

Bob: "Yeah, well, you tried to look like a big powerful, scary being. We're asking you a very simple question, and we want to help you, whether you're a part of me or not. We don't want to punish you or judge you. Are you a part of me?"

Jessie: I got a head nod, like the beetle nodded its head.

Bob: Okay. Ask it, "Please tell us directly so there's no confusion here. Are you a part of me?"

Jessie: It's trying to crawl up, like away.

Bob: Mm-hmm. Okay. So, why don't we do this and see how this goes. Surround it in a ball or egg-shaped container of light, and gently lift it off your throat and bring it out to a good conversational distance so that you and it can communicate. Let me know what happens if that works for you.

Jessie: It's like tightening its grip around my, um…

Bob: Okay. Once all your parts are ready to let it go, it can't stay. There's nothing left for its little claws to sink into. So go inside your neck and look and find the parts of you who it's hooking up to.

Jessie: Okay.

Bob: What's in there, Jessie?

Jessie: I'm just seeing like strings, you know, like…

Bob: Strings coming from that beetle thing?

Jessie: No, like that it's holding onto with its feet.

Bob: It's holding onto strings inside of you?

Jessie: Like ligaments that would be running along here.

Bob: Yeah.

Jessie: I can't see…

Bob: Okay, just ask the ligaments.

Jessie: It says, "He's got us."

Bob: Okay, okay. Ask them, "Are you ready to let go of that being, or is there some reason you need to hang onto it?"

Jessie: It's always been here.

Bob: Yeah, it's really familiar, hunh? How are you feeling toward these ligaments, where it's stuck in this terribly painful place?

Jessie: I'm curious, like what do they think it is, and why would they be okay with it?

Bob: Yeah, do you feel some compassion for how they're stuck, too? Or just curiosity?

Jessie: Yeah, like um, it makes me feel like there's some emotion behind it of, like, oh, this is just what you know.

Bob: Yeah. In desperate situations, we cling to what we know.

Jessie: Yeah.

Bob: Okay. So offer them your compassion and curiosity and see how they respond, if they can sense your presence there with them.

Jessie: Yeah, I think they can, but it's really different than what they're used to.

Bob: Yeah, I bet. How was it for them to feel you there with them?

Jessie: They were like relaxing a little. They were super tight like a violin's strings, and as they're relaxing, the beetle's kind of, like… because it's trying to hold on.

Bob: Yeah, it's not going to be able to much longer. So, offer them some more of your compassion and see if they can take in at least a few drops so they get to know from their own experience that this stuff, your compassion, really makes them stronger and safer. See if they can do that.

Jessie: I'm just feeding them drops, and they're just sort of like, melting down and, like, sort of forming into I don't know quite exactly what, but…

Bob: Okay. Ask them this: "How do the drops feel? Does it make you stronger?"

Jessie: (sighs happily)

Bob: Wonderful. Tell them this: "Those external energies always drain us and make us weaker in the end." Tell them, "If you taste my Self energy, my compassion, you'll know that it makes you stronger." Now, how do they respond to that? That was a lot of words.

Jessie: I mean, they're a little hesitant. They like how it feels now, but, you know, they don't really know.

Bob: Yeah. Ask them, "Would it be okay if I got a little closer to you?" They get to choose now; they get choice with you.

Jessie: They're looking a little hesitant about that.

Bob: Okay, so let's not do that. I want you to ask them my favorite goofy question. Ask them how old they think you are, Jessie. And the first number to come to your mind.

Jessie: Thirteen.

Bob: Okay, so give them an update from the time you were thirteen to how old you are today. And be sure to show them tough times you've gotten through, skills and strengths, and all that stuff. (long pause) What's happening?

Jessie: There's a lot of emotion.

Bob: Yeah. Is that okay with you to be feeling all that?

Jessie: Yeah.

Bob: Let them know that. Let them know all their emotion is welcome with you now. "I'm a fully adult woman with a lot of strength." How are they doing?

Jessie: They are like, looking at each other.

Bob: Yeah, figuring it out. Well, tell them this, if it's true for you, and if I say something that isn't true for you, ignore me, okay? Tell them, "I hope and I want this to be the beginning of a whole new relationship between you bunch and me. I really want that."

Jessie: I mean, they just don't understand how we got out of where we were.

Bob: Yeah, there's lots of catching up and lots of understanding to come. And tell them, if they're willing — and they get to say no… they get choices — could they come and let you hold them while we deal with that choking beetle energy? Would they be okay with that?

Jessie: Yeah, they are.

Bob: Great, wonderful, that's very courageous. In my book, that's big courage, so thank them. And now turn back to that beetle energy and remind it we do not want to judge or punish it, and put it in an egg-shaped container or a ball of light and pull it out of your body to a good conversational distance and see how that goes this time.

Jessie: It's trying to burrow up into my skull.

Bob: Yeah, it's really scared. Tell it, "We will help you… you are lost, you are in the wrong place, you are suffering terribly… we will help you. We are not here to punish or hurt you in any way." And then, when any parts of you are still connected to that can let it go, it will go out of your body.

Jessie: I have a part that says, like, "Well, what if we're wrong and it's a part of us?"

Bob: Well, we're going to check that out in a lot more detail.

Jessie: Okay.

Bob: But we just want to get it out. And that's a great question. Thank that part for asking that. It's really an intelligent concern.

Jessie: Okay, I got it in a ball of light.

Bob: And just bring it to a good conversational distance so we can get to know it a little better.

Jessie: I'm backing up a little… it's right here.

Bob: Okay.

Jessie: Okay.

Bob: Okay, great. Great. How are you feeling toward it now that it's out there in front of you?

Jessie: I mean, honestly, I'm kind of grossed out because it's like a gross beetle, you know?

Bob: Yeah. Ask that honest, grossed-out part if it would go to someplace safe and comfortable and let us deal with this thing. Okay, is it willing to do that?

Jessie: Yeah.

Bob: Okay, great. How are you feeling toward it?

Jessie: I can see stadium seats where all my parts are sitting.

Bob: Great, okay. So, ask that beetle out there, "We're going to help you, whatever you are, to the best of our ability. Are you a part of me?"

Jessie: No.

Bob: No. Okay.

Jessie: Uh, yes. What. Sorry.

Bob: That's okay. It said no and then yes.

Jessie: Yeah.

Bob: Okay, that's okay. That's not a problem. Ask this: "Is there some part of me out there who's taken this alien energy to serve it and to try and survive?"

Jessie: Yes.

Bob: Okay, that's really important. Really important. Can you ask that part of you who did that if it can sense your presence with it?

Jessie: It's really embarrassed… it's hanging its head.

Bob: And how do you feel toward it as you see its embarrassment?

Jessie: I have so much compassion for it.

Bob: Great, great. Gently offer this being your compassion and be very, very gentle, Jessie. It's probably never experienced compassion in its whole existence, so go slow and gentle now, okay? Let your breath move the way it wants and your body if it wants to move… it really can help.

Jessie: Okay.

Bob: Can this part of you feel your compassion?

Jessie: I mean, it sees it like on the floor at its feet. I've like extended it along, but it doesn't…

Bob: Okay. Ask it this… ask it, "Would you be willing to put a fingertip in the compassion and then bring that to your lips to taste?" Yeah. Is feeling this emotion okay with you, Jessie?

Jessie: Yeah.

Bob: Let the part know all its emotions are okay with you now.

Jessie: So it's just been this like dark, shadowy head hanging, and when it touched the sea of the Self energy and then it put it to its lips, like, the lips turned to, like, real, you know.

Bob: Oh, yeah.

Jessie: Yeah.

Bob: And ask it, "How did this feel to you?"

Jessie: It's almost scared of it, it's like, what…

Bob: Yeah. Tell it we're going to go real slow, and tell it, "The beetle-looking energy has tried to make you really scared of this Self energy. Because it knows that if you start getting this kind of energy in you, you won't need the beetle energy. So, what we ask is that you just taste it, which you did, and then check out from your own experience how it feels. And you'll find out it makes you stronger, calmer, and a lot warmer." And let it know there's lots more compassion here for you.

Jessie: It's sitting down with its head on its knees. It's like it wants it, but it doesn't feel worthy of it, like, "I can't — I'm not meant to have it."

Bob: Okay. Ask it this: "Do you remember when or where you took on that belief that you don't get to have this or don't deserve to have it? It's a belief you took on."

Jessie: Okay, so it just lifted up its head and looked at me with, like, a scary head.

Bob: Okay.

Jessie: That shifts my internal feeling.

Bob: Okay, let it know this: "You've been living with that external energy for a long time, and it makes sense if you go back into it and let it exist through you. It really doesn't want you to let go of that belief that you don't deserve because then it knows you'll be free and you'll get to choose, and you'll be independent." Remind this one of how it felt when it took the drop of that compassion and ask it, "Would you be willing to take in a few more?"

Jessie: It's like looking to make sure that beetle is still in the bubble out there, and then it's reaching for the seeds that I sent.

Bob: Great, great.

Jessie: Tapping them and putting it…

Bob: Great. This is big courage you got, Jessie — this is changing stuff that's been this way for a long time. And remind this one, "If big emotion comes up, that's okay."

Jessie: It's like tapping the seeds and then putting it all over.

Bob: Great. And tell it, "You could have a lot more. There's an ocean of this here for you."

Jessie: Yeah, it doesn't quite believe me, but it's…

Bob: Yeah, okay, that's fine. We want it to know from its own experience. If this is true for you, tell it this, that you want this to be the beginning of a whole new relationship between you two that this part can rest into and trust. And how's it respond to that?

Jessie: I mean, it still doesn't really believe me, but it wants to.

Bob: Mm-hmm. Yeah. We'll just ask it again, "Check how your body, how you're responding to the compassion you received from me… then you'll know."

Jessie: Yeah, it's looking at itself and how it's in color now.

Bob: Yeah. And it will grow stronger the more of this it takes in. Ask it, "Would it be okay if you got closer to it now?" And it gets to say yes or no and pick the ideal distance for it. No?

Jessie: No.

Bob: Okay. Ask it, "What are you afraid would happen if we got close?"

Jessie: "I don't know," it says… "I don't know."

Bob: It doesn't know, okay. Tell it this, if this is true for you, Jessie, that you would love to hold it in your arms, and see how it responds to that.

Jessie: It says you're going to try to take me away.

Bob: Say, "We do want you to let go of the beetle, but we don't want to take you away — we want to bring you closer."

Jessie: I think it thinks that the beetle is its mother.

Bob: Yes. Yeah. That makes sense. Ask it directly, "Do you think the beetle is your mother or your mother's spirit?"

Jessie: Yes.

Bob: Yeah.

Jessie: And it wants to be with her even if it hurts her.

Bob: Oh. Ask her this: "What if keeping your mother's spirit here was bad for your mom and bad for you — would you still want to keep connection to her?"

Jessie: Yes.

Bob: Yes?

Jessie: It's this intensity of "I just want my mom" — it's just this instinctive, like, at all costs, you know. Just that urgency of, like, "I just want my mom. It's the only thing that will make me okay."

Bob: Yeah. Does that make sense to you that this part could have those feelings?

Jessie: Totally makes sense.

Bob: Yeah, let it know, "You're really making sense." And ask it, "Could you let me be your mom?"

Jessie: You're not her.

Bob: Yeah. She wasn't really her either, you know. I think maybe this beetle energy was in her too, and, was eating her up.

Jessie: It's just crying. (Jessie is very emotional.)

Bob: Yeah. Again, is it okay with you to be feeling all this? Let her know that. It's really important she knows it's all welcome. And tell her this: how would she feel about getting the beetle energy out of her and helping get the beetle energy out of her mom?

Jessie: Yes, yes, yes, yes.

Bob: Okay.

Jessie: She wants to help Mom.

Bob: Yeah, course she does, course she does. Okay. Is she ready to let go of the beetle energy now? That's the big question. No pressure — she gets to decide.

Jessie: If it will help Mom.

Bob: Yeah. It will.

Jessie: But how? How? She doesn't understand.

Bob: Okay, that's a brilliant question. "Here's what will happen: we can get that beetle energy out of you — we can pass it back up to Mom, where it came from, and then help your mom pass it up into the light so that it's no longer in either of you. And it may go back many more generations than that — we'll have to see."

Jessie: "What if it doesn't work," she says. "What if it gets stuck in Mom?" She doesn't want it to get stuck in Mom.

Bob: "Well, I think it's stuck in Mom right now, and you know, all we really get to control is ourselves, but I think it gives Mom her best chance of healing."

Jessie: Okay.

Bob: Okay, okay. So, ask her… can you hold her while we're doing this? Or how would you like to do this?

Jessie: Yeah, she just curled into my arms.

Bob: Yeah, yeah. Oh yeah. Such a treasure, isn't she? So faithful, so kind. Okay. Now turn to the beetle energy and just check and see… it's out there in the light… see if there are any strings or tubes or cords or anything coming back to your body that connect to your body.

Jessie: Yeah.

Bob: Still in your throat?

Jessie: Mm-hmm.

Bob: Okay. Just ask in there, "Can you all let go of it now, or do you need more help? Whatever is true, we don't want any 'make nice.'"

Jessie: Yeah. There's one big tube.

Bob: Okay, great. Tell whoever is holding that, "Did you hear that we can get this out of us and help Mom get it out, too, and pass it back up and get it into the light so that it's no longer infesting our whole lineage? We can do that, but we're not going to push or try and force you. You have to be willing to turn to me and let me hold you and love you so we can get this out." See how it responds to that.

Jessie: I mean, I almost don't believe it, but it like literally let go and then like ran toward me.

Bob: Beautiful.

Jessie: Yeah.

Bob: Okay. So, pull that beetle in the light a little further away from you, just so you can see if there are any cords or tubes coming back to your body. It's okay if they're waving around in the air — that doesn't really matter. What matters is if they touch you.

Jessie: Yeah, there's one in my heart.

Bob: Yeah. The mother wound is always the deepest one. Tell that part of you in there the same thing and see if it can let go now, too.

Jessie: It's trying to, like, pass it to me to hold.

Bob: Okay. Well, tell it, "I'll take it from you, but then I'm going to let it go" and see if it's okay with that.

Jessie: No.

Bob: Okay. Ask it, "What are you afraid would happen if I let it go?"

Jessie: Empty.

Bob: Oh, oh, oh. "That's sort of true in an odd way, but it's like you become an empty glass that can get filled up with something really, really good." And ask this part to imagine what it would like to be filled with, and ask it to dream big. What's the most wonderful thing it could be filled with? Light, warmth, love, care, pleasure, joy.

Jessie: Love.

Bob: Love, yeah. Yeah. There's no room for that to come in when this attachment's there.

Jessie: Yeah.

Bob: Will it let go yet?

Jessie: It's like, "How do I know it will be filled with love and I won't just be empty?"

Bob: Okay. How are you feeling toward this part now?

Jessie: Well, confused.

Bob: Okay. Do you see it's left with this great fear of emptiness. Do you feel compassion for that fearful part of you?

Jessie: Yeah.

Bob: Offer it your compassion and say, "Here's a little tiny taste of what you can make room for," and see if it will take that in.

Jessie: You know, it has a similar idea like, "This is for other people, but this is what I have," like the...

Bob: Mm-hmm.

Jessie: "That's all I get."

Bob: No. Tell it, "That's a belief the beetle has tried to put into you and tried to put in your mother and your ancestors, and it's just not true. And as I'm offering compassion right now, if you take in a drop, you'll know from your own experience that that's not true. And see if it can do that, maybe just as an experiment at first."

Jessie: Yeah, it like wants to hold on, and then it's...

Bob: Mm-hmm, okay, yeah. Great, great.

Jessie: It did this thing — it's looking at its hand because it touched it, and the hand turned into, like, real.

Bob: Yeah. And could it take some on its lips?

Jessie: Yeah, the beetle is like trashing the thing.

Bob: Mm-hmm, that's okay. What's important is your relationship with this part. It's held so much pain and fear. How are you feeling toward it?

Jessie: I mean, I'm sending it my love and compassion in little bits to let it have that time of taking it in.

Bob: Great. And how's it doing with that?

Jessie: It's doing more, and it's turning into color, you know.

Bob: Mm-hmm, great.

Jessie: He's still holding on.

Bob: Okay. Ask it, "Are you getting ready to let go of that beetle energy? It's been lying to you, and it's been draining you. And it lied to and drained your mother."

Jessie: It let go… now it's crying.

Bob: Yeah, it's hurt. Can you hold it while it cries. Will it let you?

Jessie: He doesn't want me to hold it.

Bob: Okay, good… thank it for saying so. And if it's okay with you to feel all of this, let it know. Okay. Any more connections coming back to you?

Jessie: I don't think so.

Bob: Okay, great. So let this beetle know, "You're in the wrong place. You are lost and suffering. We're going to help you go where you can heal. And if you look up — if you have the courage to look up — you'll see something that's like a tunnel, and up at the top, there are kind beings leaning down to help you. And there is a light, and you will be welcomed to healing realms."

Jessie: It's reaching one of its little legs.

Bob: Yeah, trying to get back in. So just send it up and say, "You probably have to go back up through the generations." So turn and take this beetle energy and hand it to your mom and say, "Mom, you take this — it's not mine, I can't heal it. You take it and hand it back where you got it from so that you don't have it anymore either. It's high time all the women in our lineage got rid of this." Let me know how that goes for you.

Jessie: She said, "I don't want you to have this, and I'm so sorry."

Bob: Yeah.

Jessie: She's like running her hands to like make sure there's no, like, it's not attached to me still.

Bob: Great, great. And tell her, "Mom, it's real important you turn and pass this back where you got it from, too."

Jessie: She says she won't take it — her mom.

Bob: Her mom won't take it — your grandma? It's okay.

Jessie: My grandma is evil.

Bob: Yeah, okay. Now there's two things that can happen here, Jessie, and I want you to choose yourself as much as you can. One, your grandma can be just like a boulder in a stream, and it can just flow past her, or your mom can pass this stuff directly up into the light.

Jessie: Now she wants her to have it, she...

Bob: The grandmother?

Jessie: Yeah, my mom wants her to have it.

Bob: Okay. So hand it back to your grandma — have her hand it back to your grandma. Make sure it's all out of her. And encourage your grandmother to take this stuff and hand it back where she got it from. She doesn't need it anymore. And is grandma willing to do that?

Jessie: I can't tell.

Bob: Okay, okay. That's fine — you don't have to know. Very often this becomes like standing at a beach when a wave goes out. You know that feeling when the sand pulls away from your feet... it becomes like that — it just rolls back up the generations. And then it gets back to the first human or humans in your ancestry who got this into them. And then when it's way back there, they can send it up into the light, where it can be transformed and healed so that no one in your lineage has to carry this anymore. Let me know how all that goes for you.

Jessie: Okay.

Bob: Okay? All empty?

Jessie: Yeah, it's going back, but it's still going.

Bob: Okay, okay. Might have a very, very long way to go. And let those early ancestors know that they can pass this stuff up into the light. And you might see that beetle energy itself going up that tunnel and into the light and being welcomed.

Jessie: I do now.

Bob: You do?

Jessie: Yeah, it's far away, but it's going up now instead of just back.

Bob: Great.

Jessie: It's trying to climb back down, but it's being like sucked up.

Bob: Great, great. And you can tell the beetle energy, "They're not going to punish you — they've been missing you. You'll be welcomed like a long-lost friend. They will celebrate to have you back."

Jessie: That made it pause.

Bob: Yeah. And let it know that all its separate parts, all its slaves, employees, its army, all of that, they can all go safely now. Each one on their own can go safely to the place where they can heal.

Jessie: There's just like a whole bunch of little ones just lifting up.

Bob: Yeah, and then tell… if there's any beetle left, tell it, "Watch what happens to the little ones who went first. They're being welcomed with joy, aren't they? You too will be welcomed with joy; you have suffered too long."

Jessie: Okay, it turned. It's going toward the light.

Bob: Great, great. Yeah. They gone completely now?

Jessie: I mean, I can still see it, but it's going toward the light.

Bob: Okay. And are beings coming down to greet it in welcome? Can you see that much? Maybe not.

Jessie: I just see the light.

Bob: Okay. The light can take it now. We're just about out of time, but there's one more thing I want to do if it's okay with you.

Jessie: Okay.

Bob: As that one leaves completely, you might ask the ancestors if they want to welcome into them new energies to fill that empty space. Very often it's just light itself or warmth that comes in. I don't know what will come into your ancestors.

Jessie: Yeah.

Bob: And if they're willing to do that, ask them, "Fill with light… fill with light until you're overflowing, and then let the overflow come back down to generations, generation after generation, like a wave coming in at the beach." Yeah.

Jessie: Yeah.

Bob: And remind them, "You really do deserve this — you're worthy of this… you should have had this all along. Fill yourselves, fill yourselves. The overflow of light and life energy and warmth comes down. You might see it going into your grandmother if she'll accept it. If not, she's just a rock in the stream."

Jessie: It's like going around her.

Bob: Yeah, yeah, that's what happens sometimes. "And your mom can accept it."

Jessie: She wants it, yeah.

Bob: And then when she's full and all her parts are full, the overflow can start coming into you. Yeah. Invite all your parts to drink, too. So many of them were so courageous today.

Jessie: She said, "My mom, she said, 'I've always wanted to give this to you, Boo Boo.'" That's what she used to call me.

Bob: Yeah, yeah. And now both you and your mom are part of a great river. It's effortless and vast and deep. There's one little secret I want to say about this river: you can't grab it, keep it. The way to hold onto it is to give it away. And the more you give away, the more you'll have. You have a lot of new relationships inside to be nurturing now, right? Wonderful, wonderful, courageous group of parts.

Last question, then we gotta stop. Is there anything else that needs to happen inside today to be as healing as possible?

Jessie: No, it's just… everybody is just together like on the stadium stairs.

Bob: Wonderful, wonderful, great. Are you open to hearing some feedback?

Jessie: I would love it.

Feedback and Questions

Bob: Okay. Come back, gang. And you know, feedback from your heart first, if you can. What parts of you got triggered, what emotions you felt, how this was for you rather than technical stuff, and if there's time at the end, we'll do some technical stuff, too. Okay.

(There were a lot of warm, supportive comments. I'll only include one.)

Kerri: I don't know if I can speak because so many of my parts have just brought up so many emotions. Good emotions. I mean, it's just, such beautiful, beautiful, deep work, and at so many moments I could see, I felt like I could see… I felt the fear… all of my parts were just right there with all of your compassion and your courage. So it's hard to talk because I have so many different parts coming forward with so much emotion. It was so beautiful and I'm so honored to have been able to witness it and to… it informs so many of my parts. Thank you so much, Bob, and thank you, Jessie, so much.

Jessie: Thank you, Kerri.

Bob: Yeah, it does make a real difference, doesn't it, to have the compassion and Self energy of the group coming toward you.

Jessie: Yeah, because I tried to work with that part so many times, and I feel like I was able to do what I was able to do because we all did it together. So thank you.

Bob: I'll just say a few things. Some stuff came up that's really… first of all, a psychiatrist friend of mine, one of his favorite sayings is "The mother wound is always deepest." And I think that's sadly often true. The other thing is when we got that thing out in the ball here, there was still a part in there, and when you get that "yes, no," that at first you were going, ah, it just means that the thing… that there's still a part in there with it. So that's really valuable information. And sometimes that information will be concealed because parts think it's contradictory or unacceptable or something, so it's really important to be welcoming toward that. I had one guy describe it as, it's like there were three candles of different colors of wax that were all melted together. And two of them were him, and one wasn't, so we had to work with that. So this is fairly common that you'll get this thing sort of out of the body and still have some part of the person with it. Another image people have used is a big ball of yarn that's all tangled, and there are some things tangled in the yarn that are parts of their system. So it's very often like that.

And then the other thing is that these things are frequently passed down as a legacy burden. They get into a family somehow, and they get passed down, and very often there's tremendous grief because sometimes the parents are aware of what they're doing to their children and they don't know how to not do it, and they have this tremendous grief over what's going on. One part we didn't go to but I think it happened — and if I were working with you in an ongoing way, Jessie, what I would focus on — is very often people, when they die, don't really leave and go on where they need to go for their own soul's journey; they stay attached to a kid or some other loved one. So I'd be wanting to look at that and make sure Mom's spirit was able to go on, and I have a couple stories I could tell about that. But I'll only tell you this shorter one. A client was around twenty-eight, and her mother had died when she was twelve or thirteen, and

Mom's spirit couldn't leave, couldn't let her daughter go through blossoming into adolescence and womanhood without her being there. And she stayed and stayed and stayed, totally out of love — there were no critters involved here. But at the age of twenty-eight, the girl realized, "I can't become a full woman with my mother's spirit inside of me." And the mother's spirit realized, "This isn't good — this isn't where I belong." And they parted with incredible grief and gratitude and sadness. And it was very beautiful and very touching, but they did part. And the mother's spirit went on and the woman went on. So that's another theme that came up in your work. Okay.

There's another point I want to make. Somebody mentioned patience. It's not really patience for me because I've become convinced — deeply, deeply convinced in my bones — that the real benefit of this work is meeting those parts who let the UB attach and developing the Self-to-part connection with them. So I don't have any of this, "Oh gee, I want to get this part out of the way so we can go over here and deal with this unattached burden." So, it isn't an issue of I'm being patient with some difficult children or anything like that — I'm delighted to meet them. I think that's the real gold in this work: we get to reunite with some deep exiles whom we might never have met if it weren't for the unattached burdens showing us where they were. And I think, you know, I think parts are very intelligent and have great radar often, and if they sense back in there somewhere that you've still got that impatience thing you're struggling with, they'll know. They'll know. Especially with abuse survivors, their radar knows when parts in me are coming up before I do. They're really good at that. So I invite them, "If you sense parts of me, let me know — you're really good at this." So did that bring up any questions for anyone? I can talk forever on this subject, but…

Nina: Yeah, I just want to say that, yeah, what you said about patience, and then there's just having time. And it's interesting that when we kind of allow time now, we associate it with patience, but it's… and maybe because everything is so fast, and I think it's really beautiful in the therapy room just to have that time and the presence like an available parent, you know, but with ourselves without "Oh, I need to go do the cooking, or the cleaning needs doing, or whatever the next task." I've come to the point now of what's this about, but just allowing, and that was really noticeable and it's so valuable. I see that with my clients all the time. If I, rather than doing therapy tasks, just sit back and allow whatever to unfold and find the time to be with it, it's a real… can be a real gift to give and receive.

Bob: Yeah.

Kerri: I gave my parts just a little bit to settle down, to start to be able to process, to make, to ask a question, but they kind of keep coming back to the end, and maybe they... you could clarify at the end when the beetle was going up into the light, there was a calling, you sent out a call to all the armies of the beetle, and I was wondering did that come... was that from Jessie's lineage, because for a moment there I thought, are they coming from just other families, too? What is...

Bob: That's a great question, and that particular question is something I've developed. A lot of times, these things won't want to go to the light, and the truth is, they have free will just like us, and they can go back into the darkness. Or as they call it in Brazil, which I really like, the umbra. But very often, when they're resistant, when they want to go back to the umbra and they don't want to go to a healing realm, I say to them, "All of your parts, all of your employees, your underlings, you can't hurt them now. They know they can all safely go to the light." And very often you'll see these things just get smaller and smaller and smaller. And sometimes you even see, if it's a beetle, some of its legs start going to the light, to the healing realms. And then sometimes they just get nasty, bitter, hard, and small, and that concentrated bit of hatred and fear goes to the umbra anyway. But sometimes they realize that without all these armies and slaves, they'd be beaten badly in the umbra, so they go over to the light, too. So it's sort of a technique I've developed for when UBs are reluctant to go to the healing realms and want to go back to the darkness or whatever you want to call it. And if they do go back to the darkness, they'll be much less powerful because all the beings that they enslaved along the way can get free. But very often they'll see that these enslaved beings go to the light and are welcomed with celebration, and they decide, "Aw, me too." They often fear that if they go to the light they'll be punished, they won't be let in, all sorts of stuff like that.

Kerri: If I can make just one more comment. I also... sometimes by the reaction of these things, you can tell where you are in the healing of it all. When you commented about how like, sometimes they're cool and collected because they have the other cords there, so when there's a conversational moment, they were kind of calm. But then, when it was down to that last cord, it started to really get upset, and it's almost like you can recognize where you are getting in your own... in the process when you're down to that last part because you can see... well, they've lost their cool, the jig is up, and this is this last moment where they know that they know. Like when they're just cool, you know there's something else going on that you've gotta go for, but when they start to really freak out like that, then you know, okay, this is it.

Bob: Yeah, that's very often true, and that's an important clue, but I think the crucial, deciding factor is how her parts inside are reacting. That's the sine qua non, the bottom line, whatever you want to call it. And yes, that thing about their getting upset is a good sign. So it doesn't bother me at all when they get really angry and start threatening and saying stuff like, "I'm going to destroy the planet." All that's fine — it's actually good news.

Yeah, that's basically the way I work. Find those parts and help them connect to Self. One thing that really happens a lot is the parts take in this belief of "Oh, I don't deserve that Self, I don't deserve that compassion — that's for other people," and that comes right from the critters usually. That's one of their number one weapons. They get that belief in people, and they've got them. Well, not entirely, but it's a big part of their argument: to convince parts of that. And you can see how that locks out healing. And so many people carry that belief or have parts that carry that belief.

Jessie: So then, can I ask you, Bob, since I found so many parts that have that belief, is my… should I write that down so that I can go help them unburden that, or now that they're connected to Self is that enough, or what do you think?

Bob: I would ask them one by one.

Jessie: Okay.

Bob: And a lot of them, you're probably going to need to go do just classic IFS with. You know, one after another. If I didn't have trust in your basic healing path, I would be saying a lot of things like, "It's really important to check in with those parts every day now. At least five minutes a day — regular is what matters more than three hours once a week, and do that for at least thirty to forty days because then that will cement this idea of 'It's a whole new relationship, a whole new pattern in here. This is not a one-time thing.'" Well, the classic thing is just go inside and say, "Hi. Hi, everybody," you know. But there are other things I like, and one of them is, go out on the beach or in the forest or someplace like that, and let each part pick up a twig or a shell or something they find beautiful, and then just carry that around with you. Or a lot of times, maybe you could find a piece of jewelry that they really like and wear that. Or, I have one that I love — this really tough, tough guy with tattoos and big muscles and all of that, he stayed in touch with his parts by that satin ribbon on the edge of baby blankets. He'd run that between his fingers. So, it can be really helpful to just sit and sort of help people think and interact with their parts about how best they can stay in touch. So, often I would spend a fair amount of time doing that if there was time at the end of a session. And I love doing that because I often get new ideas from the clients as to how people can stay in touch with their parts. It is hard to come back from a session like that — enter the other realm of shifting hemispheres.

Jessie: Yeah.

Nina: I mean, maybe quickly at the end, there was… I don't know if you can say something again about the energy of the Self and then connecting to the energy of the unattached burden. There was something like… a few times, I think, in this piece of work, it was about a shifting from the beetle energy to the energy of the Self. And maybe, if you could just say again something about that and the phrases that you use. I know I wrote them down, but for me those were some key moments.

Bob: Yeah, that's the key to the whole thing. Part by part and each one, getting it to taste the Self energy, take some in, and then getting that connection strong enough so that it voluntarily, of its own free will, turns toward the Self instead of the energy of the critter, the UB, the beetle. And you can be confident that the Self energy is always going to be better, even though it might be quite a struggle sometimes — it might take many sessions with one of these parts because the critter is always, at the end of the day, a parasite. It's always taking out more energy than it's giving, and the Self always is radiating and giving more than it's taking. So ultimately, which one's going to win? You know, one feels good, and the other, at the end of the day, doesn't. So you can just rest in that confidence of "Once I get the blocks out of the way, that's going to get obvious to this part." That's why I could say things like "Just try this and see from your own experience. You know, you'll know… you don't have to trust us."

Another thing that was important for me is being super gentle with those first drops of compassion. Some of these parts have never, never, never, in their whole existence, experienced compassion. I mean, even though it's wonderful, it can be a shattering thing. And they have to let go of a whole worldview that's largely been put into them. This worldview is very pernicious, very toxic, and it's a worldview that's quite common in our culture. But that doesn't mean it's healthy. Somebody said, "Being well adjusted to an insane society is not healthy."

Jessie: Yeah.

Bob: How you doing, Jessie?

Jessie: I'm, you know, wiped out.

Bob: Good. I hope you have time to rest a little bit.

Jessie: I do, I do. And I'm still feeling some sensations. I've a part that's like, "Oh, you still have some sensation in your throat." I'm like, it's okay… I can handle the sensation.

Bob: Yeah, you're probably going to have some sensations there. I think they'll probably be a little different.

Jessie: Yeah.

Bob: And there might be. This is the last thing, and I realize we're out of time… very often you get this thing out, and it's an unattached burden — it's different from the person's parts, and it is different from regular burdens — but regular burdens are left behind because parts have been damaged by this thing being in there for years and years and years and years. So then you get the unattached burden out, but then there's sort of normal burdens in those tissues and your body that you can clean out with sort of normal, classic IFS later. I wouldn't be surprised by that at all.

Jessie: Thank you. That helps my parts that are like, "What's going on?"

Bob: Yeah. I want to mention another couple things that people have used to stay in touch with their parts: long, hot baths; playing with puppies or dogs or cats; gardening; and then there's… the list is endless, and you just have to find out what's good for you and your parts. Okay, folks, it's been wonderful being with you.

Daniel and His Father's Spirit

This case brings us to an area that is almost completely unacceptable for most modern rationalists. This is the area of contact with the spirits of dead ancestors. As we noted when we were talking about the percentages of people who believe in possession, many people believe they hear the voices of deceased loved ones, especially shortly after their death. Most often they get great consolation from these experiences. If it is within a person's belief structure, in IFS we sometimes ask the client to invite in and dialogue with the voice of the deceased parent or grandparent. This can often help provide relief and resolution. Once again it's our old friend radical pragmatism. We do not argue with a person's belief structure if it is helping them achieve emotional peace, equilibrium, and growth.

Daniel is a psychiatrist with a long-term stable practice in an upscale community. He is a very rational man who has been deeply committed to scientific materialism. His father had also been a prominent psychiatrist who had descended into alcoholism and then opioid addiction to manage his physical pain. Daniel's father eventually died of his addictions. In his decline, he had been very cold, unavailable, and mean to his son. At the time of the sessions, Daniel was approximately the age that his father had been when he died — late middle age. Daniel was not an addict of any kind, but recently he had been suffering from on-going physical pain. In IFS, we often interact with a physical symptom as though it were a part or the expression of a part that is sending a message. There are physical pains and illnesses that are purely physiological, but many have a meaning or message within them.

Daniel focused on the pain in his stomach and got curious to see if it held any messages for him. In order to do this, we had to get parts who were scared of it and angry at it to step back and give us room so that he could be genuinely curious. Focusing on the pain, he saw an image of his father as a decrepit, semi-obtunded (this is a psychiatry word that means rendered insensible) man in his cigarette-burned pajamas. His father wanted Daniel to join him in the pain and psychological illness. A part of Daniel wanted to join his father because he had so wanted this connection as a boy, and he was unwilling to let go of the father's energy. This seem to be an insurmountable impasse, but we asked the father spirit if it was carrying any energies that did not belong to it. It was. We helped the father's spirit separate from the unattached burdens of addiction, narcissism, and meanness. It was able to send them off into the light. Daniel and his guide cocooned them in a loving web and sent them off. Now the father spirit appeared as a much younger, healthy man who could offer Daniel the love and companionship he had wanted for so long. After this session, Daniel still had some physical pain, but it was much less emotionally distressing, and it did not take him over so completely. One could theorize that we'd gotten a UB out of the deceased father's spirit and this helped free the son, but I don't know the realities of the situation. I don't have to know. What I do know is this helped to reduce Daniel's suffering. Radical pragmatism. With his extensive scientific training and finely honed mind, Daniel might not have ever been willing to experiment with this strange stuff except that he was motivated by strong pain.

I've run into two other structurally similar cases. I'll describe one more — we will call her Claire. Claire had a horribly abusive childhood; her father was a sexual predator, and her mother completely failed to protect her. The only reliable male was her brother's best friend. This guy would often show up to escort her to high school and protect her from bullying there. Not long after this, he descended into addiction and died of an overdose in his early twenties. In one session, Claire found the spirit of this boy-man inside her system. It was not truly beneficial to her, but she could not bear to let it go. When she was able to be genuinely curious about it, it became clear that it carried an unattached burden of addiction. When we helped the spirit free itself of that burden, it could transform into a completely benign presence. Again in this case, I don't know what was happening, and I don't need to know the reality, but what I do know is that it helped Claire and reduced her suffering. Radical pragmatism.

CHAPTER 16

Conclusions

We reach conclusions when we tire of thinking.
—Anonymous

He who knows he is a fool is not the greatest fool.
—Chuang Tzu

To be a philosopher is to take to the road, never settling down
in someplace of satisfaction with a theory of the world.
—Henry Corbin

For me, writing a conclusion to this book is also writing a conclusion to an intense decade of research that began with the case of the woman I have called Mary. After we got that unattached burden out of her system, I really wanted to pretend that this had not happened, but I could not. I couldn't ignore it after she told me how, decades earlier, she had been medicated and given electroshock when she tried to tell people about this experience and how life-changing and freeing it was to have the UB out of her. If psychiatrists and therapists back then had been open to the existence of UBs, it would have prevented decades of suffering. This case became my personal white crow. In an undeniable way, it did not fit in with my old conceptual system. Trying to understand it, learn how to work with it, and explore what it implied for therapy has led me down many twisting paths. It has exploded my worldview. It has made my life challenging and difficult, but I am very grateful for this experience and what it has led me to.

This all reminds me of the Scottish social anthropologist Sir James Frazer. At first he just wanted to understand the priesthood of Nemi, a sacred grove where the new priest had to slay the old one. This led him in wider and wider explorations into the history of religion and mythology. His first book on this topic, *The Golden Bough*, was two thick volumes. His last edition of the book before he died was twelve volumes. For my work in the area of UBs, each bit of research opens new vistas and new areas I want to write about. Looking to understand this one case has led me to reject many assumptions and preconceptions I had taken for granted all my life. It led me to see my hard-earned understanding of trauma-oriented psychotherapy as a small part of a much larger reality. It has been profoundly humbling but also fascinating and exciting. I hope some of this excitement shines through these pages. Many of the conclusions and orientations I've come to accept are so far outside the recent Western intellectual tradition that I expect my work to be mocked and ridiculed. That's fine; perhaps some minds will be open to these realities. My hope is that any ideas or assertions that seem weird and "out there" will be attributed solely to me. Neither IFS nor Dick Schwartz is responsible for them. They are much more conservative, and I go way beyond what they teach. Let's go back and summarize some of the main implications and conclusions.

Porosity of Mind

First and foremost, mind is porous. This finding was very surprising to me. I had not thought about this subject or its significance for healing. I held the standard, unexamined Western presupposition that my mind is mine, all mine — private property. Everything inside it is mine. It is my identity. Luhrmann called this the citadel model of mind. Taylor called it the buffered self. Clarke called it the billiard ball theory. It's wrong, disastrously wrong. I've come to view it as an autoimmune disease of the soul.

This autoimmune disease of the soul, this scleroderma, is at the root of so much of our modern suffering. Charles Eisenstein, Barbara Ehrenreich, Charles Taylor, Steve Taylor, Owen Barfield, Iain McGilchrist, and Isabel Clarke point to something like this from their very different perspectives. We can use Dawkins's concept of memes and memeplexes to describe it. We can conceptualize the citadel model of mind as an especially virulent memeplex that had been around for a long time but first started spreading exponentially in Europe around the time of the Reformation. It has gathered power and momentum, and now is a pandemic that is infecting the whole world. It does great damage. While it gives us the facade of being tough and independent, it actually makes us brittle and fragile and often defensively protective. It cuts us off from human connection and relationality, which are our birthrights. It also cuts us off from our bodies.

This citadel model is a deep cause of isolation, an underlying factor in the epidemic of mental illness that plagues our modern Western world. It can also be thought of as an anorexia for deep connection. So much has been written about the alienation of our times. This core belief about our psychospiritual identity almost guarantees that we will feel lonely, isolated, and estranged from the social and natural worlds we live in. The buffered self/citadel self IS alienation. Once we stop and examine this citadel model, it is obviously and fundamentally wrong. I've reviewed some of the overwhelming evidence. But changing our thinking around this is only the first step; this underlying assumption has determined much of our implicit belief and has created or colored many of our attitudes, states of consciousness, and ways of being. Changing our cognitive structures is only a small beginning. Just as IFS and other new therapies are reaching and working with the ramifications of the realization that mind is fundamentally multiple, we will need to work with and explore the implications of a new, porous model of mind. Both multiplicity and porosity of mind are simple and even perhaps obvious ideas, but both of them change everything. To deeply integrate this realization will create tectonic shifts in our sense of who we are and our overall well-being.

Radical Pragmatism

Second is radical pragmatism. What works? William James also called this radical empiricism. What helps relieve human suffering? This basic question has guided me throughout this exploration. It seems simple, easy, and obvious, but it can be a stern taskmaster. The Holy Grail of my quest has been the relief of human suffering — nothing more, nothing less. Many times, and not always successfully, I've had to discipline myself to stay on this path and not go off chasing the ontological questions. Someone once said that one good question is worth ten good answers. Radical pragmatism has led me to ask questions of the anthropological and historical data that have not been well explored. What can we learn from other cultures' ways of holding these phenomena that can give us practical, usable help in dealing with them in a modern therapeutic framework? Or does that very framework need to be exploded and greatly expanded? Is our concept of mental distress as an illness more harmful than helpful? Many researchers have studied this field, attempting to cram the experiences of people in other cultures into our diagnostic categories. This disrespectful practice has not produced much that enlarges us or our worldview. Anthropologists have largely focused on how possession complex systems fit into societies. Historians trace timelines. The initial question determines the entire course of the inquiry.

Mircea Eliade, the great historian of religions, had a similar change in initial questions. He discussed this under the rubric of hermeneutics — the study of methods of interpretation, originally of the bible and sacred texts, and later of religious phenomena in general. There is an entire field of philosophy focused on this as well. To oversimplify, Eliade's hermeneutics led him to focus on the "how" questions: how certain religions experienced the divine, how they changed over time, how they interacted with their societies and neighbors. He rigorously avoided the ontological questions: "Is this doctrine true?" "Does this God exist?" This attitude and set of questions allowed him and other historians of religions to amass large amounts of data and understanding of the religious experience of others. It avoids all the sterile and usually angry and judgmental arguments over ultimate reality or the final meaning of a text or doctrine or behavior. William James's radical pragmatism has helped me make a similar shift.

A Biopsychological Process

Third, a basic biopsychological process occurs in almost all societies on the planet. It has occurred in every era we have records for. It can have immense impact on individuals and cultures for good or ill. The most common metaphor used to describe this process is possession. Western psychotherapy has largely ignored this process or dismissed it as mere psychopathology. As a culture, we have adamantly refused to learn from this expansive body of data.

Patrick McNamara, in his two-volume *Spirit Possession and Exorcism: History, Psychology, and Neurobiology* (2011), states that we cannot understand a culture without understanding its religion, and we cannot understand a religion without understanding possession. An overarching theme in his work is that it is a major accomplishment of a culture to learn how to relate to and channel the possession experience. "Fortunately for us, our forefathers somehow learned to cultivate and then control these possession experiences so that they enrich the personality or identity or self instead of diminishing it… The mastery of spirit possession was an important cultural achievement, and it facilitated mastery of a whole suite of other cognitive capacities" (ibid., 5).

We have lost or abandoned our society's traditional ways, and we need to re-discover them or develop new ones. Our container for these kinds of experiences has failed utterly. Euripides's play *The Bacchae* and the fate of King Pentheus can serve as a mythopoetic image of our culture's position. We, like King Pentheus, have tried to abolish and suppress these possession experiences — these eruptions of the unconscious, the divine, and their ecstasies. He paid with his life for his arrogance. We also are paying a heavy price, but hopefully we still have room to change our relationship with these powers. Some Indigenous thinkers have suggested that our King Pentheus–like attitudes are another level of colonialism. Our mental health system is a colonialism of the mind, even an imperialism in the unconscious, an imperialism of the inner world. Where colonialism and imperialism exist, rebellion is inevitable. The domineering, power-based attitudes and behaviors of the Western colonizers and conquerors are replicated in our inner world. These fractal self-similarities — as above, so below — continue to amaze me.

Luhrmann's phrase "spiritual presence experiences" is freeing and helpful. We need to stop our elitist sneering at these experiences, even though they do not fit in our current ideologies. When we stay focused on the pragmatics of healing, these experiences are significant and worthy of serious, respectful study. Dismissing them as primitive remnants or evidence of pathology precludes any real understanding. In all the psychologies that involve parts work (IFS, Gestalt, psychosynthesis, ego state therapy, Voice Dialogue, Jung's complex work, and more), there is the understanding that a part of the person can take over control of the whole person. Understanding this basic dynamic allows us to conceptualize how it can be possible for something that is not part of a person to take them over. This has been reported all over the globe, and if we are rigorously honest with ourselves, most of us can remember times when it felt as if something like this happened to us, too. This is often an important part of an individual's life path.

These phenomena have been studied widely by anthropologists and historians of religion. What I am proposing is that we approach all this data from a different perspective with new questions. This perspective is that of a modern psychotherapist. The questions are about what we can learn from these traditions that can help us lessen the human suffering we see before us. Can we adapt and apply the methods that other cultures and ages have used? From the perspective of radical pragmatism, we ask the "how" questions. How can we learn from this vast body of knowledge and experience to help us help others? The ontological questions about what spirits are and whether they're real, while fascinating, are not central to the pragmatic task of healing.

Inner World, Outer World, and More?

Fourth, we inhabit at least two separate worlds, and the ways of knowing and cognitive structures that work brilliantly in one can fail miserably in others. The simplest division of these realms is inner world/outer world, or subjective/objective, or consciousness/material. Our scientific, materialist traditions have mostly ignored the inner world, denigrating it as insubstantial and insignificant. In fact, it is all we ever experience directly. When the inner world does intrude into the scientific, materialistic frame, it is usually treated as if it were symptomatic of a broken brain, a purely biological/material problem to be done away with by biological/material means. From the two worlds perspective, this is a category error of the first degree. The mental health system we have, which is based on this stance, is failing disastrously. Dick has been working for decades to develop what he calls "laws of inner physics," which implicitly recognize that we need new cognitive structures and methods of approach for this domain. Dick also says frequently that he realizes that the "inside" we visit in therapy is the same realm shamans have been visiting for tens of thousands of years. We need to respectfully learn from this great heritage, not interpret it away. We need to let it expand us and our worldviews. The studies of interoception and Tanya Luhrmann's work clearly demonstrate that the ability to move in this inner world is learnable and valuable.

For work in the inner world, the rationalist, materialist ways of knowing are way too small. Dick is developing his laws of inner physics to free our understanding. Isabel Clarke writes about propositional and implicational cognitive structures. Iain McGilchrist focused on right and left hemispheric functions and argued brilliantly that the left-brain functions have usurped the place of the right to the detriment of our culture and of us. Some thinkers suggest three ways of knowing: logos, mythos, and bios. In a more nuanced approach, John Vervaeke suggests four. His four Ps are: propositional (theory about; materialist, scientific thinking), procedural (the "how" question, which is about action and power), perspectival (our perceptions and value systems are inextricably entwined), and participatory (the relational knowing that the new animists so emphasize). Susan Greenwood uses the classical dichotomy of the two ways of knowing: gnosis and episteme. All ways of knowing are based on value systems. They cannot be otherwise; it is our values that tell us what information is worth knowing.

Another way of thinking about our ways of knowing comes from trauma studies. These findings are especially significant. What happens when people are exposed to extreme trauma reveals much about the deep structure of the human mind and soul. Back in the 1980s, Dr. Bennett Braun developed the BASK model of dissociation. BASK stands for behavior, affect, sensation, and knowledge. He noted that highly traumatized people not only dissociate their parts, their subpersonalities, in an extreme manner, but they also often have memories that are dissociated along the BASK lines. They will have a particular behavior come back with no understanding of its significance. For example, a person could have a particular body movement that makes no sense to them. They might be flooded with intense emotion with no content. They might feel the sensations of the abuse. Or they might have clear cognitive knowledge of what happened with no other responses. The fact that these divisions appear in traumatized people suggests that they might reflect four distinct ways of knowing and perhaps four distinct memory-storage systems.

I noted earlier that some anthropologists divide cultures into monophasic (valuing information only from one state of consciousness or way of knowing) and polyphasic (valuing information from many). Our culture, or at least its elites, has become lopsidedly monophasic. This is willful blindness. While it appears strong and tough-minded, it actually makes us small, vulnerable, blind, and fragile. Anomalous experience that can be welcomed into a polyphasic system often shatters a monophasic one. Let's recall an old idea that I first met in William Blake. The imagination is not what our culture usually thinks it is: it is actually a perceptual system, like sight or hearing. It is the primary perceptual system that allows us to navigate in our internal worlds. One way to conceptualize this is to compare it to the interface on your computer screen. All the icons there are imaginal — they are not real like the software or hardware. But moving them around allows us to perceive and interact with the computer. It has real affects. If I took the icon representing the text of this book and dragged it over to the trash, it would have real consequences. Our imagination in general may be an interface.

Dick's description of the laws of inner physics focuses on the structure — the existence of the nature of Self and parts. Self cannot be damaged, it does not need to develop, it brings great energy, its presence heals, and it can handle anything in the internal world. Parts are not metaphors — they are beings. Parts are not their burdens, and they can be helped to shed these burdens. Parts are a natural and beneficial way that mind is structured. They all have precious qualities. They cannot be destroyed, but they can be exiled, hidden, or stuck in the past. All of this forms a delicate ecology that must be treated respectfully. I encourage you all to study IFS to appreciate the ramifications of these ideas. One mainstream IFS idea that is crucially important for working with UBs is the realization that when you are not afraid of something in your inner world, it loses all power.

I want to go beyond this. Inner physics has different laws from the ones that apply outside. We need something like the development of the non-Euclidean geometries or the emergence of many types of logic. Isabel Clarke has stated that in the inner world, we need a both-and logic in contrast to the either/or logic that applies in the outer world. I want to propose three other characteristics that might be helpful.

One, in the outer world, we tend to analyze things by cutting them up into smaller and smaller pieces and studying each piece until we understand it. In the inner world, it's the relationships that matter, not the pieces so much. As McGil-christ said, relationship is prior to the relata. If we use the technique of breaking things down into pieces to understand them, we lose all the relationship informa-tion, which is crucial for understanding and change in the inner world.

Two, in science in the outer world, our standard of truth is whether an experiment is reliably replicable. What if this did not apply in the inner world? What if what was really valuable and meaningful in the inner world was what was unique and could not be repeated at all? This is true of art and literature. The great and meaningful works are totally unique. If this were true inside, it would turn our research methods upside down.

Three, the quality of language and the best type of language are different in the inner world. For objective science, we want words with precise denotations; mathematics is the quintessential example. In the subjective world, we want words with rich connotations and resonant meanings. Perhaps the most powerful inner-world languages would be music and poetry. I have noticed that almost all non-Western healers use powerful imagistic language and rhythmic music and dance. They use story, not doctrine or theory. These are more potent inside. Joseph Campbell used to tell a wonderful story about a Western scholar who went to Japan to study the Shinto ceremonies, which are very colorful and involve dance and music. The scholar was moved by the ceremonies. He asked a Shinto priest, "I feel the great beauty of these ceremonies, but I don't get the philosophy or theology." The Shinto priest replied that maybe the ceremonies didn't have so much theology or philosophy — people just danced. Sadly, much Western therapy has tried to cram the vibrantly alive individual experiences of our clients into the rigid dead boxes of diagnosis.

This two-worlds, polyphasic approach may already be too much for many, but I want to push at its limits. When we go deep enough into the subjective, we encounter things that are no longer "ours" or part of us. They are autonomous. The line between inside and outside blurs and vanishes.

Many thinkers have come to believe that there is a third world between the subjective and objective. The Neoplatonists presented almost everything in terms of triads, for example, the divine-daimonic-human — the two realms mediated by a third. Luis Eduardo Luna proposed a *res fantastica* to connect Descartes's two realms of *res cogitans* and *res extensa*. The Aboriginal Australians talk of the Dreamtime and have a model of four brains (story brain, family brain, country brain, and body brain). Jungian active imagination is a special mental space where unconscious and conscious can meet on equal terms. Winnicott wrote about the "imagined internalized object" and an intermediate space where psychological healing happens. He said this space is neither objective nor subjective but something different. Laurel Kendall, the anthropologist, wrote of the oneiric space of dreams, possession, and visions. Henry Corbin wrote of the mundis imaginalis and its place in Sufi spirituality. Egil Asprem, the Swedish scholar, neuroscientist, and historian of esotericism, has extensively studied the realm of what he calls the "intermediary beings," which are beings who have access to knowledge far beyond our own but are close enough for us to contact. Jung also wrote of the "psychoid" — a realm that is between the psychological and the physical. In modern theories of consciousness, there is one model that fits well with this. It's called dual-aspect monism. This is the concept that there really is only one reality, but we cannot perceive it directly. Our categories of perception split this unity, and we experience it as two: consciousness and matter. There is evidence from many cultures and ages that learning to move in these spaces and learning how to cross the thresholds between these worlds is crucial to our emotional and spiritual health. Radical pragmatism tells us we need to become students and relearn and reintegrate these ancient skills. Thesis, antithesis, synthesis — we do not need to return to the old ways; we need a new, larger, and more inclusive way, a way that is more respectful to all.

Folk versus Elite Beliefs

Fifth, there is a wide divergence between folk and elite views of the possession complex and spiritual presence experiences in general. This is blatantly true in our society; at least half of modern Americans believe that spirit possession happens, but if you even mentioned this as worthy of respectful study in academia, you would be a pariah; you would be shunned, and it could damage your career prospects. A similar divide existed in late medieval and early modern Europe. The elite thought these phenomena were demons inside sinners and that only educated male priests could get them out. The folk beliefs held that they could be nature spirits, souls of the dead, or demons, and they often opportunistically entered whoever was near. Possession was often best healed by a woman of the village, at least until the witch-persecution epidemic pretty much wiped out these folk healers. All over the world, the possession complex has especially thrived among oppressed and marginalized people, even though it is found in all parts of society. Korea shows this tension in an interesting way. Until recently, the possessed shaman healers — the mudang — were looked down on, often despised, and their work was often illegal. Despite this, most people went to them, including the elites who were suppressing them. We have seen how Euripides's play *The Bacchae* also expresses this tension, which seems nearly universal. It deserves more attention. Institutions, domination structures, and elites do not like these eruptions of spiritual experience and often seem to perceive them as dangerous and destabilizing. This elite versus folk tension has been played out globally, and the tension between the Western intellectual tradition and other cultures can be seen as yet another incidence of this situation.

Until very recently, our Western attitudes have been appallingly arrogant. As some Indigenous people have pointed out, the very concept of "researcher and subject" is one-up and disrespectful. As a result of the elite's attitudes, we have lost an entire range of healing modalities. Most, or at least much, healing worldwide for possession involved bringing the suffering person into a circle of community and working with dance, music, and song. Movement and music in groups are essential to much of this work, and they are largely excluded from our kinds of therapy. Somehow we have come to devalue an entire range of healing that in anthropology is referred to as high-arousal cults. We've narrowed our view of spirituality and healing so much that it almost seems that we think spiritual experience is only possible in meditative, downregulated states that are so immobile as to appear catatonic. Most tribal healing, most shamanism, is very high-energy and high-arousal, with a lot of movement and loud sounds. These states also offer deep healing, yet we ignore them. They make our elite authorities very uncomfortable. Even so, the spirituality in high-arousal states does not die out; it keeps returning. Annie Dillard said, "It is madness to wear ladies' straw hats and velvet hats to church; we should all be wearing crash helmets. Ushers should issue life preservers…"

In addition to welcoming very high-energy states as potentially healing, we could also recognize groups. In the Indigenous communities I've met, the whole idea of one-on-one therapy in a private, isolated room is suspect. Their healings have traditionally occurred in groups, in circles — small circles in sweat lodges, bigger ones in ceremony. In a similar vein, let's remember that the Brazilian Spiritists, the Roman Catholic exorcists, the Protestant deliverance ministers, and many others always did their work in teams. We have largely lost modes of psychological healing that involve teams, circles, and the community.

The attitudes of the elites that are enshrined in our mental health care system also cut us off from important healing resources in another way. Considering mental-emotional distress as solely biological and treating it primarily with drugs cuts people off from the possibility of finding meaning in their suffering. This is a terrible disaster. "Whatever cuts you off from meaning is not your friend." (Sadly, I've forgotten who said this.) People who consider their suffering as spirit possession have a meaningful context and container, often with deep cultural connections. People who hold their suffering as a broken brain are cut off from finding meaning in it and are isolated from their cultures. For the radical pragmatist, meaning is crucial.

Personalism

Sixth is personalism. From the perspective of radical pragmatism, from the perspective of a clinician or healer, this is very important. Whatever these things — UBs, spirits, voices, demons — are, you get better results when you treat them as full-spectrum personalities. This is an extremely difficult proposition for many people to accept; it goes against the grain of so much of what we have been taught.

This is clearly true with parts of ourselves. Years ago when Dick was starting out, he just taught this basic truth: you'll get better results this way. When you treat parts as full-spectrum people, you automatically give them more respect, and you have more faith in their ability to transform and grow. Dick now goes further and states that parts of us ARE full-spectrum personalities. Gestalt therapy echoes this. They have a saying that you can talk to a part, or as a part, but don't talk about a part. This keeps it all relational. Animism is all about a relational stance in the world, treating others as persons, consciousnesses. Martin Buber made the spiritual/emotional/philosophical benefits of this clear. From our pragmatic viewpoint, this is all we need: this way works better. The Hearing Voices Movement encourages people to dialogue with the voices in their heads, to treat them as people. The mental health establishment considers this heresy — colluding with the delusions of the insane — but works to reduce the suffering of many. There are many theories that can explain this, including a hyperactive agency-detection cognitive mechanism or the exaptation of a social relations module for inner work, but the explanations don't matter so much. What matters is that this personalism approach helps reduce human suffering.

The Medical Model

Seventh, perhaps the entire medical model of mental distress needs to be reconsidered. Suffering seems to be an inescapable dimension of life, and to pathologize it — to deal with it under the rubric of illness — seems wrong and even disrespectful. Studying the non-Western traditions in all their vast variety has made it vividly clear to me that the whole concept of mental illness is a cultural construct of ours. I had accepted this as an obvious and undeniable basic reality, but it's not that at all. It is a cultural product whose history we can trace and whose current form is only a few hundred years old. Anthropologists speak of idioms of distress to avoid imposing our model of mental illness. Perhaps our model does us more damage than good. It cuts people off from finding meaning in their suffering, and it cuts people off from the resources of spirituality. Our disease model for dealing with mental distress is failing terribly. We need something radically new.

Humility

Eighth is humility. We know very, very little, and much of what we know is wrong. Sometimes it seems that the process of the growth of knowledge is a progressive and ever more potent lessening of our importance. Early on, Earth was flat, and wherever we lived was the center of it, with the Heavens above circling around us and an underworld below. Then we realized that the sun is the center, not us. Earth is round, and we are not at its center. We are part of a solar system, then a galaxy, then just one galaxy among billions... progressive dethronements. Most of these were fought against and resisted. Our sense of time expanded to geological and then cosmic scales. Our tininess became ever more undeniable. Now, with modern psychology, we know that we are not even the master of our own house! Our lives are largely run by our parts or our addictions or our unconscious desires, or whatever you call them. This stuff with UBs, spiritual presence experiences, and the possession complex is yet another, deeper dethronement. We cannot even claim that everything in our mind is our own. These progressive dethronements can be very hard to take, but there is a bright side: being humble also means being teachable. When we accept how precious little we know, we can learn much faster and much more deeply. Robert Kurzban, the evolutionary psychologist, compared us to the newsroom vendor in the lobby of the Empire State Building, thinking we are in charge of the entire place. David Eagleman, the neuroscientist, said we are like a stowaway hiding in a lifeboat on a big cruise ship, thinking we are the captain in control of the whole ship. The image for this that I like best comes from W. B. Yeats. Imagine that all human knowledge is a bubble, and this bubble is part of a small patch of sea-foam, one of many patches of sea-foam on a short stretch of sand in a shallow bay on the edge of a vast, dark sea.

We are on the edge of a vast, dark sea.

Afterword

What? So what? What now?

What?

Years ago, I did a session with a woman that changed my life. IFS has a theory about unattached burdens, but until I worked with this woman, I had no idea how significant they could be, and like most of us, I preferred to ignore the phenomenon. Once I dug into this area, it became clear that UBs are fairly common occurrences and often have profound effects on people. Because most IFS therapists did not want to get involved in this area, I got many referrals and gained much experience. As I have learned more and more, I have been able to flesh out the basic IFS understandings into a more fully developed pragmatic method that relieves human suffering. This method is learnable and of practical value.

So what?

This phenomenon requires us to reconsider our model of mind. Minds are porous. This is necessary and beneficial. Tanya Luhrmann talks of the Western citadel model of mind. Isabel Clarke writes about the billiard ball theory of self. Charles Taylor describes the history of the "buffered self." Whatever name we give it, our belief that our minds are private, inviolable, and sacrosanct individual fortresses is wrong, disastrously wrong. This belief appears to provide strength but actually makes us brittle and therefore fragile and weak. Some have called the citadel model of mind an imperialism of the ego. It is a fear-based domination-and-control system and is therefore structurally vulnerable. There is more than enough evidence in this book to make a strong case for the porosity of mind, but the citadel model is so deeply built into our culture that even when we intellectually know it is incorrect, we still unconsciously base our lives upon it.

This dynamic is an uncanny parallel with the idea of multiplicity of mind, which is fundamental to IFS. The unity of mind has been an unspoken assumption of our culture for at least five hundred years. Once it is dragged out into the light of day, it too is obviously and disastrously wrong (Schwartz and Falconer 2017). It has also caused a great deal of unnecessary suffering. Even after you intellectually understand that mind is multiple, it usually takes years of inner work to live from this truth. This relatively simple idea of multiplicity and the other tools of IFS are transforming psychotherapy. A similarly deep shift can occur with the acceptance of porosity of mind. Many anthropologists contrast our Western individual model of self with the non-Western dividual model. The primary characteristics of the dividual model are that it recognizes both the multiplicity and porosity of mind. Anthropologists also talk of the new animism and how we can regain some sense of participation in the cosmos. When we live from the experience of porous mind, we participate in a cosmos of deep meaning.

Now what?

Many, many thinkers from all sorts of fields have pointed to our separation and isolation as the underlying causes of our modern problems. It is this misconception of our minds and ourselves as impervious, private, and separate that underlies all these separations. The belief that our subjective experience is private and absolutely separate cuts us off at the root. It precludes deep belonging.

Johann Hari (2018) points to seven disconnections: disconnection from childhood trauma (which prevents healing), meaningful work, other people, meaningful values, status and respect, the natural world, and a hopeful future. So many thinkers have described modern alienation. Most famously, Hari attributes addiction to disconnection. He states that the opposite of addiction is not sobriety — it is human connection. When we base our lives on the unspoken assumption that our minds are totally ours and private, all these separations are almost inevitable.

The physician and neuroscientist Daniel Siegel calls this Western model of mind the solo-self. He says that this idea of a separate self is a lie — that we have been living from this lie, and it will destroy us. He calls it a cultural cancer; just as in cancer, the isolated cell or self cares only about its own existence and can therefore destroy the whole. He feels that this belief is so deeply embedded in our culture that it has shaped our language to the extent that we can't even talk about it. He has invented new words to try and describe this adequately: intraconnected, MWe, metapersonal self-construal, solo-self, and more. He states, in the more reserved language of a scientist, "An excessively differentiated self in modern culture may be at the root of our most pressing challenges today."

Charles Eisenstein is vivid in his condemnation of the illusion of a separate self. "I keep discovering a common root under all the diverse crises of the modern age. Underlying the vast swath of ruin our civilization has caused is not human nature but human nature denied… an illusion, a misconception of self and world. We define ourselves as other than we are… as discrete subjects separate from each other and separate from the world. Saints and mystics have tried for thousands of years to teach us how we are trapped in a delusion about who we are. This delusion inevitably bring suffering… you are not a skin-encapsulated ego" (Eisenstein 2007, xvii). "The root and epitome of separation is the isolated self of modern perception" (ibid., xx).

Eisenstein is talking about the citadel–billiard ball model of mind that has become an unrecognized assumption of our civilization. He optimistically sees the beginnings of an Age of Reunion where life is no longer founded on the illusion of a discrete and separate self. This age will reunite matter and spirit, humans and nature, self and other.

Steve Taylor (2010) issues a similar impassioned call for reconnection. "The sense of separation is the root cause of the constant conflict, warfare, and oppression which have blighted human history… The separate self makes it possible for us… to be violent and cruel… separateness is also the root cause of our abuse of the environment" (ibid., 1–2). Taylor blames much of this on the ego; he even describes the spread of this model of mind as the ego explosion. Unfortunately, this can be misleading because many people think of the ego as being one part of our mind. This is not a problem of one part of our mind — it is a problem with the boundaries of the whole mind. As we saw earlier, the Buddhists have been aware of this for millennia. They speak of dependent co-origination and interbeing.

D. H. Lawrence saw us all as living in solitary confinement due to our sense of separation. He wrote extensively about two aspects of this separation: our separation from our bodies and our separation from the cosmos. He wrote of our "apartness," how we are trapped in the "barbed wire enclosure of the known self." Lawrence predicted disaster if we do not change:

"If we do not rapidly open all the doors of consciousness

And freshen the putrid little space in which we are cribbed

The sky blue walls of our unventilated heaven

Will be bright red with blood."

(from the poem "Nemesis")

We cannot return to some imagined golden age of connection. The disconnection is deeply intertwined with science and all the amazing benefits it has produced. It seems more like a very slow-swinging pendulum. Participation, separation, new participation. Thesis, antithesis, synthesis. Hopefully, this book can help this new synthesis be born.

Selected & Annotated Bibliography

Modern therapists:

Soul-Centered Healing by Thomas Zinser

Spirit Releasement Therapy by William Baldwin

These two books by relatively recent therapists will probably be the most practically helpful.

An Amazing Journey into the Psychotic Mind by Jerry Marzinski and Sherry Swiney

This is the best book on unattached burdens and psychosis, even though the authors do not use IFS terminology.

William James on Exceptional Mental States: The 1896 Lowell Lectures, edited by Eugene Taylor

The great thinker tackles the more bizarre areas of study.

Shamanic Depossession by Peter Salomone

A modern shaman gives a simple and clear account of his work.

Other modern authors worth reading on this subject:

Obsession by Arthur Guirdham, MD

The Unquiet Dead by Edith Fiore, MD

Thirty Years Among the Dead by Carl Wickland, MD

Entity Possession by Samuel Sagan, MD

Egregores by Mark Stavish

Remarkable Healings: A Psychiatrist Discovers Unsuspected Roots of Mental and Physical Illness by Shakuntala Modi, MD

The Presence of Other Worlds by Wilson Van Dusen

Minds in Many Pieces by Ralph Allison, MD

Brazilian Spiritism:

The Spirits' Book by Allen Kardec

In about 1850, Kardec began writing what turned out to be six thick volumes on spirits. These he compiled by asking about 1,000 questions in each book and sending them out to a group of mediums. These books, which were written in France, became the basis of Spiritism in Brazil. Most people start with this book. It is not an easy read.

Nosso Lar by Francisco Candido Xavier aka Chico Xavier all over Brazil

Xavier was a Spiritist medium who channeled more than 400 books. Some 90 of them have been published. There are translations in more than a dozen languages, and more than 35 million copies have sold worldwide. *Nosso Lar* is perhaps his most famous novel. It is an easy read and is the basis of the film *Astral City*, available on YouTube.

Spiritism and Mental Health, edited by Emma Bragdon
An American psychologist writes about spiritism and psychiatry.

Modern exorcism:
Exorcism and Deliverance Ministry in the Twentieth Century by James Collins
This was his PhD dissertation and reads like it.

Pigs in the Parlor by Frank and Ida Mae Hammond
This book sold over 1 million copies. It is written by two very popular Texas Protestant fundamentalist ministers who did deliverance work.

History in the West:
Possession and Exorcism: Among Primitive Races, in Antiquity, the Middle Ages, and Modern Times by Traugott K. Oesterreich
This is the great text originally written in the '20s or '30s. The author, a German professor, spent his lifetime compiling cases, and this is the result.

Spirit Possession in Judaism, edited by Matt Goldish
A wonderful collection of scholarly articles

Spirit Possession and the Origins of Christianity by Stevan Davies

Discerning Spirits by Nancy Caciola

Believe Not Every Spirit by Moshe Sluhovsky

General anthropology:
(There is so much written here, it's very hard to choose.)

Possession by Erika Bourguinon
How About Demons by Felicitas Goodman
Both of these books are short, easy, and full of information.

Our Most Troubling Madness by T. M. Luhrmann and Jocelyn Marrow
This is a great book about the treatment of psychosis worldwide by an amazing woman; all of her writings are worth reading. She also has a good website. tanyaluhrmann.com/

How God Becomes Real, also by Luhrmann, is in a class by itself. It is a deep exploration of how to deepen interoception and how this has been done in many traditions.

I have picked Haiti to give a more detailed list in the hope of encouraging you to learn one other culture in some depth.

Divine Horsemen: the Living Gods of Haiti by Maya Deren

Voodoo in Haiti by Alfred Métraux

Tell My Horse by Zora Neale Hurston

Related interests:

Dispelling Wetiko by Paul Levy

Daimonic Reality by Patrick Harpur

These are both fascinating and original studies that will expand your thinking.

The Self Possessed by Frederick Smith

This is a huge, magisterial study of the history of possession states in Vedic and South Asian civilization. It will set the standard for many decades to come. It is not an easy read but is very rewarding. The author is a Sanskrit scholar, and there are many original translations in the text.

Tibetan Buddist Medicine and Psychiatry: The Diamond Healing by Terry Clifford

This is the standard text for English-speaking people; it is endorsed by the Dalai Lama.

The Mind Parasites by Colin Wilson

This novel is enjoyable and thought-provoking.

Three great classics in this field:

Ecstatic Religion by I. M. Lewis

Deep, readable, and fascinating

Shamanism by Mircea Eliade

This book has set the standard in the field for more than 50 years. All scholarly works on shamanism make reference to it. Both of these are more readable than you would expect. The conflicts in their opinions have been discussed for more than 50 years. Great books.

The Varieties of Religious Experience by William James

This may be the greatest text written in the West on psychology and religion, but I am prejudiced — I love William James.

Research Bibliography

It has been said that if you steal from one, it is plagiarism, but if you steal from many, it is research. This book is research; you may think the ideas are weird or useless, and you have every right to your views, but I want you to get how much work, study, and thought have gone into developing them. The asterisks preceding some of the listings indicate references that were especially helpful.

Abbasi, M. (2020). "Mirroring Values in Possession Ritual: A Biographic-Narrative Study of Female Participants in the Zār Ritual in the Hormozgān Province of Iran." In *The Shamaness in Asia*. Edited by D. Torri and S. Roche, 225–244. Routledge.

Abel, T. M., R. Metraux, and S. Roll. (1987). *Psychotherapy and Culture* (rev. ed.). University of New Mexico Press.

Addison, A. (2019). *Jung's Psychoid Concept Contextualized*. Routledge.

Adjaye, K. J. (2004). "Boundaries of Self and Other in Ghanaian Popular Culture." *African Studies Review*, 2004(8): 195.

Ahriman (n.d.). In *Waldorf Watch*. https://sites.google.com/site/waldorfwatch/

Alexander, B. K. (2001). "The Myth of Drug-Induced Addiction," a paper delivered to the Canadian Senate, January 2001, retrieved December 12, 2004.

Alexander, B. K., B. L. Beyerstein, P. F. Hadaway, and R. B. Coambs. (1981). "Effect of Early and Later Colony Housing on Oral Ingestion of Morphine in Rats." *Pharmacology Biochemistry and Behavior* 15 (4): 571–576.

Al-Habeeb, T. A. (2003). "A Pilot Study of Faith Healers' Views on Evil Eye, Jinn Possession, and Magic in the Kingdom of Saudi Arabia." *Journal of Family and Community Medicine* 10(3): 31–38.

Al-Krenawi, A., and J. Graham. (1997). "Spirit Possession and Exorcism in the Treatment of a Bedouin Psychiatric Patient." *Clinical Social Work Journal* 25(2): 211–222.

Allen, C., and H. S. Lustig. (1985). *Tea with Demons: A True Story*. Ballantine Books.

Allen, S. (2007). *Spirit Release: A Practical Handbook*. O Books.

*Allione, T. (2008). *Feeding Your Demons: Ancient Wisdom for Resolving Inner Conflict*. Little Brown and Company.

*Allison, R., and T. Schwarz. (1980). *Minds in Many Pieces: The Making of a Very Special Doctor*. Rawson Wade Publishers.

Ambos, E. (2011). "The Obsolescence of the Demons? Modernity and Possession in Sri Lanka." In *Health and Religious Rituals in South Asia: Disease, Possession and Healing*. Edited by F. Ferrari. Taylor & Francis Group.

American Society of Clinical Hypnosis (1965). *Religion and Hypnosis Meet*.

Amorth, G. (1999). *An Exorcist Tells His Story*. Ignatius Press.

Anderson, F. G., M. Sweezy, and R. C. Schwartz (2012). *Internal Family Systems Skills Training Manual: Trauma-Informed Treatment for Anxiety, Depression, PTSD & Substance Abuse*. PESI Publishing and Media.

Ang, A. V., and C. J. Montiel (2019). "Understanding Spirit Possession in the Philippines: A Social Representations Approach." *Mental Health, Religion & Culture* 22(7): 738–53. https://doi.org/10.1080/13674676.2019.1646232.

*Apostol, V. M. (2010). *Way of the Ancient Healer: Sacred Teachings from the Philippine Ancestral Traditions.* North Atlantic Books.

Appell-Warren, L. P. (2014). *Personhood: An Examination of the History and Use of an Anthropological Concept.* Edwin Mellen.

Ashworth, D. (2001). *Dancing with the Devil as You Channel in the Light! Survival for Healers and Therapists.* Crucible Publishers.

*Astor-Aguilera, M., and G. Harvey, eds. (2018). *Rethinking Relations and Animism: Personhood and Materiality.* Routledge.

Aukland, K. (2011). "The cult of Nakoda Bhairava: Deity worship and possession in Jainism." *Center of Jaina Studies Newsletter* (6), 31–33. https://www.duo.uio.no/handle/10852/23908.

Autry, J. Z. (2013). "Pentecostal Christianity and Church-State Relations in China: The Case of the True Jesus Church Movement." *The Review of Faith & International Affairs* 11(3): 40–51. https://doi.org/10.1080/15570274.2013.829985.

Backwoods Press (2018). *Inner Active Cards* (Cards).

Bakan, D. (1966). *The Duality of Human Existence: An Essay on Psychology and Religion.* Rand McNally & Company.

———— (1958). *Sigmund Freud and the Jewish Mystical Tradition.* Shocken.

Baker, P. (2009). *The Voice Inside.* P&P Press.

*Balcomb, A. O. (2019). "The Porous Self and the Buffered Self: The Relevance of Charles Taylor's Characterizations for the African Context." *Religion and Theology* 26(3–4): 233–254. https://doi.org/10.1163/15743012-02603007.

*Baldwin, W. J. (2003/1993). *Healing Lost Souls: Releasing Unwanted Spirits from Your Energy Body.* Hampton Roads Publishing Company.

———— (2012/1992). *Spirit Releasement Therapy* (2nd ed.). Headline Books. (Originally published in 1993)

Barbosa, O. A. P. (2003). *Hands of Faith: Healers of Brazil.* Edited by B. Keeney. Ringing Rock Press.

Barley, N. (2000). *Music and Possession in Vietnam* (10672724). (PhD diss., University of London, School of Oriental and African Studies), ProQuest.

Basso, Rebecca. (2006). "Music, Possession and Shamanism Among Khond Tribes." *Culture and Religion* 7: 177–197. 10.1080/14755610600975944.

*Bastos, M. A. V., P. R. H. O. Bastos, L. M. Gonçalves, I. H. S. Osório, and G. Lucchetti (2015). "Mediumship: Review of Quantitative Studies Published in the 21st Century." *Archives of Clinical Psychiatry (São Paulo)* 42(5).

*Bateson, G. (1979). *Mind and Nature: A Necessary Unity.* Dutton.

———— (1972). *Steps to an Ecology of Mind: Collected Essays in Anthropology, Psychiatry, Evolution, and Epistemology.* Chandler.

Battaglia, D., ed. (1995). *Rhetorics of Self-Making.* University of California Press.

*Baumeister, D., O. Sedgwick, O. Howes, and E. Peters (2017). "Auditory Verbal Hallucinations and Continuum Models of Psychosis: A Systematic Review of the Healthy Voice-Hearer Literature. *Clinical Psychology Review* 51: 125–141. https://doi.org/10.1016/j.cpr.2016.10.010.

*Beahris, J. O. (1982). *Unity and Multiplicity: Multilevel Consciousness of Self in Hypnosis, Psychiatric Disorder and Mental Health.* Brunner/Mazel.

Beeman, W. O. (2015). "The Zar in the Persian Gulf: Performative Dimensions." *Anthropology of the Contemporary Middle East and Central Eurasia,* 3(1): 1–12.

Behrend, H., and U. Luig, eds. (1999). *Spirit possession: Modernity and power in Africa.* Boydell and Brewer Ltd.

Belanger, M. (2021). *The Dictionary of Demons: Names of the Damned* (10th anniv. ed.). Llewellyn Publications.

Bell, R. (1987) *Holy Anorexia.* University of Chicago Press.

Belo, J. (1960). *Trance in Bali.* Columbia University.

Bener, A., and S. Ghuloum. (2011). "Ethnic Differences in the Knowledge, Attitude, and Beliefs Towards Mental Illness in a Traditional Fast Developing Country." *Psychiatria Danubina* 23(2): 157–64.

*Bentall, R. P. (2009). *Doctoring the Mind: Is Our Current Treatment of Mental Illness Really Any Good?* New York University Press.

———— (2003). *Madness Explained: Psychosis and Human Nature.* Penguin Books.

Benyshek, D. (2012) "Artists as Shamans: Historical Review and Recent Theoretical Model." Tenth International Society for Shamanic Research Conference, Warsaw, Poland.

Berdyaev, N. (2009) *Slavery and Freedom.* Semantron Press.

Berezkin, R., and V. Goossaert (2020). "The Wutong Cult in the Modern and Contemporary Suzhou Area." *Journal of Chinese Studies* 70: 153–203.

Berger, P. L. (1969). *A Rumor of Angels: Modern Society and the Rediscovery of the Supernatural.* Anchor Books.

Betty, S. (2020). *The Afterlife Therapist.* White Crow Books.

———— (2011). *The Afterlife Unveiled: What the Dead Are Telling Us About Their World.* O Books.

———— (2005). "The Growing Evidence for 'Demonic Possession': What Should Psychiatry's Response Be?" *Journal of Religion and Health* 44(1): 13–30.

*———— (2018, January 22). "Is Your Child's 'Imaginary Friend' Imaginary or Real? A Case Study." White Crow Books. http://whitecrowbooks.com/staffordbetty/entry/is_your_childs_imaginary_friend_imaginary_or_real_a_case_study/

Bhavsar, V., A. Ventriglio, and D. Bhugra (2016). "Dissociative Trance and Spirit Possession: Challenges for Cultures in Transition." *Psychiatry and Clinical Neurosciences* 70(12). https://doi.org/10.1111/pcn.12425.

Biehl, J., B. Good, and A. Kleinman, eds. (2007). *Subjectivity* (1st ed.). University of California Press.

Bilu, Y. (1985). "The Taming of the Deviants and Beyond: An Analysis of Dybbuk Possession and Exorcism in Judaism" in *The Psychoanalytic Study of Society.* Routledge.

Blacker, C. (1975). *The Catalpa Bow: A Study of Shamanistic Practices in Japan.* Routledge Curzon.

Blake, W. (1966). *Complete Writings.* Oxford University Press.

*Blanes, R., and D. Espirito Santo, eds. (2014). *The social life of spirits*. University of Chicago Press.

Blier, S. P. (1995). *African Vodun: Art, Psychology, and Power*. University of Chicago Press.

Blythe, C., ed. (2021). *Spirit Possession and Communication in Religious and Cultural Contexts*. Routledge.

Boddy, J. (1994). "Spirit Possession Revisited: Beyond Instrumentality." *Annual Review of Anthropology* 23(1): 407–434.

*——— (1989). *Wombs and Alien Spirits: Women, Men, and the Zar Cult in Northern Sudan* (1st ed.). University of Wisconsin Press.

*Bonheim, J. (2001). *The Hunger for Ecstasy: Fulfilling the Soul's Need for Passion and Intimacy*. Daybreak.

Borges, J. L., C. Milosz, K. Raine, D. T. Suzuki, E. Taylor, W. Van Dusen, and C. Wilson (1995). *Testimony to the Invisible: Essays on Swedenborg*. Edited by J. F. Lawrence. Chrysalis Books.

Boston, S. (2014). "Vimbuzu as a possession cult." In *Vimbuza: The Healing Dance of Northern Malawi*. Imabili Indigenous Knowledge Publications, 23–74.

*Bourguignon, E. (1976). *Possession*. Chandler and Sharp Publishers.

——— (2003). "Possession and Trance," in *Encyclopedia of Medical Anthropology: Health and Illness in the World's Cultures Topics* (2004 ed.; Vols. 1 & 2). Edited by C. R. Ember and M. Ember, 137–145. Springer.

*——— (1973). *Religion, Altered States of Consciousness and Social Change*. Ohio State University Press.

Bragdon, E. (2004). *Kardec's Spiritism: A Home for Healing and Spiritual Evolution*. Lightening Up Press.

*———, ed. (2012). *Spiritism and Mental Health: Practices from Spiritist Centers and Spiritist Psychiatric Hospitals in Brazil*. Singing Dragon.

Bragdon, E. (2002). *Spiritual Alliances: Discovering the Roots of Health at the Casa de Dom Inácio*. Lightening Up Press.

Bramly, S. (1977). *Macumba: The Teachings of Maria-Jose, Mother of the Gods*. Translated by M. Bogin. St. Martin's Press.

Brodwin, P. (2017). Technologies of the Self and Ethnographic Praxis. *Medical Anthropology* 36(1): 77–82. https://doi.org/10.1080/01459740.2015.1050491.

Brown, D. H. (2003). *Santería Enthroned: Art, Ritual, and Innovation in an Afro-Cuban Religion*. University of Chicago Press.

Bubandt, N. (2009). "Interview with an Ancestor: Spirits as Informants and the Politics of Possession in North Maluku." *Ethnography* 10(3): 291–316. https://doi.org/10.1177/1466138109339044.

Bull, G. E. (2007). "Madness or Transcendence? Tang-Ki Medium Healing in Singapore" (PhD diss., University of London), ProQuest.

Bunkenborg, M. (2012). Popular Religion Inside Out: Gender and Ritual Revival in a Hebei Township. *China Information* 26(3): 359–76. https://doi.org/10.1177/0920203X12452709.

Burnham, S. (1997). *The Ecstatic Journey: Walking the Mystical Path in Everyday Life*. Ballantine Books.

Buxton, S. (n.d.). "Compassionate Depossession Training." *The Sacred Trust*. https://sacredtrust.org/workshops/depossession-training/

*Caciola, N. (2003). *Discerning Spirits: Divine and Demonic Possession in the Middle Ages*. Cornell University Press.

*Campbell, S., and W. Campbell (2008). *Ecstatic Prophecy*. Chosen Books.

Canals, R. (2020). "Spirits Against the Law: Visual Evidence and Forms of Legal Contestation in the Practice of the Cult of María Lionza in Barcelona." *Ethnos* 85(3): 507–531. https://doi.org/10.1080/00141844.2019.1580303.

Cardeña, E., M. van Dujil, L. A. Weiner, and D. B. B. Terhune (2009). "Possession/Trance Phenomena." In *Dissociation and the Dissociative Disorders: DSM-V and Beyond*. Edited by P. F. Dell and J.A. O'Neil, 171–181. Routledge.

*Cardeña, E., S. J. Lynn, and S. Krippner, eds. (2014). *Varieties of Anomalous Experience: Examining the Scientific Evidence* (2nd ed.). American Psychological Association.

Cardeña, E., and M. Winkelman, M., eds. (2011). *Altering Consciousness: Multidisciplinary Perspectives* (Vols. 1 & 2). Praeger.

Carspecken, L. (2015). "The Unbounded Self: Peak Experiences and Border Crossings in Southern Indiana." *Anthropology of Consciousness* 26(2): 143–55. https://doi.org/10.1111/anoc.12038.

*Carter, P. (1983). *The Parts Model: A Formula for Integrity* (PhD diss., International College).

Catmur, C., E. S. Cross, and H. Over (2016). "Understanding Self and Others: From Origins to Disorders." *Philosophical Transactions of the Royal Society B* 371(1686). https://doi.org/10.1098/rstb.2015.0066.

Chan, M. (2015). "Contemporary Daoist Tangki Practice." In *Oxford Handbooks Online*. https://doi.org/10.1093/oxfordhb/9780199935420.013.11.

Chapin, B. L. (2008). "Transforming Possession: Josephine and the Work of Culture." *Ethos* 36(2): 220–245.

Chauvet, C. (2011). "Changing Spirit Identities: Rethinking the Four Palaces' Spirit Representations in Northern Vietnam." In *Engaging the Spirit World: Popular Beliefs and Practices in Modern Southeast Asia*. Edited by K. W. Endres and A. Lauser. Berghahn Books.

*Chodrow, J., ed. (1997). *Jung on Active Imagination*. Princeton University Press.

Choo, R. (2011). *The Spirit & Voodoo World of Thailand*. Wang Ci Xuan.

Choquette, S. (2006). *Ask Your Guides: Connecting to Your Divine Support System*. Hay House.

Christian, W. A. (2012). *Divine Presence in Spain and Western Europe 1500–1960*. Central European University Press.

*Christensen, P. (2013). "Modernity and Spirit Possession in Java: Horse Dance and Its Contested Magic." In *Dynamics of Religion in Southeast Asia*, 91–110. Amsterdam University Press.

Clarke, G. (1987). *Spirit Possession and Popular Religion*. Johns Hopkins University Press.

*Clarke, I. (2008). *Madness, Mystery and the Survival of God*. O Books.

*——— (2014). "The Perils of Being Porous: A Psychological View of Spirit Possession and Non-dogmatic Ways of Helping." *Self & Society* 41(4): 44–49. https://doi.org/10.1080/03060497.2014.11084387.

*————, ed. (2010). *Psychosis and Spirituality: Consolidating the New Paradigm* (2nd ed.). Wiley-Blackwell.

*———— (2016). *Schizotypy and the Experience of Transliminal Phenomena*. Royal College of Psychiatrists. https://www.isabelclarke.org/general/psychandspi_3_4247325807.pdf.

*———— (n.d.) *Science and Transcendence: Squaring the Circle*. https://www.isabelclarke. org/general/psychandspi_4_35/5238406.docx

*Clifford, T. (1987/1984). *Tibetan Buddhist Medicine & Psychiatry: The Diamond Healing*. Motilal Banarsidass.

Cline, E. M. (2010). "Female Spirit Mediums and Religious Authority in Contemporary Southeastern China." *Modern China* 36(5): 520–555. https://doi.org/10.1177/ 0097700410372921.

Cohen, E. (2007). *The Mind Possessed: The Cognition of Spirit Possession in an Afro-Brazilian Religious Tradition*. Oxford University Press.

———— (2008). "What Is Spirit Possession? Defining, Comparing, and Explaining Two Possession Forms." *Ethnos* 73(1): 101–126.

Cohen, E., and Barrett, J. L. (2008). "Conceptualizing Spirit Possession: Ethnographic and Experimental Evidence." *Ethos* 36(2): 246–67. https://doi.org/10.1111/j.1548-1352.2008.00013.x.

*Collins, J. M. (2009). *Exorcism and Deliverance Ministry in the Twentieth Century: An Analysis of the Practice and Theology of Exorcism in Modern Western Christianity*. Wipf & Stock Publishers.

Comaroff, J. L., and J. Comaroff (2001). "On Personhood: An Anthropological Perspective from Africa." *Social Identities* 7(2): 267–83. https://doi.org/10.1080/ 13504630120065310.

Conklin, B. (2001). *Consuming Grief: Compassionate Cannibalism in an Amazonian Society*. University of Texas Press.

Consentino, D. J. (1995). *Sacred Arts of Haitian Vodou*. University of California Press.

Cooley, C. H. (1922). *Human Nature and the Social Order*. Charles Scribner's Sons.

*Corbin, H. (1972). *Mundus Imaginalis or the Imaginary and the Imaginal*. Spring Publications.

*———— (1995). *Swedenborg and esoteric Islam*. Translated by L. Fox. Swedenborg Studies.

Covell, A. C. (2005). *Folk Art and Magic: Shamanism in Korea*. Hollym.

Crabtree, A. (2014). *Memoir of a Trance Therapist: Hypnosis and the Evocation of Human Potentials*. Friesen Press.

*———— (1985). *Multiple Man: Explorations in Possession & Multiple Personality*. Rinehart and Winston Ltd.

*Craffert, P. F. (2008). *The Life of a Galilean Shaman: Jesus of Nazareth in Anthropological-Historical Perspective*. Cascade Books.

Craffert, P. F., J. R. Baker, and M. J. Winkelman, eds. (2019). *The Supernatural After the Neuro-turn*. Routledge.

Crapanzano, V. (1985). *Tuhami, Portrait of a Moroccan*. University of Chicago Press.

*Csordas, T. J. (1994). *The Sacred Self: A Cultural Phenomenology of Charismatic Healing*. University of California Press.

Cumming, H., and K. Leffler (2007). *John of God: The Brazilian Healer Who's Touched the Lives of Millions*. Atria Books.

Cuneo, M. W. (2001). *American Exorcism*. Broadway Books.

Daillaire, R. (2003). *Shake Hands with the Devil: The Failure of Humanity in Rwanda*. Da Capo Press.

Dalai Lama (1999). *Freedom in Exile: an autobiography of the Dalai Lama*. Harper Collins.

Dan, J. (2002). *The Heart and the Fountain: An Anthology of Jewish Mystical Experiences*. Oxford University Press.

*Davies, S. (2014). *Spirit Possession and the Origins of Christianity*. Bardic Press.

*Davis, A. K., F. M. Clifton, E. G. Weaver, E. S. Hurwitz, M. W. Johnson, and R. R. Griffiths (2020). "Survey of Entity Encounter Experiences Occasioned by Inhaled N, N-dimethyltryptamine: Phenomenology, Interpretation, and Enduring Effects." *Journal of Psychopharmacology* 34(9): 1008–1020. https://doi.org/10.1177/0269881120916143.

Davis, W. (1985). *The Serpent and the Rainbow*. Simon & Schuster.

*Dawson, A., ed. (2011). *Summoning the Spirits: Possession and Invocation in Contemporary Religion*. Palgrave Macmillan.

*——— (2012). "Taking Possession of Santo Daime: The Growth of Umbanda within a Brazilian New Religion." In *Spirit Possession and Trance: New Interdisciplinary Perspectives*. Edited by B. E. Schmidt and L. Huskinson, 134–150. Bloomsbury Publishing.

Deardorff, D. (2004). *The Other Within: The Genius of Deformity in Myth, Culture & Psyche*. Heaven & Earth Publishing.

*DeBernardi, J. (2006). *The Way That Lives in the Heart: Chinese Popular Religion and Spirit Mediums in Penang, Malaysia*. Stanford University Press.

DeCicco, T. and Stroink, M. (2007). *International Journal of Transpersonal Studies* 26(1): 84–108.

de Heusch, L. (1962). "Cultes de possession et religions initiatiques de salut en Afrique." *Annales du Centre d'etudes des Religions*, ii. 226–44.

Dein, S., and A. S. Illaiee (2013). "Jinn and Mental Health: Looking at Jinn Possession in Modern Psychiatric Practice." *The Psychiatrist* 37: 290–293. https://doi.org/10.1192/pb.bp.113.042721.

de la Perriere, B., and P. Jackson, eds. (2022). *Spirit Possession in Buddhist Southeast Asia: Worlds Ever More Enchanted*. NiAS Press.

Delmonte, R., G. Lucchetti, A. Moreira-Almeida, and M. Farias (2016). "Can the DSM-5 Differentiate Between Nonpathological Possession and Dissociative Identity Disorder? A Case Study from an Afro-Brazilian Religion." *Journal of Trauma & Dissociation*, 17(3): 322–337. https://doi.org/10.1080/15299732.2015.1103351.

de Martino, Ernesto (1961). *The Land of Remorse: A Study of Southern Italian Tarantism*. Translated by Dorothy Zinn. Free Association Books.

Dennis, S. L. (2001). *Embrace of the Daimon: Sensuality and the Integration of Forbidden Imagery in Depth Psychology*. Nicolas Hayes.

*Deren, M. (1953). *Divine Horsemen: The Voodoo Gods of Haiti*. Thames & Hudson.

DeSteno, D. (2021). *How God Works: The Science Behind The Benefits of Religion*. Simon and Schuster.

*Diamond, S. A. (1996). *Anger, Madness, and the Daimonic: The Psychological Genesis of Violence, Evil, and Creativity*. State University of New York Press.

Dias, B., and K. Ressler (2013). "Parental Olfactory Exposure Influences Behavior and Neural Structures in Subsequent Generations." *Nature Neuroscience* 17: 89–96 (2014).

Dobbin, J. D. (1986). *The Jombee Dance of Montserrat: A Study of Trance Ritual in the West Indies.* Ohio State University Press.

*Dole, G. F. (2001). *Freedom & Evil: A Pilgrim's Guide to Hell.* Chrysalis Books.

———— (2018). *The Universe and I: Where Science & Spirituality Meet.* Swedenborg Foundation.

Dole, G., and R. Kirven (1997). *A Scientist Explores Spirit: A Biography of Emanuel Swedenborg with Key Concepts of His Theology.* The Swedenborg Foundation.

Domínguez, I. (2008). *Spirit Speak: Knowing and Understanding Spirit Guides, Ancestors, Ghosts, Angels, and the Divine.* New Page Books.

*Dossey, L. (2013). *One Mind: How Our Individual Mind Is Part of a Greater Consciousness and Why It Matters.* Hay House.

Doyle, A. C. (2003). *The History of Spiritualism.* Fredonia Books.

DuQuette, L. (1999) *My Life with the Spirits.* Weiser Books.

Duran, E. (n.d.). "The spirit of alcohol and addiction."

During, E. H., F. M. Elahi, O. Taieb, M.-R. Moro, and T. Baubet (2011). "A Critical Review of Dissociative Trance and Possession Disorders: Etiological, Diagnostic, Therapeutic, and Nosological Issues." *The Canadian Journal of Psychiatry / La Revue Canadienne de Psychiatrie* 56(4): 235–242. https://doi.org/10.1177/070674371105600407.

Durkheim, E. (1915). *The Elementary Forms of the Religious Life.* Free Press.

Dwyer, G. (2014). *The Divine and the Demonic: Supernatural Affliction and Its Treatment in North India* (1st ed.). Routledge.

Earley, J. (1999–2009). *The Best of Self to Self* (Vol. 2). Internal Family Systems.

———— (2012). *Resolving Inner Conflict: Working Through Polarization Using Internal Family Systems Therapy.* Pattern System Books.

———— (2009). *Self-Therapy* (2nd ed.). Pattern System Books.

*Ehrenreich, B. (2006). *Dancing in the Streets: A History of Collective Joy.* Metropolitan Books.

*Eisenstein, C. (2007). *The Ascent of Humanity: Civilization and the Human Sense of Self.* North Atlantic Books.

*Eldridge, M. (2007). "The Universe as Thou: William James's Religious Personalism" (unpublished conference paper). http://www.philosophy.uncc.edu/mleldrid/SAAP/USC/TP24.html.

Eliade, M. (1978). *A History of Religious Ideas* (Vols. 1–3). University of Chicago Press.

*———— (1957). *Myths, Dreams and Mysteries: The Encounter Between Contemporary Faiths and Archaic Realities.* Translated by P. Mairet. Harper Torchbooks.

*———— (1958). *Rites and Symbols of Initiation: The Mysteries of Birth and Rebirth.* Harper Torchbooks.

*———— (1987). *The Sacred and the Profane: The Nature of Religion.* Harcourt Jace Jovanovich.

*———— (1964). *Shamanism: Archaic Techniques of Ecstasy.* Translated by W. R. Trask. Pantheon Books.

*Ellenberger, H. F. (1970). *The Discovery of the Unconscious: The History and Evolution of Dynamic Psychiatry.* Basic Books.

*El-Zein, A. (2009). *Islam, Arabs, and the Intelligent World of the Jinn.* Syracuse University Press.

Endres, K. W. and A. Lauser, eds. (2011). *Engaging the Spirit World: Popular Beliefs and Practices in Modern Southeast Asia*. Berghahn Books.

Eng, K. F. (2018, March 1). "In 21ˢᵗ-Century Korea, Shamanism Is Not Only Thriving – but Evolving." TED Fellows. https://fellowsblog.ted.com/in-21st-century-korea-shamanism-is-not-only-thriving-but-evolving-f1a8862a7bc8

Evil Ones (n.d.). *Waldorf Watch*. https://sites.google.com/site/waldorfwatch/

Fadiman, J. and J. Gruber (2020). *Your Symphony of Selves: Discover and Understand More of Who We Are*. Park Street Press.

Faierstein, M. M. (1999). *Jewish Mystical Autobiographies: Book of Visions and Book of Secrets*. Paulist Press.

Falconer, R. (2021). "The Farther Reaches of IFS – Unattached Burdens and More." Master class hosted by Derek Scott.

*Farber, S. (2012). *The Spiritual Gift of Madness: The Failure of Psychiatry and the Rise of the Mad Pride Movement*. Inner Traditions.

Fardon, R., ed. (2003). *Counterworks: Managing the Diversity of Knowledge*. Routledge.

Ferrari, F. (2011). *Health and Religious Rituals in South Asia: Disease, Possession and Healing*. Taylor & Francis Group.

Fetaya, Y. (2010). *Minhat Yehuda*. Translated by A. Leader. Mechon Haktav.

*Filan, K., and Kaldera, R. (2009). *Drawing down the spirits: The traditions and techniques of spirit possession*. Destiny Books.

*Fiore, E. (1987). *The unquiet dead: A psychologist treats spirit possession*. Ballantine Books.

*Fjelstad, K., and N. T. Hien, eds. (2006). *Possessed by the Spirits: Mediumship in Contemporary Vietnamese Communities* (Southeast Asia Program). Cornell University Press.

Forbes, J. (1978). *Columbus and Other Cannibals*. Seven Stories Press.

Foucault, M. (1998). *Ethics: Subjectivity and Truth* (1st ed.). Edited by P. Rabinow. The New Press.

Franco, D. P. (2005b). *"I Love Myself, I Am Addiction-Free": Spiritual Tools to Fight Addiction: Seminar* [Album]. Spiritist Society of Baltimore.

———— (2016). *Life: Challenges and Solutions*. Leal. (Originally published in 1997)

*———— (2004). *Obsession*. Translated by E. J. Donato and H. C. Miranda. Leal. (Originally published in 1974)

———— (2005a). *Understanding Spiritual and Mental Health: Seminar* [Album]. Spiritist Society of Baltimore.

Frank, J. D. (1961). *Persuasion and Healing: A Comparative Study of Psychotherapy*. The Johns Hopkins Press.

Frazer, J. G. (1922). *The Golden Bough: A Study in Magic and Religion* (Vol 1.; abridged ed.). The Macmillan Company.

Fromm, E. (1951). *The Forgotten Language: An Introduction to the Understanding of Dreams, Fairy Tales and Myths*. Evergreen.

Furlong, D. (2003). *Working with Earth Energies: How to Tap into the Healing Powers of the Natural World*. Edited by I. Paten. Piatkus.

Galembo, P. (1998). *Vodou: Visions and Voices of Haiti*. Ten Speed Press.

Gallacher, P., ed. (1997). *The Cloud of Unknowing*, anonymous. TEAMS Middle English Texts.

*Gallagher, R. (2020). *Demonic Foes: My Twenty-Five Years as a Psychiatrist Investigating Possessions, Diabolic Attacks, and the Paranormal.* HarperOne.

*Garrett, C. (1987). *Spirit Possession and Popular Religion: from the Camisards to the Shakers.* Johns Hopkins University Press.

Gergen, K. J. (1990). "Social Understanding and the Inscription of Self." In *Cultural Psychology: Essays on Comparative Human Development* (1st ed.). Edited by J. W. Stigler, R. A. Schweder, and G. Herdt, 569–606. Cambridge University Press.

Germer, C., and R. D. Siegel, eds. (2014). *Wisdom and Compassion in Psychotherapy: Deepening Mindfulness in Clinical Practice* (1st ed). Guilford Press.

Gersi, D. (1991). *Faces in the Smoke: An Eyewitness Experience of Voodoo, Shamanism, Psychic Healing, and Other Amazing Human Powers.* Jeremy P. Tarcher.

Gill, A. (2020). *Shugendō: Pilgrimage and Ritual in a Japanese Folk Religion.* Self-published.

Giordan, G., and A. Possamai (2017). *Sociology of Exorcism in Late Modernity.* Springer.

Girma, T. (2020). *The Lived Experience of Adults with Ethiopia: of Adults with Zar Possession Among People in South Wollo: A Hermeneutic Phenomenological Study South Wollo Zon* (PhD diss., University of Gondar).

Glory to God for All Things, Glory2Godforallthings.com

*Goldish, M., ed. (2003). *Spirit Possession in Judaism: Cases and Contexts from the Middle Ages to the Present.* Wayne State University Press.

*Gonzalez-Wippler, M. (1992). *The Santeria Experience: A Journey into the Miraculous* (2nd ed.). Llewellyn Publications.

Good, M. D., S. T. Hyde, S. Pinto, and B. J. Good, eds. (2008). *Postcolonial Disorders* (1st ed.). University of California Press.

*Goodman, F. D. (2021/1992/1988). *Ecstasy, Ritual, and Alternate Reality: Religion in a Pluralistic World.* Midland Books.

*——— (1988). *How About Demons? Possession and Exorcism in the Modern World.* Indiana University Press.

——— (1997). *My Last Forty Days: A Visionary Journey Among the Pueblo Spirits.* Indiana University Press.

——— (1990). *Where the Spirits Ride the Wind: Trance Journeys and Other Ecstatic Experiences.* Indiana University Press.

Goodman, F. D., J. H. Henney, and E. Pressel (1974). *Trance, Healing, & Hallucination: Three Field Studies in Religious Experience.* John Wiley & Sons.

Goodman, F. D., and N. Nauwald (2003). *Ecstatic Trance: New Ritual Body Postures: A Workbook.* Translated by A. Altieri, J. Curran, and C. Landolt. Binkey Kok Publications.

Goulding, R. A., and R. C. Schwartz (1995). *The Mosaic Mind: Empowering the Tormented Selves of Child Abuse Survivors.* W. W. Norton & Company.

Gover, R. (1985). *Voodoo Contra.* Samuel Weiser.

Govinda, L. A. (2000/1960). Introduction to the Tibetan Book of the Dead. Translated by W. Evans-Wentz. Oxford.

Govorounova, A. (n.d.). "Pentecostalism and Shamanism in Asia and Beyond." https://www.academia.edu/35505696/Pentecostalism_and_Shamanism_in_Asia_and_Beyond

*Graf, S. J. (2000). *W. B. Yeats Twentieth-Century Magus: An In-Depth Study of Yeats's Esoteric Practices and Beliefs, Including Excerpts from His Magical Diaries.* Samuel Weiser.

Greenfield, S. (2016) *Spirits with Scalpels: The Cultural Biology of Religious Healing in Brazil.* Routledge.

Greenwood, S. (2009). *The Anthropology of Magic.* Bloomsbury Academic.

Griffiths, B. (2001). *River of Compassion.* Templegate Publishers.

*Griffiths, R. R., E. S. Hurwitz, A. K. Davis, M. W. Johnson, and R. Jesse (2019). "Survey of Subjective 'God Encounter Experiences': Comparisons Among Naturally Occurring Experiences and Those Occasioned by the Classic Psychedelics Psilocybin, LSD, Ayahuasca, or DMT. *PLOS ONE* 14(4). https://doi.org/10.1371/journal.pone.0214377.

Groop, K. (2012). "Spirit Attacks in Northern Namibia: Interpreting a New Phenomenon in an African Lutheran Context." In *Spirit Possession and Trance: New Interdisciplinary Perspectives* (B. E. Schmidt & L. Huskinson, eds.), 151–170. Bloomsbury Publishing.

*Guirdham, A. (1972). *Obsession: Psychic Forces and Evil in the Causation of Disease.* Neville Spearman Limited.

*Guisso, R., and C. Yu. (1988). *Shamanism: The Spirit World of Korea.* Asian Humanities Press.

*Gustafsson, M. (2009). *War and Shadows: The Haunting of Vietnam.* Cornell University Press.

Guthrie, E., S. Abraham, and S. Nawaz (2016). "Process of Determining the Value of Belief About Jinn Possession and Whether or Not They Are a Result of Mental Illness." *Case Reports.* https://doi.org/10.1136/bcr-2015-214005.

Hacking, I. (2006). *Mad Travelers: Reflections on the Reality of Transient Mental Ilnesses.* Harvard University Press.

——— (1995). *Rewriting the Soul: Multiple Personality and the Sciences of Memory.* Princeton University Press.

——— (1999) *The Social Construction of What?* Harvard University Press.

Hadīdī, H. (2017). *Zar: Spirit Possession, Music, and Healing Rituals in Egypt.* The American University in Cairo Press. https://doi.org/10.5743/cairo/9789774166976.001.0001.

Halliburton, M. (2005). "'Just Some Spirits': The Erosion of Spirit Possession and the Rise of 'Tension' in South India." *Medical Anthropology* 24(2): 111–144. https://doi.org/10.1080/01459740590933849.

Halloy, A. (2012). "Gods in the Flesh: Learning Emotions in the Xangô Possession Cult (Brazil)." *Ethnos* 77(2): 177–202. https://doi.org/10.1080/00141844.2011.586465.

*Hammond, F., and I. M. Hammond (1990). *Pigs in the Parlor: The Practical Guide to Deliverance.* Impact Books.

Hancock, G. (2007). *Supernatural: Meetings with the Ancient Teachers of Mankind* (rev. ed.). Disinformation Books.

Hanegraaff, W. (2012). *Esotericism and the Academy: Rejected Knowledge in Western Culture.* Cambridge University Press.

*——— (2013). *Western Esotericism.* Bloomsbury Academic.

Hanegraaff, W., and J. Kripal, eds. (2011). *Hidden Intercourse: Eros and Sexuality in the History of Western Esotericism.* Fordham University Press.

*Hannah, B. (1981). *Encounters with the Soul: Active Imagination as Developed by C. G. Jung.* SIGO Press.

Hansen, B. (2020). *Knot of the Soul: Madness, Psychoanalysis, Islam.* University of Chicago Press.

Hanwella, R., V. de Silva, A. Yoosuf, S. Karunaratne, and P. de Silva (2012). "Religious Beliefs, Possession States, and Spirits: Three Case Studies from Sri Lanka." *Case Reports in Psychiatry*. https://doi.org/10.1155/2012/232740.

Hardlife, B., and J. Taru (2014). "Dialogue with Demons: Religion, Culture and Exorcism in Christian Churches in Zimbabwe." *The International Journal of Humanities & Social Studies* 2(1): 44–50.

*Hari, J. (2018) *Lost Connections*. Bloomsbury Publishing.

Harman, W. (2011). "Possession as Protection and Affliction: The Goddess Mariyamman's Fierce Grace." In *Health and Religious Rituals in South Asia: Disease, Possession and Healing*. Translated by F. Ferrari. Taylor & Francis Group.

*Harner, M. (2013). *Cave and Cosmos: Shamanic Encounters with Another Reality*. North Atlantic Books.

*Harpur, P. (1994). *Daimonic Reality: A Field Guide to the Otherworld*. Pine Winds Press.

———— (2002). *The Philosophers' Secret Fire: A History of the Imagination*. Penguin Books.

———— (2011). *The Secret Tradition of the Soul*. Evolver Editions.

———— (2021, January 8). *Seeing Things: The Daimonic Nature of Reality*. Essentia Foundation. https://www.essentiafoundation.org/author/patrick-harpur/

*Hart, T. (2003). *The Secret Spiritual World of Children*. The New World Library.

Hassan, U. (2019). "Mind Reader: A New Brain-Machine Interface Detects What the User Wants." *Scientific American,* April 10, 2019.

Hastings, A. (1991). *With the Tongues of Men and Angels: A Study of Channeling*. Ted Buccholz.

Hecker, T., L. Braitmayer, and M. van Duijl (2015). "Global Mental Health and Trauma Exposure: The Current Evidence for the Relationship Between Traumatic Experiences and Spirit Possession." *European Journal of Psychotraumatology* 6. https://doi.org/10.3402/ejpt.v6.29126.

Heng, T. (2016). "Making 'Unofficial' Sacred Space: Spirit Mediums and House Temples in Singapore." *Geographical Review* 106(2): 215–234. https://doi.org/10.1111/j.1931-0846.2015.12156.x.

———— (2020). *Of Gods, Gifts and Ghosts: Spiritual Places in Urban Spaces*. Routledge. https://doi.org/10.4324/9780429437045.

Herbine-Blank, T., and M. Sweezy (2021). *Internal Family Systems Couple Therapy Skills Manual: Healing Relationships with Intimacy from the Inside Out*. PESI Publishing.

*Heschel, A. J. (2000). *I Asked for Wonder: A Spiritual Anthology*. Edited by S. H. Dresner. The Crossroad Publishing Company.

Hess, D. J. (1991). *Spirits and Scientists: Ideology, Spiritism, and Brazilian Culture*. Pennsylvania State University.

Hill, D. (1979). *New Testament Prophecy*. John Knox Press.

Hillman J. (1991). *A Blue Fire*. Harper Perennial.

———— (1983). *Healing Fiction*. Spring Publications.

———— (1975). *Re-Visioning Psychology*. William Morrow Paperbacks.

*Hillman, J., and Shamdasani, S. (2013). *Lament of the Dead: Psychology After Jung's Red Book*. Norton & Company.

*Hoffman, E. (1989). *The Way of Splendor: Jewish Mysticism and Modern Psychology*. Jason Aronson Inc.

Hollan, D. (2010). "Cross-Cultural Differences in the Self." In *Psychological Anthropology: A Reader on Self in Culture* (1st ed.). Edited by R. A. LeVine, 295–308. Wiley-Blackwell.

Hollis, F. (2013). *Hauntings: Dispelling the Ghosts Who Run Our Lives.* Chiron Publications.

Holm, N. G., ed. (1982). *Religious Ecstasy.* Almqvist & Wiksell International.

Homans, P., ed. (1968). *The Dialogue Between Theology and Psychology.* University of Chicago Press.

Horstmann, A. (2011). "Reconfiguring Manora Rongkru: Ancestor Worship and Spirit Possession in Southern Thailand." In *Engaging the Spirit World: Popular Beliefs and Practices in Modern Southeast Asia.* Edited by K. W. Endres and A. Lauser. Berghahn Books.

*Hsieh, S.-W. (2016). "Possession and Ritual: Daoist and Popular Healing in Taiwan." *Journal of Daoist Studies* 9(9): 73–100. https://doi.org/10.1353/dao.2016.0003.

Huang, Y.-C. (2018). "Spirit-Possession: Identities of a Master and the Rise of a Karma Kagyü Monastery in Taiwan." In *The Hybridity of Buddhism*, 159–176.

*Hufford, D. (2010). "Visionary Spiritual Experiences in an Enchanted World," *Anthropology and the Humanities* 35(2): 142–158.

*Hultkrantz, Å. (1992). *Shamanic Healing and Ritual Drama: Health and Medicine in Native North American Religious Traditions.* The Crossroad Publishing Company.

Hume, D. (1777). An Essay Concerning Human Understanding, p. 84.

Hunt, V. V. (1989). *Infinite Mind: Science of the Human Vibrations of Consciousness.* Malibu Publishing.

*Hunter, J. (2020). *Spirits, Gods, and Magic: An Introduction to the Anthropology of the Supernatural.* August Night Press.

*Hunter, J., and D. Luke, eds. (2014). *Talking with the Spirits: Ethnographies from Between the Worlds.* Daily Grail Publishing.

Hunter, R. (2016). *The Art of Spiritual Hypnosis: Accessing Divine Wisdom.* Blooming Twig Books.

——— (2005). *Hypnosis for Inner Conflict Resolution: Introducing Parts Therapy.* Crown House Publishing.

*Hurston, Z. N. (1981b). *The Sanctified Church: The Folklore Writings of Zora Neale Hurston.* Turtle Island.

*——— (1981a). *Tell My Horse.* Turtle Island. (Originally published in 1938)

Huwelmeier, G. (2018). "Trance Mediumship Takes the Stage: Reenactment and Heritagization of the Sacred in Urban Ha Noi." *Asian Ethnology* 77(1–2): 57–79.

*Huxley, A. (1952). *The Devils of London: A Study in the Psychology of Power Politics and Mystical Religion in the France of Cardinal Richelieu.* Harper Torchbooks.

Hyuk, J. N. (2004). *Shamanism in Korean Christianity.* Jimoondang International.

Igreja, V. (2018). "Spirit Possession." In H. Callan, ed., *The International Encyclopedia of Anthropology.* John Wiley & Sons. https://doi.org/10.1002/9781118924396.wbia1578.

Internal Family Systems (2016). *All Parts Are Welcome? Examining the Exiles in Our Culture and in Us* [Video]. Conference plenary session and post-conference institute. The Center for Self Leadership.

——— (2015). *Bringing Self-Leadership Out of the Office & Into the World.* Conference plenary [Video].

———— (2003a). *The Heart of Self Leadership Institute with Richard Schwartz and Cindy Libman*. Internal Family Systems 12th Annual Conference Proceedings [Video], Trailheads Publications.

———— (2003c). *IFS and Spirituality: The Center for Self Leadership* [Video]. Trailheads Publications.

———— (2014). *No Part Left Behind: The Self-Led Healing of Traumatized Inner Worlds: 2014 Conference Highlights*. Internal Family Systems 2014 Conference [Video].

———— (2003b). *Patricia* [Video]. Trailheads Publications.

———— (n.d.). *Trauma Behind Rage* [Video]. The Center for Self Leadership.

*International Society for the Study of Dissociation (1993). *Dissociation: Progress in the Dissociative Disorders,* 6(1). The Official Journal of the International Society for the Study of Dissociation.

Ireland-Frey, L. (1999). *Freeing the Captives: The Emerging Therapy of Treating Spirit Attachment*. Hampton Roads Publishing.

Irmak, K. (2014). "Schizophrenia or Possession?" *Journal of Religion and Health* Jun; 53(3): 773–7.

Irving, A. (1955). "The Self and Its Behavioral Environment." In *Culture and Experience*, 75–110. University of Pennsylvania Press.

*Isaacs, T. C. (2018). *In Bondage to Evil: A Psycho-spiritual Understanding of Possession*. Pickwick Publications.

Ishii, M. (2013). "Playing with Perspectives: Spirit Possession, Mimesis, and Permeability in the *Buuta* Ritual in South India." *Journal of the Royal Anthropological Institute* 19(4): 795–812. https://doi.org/10.1111/1467-9655.12065.

Islam, F., and R. A. Campbell (2014). "'Satan Has Afflicted Me!' Jinn-Possession and Mental Illness in the Qur'an." *Journal of Religion and Health* 53(1): 229–243.

Itzhak, N. (2015). "Making Selves and Meeting Others in Neo-shamanic Healing." *Ethos* 43(3): 286–310. https://doi.org/10.1111/etho.12086.

James, W. (1950). *The Principles of Psychology* (Vol. 1). Dover Publications. (Originally published in 1890)

*———— (1994). *The Varieties of Religious Experience*. Modern Library. (Originally published in 1936)

*Jaynes, J. (1976). *The Origin of Consciousness in the Breakdown of the Bicameral Mind*. Mariner Books.

*Jodorowsky, A. (2010). *Psychomagic: The Transformative Power of Shamanic Psychotherapy*. Translated by R. LeValley. Inner Traditions. (Originally published in 2004)

———— (2005). *The Spiritual Journey of Alejandro Jodorowsky: The Creator of El Topo*. Translated by Inner Traditions International. Park Street Press.

Jodorowsky, A., and G. Farcet (1989). *Sacred Trickery and the Way of Kindness: The Radical Wisdom of Jodo*. Translated by Inner Traditions International. Inner Traditions.

Johnson, P. J. (1996). *An Alien Occupancy: Reconsidering the Phenomenon of the Demonic for a Postmodern and Cross Cultural Pastoral Care*. (PhD diss., Emory University). ProQuest.

Johnson, R. (2013). *Spirituality in Counseling and Psychotherapy*. Wiley Press.

Johnston, W., ed. (1996). *The Cloud of Unknowing: and The Book of Privy Counseling*. Image Press.

———— (2006). *Mystical Journey: An Autobiography*. Orbis Books.

───── (1998). *Mystical Theology: The Science of Love*. Orbis Books.

The Journal of Self Leadership (2009). *The Journal of Self Leadership: Commemorative Final Edition*, 1–3.

Jung, C. G. (1967). *Alchemical Studies* (Vol. 13 of the Collected Works of Jung). Princeton University Press.

───── (1963) Letter, in the AA grapevine.

───── (1961). *Memories, Dreams, Reflections*. Edited by A. Jaffé, translated by R. Winston and C. Winston. Vintage Books.

───── (2009). *The Red Book: Liber novus*. Edited by S. Shamdasani. Philemon Foundation.

───── (1966). *The Spirit in Man, Art, and Literature* (Vol. 15 of the Collected Works of Jung). Princeton University Press.

Kalsched, D. (1996). *The Inner World of Trauma: Archetypal Defenses of the Personal Spirit*. Routledge.

───── (2013). *Trauma and the Soul: A Psycho-spiritual Approach to Human Development and its Interruption*. Routledge.

Kalweit, H. (1987). *Shamans, Healers, and Medicine Men*. Shambhala Publications.

Kapferer, B. (1991). *A Celebration of Demons: Exorcism and the Aesthetics of Healing in Sri Lanka* (2nd ed.). Berg Smithsonian Institution Press.

Kaplan, A. (1990). *Inner Space: Introduction to Kabbalah, Meditation, and Prophecy*. Edited by A. Sutton. Moznaim Publishing.

Kaplan, B., ed. (1961). *Studying Personality Cross-Culturally*. Harper & Row Publishers.

*Karamustafa, A. T. (1994). *God's Unruly Friends: Dervish Groups in the Islamic Middle Period 1200–1550*. Oneworld Publications.

Kardec, A. (2008). *The Gospel According to Spiritism* (2nd ed.). Edited by D. W. Kimble and I. Reis. International Spiritist Council. (Originally published in 1864)

───── (2009). *The Mediums' Book or Guide to Mediums and Evokers: Experimental Spiritism*. Translated by D. W. Kimble and M. M. Saiz. International Spiritist Council.

───── (2012). *Spiritism in Its Simplest Expression: Summary of the Spirits' Teachings and Their Manifestations*. Translated by D. W. Kimble and M. M. Saiz. International Spiritist Council. (Originally published in 1862)

───── (2018). *The Spiritist Book* (New English ed.). Translated by E. G. Dutrarans. Luchnos. (Originally published in 1957)

*───── (2010). *The Spirits' Book* (4th ed.). Translated by D. W. Kimble and M. M. Saiz. International Spiritist Council.

Kaspina, M. (2008). "The Dybbuk and the Ikota: Similarity and Difference in Jewish and Slavic Traditions about the Possession of an Evil Spirit." *East European Jewish Affairs* 38(1): 35–43.

Katz, P. R., and M. A. Rubinstein (2003). *Religion and the Formation of Taiwanese Identities* (1st ed.). Palgrave Macmillan.

*Katz, R. (2017). *Indigenous Healing Psychology: Honoring the Wisdom of the First Peoples*. Healing Arts Press.

───── (1983). *The Straight Path of the Spirit: Ancestral Wisdom and Healing Traditions in Fiji*. Park Street Press

Keats, J. (1899). *The Complete Poetical Works and Letters of John Keats* (Cambridge ed.). Houghton, Mifflin and Company.

*Keeney, B., ed. (1999). *Kalahari Bushmen Healers*. Ringing Rocks Press.

*———, ed. (2002). *Shakers of St. Vincent*. Ringing Rocks Press.

*——— (1994). *Shaking Out the Spirits: A Psychotherapist's Entry into the Healing Myster-ies of Global Shamanism*. Station Hill Press.

Kelly, E. F., A. Crabtree, and P. Marshall, eds. (2015). *Beyond Physicalism: Toward Recon-ciliation of Science and Spirituality*. Rowman & Littlefield.

Kendall, L. (1996). "Korean Shamans and the Spirits of Capitalism." *American Anthro-pologist* 98(3): 512–27. https://doi.org/10.1525/aa.1996.98.3.02a00060.

——— (1988). *The Life and Hard Times of a Korean Shaman: Of Tales and the Telling of Tales*. University of Hawai'i Press.

Kenyon, S. M. (1999). Zar as Modernization in Sontemporary Sudan. In *Across the Boundaries of Belief*. Routledge.

Khalifa, N., and T. Hardie (2005). "Possession and Jinn." *Journal of the Royal Society of Medicine* 98: 351–353.

*Kharitidi, O. (1996). *Entering the Circle: Ancient Secrets of Siberian Wisdom Discovered by a Russian Psychiatrist*. Harper Collins.

——— (2001). *Master of Lucid Dreams*. Hampton Roads Publishing.

Kianpoor, M., and G. F. Rhoades (2006). "Djinnati: A Possession State in Baloochistan, Iran." *Journal of Trauma Practice* 4(1–2): 147–155. https://doi.org/10.1300/J189v04n01_10.

Kiev, A., ed. (1964). *Magic, Faith, and Healing: Studies in Primitive Psychiatry Today*. The Free Press of Glencoe.

Kim, U., and J. W. Berry, eds. (1993). *Indigenous Psychologies: Research and Experience in Cultural Context*. Sage Publications.

Kingsbury, K., and A. Chesnut (2019, January 10). "Driving Out the Devil: What's Be-hind the Exorcism Boom?" *Catholic Herald*. https://catholicherald.co.uk/driving-out-the-devil-whats-behind-the-exorcism-boom/.

Kinny, J., ed. (2004). *The Inner West: An Introduction to the Hidden Wisdom of the West*. Jeremy P. Tarcher.

Kirkpatrick, S. D. (2000). *Edgar Cayce: An American Prophet*. Riverhead Books.

Kirmayer, L. J. (2007). "Psychotherapy and the Cultural Concept of Person." *Transcul-tural Psychiatry* Jun; 44(2): 232–57. https://doi.org/10.1177/1363461506070794.

——— (1992). "Taking Possession of Trance." *Transcultural Psychiatric Research Review* 29(4): 283–286.

Kitanaka, J. (2015). "The Rebirth of Secrets and the New Care of the Self in Depressed Japan." *Current Anthropology* 56(12): 251–62. https://doi.org/10.1086/683273.

*Klaniczay, G., and E. Pócs (2005). *Demons, Spirits, Witches: Communicating with the Spirits* (Vol. 1). Central European University Press.

*Klass, M. (2003). *Mind over Mind: The Anthropology and Psychology of Spirit Possession*. Rowan and Littlefield Publishers.

Kleinman, A., and E. Fitz-Henry (2007). "The Experiential Basis of Subjectivity: How In-dividuals Change in the Context of Societal Transformation." In *Subjectivity* (1st ed.). Edited by J. Biehl, B. Good, and A. Kleinman, 52–65. University of California Press.

*Knight, R. B., M. Falstein (2002). *A Man's Recovery from Traumatic Childhood Abuse*. The Haworth Press.

Knox, R. A. (1950). *Enthusiasm: A Chapter in the History of Religion*. University of Notre Dame Press.

Koch, K. E. (1973). *Demonology Past and Present: Identifying and Overcoming Demonic Strongholds*. Kregel Publications.

Koenig, H., D. King, and V. B. Carson (2012). *Handbook of Religion and Health* (2nd ed.). Oxford University Press.

Kondo, D. K. (2007). "Creating an Ideal Self: Theories of Selfhood and Pedagogy at a Japanese Ethics Retreat." In *The Anthropology of Organisations*. Edited by A. C. Jiménez. Routledge.

*Kontzevitch, I. M. (1988). *The Acquisition of the Holy Spirit in Ancient Russia* (Vol. 1). St. Herman of Alaska Brotherhood.

Koss, J. D. (2011). "Artistic Expression and Creative Process in Caribbean Possession Cult Rituals." In *The Visual Arts*. De Gruyter Mouton.

Koss-Chioino, J. (2010). "Introduction to 'Do Spirits Exist? Ways to Know.'" *Anthropology and the Humanities* 35(2): 131–141.

Kramer, K. P., (2004). *Martin Buber's I and Thou: Practicing Living Dialogue*. Paulist Press.

Kreiter, J. (2017). *Overcoming the Archon Through Alchemy*. CreateSpace Independent Publishing.

*Krippner, S. (2007). "Humanity's First Healers: Psychological and Psychiatric Stances on Shamans and Shamanism." *Archives of Clinical Psychology* 34(1): 16–22.

Krosby, A. (2014). "'Work and Strengthening': Ontological Dualism and the Ethical Treatment of Mentally Ill Patients in Madagascar." Master's thesis, University of Bergen.

*Kupperman, J. S. (2014). *Living Theurgy: A Course in Iamblichus' Philosophy, Theology, and Theurgy*. Avalonia.

Kusserow, A. S. (1999). Crossing the Great Divide: Anthropological Theories of the Western Self. *Journal of Anthropological Research* 55(4): 541–62.

Kuznetsova, A. M. (2006). "Demons versus Saints in the Early Eastern Orthodox Monastic Literature." In *Universum Hagiographicum*, 136–143. Gorgias Press.

Lacerda de Azevedo, J. (1997). *Spirits & Matter: New Horizons for Medicine*. Translated by I. Dreux. New Falcon Publications.

Lachman, G. (2016). *Beyond the Robot: The Life and Work of Colin Wilson*. Tarcher Perigee.

*——— (2017). *Lost Knowledge of the Imagination*. Floris Books.

*——— (2012). *Swedenborg: An Introduction to His Life and Ideas*. Penguin Group.

*Laing, R. D. (1967). *The Politics of Experience*. Pantheon Books.

Lamb, S. (1997). "The Making and Unmaking of Persons: Notes on Aging and Gender in North India." *Ethos* 25(3): 279–302. https://doi.org/10.1525/eth.1997.25.3.279.

*Lambek, M. (1993). *Knowledge and Practice in Mayotte: Local Discourses of Islam, Sorcery and Spirit Possession* (1st ed.). University of Toronto Press, Scholarly Publishing Division.

Laski, M. (1961). *Ecstasy in Secular and Religious Experiences*. Jeremy P. Tarcher.

*Laszlo, E., J. Houston, and L. Dossey. (2016). *What Is Consciousness? Three Sages Look Behind the Veil*. Select Books.

Laszlo, E., and A. Peake (2014). *The Immortal Mind: Science and the Continuity of Consciousness Beyond the Brain*. Inner Traditions.

Laughlin, C.D. (2020). *The Contemplative Brain: Meditation, Phenomenology and Self-Discovery from a Neuroanthropological Point of View.* Daily Grail Publishing

Lawrence, B. W., R. Carhart-Harris, R. R. Griffiths, and C. Timmermann (2022). "Phenomenology and Content of the Inhaled *N,N*-dimethyltryptamine (*N,N*-DMT) Experience." *Scientific Reports* 12(8562).

Laycock, J. P. (2015). *Spirit Possession Around the World: Possession, Communion, and Demon Expulsion Across Cultures.* ABC-CLIO.

Leavitt, J. (1993). "Are Trance and Possession Disorders?" *Transcultural Psychiatric Research Review* 30(1): 51–57. https://doi.org/10.1177/136346159303000102.

Lee, B.-O. (2007). Therapeutic Outcomes and the Process of Healing by Dang-Ki in Singapore. Master's thesis, McGill University.

Lee, B.-O., and L. J. Kirmayer (2020). "Dang-Ki Healing: An Embodied Relational Healing Practice in Singapore." *Transcultural Psychiatry* 57(6): 786–800. https://doi.org/10.1177/1363461519858448.

*Leudar, I., and P. Thomas (2000). *Voices of Reason, Voices of Insanity: Studies of Verbal Hallucinations.* Routledge.

Levy, P. (2015). *Awakened by Darkness: When Evil Becomes Your Father.* Awaken in the Dream Publishing.

*——— (2013). *Dispelling Wetiko: Breaking the Curse of Evil.* North Atlantic Books.

Levy-Bruhl, L. (1975). *The Notebooks on Primitive Mentality.* Translated by P. Rivière. Basil Blackwell & Mott.

Lewis, C. S. (1943). *The Screwtape Letters: Letters from a Senior to a Junior Devil.* Macmillan Paperbacks.

Lewis, H. S. (2005). "The Globalization of Spirit Possession." In *Social Critique and Commitment: Essays in Honor of Henry Rosenfeld.* Edited by M. Al-Haj, M. Saltman, and Z. Sobel, 169–191. University Press of America.

*Lewis, I. M. (1971). *Ecstatic Religion: An Anthropological Study of Spirit Possession and Shamanism.* Penguin Books.

Lian, X. (2010). *Redeemed by Fire: The Rise of Popular Christianity in Modern China.* Yale University Press.

Littlewood, R. (2004b). "Multiple Personality Disorder: A Clinical and Cultural Account." *Psychiatry* 3(8): 11–13.

——— (2002). *Pathologies of the West: An Anthropology of Mental Illness in Europe and America.* Cornell University Press.

——— (2004a). "Possession states." *Psychiatry* 3(8): 8–10.

——— (2001). *Religion, Agency, Restitution.* Oxford.

Liu, P.-C. (2020). "Shamanism and Gender Construction among the Kavalan of Taiwan: Men and Women's Illness Caused by Different Spirits." In *The Shamaness in Asia.* Edited by D. Torri and S. Roche, 208–224. Routledge.

Livingston, J. G. (2004). *Adversaries Walk Among Us: A Guide to the Origin, Nature, and Removal of Demons and Spirits.* Lost Coast Press.

Lucchetti, G., P. R. D. C. Aguiar, C. C. Braghetta, C. P. Vallada, A. Moreira-Almeida, and H. Vallada (2011). "Spiritist Psychiatric Hospitals in Brazil: Integration of Conventional Psychiatric Treatment and Spiritual Complementary Therapy." *Culture, Medicine, and Psychiatry* 36(1): 124–135.

*Luhrmann, T. M. (2012a). "Beyond the Brain." *The Wilson Quarterly* 36(3).

———— (2013) "Conjuring Up Our Own Gods." New York Times. (Op-ed.)

*———— (2016). "Diversity within the Psychotic Continuum." *Schizophrenia Bulletin* 43(1): 27–31. https://doi.org/10.1093/schbul/sbw137.

*———— (2011). "Hallucinations and Sensory Overrides." *Annual Review of Anthropology* 40: 71–85. https://doi.org/10.1146/annurev-anthro-081309-145819.

*———— (2007). "How Do You Learn to Know That It Is God Who Speaks?" In *Learning Religion: Anthropological Approaches,* 83–102. Berghahn Books.

*———— (2020). *How God Becomes Real: Kindling the Presence of Invisible Others.* Princeton University Press.

*———— (2012b, 1 June). "Living with Voices." *The American Scholar.* https://theamericanscholar.org/author/t-m-luhrmann/

*———— (2004). Metakinesis: How God Becomes Intimate in Contemporary U.S. Christianity. *American Anthropologist* 106(3): 518–528.

*————, ed. (2020). "Mind and Spirit: A Comparative Theory." *The Journal of the Royal Anthropological Institute* 26(1).

———— (1989). *Persuasions of the Witch's Craft: Ritual Magic in England.* Harvard University Press.

*———— (2018). "The Real Ontological Challenge." *Journal of Ethnographic Theory* 8(1–2): 79–82.

*———— (2012c). *When God Talks Back: Understanding the American Evangelical Relationship with God.* Vintage Books.

*Luhrmann, T. M., and J. Marrow, eds. (2016). *Our Most Troubling Madness: Case Studies in Schizophrenia Across Cultures.* University of California Press.

*Luhrmann, T. M., R. Padmavati, H. Tharoor, and A. Osei (2015). "Differences in Voice-Hearing Experiences of People with Psychosis in the USA, India, and Ghana: Interview-Based Study." *The British Journal of Psychiatry* 206(1): 41–44.

*Luhrmann, T.M., K. Weisman, F. Aulino, et al. (2021). "Sensing the Presence of Gods and Spirits Across Cultures and Faiths." *PNAS* 118(5). https://doi.org/10.1073/pnas.2016649118.

Luke, D. (2017) *Otherworlds.* Aeon Books.

Luke, D., and R. Spowers, eds. (2021) *DMT Entity Encounters.* Park Street Press.

*Lum, K. A. (2018). *Praising His Name in the Dance: Spirit Possession in the Spiritual Baptist Faith and Orisha Work in Trinidad, West Indies.* CRC Press.

Machingura, F. (2012). "The Shona Concept of Spirit Possession (Kusvikirwa) and the Pentecostal Phenomenon of Getting into the Spirit (Kupinda Mumweya)." *Hope's Reason: A Journal of Apologetics.*

*MacNutt, F. (2009). *Deliverance from Evil Spirits: A Practical Manual* (2nd ed.). Chosen Books.

Mageo, J. M. (2002). "Toward a Multidimensional Model of the Self." *Journal of Anthropological Research* 58(3): 339–365.

Mageo, J. M., and A. Howard (1996). *Spirits in Culture, History, and Mind.* Routledge.

Mariani, M. (2018, December). "American Exorcism." *The Atlantic.*

Maricar, N. (2018). "Malay Muslim Healers' Roles and Experiences in Treating Patients with Mental Health Issues in Singapore" (13428493). PhD thesis, The Chicago School of Professional Psychology. ProQuest.

Markus, H. R., and S. Kitayama (1991). "Culture and the Self: Implications for Cognition, Emotion, and Motivation." *Psychological Review* 98(2): 224–253. https://doi.org/10.1037/0033-295X.98.2.224.

Marovic, Z., and M. M. Machinga (2017). "African Shamanic Knowledge and Transpersonal Psychology: Spirits and Healing in Dialogue." *The Journal of Transpersonal Psychology* 49(1): 31–44.

Marshall, A. R. (2003). "Moving the Spirit on Taiwan: New Age Lingji Performance." *Journal of Chinese Religions* 31(1): 81–99. https://doi.org/10.1179/073776903804760120.

Martin, H. (1998). *The Secret Teachings of the Espiritistas: A Hidden History of Spiritual Teachings*. Metamind Publications.

Martin, M. (1976). *Hostage to the Devil: The Possession and Exorcism of Five Contemporary Americans*. Harper One.

*Marzinsky, J., and S. Swiney (2019). *An Amazing Journey into the Psychotic Mind: Breaking the Spell of the Ivory Tower*. Lulu Press Inc.

Masquelier, A. (2001). *Prayer Has Spoiled Everything: Possession, Power, and Identity in an Islamic Town of Niger*. Duke University Press. https://doi.org/10.2307/j.ctv1134dsp.

*Maté, G. (2008). *In the Realm of Hungry Ghosts: Close Encounters with Addiction*. North Atlantic Books.

Maugé, C. E. (2017). *The Yoruba Religion: Introduction to Its Practice*. Original Publications.

Mauss, M. (1985). "A Category of the Human Mind: The Notion of Person; the Notion of Self." In *The Category of the Person: Anthropology, Philosophy, History*. Edited by M. Carrithers, S. Collins, and S. Lukes. Cambridge University Press. (Originally published in 1938)

Maxwell, M., and V. Tschudin (1990). *Seeing the Invisible: Modern Religious and Other Transcendent Experiences*. Penguin Books.

McCloud, S. (2015). *American Possessions: Fighting Demons in the Contemporary United States*. Oxford University Press.

*McDaniel, J. (1989). *The Madness of the Saints: Ecstatic Religion in Bengal*. University of Chicago Press.

McFadden, J. (2020) "Integrating Information in the Brain's EM Field: The Cemi Field Theory of Consciousness." *Neuroscience of Consciousness* 2020(1), niaa 016.

*McGilchrist, I. (2009). *The Master and His Emissary: The Divided Brain and the Making of the Western World*. IDSUK.

——— (2019). *Ways of Attending*. Routledge.

Mcintosh, J. (2018). "Personhood, Self, and Individual." In *The International Encyclopedia of Anthropology*, 1–9. American Cancer Society. https://doi.org/10.1002/9781118924396.wbiea1576.

McKinney, C. (2014). "Possession Phenomena: A Critical Literature Review. Unpubl. diss., Azusa Pacific University.

*McNamara, P. (2011). *Spirit Possession and Exorcism: History, Psychology, and Neurobiology* (Vols. 1 & 2). Praeger.

McNeill, B. (2019, January). "The Centuries-Old Practice of Exorcism Is on the Rise. Why Now?" *VCU News.* https://news.vcu.edu/article/The_centuriesold_practice_of_exorcism_is_on_the_rise_Why_now.

McNeill, J. T. (1951). *A History of the Cure of Souls.* Harper & Brothers Publishers.

*McNeill, W. H. (1995). *Keeping Together in Time: Dance and Drill in Human History.* American Council of Learned Societies.

Mead, G. H., H. Joas, and D. R. Huebner (2015). *Mind, Self, and Society: The Definitive Edition* (1st enlarged ed.). Edited by C. W. Morris. University of Chicago Press. (Originally published in 1934)

Melania, M. (2020). "Insanity and demonic possession in patristic thought." *Antiochian Orthodox Christian Archdiocese of North America.* http://ww1.antiochian.org/node/22478

*Métraux, A. (1972). *Voodoo in Haiti.* Schocken.

Mianji, F., and Y. Semnani (2015). "Zār Spirit Possession in Iran and African Countries: Group Distress, Culture-Bound Syndrome or Cultural Concept of Distress?" *Iranian Journal of Psychiatry* 10(4): 225–232.

Miller, L. J., ed. (2012). *The Oxford Handbook of Psychology and Spirituality.* Oxford University Press.

Mills, A. (2010). "Understanding the Conundrum of Rebirth Experience of the Bever, Gitxsan, and Witsuwit'en." *Anthropology and the Humanities* 35(2): 172–191.

McLaughlin, E., and K. Mahler (n.d.). The Vast Influence of Interoception. Misericordia University.

Mithen, S. (1996). *The Prehistory of the Mind.* Thames and Hudson.

*Modi, S. (1997). *Remarkable Healings: A Psychiatrist Discovers Unsuspected Roots of Mental and Physical Illness.* Hampton Roads Publishing Company.

Montgomery, J. W., ed. (1975). *Demon Possession: A Medical, Historical, Anthropological and Theological Symposium.* NRP Books.

Mooney, J. (1896). *The Ghost-Dance Religion and the Sioux Outbreak of 1890.* University of Chicago Press.

*Moreira-Almeida, A., F. L. Neto, and E. Cardeña (2008). "Comparison of Brazilian Spiritist Mediumship and Dissociative Identity Disorder." *The Journal of Nervous and Mental Disease* 196(5).

Mueggler, E. (2001). *The Age of Wild Ghosts Memory, Violence, and Place in Southwest China.* University of California Press.

*Müller-Ebeling, C., C. Rätsch, and S. B. Shahi (2000). *Shamanism and Tantra in the Himalayas.* Translated by Inner Traditions. Inner Traditions.

*Murphy, J. M. (1994). *Working the Spirit: Ceremonies of the African Diaspora.* Beacon Press.

Mylonas, G. (1961). *Eleusis and the Eleusinian Mysteries.* Princeton University Press.

Naegeli-Osjord, H. (1988). *Possession & Exorcism: Understanding the Human Psyche in Turmoil.* New Frontiers Center.

*Negi, D., and R. L. Zinta (2020). "Conflicts Reconciliation Through Deity Possession: A Traditional Form of Psychotherapy." *International Journal of Engineering, Pure and Applied Sciences* 5(3).

Neuner, F., A. Pfeiffer, E. Schauer-Kaiser, M. Odenwald, T. Elbert, and V. Ertl (2012). "Haunted by Ghosts: Prevalence, Predictors and Outcomes of Spirit Possession Experiences Among Former Child Soldiers and War-Affected Civilians in Northern Uganda." *Social Science & Medicine* 75(3): 548–554. https://doi.org/10.1016/j.socscimed.2012.03.028.

*Nevius, J. L. (2020). *Demon Possession and Allied Themes* (3rd ed.). Fleming H. Revell Company.

Nickerson, P. (2001). "A Poetics and Politics of Possession: Taiwanese Spirit-Medium Cults and Autonomous Popular Cultural Space." *Positions: East Asia Cultures Critique* 9(1): 187–217.

Nielssen, H., and K. H. Skeie (2014). "Christian Revivalism and Political Imagination in Madagascar." *Journal of Religion in Africa* 44(2): 189–223. https://doi.org/10.1163/15700666-12340004.

*Noll, R. (1985). "Mental Imagery Cultivation as a Cultural Phenomenon: The Role of Visions in Shamanism." *Current Anthropology* 26(4): 443–461.

Norton , B. (2006). "'Hot-Tempered' Women and 'Effeminate Men.'" In *Possessed by the Spirits*. Edited by K. Fjelstad and H. Nguyen, 55–63. Cornell University Press.

———— (2009). *Song for the Spirits: Music and Mediums in Modern Vietnam*. University of Illinois Press.

Obeyesekere, G. (1981). *Medusa's Hair*. University of Chicago Press.

O'Brien, J. (2018). "Understanding Exorcism: An Interview with Father Jeffery Grob." *The Adoremus Bulletin*.

*Oesterreich, T. K. (1974). *Possession and Exorcism: Among Primitive Races, in Antiquity, the Middle Ages, and Modern Times*. Translated by D. Ibberson. Causeway Books.

*Oliveira, T. (2016). *Talking to Spirits in Mediumistic Meetings*. United States Spiritist Council.

Ong, A. (2007). "The Production of Possession: Spirits and the Multinational Corporation in Malaysia." In *Beyond the Body Proper: Reading the Anthropology of Material Life* (1st ed.). Edited by M. Lock and J. Farquhar. Duke University Press.

OrthodoxPhotos.com (2003). "The Nets of the Evil One." (2003). https://www.orthodoxphotos.com/readings/threshold/nets.shtml

Ortner, S. B. (2005). "Subjectivity and Cultural Critique." *Anthropological Theory* 5(1): 31–52. https://doi.org/10.1177/1463499605050867.

*Otto, R. (1923). *The Idea of the Holy*. Translated by J. W. Harvey. Oxford University Press.

*Otto, W. F. (1965). *Dionysus: Myth and Cult*. Translated by R. B. Palmer. Spring Publications. Indiana University Press.

*Page, K., and N. Nester (2007). *Energy Techniques for Spirit Releasement: Dancing with Ghosts* (2nd ed.). Clear Light Arts.

*Pagani, A. (2018). *The Secrets to Deliverance: Defeat the Toughest Cases of Demonic Bondage*. Charisma House.

*Pagels, E. (1995). *The Origin of Satan*. Vintage Books.

*Palmer, T. (2017). *The Science of Spirit Possession* (2nd ed.). Cambridge Scholars Publishing.

Palmer, T. J. (2008). "Are They Evil, Mad or Possessed? A Method of Investigation: Scientific Evaluation of Spirit Possession." *New Interpretations of Spirit Possession.*

Pandolfo, S. (2018). *Knot of the Soul: Madness, Psychoanalysis, Islam* (1st ed.). University of Chicago Press.

Papademetriou, G. C. (n.d.). Exorcism in the Orthodox Church. *Greek Orthodox Archdiocese of North America.* https://www.goarch.org/-/exorcism-in-the-orthodox-church

Parkes, G. (1996). *Composing the Soul: The Reaches of Nietzsche's Psychology.* University of Chicago Press.

Pastor, M., and J. Gauvain (2020). *Internal Family Systems Institute: Level 1 Training Manual.* Trailhead Publications.

Paxson, D. L. (2015). *The Essential Guide to Possession, Depossession, & Divine Relationships.* Weiser Books.

Pazderic, N. (2004). "Recovering True Selves in the Electro-spiritual Field of Universal Love." *Cultural Anthropology* 19(2): 196–225. https://doi.org/10.1525/can.2004.19.2.196.

Pearce, J. C. (2002). *The Biology of Transcendence: A Blueprint of the Human Spirit.* Park Street Press.

*Peck, M. S. (1983). *People of the Lie: The Hope for Healing Human Evil.* Simon & Schuster.

*——— (2005). *Glimpses of the Devil: A Psychiatrist's Personal Accounts of Possession, Exorcism, and Redemption.* Free Press.

Peebles, J. M. (2016). *The Demonism of the Ages, Spirit Obsessions, Oriental and Occidental Occultism* (4th ed.). Read Books.

Perch, Y. (2021, July 1). *Dissociation and Complexity: A Psychiatrist's Perspective.* Essentia Foundation. https://www.essentiafoundation.org/reading/dissociation-and-complexity-a-psychiatrists-perspective/

Perez, A. M. Carreiras, and J. A. Duñabeitia (2017). "Brain-to-Brain Entrainment: EEG Interbrain Synchronization While Speaking and Listening." *Scientific Reports* 7(1): 4190.

Perls, F. S. (1969). *In and Out the Garbage Pail.* Real People Press.

Perrière, B. (2011). "Being a Spirit Medium in Contemporary Burma." In *Engaging the Spirit World: Popular Beliefs and Practices in Modern Southeast Asia.* Edited by K. W. Endres and A. Lauser. Berghahn Books.

*Perry, J. W. (1974). *The Far Side of Madness.* Spring Publications.

"Personalism" (2013). *Stanford Encyclopedia of Philosophy.* https://plato.stanford.edu/entries/personalism/

*Peters, L. (2016). *Tibetan Shamanism: Ecstasy and Healing.* North Atlantic Books.

——— (1982). "Trance, Initiation, and Psychotherapy in Tamang Shamanism." *American Ethnologist* 9(1): 21–46.

Philips, A. A. B. (2001). *Spirit Possession.* [Album]. Soundknowledge Audio Publishers.

Philips, B. (2016, July 20). "Immortality and the Relentless Power of the Opponent." *Kabbalah Student.* https://kabbalahstudent.com/immortality-and-the-relentless-power-of-the-opponent/

*Pierrakos, E., and D. Thesenga (1993). *Fear No Evil: The Pathwork Method of Transforming the Lower Self.* The Pathwork Foundation.

Pinheiro, L. G. (1998). *Diary of a Counselor.* Translated by E. D'Agosto. The Spiritist Group Love and Light.

Pittman, H. O. (1995). *Demons: An Eyewitness Account* (6th ed.). Philadelphia Publishing Company.

*Plakun, E. M. (2008). "Psychiatry in Tibetan Buddhism: Madness and Its Cure Seen Through the Lens of Religious and National History." *Journal of the American Academy of Psychoanalysis and Dynamic Psychiatry* 36(3): 415–430.

Plancke, C. (2011). "The Spirit's Wish: Possession Trance and Female Power Among the Punu of Congo-Brazzaville." *Journal of Religion in Africa* 41(4): 366–395. https://doi.org/10.1163/157006611X599181.

Powell, A. "The Contribution of Spirit Release Therapy to Mental Health." *Light* 126(1).

*Prechtel, M. (2015). *The Smell of Rain on Dust: Grief and Praise.* North Atlantic Books.

Putnam, F. W. (2016). *The Way We Are: How States of Mind Influence Our Identities, Personality and Potential for Change.* Ipbooks.

Quek, T. (2002). *Distributed Cognition.* Hong Kong Polytechnic University.

Quintard, V., S. Jouffre, B. Hommel, and C. Bouquet (2021). "Embodied Self-Other Overlap in Romantic Love: A Review and Integrative Perspective." *Psychological Research* 85(3): 899–914. https://doi.org/10.1007/s00426-020-01301-8.

Quran, English Translation. Book of Signs Foundation.

Raguram, R., A. Venkateswaran, J. Ramakrishna, and M. G. Weiss (2002). "Traditional Community Resources for Mental Health: A Report of Temple Healing from India." British Medical Journal, July 6; 325(7354.38), 38–40.

*Rahardanto, M.S., and Subandi (2012). "From Acute Pain to Intense Elation: The Psychological Dynamics of Five Individuals Who Experienced Spirit Possession." *Jurnal Psikologi* 39(1): 25–45.

Ram, K. (2012). "How Is Afflictive Possession 'Learned'? Gender and Motility in South India." *Ethnos* 77(2): 203–26. https://doi.org/10.1080/00141844.2011.592952.

Rasmussen, S. J. (2012). "Spirit possession in Africa." In *The Wiley-Blackwell Companion to African Religions.* Edited by E. K. Bongmba, 184–197. John Wiley & Sons, Ltd. https://doi.org/10.1002/9781118255513.ch11.

Rausch, M. (2000). *Bodies, Boundaries, and Spirit Possession: Moroccan Women and the Revision of Tradition.* Bielefeld: transcript-Verlag.

Reimer, R. (2016). *Soul Care: 7 Transformational Principles for a Healthy Soul.* Carpenter's Son Publishing.

Rezacova, V. (2021). "Embodying Immobility: Dysphoric Geographies of Labour Migration and Their Transformations in the Therapeutic Context of 'Venda' Ancestor Possession in Post-Apartheid South Africa." In *Immobility and Medicine: Exploring Stillness, Waiting and the In-Between.* Edited by C. Vindrola-Padros, B. Vindrola-Padros, and K. Lee-Crossett, 113–134. Springer. https://doi.org/10.1007/978-981-15-4976-2_6.

Rich, J. (2014). Cultural Beliefs About Possession. *Compassionate Teacher Training Class 1.*

Rieff, P. (1968). *The Triumph of the Therapeutic: Uses of Faith after Freud.* Harper Torchbooks.

Rivas, L. H. (2016). *Spiritism 101* (1st Eng. ed.). Translated by J. Korngold. United States Spiritist Federation.

Roberts, N. (2019). "Science Says Religion Is Good for Your Health." *Forbes,* March 29.

Rogo, D. S. (1987). *The Infinite Boundary: Spirit Possession, Madness, and Multiple Personality.* The Aquarium Press.

Rojas, R. M. (2021, July). "Spiritual Sickness: A New Perspective and Approach to the Treatment of Psychosis." *Academia Letters.*

*Romme, M., S. Escher, J. Dillon, D. Corstens, and M. Morris (2009). *Living with Voices: 50 Stories of Recovery.* PCCS Books.

Rosik, C. H. (2004). "Possession Phenomena in North America: A Case Study with Ethnographic, Psychodynamic, Religious and Clinical Implications." *Journal of Trauma & Dissociation* 5(1): 49–76. https://doi.org/10.1300/J229v05n01_04.

*Ross, M. (1987). *The Fountain & the Furnace: The Way of Tears and Fire.* The Missionary Society of St. Paul the Apostle.

Rouger, G. (1985). *Music and Trance: A Theory of the Relations Between Music and Possession.* University of Chicago Press. (Originally published in 1980)

*Rowan, J., and M. Cooper, eds. (1999). *The Plural Self: Multiplicity in Everyday Life.* Sage Publications.

Roxburgh, E. C., and C. A. Roe (2011). "A Survey of Dissociation, Boundary-Thinness, and Psychological Wellbeing in Spiritualist Mental Mediumship." *Journal of Parapsychology* 75(2): 279–299.

Russell, J. B. (1988). *The Prince of Darkness: Radical Evil and the Power of Good in History.* Cornell University.

Sagan, S. (1997). *Entity Possession: Freeing the Energy Body of Negative Influences.* Destiny Books.

Salemink, O. (2014). "Spirit Worship and Possession in Vietnam and Beyond." In *Routledge Handbook of Religions in Asia.* Edited by B. Turner and O. Salemink. Routledge.

*Samuel, G. (1993). *Civilized Shamans: Buddhism in Tibetan Societies.* Smithsonian Institution Press.

Sanderson, A. (2003). "Spirit Release Therapy: What Is It and What Can It Achieve? A Clinical Presentation of Therapist and Patient Perspectives." *The Royal College of Psychiatrists.*

*Sansonese, J. N. (1994). *The Body of Myth: Mythology, Shamanic Trance, and the Sacred Geography of the Body.* Inner Traditions International.

Santo, D. E. (2016). "Clothes for Spirits: Opening and Closing the Cosmos in Brazilian Umbanda." *HAU: Journal of Ethnographic Theory* 6(3): 85–106. https://doi.org/10.14318/hau6.3.010.

*——— (2014). "Developing the Dead in Cuba: An Ethnographic Account of the Emergence of Spirits and Selves in Havana." In *Talking with the spirits.* Edited by J. Hunter and D. Luke, 191–205. Daily Grail Publishing.

——— (2017). "Possession Consciousness, Religious Individualism, and Subjectivity in Brazilian Umbanda." *Religion* 47(2): 179–202. https://doi.org/10.1080/0048721X.2016.1198839.

Sapkota, R. P., D. Gurung, D. Neupane, S. K. Shah, H. Kienzler, and L. J. Kirmayer (2014). "A Village Possessed by 'Witches': A Mixed-Methods Case-Control Study of Possession and Common Mental Disorders in Rural Nepal." *Culture, Medicine, and Psychiatry* 38(4): 642–668. https://doi.org/10.1007/s11013-014-9393-8.

Sass, L. (2017). *Madness and Modernism: Insanity in the Light of Modern Art, Literature, and Thought* (rev. ed.). Oxford University Press.

Sawyer, K. (2016). *The Dangerous Man: Conversations with Free-Thinkers and Truth-Seekers – A Collection of Alternative Research*. O Books.

*——— (2008). *Soul Companions: Conversations with Contemporary Wisdom Seekers – A Collection of Encounters with Spirit*. O Books.

Schaffler, Y., E. Cardeña, S. Reijman, and D. Haluza (2016). "Traumatic Experience and Somatoform Dissociation Among Spirit Possession Practitioners in the Dominican Republic." *Culture, Medicine, and Psychiatry* 40(1): 74–99. https://doi.org/10.1007/s11013-015-9472-5.

Scheper-Hughes, N. (2001). *Saints, Scholars, and Schizophrenics: Mental Illness in Rural Ireland*. University of California Press.

Schlottmann, D. (2018). "Spirit Possession in Korean Shaman Rituals of the Hwanghae-do-Tradition." *Journal for the Study of Religious Experience* 4(2): 3–23.

Schmidt, B. E. (2016). *Spirits and Trance in Brazil: An Anthropology of Religious Experience*. Bloomsbury Academic.

*Schmidt, B. E. and L. Huskinson, eds. (2010). *Spirit Possession and Trance: New Interdisciplinary Perspectives*. Continuum International Publishing Group.

Schumaker, J. F. (1995). *The Corruption of Reality: A Unified Theory of Religion, Hypnosis, and Psychopathology*. Prometheus Books.

Schwartz, R. C. (2018). *Greater Than the Sum of Our Parts: Discovering Your True Self Through Internal Family Systems Therapy* [Audiobook]. Sounds True.

*——— (2023). *Introduction to the Internal Family Systems Model* (2nd ed.). Trailheads Publishing.

——— (2021). *No Bad Parts: Healing Trauma and Restoring Wholeness with the Internal Family Systems Model*. Sounds True.

——— (2010). *You Are the One You've Been Waiting For: Bringing Courageous Love to Intimate Relationships*. The Center for Self Leadership.

*Schwartz, R. C., and R. R. Falconer (2017). *Many Minds, One Self: Evidence for a Radical Shift in Paradigm*. The Center for Self Leadership.

*Schwartz, R. C., and M. Sweezy (2020). *Internal Family Systems Therapy* (2nd ed.). The Guilford Press.

Scott, D. (2013). "The Integration of Spiritual Experiences." *IFSCA*. https://ifsca.ca/the-integration-of-spiritual-experiences.

Scrutton, A. P. (2015). "Schizophrenia or Possession? A Reply to Kemal Irmak and Nuray Karanci." *Journal of Religion and Health* 54(5):1963–1968. https://doi.org/10.1007/s10943-015-0027-4.

Seligman, R. (2008). "Dissociative Experience and Cultural Neuroscience: Narrative, Metaphor and Mechanism." *Culture Medicine and Psychiatry* 2008(32): 31–64. https://doi.org/10.1007/s11013-007-9077-8.

*——— (2005). "Distress, Dissociation, and Embodied Experience: Reconsidering the Pathways to Mediumship and Mental Health." *Ethos* 33(1): 71–99.

——— (2018). "Mind, Body, Brain, and the Conditions of Meaning." *Ethos* 46(3): 397–417. https://doi.org/10.1111/etho.12207.

*——— (2014). *Possessing Spirits and Healing Selves: Embodiment and Transformation in an Afro-Brazilian Religion.* Palgrave Macmillan.

Seligman, R., and L. J. Kirmayer (2008). "Dissociative Experience and Cultural Neuroscience: Narrative, Metaphor and Mechanism." *Culture, Medicine and Psychiatry* 32(1): 31–64.

Shahar, M., and R. P. Weller, eds. (1996). *Unruly Gods: Divinity and Society in China.* University of Hawai'i Press.

Shealy, C. N. (2017). *Conversations with G: A Physician's Encounter with Heaven.* Holistic Books International.

Shorto, R. (1999). *Saints and Madmen: How Pioneering Psychiatrists Are Creating a New Science of the Soul.* Henry Holt & Co.

*Sidky, H. (2011). "The State Oracle of Tibet, Spirit Possession, and Shamanism." *Numen* 58(2011): 71–99.

Siegel, D. J. (2023). *IntraConnected Mwe (me+we) as the Integration of Self, Identity, and Belonging.* W. W. Norton.

*——— (2008). *The Neurobiology of We: How Relationships, the Mind, and the Brain Interact to Shape Who We Are* [Album]. Sounds True.

*Sluhovsky, M. (2007). *Believe Not Every Spirit: Possession, Mysticism, & Discernment in Early Modern Catholicism.* University of Chicago Press.

*Smith, C. M. (2007). *Jung and Shamanism in Dialogue: Retrieving the Soul/Retrieving the Sacred.* Trafford Publishing.

*Smith, D. B. (2007). *Muses, Madmen, and Prophets: Hearing Voices and the Borders of Sanity.* Penguin Books.

Smith, F. M. (2017, April). *Possession.* Oxford Bibliographies. http://www.oxfordbibliographies.com/view/document/obo-9780195399318/obo-9780195399318-0101.xml.

——— (2010). "Possession, Embodiment, and Ritual in Mental Health Care in India." *Journal of Ritual Studies* 24(2): 21–35.

*——— (2006). *The Self Possessed: Deity and Spirit Possession in South Asian Literature and Civilization.* Columbia University Press.

Smith, G. (2009). *Developing Mediumship.* Hay House.

Smith, K. (2012). "From Dividual and Individual Selves to Porous Subjects." *The Australian Journal of Anthropology* 23(1): 50–64. https://doi.org/10.1111/j.1757-6547.2012.00167.x.

Smith, M. (2014). *Clearings: Helping Lost Souls Find the Way Home.* Balboa Press.

Snodgrass, J. G. (2002). "Imitation Is Far More Than the Sincerest of Flattery: The Mimetic Power of Spirit Possession in Rajasthan, India." *Cultural Anthropology* 17(1): 32–64.

——— (2004). "Spirit Possession in Rajasthan." In *Shamanism: An Encyclopedia of World Beliefs, Practices, and Culture.* ABC-CLIO.

——— (2002). "A Tale of Goddesses, Money, and Other Terribly Wonderful Things: Spirit Possession, Commodity Fetishism, and the Narrative of Capitalism in Rajasthan, India." *American Ethnologist* 29(3): 602–36. https://doi.org/10.1525/ae.2002.29.3.602.

Sohal, V. (2020). "Out of Sync Brain Waves May Underlie Learning Deficit Linked to Schizophrenia." *Nature Neuroscience* 23: 892–902.

Somasundaram, D., T. Thivakaran, and D. Bhugra (2008). "Possession States in Northern Sri Lanka." *Psychopathology* 41(4): 245–253. https://doi.org/10.1159/000125558.

Somer, E. (2016). "Cross-Temporal and Cross-Cultural Perspectives on Dissociative Disorders of Identity." In *Shattered But Unbroken: Voices of Triumph and Testimony.* Edited by V. Sinason and A. V. der Merwe, 89–110. Routledge.

——— (2006). "Culture-Bound Dissociation: A Comparative Analysis." *Psychiatric Clinics of North America* 29(2006): 213–226. https://doi.org/10.1016/j.psc.2005.10.009.

Somer, E., and M. Saadon (2000). "Stambali Dissociative Possession and Trance in Tunisian Healing Dance." *Transcultural Psychiatry* 37(4): 581–602.

Sood, A. (2016). "The Global Mental Health Movement and Its Impact on Traditional Healing in India." *Journal of Transcultural Psychiatry* 53(6): 766–782.

Soo-nam, K. (2005). *Gut: Korean Shamanic Ritual.* Youlhwadang Publishers.

Saint Sophrony (2021). *Saint Silouan the Athonite.* St. Vladimir's Seminary Press.

Spiegel, D., ed. (1994). *Dissociation: Culture, Mind, and Body.* American Psychiatric Press.

Spiegel, D., R. Lewis-Fernández, R. Lanius, E. Vermetten, D. Simeon, and M. Friedman (2013). "Dissociative Disorders in DSM-5." *Annual Review of Clinical Psychology* 9(1): 299–326. https://doi.org/10.1146/annurev-clinpsy-050212-185531.

Spiegel, D., R. J. Loewenstein, R. Lewis-Fernández, V. Sar, D. Simeon, E. Vermetten, E. Cardeña, and P. F. Dell (2011). "Dissociative Disorders in DSM-5." *Depression and Anxiety* 28(9), 824–852. https://doi.org/10.1002/da.20874.

Spiro, M. E. (1993). "Is the Western Conception of the Self 'Peculiar' within the Context of the World Cultures?" *Ethos* 21(2): 107–153. https://doi.org/10.1525/eth.1993.21.2.02a00010.

*Stavis, R. H., and S. Durand (2018). *Sister of Darkness: The Chronicles of a Modern Exorcist.* Dey Street.

Stolovy, T., R. Lev-Wiesel, and Z. Eisikovits (2015). "Dissociation and the Experience of Channeling: Narratives of Israeli Women Who Practice Channeling. *The International Journal of Clinical and Experimental Hypnosis* 63: 346–364. 10.1080/00207144.2015.1031555.

Stavish, M. (2018). *Egregores: The Occult Entities That Watch Over Human Destiny.* Inner Traditions.

——— (2016). *Mercury's Children: Shamanic and Hermetic Practices.* The Institute for Hermetic Studies.

*——— (2016). *Studies in Poltergeists, Obsession, & Possession.* The Institute for Hermetic Studies.

*Steege, M., and R. C. Schwartz (2008). *The Spirit-Led Life: A Christian Encounter with Internal Family Systems.* Trailheads Publications.

Steiner, R. (2000). *Guardian Angels: Connecting with Our Spiritual Guides and Helpers.* Translated by Rudolf Steiner Press. Rudolf Steiner Press.

*Stephenson, C. E. (2017). *Possession: Jung's Comparative Anatomy of the Psyche* (rev. ed.). Routledge.

Stevenson, I. (1980/1966) *Twenty Cases Suggestive of Reincarnation.* University of Virginia Press.

Stillman, W. (2018). *The Secret Language of Spirit: Understanding Spirit Communication in Our Everyday Lives.* The Career Press.

——— (2016). *Under Spiritual Siege: How Ghosts and Demons Affect Us and How to Combat Them.* Schiffer Publishing.

*St. John, G. (2015). *Mystery School in Hyperspace: A Cultural History of DMT.* Evolver Editions.

Stolovy, T., R. Lev-Wiesel, and E. Witzum (2014). "Dissociation: Adjustment or Distress? Dissociative Phenomena, Absorption and Quality of Life Among Israeli Women Who Practice Channeling Compared to Women with Similar Traumatic History." *Journal of Religion and Health* 54: 1040–1051.

*Stoyanov, Y. (2018). "Historical and Modern Eastern Orthodox Stances on Spirit Possession and Exorcism – Tradition and Innovation." International Conference, Fondazione Giorgio Cini Onlus.

Strathern, M. (1998). *The Gender of the Gift: Problems with Women and Problems with Society in Melanesia.* University of California Press.

Strauss, Claudia. (1992). "Models and Motives" In *Human Motives and Cultural Models* (Publications of the Society for Psychological Anthropology). Edited by Roy D'Andrade and Claudia Strauss, 1–20. Cambridge University Press

Subramanian, M. (2002). Travels of Possessed Women on the Brink of Memory: Embodied Faith, Nostalgia and Fear in Modern Japan. Doctoral thesis, Stanford University. ProQuest.

Sulaiman, L. (2017). *Magical Orientation of Religion Among Malay/Muslims in Singapore: A Look at Modes of Healing Pertaining to Mental Illness.* Honours BA thesis, National University of Singapore.

*Swedenborg, E. (2011). *A Swedenborg Sampler.* Translated by G. F. Dole, L. H. Cooper, and J. S. Rose. Swedenborg Foundation.

Sykes, C., M. Sweezy, and R. C. Schwartz (2023). *Internal Family Systems Therapy for Addictions: Trauma-Informed, Compassion-Based Interventions for Substance Use, Eating, Gambling and More.* PESI Publishing, Inc.

Tabberaee, W. (2009) *Prophets and Gravestones.* Baker Academic Press.

*Tart, C. T. (2009). *The End of Materialism: How Evidence of the Paranormal Is Bringing Science and Spirit Together.* New Harbinger Publications.

*Taylor, C. (2007/2018) *A Secular Age.* Harvard University Press.

——— (1989) *Sources of the Self: Making of the Modern Identity.* Harvard University Press.

*Taylor, E. (1982). *William James on Exceptional Mental States: The 1896 Lowell Lectures.* Jerry House.

Taylor, S. (2010). *The Sleep of Separateness.* December 2010, non-duality.com.

Taysom, S. (2017). "Satan Mourns Naked upon the Earth': Locating Mormon Possession and Exorcism Rituals In the American Religious Landscape, 1830–1977" in *Religion and American Culture* 27(1): 57–94.

Teasdale, J. D., and P. J. Barnard (1995). *Affect, Cognition and Change: Re-modelling Depressive Thought.* Psychology Press.

Thomas, D. (2021, February 28). *Re-thinking Identity: Children's Experiences of Self.* Essentia Foundation.

Thomas, J., N. Al-Qarni, and S. W. Furber (2015). "Conceptualizing Mental Health in the United Arab Emirates: The Perspective of Traditional Healers." *Mental Health, Religion & Culture* 18(2): 134–45. http://dx.doi.org/10.1080/13674676.2015.1010196.

Thomas, T. C. (2008). "Possession, Exorcism, and Psychotherapy." *Professional Issues in Counseling* 8(2).

Thoresen, A. (2018). *Demons and Healing: The Reality of the Demonic Threat and the Doppelgänger in the Light of Anthroposophy.* Temple Lodge. (Originally published in 2017)

Tiilikainen, M. (2012). "Somali Saar in the Era of Social and Religious Change." In *Spirit Possession and Trance: New Interdisciplinary Perspectives.* Edited by B. E. Schmidt and L. Huskinson, 117–133. Bloomsbury Publishing. http://ebookcentral.proquest.com/lib/emory/detail.action?docID=516726.

Torrey, E. F. (1972). *Witchdoctors and Psychiatrists: The Common Roots of Psychotherapy and Its Future* (rev. ed.). Perennial Library.

*Tramont, C. V. (2016). *What's Missing in Medicine: Unleashing the Healing Power of the Subconscious Mind.* Du Lac Publishing.

Turner, E. (2010). "Discussion: Ethnography as a Transformative Experience." *Anthropology and the Humanities* 35(2): 218–226.

*——— (1996). *The Hands Feel It: Healing and Spirit Presence among a Northern Alaskan People.* Northern Illinois University Press.

Turner, T. (2011). "Bodiliness: The Body Beyond the Body: Social, Material and Spiritual Dimensions of Bodiliness." In *A Companion to the Anthropology of the Body and Embodiment.* Edited by F. E. Mascia-Lees. Blackwell Publishing.

*Ustinova, Y. (2018). *Divine Mania: Alteration of Consciousness in Ancient Greece.* Routledge.

Valencia, A. V., & Froese, T. (2020). "What Binds Us? Inter-brain Neural Synchronization and Its Implications for Theories of Human Consciousness." *Neuroscience of Consciousness* 2020(1). https://doi.org/10.1093/nc/niaa010.

Vallely, A. (2011). "Ancestors, Demons and the Goddess." In *Health and Religious Rituals in South Asia: Disease, Possession and Healing.* Edited by F. Ferrari. Taylor & Francis Group.

Valliappan, R. (2011). "The Art within Madness." *Samyukta: A Journal of Women's Studies* 11(2).

van de Port, M. (2005). "Circling Around the Really Real: Spirit Possession Ceremonies and the Search for Authenticity in Bahian Candomblé." *Ethos* 33(2): 149–179. https://doi.org/10.1525/eth.2005.33.2.149.

van Duijl, M., E. Cardeña, and J. de Jong (2005). "The Validity of DSM-IV Dissociative Disorders Categories in South-West Uganda." *Transcultural Psychiatry* 42(2): 219–241. https://doi.org/10.1177/1363461505052666.

van Duijl, M., W. Kleijn, and J. de Jong (2013). "Are Symptoms of Spirit Possessed Patients Covered by the DSM-IV or DSM-5 Criteria for Possession Trance Disorder?: A Mixed-Method Explorative Study in Uganda." *Social Psychiatry and Psychiatric Epidemiology* 48: 1417–1430. https://doi.org/10.1080/15299732.2015.1103351.

——— (2014). "Unravelling the Spirits' Message: A Study of Help-Seeking Steps and Explanatory Models Among Patients Suffering from Spirit Possession in Uganda." *International Journal of Mental Health Systems* 8(1): 1–13. https://doi.org/10.1186/1752-4458-8-24.

van Duijl, M., E. Nijenhuis, I. H. Komproe, B. P. Hajo, E. Gernaat, and J. T. de Jong (2010). "Dissociative Symptoms and Reported Trauma Among Patients with Spirit Possession and Matched Healthy Controls in Uganda." *Culture, Medicine, and Psychiatry* 34(2): 380–400. https://doi.org/10.1007/s11013-010-9171-1.

Van Dusen, W. (2004). *The Presence of Other Worlds: The Psychological/Spiritual Findings of Emanuel Swedenborg* (2nd ed.). Swedenborg Foundation.

*——— (1972). *The Presence of Spirits in Madness: A Confirmation of Swedenborg in Recent Empirical Findings*. Swedenborg Foundation.

——— (1996). *Returning to the Source: The Way to the Experience of God*. Real People Press.

Varela F. J., ed. (1997). *Sleeping, Dreaming, and Dying: An Exploration of Consciousness with the Dalai Lama*. Wisdom Press

Vinea, A. (2018). "An Emergent Affliction in Today's Egypt: Islamic Healing, the Psy Sciences, and What Lies In-Between." *Medicine Anthropology Theory | An Open-Access Journal in the Anthropology of Health, Illness, and Medicine* 5(1): 50. https://doi.org/10.17157/mat.5.1.518.

Vogt, R., ed. (2012). *Perpetrator Introjects: Psychotherapeutic Diagnostics and Treatment Models*. Asanger.

Von Glahn, R. (2004). *The Sinister Way: The Divine and the Demonic in Chinese Religious Culture*. University of California Press.

Vorhölter, J. (2019). "Struggling to Be a 'Happy Self'? Psychotherapy and the Medicalization of Unhappiness in Uganda." *Current Anthropology* 60(2): 194–223. https://doi.org/10.1086/702337.

Voss, A., and W. Rowlandson, eds. (2013). *Daimonic Imagination: Uncanny Intelligence*. Cambridge Scholars Publishing.

Wainwright, E. M., P. Culbertson, and S. Smith (2010). *Spirit Possession, Theology, and Identity: A Pacific Exploration*. ATF Theology.

*Waller, J. (2009). *The Dancing Plague: The Strange, True Story of an Extraordinary Illness*. Sourcebooks.

Wallis, C. (Hareesh) (2015, September 3). "Deity Yoga: A Tantrik Technology." Tantrik Institute. https://hareesh.org/blog/2015/9/3/deity-yoga-a-tantrik-technology

Ward, C. A., ed. (1989). *Altered States of Consciousness and Mental Health: A Cross-Cultural Perspective*. Sage Publications.

Ware, K. (1995/2019). The Orthodox Way. St. Vladimir's Seminary Press.

*Watkins, M. (2000). *Invisible Guests: The Development of Imaginal Dialogues*. Spring Publications.

*Watters, E. (2011). *Crazy Like Us: The Globalization of the American Psyche*. Free Press.

*Weissman, J. (1993). *Of Two Minds: Poets Who Hear Voices*. Wesleyan University Press.

Weller, R. P. (2015). "Global Religious Changes and Civil Life in Two Chinese Societies: A Comparison of Jiangsu and Taiwan." *The Review of Faith & International Affairs* 13(2): 13–24. https://doi.org/10.1080/15570274.2015.1039305.

Wexler, B. (2008). *Brain and Culture*. Bradford Press.

*Whitaker, R. (2002). *Mad in America: Bad Science, Bad Medicine, and the Enduring Mistreatment of the Mentally Ill*. Basic Books.

Whitman, W. J. (n.d.). Berdyaev's personalism.

Wickland, C. A. (1924). *Thirty Years Among the Dead*. Self-published.

Wikipedia, s.v. "Deity Yoga," last modified June 12, 2022, 09:43, https://en.wikipedia.org/wiki/Deity_yoga.

———, s.v. "Schizotypy," last modified March 9, 2023, 20:31, https://en.wikipedia.org/wiki/Schizotypy.

————, s.v. "Distributed Cognition," last modified July 26, 2022, 06:09, https://en.wikipedia.org/wiki/Distributed_cognition.

Wikisource, s.v. "Letter to George and Thomas Keats, December 28, 1817, by John Keats," https://en.wikisource.org/wiki/Letter_to_George_and_Thomas_Keats,_December_28,_1817.

Williams, D. D. (1990). *The Demonic and the Divine.* Edited by S. A. Evans. Fortress Press.

Williamson, M. (2014). *Schizophrenia or Spirit Possession.* Tricorn Books.

*Wilson, C. (1967). *The Mind Parasites.* Monkfish Book Publishing Company.

Wilson, M. (2002). "Six Views of Embodied Cognition." *Psychonomic Bulletin & Review* 9: 625–636.

Wilson, S. (2008). *Research Is Ceremony: Indigenous Research Methods.* Fernwood Publishing.

*Winkelman, M. (2010). *Shamanism: A Biopsychosocial Paradigm of Consciousness and Healing* (2nd ed.). ABC-CLIO.

———— (2002). "Shamanism as Neurotheology and Evolutionary Psychology." *American Behavioral Scientist* 45(12): 1873–1885.

Winkelman, M., and M. E. Fortier (2019). "The Evolutionary Neuroanthropology of Consciousness: Exploring the Diversity of Conscious States Across Cultures: An Interview with Michael Winkelman." *ALIUS Bulletin* 3: 45–97. https://doi.org/10.34700/krg3-zk35.

*Winkler, H. A. (2008). *Ghost Riders of Upper Egypt.* Translated by N. S. Hopkins. The American University of Cairo Press.

Winnicott, D. W. (2005). *Playing and Reality* (2nd ed.). Routledge.

Witmer, A. (2012). *Jesus the Galilean Exorcist.* Bloomsbury.

———— (2013). "Spirit Possession, Exorcism and the Historical Jesus." The Bible and Interpretation, https://bibleinterp.arizona.edu/articles/2013/wit378019.

Wolputte, S. V. (2004). "Hang On to Your Self: Of Bodies, Embodiment, and Selves." *Annual Review of Anthropology* 33(1): 251–269. https://doi.org/10.1146/annurev.anthro.33.070203.143749.

Wood, M. (2007). *Possession, Power and the New Age: Ambiguities of Authority in Neoliberal Societies* (1st ed.). Routledge.

*Worobec, C. D. (2003). *Possession: Women, Witches, and Demons in Imperial Russia.* Northern Illinois University Press.

Xavier, F. C. (2018). *Enlightening Messages* [Album]. Spiritist Society of Baltimore and Marcelo Netto.

———— (2008). *Workers of the Life Eternal.* Translated by T. L. Wind, D. W. Kimble, and M. M. Saiz. The International Spiritist Council. (Originally published in 1946)

Xavier, F. C., and A. Luiz (2010). *Action and Reaction: Life in the Spirit World.* Translated by D. W. Kimble and I. Reis. The International Spiritist Council. (Originally published in 1956)

———— (2011). *In the Greater World: Life in the Spirit World.* Translated by D. W. Kimble and I. Reis. The International Spiritist Council (Originally published in 1944)

———— (2013). *Liberation: Life in the Spirit World.* Translated by D. W. Kimble and M. M. Saiz. The International Spiritist Council (Originally published in 1947)

*———— (2019). *Nosso Lar: Life in the Spirit World.* Translated by D. W. Kimble and M. M. Saiz. The International Spiritist Council (Originally published in 1944)

*Xavier, F. C., W. Viera, and A. Luiz (2005). *Disobsession.* Translated by T. Stevanin and J. Korngold. The International Spiritism Council.

Yang, M. M.-H. (2020). "Popular Religiosity: Deities, Spirit Mediums, Ancestors, Ghosts, and Fengshui." In *Re-enchanting Modernity: Ritual Economy and Society in Wenzhou, China,* 51–91. Duke University Press. https://doi.org/10.2307/j.ctv11sn3xd.6.

Yedor, K. (2018, June 14). *So What's Deity Yoga?* Tibetan Spirit. https://tibetanspirit.com/blogs/news/so-whats-deity-yoga

Young, D. E., and J. G. Goulet, eds. (1994). *Being Changed by Cross-Cultural Encounters: The Anthropology of Extraordinary Experience.* Broadview Press.

*Yu, C., and R. Guisso, eds. (1988). *Shamanism: The Spirit World of Korea.* Asian Humanities Press.

Zavaree, S. (2019). "'We Have Our Own Africans': Public Displays of Zār in Iran." In *Language and Tourism in Postcolonial Settings.* Edited by A. Mietzner and A. Storch, Bristol, Blue Ridge Summit: Channel View Publications, 49–65. https://www.degruyter.com/document/doi/10.21832/9781845416799-006/html.

Zhang, L. (2018). Cultivating the Therapeutic Self in China. *Medical Anthropology* 37(1): 45–58. https://doi.org/10.1080/01459740.2017.1317769.

Zhao, S. (2015). "Reconceptualizing the Self Phenomenon: Toward an Emic Conception of the Self." *Symbolic Interaction* 38(2): 235–260. https://doi.org/10.1002/symb.151.

Zigon, J. (2010). *HIV Is God's Blessing* (1st ed.). University of California Press.

*Zinser, T. (2013). *The Practice of Soul-Centered Healing* (Vol. 1). Union Street Press.

*——— (2016). *The Practice of Soul-Centered Healing* (Vol. 2). Union Street Press.

*——— (2010). *Soul-Centered Healing: A Psychologist's Extraordinary Journey into the Realms of Sub-personalities, Spirits, and Past Lives.* Union Street Press.

Zombies in Pjs (2021, April 16). *From Ghosts to Mickey Mouse: Social Content in Out-of-Body Experiences (Russian subtitles)* [Video]. Youtube.

Index

A

AA, 42, 314
Abandoned children, 94
Abe, Masao, 304
Aboriginal, 267, 410
Abram, David, 77
abstraction, 234
abuse, 4, 8, 16, 50, 111, 117, 127,
    164, 396, 408
    sexual, 7–9, 15, 50, 112, 117, 127,
    180
academia, 8–9, 26, 55, 65, 81, 181,
    186, 198–99, 248, 252, 278,
    295–96, 306, 411
Accra, 261–62
Adam, 291
addict, 4, 378, 401
addictions, 6, 8, 15, 41, 105, 181, 254,
    283, 309, 401
adorcism, 220
Adriana, 62–64, 311
Advaita Vedanta, 300
adversary, 161, 172
affective systems, primary, 75
Africa, 62, 178, 215, 217, 238,
    277–78, 340, 345, 347
afterlife, 50, 279
agency, 170, 181, 224, 258, 275, 292,
    294, 296, 338
agents, possessing, 189, 201, 235, 245
agnosia, 301
Ahriman, 259
air traffic control systems, 270
alcoholism, 6, 50, 91, 101, 252,
    314–15, 400
Alcott, Bronson, 292
Alexander, Bruce, 283
alien, 78, 159, 192–93, 238, 259, 306,
    362
alienation, 177, 264, 280, 404–5
Allah, 203, 293, 300

allies, 165, 326, 337, 370
Allison, Ralph, 9–10, 181
Allport, Gordon, 293–94
altered states, 71–72, 206, 214,
    216–18, 223, 277
Alters, 181
Amaringo, Pablo, 259
Amelia, 316–29
American belief in ghosts, 248
American Psychiatric Association, 34,
    188
amnesia, 9, 218
amputate, 91, 94, 220, 311
amulets, 54, 208
Amy, 156–58
ancestors, 19–20, 33, 62, 103, 151–53,
    155, 158, 162, 189, 238,
    279–80, 284, 341, 345, 348,
    375, 390, 393
anesthesia, 103, 144, 153
Angelou, Maya, 306
angels, 56, 63–64, 126, 145, 174,
    183–84, 203, 238–39, 248, 284,
    308, 330
anger, 6, 89–90, 146, 150, 156, 158,
    160, 162–63, 204, 252, 336
animal magnetism, 242
anima mundi, 79
animism, 205, 212, 230, 261, 274–76,
    408, 413
anomalous experiences, 216, 222, 263,
    298, 409
antipodes, 3–4, 184
antithesis, 285, 411
ants, 90, 107
anxiety, 62, 66, 89, 202, 277, 280,
    298, 309, 317, 378
anxiety disorders, 73
apocalypticism, 241
apophaticism, 105, 299–300, 302
Aquinas, Thomas, 234

Archangel Michael, 183
archetypes, 85, 153, 173, 213, 223–24,
     251, 297, 310
arrogance, 79, 180, 248, 406
ashes, 255, 358, 370
Asprem, Egil, 410
Assagioli, Roberto, 8, 169
Astier, Gabriel, 238
Astral City, 49
atheists, 67, 74, 192, 259, 269, 278,
     305, 314
atman, 19
attachments, 15, 32, 96, 110, 130,
     156–57, 267, 299, 346, 362, 390
  parasitic, 184
attentional learning, 76
Auden, 80
Auschwitz, 76
autoimmune diseases, 268, 378, 404
autonomous contents, 171
Autonomous psychic entities, 257
autonomy, 76, 232, 257–58, 280, 308
ayahuasca, 192, 252, 258–59
Azusa Street, 245–46

B
Bacchae, 228, 233, 406, 411
Bad Boll, 243
bad spirits, 54, 64–66, 153, 186, 344
Bains, Jaideep, 270
Balaji, 202, 210
Baldwin, William, 98, 103, 179,
     182–84, 186–87
Bali, 82–83, 214, 279
Balian, 83
baptism, 231, 233, 247
Baptists, 231, 240, 247
Barfield, Owen, 404
Barley Norton, 214
Barnard, 263
Basic Themes, 67, 244
BASK model of dissociation, 408
Bass, Ellen, 8
Basso, Rebecca, 219
Bateson, Gregory, 261, 272

Batin, 203
Batiste, Jean, 328
Baylor University study, 248
Beahrs, John, 289
Bede Griffiths, 293
Beelzebub, 231
befriend, 91, 103, 222
behaviorism, 69, 71, 288, 292
Bell, Rudolph, 234
Benedictine monk, 292–93
Berdyaev, Nikolai, 291
Bergstrom, Betsy, 191
Betty, Stafford, 169, 189, 220
betweenness, 282
Bhut, 203
Bigelow Foundation, 317
Bingen, 234
biolooping, 221–22
Biopsychological Process, 68, 197, 245,
     406
Bishop Kallistos Ware, 294
Blake, William, 56, 79, 81, 409
blank slate, 295
blessing, 90, 133, 150, 185, 205, 217,
     227, 265, 342, 375–76
  dangerous, 150
blockages, 53, 88, 133, 146, 175, 242,
     290, 300, 302, 313–14, 399
Blumhardt, Johann, 242–43
Boddy, Janice, 215
bodhisattva, 207, 295
bodyguards, 38–39
Bomoh, 277
Borden Parker Bowne, 293
Borges, Jorge Luis, 56
Boston personalist tradition, 293
Both/and logic, 84
boundaries, 66, 84, 103, 157, 269,
     272–73, 276, 279, 284, 291
Bounded models, 221
Bourguignon, Erika, 199
Bowmann, Elizabeth, 182
Boxer Rebellions, 200, 208
Bragdon, Emma, 47
brahman, 19, 300

Braun, Bennett, 408
Brazilian Spiritists, 49, 65, 316, 412
Brightman, Edgar, 293–94
Brother David Steindl-Rast, 292, 300, 302
bruja, 63, 311
Buber, Martin, 290–91, 413
Buchanan, Tony, 270
Buddhism, 38, 52, 56, 58–60, 95, 172, 174, 191, 205, 209–11, 213, 259, 281, 292, 302, 304, 307
buffered self, 261, 267, 272–75, 279, 284–85, 404

C
Caciola, Nancy, 234
Caldwell, Narrye, 191
California personalism, 293
Camisards, 238
Campbell, Joseph, 177, 216, 287, 289, 410
cancer, 34, 161, 240, 254, 268
Candomblé, 35, 49, 62, 199, 221
cannibals, 172–73
Cardinal Richelieu, 238
caregivers, 204, 265, 267, 274
carnival, 273, 279
carrier/host, 51
Carver, George Washington , 74
Castaneda, Carlos, 184
catatonic, 4, 412
catharsis, 58, 239
Catholicism, 46, 54–55, 65–66, 188–89, 233, 237, 240–41, 247–49, 254, 272–73, 280, 294, 304
CEMI theory, 269
central possessions, 218
ceremonies, 37, 51, 57, 59, 149, 153, 206, 208–9, 218–19, 252, 275–76, 304, 410, 412
Chabris, Christopher, 34
channeling, 47, 61, 63, 130, 182, 193, 213, 218, 244, 255, 297, 316, 406
Charcot, 171
charismatic, 247

charms, 208, 231
cheat sheet, 109
Chennai, 261–62
chöd, 97, 191
Chomsky, Noam, 295
Chopra, Deepak, 282
Chottanikkara Temple, 202
Christianity, 57, 105, 199, 209, 230, 300–301
  esoteric, 229
Christian kenosis, 303
Christian monasticism, early, 74
Christian renewal, 243
Christians, 46–47, 54, 56–57, 64, 226, 231–35, 255, 278, 298, 330
  spirit-possessed, 225
Chuang Tzu, 403
Churchill, Winston, 309
circle dances, 153
citadel model of mind, 76, 264, 267, 276, 279, 404–5
civil war, 16–17, 200, 207
Claire, 401–2
clamors, 235
Claridge, Gordon, 265
Clarke, Isabel, 83–84, 174, 216, 224, 239, 261–67, 298, 404, 408–9
Clifford, Terry, 52–53, 205
clinical outline, 87
cocaine, 121, 283
cocoon, 156–57
codependence, 8, 307
cognition, 264, 268, 270–71, 298, 405, 407–8, 413
  distributed, 270
  embodied, 73
Coleridge, 79
colluding, 68, 70, 174, 413
colonialism, 246, 264, 274, 278, 347, 406
comb, 95, 362
combative, 90, 185, 238, 248, 252, 255
community, 17, 19, 53, 218, 233, 242, 284, 294, 315, 400, 412

companionship, 94, 100, 401
compassion, 53, 57, 91, 96, 115,
      139, 142, 147, 307, 312, 314,
      321, 355–57, 359–60, 364,
      380, 382–83, 385–87, 390–91,
      394–95, 398–99
   emptiness equals, 304
   experienced, 355, 385, 399
   saintly, 84
   true, 72
compassionate dispossession, 97
compassion shine, 365
complexes, 14, 85, 170, 173, 257, 269
conflict, 94, 226, 230, 232–33, 242,
      249
confrontational, 60, 94, 99, 170, 187,
      248–49
Confucianism, 57, 207, 209
confusion, 4, 39–40, 155, 189, 263,
      381
consensus reality, 183, 233
constraint-release, 105, 298, 312
contagion, psychic, 257, 278
contagious laughter, 277
container, 41, 95–96, 119, 241, 255,
      335, 357–58, 362, 382, 384,
      406, 412
contempt, 61, 89, 94, 100, 180–81,
      197, 249, 298
contracts, 66, 300
conversion experiences, 217
converting criminal gods and demons,
      202
convulsionnaires, 240, 278
convulsions, 206, 236–37, 239–41
Corbin, Henry, 80–83, 229
cortical arousal, high, 82
Cosmides, Leda, 295
cosmocentric, 262, 274, 276
coughing, 253–54
Crapanzano, Vincent, 204
creation, 150, 258, 273, 300, 303
creativity, 14, 74, 79, 162, 176, 250,
      263, 265–66, 298
Cree, 172

critical mass of self, 87, 89, 106, 305
critters, 32, 165–66, 396, 398–99
crowds, 240, 242, 245, 247, 257, 371
Cs, 14, 17, 89, 104, 298, 300
Csordas, Tom, 100
cults
   fox, 180
   high-arousal, 412
cultural burdens, 19–20, 32
Cultural Revolution, 257
curandera, 154
curiosity, 14, 45, 72, 89, 96, 107, 109,
      115, 139, 159, 189, 260, 298,
      312–14, 319, 321–22, 330,
      333–34, 355, 381–83
   calm, 40
   real, 37, 39, 80, 239, 326
curses, 32, 62–63, 66, 112, 176, 265,
      332–33, 346–47

D
daemon, 171
daimonic, 77–83, 170, 173, 250, 253,
      259, 263
daimon-inspired books, 78
daimons, 77–79, 170–71, 173, 177,
      227, 230, 234, 298
Dalai Lama, 52, 205–7
Damascio, Antonio, 291
dance, 57, 129, 206, 209, 215,
      277–80, 345, 410
data collection, 45, 320, 322
Davies, 226, 232
Davis, 192, 259
Dawes, Gregory, 217
Dawkins, Richard, 249, 261, 269–70,
      404
de-automatization process, 216
DeCicco, 267
decolonizing trauma work, 264, 289
default mode network, 193, 217
deities, 184, 201–2, 205–6, 212
deliverance, 64, 94, 180, 247–49,
      251–55, 305, 311
Delphi, 227–28

delusions, 171, 174, 223, 413
de Martino, Ernesto, 277
demonic possession, 204, 232, 235–36, 248, 250
demonologies, 184, 188
demons, 52, 97, 100, 179, 189, 207, 231, 234, 236, 243
Dennett, Daniel, 269–70
depersonalization, 289, 291–92
depossession, 185, 190–92
depression, 73, 198, 214, 216, 280, 285, 298
Deren, Maya, 218
Derrida, Jacques, 301
Descartes, 259, 410
devekut, 55, 227
devils, 39, 65, 101, 107, 115, 135, 174, 208, 237, 239, 246, 315, 369
Dharma, 205, 337
Dhikr, 203
Di, Guan, 208
dialogues, 8, 13, 48, 66, 170, 174, 183, 213, 219, 224, 230, 288, 290, 301, 308, 316, 400, 413
Diamond Path, 205
Dias, Brian, 19
Dick, 10–15, 18–19, 21, 32–33, 38, 44, 68–72, 87, 91, 93–95, 98, 106–7, 223, 251, 284–85, 287, 290, 305, 312, 407–8, 413
Dillard, Annie, 412
Dionysian rites, 228–29, 278, 301, 303
discernment, 64–65, 235, 254–55, 306–11
disenchantment, 212, 248, 272, 285
disgust, 112, 160, 278, 311
disorder
  bipolar, 76
  dissociative identity, 9, 18, 36, 181
  dissociative trance, 35
  multiple personality, 9, 13, 18, 180–81
  obsessive-compulsive, 73, 181, 284
  posttraumatic stress, 73
dissociation, 4–5, 36, 73, 111, 171, 181–82, 199, 201, 217–18, 250, 408
dividuals, 212, 262, 273–74, 276
DMT entities, 190, 192–93, 258–59
domination structures, 232, 411
Donna, 165–66
Douglas, Mary, 266
Doyle, Arthur Conan, 244
Dreamtime, 410
drinking, 4, 6, 363
drug addict, 4, 378
druids, 256
DSM, 34–36
Dua, 204
dual-aspect monism, 411
Durkheim, Emile, 276
dybbuk, 32, 54, 226–27

E
Eagleman, David, 414
earthbounds, 61, 184, 187, 191
eating disorders, 73, 91
ecocentric, 274, 276
ecstasies, 226, 228–29, 233–34, 239, 241, 278–79, 290, 303, 406
ecstatic, 225, 228–31, 233–36, 238, 241, 250, 278–80
Edwards, Jonathan, 245
ego, 14, 60, 79–80, 82, 150, 170, 250–51, 287–89, 303–4
ego states, 61, 185
egregores, 256–57
Ehrenreich, Barbara, 278–80, 285, 404
Eisenstein, Charles, 282–83, 285, 404
Eliade, Mircea, 74, 200, 250, 405
Elkin, Mike, 33
Ellenberger, Henri, 200, 242
El-Zein, Amira, 203
Emerson, Ralph Waldo, 56, 71
emic, 36
Emperor Justinian, 233
empty chair, 70, 90
energumeni, 235

English, Joseph, 188
English Moravians, 240
enlightenment, 19, 174, 179, 238,
    241–43, 292
enthousiasmos, 229
entidades, 50
entity encounters, 175, 184, 192–93,
    257, 259
entrainment, 268
epidemic, 180, 198, 257, 280, 285,
    404
  dancing, 277
epigenetics, 19, 33
Eranos conferences, 81
Erickson, Milton, 7, 67–68, 70, 290
Erzulie, 219
Esalen Institute, 7, 11, 272
esoteric, 229, 256, 293, 410
etic, 36
Euripides, 228, 233, 406, 411
Eurocentric, 49–50, 68, 219, 221, 223,
    238
European shamans, 312
Eusebius, 233
Evans-Wentz, Walter, 257
evil spirits, 55, 171–72, 181, 188, 203,
    210, 212, 224–25, 227, 247
evolutionary psychology, 216
exaptation, 296, 413
Exeter, 249
exiles, 15–18, 77, 97, 102, 110, 206,
    210, 305, 339, 347, 349, 396
exorcism method, 46
exorcism on Newel Knight, 246
exorcisms, 48, 54–55, 59, 90, 93–94,
    180, 182, 188–89, 191, 202,
    205, 212–13, 220, 222, 226–27,
    231, 233, 235–39, 241–43,
    246–49, 254
  shamanic, 209
  traditional, 97, 187
  trial, 242
exorcists, 55, 65, 94, 188–89, 202,
    227, 231–32, 236, 249
extraction work, 191

extraterrestrials, 184, 187, 193
Ezekiel's visions, 225

F
Fage, Durand, 239
fainting, 237, 243, 277
faith, 179, 181, 250, 334–35, 342–43,
    346, 349–50, 413
faith frame, 75–76
faith healers, 204
Farber, Seth, 176–77
Father Grandier, 237
Father Johann Joseph Gassner, 242
Father Malachi Martin, 188
Father Michael Perry, 249
Father Stephen Freeman, 301
Father Tom, 65–67
Father Urbain Grandier, 237
fearlessness, 53, 110, 184
feedback, 134, 163, 344, 394
feeders, the, 97, 100, 118–19, 132,
    191, 383
Fernanda, 331–51
Fetaya, 54
Ficino, Marcilio, 259
the field of you, 17
Filan, 255
filters, 33, 77, 184, 193
Fiore, Edith, 184–86
firefighters, 15, 24, 97, 110
First Great Awakening, 245–46
Firth, Raymond, 218
Fists of Righteous Harmony, 208
Fjelstad, Karen, 214
Flewelling, Ralph, 293
folk healers, 154, 205, 236, 312, 411
Forbes, Jack, 173
fox cults in China and Korea, 180
Fox sisters, 244
fractals, 18, 406
Frank, 251
Frankl, Viktor, 66, 69, 76
Franklin, Benjamin, 246
Frazer, George, 182

free will, 41, 98–99, 121, 154, 371, 397, 399
Freud, Sigmund, 76, 170–72, 288
Froese, Tom, 268
Frost, Robert, 56
fumigation, 55, 227
function, hemispheric brain, 282, 408
Furlong, David, 182

G

Gabriel, 203
Gallagher, Richard, 188–89, 302
Gallup poll, 292
Gassner, 241–42
Gassner-Mesmer affair, 243
Geertz, Clifford, 262
Genji, 210
German Pietists, 239–40
Germer, 304
Gerod, 61
Gestalt, 7–8, 11, 62, 70, 407, 413
Al-Ghayb, 203
ghosts, 53, 213–14, 248, 348
Gid-Dim, 203
Gifford lectures, 178
Gina, 345, 349, 351
Gladis, Mariah Fenton, 7
glue, 54, 130, 226, 303
Gnostics, 253
Golden Age, 226
Golden Bough, 403
Goldish, 54, 226–27
Gottlieben Dittus, 242–43
Govinda, 205
gratitude, 42, 131, 396
Greeks, 37, 77, 79, 81, 178, 191, 203, 226–29, 232, 234, 250, 253, 278, 298, 301
Greenwood, Susan, 408
Gregory of Nyssa, 294, 301
Greyson, Bruce, 98
grief, 32, 60, 102, 151, 177, 229, 348, 373, 395–96
Griffiths, Roland, 192, 259, 293, 314–16

Grof, Stan, 95, 282
group dances, 278
group minds, 257
growth, 70, 75, 105, 134, 208, 248, 251, 296, 400, 413
growth in exorcisms and deliverance ministries, 248
growth of IFS, 251
guidance, 20, 42, 104, 106, 110, 133, 152, 154, 161, 166, 301–2, 304–5, 307–8, 310–13, 322
guidance and guides, 104, 110, 301, 304, 313
guides, 20, 101, 103–7, 110, 144–47, 149–51, 154, 158, 160, 166, 169–70, 191–93, 224, 258–59, 281, 284–85, 288, 293, 296–97, 301, 304–8, 310–14, 316, 322–23, 325–26, 329
guides and discernment, 297
Guntrip, 291
Gustafsson, 213–14
gut ceremony, 40, 57–59, 209–10
Guyon, 237

H

Hacking, Ian, 221
Haitian voodoo, 78, 177, 218, 331
Hallowell, Irving, 275
hallucinations, 82, 174, 238, 308
Hammond, Frank & Ida-Mae, 251–52, 254–55
Han, 58
Hanegraaff, Wouter, 203, 229–30
Hank, 135–49
Hanuman, 202
hard problem, the, 291
Hari, 283
    Johann, 282–83
Harner, Michael, 61, 102, 190–91, 250
Harpur, Patrick, 78–79
Harry, 14, 40–42
Hartmann, Ernest, 265, 284

Hassan, 268
  Uri, 268
hate, 5, 27, 57, 66, 100, 115, 140,
  236, 298, 307, 310, 348
Hayes, Melody, 283
head mate, 258
Hearing Voices Movement, 176–77,
  219, 413
Hegel, 285
Heidegger, 81
Helen, 27–32
hell, 5, 42, 54, 56–57, 184–85, 248,
  308, 361, 368
heresy, 237, 300, 413
hermeneutics, 405
hermeticism, 229
heroin, 41, 283
Hesse, Hermann, 14
heterarchical, 267
Heusch, 220
Hien, 214
hierarchies, 48, 99, 184, 188, 279
Hildegard, 234
Hill, David, 225
Hillman, James, 170, 288–89, 295
Hinayana, 207, 230
Hinduism, 185, 199–200, 205,
  281–82, 293, 299
Hitler, 257, 306
holiness, 55–56, 105, 207, 232, 236
Holmes, Sherlock, 244, 323
Holocaust, 20, 33, 291
holy, 55, 84, 234–35, 237, 299–300
Hong, Xiuquan, 207
Howison, George, 293
Huguenots, 238
Humanistic psychology, 294
Hume, David, 240
humility, 48–49, 152, 188, 242, 301,
  309, 368, 372, 413–14
Humphrey, Nicholas, 269–70
Hunter, Jack, 217
hunter-gatherers, 19, 222, 259,
  295–96
Huxley, Aldous, 3, 237

hyperactive agency-detection, 259, 413
hyperscanning, 268
hypnosis, 7, 61, 69, 71, 82, 182, 184,
  186, 257

I
Iamblichus, 229–30
ibburs, 32, 54
ibn Iyob, 54
ICS, 263–64
ideology, 26, 35–36, 67–68, 93, 170,
  198, 248, 251, 253, 255, 295,
  305, 407
ideomotor signaling, 61
IFS skills, 15, 17, 21, 87, 183, 312
I-it relationships, 290–91
illusion, 14, 70, 75, 94, 100, 171, 183,
  283, 294
imagery, 24, 72, 76, 82, 87, 93, 98,
  103, 109, 266, 314
images, 5, 7, 34, 37, 39, 42, 80–81,
  85, 120, 138, 140–41, 152, 161,
  289, 299–300, 302, 313, 320,
  322, 325, 328
  bizarre, 325
  central, 251
  frequent, 98
  inner-world, 70
  internal dreamlike, 24
  introjected, 288
  mythopoetic, 406
  powerful, 377
  small, 379
  visual, 156
  vivid, 41
  wonderful, 282
imaginal, 99, 203, 229, 258, 289, 409
imagination, 79–83, 229, 250, 271,
  302, 409
  active, 72, 80, 82, 410
  autonomous, 82–84, 263, 294, 301
  primary, 80, 82, 170
  secondary, 80
immeasurables, 307
impermeability, 262

impersonal, 287–89, 292–93
implicational, 216, 263–64, 408
in-betweenness, 301
incense, 51, 55, 227
incorporations, 32
Indigenous, 36, 49, 63, 83, 149–50,
    171–72, 190, 205, 215, 217,
    246, 264, 268, 275, 289, 406,
    411–12
individuals, 55, 192, 200–201, 212,
    216, 259, 262, 271, 275, 292,
    302, 406
Indra, 282
infestations, 32, 249
initiation, 35, 83, 213, 217, 219–21,
    266, 308
inner critics, 23–24
inner physics, 39, 72, 87, 146, 223,
    266, 407–9
inner sense cultivation, 74–76
insanity, 56, 170, 212, 217, 227
insect, 353–54, 356–57, 365, 370, 372
intention, 15, 17, 24, 40, 82, 90–92,
    109, 116, 119, 132, 151, 224,
    258, 381
intentionality, 275
interbeing, 281–82
interdependent coarising, 281
interdependent existence, 174
internal self-helper, 9
International Association of Exorcists,
    189, 249
interoception, 3, 71, 73, 82, 256, 265,
    408
Interpersonal neurobiology, 266
intersubjectivity, 301
intuition, 39, 60, 153, 165, 271, 345
invitation, 104, 152, 308, 342, 376
IPNB, 266–67
Irmak, Kemal, 204
Isaacs, T. Craig, 249–51
Isaiah, 225
ISH, 9–10
Islam, 169, 176, 198–99, 203–4, 292,
    300

isolation, 66, 94, 100, 107, 159, 173,
    187, 264, 280, 282–84, 377, 404
I-Thou, 290–91, 295
Itongo, 175

J
Jack, 7, 184
Jackie, 345–46, 348
jaguar breath, 103
James, Henry, 56
James, William, 26, 56, 72, 178, 182,
    185, 217, 244, 282, 310, 406
Jansenists, 240
Jensen, 214, 279, 294
Jeremiah, 225
Jessie, 378–95, 397–400
Jesus Christ, 55, 60, 64, 66–67, 70,
    174, 177, 179, 207, 225–26,
    228, 231–32, 234, 238, 251,
    300, 302–3, 369, 376
Jim, 57
jinn, 32, 45–46, 169, 198, 203–4, 277
Jnana Yoga, 299
John Paul II, 294
John Scottus Eriugena, 301
John's gospel, 231
Johns Hopkins Center, 315
Johnson, Rick, 302–4
Johnston, William, 105, 302–3
Judaism, 46, 54–55, 189, 199,
    225–27, 231, 259, 300
Julie, 158–59
Jung, Carl, 3, 14, 23, 56, 72–73, 79–
    81, 85, 169–74, 224, 250–51,
    276, 288–89, 294, 310, 314–15,
    407, 410
Jungians, 82, 107, 170, 172–73, 251,
    289, 310, 410

K
kabbalism, 54, 107, 226
Kaldera, 255
Kant, Immanuel, 292
Kardec, Allan, 48–49, 52, 244
karma, 52, 59, 64, 210, 349

Kastrup. Bernardo, 71, 78
Kathy, 163–64
Kaufmann, 290
Keats, John, 79–80
Keller, Helen, 56
Kendall, Laurel, 410
kenosis, 105, 174, 299–305, 312, 314
Kim Kum-Hwa, 58
kindling, 76, 236
kindness, 6, 48, 57, 62, 124, 192, 227,
    255, 259
Kirmayer, Lawrence, 276
Klages, Ludwig, 172
Knight, Newel, 246
Knudson, Albert, 293
Koenig, 75
Koestler, Arthur, 18
Kojiki, 210
Korea, 13, 35, 57–60, 64, 180, 197,
    207–9, 220, 222, 224, 238, 411
Kraemer, 229, 290
Kreiser, Robert, 278
Kriket, 191
Kripal, Jeffrey, 203
Kupperman, 229
Kurtz, Ernest, 73
Kurzban, Robert, 414
Kuten, 205–6

L
Laing, 176–77, 291, 293
Lama Govinda, 205
Lambeck, Michael, 217–18
Latin words for demonic possession,
    235
Lawrence, D. H., 192, 259, 285
laws of inner physics, 72, 87, 146, 223,
    266, 407–9
Laycock, Joseph, 248
LeBon, Gustav, 257
Lee Sunhwa, 59–60
legacy burdens, 19–20, 32–33, 87, 91,
    103, 153–54, 281, 346–47, 395
legacy unburdening, 33, 155, 162,
    166, 252, 346

Levy, Paul, 172–73, 212
Levy-Bruhl, Lucien, 276
Lifshitz, Michael, 258
Lifton, Robert Jay, 9, 181
liminal, 216, 266
lineage, 155, 190, 211, 340–41, 351,
    389, 391–92, 397
Lisa, 154–55
Lister's theory, 20
Littlewood, Roland, 36, 171, 221
Llinas, Rodolfo, 268
loa, 78, 102
Logical positivism, 71
loneliness, 101, 107, 158, 188, 280,
    345
Loudun, 236–37, 243
Lowell, Percival, 210
Lowell lectures, 178
Lower Order, 308
LSD, 6
Lucifer, 259
Luhrmann, Tanya, 74–77, 82, 199,
    224, 256, 258, 261–62, 283–84,
    298, 404, 407–8
Luhrmann and Inner Sense Cultiva-
    tion, 74
Luhrmann's citadel theory of mind,
    201
Luke, 192–93, 231, 259, 353–77
Luke, David, 192
Luna, Luis Eduardo, 259, 410
Luria, Isaac, 54, 226
Luther, 301
Lutheran Church, 243

M
MacMurray, John, 291
MacNutt, Francis, 64, 253–54
Madame Alexandra David-Néel, 257
madness, 55, 176, 217, 222, 226–27,
    229, 287, 412
Mad Pride, 176
maggid, 55, 226
Mahayana Buddhism, 204–5, 207,
    209, 213, 230

Mahikari, 64
Maiffret, Lisa, 214
managers, 15–16, 23, 97, 110, 134, 136, 302, 339, 347, 349
Mao Tse Tung, 213, 257, 306
Mara, 174, 205
Marion, Jean-Luc, 301
Maritan, Jacques, 294
Marsha, 43
Martin, Israel, 311
Martin Luther King Jr, 293–94
Mary, 111, 113–29, 131–34, 156, 207, 238, 403
Marzinsky, Jerry, 174–76
Maslow, Abraham, 294
mass possessions, 180, 208, 232, 237, 277
materialism, 4, 69, 71–72, 81, 169, 245, 305, 400, 408
maternal introject, 43
Maximilla, 233
May, Rollo, 173, 250
Mayahana, 207
Mayotte, 217
McAll, Kenneth, 179–80
McFadden, 269
McGilchrist, Iain, 17, 200, 216, 263, 282, 404, 408–9
McKenna, Terrence, 258
McNamara, Patrick, 406
measures of porosity, 261, 265
mechanomorphic, 264
medicalization, 83, 215, 241, 289, 312
meditation, 50, 76, 103–4, 110–12, 128, 234, 236, 257, 312–13, 344
mediums, 47–48, 178, 182, 193, 205, 210–15, 217–18, 221, 235, 244, 297, 316
MEG, 268
Meister Eckhart, 301–2, 304
melancholia, 280
Mellody, Pia, 8, 309–10
memeplexes, 256–57, 269, 404
memes, 256–57, 261, 269, 404
mental disorders, 9, 34, 176, 181, 221

mental distress, 34, 199, 405, 413
mental health care system, 49, 67, 156, 175–76, 202, 218, 222, 252, 308, 406–7, 412–13
mental health epidemic, 175
mental illness, 5, 19, 52, 74, 76, 84, 169, 176–77, 197–98, 201–5, 214–15, 221–22, 234, 241, 247, 250, 284–85, 298, 404, 413
mental imagery cultivation, 74
Merton, Thomas, 306
Mescalito, 184
Mesmer, Franz Anton, 241–42
metapersonal self-construal, 267
Methodists, 240, 247
metta, 38
Mexican healers, 62
Milarepa, 53
Millenarianism, 241
Milosz, Czeslaw, 3
mind
    billiard ball theory of, 262
    citadel model of, 262, 281, 283–84
    distributed, 271
    extended, 270
    implicational, 263
    multiple, 35
    porous, 276, 287
Mindfulness meditation, 72, 85
Minhat Yehuda, 54
minister, exorcists and deliverance, 94, 248
Mishlove, Jeffrey, 78
Mithen, Steven, 296
model
    billiard ball, 284
    biolooping, 221
    citadel mind, 269
    constraint-removal, 105
    dividual, 262
    multiple, 13–14
    predictive coding, 33, 77
modern growth of spirit possession, 208
Modi, 186

monks, 53, 59–60, 105, 206–7, 210–11
monological, 290
monophasic, 216, 408–9
Montanus, Montanists, 233, 235
Moravians, 239
Moreira-Almeida, Alexander, 217
Mormonism, 246
Morzine, 180
Moses, 177
Mother Ayahuasca, 184, 192, 258
Mount Athos, 292
Mount Qaf, 81
MPD. See Multiple personality disorder
MPIs, 277–78
mu, 304
mudang, 35, 57–60, 64, 208–9, 222, 224, 411
Mueggler, 213
Muhammad, 177, 203
Mulla Nasrudin, 297
Multiple personality disorder (MPD), 9, 13, 18, 180–82, 185
multiplicity, 13, 17, 60, 68, 170, 186, 212, 248, 261, 284–85, 294, 301, 405
    natural, 287, 311
multiplicity and IFS, 60
multiplicity and porosity of mind, 405
mundis imaginalis, 81–82, 170, 410
murti, 230, 235
music, 57, 59, 82, 202, 209, 214–16, 225, 230, 234, 279–80, 313, 322, 410, 412
Muslims, 46, 203
Muthuswamy Temple, 201–2
mysterium tremendum, 84
mystical experiences, 223, 259, 264, 266, 314–16
mysticism, 3, 8, 81, 84, 224, 238, 250, 268, 302
mythology, 67, 79, 87, 93, 102–3, 106, 109, 173, 216, 233, 250, 289, 313, 403

N
Nagas, 205
Na-Koja-Abad, 81
Nanjing, 207
narcissism, malignant, 188
Nasrudin, 298
Nazis, 69, 257, 306
near-death experiences (NDEs), 5, 98, 193, 207
Nechung Oracle, 206, 218
negative capability, 79
Neibauer, Chris, 282
neo-animism, 261
neopagans, 255–56
Neoplatonist thinking, 79–80, 229, 299, 301, 410
neo-shamanism, 97, 190–92
nested systems, 18
neuroplasticity, 217, 267
neuroscience
    affective, 75
    second-person, 269
Nicholas of Cusa, 301
Nietzsche, 76, 288
Nin, Anais, 223
Nirguna, 300
noetic, 84, 230, 315
Noll, Richard, 74
nonhumans, 212, 275
Nonviolent Communication (NVC), 97
Nosso Lar, 49–50
Novalis, 272
numinosity, 84
NVC (Nonviolent Communication), 97

O
obsessions, 3, 32, 66, 189, 249
obsessio, 235
Ojibwe, 172
oneiric space, 410
ontology, 132, 275, 284, 288, 292, 405–7
opponents, the, 107, 237, 301

Oracle of Delphi, 228
oracles, 205–7, 227, 345
Ornelas, Cáli, 50
Otto, Rudolf, 84
outsider, 4, 36, 54, 173

P

Padmasambhava, 205, 337–44,
    350–51
Pakistan, 13, 45–46
Pandolfo, 176
Panksepp, Jaak, 75
parasites, 95, 100–101, 117, 119, 163,
    173, 365, 399
Parker, Robert B., 33
Parkes, 288
participation mystique, 276
paseos, 47, 65
past-life experiences, 185–86
Pat, 7, 40, 153–54
Path Meditation, 312
pathology, 11, 17, 35, 217–18,
    222–23, 234, 241, 248, 265,
    312, 407, 413
Peck, M. Scott, 187–88
Pehar, 205–6
Pema Chödron, 304
Pentecostalism, 224, 232, 244, 247
Pentheus, 228, 406
perception, 3, 12, 33, 71, 77, 79–81,
    176, 223, 264, 266, 283, 408,
    411
perceptual disorganization, 250
perceptual systems, 33, 409
peripheral possessions, 218
perispirit, 48
permeability, 269, 274, 279, 281
perpetrator introjects, 92
Perrière, 211–12
persecution, 57, 180
person
    nonhuman, 212
    other-than-human, 275
personalism, 69–70, 287–96, 301,
    412–13

personality
    multiple, 289
    past-life, 184
personhood, 70, 230, 273, 288–89,
    291–96, 305
perspectival, 264, 408
Peterson, Jordan, 76
Pew Research Survey, 248, 292
Phaedrus, 217
phase synchronization, 268–69
phii pob, 173, 212
Philemon, 80
Philippine Spiritistism, 48
Philo, 226
Pietists, 237
Piper, Leonora, 244
pishtacos, 173
Planck, Max, 216, 263
Plato, 13, 79–80, 217, 301
Plotinus, 299
pneuma, 253
pneumatikos, 253
Poa, 337
Polanyi, Michael, 287
polarizations, 93, 112, 115, 310–11
polyphasic, 216, 408–9
Pomba Giras, 51
Pope John Paul II, 293–94
porosity of mind, 68–70, 76–77, 174,
    201, 212, 247, 250, 257, 261–
    65, 267–68, 270–71, 273–74,
    276–78, 280–82, 284–85, 287,
    404–5
portals, 23, 63, 73, 88, 160, 363
possessio, 235
possession, 32, 34–35, 54–56, 59,
    66–68, 170–74, 178–82, 185,
    188–89, 197, 199–201, 204,
    206–15, 217–20, 222, 224–34,
    236–43, 245, 247–51, 253–55,
    257, 298, 300, 311–12, 405–6,
    410–12, 414
    metaphor of, 68, 70, 174
    spiritual, 58, 181, 184, 199, 201–3,
    206, 214, 220, 230, 248

possession and exorcism, 54, 188, 226, 231, 237, 287
possession complexes, 200, 215–16, 220, 222, 225
possession cults, 169, 180, 200, 207–8, 211, 221
possession states, 36, 52, 56, 60, 173, 180, 182, 189–90, 198–99, 210, 222, 225, 230, 233–35, 238, 240, 248–50, 257, 281, 306, 406
Pratityasamutpada, 281
Prechtl, Martin, 348
predictive coding, 77
prehistory, 282, 285
Presbyterians, 240, 247
Price, Christine, 7, 161
pride, 51, 64, 130, 134, 309, 340
Prieto Velho, 51
primary process thinking, 83
Prince, Derek, 253–54, 264
Priscilla, 233
Progoff, Ira, 316
progressive dethronements, 414
prophecy, 55, 177, 193, 225–26, 228, 234, 238–39, 259, 281, 292
protection, 53, 66, 110–11, 308, 370
protective circle, 343
protectors, 8, 15–18, 23–24, 38, 90, 94, 101, 154, 161, 205, 210, 339, 349
Protestant deliverance ministries, 251, 254, 412
protoquietists, 237
Pruessner, Jens, 270
Pseudo-Dionysius, 301
psilocybin, 192, 258, 315
psyche, possessed, 171–72
psychedelics, 6, 84, 95, 192, 217, 258–59, 315
psychical research, 244
psychic contagion and porosity of mind, 278
psychography, 49, 316
psychopathology, 9, 25, 178, 189, 197, 251, 260, 265, 274, 284, 406

psychopomps, 191
psychosis, 80, 84, 170, 173, 175, 177, 252, 258, 261–64, 266, 284
psychosynthesis, 8, 290, 407
psychotic, 3, 37, 39, 50, 170, 174, 204, 219, 262, 265, 332
Psychoticism Scales, 73–74, 176, 265
PTSD, 8–9, 180–81, 216
Public Policy Polling, 248
pythia, 227–28

Q
Quan Yin, 295
quartz, smoky, 48, 344
quietism, 236
Quran, 46, 203

R
Rabbi Hayyim Vital, 226
Rabbi Isaac Luria, 226
Rabbi Laurence Kushner, 303
Rabbi Yehuda Fetaya, 54
radical empiricism, 26, 132, 178, 293, 405
radical pragmatism, 26, 67–68, 70, 132, 175, 178, 181, 183, 185, 193, 288, 310, 312, 400–402, 405–7, 411–12
Raguram, 201
Rahardanto, 219
Rajasthan, 202
real-time discernment rule, 310
recovery, 40, 175–76, 183, 298
Red Book, The, 80, 169–70
Reformation, 279–80, 285, 404
Reiki, 47, 65
reincarnation, 48–49, 54–55, 174, 186–87
relationality, 84, 404
relational systems intelligence (RSI), 271
religions, possession-based, 169, 197
repression, 231, 250, 278
reptilians, 187, 366
res cogitans, 259, 410

res extensa, 259, 410
res fantastica, 410
residues, 32, 99, 148, 151–52, 199,
  360
Ressler, Kerry, 19
revelation, 64, 73, 171, 199, 217, 254,
  307
Reverend John Nevius, 179
Reverend Rachel Rivers, 56, 174, 308
Reverend Seymour, 245
revival, 243–47
Rilke, 272
Rituale Romanum, 236
Road Less Traveled, The, 187
Roberts, Evan, 246
Rock, Chris, 297
Roel, Laura, 62
Rogers, Carl, 291, 294
Rojas, 176
Romantic poets, 79–80, 82–83
Romme, Marius, 177
Rose, Michi, 96–97
Rosenberg, Marshall, 97
Ross, Maggie, 302–3
Roth, Gabrielle, 190
RSI (relational systems intelligence),
  271
rudraksha, 53, 344
Rumi, 71, 82, 297, 299, 306
Ruqyah, 46, 203
Russell, Bertrand, 44

S
Sadhguru, 23
Safed, 226
Sai Baba, 185
Saint Anthony, 234
Saint Ignatius, 65, 75
Saint John of the Cross, 237
Saint-Medard cemetery, 240
Saint Teresa of Avila, 237, 241
Sakyamuni, 64
Sanderson, 182
Santería, 62
santero, 62

Sarah, 37–39
Schiller, 272
schizophrenia, 53, 74, 148, 176, 198,
  204, 253, 262, 264, 268, 309
schizotypy, 73–74, 176, 265
Scholem, Gershom, 55
Schooler, Jonathan, 269
Schopenhauer, Arthur, 21
Schore, Allan, 267
Schwartz, Richard, 8, 11, 61, 66, 287,
  404, 409
scleroderma, 404
Seaton, Kathleen, 47
Second Great Awakening, 245–46
secours, 241
Secular Age, 272
secularization, 241–42
Seidel, Jonathan, 225
seizures, 76, 180, 237–38, 243, 277
no self, 304
self
  buffered self/citadel, 285, 405
  multiform, 201
  semipermeable, 201, 272–73, 285
  sociocentric, 276
Self and guides, 8, 61, 105, 183, 301,
  312
self energy, 15, 17–18, 35, 52, 61, 87,
  89, 105, 113, 134, 147, 155,
  279, 283, 302, 321, 379, 383,
  386, 395, 399
Self-to-part connection, 17–18, 80, 88,
  95, 106, 109–10, 155, 284, 396
Seligman, Rebecca, 199, 221
semipermeable membrane, 68, 261,
  291
Semmelweis, Ignaz, 20
Sensory Delight Scale, 73, 265
sensory modalities, 72, 229, 313, 322,
  326, 333–34
separation, 9, 95, 173–74, 275,
  282–83, 285, 307
Seymour, William J., 245
shadow, 171, 174, 255, 326
Shakuntala Modi, 186

shamanism, 33, 52, 57, 82–83, 102–3, 190–91, 199, 208, 218, 222, 231, 250, 337, 412

shamans, 35, 57, 61, 63, 72, 82, 102, 146, 175, 190–91, 199, 208–9, 213, 219–20, 222, 231, 235–36, 263, 266, 331, 347–48

shame, 65, 91, 96, 106, 113, 198, 332, 356

shame-reduction work, initial, 312

shapeshifting, 79

Shaykh Muhammad, 46

Sheldrake, Rupert, 283

shell, 81, 103, 230, 398

Shelley, 79

Shinto, 210, 410

Siegel, Daniel, 266–68, 304

Simons, Daniel, 34

sin, 54, 65, 94, 240, 252, 254

Sir Bertrand Russell, 44

Sir Francis Crick, 268

Sir James Frazer, 403

Sister Mary Margaret Funk, 249, 254

Sluhovsky, 236–37

Smith, Frederick M., 200–202, 246, 274, 290

Smith, Joseph, 246

sociocentric, 262, 273–74, 276

Socrates, 13, 77, 79, 177, 217, 227

Sohal, Vikaas, 268

solo-self, 267–68

Solzhenitsyn, Aleksandr, 306

somebodyness, 293

somnambulistic possessions, 218

Sood, Anuba, 201–2

Sophrony, 292

Soul-Centered Healing, 60

soul fragments, 183, 186

souls, 49, 54–56, 59–60, 62, 79, 81, 151, 171–73, 181, 187, 191, 222, 226, 235, 237, 243, 250–51, 282, 285, 289, 404, 408, 411

   lost, 32, 49, 97, 131, 185, 189, 209

specie aeternitatis, 153

spell, 169, 359

Spezzano, Charles, 75

spiral movement, 152–53

spirit guides, 59, 184–85, 187, 191, 222

Spiritism, 46–50, 62, 243–44

Spiritists, 47–49, 52, 54, 62, 97, 185, 189, 222, 316

spirit mediums, 213, 215, 218–19

spirit possession phenomena, 186, 208

spirit possession prevalence, 199, 213

spirit realms, 53, 149

spirits

   ancestor, 60, 175, 209

   earthbound, 181, 184

   existence of, 57, 169

   fox, 180

   higher-order, 174

   negative, 48, 58, 60, 153, 202, 213

spirits are real, 61, 190

Spirits' Book, 48, 52

spiritual experiences, 5, 55, 59, 74, 84, 175, 177, 197, 200, 207, 236, 238, 241, 246–47, 265, 297, 299, 305, 314, 316, 411–12

Spiritualism, 243–44

spirituality, 69, 74, 84, 169, 190, 211, 229, 234, 236–37, 241, 243, 246, 269, 291, 298–99, 302, 315–16, 321, 412–13

   traditional Korean, 210

spiritual phenomena, 241, 258

spiritual practice, 234, 236, 238, 299

spiritual presence experience, 55, 199, 224, 227, 231, 245, 247

spiritus contra spiritum, 315

spirit world, 102, 184–85, 212, 214

Spowers, 192, 259

Stanford Hypnotic Susceptibility Scale, 73, 265

Staretz Silouan, 292

Stavisk, 257

St. Denis, 301

Steiner, Rudolph, 174, 259

Stephens, Michelle, 82

Stephenson, Craig, 35, 170–71, 251
Steppenwolf, 14
Stevenson, Ian, 186–87
Stolovy, 218
Stone, Hal & Sidra, 8
St. Paul, 301
Strassman, Rick, 192–93, 259
Strathern, Marilyn, 273, 276
Strauss, Claudia, 221
stray burdens, 32, 158
Stroink, 267
St. Thomas Aquinas, 301
Subandi, 219
subjectivity, 5, 35, 69, 72–73, 78,
    85, 188, 197, 214, 223, 270,
    284–85, 288–89, 291, 293, 295,
    297, 326, 330, 407, 410
subordinates, 41, 160, 165
subpersonalities, 7, 14–15, 61, 70,
    170, 284, 408
Sufis, 129, 410
Sugawara, 210
Suhrawardi, 81
suicide, 5, 50, 159, 237, 243, 258,
    269, 280, 298
supernatural, 178, 189, 213, 234,
    236–37, 239, 241, 279
superstitions, 19, 180, 197, 236, 296
supervision, 6, 23, 73, 153, 164, 243,
    252, 329–30, 378
Surin, Jean-Joseph, 237
survivors movement, 8
Suryani, Luh Ketut, 82–84
Sutherland, Jim, 56
Suzuki, 56
sweat lodges, 152, 412
Swedenborg, Emanuel, 56–57, 174,
    300, 308
symptoms, 3, 11, 186, 220, 226,
    241–43, 246, 277, 401

T
Tabberaee, 233
tabernacles, 246
Taiping Rebellion, 207

Taiwan, 198, 207–8
talismans, 213, 231
Tamil rituals, 220
tantra, 200–201
Taoism, 57, 209, 300, 304
Taylor, Charles, 261, 272, 279, 285,
    404
Taylor, Eugene, 178
Taylor, Steve, 404
Taysom, 246
Teasdale, 263
Tellegen Absorption Scale, 73, 265
Tertullian, 233
Thailand, 173, 211–13, 215, 238
Thalbourne, Michael, 266
Thebes, 228
theology, 18, 74, 105, 254, 290–91,
    293–94, 299–300, 303, 410
theory
    actor-network, 271
    billiard ball, 404
    citadel, 283, 404
    distributed cognition, 261, 270
theosophists, 257
therapy
    cognitive behavioral, 16, 290
    decolonizing, 36, 171, 264
    ego state, 7, 61, 184, 407
    spirit releasement, 98, 182–83
    work post-induction, 8
Theravada, 205, 207, 211, 213
theurgy, 229–30, 235
Thich Nhat Hanh, 281, 306
thou art that, 19
threshold, 174, 223, 263, 266, 285,
    411
Thupten Ngodup, 206
Tibet, 50, 52–53, 74, 97, 173, 205–6,
    218, 257–58, 337, 345
Tolstoy, Leo, 208
Tooby, John, 295
torture, 5, 142, 148, 241
trailheads, 103, 128, 313
Tramont, Charles, 181, 186–87, 311

trance, 35, 55, 58, 61, 202, 206–9, 213–14, 223, 225, 228, 233, 235–36, 239, 244, 250, 277
  insensible, 82, 218, 234–35
transcendence, 18, 72, 84, 224, 279, 315
transliminal, 83–84, 170, 174, 223–24, 247, 265–66
Transliminality Scale, 73, 265
transrational, 216
trauma, 4, 7–9, 13, 15–16, 20, 25, 87, 96, 103, 105–6, 134, 149, 173, 180–82, 213, 215, 218, 254, 408
  intergenerational, 180
triads, 23, 301, 410
tricksters, 79, 102, 203, 272
Trilling, Lionel, 280
tsimtsum, 300
Tsultrim Allione, 97
Tuhami, 204
tulpas, 257–58
Turner, Edith, 266
Turner, Victor, 266
Twain, Mark, 208
twelve-step, 220, 283, 305
TWIT, 293, 295
Tyringham Hall, 192, 259

U
ubuntu, 282
Umbanda, 35, 49, 62, 177
umbra, 397
unblend, 88, 159, 166, 299, 302–3, 305, 321–22, 380
unburden, 38–39, 117, 146, 154–55, 160, 192, 305, 360, 362, 398
unconscious cognition, 217
unconscious predictive filter systems, 33
underlings, 99–100, 110, 120–21, 397
unifications, 54
Upper Paleolithic revolution, 296
Upton, Charles, 101
Ustinova, 228–29
utilization principle, 67–68

V
Vachss, Andrew, 5, 33
Vajrayana, 205
Valencia, Anna, 268–69
Van Dusen, Wilson, 174–75, 308
van Gennep, 216
Varela, 205
Vedic tradition, 201, 281–82, 299
Veissière, Samuel, 258
Ventura, Michael, 17
Vervaeke, John, 216, 264, 408
Verzegnis, Monte, 180
Vietnam, 8, 13, 181, 211, 213–14, 217, 281
visions, 25, 43, 53, 56, 64, 66, 69, 73, 81–82, 170, 176–77, 207, 224–25, 236, 238–39, 241, 246, 253, 283, 298, 410
  limited, 276
  powerful, 235
visualizations, 103, 257
voice dialogue, 8, 290, 407
Voltaire, 172, 241
voodoo, 102, 177
Voss, 170

W
Waller, John, 198, 277
Warner, Richard, 264
Waterboarding, 5
Watkins, Helen & Jack, 7, 61, 184
Watkins, Mary, 289
Wattanagan, Kanya, 212
Watters, Ethan, 198
Weber, Max, 211, 248, 272–73, 285
webs, 262–63, 265, 271, 274
WEIRD culture, 216
Weller, Francis, 17, 74
Weller, Robert, 208
Welsh Revival, 246–47
wetiko, 172–74
white crow, personal, 244–45, 403
White Darkness, 218–19
Whitefield, George, 239, 245–46
Whitehead, Alfred North, 44

Whitman, Walt, 292
Wicca, modern, 153
Wickland, Carl, 180
Wilson, Colin, 4, 271
Wilson, Margaret, 271
Wilson, Shawn, 275
Winkelman, Michael, 217
Winnicott, Donald, 75, 410
witchcraft, 51, 62–63, 76, 181,
    236–37, 312
witch doctors, 198, 331–32, 335,
    338–39, 345, 348
witnessing, 58, 64, 80, 160, 176, 193,
    209–10, 239, 305, 346
Wordsworth, 272
wu-wei, 304

X
Xavier, Chico, 49

Y
Yang illnesses, 213
yawning, 63, 253
Yeats, 56, 80, 414
Yehuda, Rachel, 20
Yin diseases, 213
Yoram Bilu, 226
Yoruba religion, 62
Yunkaporta, Tyson, 267

Z
Zahir, 203
zebras, 91, 109
Zen, 193, 292, 303
Zinser, Tom, 60–61, 187

Acknowledgments

First of all, thanks to Nikki Fryn — friend, IT wizard, website designer, and more. Without her steady support, this book might not exist.

To Kira Freed — a wonderful and patient editor.

To Richard Schwartz — for IFS and his friendship and support all these years.

To Bo Shao, Oleg Gorelik, Yuyang Zou, and the Evolve Foundation for their encouragement and help.

To Jim Sutherland — for his unfailing friendship and understanding.

To Rachel Rivers, Peter Nielsen, and all the others who gave me valuable feedback and lent me some of their courage when I faltered.

To Pat — for decades of healing work.

About the Author

Robert Falconer MA, CHT

For the past decade or more, Bob Falconer has devoted himself full-time to Internal Family Systems (IFS) Therapy. In that time, he has attended all the levels of IFS training offered, has been a program assistant more than twenty times, and has attended many workshops and events with Richard Schwartz as both an assistant and a participant. He has helped train well over one thousand therapists worldwide, including those from Pakistan, China, Korea, Australia, Spain, Poland, Mexico, Canada, and the UK. He is perhaps best known in the IFS world for having coauthored the book *Many Minds, One Self* with Richard Schwartz.

Bob's own history is one of extreme sadistic child abuse: sexual, physical, emotional, and spiritual. Both parents were addicts and offenders. His mother was hospitalized several times for mental illness. His brother committed suicide when they were teenagers. And his father was murdered when Bob was twenty-one. His interest in therapy stems from his own determination to heal himself and then help others with histories like his.

In the '70s and '80s, therapists often pretended that child sexual abuse hardly ever occurred. There was no diagnosis of PTSD until the Vietnam veterans' rap groups got together and used political action to force the therapeutic establishment to recognize this diagnosis. Bob was one of the first men to publicly identify as a survivor of childhood sexual abuse, and he was very active in the survivors movement. For over ten years, he was the director of the Institute for Trauma Oriented Psychotherapy and, in this capacity, coedited a series of four books on childhood abuse with Robert Geffner of the Family Violence Institute. At this time, Bob also published an autobiographical account of his own abuse under the pseudonym Robert Blackburn Knight. Bob still consults with a few complex trauma clients, but his focus shifted to teaching IFS and now to exploring the others within us: unattached burdens and guides.

In his pursuit of healing for himself and others, Bob has explored many modalities. His undergraduate degree was in anthropology, and he has been fascinated by shamanism ever since. He had the great good fortune to study with Michael Harner and Sandra Ingerman, among others. His first love in the therapy world was Ericksonian hypnotherapy. This led him to Jack and Helen Watkins' ego state therapy.

Since 1971, Bob has been regularly attending workshops and trainings at the Esalen Institute. He has taken over 140 seminars there. The Gestalt therapy of Mariah Fenton Gladis and Christine Price made a deep impression on him. Bob also studied codependency and addiction with Pia Mellody in the '80s and '90s. He had the privilege of learning nonviolent communication from Marshall Rosenberg and studied expressive arts and dance with Anna Halprin, Stuart Cubley, Andrea Juhan, and many others.

Psychedelics have helped Bob's healing since he first became involved with them in 1967. He is very grateful for the current psychedelic renaissance and enjoys training people who know how to use IFS in psychedelic-assisted therapy.

Bob is producing a series of online courses teaching how to work with the others within us — unattached burdens and guides. You will be able to find links to these on his website as soon as they are available. He will also be offering small experiential consultation groups on this subject.

Robert Falconer's website: https://robertfalconer.us

YouTube Channel: https://www.youtube.com/@bobfalconer

Facebook: https://www.facebook.com/theotherswithinus

IFS Institute website: https://ifs-institute.com
to learn more about Internal Family Systems

Printed in Great Britain
by Amazon

24273794R00278